Thesaurus of Sociological Indexing Terms

Second Edition

Barbara Booth
Principal Lexicographer
and
Michael Blair
Thesaurus Development & Indexing Editor

sociological abstracts, inc.
P.O. Box 22206
San Diego, California 92122

Copyright © 1989 by **sociological abstracts inc.**
P.O. Box 22206
San Diego, CA 92122-0206

All rights reserved
No part of this publication may be reproduced or transmitted in any form or by any means, electronic or mechanical, including photocopying, recording or by any information storage and retrieval system, without permission in writing from **sociological abstracts inc.**

Library of Congress Catalog Card Number: LC 89-60757
ISBN 0-930710-06-1
Printed and bound in the United States of America

First Edition 1986
Second Edition 1989

Contents

Acknowledgements iv

Introduction to the First Edition v

Introduction to the Second Edition vi

Thesaurus Structure vi

Search Guidelines viii

Sample Entries x

Descriptors Added, Second Edition xi

Alphabetical List of Terms 1-275

Rotated Descriptor Display 277-317

Classification Scheme 318-319

Bibliography 319-320

Acknowledgement, First Edition

The *Thesaurus of Sociological Indexing Terms* was developed to retrieve information contained in the *Sociological Abstracts* and *Social Planning, Policy and Development Abstracts* databases, and has been used to index documents included since January 1986.

Plans for the second edition, to be published in three years, include updated descriptor entries, additional scope notes, and a rotated index display.

The Thesaurus project director was Barbara Booth, an outstanding lexicographer with extensive experience in thesaurus development. The Thesaurus could not have been completed without her expertise, creativity, thoroughness, and sensitivity to the problems of sociological terminology. Barbara was assisted ably through all phases of the project by Alex Rubins of the Sociological Abstracts indexing department. Special thanks are also extended to Anita Colby, Cara Birardi, and Lizette LeSavage of Barbara Booth's staff, and to Michael Blair, and the other members of the production and editorial departments at Sociological Abstracts, Inc.

We invite interested scholars and users to send us their comments and suggestions.

Acknowledgement, Second Edition

Special thanks are due again to lexicographical consultant Barbara Booth, who not only reviewed each proposed change to the Thesaurus, but produced a new crop of thesaurus specialists in her classes at UCLA's Graduate School of Library and Information Science. David Acheson researched and worked up many of the new main terms added in the Second Edition and wrote a substantial number of new scope notes, and several current students made significant contributions as part of their course work. Thanks are due also to the ongoing efforts of Michael Blair in developing and using the Thesaurus, to Lynette Hunter who managed the computers, databases and other related software used to contain and structure the work, to Terry Owen of SA Education Services, who helped with online database searches, and to the editorial staff at SA Inc., especially, Publications Manager Sandra Stanton, and assistant editors Jill Ireland and Julie Taylor, all of whom contributed many hours and their considerable skills to proofreading and correcting the final product.

Introduction to the First Edition

The 34 years of **sociological abstracts**' history have seen revolutionary changes in the methods and principles of information management. The "information explosion" of the 1950s and 1960s demanded new ways of organizing and accessing bibliographic information, while advances in automation and computer science made possible the compilation of vast databases of information. The 1970s saw the formation of online vendors of bibliographic databases, such as DIALOG and BRS Information Technologies, which made these databases centrally available to anyone with a terminal and telecommunications capability. Today the pace of change in information technology continues unabated. In the last five years, the personal computer has redefined the methods of the online information user. The online services have introduced new search capabilities in response to the growing number of full-text information files. In the near future, technological innovations such as the new optical media may further alter the way in which information is delivered to the user.

When **sociological abstracts** (**sa**) was launched in 1952, the computer was just beginning to impact bibliography. Researchers such as Mortimer Taube proposed that the best way to deal with the growing flood of scientific, technical, and scholarly literature would be to let the author's original words — the "natural language" of the document — be the index terms. The computer could manipulate and associate the words ("uniterms") in the retrieval process. In retrieval, the searcher would pair ("coordinate") words to identify pertinent material. This idea led to a movement away from traditional subject headings based on ideas, and toward "post-coordinate" natural language indexing systems. Post-coordinate principles remain today as the basis of Boolean search logic and proximity (word position) searching.

Such a post-coordinate indexing system was adopted for **sa**. In 1963, **sa** created a Descriptor Authority File consisting of 800 index terms that had appeared at least five times in several previous volumes. In 1964, variant prefixes and suffixes were added to the root uniterms to broaden their applicability. creating a system of "descriptor strings" (e.g., Profession/Professions/Professional/Professionalism). Over the years, many new descriptor strings were added to the Descriptor Authority File, until, by 1985, it totalled 4,838 terms.

The mission of **sa** remains the same as it was in 1952: to document the world's sociological literature — journal articles, conference papers, proceedings, books, and book reviews. But information technology has changed. Powerful new full-text capabilities are available for the manipulation of natural language. In addition, the sheer number of documents in the **sa** databases and the number of years to be searched in the printed indexes have burdened the search process. Changes in sociological terminology have intensified the problems of imprecision in natural language and this type of indexing has become less useful.

In 1984, **sa** determined to improve its indexing system by developing an authoritative thesaurus of subject descriptors for sociology, based on the concepts found in the literature. But development of a thesaurus was complicated by the need to maintain continuity between the new indexing system and the old. Therefore, this massive undertaking had multiple objectives: to develop a concept-based sociological indexing vocabulary using standard lexicographic principles and notation; to maintain the integrity and cohesiveness of the **sa** files, both in print and online, through appropriate notes and cross-referencing; and to thoroughly document prior indexing practice and usage. The resulting thesaurus is based on the existing Descriptor Authority File and the 22 years of sociological literature available for research in the **sa** databases.

Two years were spent in research and development. The result — this first edition of the *Thesaurus of Sociological Indexing Terms* — includes 6,748 vocabulary terms, of which 3,563 are Main Term descriptors and 3,185 are nonindexable Use references and discontinued terms. A total of 2,697 terms from the Descriptor Authority File were retained and incorporated into the Thesaurus, including 762 retained in their existing form, 1,689 retained with some change in word form, and 123 terms representing multiple concepts split into two or more new descriptors. Over 1,500 Descriptor Authority File terms were discontinued: 366 were deleted outright and appear in the Thesaurus only with a History Note; 1,160 were converted to Use references or appear with a "see now" note pointing to appropriate descriptors. New terms developed in the course of research include 866 descriptors and 1,659 Use references.

Thesaurus Development

The first step in the Thesaurus project was the development of a Descriptor Input Form. The form was designed for flexible recording of Thesaurus entries and allowed for the documentation of lexicographic research. A form was prepared for each of the 4,838 terms in the Descriptor Authority File. The forms were then grouped into 30 major subject categories, such as Health, Marriage and Family, and Religion.

The work proceeded group by group. Each term was searched against the database to determine the number of postings (instances of use) since 1963 and the year of first usage. Descriptive phrases (identifier entries) from the latest three annual **sa** subject indexes were then analyzed, supplemented by database searches of the backfile to identify trends in meaning or usage over time. Lightly posted terms — those with few entries in the printed indexes — were researched online. Lexicographic authorities, including other social science thesauri and a broad range of dictionaries from many disciplines, were consulted to establish preferred word forms, document synonyms, and gather definitions. Subject terms, personal names, and geographic place names each received special treatment.

Subject Terms

Particular attention was paid to the number of postings and the scope of the concept in selecting subject descriptors. Authority File descriptor strings with more than a page of entries in the annual indexes were exhaustively analyzed to identify specific concepts as new candidate descriptors. Conversely, descriptor strings with few entries were merged wherever possible into a more generic term. In general, the objective was to establish many, very specific descriptors in core areas of the vocabulary and fewer, more general descriptors in peripheral areas in order to improve the readability of the printed indexes and retrievability in online searching. New descriptors were established for concepts containing words that are common in sociology, but where natural language is ineffective for accurate retrieval. The many new "Class" and "Occupational" terms are examples of the results of this analysis.

Geographic Place Names

Geographic descriptors entered into the Thesaurus include all countries, and those cities that are frequently discussed in the sociological literature. Existing geographic terms not meeting these criteria were entered only as discontinued descriptors.

In addition to assigning geographic descriptors for locations that are the focus of research, the following **sa** indexing practices are noted:

1. Tribes are assigned two descriptors: Traditional Societies and an appropriate geographic descriptor.
2. Immigrant groups are assigned a geographic descriptor for their place of residence and a "Cultural Group" term for their place of origin (e.g., for Italians living in New Jersey, the descriptors are New Jersey and European Cultural Groups).
3. Research conducted outside the United States is assigned a geographic descriptor even when the location is not the topic or focus.
4. To facilitate retrieval, both a city or province and country descriptor may be assigned to the same document.

Personal Names

Personal names were entered selectively, based on frequency of occurrence as the focus of sociological literature. All names are displayed in their fullest form and include dates of birth and death whenever possible.

Introduction to the Second Edition

In preparation for the Second Edition, proposed new descriptors were collected and submitted to the lexicographers for research and development consistent with procedures used to create the first edition. For each, the database was searched to assess the frequency and kinds of usage, and a variety of reference materials were used to establish current definitions.

"Use" Terms

Seventy-two of the 249 candidates that were approved are entered as nonpostable main terms. These appear in the list of main terms in light typeface, with the instruction to use a specific already existing entry. "Birthdays," for example, is entered with a note to use "Celebrations" (D113800).

Personal Names

Twenty-seven new entries are provided for persons of particular significance to sociology, bringing the total to 252. The criterion was that a subject search on the individual's name indicate that the person is not only a published author but also a topic of interest in the works of other social scientists.

Geographical Place Names

Forty-eight new descriptors are included for cities throughout the world, including Beirut, Lebanon, Pretoria, South Africa, and Managua, Nicaragua, in step with the growing literature on developing countries.

Cultural Groups

Several descriptors were added to the list of terms for geographically defined cultural groups, to facilitate more precise research on refugees and other immigrant populations. Examples include Middle Eastern Cultural Groups, South Asian Cultural Groups, Southern African Cultural Groups, and Soviet Union Cultural Groups.

General Subject Terms

One-hundred seventy-nine postable descriptors are provided for new concepts, variables, methods, and relationships now current in the literature. A list of these is appended, and their complete displays can be found in the main term list.

Scope Notes

Two-hundred eighty-nine new scope notes are added to old and new descriptors, and 70 of the original notes are revised and clarified. Special effort was made to make all technical and obscure terminology instantly meaningful, including statistical concepts and concepts tied to specific theoretical orientations such as Marxist analysis, symbolic interactionism, and ethnomethodology.

"Relation" Terms

Several additions are made to the list of descriptors for interrelations of complex variables such as Intergenerational Relations and Practitioner Patient Relationship. These include Police Community Relations, Family Work Relationship, and Soviet American Relations, and will add significantly to search precision on highly complicated and multifaceted topics.

Rotated Descriptor Display

A rotated term display is included following the main term list, allowing users to find multiword descriptors alphabetically by each meaningful component. This will enhance searches for Personal Names and Geographical Place Names, as well as for concepts beginning with recurrent words such as Social –, Political –, Urban –, etc.

Other improvements in the Second Edition include relocation of the bibliography used in terminological research to the rear of the volume, a separate list of the new descriptors, addition of a list of subject matter classification elements used in the **sa** table of contents, and new Sample Thesaurus Entries.

Thesaurus Structure

This second edition of the *Thesaurus of Sociological Indexing Terms* contains an alphabetical listing of Main Term descriptors used for indexing and searching the **sa** databases and printed indexes, beginning with the April 1986 issue. It also references discontinued terms from the former Descriptor Authority File, which are used for accessing information prior to 1986. Associated term relationships are displayed under each Main Term. These may include a Descriptor Code (DC), Scope Note (SN), History Note (HN), Used For (UF) and Use references, Broader Terms (BT), Narrower Terms (NT), and Related Terms (RT). Each of these elements of the Thesaurus display is explained below.

Main Terms (MT)

Main Terms appear in boldface letters. Nouns and noun phrases are preferred for Main Terms, with plural word forms used with nouns that can be quantified (Institutions, Values, Workers) and singular word forms used with nouns representing processes, properties, and conditions (Employment, Migration, Validity). The gerund or verbal noun is also used with process terms (Data Processing, Marketing).

Main Term descriptors are limited to 60 characters. Punctuation is used minimally. Hyphens are used where needed for clarity. In cases where ambiguity may occur, and to distinguish the meaning of homographs, Main Terms and Use reference terms appear with qualifying expressions in parentheses.

Authoritarianism (Political Ideology)
Authoritarianism (Psychology)

Repression (Defense Mechanism)
Represssion (Political)

Descriptor Codes (DC)

Descriptor Codes are seven-character, alpha-numeric authority numbers for Thesaurus terms. New Descriptor Codes have been assigned to all Main Terms. These are distinguished from former Descriptor Codes by the "D" prefix. Since a Descriptor Code is a unique number representing a specific Main Term, it may be used in online searching as an alternative to specifying the Main Term itself.

Community Organizations
DC D155100

Scope Notes (SN)

Scope Notes are brief statements of the intended meaning or usage of a Main Term. They may provide definitions, user instructions, or both.

Dependency Theory
SN Theory that perceives the social and economic development of underdeveloped countries as being conditioned by the domination of more powerful countries through the extraction of surplus value or the repatriation of profit.

Scientists
SN Coordinate with specific scientific disciplines to locate information about personnel in that discipline, e.g., for Chemists, use Scientists and Chemistry.

Residential Mobility
SN Movement from residence to residence within the same community or geographical area. Do not confuse with Geographic Mobility.

Context-Dependent Terms

Certain descriptors representing the broadest concepts and/or standing at the head of a conceptual hierarchy have been designated as "context-dependent." These terms are used in indexing in coordination with other terms to specify concepts not yet represented in the Thesaurus. For example, a term that belongs in a set of closely related terms may not yet have achieved currency in the literature and may not therefore be included as a Main Term entry in the Thesaurus. It may then be necessary to coordinate the broad context-related term with related entries for optimal retrievability. More specific (narrower) terms are always preferred in indexing; however, there are cases in which the most appropriate choice of descriptor may not be obvious. The context-dependent designation serves to alert the user of the need to examine the Scope Notes and other display features of comparable or closely related terms carefully in order to select the best descriptor.

Conflict
SN A context-dependent term for strife, mental or physical, among individuals or groups. Select a more specific entry or coordinate with other terms.

History Notes (HN)

History Notes link Thesaurus descriptors with the Descriptor Authority File terms used in indexing prior to 1986. They are the key to searching the printed indexes and the online databases from 1963 through 1985. History Notes provide the range of years in which a term was in use, its former Descriptor Code, and the word form of the term if it has changed. Often they provide search instructions. History Notes appear for both Main Terms and discontinued terms.

History Notes are standardized according to the disposition of or action taken on the former Descriptor Authority File term. Examples of the several types of History Notes are given below.

Religiosity
HN Formerly (1963-1985) DC 383175.

This term was used in indexing between 1963 and 1985 and was retained in the Thesaurus in its exact form. The History Note references the former Descriptor Code assigned to the term.

Phonetics
HN Formerly (1964-1985) DC 334050, Phonetic/Phonetics.

This History Note documents the former descriptor string Phonetic/Phonetics, which was used in indexing between 1964 and 1985. The word form has been collapsed to a preferred form.

Citizenship
HN Formerly (1963-1985) included in DC 090600, Citizen/Citizens/Citizenship.

The "included in" note identifies a "term split." In this case, two distinct concepts — citizens and citizenship — were contained within a single descriptor string. Each was established as a separate Thesaurus descriptor.

Chronic Illness
HN Added, 1986. Prior to 1986 use Chronic/Chronically (DC 090520) and Illness/Illnesses (DC 223700).

This descriptor was newly added in 1986. The History Note specifies how this concept was formerly coordinately indexed. The user of the printed indexes will find this concept prior to 1986 under either of the former terms Chronic/Chronically or Illness/Illnesses, while the online searcher should specify both terms in an "AND" search statement.

Chromosome/Chromosomic (1969-1985)
HN DC 090517, deleted 1986

Discontinued terms appear in the Thesaurus with a qualifying range of years indicating their period of active use in indexing. The History Note provides the former Descriptor Code and notes that it was deleted from use in 1986.

Confinement (1964-1985)
HN DC 110940, deleted 1986. See now Detention, Institutionalization (Persons), or Hospitalization.

Many discontinued terms appear with "see now" notes pointing to Thesaurus descriptors that are closely related to the concept represented by the discontinued term. This type of History Note is used when two or more descriptors are referenced.

Fairness (1984-1985)
HN DC 171147.
Use Equity

"Use" references direct the indexer or searcher from non-preferred synonyms or variant expressions to preferred Main Terms. When terms from the Descriptor Authority File were downgraded to the status of Use references, the History Note records the former Descriptor Code.

Used For (UF)

Terms referenced by the Used For designation are non-preferred terms. They include synonyms and variants of the Main Term and specific terms indexed under a more generic descriptor. Often they include discontinued terms from the Descriptor Authority File; these appear with a qualifying range of years indicating their period of active use in indexing. For every Used For term, a reciprocal Use reference is generated, pointing to the preferred Main Term.

Academic Achievement
UF Academic Performance
Educational Achievement
Scholastic Achievement
School Performance
Student Achievement

Films
UF Cinema (1963-1985)
Motion Pictures
Movie/Movies (1963-1985)

Reference Materials
UF Atlas/Atlases (1972-1985)
Dictionary/Dictionaries (1963-1985)
Encyclopedia/Encyclopedias (1963-1985)
Guide/Guiding (1963-1985)

Use

"Use" references direct the user from synonyms and other non-preferred expressions to the preferred Main Term. They are the reciprocal entries of terms referenced by the Used For designation. Discontinued terms appearing as Use references are shown with a qualifying range of years of active use and History Notes recording the former Descriptor Code.

Student Achievement
Use Academic Achievement

Cinema (1963-1985)
HN DC 090570
Use Films

Encyclopedia/Encyclopedias (1963-1985)
HN DC 154600
Use Reference Materials

Broader Terms (BT) and Narrower Terms (NT)

Broader Terms indicate the more general class or classes to which the Main Term logically belongs. Narrower Terms indicate the more specific sub-classes of the Main Term. The Broader Term/Narrower Term relationship is reciprocal — for every Broader Term reference there is a corresponding reciprocal Narrower Term reference.

Communes
BT Collectives

Collectives
NT Communes

Broader Term/Narrower Term relationships create thesaurus *hierarchies*, sequences of class relationships that may extend upward more generally or downward more specifically through several levels. At any point in the hierarchy, Broader Term/Narrower Term designations refer upward or downward only to the next most general or specific level. However, by tracing these references, a complete hierarchy or "family tree" can be approximated.

Broader	Groups
	. Organizations (Social)
	. . Collectives
	. . . Communes
Narrower	. . . . Kibbutz

Note: Searching a Broader Term in the **sa** online databases will not automatically retrieve abstracts representing the concepts of its Narrower Terms *unless those Narrower Terms have also been assigned to the documents in indexing* (e.g., searching Collectives will not automatically retrieve Communes).

Related Terms (RT)

Terms referenced by the Related Term designation bear a close conceptual relationship to the Main Term, but they do not share the direct class/sub-class relationship described by the Broader Term/Narrower Term relationship. Related Terms are always entered reciprocally. They should be considered for use as other appropriate search terms.

Class Politics
RT Class Relations
Labor Movements
Social Class
Syndicalism
Worker Consciousness
Working Class

Search Guidelines

Until you become familiar with the *Thesaurus of Sociological Indexing Terms* and its indexing vocabulary, your success in using the Thesaurus for effective searches of the **sa** databases and printed indexes will be aided if you follow the steps outlined below. A basic point to remember is that you may need to search *different* or *additional* index terms before 1986 than after 1986.

1. Make a list of words or phrases that clearly and briefly describes your research topic. The first few times, you may find it helpful to do this on paper.
2. Locate the descriptors (Main Terms) most specifically describing your topic. Carefully review Scope Notes for the intended meaning of terms and instructional notes. Check the Broader Terms, Narrower Terms, and Related Terms to identify any other descriptors pertinent to the topic. These will help you broaden or narrow the focus of your search. Then check History Notes and Used For references to identify corresponding terms for searching prior to 1986. In the example below, you would need to search the term Alienation for 1986 and thereafter, but three terms prior to 1986: Alienation/Alienated, Estrangement, and Powerless/Powerlessness.

Alienation
HN Formerly (1963-1985) DC 027440.
Alienation/Alienated.
UF Estrangement (1965-1985)
Powerless/Powerlessness (1970-1985)

Keep in mind that information pertinent to your research may be indexed under a broader descriptor. Specific articles indexed under narrower concepts may also be directly applicable.

3. Repeat step 2 for other terms you have identified as appropriate to your topic. You should end up with two lists of terms, one for searching prior to 1986 and another for searching after 1986.
4. Turn to the annual cumulative indexes of **sa** or access the **sa** databases through DIALOG, BRS Information Technologies, or Data Star.

Searching the Printed Indexes

Begin with the Subject Index section of individual issues or annual cumulative indexes published in 1986 or thereafter. Consult several or all of the Thesaurus descriptors you have listed; then focus your search on those descriptors found to be the most productive for your topic. Usually these will represent the most concrete or central aspect of the topic.

Examine the entries under the descriptors to locate pertinent material, noting the abstract accession numbers. Follow up by reading the abstracts and obtaining journal citations in the Main Section.

Then turn to the annual indexes published prior to 1986. Repeat the steps outlined above, using the Descriptor Authority File terms referenced in History Notes and discontinued Used For terms. In a comprehensive search, be alert to the range of years during which the terms were in use.

Searching Online

Frequently, Main Term descriptors in the Thesaurus are identical to one of the component words in a former descriptor string. Since the online services make each of the variant terms delineated by the slashes (/) in descriptor strings searchable separately, you need only specify the current descriptor in searching both before and after 1986 in these cases. In the example of Alienation, above, only the term Alienation, and not the variant form Alienated, need be specified. However, you must also search any discontinued terms appearing as Used For references. This should be expressed as an "OR" statement (use the appropriate commands and protocols of your online service):

Alienation OR Estrangement OR Powerlessness

Where the new and old forms of a term have changed greatly, you may find it easier to search using the respective Descriptor Codes rather than the index terms.

College Students
- **DC** D147600
- **HN** Formerly (1985) DC 448300, Student, College.

Again, the Descriptor Code search is expressed as an "OR" statement.

D147600 OR 448300

History Notes often specify how the concept represented by a new Main Term descriptor was formerly coordinately indexed. In these cases a more complex search statement is required.

Ancestor Worship
- **DC** D030600
- **HN** Added, 1986. Prior to 1986 use Ancestor/Ancestors/Ancestral (DC 031500) and Worship (DC 493440).

Here an "OR" and an "AND" statement should be combined. Using the commands and protocols of your online service, this can be done as a single complex search statement or in separate steps:

Ancestor Worship OR (Ancestor AND Worship)

Alternatively:

D030600 OR (031500 AND 493440)

Keep in mind that both old and new index terms can be combined flexibly with words in titles, identifier phrases, and abstracts in search strategies. Online search capabilities give you powerful tools for precision and recall in retrieval.

Using the Online Thesaurus

The **sa** thesaurus may now be accessed online in DIALOG File 37. EXPANDing a search term during an online session yields an alphabetical list of terms in sequence, displayed by set number for easy selection, and indicating which are listed and displayed fully in the Thesaurus [Illustrated in Step 1 below].

Step 1

?expand ethnic

Ref	Items	RT	Index-term
E1	1		ETHNIA
E2	9116		*ETHNIC
E3	0	1	ETHNIC BUSINESSES
E4	93	34	ETHNIC GROUPS
E5	185	12	ETHNIC IDENTITY

An item from such a listing produces a thesaurus-level display of the descriptor, including an excerpt from the history note and a list of broader, related, and narrower terms [Step 2 below].

Step 2

?expand E5

Ref	Items	Type	RT	Index-term
R1	185		12	*ETHNIC IDENTITY
R2	0	S		(FORMERLY (1985) DC 160130.)
R3	0	F	1	RACIAL IDENTITY
R4	5149	B	11	IDENTITY (A CONTEXT-DEPENDEN.
R5	54	R	14	BLACK POWER
R6	137	R	24	CULTURAL IDENTITY
R7	93	R	34	ETHNIC GROUPS
R8	5807	R	17	ETHNICITY
R9	305	R	18	ETHNOCENTRISM

These are presented with new reference-set numbers. Expanding any of these sets will produce a full thesaurus-level display [Step 3].

Step 3

?expand R9

Ref	Items	Type	RT	Index-term
R1	305		18	*ETHNOCENTRISM
R2	0	S		(FORMERLY (1964-1985) DC . . .
R3	0	F	1	CULTURAL BIAS
R4	157	B	39	SOCIAL ATTITUDES
R5	1984	R	15	BIAS
R6	53	R	25	CULTURAL CONFLICT
R7	137	R	24	CULTURAL IDENTITY

The online searcher can thus move from term to term, from the generic to the most specific, gathering facts about the frequencies of postings and finding new appropriate search terms along the way.

Sample Thesaurus Entries

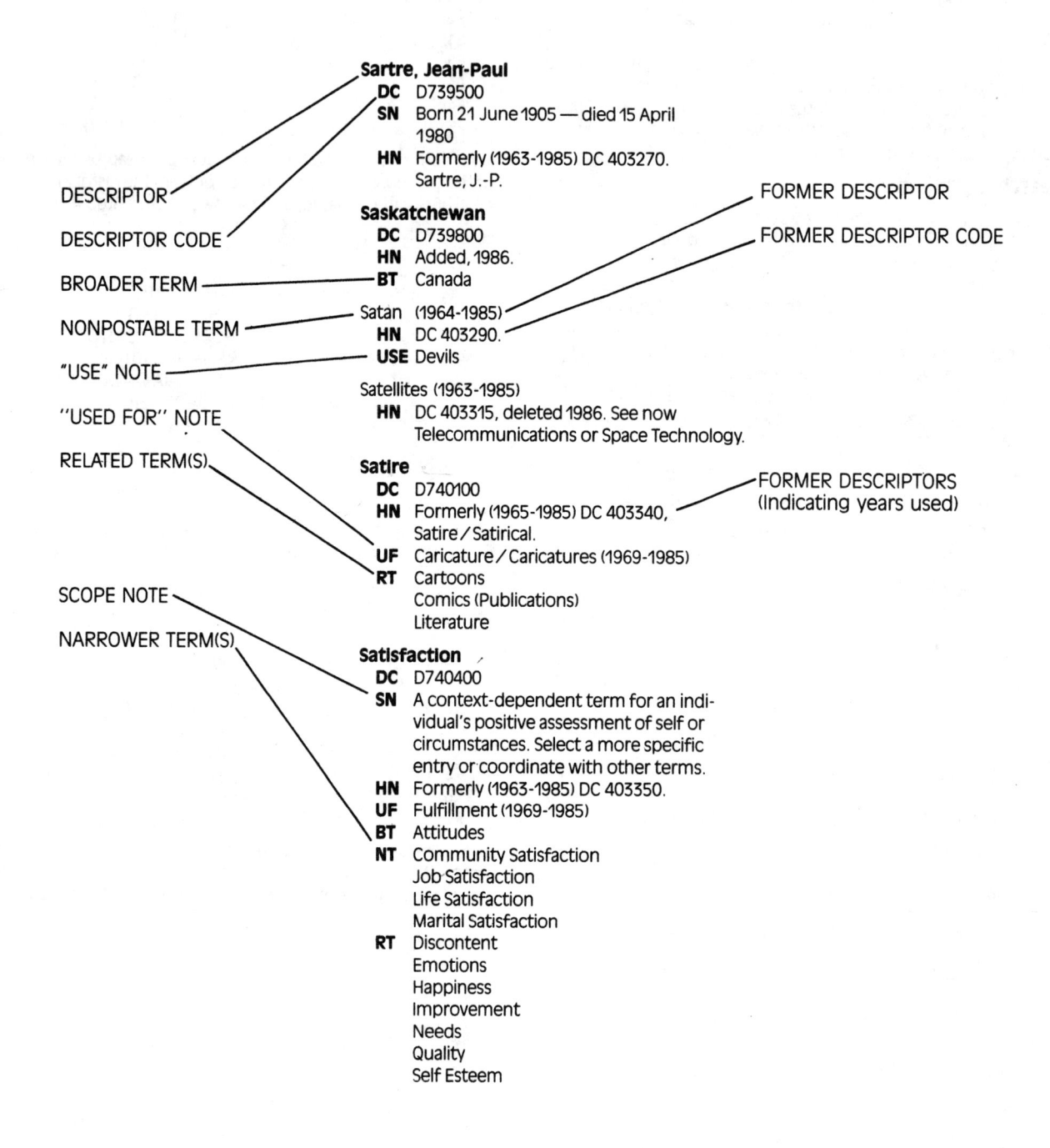

Sartre, Jean-Paul
- **DC** D739500
- **SN** Born 21 June 1905 — died 15 April 1980
- **HN** Formerly (1963-1985) DC 403270. Sartre, J.-P.

Saskatchewan
- **DC** D739800
- **HN** Added, 1986.
- **BT** Canada

Satan (1964-1985)
- **HN** DC 403290.
- **USE** Devils

Satellites (1963-1985)
- **HN** DC 403315, deleted 1986. See now Telecommunications or Space Technology.

Satire
- **DC** D740100
- **HN** Formerly (1965-1985) DC 403340, Satire / Satirical.
- **UF** Caricature / Caricatures (1969-1985)
- **RT** Cartoons
  Comics (Publications)
  Literature

Satisfaction
- **DC** D740400
- **SN** A context-dependent term for an individual's positive assessment of self or circumstances. Select a more specific entry or coordinate with other terms.
- **HN** Formerly (1963-1985) DC 403350.
- **UF** Fulfillment (1969-1985)
- **BT** Attitudes
- **NT** Community Satisfaction
  Job Satisfaction
  Life Satisfaction
  Marital Satisfaction
- **RT** Discontent
  Emotions
  Happiness
  Improvement
  Needs
  Quality
  Self Esteem

Labels:
- DESCRIPTOR
- DESCRIPTOR CODE
- BROADER TERM
- NONPOSTABLE TERM
- "USE" NOTE
- "USED FOR" NOTE
- RELATED TERM(S)
- SCOPE NOTE
- NARROWER TERM(S)
- FORMER DESCRIPTOR
- FORMER DESCRIPTOR CODE
- FORMER DESCRIPTORS (Indicating years used)

Descriptors Added, Second Edition

Addis Ababa, Ethiopia
Adult Children
Alcohol Abuse
Alexander, Jeffrey C.
Algiers, Algeria
Alzheimer's Disease
Animal Human Relations
Athens, Greece
Baghdad, Iraq
Bangkok, Thailand
Barcelona, Spain
Behavior Problems
Beirut, Lebanon
Bellah, Robert N.
Berger, Peter
Bisexuality
Black White Relations
Bogota, Colombia
Borders
Borgatta, Edgar F.
Boulding, Kenneth Ewart
Brisbane, Australia
Cairo, Egypt
Canberra, Australia
Cape Town, South Africa
Caplow, Theodore
Caracas, Venezuela
Caregivers
Career Criminals
Celebrations
Child Mortality
Child Sex Preferences
Child Sexual Abuse
Child Support
Childhood Factors
China
Cicourel, Aaron V.
Clinical Social Work
Cocaine
Collins, Randall
Communicative Action
Computer Software
Conversational Analysis
Cottage Industries
Crisis Intervention
Damascus, Syria
Decriminalization
Defense Spending
Deindustrialization
Denzin, Norman K.
Development Policy
Discretionary Power
Drug Trafficking
Ecological Models
Elderly Women
Employee Assistance Programs
Energy Development
Entertainment Industry
Expert Witnesses
Family Businesses

Family Conflict
Family Stability
Family Work Relationship
Female Headed Households
Fertility Decline
Feyerabend, Paul Karl
Figuration Sociology
Food Industry
Giddens, Anthony
Government Spending
Graduate Schools
Gusfield, Joseph Robert
Hanoi, Vietnam
Hauser, Robert Mason
Havana, Cuba
Heads of Households
Health Behavior
High Technology Industries
Historical Development
Ho Chi Minh City, Vietnam
Home Health Care
Home Workplaces
Homosexual Relationships
Housing Costs
Information Technology
Interpersonal Conflict
Interpretive Sociology
Jakarta, Indonesia
Janowitz, Morris
Kabul, Afghanistan
Kampala, Uganda
Karachi, Pakistan
Kiev, Union of Soviet Socialist Republics
Kinshasa, Zaire
König, René
Kuala Lumpur, Malaysia
Lagos, Nigeria
Landlord Tenant Relations
Language Social Class Relationship
Lee, Alfred McClung
Leningrad, Union of Soviet Socialist Republics
Lowenthal, Leo
Managua, Nicaragua
Marital Status
Matza, David
Medical Decision Making
Medical Model
Melbourne, Australia
Mental Health Services
Merleau-Ponty, Maurice
Middle Eastern Cultural Groups
Milan, Italy
Militarization
Mother Absence
Naples, Italy
Nonprofit Organizations
North African Cultural Groups
Organizational Dissolution
Police Community Relations
Political Action Committees

Political Factors
Porto Alegre, Brazil
Postmodernism
Pretoria, South Africa
Primary Health Care
Privatization
Protectionism
Psychological Development
Psychological Factors
Psychosocial Factors
Public Relations
Public Sector Private Sector Relations
Public Transportation
Racial Differences
Rangoon, Burma
Rastafarians
Rational Choice
Religion Politics Relationship
Reproductive Technologies
Resource Mobilization
Rio de Janeiro, Brazil
Risk Assessment
Rokkan, Stein
Role Satisfaction
San Juan, Puerto Rico
Schism
Self Destructive Behavior
Self Employment
Self Help Groups
Seoul, South Korea
Sikhism
Sikhs
Single Fathers
Socialized Medicine
Sofia, Bulgaria
South Asian Cultural Groups
Southeast Asian Cultural Groups
Southern African Cultural Groups
Soviet American Relations
Soviet Union Cultural Groups
Stockholm, Sweden
Structuration
Sydney, Australia
Teacher Education
Tel Aviv, Israel
Tilly, Charles
Treatment Methods
Turn Taking
Unwanted Pregnancy
Van den Berghe, Pierre Louis
Verbal Accounts
Victim Offender Relations
Vigilantism
Welfare Dependency
Welfare Reform
Womens Roles
Working Mothers
Youth Culture

Alphabetical List of Terms

Ability — Academic

Ability
- DC D000300
- HN Formerly (1963-1985) DC 000100, Ability/Abilities.
- UF Capacity (1971-1985)
  Talent (1963-1985)
- NT Competence
  Skills
- RT Academic Aptitude
  Achievement
  Aspiration
  Creativity
  Genius
  Gifted
  Intelligence
  Leadership
  Learning
  Performance
  Qualifications
  Tracking (Education)

Abnormal Psychology
- Use Psychopathology

Abnormal/Abnormality/Abnormalities (1963-1985)
- HN DC 000200, deleted 1986.

Abolition/Abolitionist/Abolitionists (1972-1985)
- HN DC 000220.
- Use Slavery

Aboriginal Australians
- DC D000600
- HN Formerly (1963-1985) DC 000230, Aborigine/Aborigines/Aboriginal.
- BT Australasian Cultural Groups
- RT Acculturation
  Biculturalism
  Indigenous Populations
  Traditional Societies

Abortion
- DC D000900
- HN Formerly (1963-1985) DC 000320.
- BT Surgery
- RT Birth
  Birth Control
  Family Planning
  Fetus
  Infanticide
  Miscarriage
  Population Policy
  Pregnancy
  Unwanted Pregnancy

Abroad (1963-1985)
- HN DC 000460, deleted 1986.

Absence/Absences (1964-1985)
- HN DC 000490, deleted 1986. See now Absenteeism, Father Absence, or Single Parent Family.

Absent Without Leave
- Use Military Desertion

Absenteeism
- DC D001200
- SN Persistent absense from work or school.
- HN Formerly (1965-1985) DC 000500.
- UF Employee Absenteeism
  School Absenteeism
- RT Attendance
  Dropouts
  Personnel Management
  Students
  Truancy

Absolutes/Absolutism (1966-1985)
- HN DC 000650, deleted 1986. See now Totalitarianism or Relativism.

Abstention/Abstentionism/Abstinence (1967-1985)
- HN DC 000750, deleted 1986.

Abstraction
- DC D001300
- HN Formerly (1963-1985) DC 001000, Abstract/Abstracts/Abstraction/Abstracting.
- BT Cognition
- RT Concepts
  Constructs
  Generalization
  Reality
  Reasoning

Absurd/Absurdity (1969-1985)
- HN DC 001010, deleted 1986.

Abundance (1969-1985)
- HN DC 001025.
- Use Affluence

Abuse
- DC D001400
- SN A context-dependent term; select a more specific entry or coordinate with other terms.
- HN Formerly (1979-1985) DC 001050, Abuse/Abuses/Abusing/Abusive.
- UF Cruelty (1975-1985)
- NT Child Abuse
  Elder Abuse
  Sexual Abuse
  Spouse Abuse
  Substance Abuse
- RT Battered Women
  Coercion
  Deviant Behavior
  Family Violence
  Offenses
  Sexual Harassment
  Threat
  Torture
  Victimization
  Violence

Academic Achievement
- DC D001500
- HN Added, 1986.
- UF Academic Performance
  Educational Achievement
  Scholastic Achievement
  School Performance
  Student Achievement
- BT Achievement
- RT Academic Aptitude
  Educational Attainment
  Educational Research
  Grades (Scholastic)
  Learning
  Project Head Start
  Scholarship
  Students

Academic Aptitude
- DC D001800
- HN Formerly (1963-1985) DC 035400, Aptitude/Aptitudes.
- UF Aptitude (Academic)
  Educability (1965-1985)
- RT Ability
  Academic Achievement
  Cognitive Development
  Gifted

Academic Aptitude (cont'd)
- RT Intelligence
  Intelligence Tests
  Learning
  Students
  Tracking (Education)

Academic Careers
- DC D002100
- HN Added, 1986.
- BT Careers
- RT Academic Tenure
  College Faculty
  Researchers
  Scholarship

Academic Deans
- Use Deans

Academic Degrees
- DC D002400
- HN Formerly (1971-1985) DC 125635, Degree/Degrees.
- UF Degrees (Academic)
  Educational Degrees
- NT Baccalaureate Degrees
  Doctoral Degrees
  Masters Degrees
- RT Academic Disciplines
  College Graduates
  College Majors
  College Students
  Educational Attainment
  Educational Plans
  Higher Education
  Occupational Qualifications
  Professional Training

Academic Departments
- DC D002700
- HN Added, 1986.
- UF University Departments
- BT Departments
- RT College Majors
  Colleges
  Curriculum
  Educational Administration
  Universities

Academic Disciplines
- DC D003000
- SN Branches of knowledge or fields of study or instruction.
- HN Formerly (1963-1985) part of DC 133000, Discipline/Disciplines.
- UF Disciplines (Academic)
  Intellectual Disciplines
  Scientific Disciplines
  University Disciplines
- RT Academic Degrees
  College Majors
  Higher Education
  Humanities
  Interdisciplinary Approach
  Knowledge
  Mathematics
  Medicine
  Natural Sciences
  Research
  Social Sciences

Academic Freedom
- DC D003300
- HN Added, 1986.
- UF Teaching Freedom
- BT Freedom
- RT Censorship
  College Faculty
  Educational Policy
  Information Dissemination

Academic

Academic Performance
  Use Academic Achievement

Academic Tenure
  DC D003600
  SN Refers to a status granted to the most highly qualified and accomplished teachers, conferring prestige and job protection.
  HN Added, 1986.
  UF Faculty Tenure
    Tenure (Academic)
  BT Tenure
  RT Academic Careers
    College Faculty
    Personnel Policy
    Seniority
    Teachers

Academic/Academics/Academy/Academia (1963-1985)
  HN DC 002000, deleted 1986. See now appropriate "Academic," "College," or "Teacher" terms.

Acceptance
  DC D003900
  SN A context-dependent term; select a more specific entry or coordinate with other terms.
  HN Formerly (1963-1985) DC 003500.
  BT Social Behavior
  NT Social Acceptance
  RT Affiliation Need
    Approval
    Interpersonal Relations
    Membership
    Peer Relations
    Rejection
    Resistance
    Social Attitudes
    Social Desirability
    Social Response

Access
  DC D004000
  HN Formerly (1983-1985) DC 003555.
  UF Availability
    Equal Access
  RT Boundaries
    Constraints
    Discrimination
    Equality
    Opportunities
    Rights
    Services
    Social Closure

Accidents
  DC D004200
  HN Formerly (1963-1985) DC 004000, Accident/Accidents.
  RT Air Transportation
    Automobiles
    Drunk Driving
    Emergencies
    Fire
    Hazards
    Health
    Injuries
    Occupational Safety And Health
    Safety
    Survival
    Traffic

Accommodation/Accommodations (1963-1985)
  HN DC 004750.
  Use Adjustment

Accomplish/Accomplished/Accomplishment (1972-1985)
  HN DC 004755.
  Use Achievement

Accountability
  DC D004500
  SN Liability for results or outcomes obtained through the exercise of delegated authority.
  HN Formerly (1984-1985) DC 004762, Accountability/Accountable.
  BT Responsibility
  RT Competence
    Effectiveness
    Ethics
    Performance
    Productivity
    Professional Malpractice

Accountants
  DC D004800
  HN Formerly (1969-1985) DC 004798, Accountant/Accountants.
  BT Professional Workers
  RT Accounting

Accounting
  DC D005100
  HN Formerly (1963-1985) DC 004800.
  UF Bookkeeping
  RT Accountants
    Budgets
    Management
    Service Industries

Accreditation (1984-1985)
  HN DC 004900.
  Use Certification

Acculturation
  DC D005400
  SN Psychological and social adjustment to a new culture, often following immigration.
  HN Formerly (1963-1985) DC 006000, Acculturation/Acculturated/Acculturative.
  UF Americanization (1963-1985)
  BT Social Processes
  RT Aboriginal Australians
    Assimilation
    Biculturalism
    Civilization
    Cultural Change
    Cultural Conflict
    Cultural Groups
    Cultural Identity
    Cultural Pluralism
    Cultural Transmission
    Cultural Values
    Culture
    Culture Contact
    Ethnic Groups
    Ethnicity
    Indigenous Populations
    Intercultural Communication
    Language Shift
    Mestizos
    Refugees
    Social Integration
    Subcultures

Acquired

Accumulation
  DC D005700
  HN Formerly (1969-1985) DC 006009, Accumulation/Accumulations.
  RT Capital
    Marxist Economics
    Political Economy
    Property
    Saving
    Wealth

Accuracy
  DC D005800
  HN Formerly (1969-1985) DC 006050.
  RT Bias
    Errors
    Judgment
    Measurement
    Quality
    Reliability
    Truth
    Validity
    Verification

Accusatorial Legal System
  Use Adversary Legal System

Achievement
  DC D006000
  HN Formerly (1963-1985) DC 008000, Achieve/Achiever/Achieved/Achievement/Achievements.
  UF Accomplish/Accomplished/Accomplishment (1972-1985)
    Merit/Merits (1963-1985)
  NT Academic Achievement
    Occupational Achievement
  RT Ability
    Achievement Tests
    Ascription
    Aspiration
    Attainment
    Awards
    Effectiveness
    Evaluation
    Expectations
    Failure
    Genius
    Goals
    Improvement
    Motivation
    Performance
    Pragmatism
    Quality
    Recognition (Achievement)
    Social Mobility
    Standards
    Success

Achievement Tests
  DC D006300
  HN Added, 1986.
  BT Tests
  RT Achievement
    Placement

Acquaintance/Acquaintances (1965-1985)
  HN DC 009500, deleted 1986. See now Friendship or Social Contact.

Acquiescence (1963-1985)
  HN DC 010800, deleted 1986.

Acquired Immune Deficiency Syndrome
  DC D006400
  SN Collapse of the immune system due to viral infection during sexual intercourse and transfusions of infected blood, leading to death by ensuing opportunistic infections, particularly Kaposi's sarcoma and pneumosystic pneumonia.

Acquisitions

Acquired Immune Deficiency Syndrome (cont'd)
- **HN** Added, 1986.
- **UF** AIDS
- **BT** Diseases
- **RT** Health Problems

Acquisitions And Mergers
- **Use** Mergers

Acquit/Acquittal/Acquitting (1965-1985)
- **HN** DC 011000.
- **Use** Verdicts

Acting (Dramatic)
- **Use** Theater Arts

Action
- **DC** D006450
- **SN** A context-dependent term; select a more specific entry or coordinate with other terms.
- **HN** Formerly (1963-1985) part of DC 011700, Act/Acts/Action/Actionalism.
- **NT** Affirmative Action
  Communicative Action
  Political Action
  Social Action
- **RT** Action Research
  Action Theory
  Activism
  Behavior
  Intentionality
  Norms
  Praxis
  Symbolic Interactionism
  Will

Action Research
- **DC** D006500
- **SN** Study of social phenomena in a real context, rather than under artificially controlled conditions.
- **HN** Added, 1986.
- **BT** Research
- **NT** Evaluation Research
- **RT** Action
  Community Research
  Social Action
  Social Change
  Social Science Research

Action Theory
- **DC** D006550
- **SN** Initiated by Talcott Parsons, a theoretical framework linking deliberate and meaningful behavior to social and cultural structures through focus on goal orientation and normatively regulated social relations.
- **HN** Added, 1986.
- **UF** General Theory of Action
  Theory of Action
- **BT** Social Theories
- **RT** Action
  Communicative Action
  Figuration Sociology
  Functionalism
  Hermeneutics
  Holism
  Intentionality
  Interpretive Sociology
  Phenomenology
  Social Action
  Social Equilibrium
  Structuration
  Symbolic Interactionism
  Verstehen
  Voluntarism

Activism
- **DC** D006600
- **SN** Participation in movements espousing direct action to promote or hasten political or social change.
- **HN** Formerly (1964-1985) DC 012990, Active/Activist/Activists/Activism/Activeness.
- **UF** Militant/Militants/Militancy (1968-1985)
- **BT** Participation
- **RT** Action
  Agitation
  Citizen Participation
  Civil Disobedience
  Civil Rights Organizations
  Interest Groups
  Lobbying
  Movements
  Political Action
  Political Movements
  Progressivism
  Protest Movements
  Social Action
  Social Attitudes
  Social Change
  Social Criticism
  Social Interest
  Social Movements
  Volunteers

Activities
- **DC** D006900
- **SN** A context-dependent term; select a more specific entry or coordinate with other terms.
- **HN** Formerly (1963-1985) DC 013000, Activity/Activities.
- **UF** Activity Participation
- **NT** Camping
  Cultural Activities
  Games
  Physical Fitness
  Play
  Sports
  Tasks
  Television Viewing
- **RT** Amateurs
  Function
  Implementation
  Leisure
  Participation
  Praxis
  Recreation
  Services
  Travel
  Volunteers

Activity Participation
- **Use** Activities

Actors
- **DC** D007200
- **SN** Persons who perform in plays, motion pictures, etc.
- **HN** Formerly (1966-1985) DC 013100, Actor/Actors/Actresses.
- **UF** Actresses
- **BT** Artists
- **RT** Drama
  Films
  Television
  Theater Arts

Actresses
- **Use** Actors

Administration

Acts (Statutes)
- **Use** Statutes

Actualization (Self)
- **Use** Self Actualization

Actuary/Actuarial (1968-1985)
- **HN** DC 013220.
- **Use** Insurance

Adapt/Adaptive/Adaptability/Adaptation (1963-1985)
- **HN** DC 013300.
- **Use** Adjustment

Addict/Addicts/Addicted/Addictive/Addiction (1963-1985)
- **HN** DC 013500.
- **Use** Drug Addiction

Addis Ababa, Ethiopia
- **DC** D007400
- **HN** Added, 1989.
- **BT** Ethiopia

Aden (1972-1985)
- **HN** DC 013550.
- **Use** Yemen (Peoples Democratic Republic)

Adequacy (1963-1985)
- **HN** DC 013600, deleted 1986.

Adjustment
- **DC** D007500
- **SN** Refers broadly to psychological changes induced by a challenge, adversity, or growth process.
- **HN** Formerly (1963-1985) DC 013800, Adjustment/Adjustments.
- **UF** Accommodation/Accommodations (1963-1985)
  Adapt/Adaptive/Adaptability/Adaptation (1963-1985)
  Maladjustment/Maladjusted (1964-1985)
  Psychological Adjustment
  Readjustments (1967-1985)
  Social Maladaptation (1964-1985)
- **NT** Marital Adjustment
- **RT** Behavior
  Change
  Chronic Illness
  Conformity
  Cooptation
  Coping
  Counseling
  Deinstitutionalization
  Flexibility
  Life Events
  Life Stage Transitions
  Mental Health
  Orientation
  Problems
  Rehabilitation
  Socialization
  Well Being

Adler, Alfred
- **DC** D007650
- **SN** Born 7 February 1870 - died 28 May 1937.
- **HN** Formerly (1963-1985) DC 014050, Adler, A./Adlerian.

Administration
- **Use** Management

Administrative

Administrative Districts
 Use Districts

Administrators
 DC D007800
 HN Formerly (1963-1985) part of DC 014200, Administration/ Administrative/Administrator/ Administrators.
 BT Professional Workers
 NT Deans
   Directors
   Executives
   Managers
   Principals
   Superintendents
 RT Leadership
   Management
   Planners
   Policy Making
   Public Officials

Admissions
 DC D008100
 SN Admissions to health, educational, or other institutions or facilities.
 HN Formerly (1964-1985) DC 014300.
 UF Readmissions
 RT Discharge
   Hospitalization
   Institutionalization (Persons)
   Patients
   Schools

Adolescent Delinquency
 Use Juvenile Delinquency

Adolescents
 DC D008400
 SN Persons aged 13 to 17.
 HN Formerly (1963-1985) DC 014600, Adolescence/Adolescent/ Adolescents.
 UF Teenage/Teenagers (1963-1985)
 BT Age Groups
 RT Children
   Dating (Social)
   Family Relations
   High School Students
   Juvenile Delinquency
   Juvenile Offenders
   Parent Child Relations
   Premarital Sex
   Puberty
   Runaways
   Unwanted Pregnancy
   Unwed Mothers
   Young Adults
   Youth
   Youth Culture
   Youth Employment
   Youth Organizations

Adopted Children
 DC D008700
 HN Formerly (1963-1985) part of DC 014800, Adopt/Adoption/Adopted/ Adoptive.
 BT Children
 RT Foster Children
   Orphans
   Parent Child Relations
   Permanency Planning
   Placement
   Stepfamily

Adoption of Innovations
 DC D009000
 HN Added, 1986.
 UF Integration of Innovations
 RT Agricultural Mechanization
   Diffusion
   High Technology Industries
   Innovations
   Research Applications
   Sociology of Science
   Technological Innovations
   Technological Progress
   Technology Transfer
   Traditionalism
   Traditions

Adorno, Theodor Wiesengrund
 DC D009300
 SN Born 11 September 1903 - died 6 August 1969.
 HN Formerly (1964-1985) DC 014900, Adorno, T. W.

Adult Children
 DC D009500
 SN Adults in relationship to their parents, eg, as caregivers of elderly parents, or as affected by parental characteristics, for example, adult children of alcoholics.
 HN Added, 1989.
 UF Adult Offspring
 BT Children
 RT Adults
   Family Life
   Family Relations
   Family Role
   Filial Responsibility
   Intergenerational Relations
   Parent Child Relations
   Parents

Adult Development
 DC D009600
 SN Psychosocial growth and change during adulthood, distinguished from that determined by biological growth during childhood.
 HN Added, 1986.
 BT Development
 RT Adults
   Aging
   Cognitive Development
   Developmental Stages
   Individuals
   Life Stage Transitions
   Moral Development
   Psychological Development

Adult Dropouts
 Use Dropouts

Adult Education
 DC D009900
 HN Added, 1986.
 UF Continuing Education
   Further Education
 BT Education
 RT Adults
   Elementary Education
   Higher Education
   Literacy Programs
   Secondary Education

Adult Offspring
 Use Adult Children

Advisors

Adult Runaways
 Use Runaways

Adultery (1968-1985)
 HN DC 015500.
 Use Extramarital Sexuality

Adulthood
 Use Adults

Adults
 DC D010500
 SN Persons aged 18 years or older.
 HN Formerly (1963-1985) DC 015000, Adult/Adults/Adulthood.
 UF Adulthood
 BT Age Groups
 NT Elderly
   Middle Aged Adults
   Young Adults
 RT Adult Children
   Adult Development
   Adult Education
   Family Life
   Filial Responsibility
   Parents

Advancement/Advancements (1968-1985)
 HN DC 015550, deleted 1986. See now Promotion (Occupational), Technological Progress, or Social Mobility.

Advantage/Advantages/Advantaged (1969-1985)
 HN DC 015563.
 Use Privilege

Adversary Legal System
 DC D010800
 HN Formerly (1965-1985) DC 015575, Adversary/Adversaries.
 UF Accusatorial Legal System
 BT Legal System
 RT Arbitration
   Criminal Proceedings
   Litigation
   Sociology of Law

Advertisements
 Use Advertising

Advertising
 DC D011100
 HN Formerly (1963-1985) DC 016000, Advertise/Advertising/ Advertisement/Advertisements.
 UF Advertisements
 BT Publicity
 RT Brand Names
   Discourse
   Fashions
   Marketing
   Mass Media
   Mass Media Effects
   Public Relations
   Purchasing
   Retail Industry
   Sales

Advisors
 DC D011400
 HN Formerly (1964-1985) part of DC 016200, Advise/Advisor/Advisors/ Advisory/Advising/Advice.
 BT Specialists
 RT Advisory Committees
   Consultants
   Experts
   Professional Consultation

Advisory — Age

Advisory Committees
- DC D011700
- HN Added, 1986.
- UF Advisory Organizations
- BT Committees
- RT Advisors
  Governing Boards

Advisory Organizations
- Use Advisory Committees

Advocacy
- DC D012000
- SN Support or defense of a particular individual, group, or cause.
- HN Formerly (1982-1985) DC 016205.
- UF Advocate (1971-1985)
- RT Legal Profession
  Representation
  Services

Advocate (1971-1985)
- HN DC 016225.
- Use Advocacy

Aesthetics
- DC D012300
- HN Formerly (1970-1985) DC 016250, Aesthetic/Aesthetics.
- UF Esthetic/Esthetics/Estheticism/ Esthete (1963-1985)
- NT Marxist Aesthetics
- RT Art
  Artistic Styles
  Cultural Values
  Literary Criticism
  Social Values
  Sociology of Art
  Sociology of Literature

AFDC/Aid for Families of Dependent Children (1965-1985)
- HN DC 016275.
- Use Welfare Services

Affair/Affairs (1963-1985)
- HN DC 016300, deleted 1986. See now Extramarital Sexuality or International Relations.

Affect/Affects/Affected (1963-1985)
- HN DC 017000.
- Use Emotions

Affection (1964-1985)
- HN DC 017295.
- Use Love

Affective Illness
- DC D012450
- HN Added, 1986.
- UF Emotional Illness
- NT Depression (Psychology)
- RT Anxiety
  Mental Illness

Affectivity/Affective (1963-1985)
- HN DC 017320.
- Use Emotions

Affiliation
- Use Membership

Affiliation Need
- DC D012600
- HN Formerly (1963-1985) part of DC 017600, Affiliate/Affiliates/Affiliated/ Affiliation/Affiliative.
- UF Affiliative Need
- BT Needs
- RT Acceptance
  Approval

Affiliation Need (cont'd)
- RT Friendship
  Membership
  Peer Groups
  Social Acceptance
  Social Groups
  Social Identity
  Social Isolation
  Social Participation
  Social Support

Affiliative Need
- Use Affiliation Need

Affinity (Attraction)
- Use Interpersonal Attraction

Affinity (Kinship)
- DC D012700
- SN A social relationship based on marriage or adoption (eg, inlaws) rather than blood ties. Contrasted with Consanguinity.
- HN Formerly (1964-1985) DC 018200, Affinity/Affinal.
- RT Consanguinity
  Kinship
  Marriage
  Relatives

Affirmative Action
- DC D012900
- SN Programs and policies designed to overcome underrepresentation of women and minority groups in employment and post-secondary education, relative to the composition of the area population.
- HN Formerly (1977-1985) DC 018352.
- BT Action
- RT Disadvantaged
  Discrimination
  Educational Policy
  Employment Discrimination
  Employment Opportunities
  Females
  Hiring Practices
  Minority Groups
  Occupational Segregation
  Opportunities
  Personnel Policy
  Quotas
  Social Action
  Social Reform
  Tokenism

Affluence
- DC D013200
- HN Formerly (1963-1985) DC 018355, Affluent/Affluence.
- UF Abundance (1969-1985)
  Prosperity (1964-1985)
- BT Economic Conditions
- RT Living Conditions
  Poverty
  Quality of Life
  Socioeconomic Status
  Standard of Living
  Wealth
  Well Being

Afghanistan
- DC D013500
- HN Formerly (1964-1985) DC 018360, Afghan/Afghanistan/Afghanistani/ Afghanistanis.
- BT Middle East
- NT Kabul, Afghanistan

Africa
- DC D013800
- SN See also specific countries, eg, Ethiopia, Sudan.
- HN Formerly (1963-1985) DC 018500, Africa/African/Africans.
- NT North Africa
  Sub Saharan Africa
- RT African Cultural Groups
  Pan-Africanism

African Cultural Groups
- DC D014100
- HN Added, 1986. Prior to 1986, concepts representing specific African cultural groups, eg, Kenyans, were often indexed under terms representing the geographic place name, eg, Kenya/Kenyan/Kenyans.
- BT Cultural Groups
- NT African Cultural Groups
  North African Cultural Groups
  Southern African Cultural Groups
- RT Africa
  African Languages
  Arab Cultural Groups
  Traditional Societies

African Languages
- DC D014400
- HN Added, 1986.
- UF Bantu Languages
  Bantuide Languages
  Igbo
  Khoin Languages
  Sudanic Languages
- BT Languages
- NT Swahili
- RT African Cultural Groups

Afrikaans
- Use Germanic Languages

Afrikaner/Afrikaners (1970-1985)
- HN DC 018502, deleted 1986. See now African Cultural Groups.

Afro (1963-1985)
- HN DC 018505.
- Use Blacks

After Care
- DC D014700
- SN Continuing program of follow-up and rehabilitation designed to reinforce the effects of treatment and promote adjustment.
- HN Formerly (1967-1985) DC 018600.
- UF Followup Treatment
- RT Discharge
  Health Care
  Home Health Care
  Institutionalization (Persons)
  Outpatients
  Self Care
  Treatment Programs

Age
- DC D014850
- HN Formerly (1963-1985) part of DC 019998, Age/Ageism.
- BT Physical Characteristics
- RT Age Differences
  Age Groups
  Aging
  Demographic Characteristics
  Time

Age

Age Cohorts
  Use Age Groups

Age Differences
  DC D015000
  SN Used in analyses in which a social problem or phenomenon is explained as a consequence or correlate of differences in the ages of a similar subject population.
  HN Added, 1986.
  BT Differences
  RT Age
      Age Groups
      Child Development
      Generational Differences
      Individual Differences
      Physical Characteristics
      Sex Differences

Age Groups
  DC D015300
  SN The narrower terms listed below refer to groups with fixed age ranges, which are specified in their scope notes.
  HN Added, 1986.
  UF Age Cohorts
  BT Groups
  NT Adolescents
      Adults
      Children
      Elderly
      Infants
      Middle Aged Adults
      Young Adults
  RT Age
      Age Differences
      Childhood
      Cohort Analysis
      Demographic Characteristics
      Generational Differences
      Individuals
      Intergenerational Relations
      Peer Groups
      Peers
      Youth

Aged (1963-1985)
  HN DC 020000.
  Use Elderly

Ageism
  DC D015400
  SN Entrenched prejudices about people based on perceived age, particularly negative perceptions of the elderly.
  HN Formerly (1971-1985) part of DC 019998, Age/Ageism.
  BT Discrimination
  RT Aging
      Bias
      Elderly
      Prejudice
      Retirement
      Social Attitudes

Agencies
  DC D015500
  SN Do not confuse with 'agency', which may refer to the power to exert a causal influence.
  HN Formerly (1963-1985) DC 020200, Agency/Agencies.
  BT Organizations (Social)
  NT Government Agencies
      Social Agencies
  RT Associations
      Centers

Agencies (cont'd)
  RT Charities
      Clinics
      Delivery Systems
      Nonprofit Organizations
      Services

Agency
  Use Causality

Agents (Change)
  Use Change Agents

Agents (Socialization)
  Use Socialization Agents

Aggregate Data
  DC D015550
  HN Formerly (1963-1985) DC 020400, Aggregate/Aggregation/Aggregative.
  UF Aggregative Analysis
  BT Data
  RT Profiles
      Quantitative Methods
      Secondary Analysis

Aggregative Analysis
  Use Aggregate Data

Aggression
  DC D015600
  HN Formerly (1963-1985) DC 020800, Aggression/Aggressive/Aggressiveness.
  UF Aggressive Behavior
  BT Social Behavior
  RT Assertiveness
      Behavior Problems
      Competition
      Conflict
      Crime
      Delinquency
      Dominance
      Frustration
      Hostility
      Interpersonal Conflict
      Invasion
      Social Interaction
      Threat
      Violence
      War

Aggressive Behavior
  Use Aggression

Aging
  DC D015900
  HN Formerly (1963-1985) DC 021000.
  UF Old Age (1963-1985)
  BT Life Cycle
  RT Adult Development
      Age
      Ageism
      Elder Abuse
      Elderly
      Gerontology
      Life Stage Transitions
      Middle Aged Adults
      Senility

Agitation
  DC D016150
  HN Formerly (1965-1985) DC 021030, Agitation/Agitator/Agitators.
  UF Political Agitation
      Social Agitation
  RT Activism
      Mobilization
      Persuasion

Agrarian

Agitation (cont'd)
  RT Political Action
      Propaganda
      Social Action
      Social Change
      Social Movements
      Social Unrest

Agnate/Agnation (1967-1985)
  HN DC 021065.
  Use Patrilineality

Agnosticism
  DC D016200
  HN Formerly (1966-1985) DC 021075, Agnostic/Agnostics/Agnosticism.
  UF Agnostics
  BT Philosophical Doctrines
      Religious Beliefs
  RT Atheism
      Heresy
      Humanism
      Rationalism
      Skepticism

Agnostics
  Use Agnosticism

Agrarian Reform
  Use Land Reform

Agrarian Societies
  DC D016500
  HN Formerly (1963-1985) part of DC 021100, Agrarian/Agrarianism.
  BT Traditional Societies
  RT Agricultural Economics
      Agriculture
      Dual Economy
      Economic Underdevelopment
      Peasant Societies

Agrarian Structures
  DC D016800
  SN Patterns or interrelationships of agricultural institutions, including land tenure, production, and supporting services.
  HN Formerly (1963-1985) part of DC 021100, Agrarian/Agrarianism.
  UF Agrarian Systems
      Agricultural Structures
      Farming Systems
  NT Crofting
      Homesteading
      Sharecropping
  RT Agricultural Collectives
      Agricultural Economics
      Agricultural Enterprises
      Agricultural Policy
      Agricultural Research
      Agriculture
      Common Lands
      Economic Structure
      Economic Systems
      Feudalism
      Land Reform
      Land Tenure
      Land Use
      Peasant Societies
      Plantations
      Rural Areas
      Small Farms
      Structure

Agrarian

Agrarian Systems
  Use Agrarian Structures

Agreement
  DC D017100
  HN Formerly (1963-1985) DC 021108, Agreement/Agreements.
  NT Consensus
  RT Alliance
      Disputes
      Informed Consent
      Interpersonal Communication
      Persuasion
      Rapport
      Similarity

Agreements
  Use Contracts

Agribusiness
  DC D017400
  HN Added, 1986.
  BT Business
  RT Agricultural Economics
      Agricultural Enterprises
      Agricultural Mechanization
      Agricultural Production
      Agricultural Technology
      Agriculture
      Farms
      Rural Development

Agricultural Collectives
  DC D017700
  HN Added, 1986.
  UF Collective Farms
      Kolkhoz/Kolkhozes (1965-1985)
      Moshav (1964-1985)
  BT Agricultural Enterprises
      Collectives
  RT Agrarian Structures
      Communes
      Kibbutz
      Maoism
      Stalinism

Agricultural Communities
  Use Rural Communities

Agricultural Development
  DC D018000
  HN Added, 1986.
  BT Economic Development
  NT Agricultural Mechanization
  RT Agricultural Economics
      Agricultural Policy
      Agricultural Production
      Agricultural Research
      Agricultural Technology
      Agriculture
      Extension Services
      Land Use
      Livestock
      Natural Resources
      Rural Development

Agricultural Economics
  DC D018300
  HN Added, 1986.
  BT Economics
  RT Agrarian Societies
      Agrarian Structures
      Agribusiness
      Agricultural Development
      Agricultural Enterprises
      Agricultural Policy
      Agricultural Production
      Agricultural Research
      Agricultural Workers

Agricultural Economics (cont'd)
  RT Agriculture
      Land Tenure
      Part Time Farming
      Small Farms
      Subsistence Economy

Agricultural Engineering
  Use Agricultural Technology

Agricultural Enterprises
  DC D018600
  HN Added, 1986.
  BT Enterprises
  NT Agricultural Collectives
      Farms
      Plantations
  RT Agrarian Structures
      Agribusiness
      Agricultural Economics
      Agricultural Production
      Agriculture
      Farmers
      Homesteading
      Land Tenure

Agricultural Extension
  Use Extension Services

Agricultural Mechanization
  DC D018900
  HN Added, 1986.
  UF Farm Mechanization
  BT Agricultural Development
  RT Adoption of Innovations
      Agribusiness
      Agricultural Policy
      Agricultural Production
      Agricultural Research
      Agricultural Technology
      Agriculture
      Automation
      Farms
      Innovations
      Machinery
      Technological Change

Agricultural Policy
  DC D019200
  HN Added, 1986.
  BT Economic Policy
  RT Agrarian Structures
      Agricultural Development
      Agricultural Economics
      Agricultural Mechanization
      Agriculture
      Government Policy
      Hunting
      Land Reform
      Land Use
      Public Policy
      Rural Development
      Soil Conservation

Agricultural Production
  DC D019500
  HN Added, 1986.
  UF Crop Production
      Farm Production
  BT Production
  RT Agribusiness
      Agricultural Development
      Agricultural Economics
      Agricultural Enterprises
      Agricultural Mechanization
      Agricultural Research
      Agriculture
      Animal Husbandry

Agriculture

Agricultural Production (cont'd)
  RT Commodities
      Farmers
      Farms
      Livestock

Agricultural Research
  DC D019800
  HN Added, 1986.
  BT Research
  RT Agrarian Structures
      Agricultural Development
      Agricultural Economics
      Agricultural Mechanization
      Agricultural Production
      Agricultural Technology
      Agriculture
      Animal Husbandry
      Eugenics

Agricultural Structures
  Use Agrarian Structures

Agricultural Technology
  DC D020100
  HN Added, 1986.
  UF Agricultural Engineering
      Farm Technology
  BT Technology
  NT Irrigation
  RT Agribusiness
      Agricultural Development
      Agricultural Mechanization
      Agricultural Research
      Agriculture
      Chemistry
      Extension Services
      Farms
      Land Use
      Machinery
      Pesticides
      Small Farms
      Soil Conservation

Agricultural Workers
  DC D020400
  SN Unskilled manual laborers employed to work on farms, ranches, or other agricultural operations.
  HN Added, 1986.
  UF Farm Workers
  BT Blue Collar Workers
  NT Peasants
  RT Agricultural Economics
      Agriculture
      Animal Husbandry
      Farmers
      Farms
      Migrant Workers
      Plantations
      Rural Population

Agriculture
  DC D020700
  HN Formerly (1963-1985) DC 021120, Agriculture/Agricultural.
  UF Agronomy/Agronomists (1969-1985)
      Farming
  NT Animal Husbandry
      Part Time Farming
  RT Agrarian Societies
      Agrarian Structures
      Agribusiness
      Agricultural Development
      Agricultural Economics
      Agricultural Enterprises
      Agricultural Mechanization
      Agricultural Policy

Agriculturists

Agriculture (cont'd)
- RT Agricultural Production
  Agricultural Research
  Agricultural Technology
  Agricultural Workers
  Agriculture
  Commodities
  Economic Sectors
  Farmers
  Farms
  Food
  Food Industry
  Gardening
  Industry
  Land Use
  Plants (Botanical)
  Rural Areas
  Soil Conservation

Agriculturists (1963-1985)
- HN DC 021140.
- Use Farmers

Agronomy/Agronomists (1969-1985)
- HN DC 021150.
- Use Agriculture

Aid (1963-1985)
- HN DC 021160.
- Use Assistance

AIDS
- Use Acquired Immune Deficiency Syndrome

Aims (1968-1985)
- HN DC 021170.
- Use Goals

Air Force (1963-1985)
- HN DC 022000.
- Use Armed Forces

Air Pollution
- DC D021000
- HN Added, 1986.
- UF Atmospheric Contamination
  Smog
- BT Pollution
- RT Human Ecology
  Pollution Control
  Urban Areas
  Wastes

Air Transportation
- DC D021300
- HN Added, 1986.
- UF Aircraft (1970-1985)
  Airline Traffic (1977-1985)
  Aviation (1970-1985)
- BT Transportation
- RT Accidents
  Public Transportation
  Traffic

Aircraft (1970-1985)
- HN DC 021400.
- Use Air Transportation

Airline Traffic (1977-1985)
- HN DC 022500.
- Use Air Transportation

Alabama
- DC D021600
- HN Formerly (1963-1985) DC 023400, Alabama/Alabaman/Alabamans.
- BT Southern States
  United States of America
- RT Appalachia

Alaska
- DC D021900
- HN Formerly (1964-1985) DC 024000, Alaska/Alaskan/Alaskans.
- BT United States of America
- RT Arctic Regions

Albania
- DC D022200
- HN Formerly (1966-1985) DC 024400, Albania/Albanian/Albanians.
- BT Balkan States
  Eastern Europe

Alberta
- DC D022500
- HN Added, 1986.
- BT Canada

Alcohol (1963-1985)
- HN DC 025000, deleted 1986. See now specific "Alcohol" terms.

Alcohol Abuse
- DC D022700
- SN Overuse or misuse of alcoholic beverages. Do not confuse with Alcoholism.
- HN Added, 1989.
- BT Alcohol Use
  Substance Abuse
- NT Alcoholism
- RT Drinking Behavior
  Drug Abuse
  Drunkenness

Alcohol Consumption
- Use Alcohol Use

Alcohol Dependency
- Use Alcoholism

Alcohol Detoxification
- Use Detoxification

Alcohol Intoxication
- Use Drunkenness

Alcohol Use
- DC D022800
- HN Added, 1986. Prior to 1986 use DC 025000, Alcohol.
- UF Alcohol Consumption
  Drinking/Drinkers (1963-1985)
  Social Drinking
- NT Alcohol Abuse
- RT Alcoholic Beverages
  Alcoholism
  Behavior
  Drinking Behavior
  Drug Use
  Drunk Driving
  Drunkenness
  Health
  Temperance Movements

Alcoholic Beverages
- DC D023100
- HN Added, 1986.
- UF Beverages (Alcoholic)
  Liquor (1966-1985)
- RT Alcohol Use
  Drugs

Alcoholics
- Use Alcoholism

Alienation

Alcoholism
- DC D023400
- HN Formerly (1963-1985) DC 027000, Alcoholic/Alcoholics/Alcoholism.
- UF Alcohol Dependency
  Alcoholics
- BT Alcohol Abuse
  Diseases
- RT Alcohol Use
  Detoxification
  Deviant Behavior
  Drinking Behavior
  Drug Addiction
  Drunkenness
  Mental Illness
  Temperance Movements

Alexander, Jeffrey C.
- DC D023600
- SN Born 30 May 1974 - .
- HN Added, 1989.

Algebra/Algebraic (1964-1985)
- HN DC 027330.
- Use Mathematics

Algeria
- DC D023700
- HN Formerly (1963-1985) DC 027400, Algeria/Algerian/Algerians.
- BT Arab Countries
  Mediterranean Countries
  North Africa
- NT Algiers, Algeria

Algiers, Algeria
- DC D023750
- HN Added, 1989.
- BT Algeria

Algorithms
- DC D023800
- SN Sequences of steps in a procedure with known results.
- HN Formerly (1983-1984) DC 027420, Algorithm/Algorithms.
- RT Computation
  Mathematics
  Methods

Alien/Aliens (1984-1985)
- HN DC 027432.
- Use Foreigners

Alienation
- DC D024000
- SN In Marxist analysis, estrangement from self or society due to loss of control over the means of making a living in capitalist systems. In other contexts, the sense of powerlessness produced by rapid diffusion of new technologies and other social changes.
- HN Formerly (1963-1985) DC 027440, Alienation/Alienated.
- UF Estrangement (1965-1985)
  Meaninglessness
  Powerless/Powerlessness (1970-1985)
- BT Emotions
- RT Anomie
  Apathy
  Depersonalization
  Disengagement
  Disorders
  Existentialism
  Hostility
  Individual Collective Relationship

Alienation (cont'd)
- **RT** Loneliness
  Marginality
  Marxist Analysis
  Mass Society
  Pessimism
  Reification
  Role Conflict
  Social Attitudes
  Social Isolation

Alignment/Alignments (1975-1985)
- **HN** DC 027470, deleted 1986.

Alimony
- **DC** D024300
- **HN** Formerly (1967-1985) DC 027500.
- **RT** Annulment
  Child Support
  Divorce
  Financial Support

Alinsky, Saul David
- **DC** D024600
- **SN** Born 30 January 1909 - died 12 June 1972.
- **HN** Formerly (1974-1985) DC 027560, Alinsky, Saul.

Aliyah
- **DC** D024900
- **HN** Formerly (1964-1985) DC 027600.
- **RT** Jews
  Zionism

Alliance
- **DC** D025200
- **HN** Formerly (1963-1985) DC 027725, Alliance/Alliances.
- **UF** Social Alliance/Social Alliances (1985)
- **BT** Interaction
- **RT** Agreement
  Coalitions
  Conflict
  Cooperation
  Intergroup Relations
  International Alliances
  International Relations
  Social Behavior
  War

Allied Countries
- **Use** International Alliances

Allied Health Personnel
- **Use** Paramedical Personnel

Allocation
- **DC** D025500
- **HN** Formerly (1972-1985) DC 027740.
- **NT** Resource Allocation
- **RT** Appropriation
  Distribution
  Distributive Justice

Allocation of Resources
- **Use** Resource Allocation

Allport, Gordon Willard
- **DC** D025800
- **SN** Born 11 November 1897 - died 9 October 1967.
- **HN** Formerly (1966-1985) DC 027770, Allport, G. W.

Alpine (1964-1985)
- **HN** DC 027900.
- **Use** Mountain Regions

Alsace, France (1965-1985)
- **HN** DC 028000, deleted 1986.

Altaic Language (1965-1985)
- **HN** DC 029000.
- **Use** Oriental Languages

Altercasting (1964-1985)
- **HN** DC 029400.
- **Use** Impression Management

Alternative Approaches
- **DC** D026000
- **SN** Programs, systems, or procedures offered as alternatives to established or traditional forms or methods. Do not confuse with Choices.
- **HN** Formerly (1963-1985) DC 029600, Alternative/Alternatives.
- **UF** Nontraditional Approaches
- **RT** Appropriate Technologies
  Innovations
  Methods

Alternative Lifestyle
- **Use** Lifestyle

Althusser, Louis
- **DC** D026100
- **SN** Born 16 October 1918 - .
- **HN** Formerly (1971-1985) DC 029610.

Altitude Effects
- **DC** D026400
- **HN** Formerly (1972-1985) DC 029620, Altitude/Altitudes.
- **UF** Elevation Effects
- **BT** Effects
- **RT** Environmental Factors
  Mountain Regions

Altruism
- **DC** D026700
- **SN** Principle of regard for the interests and needs of others, including social groups. Often contrasted with Egoism and Individualism.
- **HN** Formerly (1963-1985) DC 029650, Altruism/Altruistic.
- **BT** Social Behavior
- **RT** Charities
  Cooperation
  Egoism
  Ethics
  Gift Giving
  Helping Behavior
  Humanitarianism
  Interpersonal Relations
  Philanthropy
  Sharing
  Social Attitudes
  Social Interest
  Social Values
  Volunteers

Alumnus/Alumnae (1967-1985)
- **HN** DC 029800, deleted 1986. See now Graduates or College Graduates.

Alzheimer's Disease
- **DC** D026800
- **SN** A disease of old age characterized by progressive loss of memory and of mental and social competence.
- **HN** Added, 1989.
- **BT** Diseases
- **RT** Brain
  Neurology
  Senility

Amateur Athletes
- **Use** Athletes

Amateur Status
- **Use** Amateurs

Amateurs
- **DC** D027000
- **HN** Formerly (1984-1985) DC 029816, Amateur.
- **UF** Amateur Status
- **RT** Activities
  Interests
  Laymen
  Leisure
  Sports

Amazon
- **DC** D027300
- **HN** Formerly (1969-1985) DC 029820.
- **RT** Brazil
  South America

Ambiguity
- **DC** D027400
- **HN** Formerly (1963-1985) DC 030000, Ambiguity/Ambiguities.
- **UF** Double Meaning
- **NT** Role Ambiguity
- **RT** Communication
  Concepts
  Meaning
  Stress

Ambilineal (1964-1985)
- **HN** DC 030040, deleted 1986.

Ambition/Ambitions (1964-1985)
- **HN** DC 030102.
- **Use** Aspiration

Ambivalence
- **DC** D027600
- **HN** Formerly (1964-1985) DC 030104, Ambivalence/Ambivalent.
- **BT** Social Behavior
- **RT** Decision Making
  Emotions

Amendments (Constitutional)
- **Use** Constitutional Amendments

America/American/Americans (1963-1985)
- **HN** DC 030150, deleted 1986. See now North American Cultural Groups, Latin American Cultural Groups, or appropriate geographic terms, eg, North America, Latin America, United States of America, and their associated terms.

American Anthropological Association (1969-1985)
- **HN** DC 030180.
- **Use** Professional Associations

American Fed of Labor & Cong of Ind Orgs (1963-1985)
- **HN** DC 030185. Abbreviated here due to character restrictions. Formerly used in indexing under its full name American Federation of Labor & Congress of Industrial Organizations.
- **Use** Unions

American Indian Reservations
- **DC** D027900
- **HN** Formerly (1963-1985) DC 385730, Reservation.
- **UF** Reservations (American Indian)
- **RT** American Indians
  Relocation

American   Andes

American Indian Reservations
(cont'd)
- **RT** Separatism
  Social Isolation
  Traditional Societies
  Treaties

American Indians
- **DC** D028200
- **SN** Indigenous social groups of North, Central, and South America. For specific tribes, use Traditional Societies and the appropriate geographical descriptor.
- **HN** Formerly (1984-1985) DC 030160, American Indian/American Indians.
- **UF** Amerind/Amerinds/Amerindian (1979-1985)
  Indian/Indians (1964-1985)
  Native American/Native Americans (1979-1985)
- **BT** Latin American Cultural Groups
  North American Cultural Groups
- **NT** Mayans
- **RT** American Indian Reservations
  Amerindian Languages
  Indigenous Populations
  Mestizos
  Potlatches
  Traditional Societies

American Psychological Association
(1965-1985)
- **HN** DC 030200.
- **Use** Professional Associations

American Samoa
- **DC** D028500
- **HN** Added, 1986. Prior to 1986 use Samoa (DC 400800).
- **BT** Polynesia

American Sociological Association
(1963-1985)
- **HN** DC 030340.
- **Use** Sociological Associations

American Statistical Association
(1966-1985)
- **HN** DC 030350.
- **Use** Professional Associations

Americanization (1963-1985)
- **HN** DC 030170.
- **Use** Acculturation

Americas, The (1963-1985)
- **HN** DC 030360, deleted 1986. See now North America, Latin America, South America, Central America, or United States of America.

Amerind/Amerinds/Amerindian
(1979-1985)
- **HN** DC 030370.
- **Use** American Indians

Amerindian Languages
- **DC** D028800
- **HN** Added, 1986.
- **UF** Central American Indian Languages
  North American Indian Languages
  South American Indian Languages
- **BT** Languages
- **RT** American Indians

Amharic
- **Use** Semitic Languages

Amish
- **DC** D029100
- **HN** Formerly (1964-1985) DC 030380.
- **UF** Old Order Amish
- **BT** Protestants
- **RT** Mennonites
  Protestantism

Amniocentesis
- **DC** D029400
- **SN** Medical procedure for ascertaining the gender and health of the fetus by analysis of the mother's amniotic fluid.
- **HN** Formerly (1985) DC 030600.
- **RT** Fetus
  Pregnancy
  Reproductive Technologies

Amsterdam, Netherlands
- **DC** D029700
- **HN** Formerly (1963-1985) DC 030700, Amsterdam, Holland.
- **BT** Netherlands

Amusement Industry
- **Use** Entertainment Industry

Amusement/Amusements (1967-1985)
- **HN** DC 030800.
- **Use** Recreational Facilities

Anabaptist Church
- **Use** Anabaptists

Anabaptists
- **DC** D030000
- **HN** Formerly (1963-1985) DC 030807, Anabaptist/Anabaptists.
- **UF** Anabaptist Church
- **BT** Protestants
- **RT** Millenarianism
  Protestantism

Analogy
- **DC** D030100
- **HN** Formerly (1963-1985) DC 030810, Analogue/Analogy/Analogies.
- **RT** Comparative Analysis
  Inference
  Logic
  Reasoning

Analysis
- **DC** D030200
- **SN** A context-dependent term; select a more specific entry or coordinate with other terms.
- **HN** Formerly (1963-1985) DC 031400, Analysis/Analyses/Analyzing.
- **UF** Analytic/Analytical (1963-1985)
- **NT** Class Analysis
  Cohort Analysis
  Comparative Analysis
  Componential Analysis
  Content Analysis
  Conversational Analysis
  Discourse Analysis
  Latent Structure Analysis
  Marxist Analysis
  Network Analysis
  Policy Analysis
  Principal Components Analysis
  Secondary Analysis
  Social Area Analysis

Analysis (cont'd)
- **NT** Spatial Analysis
  Structural-Functional Analysis
  Time Series Analysis
- **RT** Classification
  Constructs
  Dramaturgical Approach
  Evaluation
  Hermeneutics
  Ideal Types
  Methodology (Data Analysis)
  Methodology (Philosophical)
  Profiles
  Qualitative Methods
  Quantitative Methods
  Research
  Trends
  Typology
  Verstehen

Analysis of Variance
- **Use** Variance (Statistics)

Analytic/Analytical (1963-1985)
- **HN** DC 031420.
- **Use** Analysis

Anarchism
- **DC** D030300
- **HN** Formerly (1964-1985) DC 031440, Anarchy/Anarchism/Anarchist/Anarchists/Anarchic/Anarchistic.
- **BT** Political Ideologies
- **RT** Nihilism
  Syndicalism
  Vigilantism

Anatolia, Turkey (1963-1985)
- **HN** DC 031450.
- **Use** Turkey

Anatomy/Anatomical (1964-1985)
- **HN** DC 031470, deleted 1986.

Ancestor Worship
- **DC** D030600
- **HN** Added, 1986. Prior to 1986 use Ancestor/Ancestors/Ancestral (DC 031500) and Worship (DC 493440).
- **BT** Worship
- **RT** Asian Cultural Groups
  Confucianism
  Ghosts
  Religions
  Shintoism
  Spirits
  Traditional Societies
  Voodooism

Ancient Greek Philosophy
- **DC** D030750
- **HN** Added, 1986.
- **UF** Aristotle/Aristotelian (1964-1985)
  Greek Philosophy
  Plato/Platonic (1964-1985)
  Socrates/Socratic (1966-1985)
  Stoicism (1964-1985)
- **BT** Philosophy
- **RT** Antiquity
  Philosophers

Ancient Times (1963-1985)
- **HN** DC 031530.
- **Use** Antiquity

Andes
- **DC** D030900
- **HN** Formerly (1964-1985) DC 031550, Andes/Andean.
- **RT** Mountain Regions

Andhra

Andes (cont'd)
- RT South America

Andhra Pradesh, India
- DC D031200
- HN Formerly (1966-1985) DC 031555.
- BT India

Andorra
- DC D031500
- HN Added, 1986.
- BT Western Europe

Androgyny
- DC D031800
- SN Integration of traditional male and female characteristics, including both biological/physical and psychological/behavioral traits.
- HN Formerly (1982-1985) DC 031558, Androgyny/Androgynous.
- RT Bisexuality
  Femininity
  Masculinity
  Personality Traits
  Sex Role Identity
  Sex Roles
  Womens Roles

Anemia/Anemic (1964-1985)
- HN DC 031560, deleted 1986.

Anesthetic (1963-1985)
- HN DC 031565, deleted 1986.

Anger
- DC D032100
- HN Formerly (1964-1985) DC 031600.
- BT Emotions
- NT Hostility
- RT Frustration
  Hate
  Social Behavior

Anglicans
- DC D032400
- HN Formerly (1967-1985) DC 031650, Anglican/Anglicans.
- UF Church of England
- BT Protestants
- RT Protestantism

Anglo Americans
- DC D032700
- HN Formerly (1963-1985) DC 031660, Anglo.
- BT Ethnic Groups
- RT Black White Differences
  North American Cultural Groups
  Whites

Anglophone/Anglophones (1982-1985)
- HN DC 031680.
- Use Ethnolinguistic Groups

Angola
- DC D033000
- HN Formerly (1982-1985) DC 031690.
- BT Sub Saharan Africa

Anguilla
- DC D033300
- HN Added, 1986.
- BT Caribbean

Anguish
- Use Psychological Distress

Animal Breeding
- Use Animal Husbandry

Animal Human Relations
- DC D033500
- SN Encompasses studies of the role of animals in human social life and culture.
- HN Added, 1989.
- UF Animal Rights
- BT Relations
- RT Animal Husbandry
  Animals
  Environmental Protection
  Natural Environment
  Pets

Animal Husbandry
- DC D033600
- HN Added, 1986.
- UF Animal Breeding
  Stock Farming
- BT Agriculture
- RT Agricultural Production
  Agricultural Research
  Agricultural Workers
  Animal Human Relations
  Animals
  Dairy Farms
  Eugenics
  Livestock
  Water Supply

Animal Rights
- Use Animal Human Relations

Animals
- DC D033900
- HN Formerly (1963-1985) DC 031800, Animal/Animals.
- UF Fauna
  Predators
- NT Livestock
  Pets
  Primates
- RT Animal Human Relations
  Animal Husbandry
  Hunting
  Natural Resources

Animism
- DC D034200
- SN Belief that natural phenomena and animate and inanimate objects in the environment possess an innate spirit.
- HN Formerly (1964-1985) DC 031840.
- RT Myths
  Paganism
  Religions
  Soul
  Spirits
  Totemism
  Traditional Societies

Annals (1969-1985)
- HN DC 031845.
- Use Records (Documents)

Annexation
- DC D034500
- HN Formerly (1965-1985) DC 031850, Annex/Annexes/Annexation/Annexed.
- UF Municipal Annexation
  Territorial Annexation
- RT City Planning
  Suburbs
  Urban Areas

ANOVA

Annihilate/Annihilation/Annihilated (1966-1985)
- HN DC 031860, deleted 1986.

Anniversaries
- Use Celebrations

Annotated Bibliographies
- Use Bibliographies

Annulment
- DC D034800
- HN Formerly (1964-1985) DC 031875.
- BT Marital Disruption
- RT Alimony
  Divorce
  Marital Satisfaction
  Remarriage

Anomia (1967-1985)
- HN DC 031895.
- Use Anomie

Anomie
- DC D035100
- SN French for normlessness, the term coined by Emile Durkheim to describe the disorientation brought about by rapid social change, for example, following rural to urban migration.
- HN Formerly (1963-1985) DC 031900, Anomie/Anomic.
- UF Anomia (1967-1985)
  Normless/Normlessness (1971-1985)
- RT Alienation
  Deviance
  Disorders
  Egoism
  Existentialism
  Goals
  Mass Society
  Social Behavior
  Social Cohesion
  Social Isolation
  Social Segmentation
  Social Values

Anonymity
- DC D035400
- HN Formerly (1963-1985) DC 031995, Anonymity/Anonymous.
- RT Privacy
  Public Behavior
  Self Disclosure
  Social Identity
  Social Perception

Anorexia Nervosa
- DC D035700
- SN Eating disorder primarily affecting young women, characterized by distorted body self-image and excessive dieting, sometimes to the point of starvation.
- HN Formerly (1984-1985) DC 032005, Anorexia.
- BT Eating Disorders
- RT Body Weight
  Bulimia
  Malnutrition
  Mental Illness

ANOVA
- Use Variance (Statistics)

Antagonism

Antagonism/Antagonize/Antagonist/Antagonists (1971-1985)
- **HN** DC 032300.
- **Use** Hostility

Antarctica
- **DC** D035900
- **HN** Added, 1986.

Antecedent/Antecedents (1969-1985)
- **HN** DC 032600, deleted 1986. See now Causality or Etiology.

Anthrobiology/Anthrobiological (1965-1985)
- **HN** DC 032700.
- **Use** Anthropology

Anthropologists
- **DC** D036000
- **HN** Formerly (1963-1985) DC 032900, Anthropologist/Anthropologists.
- **UF** Archaeologist/Archaeologists (1963-1985)
  Ethnologist/Ethnologists (1964-1985)
- **BT** Social Scientists
- **RT** Anthropology

Anthropology
- **DC** D036300
- **HN** Formerly (1963-1985) DC 033000, Anthropology/Anthropological.
- **UF** Anthrobiology/Anthrobiological (1965-1985)
  Physical Anthropology
- **BT** Social Sciences
- **NT** Archaeology
  Ethnography
  Ethnology
  Social Anthropology
- **RT** Anthropologists
  Comparative Sociology
  Crosscultural Analysis
  Cultural Pluralism
  Folk Culture
  Museums
  Prehistory
  Race

Anthropometry (1963-1985)
- **HN** DC 033200, deleted 1986.

Anticipation/Anticipatory (1964-1985)
- **HN** DC 033390.
- **Use** Expectations

Antigua
- **DC** D036600
- **HN** Added, 1986.
- **BT** Caribbean

Antilles (1964-1985)
- **HN** DC 033393.
- **Use** Caribbean

Antinuclear Movements
- **DC** D036900
- **HN** Formerly (1981-1985) DC 033394, Antinuclear.
- **UF** Nuclear Freeze Movement
- **BT** Peace Movements
- **RT** Disarmament
  Movements
  Nuclear Energy
  Nuclear War
  Nuclear Weapons
  Protest Movements

Antipoverty Programs
- **DC** D037200
- **HN** Formerly (1965-1985) DC 033395, Antipoverty.
- **UF** Poverty Programs
- **BT** Programs
  Social Programs
- **RT** Disadvantaged
  Government Policy
  Improvement
  Income Maintenance Programs
  Low Income Groups
  Poverty
  Social Policy
  Urban Renewal
  Welfare Services

Antiquity
- **DC** D037500
- **SN** Early period of history, especially before the Middle Ages.
- **HN** Formerly (1966-1985) DC 033398, Antique/Antiquity.
- **UF** Ancient Times (1963-1985)
  Assyria (1971-1985)
  Babylonia/Babylonian/Babylonians (1970-1985)
  Mesopotamia/Mesopotamian/Mesopotamians (1963-1985)
  Peloponnesia/Peloponnesian/Peloponnesians (1964-1985)
- **BT** Time Periods
- **RT** Ancient Greek Philosophy
  Archaeology
  Civilization
  History

Anti-Semitism
- **DC** D037800
- **SN** Economic, religious, or racial discrimination or prejudice against Jews.
- **HN** Formerly (1963-1985) DC 033400, Anti-Semitism/Anti-Semitic.
- **BT** Prejudice
- **RT** Holocaust
  Jews
  Nazism
  Racism
  Stereotypes

Antisocial (1981-1985)
- **HN** DC 033490.
- **Use** Deviant Behavior

Antisocial Personality
- **Use** Sociopathic Personality

Antwerp, Belgium
- **DC** D038100
- **HN** Formerly (1983-1985) DC 033535.
- **BT** Belgium

Anxiety
- **DC** D038400
- **HN** Formerly (1963-1985) DC 033600.
- **UF** Apprehension (1971-1985)
- **BT** Emotions
- **RT** Affective Illness
  Certainty
  Cognitive Dissonance
  Depression (Psychology)
  Fear
  Guilt
  Personality Traits
  Psychological Stress
  Tension
  Threat

Apartheid
- **DC** D038700
- **SN** System of racial segregation and political and economic discrimination against non-Europeans which has operated in the Republic of South Africa since 1948.
- **HN** Formerly (1964-1985) DC 035020.
- **RT** Blacks
  Government Policy
  Racial Segregation
  Racism
  Separatism
  Social Policy

Apartment/Apartments (1963-1985)
- **HN** DC 035070.
- **Use** Housing

Apathy
- **DC** D039000
- **HN** Formerly (1963-1985) DC 035080, Apathy/Apathetic.
- **UF** Indifference (1971-1985)
- **BT** Emotions
- **RT** Alienation
  Aspiration
  Boredom
  Disengagement
  Passiveness
  Political Attitudes
  Social Attitudes

Aphasia
- **DC** D039300
- **SN** Partial or complete loss of the ability to speak, as the result of a developmental disorder, disease, or brain injury.
- **HN** Formerly (1984-1985) DC 035087, Aphasia/Aphasic.
- **BT** Language Disorders
- **RT** Learning Disabilities

Apocalypse
- **DC** D039600
- **SN** Refers to the Book of Revelations in the New Testament and to fulfillment of the prophesies made there.
- **HN** Formerly (1963-1986) DC 035100, Apocalypse/Apocalyptic.
- **RT** Bible
  Prophecy
  Religious Beliefs

Apostasy
- **DC** D039900
- **SN** Abandonment or renunciation of a previous belief, loyalty, or religious faith.
- **HN** Formerly (1985) DC 035117, Apostasy/Aspostate/Apostatize.
- **RT** Heresy
  Political Defection
  Religions
  Religious Conversion
  Schism

Appalachia
- **DC** D040200
- **HN** Formerly (1964-1985) DC 035125, Appalachia/Appalachian/Appalachians.
- **RT** Alabama
  Georgia
  Kentucky
  Pennsylvania
  South Carolina
  Tennessee

Apparel

Appalachia (cont'd)
- RT Virginia
- West Virginia

Apparel Industry
- Use Garment Industry

Appearance/Appearances (1967-1985)
- HN DC 035130, deleted 1986. See now Attractiveness, Impression Management, or Self Presentation.

Appendectomy (1967-1985)
- HN DC 035133.
- Use Surgery

Applicability
- Use Relevance

Application of Theories
- Use Theory Practice Relationship

Application/Applications (1965-1985)
- HN DC 035140, deleted 1986. See now Job Application, Relevance, Research Applications, or Theory Practice Relationship.

Applications of Research
- Use Research Applications

Applied (1963-1985)
- HN DC 035160, deleted 1986. See now Applied Sociology, Social Science Research, or Psychology.

Applied Research
- Use Research

Applied Sciences
- Use Technology

Applied Sociology
- DC D040500
- SN Methods based on the results of sociological research, used to help in implementing social policies or achieving desidred social change.
- HN Formerly (1985) DC 035165.
- UF Clinical Sociology (1985)
- BT Sociology
- RT Community Mental Health
- Research Applications

Apportionment (Legislative)
- Use Legislative Apportionment

Appraisal/Appraisals (1965-1985)
- HN DC 035200.
- Use Evaluation

Apprehension (1971-1985)
- HN DC 035260.
- Use Anxiety

Apprenticeships
- DC D040800
- HN Formerly (1964-1985) DC 035300, Apprentice/Apprentices/Apprenticeship.
- BT Job Training
- RT Vocational Education

Approach/Approaches (1964-1985)
- HN DC 035310.
- Use Methods

Appropriate Technologies
- DC D041100
- SN Technologies suited to the specific economic, sociocultural, political, and biophysical needs of a given society at a particular time. Often implies locally produced, labor-intensive, reparable, ecologically sound, and community-building technologies.
- HN Added, 1986.
- BT Technology
- RT Alternative Approaches
- High Technology Industries
- Sociology of Science
- Solar Energy
- Technical Assistance
- Technological Progress
- Technology Assessment
- Technology Transfer

Appropriation
- DC D041400
- HN Formerly (1981-1985) DC 035340, Appropriation/Appropriations.
- NT Expropriation
- RT Allocation
- Budgets
- Resource Allocation

Approval
- DC D041700
- HN Formerly (1966-1985) DC 035350.
- UF Popularity
- Social Approval
- BT Social Behavior
- RT Acceptance
- Affiliation Need
- Criticism
- Motivation
- Resistance
- Social Acceptance
- Social Attitudes
- Social Desirability

Aptitude (Academic)
- Use Academic Aptitude

Arab Countries
- DC D041900
- HN Added, 1986.
- BT Countries
- NT Algeria
- Bahrain
- Egypt
- Iraq
- Jordan
- Kuwait
- Lebanon
- Libya
- Morocco
- Palestine
- Qatar
- Saudi Arabia
- Sudan
- Syria
- Tunisia
- United Arab Emirates
- Yemen Arab Republic
- Yemen (Peoples Democratic Republic)
- RT Arab Cultural Groups
- Mediterranean Countries
- Middle East
- North Africa

Architects

Arab Cultural Groups
- DC D042000
- HN Added, 1986. Prior to 1986, concepts representing specific Arab cultural groups, eg, Tunisians, were often indexed under terms representing the geographic place name, eg, Tunisia/Tunisian/Tunisians.
- BT Cultural Groups
- NT Palestinians
- RT African Cultural Groups
- Arab Countries
- Arab Cultural Groups
- Islam
- Islamic Law
- Middle Eastern Cultural Groups
- Muslims
- Nomadic Societies
- North African Cultural Groups
- Semitic Languages

Arab/Arabs/Arabia/Arabian/Arabic (1963-1985)
- HN DC 035650, deleted 1986. See now Saudi Arabia, Arab Cultural Groups, or Semitic Languages.

Arabic
- Use Semitic Languages

Arbitration
- DC D042300
- HN Formerly (1963-1985) DC 035690, Arbitration/Arbitrator.
- RT Adversary Legal System
- Collective Bargaining
- Conflict Resolution
- Litigation
- Negotiation

Archaeologist/Archaeologists (1963-1985)
- HN DC 035718.
- Use Anthropologists

Archaeology
- DC D042600
- HN Formerly (1963-1985) DC 035720, Archaeology/Archaeological.
- BT Anthropology
- RT Antiquity
- History
- Prehistoric Man
- Prehistory

Archaism/Archaic (1964-1985)
- HN DC 035730.
- Use Traditional Societies

Archetype/Archetypes/Archetypical (1975-1985)
- HN DC 035765.
- Use Types

Archipelago (1969-1985)
- HN DC 035800.
- Use Islands

Architects
- DC D042900
- HN Formerly (1964-1985) DC 035825, Architect/Architects.
- BT Professional Workers
- RT Architecture
- Construction Industry

13

Architecture

Architecture
- DC D043200
- HN Formerly (1963-1985) DC 035830, Architecture/Architectural.
- BT Fine Arts
- RT Architects
       Art
       Buildings
       Design
       Environmental Design
       Fashions
       Postmodernism
       Renaissance
       Visual Arts

Archival Research
- DC D043450
- HN Added, 1986.
- BT Research
- RT Archives
       Methodology (Data Collection)
       Records (Documents)

Archives
- DC D043500
- HN Formerly (1964-1985) DC 035835, Archive/Archives/Archival.
- RT Archival Research
       Data Banks
       Documentation
       Information Sources
       Libraries

Arctic Regions
- DC D043800
- HN Formerly (1964-1985) DC 035848, Arctic.
- BT Geographic Regions
- RT Alaska
       Arid Zones
       Earth (Planet)
       Eskimos
       Greenland
       Lapland
       Mountain Regions
       Northwest Territories
       Siberia
       Tropical Regions
       Yukon

Area/Areas (1963-1985)
- HN DC 035860.
- Use Geographic Regions

Arendt, Hannah
- DC D044100
- SN Born 14 October 1906 - died 4 December 1975.
- HN Formerly (1979-1985) DC 035895, Arendt, H.

Argentina
- DC D044400
- HN Formerly (1963-1985) DC 035920, Argentina/Argentinean/Argentine.
- BT South America
- NT Buenos Aires, Argentina

Argot (1968-1985)
- HN DC 035940.
- Use Slang

Argument/Arguments/Argumentation (1963-1985)
- HN DC 035950.
- Use Debate

Arid Lands
- Use Arid Zones

Arid Zones
- DC D044700
- HN Formerly (1963-1985) DC 035970, Arid.
- UF Arid Lands
       Deserts
       Semi Arid Lands
- BT Geographic Regions
- RT Arctic Regions
       Earth (Planet)
       Mountain Regions
       Nomadic Societies
       Tropical Regions

Aristocracy
- DC D045000
- HN Formerly (1963-1985) DC 035975, Aristocracy/Aristocratic/Aristocrat/Aristocrats.
- UF Nobility (1963-1985)
- RT Elites
       Elitism
       Feudalism
       Monarchy
       Oligarchy
       Peasants
       Political Systems
       Royalty
       Ruling Class
       Upper Class

Aristotle/Aristotelian (1964-1985)
- HN DC 036000.
- Use Ancient Greek Philosophy

Arizona
- DC D045300
- HN Formerly (1971-1985) DC 036050.
- BT United States of America
       Western States
- NT Phoenix, Arizona

Arkansas
- DC D045600
- HN Formerly (1963-1985) DC 036250.
- BT Southern States
       United States of America
- RT Ozark Mountains

Armaments
- DC D045900
- HN Formerly (1963-1985) DC 036450, Armament/Armaments.
- UF Arms Race
       Munitions
       Rearmament
- NT Weapons
- RT Armed Forces
       Defense Spending
       Disarmament
       Militarism
       Military Personnel
       National Security
       Nuclear War
       Space Technology
       War

Armed Forces
- DC D046200
- HN Formerly (1964-1985) DC 036460.
- UF Air Force (1963-1985)
       Army/Armies (1963-1985)
       Military Forces
       Navy (1965-1985)
- RT Armaments
       Civil Defense

Art

Armed Forces (cont'd)
- RT Defense Spending
       Militarism
       Militarization
       Military Civilian Relations
       Military Personnel
       Military Service
       Military Sociology
       Paramilitary Forces
       War

Armenian Soviet Socialist Republic
- DC D046500
- HN Formerly (1967-1985) DC 036470, Armenia/Armenian/Armenians.
- BT Union of Soviet Socialist Republics

Arms Control
- Use Disarmament

Arms Race
- Use Armaments

Army/Armies (1963-1985)
- HN DC 036500.
- Use Armed Forces

Aron, Raymond Claude Ferdinand
- DC D046800
- SN Born 14 March 1905 - died 17 October 1983.
- HN Formerly (1965-1985) DC 036550, Aron, R.

Arouse/Arousal/Aroused (1963-1985)
- HN DC 036575.
- Use Sexual Arousal

Arrests
- DC D047100
- HN Formerly (1963-1985) DC 037500, Arrest/Arrests.
- RT Detention
       Offenders
       Offenses
       Pretrial Release

Arson
- DC D047400
- HN Formerly (1972-1985) DC 037950, Arson/Arsonist/Arsonists.
- BT Offenses
- RT Fire

Art
- DC D047700
- HN Formerly (1963-1985) DC 038000, Art/Arts/Artistic.
- UF Art Works
       Commercial Art
       Creative Art
       Works of Art
- RT Aesthetics
       Architecture
       Art History
       Artistic Styles
       Artists
       Crafts
       Cultural Values
       Culture
       Dance
       Design
       Drama
       Fine Arts
       Humanities
       Images
       Literature
       Marxist Aesthetics

Art

Art (cont'd)
- **RT** Material Culture
  Monuments
  Museums
  Music
  Naturalism
  Sociology of Art
  Symbolism
  Theater Arts
  Visual Arts

Art History
- **DC** D048000
- **HN** Added, 1986.
- **BT** History
- **RT** Art
  Artistic Styles
  Artists
  Fine Arts
  Postmodernism
  Renaissance
  Romanticism
  Sociology of Art
  Visual Arts

Art Works
- **Use** Art

Arthritis
- **DC** D048300
- **HN** Formerly (1969-1985) DC 038490.
- **UF** Rheumatism
- **BT** Diseases

Articles
- **DC** D048600
- **HN** Formerly (1972-1985) DC 038495, Article/Articles.
- **UF** Journal Articles
  Newspaper Articles
- **BT** Publications
- **NT** Obituaries
- **RT** Bibliographies
  Citations (References)
  Periodicals
  Writing for Publication

Articulate/Articulateness/Articulation (1972-1985)
- **HN** DC 038500, deleted 1986. See now Social Integration or Speech.

Artifacts
- **DC** D048900
- **HN** Formerly (1964-1985) DC 038590, Artifact/Artifacts.
- **BT** Material Culture
- **RT** Crafts
  Masks
  Tools

Artificial Insemination
- **DC** D049200
- **HN** Formerly (1963-1985) DC 038600.
- **UF** In Vitro Fertilization
  Insemination (1968-1985)
- **BT** Reproductive Technologies
- **RT** Pregnancy
  Sexual Reproduction
  Surrogate Parents

Artificial Intelligence
- **DC** D049500
- **SN** Computer systems that simulate creative thought processes, including learning from experience and decision making based on anticipated consequences.
- **HN** Formerly (1985) DC 038602.

Artificial Intelligence (cont'd)
- **RT** Cognition
  Computers
  Cybernetics
  Intelligence

Artisans
- **DC** D049800
- **HN** Formerly (1968-1985) DC 038605, Artisan/Artisans.
- **UF** Craftsmen (1964-1985)
- **RT** Artists
  Crafts
  Guilds

Artistic Styles
- **DC** D050100
- **HN** Added, 1986.
- **UF** Classicism (1963-1985)
  Impressionism
  Realism (Art)
- **BT** Styles
- **NT** Postmodernism
  Romanticism
- **RT** Aesthetics
  Art
  Art History
  Artists
  Music
  Naturalism
  Sociology of Art

Artists
- **DC** D050400
- **HN** Formerly (1967-1985) DC 038610, Artist/Artists.
- **BT** Professional Workers
- **NT** Actors
  Musicians
- **RT** Art
  Art History
  Artisans
  Artistic Styles
  Fine Arts

Arts
- **Use** Humanities

Aruba
- **DC** D050700
- **HN** Added, 1986.
- **BT** Netherlands Antilles

Ascendancy
- **Use** Dominance

Asceticism
- **DC** D051000
- **SN** Practice of self-denial of sensual gratification for enhancement of the spiritual self.
- **HN** Formerly (1968-1985) DC 039100, Ascetic/Asceticism.
- **BT** Religious Behavior
- **RT** Cathari
  Manicheism
  Monasticism
  Monks
  Mysticism
  Religious Beliefs
  Sadhus

Asch, Solomon Elliott
- **DC** D051300
- **SN** Born 1907 - .
- **HN** Formerly (1964-1985) DC 039400, Asch, S.

Aspiration

Ascription
- **DC** D051400
- **SN** The arbitrary attribution of statuses, roles, occupations, or other qualities to individuals based on the social circumstances under which they are born, rather than their abilities and achievements.
- **HN** Formerly (1969-1985) DC 039450.
- **RT** Achievement
  Caste Systems
  Inheritance And Succession
  Roles
  Social Status

Ashkenazic Jews
- **Use** Jewish Cultural Groups

Asia
- **DC** D051600
- **HN** Formerly (1963-1985) DC 039500, Asia/Asian/Asians/Asiatic.
- **BT** Eurasia
- **NT** China
  Far East
  Middle East
  South Asia
  Southeast Asia
- **RT** Asian Cultural Groups

Asian Cultural Groups
- **DC** D051900
- **HN** Added, 1986. Prior to 1986, concepts representing specific Asian cultural groups, eg, Japanese, were often indexed under terms representing the geographic place name, eg, Japan/Japanese.
- **UF** Oriental Cultural Groups
- **BT** Cultural Groups
- **NT** South Asian Cultural Groups
  Southeast Asian Cultural Groups
- **RT** Ancestor Worship
  Asia
  Buddhists
  Confucianism
  Oriental Languages
  Samurai
  Shintoism
  Soviet Union Cultural Groups

Asian Languages
- **Use** Oriental Languages

Aspect/Aspects (1969-1985)
- **HN** DC 039590, deleted 1986.

Aspiration
- **DC** D052200
- **HN** Formerly (1963-1985) DC 040000, Aspiration/Aspirational/Aspirations.
- **UF** Ambition/Ambitions (1964-1985)
  Striving (1972-1985)
- **NT** Occupational Aspiration
- **RT** Ability
  Achievement
  Apathy
  Expectations
  Failure
  Goals
  Life Plans
  Motivation
  Performance
  Self Actualization
  Self Concept
  Success

Assamese

Assamese (Language)
Use Indic Languages

Assassination
DC D052500
HN Formerly (1965-1985) DC 040200, Assassin/Assassins/Assassinate/ Assassination/Assassinations.
BT Homicide
    Political Violence
RT Offenses
    Terrorism

Assault
DC D052800
HN Formerly (1966-1985) DC 040210, Assault/Assaults/Assaulting/ Assaultive.
BT Offenses
    Violence
NT Sexual Assault
RT Family Violence
    Homicide
    Lynching
    Robbery

Assembly/Assemblies (1963-1985)
HN DC 040215, deleted 1986.

Assertiveness
DC D053100
HN Formerly (1963-1985) DC 040225, Assertion/Assertions/Assertive.
UF Self Assertion
BT Social Behavior
RT Aggression
    Interpersonal Communication
    Interpersonal Relations
    Personality Traits
    Self Expression
    Self Presentation
    Social Interaction

Assess/Assesses/Assessment/ Assessments/Assessing (1964-1985)
HN DC 040235.
Use Evaluation

Assessment of Technology
Use Technology Assessment

Assignment/Assignments (1963-1985)
HN DC 040350, deleted 1986.

Assimilation
DC D053400
SN The process whereby a minority or immigrant group gives up its cultural traits and embraces those of the dominant society. Assimilation can either be a one-way or mutual process. Closely related to Acculturation.
HN Formerly (1963-1985) DC 040500.
BT Social Processes
RT Acculturation
    Biculturalism
    Cooptation
    Cultural Change
    Cultural Groups
    Cultural Pluralism
    Culture
    Ethnic Groups
    Immigrants
    Indigenous Populations
    Minority Groups
    Nativism

Assimilation (cont'd)
RT Newcomers
    Social Cohesion
    Social Integration
    Strangers
    Subcultures

Assistance
DC D053700
HN Formerly (1963-1985) part of DC 041000, Assistance/Assistant/ Assistants/Assistantship.
UF Aid (1963-1985)
NT Foreign Aid
    Technical Assistance
RT Charities
    Contributions (Donations)
    Disaster Relief
    Emergencies
    Employee Assistance Programs
    Financial Support
    Guidance
    Help Seeking Behavior
    Helping Behavior
    Human Services
    Intervention
    Needs
    Professional Consultation
    Shelters
    Social Services
    Sponsorship
    Support

Association Measures (Statistical)
Use Correlation

Associations
DC D054000
HN Formerly (1963-1985) DC 043400, Association/Associations/ Associational.
UF Voluntary Associations (1985)
    Young Men's-Women's Christian Assn/YM & YWCA (1964-1985)
BT Organizations (Social)
NT Employers Associations
    Professional Associations
    Secret Societies
RT Agencies
    Clubs
    Institutions
    Membership
    Nonprofit Organizations
    Social Contact
    Social Participation

Assortative (1964-1985)
HN DC 043450.
Use Homogamy

Assumption/Assumptions (1984-1985)
HN DC 043455.
Use Postulates

Assyria (1971-1985)
HN DC 043460.
Use Antiquity

Astrology
DC D054300
HN Formerly (1969-1986) DC 043465, Astrology/Astrologers.
UF Horoscope (1983-1985)
    Zodiac
BT Divination
RT Fate
    Occultism

Atmospheric

Astronautics
Use Space Technology

Astronomy
DC D054600
HN Formerly (1984-1985) DC 043488.
BT Physical Sciences
RT Scientific Research
    Space Technology

Asylum/Asylums (1969-1985)
HN DC 043495.
Use Mental Hospitals

Asymmetry/Asymmetric/ Asymmetrical (1963-1985)
HN DC 043500, deleted 1986.

Atheism
DC D054900
HN Formerly (1964-1985) DC 043540, Atheism/Atheist/Atheists/Atheistic.
UF Atheists
BT Philosophical Doctrines
    Religious Beliefs
RT Agnosticism
    Deities
    Heresy
    Humanism
    Materialism
    Rationalism

Atheists
Use Atheism

Athens, Greece
DC D054950
HN Added, 1989.
BT Greece

Athletes
DC D055200
HN Formerly (1964-1985) part of DC 043550, Athlete/Athletic/Athletics.
UF Amateur Athletes
    Professional Athletes
RT Olympic Games
    Sports

Athletic Teams
Use Sports Teams

Athletics
Use Sports

Atlanta, Georgia
DC D055500
HN Formerly (1965-1985) DC 043560, Atlanta, Ga.
BT Georgia

Atlantic Ocean
DC D055800
HN Formerly (1977-1985) DC 043565, Atlantic.
BT Oceans
NT North Atlantic Ocean
    South Atlantic Ocean
RT Pacific Ocean

Atlas/Atlases (1972-1985)
HN DC 043580.
Use Reference Materials

Atmospheric Contamination
Use Air Pollution

Art

Art (cont'd)
- RT Material Culture
- Monuments
- Museums
- Music
- Naturalism
- Sociology of Art
- Symbolism
- Theater Arts
- Visual Arts

Art History
- DC D048000
- HN Added, 1986.
- BT History
- RT Art
- Artistic Styles
- Artists
- Fine Arts
- Postmodernism
- Renaissance
- Romanticism
- Sociology of Art
- Visual Arts

Art Works
- Use Art

Arthritis
- DC D048300
- HN Formerly (1969-1985) DC 038490.
- UF Rheumatism
- BT Diseases

Articles
- DC D048600
- HN Formerly (1972-1985) DC 038495, Article/Articles.
- UF Journal Articles
- Newspaper Articles
- BT Publications
- NT Obituaries
- RT Bibliographies
- Citations (References)
- Periodicals
- Writing for Publication

Articulate/Articulateness/ Articulation (1972-1985)
- HN DC 038500, deleted 1986. See now Social Integration or Speech.

Artifacts
- DC D048900
- HN Formerly (1964-1985) DC 038590, Artifact/Artifacts.
- BT Material Culture
- RT Crafts
- Masks
- Tools

Artificial Insemination
- DC D049200
- HN Formerly (1963-1985) DC 038600.
- UF In Vitro Fertilization
- Insemination (1968-1985)
- BT Reproductive Technologies
- RT Pregnancy
- Sexual Reproduction
- Surrogate Parents

Artificial Intelligence
- DC D049500
- SN Computer systems that simulate creative thought processes, including learning from experience and decision making based on anticipated consequences.
- HN Formerly (1985) DC 038602.

Artificial Intelligence (cont'd)
- RT Cognition
- Computers
- Cybernetics
- Intelligence

Artisans
- DC D049800
- HN Formerly (1968-1985) DC 038605, Artisan/Artisans.
- UF Craftsmen (1964-1985)
- RT Artists
- Crafts
- Guilds

Artistic Styles
- DC D050100
- HN Added, 1986.
- UF Classicism (1963-1985)
- Impressionism
- Realism (Art)
- BT Styles
- NT Postmodernism
- Romanticism
- RT Aesthetics
- Art
- Art History
- Artists
- Music
- Naturalism
- Sociology of Art

Artists
- DC D050400
- HN Formerly (1967-1985) DC 038610, Artist/Artists.
- BT Professional Workers
- NT Actors
- Musicians
- RT Art
- Art History
- Artisans
- Artistic Styles
- Fine Arts

Arts
- Use Humanities

Aruba
- DC D050700
- HN Added, 1986.
- BT Netherlands Antilles

Ascendancy
- Use Dominance

Asceticism
- DC D051000
- SN Practice of self-denial of sensual gratification for enhancement of the spiritual self.
- HN Formerly (1968-1985) DC 039100, Ascetic/Asceticism.
- BT Religious Behavior
- RT Cathari
- Manicheism
- Monasticism
- Monks
- Mysticism
- Religious Beliefs
- Sadhus

Asch, Solomon Elliott
- DC D051300
- SN Born 1907 - .
- HN Formerly (1964-1985) DC 039400, Asch, S.

Aspiration

Ascription
- DC D051400
- SN The arbitrary attribution of statuses, roles, occupations, or other qualities to individuals based on the social circumstances under which they are born, rather than their abilities and achievements.
- HN Formerly (1969-1985) DC 039450.
- RT Achievement
- Caste Systems
- Inheritance And Succession
- Roles
- Social Status

Ashkenazic Jews
- Use Jewish Cultural Groups

Asia
- DC D051600
- HN Formerly (1963-1985) DC 039500, Asia/Asian/Asians/Asiatic.
- BT Eurasia
- NT China
- Far East
- Middle East
- South Asia
- Southeast Asia
- RT Asian Cultural Groups

Asian Cultural Groups
- DC D051900
- HN Added, 1986. Prior to 1986, concepts representing specific Asian cultural groups, eg, Japanese, were often indexed under terms representing the geographic place name, eg, Japan/Japanese.
- UF Oriental Cultural Groups
- BT Cultural Groups
- NT South Asian Cultural Groups
- Southeast Asian Cultural Groups
- RT Ancestor Worship
- Asia
- Buddhists
- Confucianism
- Oriental Languages
- Samurai
- Shintoism
- Soviet Union Cultural Groups

Asian Languages
- Use Oriental Languages

Aspect/Aspects (1969-1985)
- HN DC 039590, deleted 1986.

Aspiration
- DC D052200
- HN Formerly (1963-1985) DC 040000, Aspiration/Aspirational/Aspirations.
- UF Ambition/Ambitions (1964-1985)
- Striving (1972-1985)
- NT Occupational Aspiration
- RT Ability
- Achievement
- Apathy
- Expectations
- Failure
- Goals
- Life Plans
- Motivation
- Performance
- Self Actualization
- Self Concept
- Success

Assamese

Assamese (Language)
- Use Indic Languages

Assassination
- DC D052500
- HN Formerly (1965-1985) DC 040200, Assassin/Assassins/Assassinate/ Assassination/Assassinations.
- BT Homicide
  Political Violence
- RT Offenses
  Terrorism

Assault
- DC D052800
- HN Formerly (1966-1985) DC 040210, Assault/Assaults/Assaulting/ Assaultive.
- BT Offenses
  Violence
- NT Sexual Assault
- RT Family Violence
  Homicide
  Lynching
  Robbery

Assembly/Assemblies (1963-1985)
- HN DC 040215, deleted 1986.

Assertiveness
- DC D053100
- HN Formerly (1963-1985) DC 040225, Assertion/Assertions/Assertive.
- UF Self Assertion
- BT Social Behavior
- RT Aggression
  Interpersonal Communication
  Interpersonal Relations
  Personality Traits
  Self Expression
  Self Presentation
  Social Interaction

Assess/Assesses/Assessment/ Assessments/Assessing (1964-1985)
- HN DC 040235.
- Use Evaluation

Assessment of Technology
- Use Technology Assessment

Assignment/Assignments (1963-1985)
- HN DC 040350, deleted 1986.

Assimilation
- DC D053400
- SN The process whereby a minority or immigrant group gives up its cultural traits and embraces those of the dominant society. Assimilation can either be a one-way or mutual process. Closely related to Acculturation.
- HN Formerly (1963-1985) DC 040500.
- BT Social Processes
- RT Acculturation
  Biculturalism
  Cooptation
  Cultural Change
  Cultural Groups
  Cultural Pluralism
  Culture
  Ethnic Groups
  Immigrants
  Indigenous Populations
  Minority Groups
  Nativism

Assimilation (cont'd)
- RT Newcomers
  Social Cohesion
  Social Integration
  Strangers
  Subcultures

Assistance
- DC D053700
- HN Formerly (1963-1985) part of DC 041000, Assistance/Assistant/ Assistants/Assistantship.
- UF Aid (1963-1985)
- NT Foreign Aid
  Technical Assistance
- RT Charities
  Contributions (Donations)
  Disaster Relief
  Emergencies
  Employee Assistance Programs
  Financial Support
  Guidance
  Help Seeking Behavior
  Helping Behavior
  Human Services
  Intervention
  Needs
  Professional Consultation
  Shelters
  Social Services
  Sponsorship
  Support

Association Measures (Statistical)
- Use Correlation

Associations
- DC D054000
- HN Formerly (1963-1985) DC 043400, Association/Associations/ Associational.
- UF Voluntary Associations (1985)
  Young Men's-Women's Christian Assn/YM & YWCA (1964-1985)
- BT Organizations (Social)
- NT Employers Associations
  Professional Associations
  Secret Societies
- RT Agencies
  Clubs
  Institutions
  Membership
  Nonprofit Organizations
  Social Contact
  Social Participation

Assortative (1964-1985)
- HN DC 043450.
- Use Homogamy

Assumption/Assumptions (1984-1985)
- HN DC 043455.
- Use Postulates

Assyria (1971-1985)
- HN DC 043460.
- Use Antiquity

Astrology
- DC D054300
- HN Formerly (1969-1986) DC 043465, Astrology/Astrologers.
- UF Horoscope (1983-1985)
  Zodiac
- BT Divination
- RT Fate
  Occultism

Atmospheric

Astronautics
- Use Space Technology

Astronomy
- DC D054600
- HN Formerly (1984-1985) DC 043488.
- BT Physical Sciences
- RT Scientific Research
  Space Technology

Asylum/Asylums (1969-1985)
- HN DC 043495.
- Use Mental Hospitals

Asymmetry/Asymmetric/ Asymmetrical (1963-1985)
- HN DC 043500, deleted 1986.

Atheism
- DC D054900
- HN Formerly (1964-1985) DC 043540, Atheism/Atheist/Atheists/Atheistic.
- UF Atheists
- BT Philosophical Doctrines
  Religious Beliefs
- RT Agnosticism
  Deities
  Heresy
  Humanism
  Materialism
  Rationalism

Atheists
- Use Atheism

Athens, Greece
- DC D054950
- HN Added, 1989.
- BT Greece

Athletes
- DC D055200
- HN Formerly (1964-1985) part of DC 043550, Athlete/Athletic/Athletics.
- UF Amateur Athletes
  Professional Athletes
- RT Olympic Games
  Sports

Athletic Teams
- Use Sports Teams

Athletics
- Use Sports

Atlanta, Georgia
- DC D055500
- HN Formerly (1965-1985) DC 043560, Atlanta, Ga.
- BT Georgia

Atlantic Ocean
- DC D055800
- HN Formerly (1977-1985) DC 043565, Atlantic.
- BT Oceans
- NT North Atlantic Ocean
  South Atlantic Ocean
- RT Pacific Ocean

Atlas/Atlases (1972-1985)
- HN DC 043580.
- Use Reference Materials

Atmospheric Contamination
- Use Air Pollution

Atomic

Atomic Power
   Use Nuclear Energy

Atomic War
   Use Nuclear War

Atomic Weapons
   Use Nuclear Weapons

Atomic/Atomicism (1963-1985)
   HN DC 043600, deleted 1986. See now appropriate "Nuclear" terms.

Attachment
   DC D056100
   SN The formation of significant emotional, social, or organizational bonds.
   HN Formerly (1972-1985) DC 043675, Attach/Attachment/Attachments.
   UF Bond/Bonds/Bonding (1983-1985)
   RT Family Relations
      Interpersonal Attraction
      Interpersonal Relations
      Intimacy
      Love
      Parent Child Relations
      Symbiotic Relations

Attack (1971-1985)
   HN DC 043680, deleted 1986.

Attainment
   DC D056400
   HN Formerly (1968-1985) DC 043700, Attain/Attainment/Attained.
   NT Educational Attainment
      Status Attainment
   RT Achievement

Attendance
   DC D056700
   HN Formerly (1963-1985) DC 043750.
   NT Church Attendance
      School Attendance
   RT Absenteeism
      Dropouts

Attention
   DC D057000
   SN A context-dependent term; select a more specific entry or coordinate with other terms.
   HN Formerly (1967-1985) DC 044000.
   UF Distraction/Distractions (1969-1985)
   BT Consciousness
   RT Behavior
      Cognition
      Redundancy

Attitude Change
   DC D057300
   HN Formerly (1963-1985) DC 045000, Attitude Change/Attitude Changes.
   BT Change
   RT Attitudes
      Change Agents
      Indoctrination

Attitude Measures
   DC D057450
   HN Formerly (1963-1985) DC 046000, Attitude Scale.
   UF Opinion Scales
      Scales (Attitude)
   BT Measures (Instruments)
   NT Semantic Differential
   RT Attitudes
      Beliefs
      F Scale

Attitude Measures (cont'd)
   RT Guttman Scales
      Latent Structure Analysis
      Opinions
      Personality Measures
      Projective Techniques
      Questionnaires
      Scales
      Social Desirability Scales
      Surveys

Attitudes
   DC D057600
   SN A context-dependent term; select a more specific entry or coordinate with other terms. Refers to the thoughts, feelings, perceptions, opinions, or mind-set of an individual or group as measured with psychometric instruments. Social Attitudes is preferred in sociological analyses.
   HN Formerly (1963-1985) DC 044500, Attitude/Attitudes/Attitudinal.
   UF Predispositions (1967-1985)
      Sentiment/Sentiments (1963-1985)
   NT Death Attitudes
      Discontent
      Environmental Attitudes
      Language Attitudes
      Opinions
      Parental Attitudes
      Political Attitudes
      Prejudice
      Religious Attitudes
      Satisfaction
      Sex Role Attitudes
      Skepticism
      Social Attitudes
      Student Attitudes
      Teacher Attitudes
      Tolerance
      Work Attitudes
      Worker Attitudes
   RT Attitude Change
      Attitude Measures
      Behavior
      Beliefs
      Bias
      Cognitive Dissonance
      Congruence (Psychology)
      Dogmatism
      Emotions
      Expectations
      Human Dignity
      Interests
      Judgment
      Latent Structure Analysis
      Orientation
      Perceptions
      Preferences
      Sexual Permissiveness
      Stereotypes

Attorney Client Relationship
   Use Client Relations

Attorneys
   Use Lawyers

Attorneys (Prosecuting)
   Use Prosecutors

Attractiveness
   DC D057900
   HN Formerly (1963-1985) DC 046420, Attract/Attractive/Attractiveness/Attraction/Attractions.
   UF Beauty (1971-1985)
      Physical Attractiveness
   RT Human Body
      Interpersonal Attraction
      Physical Characteristics
      Social Desirability

Australasia

Attribution
   DC D058200
   SN A context-dependent term for the process by which individuals assign meaning and value to external phenomena.
   HN Formerly (1981-1985) DC 046435, Attribution/Attributions.
   UF Causal Attribution
   RT Causality
      Impression Formation
      Locus of Control
      Personality
      Self Concept
      Social Behavior
      Social Perception

Attrition
   DC D058300
   HN Formerly (1965-1985) DC 046460.
   RT Cohort Analysis
      Dropouts
      Labor Turnover
      Longitudinal Studies
      Panel Data

Audiences
   DC D058500
   HN Formerly (1963-1985) DC 046500, Audience/Audiences.
   UF Listener (1965-1985)
      Viewers
   BT Groups
   RT Communication
      Communication Research
      Drama
      Entertainment Industry
      Mass Media
      Mass Media Effects
      Messages
      Radio
      Spectators
      Television Viewing
      Theater Arts

Audio Recordings
   Use Recordings

Audiovisual Media
   DC D058800
   HN Formerly (1964-1985) DC 047100, Audiovisual.
   UF Nonbook Materials
      Nonprint Media
   NT Cartoons
      Films
      Photographs
      Recordings
   RT Education
      Graffiti
      Images
      Mass Media
      Publications
      Telecommunications

Audition
   Use Hearing

Auditory (1979-1985)
   HN DC 047110, deleted 1986.

Australasia
   DC D059100
   SN Australia, New Zealand, and neighboring islands in the South Pacific Ocean.
   HN Added, 1986.
   NT Australia
      New Zealand
   RT Australasian Cultural Groups

Australasian

Australasian Cultural Groups
- DC D059400
- HN Added, 1986. Prior to 1986, concepts representing specific Australasian cultural groups, eg, Australians, were often indexed under terms representing the geographic place name, eg, Australia/Australian/Australians.
- BT Cultural Groups
- NT Aboriginal Australians
- RT Australasia
    Austronesian Languages

Australia
- DC D059700
- HN Formerly (1963-1985) DC 047700, Australia/Australian/Australians.
- BT Australasia
- NT Brisbane, Australia
    Canberra, Australia
    Melbourne, Australia
    Sydney, Australia
    Tasmania

Australian Aboriginal Languages
- Use Austronesian Languages

Austria
- DC D060000
- HN Formerly (1963-1985) DC 047800, Austria/Austrian/Austrians.
- BT Western Europe
- NT Vienna, Austria

Austronesian Languages
- DC D060300
- HN Added, 1986.
- UF Australian Aboriginal Languages
    Malayo Polynesian Languages
    Melanesian (Language)
    Micronesian (Language)
    Papuan Languages
    Tasmanian Languages
- BT Languages
- RT Australasian Cultural Groups
    Oceanic Cultural Groups

Autarchy/Autarchies (1970-1985)
- HN DC 047855, deleted 1986.

Authenticity (1967-1985)
- HN DC 047870.
- Use Credibility

Authoritarian Personality
- Use Authoritarianism (Psychology)

Authoritarianism (Political Ideology)
- DC D060600
- HN Formerly (1963-1985) part of DC 048000, Authoritarian/Authoritarianism.
- BT Political Ideologies
- RT Despotism
    Dictatorship
    Fascism
    Political Elites
    Repression (Political)
    Totalitarianism

Authoritarianism (Psychology)
- DC D060900
- SN Pattern of personality traits characterized by the desire for unquestioning obedience, servile acceptance of superior authority, rigidity, intolerance of opposing views, conventionality, and cynicism. The term is associated with the work of Theodor W. Adorno, among others.

Authoritarianism (Psychology) (cont'd)
- HN Formerly (1963-1985) part of DC 048000, Authoritarian/Authoritarianism.
- UF Authoritarian Personality
- BT Personality Traits
- RT Dogmatism
    Dominance
    Egalitarianism
    F Scale
    Obedience
    Traditionalism

Authority
- DC D061200
- SN Power that is recognized as legitimate, or morally just, by members of a society or social group. Also, power that is institutionalized and thus routinely obeyed. See also Power and Legitimacy.
- HN Formerly (1963-1985) DC 049000, Authority/Authorities/Authoritative.
- UF Command/Commands (1964-1985)
- BT Power
- RT Charisma
    Chieftaincies
    Dominance
    Influence
    Leadership
    Legitimacy
    Obedience
    Responsibility
    Social Power
    Sovereignty
    State
    State Power

Authors
- Use Writers

Authorship
- DC D061500
- HN Formerly (1964-1985) part of DC 047900, Author/Authorship.
- UF Multiple Authorship
    Plagiarize/Plagiarism/Plagiarists (1967-1985)
    Pseudonyms (1964-1985)
- RT Literature
    Publications
    Scholarship
    Writers
    Writing
    Writing for Publication

Autism
- DC D061800
- SN A cognitive disorder characterized by extreme self-absorbtion and inability to relate socially.
- HN Formerly (1964-1985) DC 049400, Autistic.
- UF Autistic
    Infantile Autism
- RT Child Development
    Mental Illness
    Schizophrenia

Autistic
- Use Autism

Autobiographical Materials
- DC D062100
- HN Formerly (1963-1985) DC 050240, Autobiography/Autobiographies.
- UF Autobiographies
    Diary/Diaries (1972-1985)

Autonomy

Autobiographical Materials (cont'd)
- UF Memoir/Memoirs (1969-1985)
- RT Biographies
    Letters (Correspondence)
    Literature
    Narratives

Autobiographies
- Use Autobiographical Materials

Autocracy/Autocratic/Autocrat/Autocrats (1964-1985)
- HN DC 050250.
- Use Dictatorship

Autoeroticism
- Use Masturbation

Automatic Data Processing
- Use Data Processing

Automation
- DC D062400
- HN Formerly (1963-1985) DC 050600, Automation/Automator/Automated.
- UF Mechanization
- BT Technology
- NT Industrial Automation
    Office Automation
- RT Agricultural Mechanization
    Computers
    Cybernetics
    Data Processing
    Electronic Technology
    Machinery
    Metallurgical Technology
    Technology Transfer

Automobile Industry
- DC D062700
- HN Added, 1986.
- UF Automotive Industry
- BT Manufacturing Industries
- RT Automobiles

Automobiles
- DC D063000
- HN Formerly (1963-1985) part of DC 050700, Automobile/Automobiles.
- UF Buses
    Cars
    Motor Vehicles
    Motorcycles
    Recreational Vehicles
- RT Accidents
    Automobile Industry
    Commuting (Travel)
    Drunk Driving
    Highways
    Machinery
    Public Transportation
    Traffic
    Transportation

Automotive Industry
- Use Automobile Industry

Autonomic (1965-1985)
- HN DC 050775, deleted 1986.

Autonomy
- DC D063300
- HN Formerly (1964-1985) DC 050800, Autonomous/Autonomy.
- UF Heteronomy (1983-1985)
- RT Independence
    Self Determination
    Sovereignty
    State

Autopsy

Autopsy/Autopsies (1963-1985)
  HN DC 050805, deleted 1986.

Availability
  Use Access

Aviation (1970-1985)
  HN DC 050900.
  Use Air Transportation

Avoidance
  DC D063600
  SN Defense mechanism characterized by refusal to encounter situations, objects, or activities.
  HN Formerly (1963-1985) DC 050960.
  RT Coping
      Repression (Defense Mechanism)

Awards
  DC D063700
  HN Formerly (1980-1985) DC 050985, Award/Awards.
  UF Nobel Prize (1963-1985)
      Prize/Prizes (1963-1985)
  BT Recognition (Achievement)
  RT Achievement
      Fellowships And Scholarships
      Incentives
      Performance
      Prestige
      Rewards
      Sanctions

Awareness (1963-1985)
  HN DC 051000.
  Use Consciousness

Axiology (1971-1985)
  HN DC 051030.
  Use Values

Azores
  DC D063900
  HN Added, 1986.
  BT Western Europe
  RT North Atlantic Ocean

Baby/Babies (1984-1985)
  HN DC 051064.
  Use Infants

Babylonia/Babylonian/Babylonians (1970-1985)
  HN DC 051066.
  Use Antiquity

Baccalaureate Degrees
  DC D064200
  HN Formerly (1963-1985) DC 051074, Baccalaureate/Baccalaureates.
  UF Bachelors Degrees
  BT Academic Degrees
  RT Doctoral Degrees
      Masters Degrees
      Undergraduate Programs
      Undergraduate Students

Bachelor/Bachelors/Bachelorhood (1969-1985)
  HN DC 051082.
  Use Single Persons

Bachelors Degrees
  Use Baccalaureate Degrees

Bachofen, Johann Jakob
  DC D064500
  SN Born 22 December 1815 - died 25 November 1887.

Bachofen, Johann Jakob (cont'd)
  HN Formerly (1964-1985) DC 051090, Bachofen, J. J.

Background/Backgrounds (1963-1985)
  HN DC 051098.
  Use Social Background

Backlash (1966-1985)
  HN DC 051106.
  Use Countermovements

Backwardness (Economic)
  Use Economic Underdevelopment

Baghdad, Iraq
  DC D064700
  HN Added, 1989.
  BT Iraq

Bahai Religious Movement
  Use Bahaism

Bahaism
  DC D064800
  HN Formerly (1963-1985) DC 051114, Bahai/Bahaism.
  UF Bahai Religious Movement
  BT Religions
  RT Religious Movements

Bahamas
  DC D065100
  HN Formerly (1967-1985) DC 051117, Bahamas/Bahamian/Bahamians.
  BT Caribbean

Bahrain
  DC D065400
  HN Added, 1986.
  BT Arab Countries
      Middle East

Bail Decisions
  Use Pretrial Release

Bail/Bailbond/Bailbondsman/Bailbondsmen (1972-1985)
  HN DC 051119, deleted 1986.

Balance Theory
  DC D065600
  SN A social psychological theory, developed by Fritz Heider, that focuses on the relationships between cognitive structures and social interaction. These cognitive structures are characterized in terms of balance, imbalance, and resulting tensions.
  HN Formerly (1963-1985) DC 051122, Balance.
  BT Social Theories
  RT Group Dynamics
      Interaction
      Interpersonal Relations
      Organizational Structure
      Power
      Social Equilibrium
      Social Psychology
      Social Structure

Bales, Robert Freed
  DC D065700
  SN Born 9 September 1916 - .
  HN Formerly (1964-1985) DC 051130, Bales, R.

Bankruptcy

Bali
  DC D066000
  HN Formerly (1967-1985) DC 051135.
  BT Indonesia

Balkan States
  DC D066300
  HN Formerly (1972-1985) DC 051138, Balkan/Balkans.
  BT Europe
  NT Albania
      Bulgaria
      Greece
      Romania
      Turkey
      Yugoslavia

Ballet
  Use Dance

Baltic States
  DC D066600
  HN Formerly (1969-1985) DC 051148, Baltic Sea.
  BT Western Europe
  NT Estonian Soviet Socialist Republic
      Finland
      Latvian Soviet Socialist Republic

Baltimore, Maryland
  DC D066900
  HN Formerly (1963-1985) DC 051160, Baltimore, Md.
  BT Maryland

Banditry
  DC D067200
  HN Formerly (1980-1985) DC 051161a, Bandit/Bandits/Banditism/Banditry.
  RT Offenses
      Robbery

Banfield, Edward Christie
  DC D067500
  SN Born 19 November 1916 - .
  HN Formerly (1985) DC 051161b, Banfield, E.

Bangkok, Thailand
  DC D067700
  HN Added, 1989.
  BT Thailand

Bangladesh
  DC D067800
  HN Formerly (1979-1985) DC 051164.
  BT South Asia
  NT Bengal

Banking
  DC D068100
  HN Formerly (1971-1985) DC 051165, Bank/Banks/Banking.
  UF Banking Industry
  BT Service Industries
  RT Capital
      Credit
      Finance
      International Economic Organizations
      Investment
      Loans
      Saving

Banking Industry
  Use Banking

Bankruptcy
  DC D068400
  HN Formerly (1984-1985) DC 051167.

Bankruptcy (cont'd)
    UF   Insolvency
           Receivership
    RT   Debts
           Economic Problems
           Finance
           Organizational Dissolution

Bantu (1965-1985)
    HN   DC 051170, deleted 1986. See now African Cultural Groups or African Languages.

Bantu Languages
    Use African Languages

Bantuide Languages
    Use African Languages

Baptism
    DC   D068700
    HN   Formerly (1963-1985) part of DC 051178, Baptist/Baptists/Baptism.
    UF   Baptismal Rites
    BT   Religious Rituals
    RT   Salvation

Baptismal Rites
    Use Baptism

Baptist Churches
    Use Baptists

Baptists
    DC   D069000
    HN   Formerly (1963-1985) part of DC 051178, Baptist/Baptists/Baptism.
    UF   Baptist Churches
           Southern Baptist Church
    BT   Protestants
    RT   Protestantism

Bar/Bars (1983-1985)
    HN   DC 051180.
    Use Eating And Drinking Establishments

Barbados
    DC   D069300
    HN   Formerly (1964-1985) DC 051202.
    BT   Caribbean

Barbuda
    DC   D069600
    HN   Added, 1986.
    BT   Caribbean

Barcelona, Spain
    DC   D069700
    HN   Added, 1989.
    BT   Spain

Bards
    Use Poets

Bargain/Bargains/Bargaining (1963-1985)
    HN   DC 051210.
    Use Negotiation

Barriers
    Use Constraints

Barrio/Barrios (1964-1985)
    HN   DC 051218.
    Use Ethnic Neighborhoods

Barter
    Use Exchange (Economics)

Barthes, Roland
    DC   D069900
    SN   Born 12 November 1915 - died 25 March 1980.
    HN   Formerly (1984-1985) DC 051219a.

Base And Superstructure
    DC   D070100
    SN   In Marxist theory, the economy (base) of a society determines the character of its ideas and social institutions (superstructure).
    HN   Added, 1986.
    UF   Superstructure/Superstructures (1972-1985)
    RT   Economic Structure
           Economics
           Family Structure
           Forces And Relations of Production
           Ideologies
           Labor Theory of Value
           Marxism
           Marxist Sociology
           Modes of Production
           Social Structure
           State

Baseline (1984-1985)
    HN   DC 051222, deleted 1986.

Basic Research
    Use Research

Basque Provinces
    DC   D070200
    SN   A region in northern Spain south of the Bay of Biscay comprising the provinces of Alava, Guipuzcoa, and Vizcaya.
    HN   Formerly (1984-1985) DC 051223, Basque region, Spain.
    BT   Spain

Bateson, Gregory
    DC   D070350
    SN   Born 9 May 1904 - died 4 July 1980.
    HN   Added, 1986.

Bathe/Bathing (1981-1985)
    HN   DC 051226, deleted 1986.

Battered (1981-1985)
    HN   DC 051240, deleted 1986. See now Battered Women and specific "Abuse" terms.

Battered Children
    Use Child Abuse

Battered Women
    DC   D070500
    HN   Added, 1986.
    BT   Females
    RT   Abuse
           Child Abuse
           Elder Abuse
           Family Violence
           Shelters
           Spouse Abuse
           Victimization
           Victims

Battery/Batteries (1975-1985)
    HN   DC 051242, deleted 1986. See now Assault, Battered Women, or appropriate "Measurement" terms.

Bavaria/Bavarian/Bavarians (1969-1985)
    HN   DC 051246, deleted 1986.

Beatnik/Beatniks (1966-1985)
    HN   DC 051258.
    Use Countercultures

Beauty (1971-1985)
    HN   DC 051268.
    Use Attractiveness

de Beauvoir, Simone
    DC   D070800
    SN   Born 9 January 1908 - died 14 April 1986.
    HN   Formerly (1967-1985) DC 121175, De Beauvoir, Simone.

Becker, Howard Saul
    DC   D071400
    SN   Born 18 April 1928 - .
    HN   Formerly (1973-1985) DC 051283, Becker, Howard S.

Bedouin/Bedouins (1971-1985)
    HN   DC 051293, deleted 1986. See now Arab Cultural Groups or Nomadic Societies.

Beggary
    DC   D071700
    SN   Condition of extreme poverty accompanied by begging for money, food, etc.
    HN   Formerly (1963-1985) part of DC 051297, Beggar/Beggars/Begging.
    UF   Begging
    RT   Poverty

Begging
    Use Beggary

Behavior
    DC   D072000
    SN   A context-dependent term; select a more specific entry or coordinate with other terms. Refers to specific actions attributed to individuals or groups, particularly as measured psychometrically. See also Social Behavior and Social Interaction, which are preferred in sociological analyses.
    HN   Formerly (1963-1985) DC 051300, Behavior/Behavioral.
    UF   Conduct (1977-1985)
           Human Actions
    NT   Deviant Behavior
           Drinking Behavior
           Habits
           Health Behavior
           Helping Behavior
           Illness Behavior
           Imitation
           Instinct
           Organizational Behavior
           Participation
           Performance
           Political Behavior
           Public Behavior
           Responses
           Self Destructive Behavior
           Sexual Behavior
           Social Behavior
           Spatial Behavior
           Spontaneity
           Student Behavior
           Territoriality
    RT   Action
           Adjustment

Behavior

Behavior (cont'd)
- **RT** Alcohol Use
  - Attention
  - Attitudes
  - Behavior Modification
  - Behavior Problems
  - Behavioral Sciences
  - Behaviorism
  - Codes of Conduct
  - Compulsivity
  - Conditioning
  - Congruence (Psychology)
  - Coping
  - Customs
  - Drug Use
  - Ethology
  - Function
  - Health Care Utilization
  - Human Nature
  - Impulsiveness
  - Individual Differences
  - Interaction
  - Internalization
  - Language
  - Life Stage Transitions
  - Lifestyle
  - Mental Illness
  - Norms
  - Personality
  - Play
  - Psychological Factors
  - Psychological Research
  - Psychology
  - Roles
  - Safety
  - Sanctions
  - Skills
  - Smoking
  - Social Control
  - Styles
  - Traditions
  - Violence

Behavior Modification
- **DC** D072300
- **SN** Training or learning methods based on Behaviorism, often as an alternative to Psychotherapy.
- **HN** Formerly (1969-1985) DC 274544, Modify/Modified/Modification/Modifications.
- **UF** Behavior Therapy
  - Modification (Behavior)
- **BT** Conditioning
- **RT** Behavior
  - Counseling
  - Delinquency Prevention
  - Family Therapy
  - Intervention
  - Psychotherapy
  - Reinforcement
  - Self Help
  - Transcendental Meditation

Behavior Problems
- **DC** D072400
- **SN** Unwillingness or inability to adhere to social norms and expectations, eg, hyperactivity and impulsiveness in social interaction.
- **HN** Added, 1989.
- **UF** Misbehavior
  - Misconduct
- **BT** Problems
- **RT** Aggression
  - Behavior
  - Deviant Behavior
  - Obedience
  - Social Behavior

Behavior Therapy
- **Use** Behavior Modification

Behavioral Science Research
- **Use** Social Science Research

Behavioral Sciences
- **DC** D072600
- **HN** Formerly (1963-1985) DC 051310, Behavioral Science/Behavioral Sciences/Behavioral Scientist/Behavioral Scientists.
- **BT** Social Sciences
- **NT** Ethology
  - Psychology
  - Sociobiology
- **RT** Behavior
  - Biology
  - Psychiatry
  - Science
  - Sociology

Behavioral Scientists
- **Use** Social Scientists

Behaviorism
- **DC** D072900
- **SN** Psychological theory focusing on observable, measurable behavior as the only appropriate subject matter for scientific psychological investigation.
- **HN** Formerly (1963-1985) DC 051500, Behaviorism/Behaviorist/Behaviorists.
- **BT** Philosophical Doctrines
  - Psychology
- **RT** Behavior
  - Empiricism
  - Positivism
  - Praxeology
  - Reductionism
  - Stimuli

Beirut, Lebanon
- **DC** D073100
- **HN** Added, 1989.
- **BT** Lebanon

Belgium
- **DC** D073200
- **HN** Formerly (1963-1985) DC 051850, Belgium/Belgian/Belgians.
- **BT** Western Europe
- **NT** Antwerp, Belgium
  - Brussels, Belgium
  - Flanders

Belief Systems
- **Use** Beliefs

Beliefs
- **DC** D073500
- **SN** A context-dependent term for an individual's or group's internalized concepts about the outside world.
- **HN** Formerly (1963-1985) DC 051870, Belief/Beliefs.
- **UF** Belief Systems
  - Creed/Creeds (1971-1985)
- **NT** Fatalism
  - Religious Beliefs
  - Superstitions
- **RT** Attitude Measures
  - Attitudes
  - Certainty
  - Cognitive Dissonance
  - Common Sense
  - Culture
  - Dogmatism

Bengal

Beliefs (cont'd)
- **RT** Epistemological Doctrines
  - Ethics
  - Ideologies
  - Irrationality
  - Magic
  - Mysticism
  - Norms
  - Occultism
  - Opinions
  - Perceptions
  - Philosophical Doctrines
  - Rationality
  - Reality
  - Religions
  - Skepticism
  - Social Attitudes
  - Social Values
  - Truth
  - Values
  - Worldview

Believability
- **Use** Credibility

Belize
- **DC** D073800
- **HN** Formerly (1984-1985) DC 051870c.
- **BT** Central America

Bell, Daniel
- **DC** D074100
- **SN** Born 10 May 1919 - .
- **HN** Formerly (1970-1985) DC 051871, Bell, D.

Bellah, Robert N.
- **DC** D074200
- **SN** Born 23 February 1927 - .
- **HN** Added, 1989.

Bendix, Reinhard
- **DC** D074400
- **SN** Born 25 February 1916 - .
- **HN** Formerly (1963-1985) DC 051875.

Benedict, Ruth Fulton
- **DC** D074700
- **SN** Born 5 June 1887 - died 17 September 1948.
- **HN** Formerly (1964-1985) DC 051880, Benedict, Ruth.

Benefits
- **DC** D075000
- **SN** Broad term incorporating any compensation or advantage received due to age, injury, illness, unemployment, death, or other special life circumstance, often under government, employer, or private insurance programs.
- **HN** Formerly (1968-1985) DC 051950.
- **UF** Employee Benefits
- **BT** Compensation
- **RT** Disability Recipients
  - Insurance
  - Pensions
  - Social Security
  - Social Welfare
  - Welfare Recipients
  - Welfare Services

Bengal
- **DC** D075300
- **HN** Added, 1986.
- **BT** Bangladesh
  - India

Bengal/Bengali/Bengalese (1963-1985)
  HN DC 052100, deleted 1986. See now Indic Languages, Bengal, or West Bengal.

Bengali (Language)
  Use Indic Languages

Benin
  DC D075600
  HN Added, 1986.
  BT Sub Saharan Africa

Berber/Berbers (1969-1985)
  HN DC 052160, deleted 1986. See now African Cultural Groups.

Bereavement
  Use Grief

Berger, Peter
  DC D075800
  SN Born 1929 - .
  HN Added, 1989.

Bergson, Henri Louis
  DC D075900
  SN Born 18 October 1859 - died 3 January 1941.
  HN Formerly (1964-1985) DC 052200, Bergson, Henri.

Berkeley, Calif. (1964-1985)
  HN DC 052220, deleted 1986.

Berlin, Federal Republic of Germany
  DC D076200
  HN Formerly (1964-1985) DC 052229, Berlin, West.
  UF West Berlin
  BT Federal Republic of Germany

Berlin, German Democratic Republic
  DC D076500
  HN Formerly (1980-1985) DC 052227, Berlin, East.
  UF East Berlin
  BT German Democratic Republic

Berlin, Germany
  DC D076800
  SN Use limited to Berlin, Germany, prior to 1945. See also Berlin, German Democratic Republic, or Berlin, Federal Republic of Germany.
  HN Formerly (1963-1985) DC 052225, Berlin/Berliner/Berliners.
  BT Germany

Berlin, Sir Isaiah
  DC D077100
  SN Born 6 June 1909 - .
  HN Formerly (1971-1985) DC 052226, Berlin, Isaiah.

Bermuda
  DC D077400
  HN Added, 1986.
  BT North America
  RT North Atlantic Ocean

Bet/Bets/Bettor/Betting (1964-1985)
  HN DC 052320.
  Use Gambling

Beverages (Alcoholic)
  Use Alcoholic Beverages

Bhutan
  DC D077700
  HN Added, 1986.
  BT Himalayan States
       South Asia

Biafra/Biafran/Biafrans (1970-1985)
  HN DC 052420, deleted 1986.

Bias
  DC D077900
  HN Formerly (1963-1985) DC 052500, Bias/Biases/Biased.
  NT Prejudice
       Statistical Bias
       Test Bias
  RT Accuracy
       Ageism
       Attitudes
       Discrimination
       Egocentrism
       Equity
       Ethnocentrism
       Racism
       Sectarianism
       Sexism
       Subjectivity

Bible
  DC D078000
  HN Formerly (1963-1985) DC 052800, Bible/Biblical.
  UF Gospel/Gospels (1967-1985)
       New Testament
       Old Testament
  BT Religious Literature
  RT Apocalypse
       Christianity
       Devils
       Evangelism
       God (Judeo-Christian)
       Hermeneutics
       Jesus Christ
       Judaism
       Judeo-Christian Tradition
       Millenarianism
       Rabbinical Literature

Bibliographic Citations
  Use Citations (References)

Bibliographies
  DC D078300
  SN Discussions of Bibliographies as methodological tools in social science research.
  HN Formerly (1963-1985) DC 053000, Bibliography/Bibliographies/Bibliographic.
  UF Annotated Bibliographies
  BT Reference Materials
  RT Articles
       Books
       Citations (References)
       Literature Reviews

Biculturalism
  DC D078600
  HN Formerly (1985) DC 053100.
  BT Cultural Pluralism
  RT Aboriginal Australians
       Acculturation
       Assimilation
       Bilingual Education
       Bilingualism
       Crosscultural Analysis

Biculturalism (cont'd)
  RT Cultural Conflict
       Cultural Groups
       Cultural Identity
       Cultural Values
       Culture
       Culture Contact
       Ethnic Groups
       Ethnic Minorities
       Ethnic Relations
       Immigrants
       Language Maintenance
       Language Policy
       Minority Groups
       Multicultural Education
       Plural Societies

Bigotry (1965-1985)
  HN DC 054100.
  Use Prejudice

Bihar, India
  DC D078900
  HN Formerly (1968-1985) DC 054200.
  BT India

Bilingual Education
  DC D079200
  HN Added, 1986.
  BT Education
  RT Biculturalism
       Bilingualism
       Cultural Identity
       Educational Policy
       Language Maintenance
       Language Planning
       Language Policy
       Multicultural Education
       Multilingualism
       Second Language Learning

Bilingualism
  DC D079500
  HN Formerly (1963-1985) DC 054300, Bilingual/Bilingualism.
  RT Biculturalism
       Bilingual Education
       Code Switching
       Crosscultural Analysis
       Cultural Pluralism
       Diglossia
       Intercultural Communication
       Language Maintenance
       Language Planning
       Language Policy
       Language Social Class Relationship
       Languages
       Monolingualism
       Multilingualism
       Psycholinguistics
       Second Language Learning
       Sociolinguistics
       Translation

Bimodal (1981-1985)
  HN DC 054400, deleted 1986.

Binet, Alfred
  DC D079800
  SN Born 1857 - died 1911.
  HN Formerly (1971-1985) DC 054420, Binet, A.

Binomial/Binomialism (1963-1985)
  HN DC 054450, deleted 1986.

Bio- / Bisexuality

Bio- (1971-1985)
- HN DC 054465, deleted 1986. See now specific terms.

Bioethics
- DC D080100
- HN Added, 1986.
- BT Research Ethics
- RT Biological Sciences
  Eugenics
  Medical Research
  Medical Technology
  Medicine
  Morality
  Personhood
  Scientific Research

Biographies
- DC D080400
- SN Refers to Biographies as topics of analysis, not as types of documents.
- HN Formerly (1965-1985) DC 054485, Biography/Biographies/Biographic.
- BT Literature
- RT Autobiographical Materials
  Narratives
  Psychohistory

Biological Factors
- DC D080700
- SN Characteristics of the human body, including appearance, drives, instincts, and more subtle aspects of the individual genetic makeup, that play a role in analyses of social phenomena.
- HN Formerly (1963-1985) part of DC 054500, Biology/Biological.
- RT Biological Sciences
  Biology
  Environmental Factors
  Evolution
  Family
  Genetics
  Influence
  Social Factors
  Sociocultural Factors
  Sociodemographic Factors

Biological Sciences
- DC D081000
- HN Added, 1986.
- UF Life Sciences
- BT Natural Sciences
- NT Biology
  Biomedicine
  Ecology
  Ethology
  Genetics
  Physiology
- RT Bioethics
  Biological Factors
  Human Body

Biology
- DC D081300
- HN Formerly (1963-1985) part of DC 054500, Biology/Biological.
- BT Biological Sciences
- NT Sociobiology
- RT Behavioral Sciences
  Biological Factors
  Biomedicine
  Biotechnology
  Darwinism
  Eugenics
  Evolution
  Evolutionary Theories
  Genetics

Biology (cont'd)
- RT Human Body
  Life
  Physiology
  Plants (Botanical)
  Race
  Scientific Research
  Sex
  Sexual Reproduction

Biomedical Research
- Use Medical Research

Biomedicine
- DC D081600
- SN Branch of clinical medicine dealing with the relationship between body chemistry and physiological functions.
- HN Formerly (1985) DC 054502.
- BT Biological Sciences
  Medicine
- RT Biology

Biometric/Biometrics (1963-1985)
- HN DC 054503, deleted 1986.

Biosocial Theory
- DC D081900
- SN Closely related to Sociobiology.
- HN Formerly (1964-1985) DC 054505, Biosocial.
- BT Theories
- RT Social Theories
  Sociobiology
  Sociological Theory

Biosociology
- Use Sociobiology

Biotechnology
- DC D082200
- SN Use of biological organisms, systems, processes, or data to make or modify products, or address problems associated with the relationship between humans and machines.
- HN Added, 1986.
- UF Ergonomy/Ergonomic/Ergonomics (1969-1985)
  Human Factors Engineering
- BT Technology
- RT Biology
  Cybernetics
  Engineering
  Industrial Automation
  Scientific Research
  Work Environment
  Worker Machine Relationship

Birth
- DC D082500
- SN Refers to the process of childbirth, including both biological and sociocultural aspects.
- HN Formerly (1963-1985) DC 055200, Birth/Births.
- UF Childbearing/Childbirth (1964-1985)
  Parturition
- BT Life Cycle
- RT Abortion
  Birth Control
  Birth Order
  Birth Spacing
  Couvade
  Existence
  Fecundity
  Fertility
  Fertility Decline

Birth (cont'd)
- RT First Birth Timing
  Gynecology
  Illegitimacy
  Inbreeding
  Infant Mortality
  Infants
  Midwifery
  Physiology
  Pregnancy
  Reproductive Technologies
  Sexual Reproduction
  Twins
  Unwed Mothers

Birth Control
- DC D082800
- SN Refers both to specific contraceptive methods and devices and to related policies and beliefs.
- HN Formerly (1963-1985) DC 055210.
- UF Contraceptive/Contraceptives/Contraception (1963-1985)
- BT Family Planning
- NT Intrauterine Devices
- RT Abortion
  Birth
  Fertility
  Fertility Decline
  Population
  Population Policy
  Premarital Sex
  Sex Information
  Sterilization
  Vasectomy

Birth Defects
- Use Congenitally Handicapped

Birth Order
- DC D083100
- SN Implies culturally defined status ascribed to siblings according to relative birth order.
- HN Formerly (1969-1985) DC 055211.
- UF Primogeniture (1972-1985)
- RT Birth
  Birth Spacing
  First Birth Timing
  Inheritance And Succession
  Only Children
  Siblings

Birth Spacing
- DC D083400
- SN Time elapsed between births, determined both by physical and health characteristics of the mother and by Family Planning.
- HN Added, 1986.
- UF Child Spacing
- RT Birth
  Birth Order
  Family Planning
  Fecundity
  First Birth Timing
  Lactation
  Siblings

Birthdays
- Use Celebrations

Bisexuality
- DC D083600
- SN Sexual attraction to and/or intercourse with both opposite and same sex partners.
- HN Added, 1989.
- BT Sexual Behavior

Bivariate / Body

Bisexuality (cont'd)
- BT Sexuality
- RT Androgyny
  Heterosexuality
  Homosexuality
  Lesbianism
  Sex Roles
  Sexual Preferences
  Transsexualism

Bivariate (1971-1985)
- HN DC 055213, deleted 1986.

Black Community
- DC D083700
- HN Added, 1986.
- RT Blacks
  Communities
  Ethnic Groups
  Ethnic Neighborhoods
  Group Identity

Black Death
- Use Plague

Black Family
- DC D084000
- HN Added, 1986.
- BT Family
- RT Blacks
  Family Life
  Family Structure

Black Muslims
- DC D084300
- HN Formerly (1963-1985) DC 055225, Black Muslim/Black Muslims.
- UF Nation of Islam
- BT Muslims
- RT Blacks
  Islam

Black Nationalism (1964-1985)
- HN DC 055230.
- Use Black Power

Black Power
- DC D084600
- HN Formerly (1969-1985) DC 055235.
- UF Black Nationalism (1964-1985)
- RT Black White Relations
  Blacks
  Civil Rights
  Civil Rights Organizations
  Ethnic Identity
  Movements
  Nationalism
  Pan-Africanism
  Political Movements
  Political Power
  Self Determination
  Social Movements

Black White Differences
- DC D084900
- SN Used in analyses in which a social problem or phenomenon is explained as a consequence or correlate of differences between whites and blacks.
- HN Added, 1986.
- UF White Black Differences
- BT Racial Differences
- RT Anglo Americans
  Black White Relations
  Blacks
  Comparative Sociology
  Regional Differences
  Social Inequality
  Sociocultural Factors
  Whites

Black White Relations
- DC D085000
- HN Added, 1989.
- BT Racial Relations
- RT Black Power
  Black White Differences
  Blacks
  Majority Groups
  Minority Groups
  Whites

Blackmail/Blackmailing (1964-1985)
- HN DC 055223.
- Use Offenses

Blacks
- DC D085200
- HN Formerly (1966-1985) part of DC 055218, Black/Blacks.
- UF Afro (1963-1985)
  Negro/Negroes (1963-1985)
- RT Apartheid
  Black Community
  Black Family
  Black Muslims
  Black Power
  Black White Differences
  Black White Relations
  Ethnic Groups
  Race
  Racial Relations
  Slavery

Blau, Peter Michael
- DC D085500
- SN Born 7 February 1918 - .
- HN Formerly (1966-1985) DC 055250, Blau, Peter.

Blind
- DC D085800
- HN Formerly (1964-1985) DC 055300, Blind/Blindness.
- BT Handicapped
- RT Deaf
  Vision

Bloch, Ernst
- DC D086100
- SN Born 8 July 1885 - died 1977.
- HN Formerly (1984-1985) DC 056900.

Block/Blocks (1966-1985)
- HN DC 057000, deleted 1986.

Blood
- DC D086400
- HN Formerly (1963-1985) DC 057400.
- RT Blood Groups
  Blood Pressure
  Heart
  Human Body
  Leukemia
  Physiology

Blood Feuds
- Use Feuds

Blood Groups
- DC D086700
- HN Formerly (1963-1985) DC 057500.
- RT Blood
  Genetics

Blood Pressure
- DC D086800
- HN Added, 1986.
- UF Hypertension
- BT Pressure
- RT Blood
  Health
  Human Body

Blood Sacrifices
- Use Sacrificial Rites

Blue Collar Workers
- DC D087000
- SN Skilled, semiskilled, or unskilled workers engaged in physical, rather than mental or social, work. Contrasted with White Collar Workers.
- HN Formerly (1964-1985) DC 058470, Blue-Collar.
- BT Workers
- NT Agricultural Workers
  Domestics
  Farmers
  Fishermen
  Foremen
  Industrial Workers
  Longshoremen
  Manual Workers
  Miners
- RT Lower Class
  Occupational Classifications
  Occupations
  Professional Workers
  Unions
  White Collar Workers
  Working Class

Blue Cross Blue Shield Plans (1964-1985)
- HN DC 058500, deleted 1986.

Blumer, Herbert George
- DC D087300
- SN Born 7 March 1900 - died 13 April 1987.
- HN Formerly (1967-1985) DC 058503, Blumer, Herbert.

Boards of Directors
- Use Directors

Boards of Education
- Use School Boards

Boards of Trustees
- Use Governing Boards

Boas, Franz
- DC D087600
- SN Born 9 July 1858 - died 21 December 1942.
- HN Formerly (1964-1985) DC 058510.

Bodily Contact
- Use Physical Contact

Body Care
- Use Hygiene

Body Height
- DC D087900
- HN Added, 1986.
- UF Height (1963-1985)
  Stature (1965-1985)
- BT Physical Characteristics
- RT Body Weight
  Human Body

Body Image
- Use Self Concept

Body Language
- Use Nonverbal Communication

Body Weight
- DC D088200
- HN Added, 1986.
- UF Weight (1963-1985)
- BT Physical Characteristics
- RT Anorexia Nervosa
  Body Height
  Human Body
  Malnutrition
  Obesity

Body / Bourgeoisie

Body/Bodies (1963-1985)
- HN DC 059000.
- Use Human Body

Bogota, Colombia
- DC D088400
- HN Added, 1989.
- BT Colombia

Bohemia/Bohemian/Bohemians/ Bohemianism (1965-1985)
- HN DC 059990, deleted 1986. See now Czechoslovakia, Countercultures, or appropriate "Social Class" terms.

Bolivia
- DC D088500
- HN Formerly (1963-1985) DC 063130, Bolivia/Bolivian/Bolivians.
- BT South America

Bolshevism
- DC D088800
- SN Marxist Communism of the type practiced in the USSR during the period culminating in the Russian Revolution.
- HN Formerly (1964-1985) DC 063200, Bolshevism/Bolshevik.
- BT Marxism
- RT Communism
  Leninism
  Stalinism

Bombay, India
- DC D089100
- HN Formerly (1963-1985) DC 063275.
- BT India

Bombs
- DC D089400
- HN Formerly (1965-1985) DC 063325, Bomb/Bombs/Bombing/Bombings/ Bomber/Bombers.
- BT Weapons
- RT Terrorism

Bond/Bonds/Bonding (1983-1985)
- HN DC 063414.
- Use Attachment

Book Industry
- Use Publishing Industry

Book Reviews
- DC D089700
- SN Discussions of Book Reviews as methods of sociological analysis.
- HN Added, 1986.
- BT Publications
- RT Books
  Literary Criticism
  Literature Reviews

Bookkeeping
- Use Accounting

Books
- DC D090000
- HN Formerly (1963-1985) DC 063700, Book/Books.
- UF Monograph/Monographs/ Monographic (1964-1985)
- BT Publications
- RT Bibliographies
  Book Reviews
  Literature
  Novels
  Short Stories
  Writing for Publication

Boom Towns
- DC D090300
- HN Formerly (1984-1985) DC 063705, Boom Town/Boom Towns.
- BT Towns
- RT Community Change
  Community Development

Borders
- DC D090500
- SN Boundaries between countries, usually including some of the adjacent territory on both sides.
- HN Added, 1989.
- UF Territorial Boundaries
- BT Boundaries
- RT Countries
  Emigration
  Geographic Regions
  Immigrants
  Immigration
  International Conflict
  International Relations
  Invasion
  Regional Differences
  States (Political Subdivisions)
  Undocumented Immigrants
  War

Boredom
- DC D090600
- HN Formerly (1968-1985) DC 063750.
- BT Emotions
- RT Apathy

Borgatta, Edgar F.
- DC D090700
- SN Born 1 Sept 1924 - .
- HN Reinstated, 1989. Formerly (1963-1985) DC 063758.

Born (1963-1985)
- HN DC 063770, deleted 1986.

Borneo (1963-1985)
- HN DC 063775.
- Use Indonesia

Borstal
- DC D090900
- SN British reform school system for adolescent delinquents aged 16 through 23.
- HN Formerly (1966-1985) DC 063786.
- RT Juvenile Correctional Institutions

Boston, Massachusetts
- DC D091200
- HN Formerly (1964-1985) DC 063825, Boston, Mass.
- BT Massachusetts

Botswana
- DC D091500
- HN Formerly (1984-1985) DC 063900.
- BT Sub Saharan Africa

Boulding, Kenneth Ewart
- DC D091700
- SN Born 18 January 1910 - .
- HN Added, 1989.

Boundaries
- DC D091800
- SN Socially and culturally defined parameters separating the individual and the group, and separating other abstractions such as kinship groups, families, ethnic groups, races, and nations.

Boundaries (cont'd)
- HN Formerly (1963-1985) DC 063910, Boundary/Boundaries.
- UF Social Boundaries
- NT Borders
- RT Access
  Boundary Maintenance
  Constraints
  Social Stratification
  Social Structure
  Space
  Territoriality

Boundary Maintenance
- DC D092100
- SN In action theory and functionalism, the tendency of a social system to perpetuate its existence as a self-contained unit by maintaining constant patterns of integration among its components relative to the external environment.
- HN Added, 1986.
- RT Boundaries
  Social Closure
  Social Processes
  Social Systems

Bourdieu, Pierre
- DC D092400
- SN Born 1 August 1930 - .
- HN Formerly (1985) DC 063925.

Bourgeois Ideologies
- DC D092700
- SN Belief systems originating with and supporting the interests of the Bourgeoisie.
- HN Added, 1986.
- BT Ideologies
- RT Bourgeoisie
  Political Ideologies

Bourgeois Societies
- DC D093000
- HN Added, 1986.
- BT Society
- RT Bourgeoisie
  Capitalist Societies
  Marxism
  Western Society

Bourgeois Sociology
- DC D093100
- SN Sociology in capitalist societies, seen from a Marxist point of view as serving the interests of the bourgeoisie and ruling class.
- HN Added, 1986.
- BT Sociology
- RT Marxist Sociology
  Radical Sociology

Bourgeoisie
- DC D093300
- SN In Marxist analysis, the social class made up of entrepreneurs, merchants, and industrialists active in the early stages of capitalist development, distinguished from the Ruling Class and Aristocracy above and the Proletariat and Peasants below.
- HN Formerly (1963-1985) DC 063940, Bourgeois/Bourgeoisie/ Bourgeoisification.
- UF Petite Bourgeoisie
- RT Bourgeois Ideologies
  Bourgeois Societies
  Embourgeoisement
  Forces And Relations of Production
  Middle Class

Boy

Boy/Boys (1963-1985)
- HN DC 064000.
- Use Children

Boycotts
- DC D093600
- HN Formerly (1964-1985) DC 064004, Boycott/Boycotts/Boycotting.
- BT Protest Movements
- RT Social Action
  Strikes

Brahmans
- Use Brahmins

Brahmins
- DC D093900
- HN Formerly (1964-1985) DC 064900, Brahmin/Brahmins.
- UF Brahmans
- BT Hindus
- RT Hinduism

Brain
- DC D094200
- HN Formerly (1964-1985) DC 065500, Brain/Brains.
- RT Alzheimer's Disease
  Cerebral Palsy
  Epilepsy
  Human Body
  Neurology
  Senility

Brain Drain
- DC D094500
- SN Migration of professionals (eg, scientists, professors, and physicians) from one country to another, usually for higher salaries and better living conditions.
- HN Formerly (1978-1985) DC 065510.
- BT Emigration
- RT Professions
  Scientists

Brainwashing
- DC D094800
- SN Forcible manipulation of an individual's will, often by means of physical or psychological duress, to induce a radical departure from former behavior patterns or beliefs.
- HN Formerly (1976-1985) DC 065550.
- UF Coercive Persuasion
  Menticide
  Thought Control
- BT Indoctrination
  Torture
- RT Coercion

Brand Names
- DC D095100
- HN Formerly (1972-1985) DC 065580, Brand/Brands.
- RT Advertising
  Consumers
  Purchasing
  Retail Industry

Brazil
- DC D095400
- HN Formerly (1963-1985) DC 065700, Brazil/Brazilian/Brazilians.
- BT South America
- NT Porto Alegre, Brazil
  Rio de Janeiro, Brazil
  Sao Paulo, Brazil
- RT Amazon

Breaking and Entering
- Use Burglary

Breast Feeding
- DC D095700
- HN Formerly (1969-1985) DC 065800.
- BT Feeding Practices
- RT Childrearing Practices
  Lactation

Breed/Breeding (1965-1985)
- HN DC 065815, deleted 1986. See now Inbreeding, Eugenics, or Animal Husbandry.

Bribery (1964-1985)
- HN DC 065900.
- Use Offenses

Brideprice
- Use Bridewealth

Bridewealth
- DC D096000
- HN Formerly (1965-1985) DC 066000.
- UF Brideprice
- RT Dowry
  Marriage

Brisbane, Australia
- DC D096200
- HN Added, 1989.
- BT Australia

Britain/British (1963-1985)
- HN DC 067100, deleted 1986. See now Great Britain or England.

British Columbia
- DC D096300
- HN Added, 1986.
- BT Canada
- NT Vancouver, British Columbia

Brittany, France (1967-1985)
- HN DC 067120, deleted 1986.

Broadcast Communications
- Use Telecommunications

Broadcast Scheduling
- Use Programming (Broadcast)

Broadcast Television
- Use Television

Broadcast/Broadcasts/ Broadcasting/Broadcasters (1963-1985)
- HN DC 067175.
- Use Mass Media

Bronze Age (1971-1985)
- HN DC 067180.
- Use Prehistory

Brooklyn, N.Y. (1969-1985)
- HN DC 067250.
- Use New York City, New York

Brother/Brothers (1985)
- HN DC 067300.
- Use Siblings

Brotherhoods (Religious)
- Use Religious Brotherhoods

Buildings

Brussels, Belgium
- DC D096600
- HN Formerly (1967-1985) DC 067425.
- BT Belgium

Buber, Martin
- DC D096900
- SN Born 8 February 1878 - died 13 June 1965.
- HN Formerly (1966-1985) DC 067450.

Bucharest, Romania
- DC D097200
- HN Formerly (1967-1985) DC 067475, Bucharest, Rumania.
- BT Romania

Buddhism
- DC D097500
- HN Formerly (1963-1985) part of DC 067500, Buddhism/Buddhist/ Buddhists.
- BT Religions
- NT Zen Buddhism
- RT Buddhists
  Dharma
  Karma

Buddhists
- DC D097800
- HN Formerly (1963-1985) part of DC 067500, Buddhism/Buddhist/ Buddhists.
- BT Religious Cultural Groups
- RT Asian Cultural Groups
  Buddhism
  Lamaism

Budgets
- DC D098100
- HN Formerly (1963-1985) DC 067510, Budget/Budgets/Budgeting.
- RT Accounting
  Appropriation
  Cost Containment
  Expenditures
  Finance
  Income
  Management
  Public Debt
  Resource Allocation

Buenos Aires, Argentina
- DC D098400
- HN Formerly (1964-1985) DC 067550.
- BT Argentina

Buffalo, New York
- DC D098700
- HN Formerly (1963-1985) DC 067575, Buffalo, N.Y.
- BT New York

Building Industry
- Use Construction Industry

Buildings
- DC D099000
- HN Formerly (1965-1985) DC 067600, Building/Buildings.
- BT Facilities
- RT Architecture
  Construction Industry
  Hostels
  Hotels
  Housing
  Shelters

Bulgaria

Bulgaria
- DC D099300
- HN Formerly (1963-1985) DC 067700, Bulgaria/Bulgarian/Bulgarians.
- BT Balkan States
  Eastern Europe
- NT Sofia, Bulgaria

Bulimia
- DC D099400
- SN Eating disorder primarily affecting young women, characterized by extreme overeating followed by self-induced vomiting.
- HN Added, 1986.
- BT Eating Disorders
- RT Anorexia Nervosa
  Mental Illness

Bund/Bunds/Bundist/Bundists (1970-1985)
- HN DC 067720, deleted 1986.

Bureau of Indian Affairs (1963-1985)
- HN DC 067855.
- Use Government Agencies

Bureaucracy
- DC D099600
- SN Highly structured organizations designed to accomplish explicit purposes efficiently, but often characterized by inefficiency due to excessive size, internal complexity, and inability to adjust to changing external circumstances.
- HN Formerly (1963-1985) DC 067800, Bureaucracy/Bureaucracies/Bureaucrat/Bureaucratic.
- UF Bureaucratic Organization
- BT Organizational Structure
- RT Bureaucratization
  Civil Service
  Complex Organizations
  Hierarchy
  Organizations (Social)
  Public Administration

Bureaucratic Organization
- Use Bureaucracy

Bureaucratization
- DC D099900
- SN The process whereby a social organization acquires the formality and regimentation of a bureaucracy.
- HN Formerly (1963-1985) DC 067850.
- BT Social Processes
- RT Bureaucracy
  Rationalization

Burgher (1964-1985)
- HN DC 067860, deleted 1986.

Burglary
- DC D100200
- HN Formerly (1971-1985) DC 067863, Burglar/Burglars/Burglary.
- UF Breaking and Entering
- BT Offenses
- RT Larceny
  Robbery

Burials
- DC D100500
- HN Formerly (1963-1985) DC 067870, Burial/Burials.
- UF Interments
  Mortuary Rites
- BT Death Rituals
- RT Cemeteries
  Cremation

Burials (cont'd)
- RT Death
  Death Attitudes
  Funerals
  Religious Rituals

Burke, Edmund
- DC D100800
- SN Born 12 January 1729 - died 9 July 1797.
- HN Formerly (1966-1985) DC 067876.

Burkina Faso
- DC D101100
- HN Added, 1986.
- UF Upper Volta (1971-1985)
- BT Sub Saharan Africa

Burma
- DC D101400
- HN Formerly (1963-1985) DC 067890, Burma/Burmese.
- BT Southeast Asia
- NT Rangoon, Burma

Burnout (1983-1985)
- HN DC 067892a.
- Use Occupational Stress

Burt, Sir Cyril Lodowic
- DC D101700
- SN Born 1883 - died 1971.
- HN Formerly (1963-1985) DC 067893, Burt, Sir Cyril.

Burundi
- DC D102000
- HN Formerly (1968-1985) DC 067900.
- BT Sub Saharan Africa

Buses
- Use Automobiles

Bushmen (1969-1985)
- HN DC 067970, deleted 1986. See now Traditional Societies or African Cultural Groups.

Business
- DC D102300
- HN Formerly (1963-1985) DC 068000, Business/Businesses.
- NT Agribusiness
- RT Business Cycles
  Business Society Relationship
  Businessmen
  Capitalism
  Commodities
  Contracts
  Corporations
  Depression (Economics)
  Economic Sectors
  Economics
  Employers
  Employment
  Enterprises
  Entrepreneurship
  Executives
  Finance
  Industry
  Investment
  Labor
  Markets
  Minority Businesses
  Oligopolies
  Private Sector
  Products
  Profits
  Purchasing

Byzantium

Business (cont'd)
- RT Retail Industry
  Sales
  Small Businesses
  Trade
  Unions

Business Cycles
- DC D102600
- HN Added, 1986.
- UF Economic Cycles
  Economic Fluctuations
- RT Business
  Cyclical Processes
  Depression (Economics)
  Econometric Analysis
  Economic Change
  Economic Conditions
  Economic History
  Economic Problems
  Inflation
  Market Economy

Business Elite
- Use Economic Elites

Business Enterprises
- Use Enterprises

Business Organizations
- Use Enterprises

Business Society Relationship
- DC D102900
- SN Studies focusing on social institutions related to business and commerce and their effects on and interactions with other aspects of society.
- HN Added, 1986.
- BT Social Relations
- RT Business
  Corporatism
  Employment
  Employment Changes
  Labor
  Occupational Structure
  Public Relations
  Public Sector Private Sector Relations
  Society

Businessmen
- DC D103200
- HN Formerly (1963-1985) DC 068025, Businessmen/Businessman.
- NT Merchants
- RT Business
  Enterprises
  Entrepreneurship
  Executives
  Professional Workers
  Profit Motive

Busing (1981-1985)
- HN DC 068032.
- Use School Desegregation

Buyer (1971-1985)
- HN DC 068050, deleted 1986. See now Consumers or Purchasing.

Buying
- Use Purchasing

Byzantium/Byzantine (1967-1985)
- HN DC 068100.
- Use Middle Ages

27

Cabala

Cabala
- DC D103500
- HN Formerly (1964-1986) DC 068200.
- BT Occultism
- RT Judaism
     Mysticism

Cable Television
- Use Television

Cadres
- DC D103600
- SN The white-collar labor force manning contemporary bureaucracies, particularly managers and upper-level technicians.
- HN Formerly (1964-1985) DC 068400, Cadre/Cadres.
- BT Groups
- RT Leadership
     Management
     Managers

Cafe/Cafes (1964-1985)
- HN DC 068450.
- Use Eating And Drinking Establishments

CAI
- Use Computer Assisted Instruction

Cairo, Egypt
- DC D103700
- HN Added, 1989.
- BT Egypt

Cajun/Cajuns (1983-1985)
- HN DC 068530, deleted 1986. See now North American Cultural Groups or Ethnic Groups.

Calculation
- Use Computation

Calcutta, India
- DC D103800
- HN Formerly (1964-1985) DC 068600.
- BT India

Calendars
- DC D104100
- HN Formerly (1964-1985) DC 068670, Calendar.
- RT Holidays
     Time

Calibrate/Calibration (1971-1985)
- HN DC 068575, deleted 1986.

California
- DC D104400
- HN Formerly (1963-1985) DC 068950, California/Californian/Californians.
- BT United States of America
     Western States
- NT Los Angeles, California
     San Diego, California
     San Francisco, California

California F-Scale (1969-1985)
- HN DC 069000.
- Use F-Scale

Calvinism
- DC D104700
- HN Formerly (1963-1985) part of DC 069100, Calvin/Calvinist/Calvinists/Calvinism.
- BT Protestantism
- RT Calvinists

Calvinists
- DC D105000
- HN Formerly (1963-1985) part of DC 069100, Calvin/Calvinist/Calvinists/Calvinism.
- BT Protestants
- RT Calvinism

Cambodia/Cambodian/Cambodians (1963-1985)
- HN DC 069143.
- Use Kampuchea

Camera/Cameras (1972-1985)
- HN DC 069157.
- Use Photographs

Cameroons
- DC D105300
- HN Formerly (1963-1985) DC 069160.
- BT Sub Saharan Africa

Campaigns (Political)
- Use Political Campaigns

Camping
- DC D105600
- HN Formerly (1964-1985) DC 069165, Camp/Camps/Camping.
- BT Activities
- RT Recreational Facilities

Campus/Campuses (1964-1985)
- HN DC 069169, deleted 1986. See now Colleges, Universities, or Higher Education.

Camus, Albert
- DC D105900
- SN Born 7 November 1913 - died 4 January 1960.
- HN Formerly (1964-1985) DC 069170.

Canada
- DC D106200
- HN Formerly (1963-1985) DC 069175, Canada/Canadian/Canadians.
- BT North America
- NT Alberta
     British Columbia
     Manitoba
     New Brunswick
     Newfoundland
     Northwest Territories
     Nova Scotia
     Ontario
     Prince Edward Island
     Quebec
     Saskatchewan
     Yukon

Canary Islands
- DC D106500
- HN Added, 1986.
- BT Western Europe
- RT North Africa
     North Atlantic Ocean

Canberra, Australia
- DC D106600
- HN Added, 1989.
- BT Australia

Cancer
- DC D106800
- HN Formerly (1963-1985) DC 069200.
- UF Carcinogen/Carcinogens/Carcinogenic (1980-1985)
     Neoplasms
- BT Diseases
- NT Leukemia
- RT Smoking
     Terminal Illness

Capital

Candidates
- DC D107100
- HN Formerly (1963-1985) DC 069210, Candidate/Candidates.
- UF Political Candidates
- RT Elections
     Political Campaigns
     Political Parties
     Political Power
     Politicians
     Politics
     Public Officials

Cannabis
- Use Marijuana

Cannibalism
- DC D107400
- HN Formerly (1964-1985) DC 069230, Cannibal/Cannibals/Cannibalism.
- UF Windigo Psychosis
- RT Death Rituals
     Myths
     Rituals
     Sacrificial Rites
     Taboos
     Totemism

Canonical Correlation
- Use Discriminant Analysis

Canonization
- Use Saints

Canons
- DC D107700
- SN Laws or rules of doctrine decreed by church councils and approved by the highest ecclesiastical authority. Also lists of those books officially recognized as Christian Holy Scripture.
- HN Formerly (1972-1985) part of DC 069234, Canon/Canons/Canonize/Canonized/Canonization.
- BT Religious Doctrines
- RT Christianity
     Ecclesiastical Law
     Religious Beliefs
     Religious Literature

Cantril, Albert Hadley
- DC D108000
- SN Born 1906 - died 1969.
- HN Formerly (1965-1985) DC 069250, Cantril, Hadley.

Capacity (1971-1985)
- HN DC 069370.
- Use Ability

Cape Town, South Africa
- DC D108250
- HN Added, 1989.
- BT South Africa

Cape Verde Islands
- DC D108300
- HN Added, 1986.
- BT Sub Saharan Africa
- RT North Atlantic Ocean

Capital
- DC D108600
- HN Formerly (1963-1985) DC 069390.
- RT Accumulation
     Banking
     Capitalism
     Economics
     Finance
     Income

Capital

Capital (cont'd)
- **RT** Investment
  Labor
  Marxist Economics
  Money
  Production
  Profits
  Property
  Saving
  Wealth

Capital Punishment
- **DC** D108900
- **HN** Formerly (1971-1985) DC 069395.
- **UF** Death Penalty (1979-1985)
- **BT** Punishment
- **RT** Deterrence

Capitalism
- **DC** D109200
- **HN** Formerly (1963-1985) DC 069400, Capitalism/Capitalist/Capitalistic.
- **BT** Economic Systems
  Political Ideologies
- **NT** Monopoly Capitalism
  State Capitalism
- **RT** Business
  Capital
  Capitalist Societies
  Communism
  Conflict Theory
  Democracy
  Forces And Relations of Production
  Imperialism
  Labor
  Labor Process
  Market Economy
  Marxism
  Marxist Economics
  Marxist Sociology
  Modes of Production
  Political Economy
  Profit Motive
  Socialism
  World System Theory

Capitalist Countries
- **Use** Capitalist Societies

Capitalist Societies
- **DC** D109500
- **HN** Added, 1986.
- **UF** Capitalist Countries
- **BT** Society
- **RT** Bourgeois Societies
  Capitalism
  Communist Societies
  Industrial Societies
  Liberal Democratic Societies
  Political Ideologies
  Rationalization
  Socialist Societies
  Western Society
  Working Class

Capitalist World System
- **Use** World System Theory

Caplow, Theodore
- **DC** D109525
- **SN** Born 1 May 1920 - .
- **HN** Added, 1989.

Captivity (1966-1985)
- **HN** DC 069500.
- **Use** Prisoners of War

Caracas, Venezuela
- **DC** D109550
- **HN** Added, 1989.
- **BT** Venezuela

Carcinogen/Carcinogens/Carcinogenic (1980-1985)
- **HN** DC 069600.
- **Use** Cancer

Cardiovascular Diseases
- **Use** Heart Diseases

Care (1984-1985)
- **HN** DC 069640, deleted 1986. See now Child Care Services, Day Care, Foster Care, Health Care, After Care, or Self Care.

Career Choice
- **Use** Occupational Choice

Career Criminals
- **DC** D109700
- **SN** Individuals whose primary, long-term occupational identity is as a specialist in some area of criminal activity. Do not confuse with White Collar Crime.
- **HN** Added, 1989.
- **UF** Professional Criminals
- **BT** Offenders
- **RT** Deviant Behavior
  Organized Crime
  Recidivism

Career Decisions
- **Use** Occupational Choice

Career Goals
- **Use** Occupational Aspiration

Career Mobility
- **Use** Occupational Mobility

Career Patterns
- **DC** D109800
- **HN** Added, 1986.
- **RT** Careers
  Occupational Mobility
  Work Experience

Career Plans
- **Use** Life Plans

Careers
- **DC** D110100
- **SN** Sequences of related occupational roles through which individuals progress or plan to progress during their working lives, often with increasing prestige and financial benefits.
- **HN** Formerly (1963-1985) DC 069700, Career/Careers.
- **NT** Academic Careers
- **RT** Career Patterns
  Dual Career Family
  Employment
  Life Plans
  Occupational Achievement
  Occupational Aspiration
  Occupational Choice
  Occupational Mobility
  Occupational Status
  Occupations
  Professions
  Promotion (Occupational)

Caribbean

Caregivers
- **DC** D110200
- **HN** Reinstated 1989. Formerly (1984-1985) DC 069660.
- **RT** Child Care Services
  Day Care
  Foster Care
  Health Care
  Health Professions
  Social Services
  Social Workers

Cargo Cults
- **DC** D110400
- **SN** Tribal religious groups that emerged in New Guinea following initial contacts with Western culture. Ancient beliefs and symbols took the form of explorers, aircraft, and landing strips, and rituals were adapted to induce supply planes to return from "the other world."
- **HN** Formerly (1963-1985) DC 069750.
- **BT** Cults
- **RT** Messianic Movements
  Millenarianism
  Oceanic Cultural Groups
  Traditional Societies

Caribbean
- **DC** D110700
- **HN** Formerly (1963-1985) DC 069800.
- **UF** Antilles (1964-1985)
  Greater Antilles
  Indies, West/Indian, West/Indians, West (1964-1985)
  Leeward Islands
  Lesser Antilles
  West Indies
  Windward Islands
- **BT** Latin America
- **NT** Anguilla
  Antigua
  Bahamas
  Barbados
  Barbuda
  Cayman Islands
  Cuba
  Dominica
  Dominican Republic
  Grenada
  Guadeloupe
  Haiti
  Jamaica
  Martinique
  Montserrat
  Netherlands Antilles
  Puerto Rico
  Saba
  Saint Barthelemy
  Saint Eustatius
  Saint Kitts Nevis
  Saint Lucia
  Saint Martin
  Saint Vincent
  Trinidad And Tobago
  Turks And Caicos Islands
  Virgin Islands
- **RT** Caribbean Cultural Groups
  Central America

Caribbean Cultural Groups
- **DC** D110725
- **HN** Added 1986. Prior to 1986, concepts representing specific Caribbean cultural groups, eg, Haitians, were often indexed under terms representing the geographic place name, eg, Haiti/Haitian/Haitians.
- **BT** Latin American Cultural Groups
- **RT** Caribbean
  North American Cultural Groups

Caricature

Caricature/Caricatures (1969-1985)
HN DC 069810.
Use Satire

Carnival/Carnivals (1970-1985)
HN DC 069865.
Use Festivals

Caroline Islands
DC D111000
HN Formerly (1964-1985) DC 069872, Carolines.
BT Micronesia

Cars
Use Automobiles

Carter Administration
DC D111300
HN Formerly (1981-1985) DC 069878, Carter, James Earl.
RT Presidents

Cartoons
DC D111600
HN Formerly (1963-1985) DC 069900, Cartoon/Cartoons/Cartoonist.
BT Audiovisual Media
RT Children
Comics (Publications)
Films
Humor
Mass Media Effects
Mass Media Violence
Satire
Television

Case Disposition
Use Disposition

Case Studies
DC D111750
HN Formerly (1963-1985) DC 070200, Case Study/Case Studies.
BT Methodology (Data Collection)
RT Longitudinal Studies
Qualitative Methods
Research

Cases (Legal)
Use Legal Cases

Cases (Social Work)
Use Social Work Cases

Casework/Caseworker/Caseworkers (1963-1985)
HN DC 070250.
Use Social Work

Caste Systems
DC D111900
SN A system of social stratification in which the strata are arranged hierarchically according to relative spiritual purity. Associated primarily with traditional Hindu society in and around India, these systems are characterized by strict rules and highly structured rituals preserving caste boundaries.
HN Formerly (1963-1985) DC 070350, Caste/Castes.
UF Jajmani System (1964-1985)
Subcaste (1984-1985)
Untouchable/Untouchables/
Untouchability (1963-1985)
BT Social Systems
RT Ascription
Ethnic Groups

Caste Systems (cont'd)
RT Hinduism
Panchayats
Social Control
Social Status
Social Stratification
Social Structure
Traditional Societies

Castration
DC D112200
HN Formerly (1963-1985) DC 070375.
BT Surgery
RT Genitals
Sterilization

Casualty/Casualties (1963-1985)
HN DC 070500, deleted 1986.

Catalan (Language)
Use Romance Languages

Catalonia, Spain
DC D112500
SN A region in northeastern Spain extending along the Mediterranean Sea from the French border.
HN Formerly (1964-1985) DC 070515, Catalan/Catalonia, Spain.
BT Spain

Catastrophe/Catastrophes (1966-1985)
HN DC 070700.
Use Disasters

Categorical Data
DC D112650
HN Added, 1986.
BT Data
RT Qualitative Methods

Category/Categories/Categorical/
Categorization (1963-1985)
HN DC 071000.
Use Classification

Cathari
DC D112800
HN Formerly (1969-1985) DC 071600.
BT Religious Cultural Groups
RT Asceticism
Christianity
Manicheism

Catholic Charities
Use Charities

Catholicism
DC D113100
HN Formerly (1963-1985) part of DC 073000, Catholic/Catholics/Catholicism.
BT Christianity
NT Roman Catholicism
RT Catholics
Religious Orthodoxy

Catholics
DC D113400
HN Formerly (1963-1985) part of DC 073000, Catholic/Catholics/Catholicism.
BT Christians
NT Roman Catholics
RT Catholicism

Celebrations

Cattle/Cattlebreeding (1964-1985)
HN DC 073500.
Use Livestock

Caucasian/Caucasians (1966-1985)
HN DC 073800.
Use Whites

Caucus/Caucuses (1972-1985)
HN DC 073850, deleted 1986.

Causal Analysis
Use Causality

Causal Attribution
Use Attribution

Causal Models
DC D113500
SN Systematic representations of possible causal connections among variables.
HN Added, 1986.
BT Models
RT Causality
Explanation
Loglinear Analysis
Methodology (Philosophical)
Path Analysis
Regression Analysis

Causality
DC D113550
HN Formerly (1963-1985) DC 074050.
UF Agency
Causal Analysis
RT Attribution
Causal Models
Determinism
Disorders
Effects
Etiology
Explanation
Influence
Interaction
Methodology (Philosophical)
Path Analysis
Randomness

Cause/Causes/Causal/Causation (1963-1985)
HN DC 074000, deleted 1986. See now Causal Models or Causality.

Cayman Islands
DC D113700
HN Added, 1986.
BT Caribbean

Celebrations
DC D113800
SN Festivities or observances held in honor of anniversaries, birthdays, reunions, etc.
HN Added, 1989.
UF Anniversaries
Birthdays
RT Customs
Festivals
Gift Giving
Holidays
Life Events
Rituals
Sociability
Social Life
Weddings

Celibacy

Celibacy
- **DC** D114000
- **HN** Formerly (1964-1985) DC 074200, Celibate/Celibates/Celibacy.
- **UF** Chastity (1970-1985)
  Sexual Abstinence
- **BT** Sexual Behavior
- **RT** Virginity

Cemeteries
- **DC** D114300
- **HN** Formerly (1977-1985) DC 074250, Cemetery/Cemeteries.
- **UF** Graveyards
- **NT** Ossuaries
- **RT** Burials
  Death
  Death Attitudes
  Death Rituals

Censorship
- **DC** D114600
- **HN** Formerly (1963-1985) DC 074350, Censor/Censors/Censored/Censorship.
- **UF** Political Censorship
- **RT** Academic Freedom
  Information Dissemination
  Morality
  Publications
  Repression (Political)
  Sanctions
  Social Values
  State Power

Census
- **DC** D114900
- **HN** Formerly (1963-1985) DC 074400, Census/Censuses.
- **UF** Population Statistics
- **BT** Methodology (Data Collection)
- **RT** Demography
  Population
  Social Area Analysis
  Statistics

Center And Periphery
- **DC** D115200
- **SN** Refers to both the relations between the power and cultural core of a society and its subordinate, peripheral social groups; and, in the global economy, the relations between the economic core (ie, the highly developed industrialized countries) and underdeveloped peripheral economies (ie, countries trading primary products for manufactured goods).
- **HN** Added, 1986.
- **UF** Core (1984-1985)
  Peripheral/Periphery (1983-1985)
- **RT** Centrality
  Dependency Theory
  Developing Countries
  Dual Economy
  Economic Structure
  Economic Theories
  Economic Underdevelopment
  Imperialism
  Intergroup Relations
  International Division of Labor
  Labor Market Segmentation
  Majority Groups
  Marginality
  Metropolitan Areas
  Minority Groups
  Social Structure
  Trade
  World System Theory

Centers
- **DC** D115500
- **SN** Facilities serving as a focal point for activities or services.
- **HN** Formerly (1963-1985) DC 074440, Center/Centers.
- **BT** Facilities
- **NT** Community Mental Health Centers
- **RT** Agencies

Central African Republic
- **DC** D115800
- **HN** Added, 1986.
- **BT** Sub Saharan Africa

Central America
- **DC** D116100
- **HN** Formerly (1984-1985) DC 074504.
- **BT** Latin America
- **NT** Belize
  Costa Rica
  El Salvador
  Guatemala
  Honduras
  Nicaragua
  Panama
- **RT** Caribbean
  Mexico

Central American Indian Languages
- **Use** Amerindian Languages

Central Cities
- **DC** D116400
- **HN** Added, 1986.
- **UF** Inner City
- **BT** Cities
- **RT** Commuting (Travel)
  Ethnic Neighborhoods
  Ghettos
  Metropolitan Areas
  Skid Row
  Slums
  Suburbs
  Urban Poverty
  Urban Renewal

Central Government
- **DC** D116700
- **HN** Added, 1986.
- **UF** National Government
- **BT** Government
- **NT** Federal Government
- **RT** Local Government
  Presidents
  Provinces

Centrality
- **DC** D116900
- **HN** Formerly (1963-1985) DC 074510.
- **RT** Center And Periphery
  Communication
  Group Dynamics
  Marginality
  Organizational Structure
  Social Networks
  Social Structure

Centralization
- **DC** D117000
- **HN** Formerly (1963-1985) DC 074500, Central/Centralism/Centralization/Centralized.
- **BT** Organizational Structure
- **RT** Decentralization
  Organizational Change

Change

Century/Centuries (1963-1985)
- **HN** DC 074600.
- **Use** Time Periods

Ceramics (1965-1985)
- **HN** DC 076500.
- **Use** Crafts

Cerebral Palsy
- **DC** D117300
- **HN** Formerly (1980-1985) DC 077000.
- **RT** Brain
  Congenitally Handicapped
  Handicapped
  Mentally Retarded
  Neurology

Ceremony/Ceremonial/Ceremonialism (1963-1985)
- **HN** DC 077200.
- **Use** Rituals

Certainty
- **DC** D117600
- **HN** Formerly (1963-1985) DC 077400.
- **UF** Doubt (1969-1985)
  Uncertainty (1964-1985)
- **RT** Anxiety
  Beliefs
  Morale
  Security
  Skepticism

Certification
- **DC** D117900
- **HN** Formerly (1964-1985) DC 077440, Certification/Certifications.
- **UF** Accreditation (1984-1985)
  Credentialing
  Professional Certification
- **RT** Licenses
  Occupational Qualifications
  Qualifications

Ceylon/Ceylonese (1963-1985)
- **HN** DC 077600.
- **Use** Sri Lanka

Chad
- **DC** D118200
- **HN** Added, 1986.
- **BT** Sub Saharan Africa

Chains (Markov)
- **Use** Markov Process

Chance
- **DC** D118400
- **HN** Formerly (1963-1985) DC 077775, Chance/Chances.
- **UF** Luck (1969-1985)
- **RT** Fate
  Gambling
  Probability
  Randomness
  Risk

Change
- **DC** D118500
- **SN** A context-dependent term; select a more specific entry or coordinate with other terms. In contexts where Change is closely related to the narrower term Social Change, select the latter.
- **HN** Formerly (1963-1985) DC 077800, Change/Changes.
- **NT** Attitude Change
  Community Change

Change

Change (cont'd)
- **NT** Cooptation
  Cultural Change
  Demographic Change
  Economic Change
  Employment Changes
  Historical Development
  Job Change
  Language Shift
  Organizational Change
  Reform
  Revolutions
  Social Change
  Technological Change
- **RT** Adjustment
  Change Agents
  Development
  Developmental Stages
  History
  Improvement
  Means-Ends Rationality
  Mobility
  Preservation
  Resistance
  Stability
  Strategies
  Trends

Change Agents
- **DC** D118800
- **SN** In analyses of social and community development, persons and social groups responsible for implementing new policies and programs.
- **HN** Formerly (1963-1985) part of DC 020250, Agent/Agents.
- **UF** Agents (Change)
- **RT** Attitude Change
  Change
  Community Change
  Methods
  Organizational Change
  Social Change

Channel Islands
- **DC** D119100
- **HN** Added, 1986.
- **BT** Western Europe

Chapel/Chapels (1964-1985)
- **HN** DC 077850.
- **Use** Places of Worship

Character
- **Use** Personality

Character/Characters/ Characterization (1963-1985)
- **HN** DC 077990, deleted 1986. See now Personality or Fictional Characters.

Characteristic/Characteristics (1963-1985)
- **HN** DC 078050, deleted 1986. See now Client Characteristics, Demographic Characteristics, Interviewer Characteristics, Job Characteristics, or Physical Characteristics.

Charisma
- **DC** D119400
- **SN** Ability to charm, influence, or control people, especially in large groups, by the force of one's personality.
- **HN** Formerly (1963-1985) DC 078100, Charisma/Charismatic.
- **BT** Personality Traits
- **RT** Authority
  Cults
  Leadership
  Messianic Figures
  Religious Movements

Charitable Agencies
- **Use** Charities

Charitable Contributions
- **Use** Contributions (Donations)

Charities
- **DC** D119700
- **HN** Formerly (1963-1985) DC 078150, Charity/Charities.
- **UF** Catholic Charities
  Charitable Agencies
- **BT** Organizations (Social)
- **RT** Agencies
  Altruism
  Assistance
  Contributions (Donations)
  Financial Support
  Foundations
  Gift Giving
  Human Service Organizations
  Humanitarianism
  Nonprofit Organizations
  Philanthropy
  Social Action
  Social Agencies
  Social Interest
  Volunteers

Charter/Charters (1964-1985)
- **HN** DC 078190, deleted 1986.

Charts
- **Use** Graphs

Chassidim
- **Use** Hassidim

Chassidism
- **Use** Hassidism

Chastity (1970-1985)
- **HN** DC 078275.
- **Use** Celibacy

Chauvinism/Chauvinistic (1977-1985)
- **HN** DC 078400.
- **Use** Sexism

Cheating
- **DC** D120000
- **HN** Formerly (1966-1985) DC 078500, Cheat/Cheats/Cheater/Cheaters/ Cheating.
- **BT** Deviant Behavior
- **RT** Deception
  Fraud
  Offenses

Chemical Industry
- **DC** D120300
- **HN** Added, 1986.
- **BT** Manufacturing Industries
- **RT** Chemistry
  Petroleum Industry

Chemistry
- **DC** D120600
- **HN** Formerly (1963-1985) DC 079500, Chemist/Chemists/Chemistry/ Chemical.
- **UF** Inorganic Chemistry
  Organic Chemistry
- **BT** Physical Sciences
- **RT** Agricultural Technology
  Chemical Industry
  Metallurgical Technology
  Radiation
  Scientific Research

Child

Chi Square Test
- **DC** D120800
- **SN** In statistics, a test measuring how well actual data fit within a hypothetical normal distribution; often used for testing the presence of bias in a data sample.
- **HN** Formerly (1963-1985) DC 090100, Chi-Square.
- **RT** Quantitative Methods
  Statistical Significance
  Statistics

Chicago, Illinois
- **DC** D120900
- **HN** Formerly (1963-1985) DC 080400, Chicago, Ill.
- **BT** Illinois

Chicago School of Sociology
- **DC** D121200
- **SN** Form of interpretive sociology developed at the University of Chicago between 1918 and 1939, best known for its urban sociology and the development of the symbolic interactionist approach.
- **HN** Formerly (1985) DC 080405, Chicago School.
- **RT** History of Sociology
  Life History
  Social Psychology
  Sociological Research
  Sociological Theory
  Sociology
  Symbolic Interactionism
  Urban Sociology

Chicano/Chicanos (1972-1985)
- **HN** DC 080410.
- **Use** Mexican Americans

Chief/Chiefs (1964-1985)
- **HN** DC 080500.
- **Use** Chieftaincies

Chieftaincies
- **DC** D121500
- **HN** Formerly (1964-1985) DC 080510, Chieftain/Chieftaincy.
- **UF** Chief/Chiefs (1964-1985)
- **BT** Political Systems
- **RT** Authority
  Clans
  Traditional Societies

Child Abuse
- **DC** D121800
- **HN** Formerly (1981-1985) DC 081235.
- **UF** Battered Children
- **BT** Abuse
  Family Violence
- **NT** Child Sexual Abuse
- **RT** Battered Women
  Child Custody
  Child Neglect
  Children
  Parent Child Relations
  Spouse Abuse
  Victims

Child Care Services
- **DC** D122100
- **SN** Services such as baby-sitting, preschool, day care, or after-school care. Includes staff and child care facilities.
- **HN** Formerly (1979-1985) DC 081250, Child Care.
- **BT** Human Services
- **RT** Caregivers
  Childrearing Practices
  Children
  Day Care
  Foster Care

32

Child   Children

Child Custody
- **DC** D122400
- **SN** Judicial arrangement for the care of a child, usually as a result of divorce, abuse, or neglect.
- **HN** Formerly (1969-1985) DC 119875, Custody/Custodial.
- **UF** Joint Custody
  Shared Custody
- **RT** Child Abuse
  Child Neglect
  Child Support
  Divorce
  Family Policy
  Guardianship
  Mother Absence
  Parent Child Relations
  Placement
  Single Fathers
  Single Parent Family
  Visitation

Child Development
- **DC** D122700
- **SN** The physiological, psychological, cognitive, and social growth of the individual from birth to age 12.
- **HN** Added, 1986.
- **BT** Development
- **RT** Age Differences
  Autism
  Childhood
  Children
  Cognitive Development
  Developmental Stages
  Egocentrism
  Individual Differences
  Individuals
  Infants
  Life Cycle
  Oedipal Complex
  Parent Child Relations
  Pediatrics
  Psychological Development
  Socialization

Child Guidance
  Use Guidance

Child Mortality
- **DC** D122800
- **SN** Deaths of persons aged 24 months to 12 years.
- **HN** Added, 1989.
- **NT** Infant Mortality
- **RT** Children
  Death
  Health Policy
  Mortality Rates
  Survival

Child Neglect
- **DC** D123000
- **HN** Formerly (1984-1985) DC 088050.
- **RT** Child Abuse
  Child Custody
  Child Sexual Abuse
  Child Welfare Services
  Children
  Family Policy
  Family Violence
  Juvenile Delinquency
  Placement

Child Sex Preferences
- **DC** D123200
- **SN** Parents' preferences regarding offspring gender. Do not confuse with Sexual Preferences.
- **HN** Added, 1989.

Child Sex Preferences (cont'd)
- **UF** Male Child Preferences
  Parental Sex Preferences
  Sex Preferences (Children)
- **BT** Preferences
- **RT** Children
  Daughters
  Females
  Males
  Parental Attitudes
  Sex Role Attitudes
  Sons

Child Sexual Abuse
- **DC** D123225
- **HN** Added, 1989.
- **BT** Child Abuse
  Sexual Abuse
- **RT** Child Neglect
  Children
  Incest
  Parent Child Relations
  Victimization

Child Spacing
  Use Birth Spacing

Child Support
- **DC** D123250
- **SN** Financial support provided by a non-custodial parent, often required by the court in divorce cases.
- **HN** Added, 1989.
- **BT** Financial Support
- **RT** Alimony
  Child Custody
  Children
  Divorce
  Family Policy
  Payments

Child Welfare Services
- **DC** D123300
- **HN** Added, 1986.
- **BT** Welfare Services
- **RT** Child Neglect
  Children
  Food Stamps
  Foster Children
  Intervention
  Permanency Planning

Childbearing/Childbirth (1964-1985)
- **HN** DC 081500.
  Use Birth

Childhood
- **DC** D123600
- **HN** Formerly (1963-1985) part of DC 081000, Child/Children/Childhood.
- **UF** Latency Period
- **RT** Age Groups
  Child Development
  Childhood Factors
  Children
  Life Stage Transitions
  Puberty
  Youth

Childhood Factors
- **DC** D123700
- **SN** Childhood events or experiences used to explain patterns observed in adult social behavior.
- **HN** Added, 1989.
- **RT** Childhood
  Childrearing Practices
  Developmental Stages
  Home Environment

Childhood Factors (cont'd)
- **RT** Parent Child Relations
  Parental Attitudes
  Psychological Factors
  Role Models
  Significant Others
  Social Background

Childlessness
- **DC** D123900
- **HN** Formerly (1963-1985) DC 088000, Childless/Childlessness.
- **UF** Infertility (1966-1985)
  Sterility/Fertility (1966-1985)
- **RT** Family Planning
  Family Structure
  Gynecology
  Parenthood
  Surrogate Parents

Childrearing Attitudes
  Use Parental Attitudes

Childrearing Practices
- **DC** D124200
- **SN** Beliefs about and specific methods of raising children in a given parent-child relationship, family, or social group.
- **HN** Formerly (1963-1985) DC 088100, Childrearing.
- **UF** Parenting Methods
  Rearing/Reared (1966-1985)
- **BT** Methods
- **RT** Breast Feeding
  Child Care Services
  Childhood Factors
  Children
  Corporal Punishment
  Cultural Transmission
  Discipline
  Fathers
  Guidance
  Mothers
  Nurturance
  Parent Child Relations
  Parental Attitudes
  Parents
  Physical Contact
  Socialization
  Working Mothers

Children
- **DC** D124500
- **SN** Persons aged 24 months to 12 years.
- **HN** Formerly (1963-1985) part of DC 081000, Child/Children/Childhood.
- **UF** Boy/Boys (1963-1985)
  Girl/Girls (1963-1985)
- **BT** Age Groups
- **NT** Adopted Children
  Adult Children
  Foster Children
  Grandchildren
  Infants
  Only Children
  Preschool Children
- **RT** Adolescents
  Cartoons
  Child Abuse
  Child Care Services
  Child Development
  Child Mortality
  Child Neglect
  Child Sex Preferences
  Child Sexual Abuse
  Child Support
  Child Welfare Services

Children

Children (cont'd)
- RT Childhood
  - Childrearing Practices
  - Daughters
  - Dependents
  - Elementary School Students
  - Family Life
  - Family Role
  - Home Environment
  - Intergenerational Mobility
  - Orphans
  - Parent Child Relations
  - Pediatrics
  - Play
  - Relatives
  - Siblings
  - Sons
  - Twins

Children (Illegitimate)
- Use Illegitimacy

Chile
- DC D124800
- HN Formerly (1963-1985) DC 089900, Chile/Chilean/Chileans.
- BT South America

China
- DC D125000
- SN Use limited to China prior to 1949. See also Peoples Republic of China and Taiwan.
- HN Added, 1989. Formerly (1973-1985) DC 090050, China/Chinese.
- BT Asia
  - Far East
- RT Hong Kong
  - Macao
  - Mongolia

China/Chinese (1963-1985)
- HN DC 090050, deleted 1986.

Chinatown/Chinatowns (1973-1985)
- HN DC 090053.
- Use Ethnic Neighborhoods

Chiropractors
- DC D125100
- HN Formerly (1963-1985) DC 090075, Chiropractor/Chiropractors/Chiropractic.
- BT Professional Workers
- RT Health Professions

Choices
- DC D125400
- SN A context-dependent term for the options in decision-making processes; select a more specific entry or coordinate with other terms.
- HN Formerly (1963-1985) DC 090400, Choice/Choices.
- BT Decisions
- NT Dilemmas
  - Occupational Choice
  - Rational Choice
- RT Decision Making
  - Game Theory
  - Group Decision Making
  - Judgment
  - Mate Selection
  - Preferences
  - Selection Procedures

Choreography
- Use Dance

Chou En-lai
- DC D125700
- SN Born 1898 - died 8 January 1976.
- HN Formerly (1971-1985) DC 090430.

Christ (1964-1985)
- HN DC 090500.
- Use Jesus Christ

Christianity
- DC D126000
- HN Formerly (1963-1985) part of DC 090510, Christian/Christians/Christianity/Christianization.
- BT Religions
- NT Catholicism
  - Protestantism
- RT Bible
  - Canons
  - Cathari
  - Christians
  - Christmas
  - Devils
  - Ecumenical Movement
  - Ecumenicism
  - God (Judeo-Christian)
  - Jesus Christ
  - Jesus Movement
  - Judeo-Christian Tradition
  - Liturgy
  - Millenarianism
  - Paganism
  - Passion Plays
  - Seminarians
  - Western Civilization

Christianization
- Use Religious Conversion

Christians
- DC D126300
- HN Formerly (1963-1985) part of DC 090510, Christian/Christians/Christianity/Christianization.
- BT Religious Cultural Groups
- NT Catholics
  - Protestants
- RT Christianity
  - Gentiles
  - Judeo-Christian Tradition

Christmas
- DC D126600
- HN Formerly (1964-1985) DC 090515.
- BT Holidays
- RT Christianity
  - Gift Giving
  - Jesus Christ
  - Religious Rituals

Chromosome/Chromosomic (1969-1985)
- HN DC 090517, deleted 1986.

Chronic Illness
- DC D126900
- HN Added, 1986. Prior to 1986 use Chronic/Chronically (DC 090520) and Illness/Illnesses (DC 223700).
- BT Illness
- RT Adjustment
  - Pain
  - Physically Handicapped

Churches

Chronologies
- DC D127200
- HN Formerly (1964-1985) DC 090525, Chronology/Chronologies/Chronological.
- BT History
- RT Genealogy
  - Records (Documents)
  - Time
  - Time Periods

Church Attendance
- DC D127500
- HN Added, 1986.
- BT Attendance
  - Religious Behavior
- RT Church Membership
  - Churches
  - Places of Worship
  - Religiosity
  - Religious Rituals

Church Buildings
- Use Places of Worship

Church Doctrines
- Use Religious Doctrines

Church Membership
- DC D127800
- SN Refers broadly to membership in any religious congregation.
- HN Added, 1986.
- UF Religious Affiliation
- BT Membership
- RT Church Attendance
  - Churches
  - Congregations
  - Denominations
  - Laity (Religious)
  - Religious Behavior
  - Religious Beliefs

Church of England
- Use Anglicans

Church State Relationship
- DC D128100
- SN Relations between religious and political institutions.
- HN Added, 1986.
- BT Social Relations
- RT Churches
  - Ecclesiastical Law
  - Religion Politics Relationship
  - Religious Education
  - Secularization
  - State
  - State Society Relationship

Churches
- DC D128400
- HN Formerly (1963-1985) DC 090353, Church/Churches.
- BT Organizations (Social)
- RT Church Attendance
  - Church Membership
  - Church State Relationship
  - Community Organizations
  - Congregations
  - Denominations
  - Institutions
  - Nonprofit Organizations
  - Parishioners
  - Places of Worship
  - Religions
  - Sects
  - Secularization
  - Tithing

Cicourel

Cicourel, Aaron V.
- **DC** D128500
- **SN** Born 29 August 1928 - .
- **HN** Added, 1989.

Cigarette/Cigarettes (1964-1985)
- **HN** DC 090545.
- **Use** Smoking

Cincinnati, Ohio
- **DC** D128700
- **HN** Formerly (1969-1985) DC 090560.
- **BT** Ohio

Cinema (1963-1985)
- **HN** DC 090570.
- **Use** Films

Circulatory (1965-1985)
- **HN** DC 090585, deleted 1986.

Circumcision
- **DC** D129000
- **HN** Formerly (1964-1985) DC 090586.
- **UF** Ritual Circumcision
- **BT** Surgery
- **RT** Genital Mutilation
  Genitals

Circumstance/Circumstances (1971-1985)
- **HN** DC 090587.
- **Use** Environment

Cirrhosis (1964-1985)
- **HN** DC 090590.
- **Use** Diseases

Citations (References)
- **DC** D129300
- **SN** Published references by a scholar to the contributions of another. Includes studies of scientific productivity based on statistical analyses of publication patterns.
- **HN** Formerly (1972-1985) DC 090598, Cite/Cites/Cited/Citing/Citation.
- **UF** Bibliographic Citations
  Footnotes (References)
- **BT** Reference Materials
- **RT** Articles
  Bibliographies
  Literature Reviews

Cities
- **DC** D129600
- **HN** Formerly (1963-1985) DC 090610, City/Cities.
- **UF** Municipal/Municipality/Municipalities (1963-1985)
- **BT** Communities
- **NT** Central Cities
- **RT** City Planning
  Community Size
  Local Government
  Local Politics
  Mayors
  Metropolitan Areas
  Neighborhoods
  Public Administration
  Suburbs
  Towns
  Urban Areas
  Urban Development
  Urban Policy
  Urban Renewal
  Urban Sociology
  Urbanism
  Urbanization

Citizen Involvement
- **Use** Citizen Participation

Citizen Participation
- **DC** D129900
- **HN** Added, 1986.
- **UF** Citizen Involvement
  Public Participation
- **BT** Participation
- **RT** Activism
  Citizens
  Community Development
  Community Involvement
  Police Community Relations
  Political Participation
  Representation
  Social Action

Citizens
- **DC** D130200
- **HN** Formerly (1963-1985) part of DC 090600, Citizen/Citizens/Citizenship.
- **UF** Civilian/Civilians (1963-1985)
- **RT** Citizen Participation
  Citizenship
  Civil Defense
  Civil Rights
  Countries
  General Public
  Military Civilian Relations
  Political Participation
  Public Opinion
  State Society Relationship
  Voters

Citizenship
- **DC** D130500
- **HN** Formerly (1963-1985) part of DC 090600, Citizen/Citizens/Citizenship.
- **RT** Citizens
  Civil Rights
  Foreigners
  Military Service
  Political Defection
  Social Responsibility
  Voting

City Planners
- **Use** Planners

City Planning
- **DC** D130800
- **HN** Formerly (1964-1985) DC 090612.
- **UF** Urban Planning
- **BT** Local Planning
- **RT** Annexation
  Cities
  Community Development
  Government Policy
  Housing
  Local Government
  Neighborhood Change
  Public Transportation
  Urban Areas
  Urban Development
  Urban Renewal
  Zoning

City States (1964-1985)
- **HN** DC 090614, deleted 1986.

Civic/Civics (1963-1985)
- **HN** DC 090620, deleted 1986. See now Social Studies, Citizenship, Citizen Participation, or other appropriate "City" and "Social" terms.

Civil

Civil Codes
- **Use** Statutes

Civil Courts
- **Use** Courts

Civil Defense
- **DC** D131100
- **HN** Formerly (1963-1985) DC 090627.
- **RT** Armed Forces
  Citizens
  Military Civilian Relations
  Natural Disasters
  Survival
  War

Civil Disobedience
- **DC** D131400
- **HN** Formerly (1970-1985) DC 134508, Disobedience.
- **UF** Disobedience (Civil)
- **BT** Political Behavior
- **RT** Activism
  Civil Disorders
  Civil Rights
  Civil Rights Organizations
  Dissent
  Nonviolence
  Political Action
  Political Movements
  Political Power
  Protest Movements

Civil Disorders
- **DC** D131700
- **HN** Added, 1986.
- **UF** Civil Disturbances
- **BT** Disorders
  Violence
- **RT** Civil Disobedience
  Collective Behavior
  Conflict
  Emergencies
  Movements
  Political Violence
  Protest Movements
  Repression (Political)
  Riots
  Social Conflict
  Social Disorganization
  Social Unrest

Civil Disturbances
- **Use** Civil Disorders

Civil Law
- **Use** Law

Civil Liberties (1965-1985)
- **HN** DC 090629.
- **Use** Human Rights

Civil Procedure
- **Use** Legal Procedure

Civil Proceedings
- **Use** Litigation

Civil Religion
- **DC** D132000
- **SN** Sociocultural beliefs, symbols, and institutions that serve to legitimate a social system, create solidarity, and politically mobilize the society, and that exhibit many of the attributes and functions traditionally ascribed to religion.
- **HN** Added, 1986.
- **RT** National Identity
  Political Ideologies

Civil

Civil Religion (cont'd)
- RT Religions
- Secularization

Civil Rights
- DC D132300
- HN Formerly (1963-1985) DC 090632.
- BT Human Rights
- NT Property Rights
- Voting Rights
- RT Black Power
- Citizens
- Citizenship
- Civil Disobedience
- Civil Rights Organizations
- Constitutional Amendments
- Constitutions
- Democracy
- Discrimination
- Due Process
- Law
- Liberalism
- Privacy
- Racial Segregation
- Social Justice
- Social Movements
- Voting
- Womens Rights

Civil Rights Organizations
- DC D132600
- HN Added, 1986.
- UF Congress of Racial Equality/CORE (1969-1985)
- NAACP/National Assn Advancement Colored People (1966-1985)
- Southern Christian Leadership Conference/SCLC (1969-1985)
- BT Organizations (Social)
- RT Activism
- Black Power
- Civil Disobedience
- Civil Rights
- Interest Groups
- Political Action
- Protest Movements
- Racial Relations
- Social Action

Civil Service
- DC D132900
- HN Formerly (1981-1985) DC 090633.
- RT Bureaucracy
- Public Administration
- Public Officials

Civil Society
- DC D133200
- HN Added, 1986.
- BT Society
- RT General Public
- Mass Society
- Modern Society
- Social Relations
- State Society Relationship

Civil Unrest
- Use Social Unrest

Civil War
- DC D133500
- HN Formerly (1965-1985) DC 090634.
- BT War
- RT Guerrillas
- Political Violence
- Rebellions
- Revolutions

Civil/Civilized/Civilizing/Civility (1963-1985)
- HN DC 090625, deleted 1986. See now appropriate "Civil," "Law," or "Legal" terms.

Civilian Military Relations
- Use Military Civilian Relations

Civilian/Civilians (1963-1985)
- HN DC 090638.
- Use Citizens

Civilization
- DC D133800
- HN Formerly (1963-1985) DC 090640, Civilization/Civilizations.
- NT Western Civilization
- RT Acculturation
- Antiquity
- Cultural Values
- Culture
- Figuration Sociology
- History
- Industrial Societies
- Social Values
- Society
- Sociocultural Factors
- Traditional Societies

Clairvoyance
- Use Extrasensory Perception

Clans
- DC D134100
- SN Social groups, especially in tribal organizations, regarded as being descended from a common ancestor.
- HN Formerly (1963-1985) DC 090660, Clan/Clans.
- UF Gens (1972-1985)
- Moiety/Moieties (1976-1985)
- Phratries
- RT Chieftaincies
- Family
- Intermarriage
- Kinship
- Lineage
- Situses
- Totemism
- Traditional Societies

Class Analysis
- DC D134400
- HN Added, 1986.
- UF Social Class Analysis
- BT Analysis
- RT Class Differences
- Class Formation
- Class Relations
- Marxism
- Marxist Analysis
- Social Class
- Social Stratification
- Social Structure

Class Conflict
- Use Class Struggle

Class Consciousness
- DC D134700
- HN Added, 1986.
- BT Social Consciousness
- RT Class Identity
- Class Struggle
- Critical Theory
- Leninism
- Marxism
- Marxist Sociology
- Social Class
- Worker Consciousness

Class

Class Differences
- DC D135000
- SN Used in analyses in which a social problem or phenomenon is explained as a consequence or correlate of differences of social class in an otherwise similar population.
- HN Added, 1986.
- BT Differences
- RT Class Analysis
- Comparative Sociology
- Language Social Class Relationship
- Minority Groups
- Social Class
- Social Inequality
- Socioeconomic Status

Class Formation
- DC D135300
- HN Added, 1986.
- BT Group Formation
- RT Class Analysis
- Social Class
- Social Processes

Class Identification
- Use Class Identity

Class Identity
- DC D135600
- SN An internalized sense of belonging to a particular socal class.
- HN Added, 1986.
- UF Class Identification
- BT Group Identity
- RT Class Consciousness
- Social Class
- Social Identity

Class Mobility
- Use Social Mobility

Class Politics
- DC D135900
- SN Political activities arising from social-class concerns and conflicts.
- HN Added, 1986.
- BT Politics
- RT Class Relations
- Labor Movements
- Social Class
- Syndicalism
- Worker Consciousness
- Working Class

Class Relations
- DC D136200
- HN Added, 1986.
- BT Intergroup Relations
- RT Class Analysis
- Class Politics
- Class Society
- Class Struggle
- Ethnic Relations
- Forces And Relations of Production
- Language Social Class Relationship
- Racial Relations
- Social Class

Class Society
- DC D136500
- HN Added, 1986.
- UF Class System
- BT Society
- RT Class Relations
- Social Class
- Social Stratification
- Social Structure

Class

Class Status
  Use Social Status

Class Stratification
  Use Social Stratification

Class Structure
  Use Social Structure

Class Struggle
  DC D136800
  SN In Marxist analysis, the friction characteristic of relations between the Bourgeoisie and Proletariat leading ultimately to Social Revolution.
  HN Added, 1986.
  UF Class Conflict
    Struggle/Struggles (1963-1985)
  BT Social Conflict
  RT Class Consciousness
    Class Relations
    Ideological Struggle
    Marxism
    Marxist Sociology
    Proletariat
    Social Class
    Working Class

Class System
  Use Class Society

Class/Classes (1963-1985)
  HN DC 090670, deleted 1986. See now appropriate "Social Class" or "Education" terms.

Classic/Classics/Classical (1963-1985)
  HN DC 090680, deleted 1986.

Classical Literature
  Use Literature

Classicism (1963-1985)
  HN DC 090690.
  Use Artistic Styles

Classification
  DC D136950
  HN Formerly (1963-1985) DC 090700, Classification/Classified/Classificatory.
  UF Category/Categories/Categorical/Categorization (1963-1985)
    Taxonomy/Taxonomies/Taxonomic/Taxonomical (1963-1985)
  NT Coding
    Occupational Classifications
    Types
    Typology
  RT Analysis
    Hierarchy
    Labeling
    Operational Definitions
    Relations
    Stratification
    Structure

Classroom Discipline
  Use Discipline

Classroom Environment
  DC D137100
  HN Formerly (1963-1985) DC 091000, Classroom.
  BT Environment
  RT Student Teacher Relationship
    Students
    Teachers

Clausewitz, Karl von
  DC D137400
  SN Born 1 June 1780 - died 1831.
  HN Formerly (1966-1985) DC 091040, Clausewitz, Karl.

Cleavage
  DC D137600
  HN Formerly (1963-1985) DC 091100.
  UF Social Cleavage
  NT Schism
  RT Cliques
    Cultural Pluralism
    Dissent
    Factionalism
    Polarization
    Separatism
    Social Cohesion
    Social Conflict
    Social Segmentation
    Subcultures

Clergy
  DC D137700
  HN Formerly (1963-1985) DC 091550, Clergy/Clergyman/Clergymen/Clericalism.
  UF Clergymen
    Clericalism
    Ministry (Religion)
    Pastorate (1969-1985)
  BT Professional Workers
  NT Deacons
    Ministers (Clergy)
    Missionaries
    Monks
    Nuns
    Pastors
    Preachers
    Priests
    Rabbis
  RT Congregations
    Laity (Religious)
    Papacy
    Religions
    Religious Orders
    Seminarians
    Sermons

Clergymen
  Use Clergy

Clerical Workers
  DC D138000
  HN Formerly (1965-1985) DC 091575, Clerk/Clerks/Clerking/Clerical.
  UF Office Workers
  BT White Collar Workers
  RT Office Automation

Clericalism
  Use Clergy

Cleveland, Ohio
  DC D138300
  HN Formerly (1964-1985) DC 091585.
  BT Ohio

Client Characteristics
  DC D138600
  SN Physical, socioeconomic, psychological, and other traits of patients or users of legal and other professional services.
  HN Added, 1986.
  UF Client Selection
  RT Clients
    Patients
    Personality
    Practitioner Patient Relationship

Clinics

Client Relations
  DC D138900
  SN Interaction between provider and user of professional, legal, or human services. For this concept in a health services context, use Practitioner Patient Relationship.
  HN Added, 1986.
  UF Attorney Client Relationship
    Counselor Client Relationship
    Lawyer Client Relationship
    Therapist Client Relationship
  BT Interpersonal Relations
  NT Practitioner Patient Relationship
  RT Clients
    Confidentiality
    Counseling
    Helping Behavior
    Legal Profession
    Professional Malpractice
    Psychotherapy
    Social Workers
    Therapists
    Treatment Methods

Client Selection
  Use Client Characteristics

Clients
  DC D139200
  HN Formerly (1963-1985) DC 091625, Client/Clients/Clientele.
  RT Client Characteristics
    Client Relations
    Counseling
    Lawyers
    Patients
    Psychotherapy
    Transference (Psychology)

Climate/Climates (1963-1985)
  HN DC 091650, deleted 1986. See now Weather or Environment and its associated terms.

Clinical Social Work
  DC D139400
  SN Specialization in social work in which practitioners are trained, certified, and licensed to administer psychological testing and individual, conjoint, and group psychotherapy.
  HN Added, 1989.
  UF Psychiatric Social Work
  BT Social Work
  RT Conjoint Therapy
    Family Therapy
    Group Therapy
    Intervention
    Psychometric Analysis
    Psychotherapy

Clinical Sociology (1985)
  HN DC 092000.
  Use Applied Sociology

Clinics
  DC D139500
  HN Formerly (1963-1985) DC 091700, Clinic/Clinics/Clinical/Clinician.
  BT Facilities
  RT Agencies
    Health Care
    Outpatients

Cliques

Cliques
- **DC** D139800
- **HN** Formerly (1963-1985) DC 093100, Clique/Cliques.
- **BT** Primary Groups
- **RT** Cleavage
  Friendship
  Peer Groups
  Small Groups

Closure
- **DC** D140100
- **HN** Formerly (1983-1985) DC 093200.
- **NT** Plant Closure
  Social Closure

Cloth Manufacturing
- **Use** Textile Industry

Clothing
- **DC** D140400
- **HN** Formerly (1963-1985) DC 093500, Clothes/Clothing.
- **UF** Costume
  Dress/Dresses/Dressed/Dressing (1972-1985)
  Uniforms
- **RT** Customs
  Fashions
  Garment Industry
  Masks
  Material Culture
  Nonverbal Communication

Clothing Industry
- **Use** Garment Industry

Clubs
- **DC** D140700
- **HN** Formerly (1964-1985) DC 093575, Club/Clubs.
- **BT** Organizations (Social)
- **RT** Associations
  Community Organizations
  Leisure
  Social Participation
  Sports Teams
  Youth Organizations

Cluster Analysis
- **DC** D140800
- **SN** Statistical techniques used in multivariate analysis to group together similar measures or variables.
- **HN** Formerly (1963-1985) DC 093650, Cluster/Clustering/Clusters.
- **BT** Multivariate Analysis
- **RT** Correlation
  Dimensional Analysis
  Discriminant Analysis
  Factor Analysis

Coal
- **DC** D141000
- **HN** Formerly (1984-1985) DC 093690.
- **BT** Fuels
  Natural Resources
- **RT** Energy
  Energy Policy
  Geology
  Mining Industry
  Raw Materials

Coal Miners
- **Use** Miners

Coalition Formation
- **DC** D141300
- **SN** In task-oriented groups, processes involved in formation of informal partnerships.
- **HN** Added, 1986.
- **BT** Group Formation
- **RT** Coalitions

Coalitions
- **DC** D141600
- **SN** Temporary alliances of two or more parties, persons, groups, or states for cooperative action.
- **HN** Formerly (1963-1985) DC 093700, Coalition/Coalitions.
- **BT** Groups
- **NT** International Alliances
- **RT** Alliance
  Coalition Formation
  Cooperation
  Federations
  Intergroup Relations
  Political Action

Cocaine
- **DC** D141700
- **HN** Added, 1989.
- **RT** Drug Abuse
  Drug Addiction
  Narcotic Drugs
  Psychedelic Drugs

Cocoa (1967-1985)
- **HN** DC 094377.
- **Use** Food

Code Switching
- **DC** D141900
- **SN** Alternating from the use of one language or language variety to another depending on the situation.
- **HN** Added, 1986.
- **UF** Switching (Language)
- **RT** Bilingualism
  Diglossia
  Language
  Language Social Class Relationship
  Language Usage
  Language Varieties
  Morphology (Language)
  Multilingualism
  Phonetics
  Sociolinguistics
  Vocabularies

Codes of Conduct
- **DC** D142000
- **SN** Formal or informal systems of group standards that regulate the behavior of group members.
- **HN** Formerly (1963-1985) part of DC 094400, Code/Codes/Coding.
- **UF** Codes of Ethics
- **RT** Behavior
  Ethics
  Group Norms
  Professional Ethics

Codes of Ethics
- **Use** Codes of Conduct

Codes (Symbols)
- **Use** Coding

Codification/Codifications (1966-1985)
- **HN** DC 094500, deleted 1986.

Cognition

Coding
- **DC** D142100
- **HN** Formerly (1963-1985) part of DC 094400, Code/Codes/Coding.
- **UF** Codes (Symbols)
  Notation (1982-1985)
- **BT** Classification
  Information Processing
- **RT** Data
  Items (Measures)

Coeds
- **Use** College Students

Coefficient/Coefficients (1963-1985)
- **HN** DC 094600.
- **Use** Correlation

Coercion
- **DC** D142200
- **HN** Formerly (1966-1985) Coercion/Coercive/Coerciveness.
- **RT** Abuse
  Brainwashing
  Conflict
  Control
  Dominance
  Hegemony
  Obedience
  Oppression
  Power
  Punishment
  Torture
  Violence

Coercive Persuasion
- **Use** Brainwashing

Coexistence (International Relations)
- **Use** Peaceful Coexistence

Coffee House (1966-1985)
- **HN** DC 094925.
- **Use** Eating And Drinking Establishments

Cognatic Descent
- **DC** D142500
- **SN** Bilateral principle of descent that recognizes both male and female ancestors in determining kinship.
- **HN** Formerly (1967-1985) DC 094950, Cognate/Cognation/Cognatic.
- **BT** Descent
- **RT** Kinship
  Unilineality

Cognition
- **DC** D142800
- **HN** Formerly (1963-1985) DC 095000, Cognition/Cognitive.
- **UF** Cognitive Factors
  Cognitive Processes
- **NT** Abstraction
  Decision Making
  Imagination
  Intuition
  Judgment
  Memory
  Problem Solving
  Thinking
- **RT** Artificial Intelligence
  Attention
  Cognitive Development
  Cognitive Dissonance
  Cognitive Mapping
  Comprehension
  Concepts
  Consciousness
  Epistemological Doctrines

Cognitive

Cognition (cont'd)
- **RT** Epistemology
  Information Processing
  Intelligence
  Intelligence Tests
  Knowledge
  Learning
  Learning Disabilities
  Mind
  Phenomenology
  Psychology
  Rationalism
  Synthesis
  Theory Formation

Cognitive Development
- **DC** D143100
- **SN** Development of human mental capabilities through stages of sophistication, linked to maturation and learning from experience.
- **HN** Added, 1986.
- **UF** Mental Development
- **BT** Psychological Development
- **NT** Intellectual Development
  Language Acquisition
  Psychological Development
- **RT** Academic Aptitude
  Adult Development
  Child Development
  Cognition
  Cognitive Dissonance
  Concept Formation
  Developmental Stages
  Egocentrism
  Epistemology
  Experience
  Judgment
  Psychodynamics

Cognitive Dissonance
- **DC** D143200
- **SN** The theory, developed by Leon Festinger, that the psychological discomfort caused by inconsistencies in perceptions, beliefs, ideas, or other forms of knowledge motivate individuals to seek consistency through a change in attitude or belief, action, or selective perception. Cognitive dissonance might, for example, be felt by followers of a cult whose leader's predictions are proved false.
- **HN** Added, 1986.
- **RT** Anxiety
  Attitudes
  Beliefs
  Cognition
  Cognitive Development
  Conflict
  Congruence (Psychology)
  Psychological Stress
  Self Concept
  Self Esteem

Cognitive Factors
- **Use** Cognition

Cognitive Mapping
- **DC** D143300
- **SN** The formation of mental pictures of external reality that allow the processing of social and spatial surroundings, and cause-effect and means-end relationships.
- **HN** Formerly (1963-1985) part of DC 258400, Map/Maps/Mapped/Mapping.
- **RT** Cognition

Cognitive Mapping (cont'd)
- **RT** Expectations
  Learning
  Spatial Analysis

Cognitive Processes
- **Use** Cognition

Cohabitation
- **DC** D143400
- **SN** Shared domestic living arrangements of unmarried couples.
- **HN** Formerly (1981-1985) DC 095150, Cohabit/Cohabitation.
- **RT** Couples
  Family Life
  Marriage
  Premarital Sex
  Residential Preferences
  Single Persons

Coherent/Coherence (1970-1985)
- **HN** DC 095375, deleted 1986.

Cohesion/Cohesive/Cohesiveness (1963-1985)
- **HN** DC 095400.
- **Use** Social Cohesion

Cohort Analysis
- **DC** D143500
- **SN** The study of the changes over an extended period among groups of people who share a common characteristic or experience (eg, those born in a specific year).
- **HN** Formerly (1968-1985) DC 095422, Cohort/Cohorts.
- **BT** Analysis
- **RT** Age Groups
  Attrition
  Demographic Characteristics
  Longitudinal Studies
  Panel Data

Cohort Life Tables (1965-1985)
- **HN** DC 095425.
- **Use** Life Tables

Coitus/Coital (1963-1985)
- **HN** DC 095500.
- **Use** Sexual Intercourse

Cold War
- **DC** D143700
- **HN** Formerly (1963-1985) DC 095775.
- **RT** Cold War
  International Relations
  Peaceful Coexistence
  War

Coleman, James Samuel
- **DC** D144000
- **SN** Born 12 May 1926 - .
- **HN** Formerly (1964-1985) DC 095795, Coleman, J. S.

Collaborate/Collaboration/Collaborative (1963-1985)
- **HN** DC 095825.
- **Use** Cooperation

Collateral (1969-1985)
- **HN** DC 095850, deleted 1986.

Collect/Collecting/Collection/Collections (1963-1985)
- **HN** DC 095895, deleted 1986. See now Data Collection.

Collectives

Collective Action
- **DC** D144300
- **HN** Added, 1986.
- **BT** Social Action
- **RT** Collective Behavior
  Political Action
  Solidarity Movements

Collective Bargaining
- **DC** D144600
- **HN** Added, 1986.
- **BT** Negotiation
- **RT** Arbitration
  Contracts
  Employers
  Employers Associations
  Industrial Democracy
  Labor
  Labor Disputes
  Labor Relations
  Unions

Collective Behavior
- **DC** D144900
- **SN** The relatively spontaneous and unstructured thoughts, feelings, and actions of a collectivity of people responding to similar stimuli. Forms of collective behavior include fads, public opinion formation, panics, crazes, and the rise of social movements. Compare with Mass Behavior.
- **HN** Formerly (1979-1985) DC 095915, Collective Behavior/Collective Behaviors.
- **BT** Social Behavior
- **NT** Mass Behavior
  Riots
- **RT** Civil Disorders
  Collective Action
  Contagion Theory
  Crowds
  Discontent
  Individual Collective Relationship
  Social Movements
  Social Response
  Spontaneity

Collective Farms
- **Use** Agricultural Collectives

Collective Identity
- **Use** Group Identity

Collective Individual Relationship
- **Use** Individual Collective Relationship

Collective Representation
- **DC** D145200
- **SN** Concept or symbol that has a common meaning to the members of a group.
- **HN** Added, 1986.
- **UF** Representation (Collective)
- **RT** Concepts
  Meaning
  Signs
  Social Cohesion
  Social Determination of Meaning
  Symbolism

Collective Settlements
- **Use** Communes

Collectives
- **DC** D145500
- **SN** A context-dependent term for goal-oriented social organizations with shared, usually socialistic, political ideologies.
- **HN** Formerly (1963-1985) part of DC 095900, Collective/Collectives/Collectivism/Collectivist.

Collectivism / Comics

Collectives (cont'd)
- UF Labor Collectives
       Work Collectives
- BT Organizations (Social)
- NT Agricultural Collectives
       Communes
       Industrial Collectives
- RT Collectivism
       Collectivization
       Common Lands
       Enterprises
       Marxism

Collectivism
- DC D145800
- SN Centralized political control of social and especially economic activity.
- HN Formerly (1963-1985) part of DC 095900, Collective/Collectives/Collectivism/Collectivist.
- BT Economic Systems
- RT Collectives
       Collectivization
       Communism
       Corporatism
       Forces And Relations of Production
       Individualism
       Maoism
       Socialism

Collectivization
- DC D146100
- HN Formerly (1963-1985) DC 095925, Collectivity/Collectivities/Collectivization.
- RT Collectives
       Collectivism
       Communist Societies
       Expropriation

College Administration
- Use Educational Administration

College Curriculum
- Use Curriculum

College Faculty
- DC D146400
- HN Formerly (1964-1985) DC 171050, Faculty/Faculties.
- UF Faculty (College)
       Professor/Professors/Professorial (1963-1985)
- BT Teachers
- RT Academic Careers
       Academic Freedom
       Academic Tenure
       College Students
       Colleges
       Community Colleges
       Deans
       Doctoral Degrees
       Educational Administration
       Higher Education
       Scholarship
       Universities

College Graduates
- DC D146700
- HN Added, 1986.
- UF University Graduates
- BT Graduates
- RT Academic Degrees
       College Students
       Graduate Students
       Undergraduate Students

College Majors
- DC D147000
- HN Formerly (1983-1985) DC 096025, College Major/College Majors.
- UF Majors (Students)
- RT Academic Degrees
       Academic Departments
       Academic Disciplines
       College Students
       Higher Education
       Sociology Education
       Undergraduate Programs

College Sports
- DC D147300
- HN Added, 1986.
- UF Intercollegiate Sports
- BT Sports
- RT College Students
       Colleges
       Universities

College Students
- DC D147600
- HN Formerly (1985) DC 448300, Student, College.
- UF Coeds
       Student, College (1985)
       University Students
- BT Students
- NT Graduate Students
       Seminarians
       Undergraduate Students
- RT Academic Degrees
       College Faculty
       College Graduates
       College Majors
       College Sports
       Colleges
       Community Colleges
       Fraternities And Sororities
       Higher Education
       Married Students
       Polytechnic Schools
       Universities
       Young Adults

Colleges
- DC D147900
- HN Formerly (1963-1985) part of DC 096000, College/Colleges/Collegians.
- BT Schools
- NT Community Colleges
       Graduate Schools
       Polytechnic Schools
       Universities
- RT Academic Departments
       College Faculty
       College Sports
       College Students
       Higher Education
       Private Schools
       Public Schools
       Undergraduate Programs

Collins, Randall
- DC D148000
- SN Born 1941 - .
- HN Added, 1989.

Colloquium/Colloquia (1969-1985)
- HN DC 096075.
- Use Symposia

Colombia
- DC D148200
- HN Formerly (1963-1985) DC 097000, Colombia/Colombian.
- BT South America
- NT Bogota, Colombia

Colonialism
- DC D148500
- SN Enduring effects in a society or culture of past colonization and the specific ideology used to justify colonization by force.
- HN Formerly (1963-1985) DC 097500, Colonial/Colonials/Colonialism/Colonialist.
- UF Colonies/Colonist (1963-1985)
- BT Imperialism
- RT Culture Contact
       Empires
       Exploitation
       Indigenous Populations
       Nativistic Movements

Colonies/Colonist (1963-1985)
- HN DC 098500.
- Use Colonialism

Colonization
- DC D148800
- HN Formerly (1963-1985) DC 099200.
- BT Land Settlement
- RT Decolonization
       Frontiers
       Immigration
       Invasion
       Migration
       Settlement Patterns
       Settlers

Color/Colored (1963-1985)
- HN DC 100000, deleted 1986.

Colorado
- DC D149100
- HN Formerly (1964-1985) DC 100100.
- BT United States of America
       Western States
- NT Denver, Colorado

Columnists
- Use Journalists

Combat
- DC D149400
- HN Formerly (1963-1985) DC 101000.
- BT Violence
- RT Invasion
       Military Desertion
       War

Comedy (Drama)
- Use Drama

Comedy/Comedies (1963-1985)
- HN DC 101200, deleted 1986. See now Drama, Programming (Broadcast), or Humor.

Comfort (1968-1985)
- HN DC 102700, deleted 1986.

Comic Books
- Use Comics (Publications)

Comic Strips
- Use Comics (Publications)

Comics (Publications)
- DC D149700
- HN Formerly (1964-1985) DC 102730, Comic/Comics.
- UF Comic Books
       Comic Strips
- BT Publications
- RT Cartoons
       Fiction

Command　　　　　　　　　　　　　　　　　　　　　　　　　Communicative

Comics (Publications) (cont'd)
- RT Humor
  - Newspapers
  - Popular Culture
  - Satire

Command/Commands (1964-1985)
- HN DC 102775.
- Use Authority

**Comment/Comments/
Commentator/Commentary
(1964-1985)**
- HN DC 102780, deleted 1986.

Commerce (1963-1985)
- HN DC 102800.
- Use Trade

Commercial Art
- Use Art

Commercial Enterprises
- Use Enterprises

**Commercial/Commercialism/
Commercialization (1963-1985)**
- HN DC 102850, deleted 1986. See now Advertising, Business, Enterprises, and their associated terms.

Commissions
- DC D150000
- SN Groups officially empowered to perform some duty or execute some trust.
- HN Formerly (1963-1985) DC 102865, Commission/Commissions/Commissioner.
- BT Organizations (Social)
- RT Councils
  - Governing Boards
  - Government
  - Planners

Commitment
- DC D150300
- SN State of obligation or devotion to a task, objective, or personal relationship.
- HN Formerly (1963-1985) DC 102870, Commitment/Commitments.
- BT Loyalty
- NT Organizational Commitment
- RT Goals
  - Intentionality
  - Motivation
  - Obligation

Commitment (Civil)
- Use Institutionalization (Persons)

Committees
- DC D150600
- HN Formerly (1963-1985) DC 102880, Committee/Committees.
- BT Organizations (Social)
- NT Advisory Committees
  - Political Action Committees
- RT Governing Boards

Commodities
- DC D150900
- SN Broad term incorporating any articles of commerce, including goods and services. Often used in the more limited sense of raw or semi-processed bulk goods.
- HN Formerly (1972-1985) DC 102930, Commodity/Commodities.

Commodities (cont'd)
- RT Agricultural Production
  - Agriculture
  - Business
  - Consumption
  - Distributive Justice
  - Economics
  - Exchange (Economics)
  - Industry
  - Production Consumption Relationship
  - Products
  - Raw Materials
  - Scarcity
  - Trade

Commodity Fetishism
- Use Reification

Common Knowledge
- Use Common Sense

Common Lands
- DC D151200
- HN Formerly (1963-1985) part of DC 102940, Common.
- UF Commons
  - Communal Lands
- BT Land
- RT Agrarian Structures
  - Collectives
  - Cooperatives
  - Land Ownership
  - Land Use
  - Parks
  - Recreational Facilities
  - Traditional Societies

Common Market (1964-1985)
- HN DC 102945.
- Use European Economic Community

Common Sense
- DC D151300
- HN Formerly (1963-1985) part of DC 102940, Common.
- UF Common Knowledge
- BT Knowledge
- RT Beliefs
  - Everyday Life
  - Folklore
  - Lebenswelt
  - Traditions
  - Worldview

Commons
- Use Common Lands

Communal Lands
- Use Common Lands

Communal Living
- Use Communes

Communes
- DC D151500
- HN Formerly (1963-1985) DC 102960, Commune/Communes/Communal/Communalism/Communality.
- UF Collective Settlements
  - Communal Living
- BT Collectives
- NT Kibbutz
- RT Agricultural Collectives
  - Communities

Communication
- DC D151800
- HN Formerly (1963-1985) DC 103000, Communication/Communications/Communicative/Communicational.
- UF Communication Theory
- NT Intercultural Communication
  - Interpersonal Communication
  - Manual Communication
  - Nonverbal Communication
  - Persuasion
  - Propaganda
  - Publicity
  - Verbal Communication
- RT Ambiguity
  - Audiences
  - Centrality
  - Communication Research
  - Communicative Action
  - Content Analysis
  - Cybernetics
  - Diffusion
  - Discourse Analysis
  - Feedback
  - Information
  - Information Processing
  - Information Technology
  - Information Theory
  - Interaction
  - Linguistics
  - Meaning
  - Messages
  - Noise
  - Signs
  - Social Networks
  - Telecommunications
  - Translation

Communication (Nonverbal)
- Use Nonverbal Communication

Communication (Privileged)
- Use Confidentiality

Communication Research
- DC D151900
- HN Added, 1986.
- UF Mass Communication Research
- BT Research
- RT Audiences
  - Communication
  - Content Analysis
  - Discourse Analysis
  - Mass Media
  - Social Science Research
  - Telecommunications

Communication Style
- Use Interpersonal Communication

Communication Theory
- Use Communication

Communications Media
- Use Mass Media

Communications Systems
- Use Telecommunications

Communications Technology
- Use Telecommunications

Communicative Action
- DC D152000
- SN Introduced by Jurgen Habermas, a theoretical perspective linking languages, symbols, and communication media to social and political processes.
- HN Added, 1989.

Communicative Action (cont'd)
- **BT** Action
- **RT** Action Theory
  - Communication
  - Language Usage
  - Mass Media
  - Social Interaction
  - Sociolinguistics
  - Symbolic Interactionism

Communism
- **DC** D152100
- **HN** Formerly (1963-1985) DC 103800, Communist/Communists/Communism.
- **BT** Economic Systems
  - Marxism
  - Political Ideologies
- **RT** Bolshevism
  - Capitalism
  - Collectivism
  - Communist Parties
  - Communist Societies
  - Leninism
  - Maoism
  - Marxist Economics
  - McCarthyism
  - Modes of Production
  - Revisionism
  - Socialism
  - Stalinism
  - Totalitarianism

Communist Countries
- **Use** Communist Societies

Communist Parties
- **DC** D152400
- **HN** Added, 1986.
- **BT** Political Parties
- **RT** Communism
  - Communist Societies
  - Left Wing Politics
  - Socialist Parties

Communist Revisionism
- **Use** Revisionism

Communist Societies
- **DC** D152700
- **HN** Added, 1986.
- **UF** Communist Countries
- **BT** Society
- **RT** Capitalist Societies
  - Collectivization
  - Communism
  - Communist Parties
  - Liberal Democratic Societies
  - Political Ideologies
  - Socialist Societies

Communities
- **DC** D153000
- **SN** A context-dependent term; select a more specific entry or coordinate with other terms. Collectivities of people living in specific geographic areas in which they satisfy many of their social and economic needs through a complex of interdependent social relationships. Community members often share a common social identity and common interests.
- **HN** Formerly (1963-1985) DC 104000, Community/Communities/Communitarian.
- **UF** Local Communities
- **BT** Groups
- **NT** Cities
  - Fishing Communities

Communities (cont'd)
- **NT** Neighborhoods
  - Retirement Communities
  - Rural Communities
  - Suburbs
  - Towns
  - Villages
- **RT** Black Community
  - Communes
  - Community Change
  - Community Colleges
  - Community Development
  - Community Involvement
  - Community Mental Health
  - Community Organizations
  - Community Power
  - Community Research
  - Community Satisfaction
  - Community Services
  - Community Size
  - Community Structure
  - Districts
  - Environment
  - Everyday Life
  - Gemeinschaft And Gesellschaft
  - Group Composition
  - Human Ecology
  - Land Settlement
  - Living Conditions
  - Local Government
  - Local Planning
  - Local Politics
  - Localism
  - Neighbors
  - Newcomers
  - Police Community Relations
  - Residence
  - Residential Mobility
  - Residents
  - Scientific Community
  - Social Cohesion
  - Social Contact
  - Social Dynamics
  - Social Interaction

Community Change
- **DC** D153300
- **HN** Added, 1986.
- **BT** Change
- **NT** Neighborhood Change
- **RT** Boom Towns
  - Change Agents
  - Communities
  - Community Development
  - Community Satisfaction
  - Demographic Change
  - Social Change
  - Urban Renewal
  - Urbanization

Community Colleges
- **DC** D153600
- **HN** Added, 1986.
- **UF** Junior Colleges
- **BT** Colleges
- **RT** College Faculty
  - College Students
  - Communities
  - Higher Education
  - Public Schools
  - Undergraduate Programs

Community Development
- **DC** D153900
- **SN** The solution or amelioration of a community's social problems through actions organized and controlled by the community itself.
- **HN** Formerly (1963-1985) DC 104100.

Community Development (cont'd)
- **BT** Development
- **RT** Boom Towns
  - Citizen Participation
  - City Planning
  - Communities
  - Community Change
  - Community Involvement
  - Community Organizations
  - Community Services
  - Development Policy
  - Development Strategies
  - Economic Development
  - Extension Services
  - Local Planning
  - Neighborhood Change
  - New Towns
  - Rural Development
  - Urban Development
  - Urban Renewal

Community Health Services
- **Use** Health Services

Community Involvement
- **DC** D154200
- **SN** Involvement of the community in activities or programs.
- **HN** Added, 1986.
- **UF** Community Participation
- **BT** Participation
- **RT** Citizen Participation
  - Communities
  - Community Development
  - Social Action
  - State Intervention

Community Mental Health
- **DC** D154500
- **SN** Community activities contributing toward mental health, usually not institutionally based, with emphasis on preventive services such as consultation or education, and often employing innovative strategies.
- **HN** Added, 1986.
- **BT** Mental Health
- **RT** Applied Sociology
  - Communities
  - Community Mental Health Centers
  - Deinstitutionalization
  - Delinquency Prevention
  - Mental Health Services

Community Mental Health Centers
- **DC** D154800
- **HN** Formerly (1984-1985) DC 104160, Community Mental Health Center/CMHC.
- **BT** Centers
- **RT** Community Mental Health
  - Community Organizations
  - Mental Patients
  - Social Agencies

Community Organization
- **Use** Community Structure

Community Organizations
- **DC** D155100
- **HN** Formerly (1963-1985) DC 104175, Community Organization/Community Organizations.
- **UF** Local Organizations
  - Neighborhood Organizations
- **BT** Organizations (Social)
- **RT** Churches
  - Clubs
  - Communities

Community

Community Organizations (cont'd)
- RT Community Development
- Community Mental Health Centers
- Community Services
- Information And Referral Services

Community Participation
- Use Community Involvement

Community Planning
- Use Local Planning

Community Politics
- Use Local Politics

Community Power
- DC D155400
- HN Formerly (1963-1985) DC 104190, Community Power Structure.
- BT Power
- RT Communities
- Community Structure
- Local Politics
- Social Power

Community Research
- DC D155700
- HN Added, 1986.
- BT Research
- RT Action Research
- Communities
- Middletown Studies
- Social Science Research
- Sociological Research

Community Residents
- Use Residents

Community Response
- Use Social Response

Community Sanitation
- Use Sanitation

Community Satisfaction
- DC D156000
- HN Added, 1986.
- UF Neighborhood Satisfaction
- Resident Satisfaction
- BT Satisfaction
- RT Communities
- Community Change
- Housing
- Living Conditions
- Police Community Relations
- Residential Preferences
- Social Conditions

Community Services
- DC D156300
- HN Formerly (1964-1985) DC 104200, Community Service/Community Services.
- BT Services
- NT Information And Referral Services
- RT Communities
- Community Development
- Community Organizations
- Local Government
- Public Services
- Social Services

Community Size
- DC D156600
- HN Added, 1986.
- BT Size
- RT Cities
- Communities
- Community Structure

Community Size (cont'd)
- RT Demography
- Group Size
- Population Density
- Rural Urban Continuum
- Towns
- Villages

Community Structure
- DC D156900
- HN Added, 1986.
- UF Community Organization
- BT Structure
- RT Communities
- Community Power
- Community Size
- Ghettos
- Social Structure
- Suburbs

Commuting (Travel)
- DC D157200
- HN Formerly (1963-1985) DC 104210, Commuting/Commuter/Commuters.
- BT Travel
- RT Automobiles
- Central Cities
- Employment
- Public Transportation
- Residential Patterns
- Suburbs
- Urbanism
- Workplaces

Comoro Islands
- DC D157500
- HN Added, 1986.
- BT Sub Saharan Africa

Compadrazgo
- DC D157800
- SN The spiritual relationship in Spanish-speaking countries between a godparent or godparents and a godchild and its parents.
- HN Formerly (1964-1985) DC 104280.
- RT Godparenthood
- Kinship

Companion/Companions/Companionship (1963-1985)
- HN DC 104300.
- Use Friendship

Company/Companies (1963-1985)
- HN DC 104340.
- Use Firms

Comparative Analysis
- DC D158000
- HN Formerly (1963-1985) DC 104450, Comparison/Comparisons/Comparative/Comparability.
- UF Comparative Research
- BT Analysis
- NT Crosscultural Analysis
- RT Analogy
- Comparative Sociology
- Differences

Comparative Research
- Use Comparative Analysis

Comparative Sociology
- DC D158100
- SN Study of societies or social groups in comparison with one another, for purposes of discovering similarities and differences.
- HN Formerly (1985) DC 104455.

Complementary

Comparative Sociology (cont'd)
- BT Sociology
- RT Anthropology
- Black White Differences
- Class Differences
- Comparative Analysis
- Crosscultural Analysis
- Regional Differences
- Rural Urban Differences

Compassion
- DC D158400
- HN Formerly (1972-1985) DC 104460, Compassion/Compassionate.
- UF Sympathy/Sympathetic (1964-1985)
- BT Emotions
- RT Empathy
- Interpersonal Relations

Compensation
- DC D158700
- SN Payment given or received in return for goods or services, or as settlement of a debt or injury.
- HN Formerly (1963-1985) DC 104500, Compensation/Compensative/Compensatory/Compensating.
- UF Remuneration (1964-1985)
- Reparations (1972-1985)
- Tip/Tipping (1963-1985)
- NT Benefits
- Pensions
- Restitution (Corrections)
- Salaries
- Wages
- RT Costs
- Expenditures
- Income
- Payments

Competence
- DC D159000
- HN Formerly (1963-1985) DC 104600, Competence/Competency.
- UF Proficiency (1978-1985)
- BT Ability
- RT Accountability
- Performance

Competition
- DC D159300
- HN Formerly (1963-1985) DC 104700, Competition/Competitive.
- BT Social Behavior
- RT Aggression
- Conflict
- Conflict Theory
- Cooperation
- Family Conflict
- Game Theory
- Goals
- Intergroup Relations
- Interpersonal Relations
- Monopolies
- Oligopolies
- Performance
- Social Darwinism
- Social Interaction

Complaint/Complaints (1966-1985)
- HN DC 104730.
- Use Grievances

Complementary Needs
- DC D159500
- SN Different needs that are satisfied by each partner in a close personal relationship, especially between spouses or sexual partners.
- HN Formerly (1963-1985) DC 104740, Complementary/Complementarity.

Complex

Complementary Needs (cont'd)
- BT Needs
- RT Homogamy
  Marital Satisfaction
  Mate Selection
  Personality Traits

Complex Organizations
- DC D159600
- HN Added, 1986.
- BT Organizations (Social)
- RT Bureaucracy
  Federations
  Interorganizational Relations
  Organization Size
  Organizational Culture

Complex Societies
- DC D159900
- SN Societies in which the social activities carried out by one institution (eg, the family) have been divided among other, more specialized institutions (eg, the educational and work systems). See also Division of Labor.
- HN Added, 1986.
- BT Society
- RT Industrial Societies
  Modern Society
  Postindustrial Societies
  Specialization

Complex/Complexity (1963-1985)
- HN DC 104750, deleted 1986.

Compliance
- DC D160200
- HN Formerly (1963-1985) DC 104775.
- BT Social Behavior
- NT Treatment Compliance
- RT Cooperation
  Law Enforcement
  Legislation
  Obedience
  Social Control

Componential Analysis
- DC D160350
- SN A formal methodology for analyzing ethnographic data that focuses on systems of terminology and their inherent organizational and logical properties.
- HN Formerly (1969-1985) DC 104850, Component/Components/Componential.
- BT Analysis
- RT Quantitative Methods

Composite Indexes
- Use Indexes (Measures)

Composition/Compositions/Compositional (1963-1985)
- HN DC 105000, deleted 1986. See now Group Composition or Membership.

Comprehension
- DC D160500
- SN Knowledge or understanding of the meaning, significance, or principles of an object, situation, event, or printed or spoken language.
- HN Formerly (1963-1985) DC 105200.
- UF Understanding (1967-1985)
- RT Cognition
  Intelligence
  Intuition
  Knowledge
  Meaning
  Verstehen

Comprehensive (1966-1985)
- HN DC 105210, deleted 1986.

Compromise/Compromises (1964-1985)
- HN DC 105300.
- Use Negotiation

Compulsive Behavior
- Use Compulsivity

Compulsive Gambling
- Use Gambling

Compulsivity
- DC D160800
- HN Formerly (1963-1985) part of DC 105500, Compulsion/Compulsive/Compulsivity/Compulsory.
- UF Compulsive Behavior
- BT Personality Traits
- RT Behavior
  Flexibility
  Impulsiveness
  Spontaneity

Compulsory Involvement
- Use Compulsory Participation

Compulsory Participation
- DC D161100
- HN Formerly (1963-1985) part of DC 105500, Compulsion/Compulsive/Compulsivity/Compulsory.
- UF Compulsory Involvement
- BT Participation
- RT Education
  State Power

Computation
- DC D161300
- HN Formerly (1963-1985) DC 105990, Compute/Computing/Computed/Computation.
- UF Calculation
- RT Algorithms
  Computers
  Estimation
  Mathematics
  Measurement
  Ratios
  Statistics

Computer Assisted Instruction
- DC D161400
- HN Added, 1986.
- UF CAI
  Programmed Learning (1963-1985)
  Teaching Machines (1964-1985)
- BT Teaching
- RT Computers
  Teaching Methods

Computer Assisted Research
- DC D161700
- HN Added, 1986.
- BT Research
- RT Computer Software
  Computers
  Data Banks
  Data Processing
  Models
  Simulation
  Telephone Surveys

Concentration

Computer Programs
- Use Computer Software

Computer Software
- DC D161900
- SN Programs or instructions used to direct the operation of a computer.
- HN Added, 1989.
- UF Computer Programs
  Programming (Computers)
  Software (Computers)
- RT Computer Assisted Research
  Computers
  Data Banks
  Data Processing
  High Technology Industries

Computer Technology
- Use Electronic Technology

Computers
- DC D162000
- HN Formerly (1963-1985) DC 106000, Computer/Computers/Computerization/Computerized.
- NT Microcomputers
- RT Artificial Intelligence
  Automation
  Computation
  Computer Assisted Instruction
  Computer Assisted Research
  Computer Software
  Cybernetics
  Data Banks
  Data Processing
  Electronic Technology
  High Technology Industries
  Industrial Automation
  Information Technology
  Machinery
  Scientific Technological Revolution
  Systems
  Telecommunications

Comte, Auguste Isidore-Marie-Francois-Xavier
- DC D162100
- SN Born 19 January 1798 - died 5 September 1857.
- HN Formerly (1963-1985) DC 106500, Comte, A./Comteian/Comteist/Comteists.

Conceit/Conceits/Conceited (1972-1985)
- HN DC 106840.
- Use Egoism

Conceive (1965-1985)
- HN DC 106850.
- Use Pregnancy

Concentrate/Concentrates/Concentrations (1972-1985)
- HN DC 106890, deleted 1986. See now Oligopolies, Population Distribution, or Geographic Distribution.

Concentration Camps
- DC D162300
- HN Formerly (1963-1985) DC 106900.
- UF Internment Camps
- BT Prisons
- RT Holocaust
  World War II

44

Concept

Concept Formation
- **DC** D162600
- **HN** Added, 1986.
- **UF** Conceptualization
  Ideation
- **BT** Formation
- **RT** Cognitive Development
  Concepts
  Creativity
  Epistemological Doctrines
  Epistemology
  Generalization
  Methodology (Philosophical)
  Mind
  Reasoning
  Theory Formation

Conception (Biology)
- **Use** Pregnancy

Concepts
- **DC** D162900
- **SN** A context-dependent term for ideas or thoughts that are not directly observed in nature but mentally constructed through generalization and abstraction.
- **HN** Formerly (1963-1985) DC 107000, Concept/Concepts/Conceptual/Conceptualization.
- **UF** Idea/Ideas/Ideational (1963-1985)
- **RT** Abstraction
  Ambiguity
  Cognition
  Collective Representation
  Concept Formation
  Conscience
  Constructs
  Images
  Methodology (Philosophical)
  Mind
  Nominalism
  Operational Definitions
  Phenomena
  Sociology of Knowledge
  Space And Time
  Theories
  Thinking

Conceptual Issues
- **Use** Theoretical Problems

Conceptualization
- **Use** Concept Formation

Concert/Concerts (1972-1985)
- **HN** DC 107010.
- **Use** Music

Concession/Concessions (1970-1985)
- **HN** DC 107080.
- **Use** Negotiation

Conciliation (1976-1985)
- **HN** DC 108030.
- **Use** Mediation

Conditioning
- **DC** D163200
- **SN** Process by which a specific pattern of responses to a certain stimulus is learned, conceptualized from the viewpoint of Behaviorism.
- **HN** Formerly (1963-1985) part of DC 108800, Condition/Conditions/Conditioning/Conditional/Conditioned.
- **UF** Operant (1971-1985)

Conditioning (cont'd)
- **UF** Social Conditioning
- **NT** Behavior Modification
- **RT** Behavior
  Learning
  Psychological Factors
  Psychology
  Reinforcement
  Responses
  Stimuli

Condorcet, Marie Jean Antoine Nicolas de Caritat
- **DC** D163500
- **SN** Born 17 September 1743 - died 28 March 1794.
- **HN** Formerly (1973-1985) DC 122240, De Condorcet, A.

Condorcet Paradox (1969-1985)
- **HN** DC 109000.
- **Use** Voting Behavior

Conduct (1977-1985)
- **HN** DC 110500.
- **Use** Behavior

Conference/Conferences (1963-1985)
- **HN** DC 110800.
- **Use** Congresses And Conventions

Confession
- **DC** D163800
- **HN** Formerly (1972-1985) DC 110850, Confess/Confession/Confessor.
- **UF** Confessors
- **RT** Guilt
  Religious Rituals
  Roman Catholicism
  Sins

Confessors
- **Use** Confession

Confidence (1975-1985)
- **HN** DC 110870.
- **Use** Trust

Confidential Information
- **Use** Confidentiality

Confidentiality
- **DC** D164100
- **HN** Formerly (1964-1985) DC 110920, Confidential/Confidentiality.
- **UF** Communication (Privileged)
  Confidential Information
  Privileged Communications
- **BT** Privacy
- **RT** Client Relations
  Interpersonal Communication
  Practitioner Patient Relationship
  Self Disclosure

Configuration/Configurations/Configurational (1963-1985)
- **HN** DC 110930.
- **Use** Structure

Confinement (1964-1985)
- **HN** DC 110940, deleted 1986. See now Detention, Institutionalization (Persons), or Hospitalization.

Conflict

Conflict
- **DC** D164400
- **SN** A context-dependent term for strife, mental or physical, among individuals or groups. Select a more specific entry or coordinate with other terms.

Conflict (cont'd)
- **HN** Formerly (1963-1985) DC 111000, Conflict/Conflicts.
- **UF** Confront/Confrontation (1969-1985)
  Contest/Contests/Contestation (1970-1985)
  Rivalry (1964-1985)
- **BT** Interaction
- **NT** Conflict
  Cultural Conflict
  Disputes
  Family Conflict
  Ideological Struggle
  International Conflict
  Interpersonal Conflict
  Role Conflict
  Social Conflict
- **RT** Aggression
  Alliance
  Civil Disorders
  Coercion
  Cognitive Dissonance
  Competition
  Conflict Resolution
  Conflict Theory
  Consensus
  Dissent
  Hostility
  Intergroup Relations
  Power
  Problems
  Repression (Political)
  Resistance
  Social Behavior
  Threat
  Violence
  War

Conflict Resolution
- **DC** D164700
- **HN** Added, 1986.
- **UF** Dispute Settlement
  Reconcile/Reconciliation (1972-1985)
  Resolution/Resolutions (1963-1985)
- **NT** Mediation
- **RT** Arbitration
  Conflict
  Decision Making
  Intergroup Relations
  Interpersonal Conflict
  Negotiation
  Peace
  Persuasion

Conflict Theory
- **DC** D164800
- **SN** Theories that examine the role of conflict in social phenomena. Conflict, competition, and aggressiveness are seen as inherent in social processes.
- **HN** Added, 1986.
- **UF** Social Conflict Theory
- **BT** Social Theories
- **RT** Capitalism
  Competition
  Conflict
  Consensus
  Functionalism
  Macrosociology
  Marxist Sociology
  Microsociology
  Political Sociology
  Social Conflict
  Social Order
  Structural-Functional Analysis

Conformity

Conformity
- DC D165000
- HN Formerly (1963-1985) DC 112000, Conform/Conforming/Conformist/Conformists/Conformity.
- UF Nonconformity
  Social Conformity (1969-1985)
- BT Social Behavior
- RT Adjustment
  Deviance
  Norms
  Peer Groups
  Peer Influence
  Personality Traits
  Similarity
  Social Control
  Social Influence
  Social Pressure
  Socialization
  Uniformity

Confront/Confrontation (1969-1985)
- HN DC 112006.
- Use Conflict

Confucianism
- DC D165300
- HN Formerly (1963-1985) part of DC 112027, Confucius/Confucian/Confucianism.
- BT Religions
- RT Ancestor Worship
  Asian Cultural Groups

Confusion (1963-1985)
- HN DC 112030, deleted 1986.

Congenitally Handicapped
- DC D165600
- HN Formerly (1968-1985) DC 112040, Congenital.
- UF Birth Defects
- BT Handicapped
- RT Cerebral Palsy
  Downs Syndrome
  Genetics

Conglomerate/Conglomerates (1972-1985)
- HN DC 112050, deleted 1986.

Congo
- DC D165900
- HN Formerly (1963-1985) DC 112055, Congo/Congolese.
- BT Sub Saharan Africa

Congregations
- DC D166200
- HN Formerly (1963-1985) DC 112064, Congregation/Congregations/Congregational.
- BT Laity (Religious)
- RT Church Membership
  Churches
  Clergy
  Parishioners

Congress (Legislative Body)
- Use Legislative Bodies

Congress of Industrial Organizations/CIO (1969-1985)
- HN DC 112072.
- Use Unions

Congress of Racial Equality/CORE (1969-1985)
- HN DC 112075.
- Use Civil Rights Organizations

Congress/Congresses/Congressional (1963-1985)
- HN DC 112070, deleted 1986. See now Legislative Bodies or Congresses And Conventions.

Congresses And Conventions
- DC D166500
- HN Added, 1986. Prior to 1986 use DC 112070, Congress/Congresses/Congressional.
- UF Conference/Conferences (1963-1985)
  Conventions (Congresses)
  International Congresses And Conventions
  World Congress of Sociology (1970-1985)
- BT Meetings
- RT Institutes
  Seminars
  Symposia

Congressmen/Congressman (1963-1985)
- HN DC 112080.
- Use Legislators

Congruence (Psychology)
- DC D166600
- SN A state of accord with oneself or others. Self-congruence is agreement between one's real and ideal selves, or between one's experience and self-concept.
- HN Formerly (1963-1985) DC 112095, Congruence/Congruency.
- UF Congruity (1963-1985)
  Discrepancy (Psychology)
  Self Congruence
- RT Attitudes
  Behavior
  Cognitive Dissonance
  Role Conflict
  Self Concept
  Status Inconsistency

Congruity (1963-1985)
- HN DC 112110.
- Use Congruence (Psychology)

Conjoint Therapy
- DC D166800
- HN Formerly (1964-1985) DC 112112, Conjoint.
- BT Treatment
- RT Clinical Social Work
  Family Therapy
  Group Therapy
  Psychotherapy

Conjugal (1963-1985)
- HN DC 112115, deleted 1986. See now specific "Marriage," "Marital," or "Family" terms.

Conjugal Family
- Use Nuclear Family

Conjugal Relations
- Use Marital Relations

Consensus

Conjugal Violence
- Use Family Violence

Conjugal Visitation
- Use Visitation

Connecticut
- DC D167100
- HN Formerly (1963-1985) DC 112120.
- BT Northern States
  United States of America
- NT Hartford, Connecticut

Consanguinity
- DC D167400
- HN Formerly (1963-1985) DC 112180, Consanguinity/Consanguineous.
- RT Affinity (Kinship)
  Cousin Marriage
  Endogamy
  Inbreeding
  Incest
  Kinship
  Marriage

Conscience
- DC D167700
- HN Formerly (1963-1985) DC 112200.
- UF Superego
- RT Concepts
  Consciousness
  Guilt
  Individuals
  Mind
  Moral Judgment
  Morality
  Obligation
  Shame
  Values

Conscience Development
- Use Moral Development

Conscientious Objectors
- DC D168000
- HN Formerly (1964-1985) DC 112250, Conscientious.
- RT Draft (Military)
  Military Service
  Nonviolence
  Pacifism

Consciousness
- DC D168300
- HN Formerly (1963-1985) DC 112400, Conscious/Consciousness.
- UF Awareness (1963-1985)
- NT Attention
  Perceptions
  Social Consciousness
- RT Cognition
  Conscience
  Intentionality
  Intuition
  Mind
  Phenomenology
  Transcendental Meditation
  Unconscious (Psychology)
  Will

Consensus
- DC D168600
- HN Formerly (1963-1985) DC 112475, Consensus/Consensual.
- BT Agreement
- RT Conflict
  Conflict Theory
  Disputes
  Dissent

Consent

Consensus (cont'd)
  RT Group Decision Making
      Group Dynamics
      Public Opinion
      Social Cohesion

Consent (Informed)
  Use Informed Consent

Consequence/Consequences (1964-1985)
  HN DC 112482.
  Use Effects

Conservation
  DC D168900
  HN Formerly (1963-1985) DC 112550.
  BT Resource Management
  NT Energy Conservation
      Soil Conservation
  RT Ecology
      Energy Consumption
      Environmental Attitudes
      Environmental Protection
      Human Ecology
      Land Use
      Natural Environment
      Natural Resources
      Pollution
      Preservation
      Wastes
      Water Supply

Conservatism
  DC D169200
  HN Formerly (1963-1985) DC 112600, Conservative/Conservatives/Conservatism.
  UF Tory/Tories/Toryism (1963-1985)
  BT Political Ideologies
  RT Liberalism
      McCarthyism
      Religious Fundamentalism
      Right Wing Politics
      Traditionalism

Consideration/Considerations (1965-1985)
  HN DC 112700, deleted 1986.

Consistency (1963-1985)
  HN DC 112800, deleted 1986. See now Reliability, Similarity, Congruence (Psychology), or Status Inconsistency.

Consolidate/Consolidating/Consolidation (1972-1985)
  HN DC 112810.
  Use Mergers

Conspiracy/Conspiracies (1971-1985)
  HN DC 112950, deleted 1986.

Constituent/Constituents/Constituency (1972-1985)
  HN DC 113340, deleted 1986.

Constitutional Amendments
  DC D169500
  HN Formerly (1971-1985) DC 030140, Amend/Amends/Amended/Amending/Amendment/Amendments.
  UF Amendments (Constitutional)
      Equal Rights Amendment/ERA (1984-1985)
      First Amendment (1971-1985)
  RT Civil Rights
      Constitutions
      Legislation
      Statutes

Constitutions
  DC D169800
  HN Formerly (1963-1985) DC 113350, Constitution/Constitutions/Constitutional/Constitutionality.
  RT Civil Rights
      Constitutional Amendments
      Government
      Law
      Political Systems
      State

Constraints
  DC D170000
  HN Formerly (1963-1985) DC 113405, Constraint/Constraints.
  UF Barriers
      Restraint/Restraints (1964-1985)
      Restriction/Restrictions (1963-1985)
  RT Access
      Boundaries
      Development
      Freedom
      Limitations
      Needs
      Opportunities
      Problems
      Resources

Construct/Constructs/Constructions/Constructionist (1963-1985)
  HN DC 113406, deleted 1986. See now Construction Industry or Constructs.

Constructed Types
  Use Ideal Types

Construction Industry
  DC D170100
  HN Formerly (1963-1985) part of DC 113406, Construct/Constructs/Construction/Constructionist.
  UF Building Industry
  BT Industry
  RT Architects
      Buildings
      Engineering

Constructivism
  Use Interpretive Sociology

Constructs
  DC D170200
  SN Hypothetical models or concepts (eg, status, rational action) that are used as an aid or guide to research and not intended to be accurate descriptions of observable reality.
  HN Formerly (1966-1985) part of DC 113406, Construct/Constructs/Construction/Constructionist.
  RT Abstraction
      Analysis
      Concepts
      Generalization
      Heuristics
      Ideal Types
      Inference
      Models
      Paradigms
      Research
      Types

Consultants
  DC D170400
  HN Formerly (1963-1985) part of DC 113410, Consult/Consults/Consultation/Consultant/Consulting.
  BT Specialists
  RT Advisors
      Experts
      Professional Consultation
      Professional Workers
      Services

Consumption

Consultation (Professional)
  Use Professional Consultation

Consumer Behavior
  Use Consumers

Consumer Cooperatives
  Use Cooperatives

Consumer Goods
  Use Products

Consumer Protection
  Use Consumerism

Consumerism
  DC D170700
  SN Movement to protect the rights of consumers against useless, inferior, or dangerous products; misleading advertising; and unfair pricing.
  HN Formerly (1963-1985) part of DC 114000, Consumer/Consumers/Consumerism.
  UF Consumer Protection
  BT Protection
  RT Commercialization
      Consumers
      Marketing
      Purchasing
      Retail Industry
      Safety
      Sales

Consumers
  DC D171000
  HN Formerly (1963-1985) part of DC 114000, Consumer/Consumers/Consumerism.
  UF Consumer Behavior
      Customer/Customers (1972-1985)
  RT Brand Names
      Consumerism
      Consumption
      General Public
      Market Research
      Marketing
      Merchants
      Products
      Purchasing
      Retail Industry
      Sales
      Stores

Consumption
  DC D171300
  HN Formerly (1963-1985) DC 114215, Consumption/Consumptive.
  NT Energy Consumption
  RT Commodities
      Consumers
      Distributive Justice
      Economics
      Expenditures
      Prices
      Production
      Purchasing
      Saving
      Scarcity
      Standard of Living
      Trade
      Utilization
      Wealth

Consumption Production Relationship
  Use Production Consumption Relationship

Contact

Contact (1963-1985)
- HN DC 114250, deleted 1986. See now Culture Contact, Eye Contact, Physical Contact, or Social Contact.

Contagion Theory
- DC D171400
- SN Explanations of how moods, thoughts, and behavior are communicated in a group or crowd and accepted by individual participants as a result of emotional contagion.
- HN Formerly (1966-1985) DC 114260, Contagion.
- UF Social Contagion Theory
- BT Social Theories
- RT Collective Behavior
    Crowds

Containment of Costs
- Use Cost Containment

Contemporary Society
- Use Modern Society

Contemporary/Contemporaries (1963-1985)
- HN DC 114285, deleted 1986.

Contempt (1969-1985)
- HN DC 114290.
- Use Hate

Content Analysis
- DC D171450
- SN A research technique that systematically, objectively, and quantitatively describes the content of print or non-print communications.
- HN Formerly (1963-1985) DC 114300, Content/Contents.
- BT Analysis
    Methodology (Data Collection)
- RT Communication
    Communication Research
    Discourse Analysis
    Literary Criticism
    Literature
    Mass Media
    Messages

Contest/Contests/Contestation (1970-1985)
- HN DC 114350.
- Use Conflict

Context/Contexts/Contextual/Contextualist (1963-1985)
- HN DC 114400.
- Use Environment

Contingency Analysis
- DC D171500
- SN A statistical technique used to analyze the interrelationships between two variables.
- HN Formerly (1971-1985) DC 114413, Contingent/Contingents/Contingency.
- UF Contingency, Mean, Square (1963-1985)
- BT Methodology (Data Analysis)
    Quantitative Methods
- RT Correlation
    Loglinear Analysis
    Tables
    Variables

Contingency, Mean, Square (1963-1985)
- HN DC 114412.
- Use Contingency Analysis

Contingency Theory
- Use Organization Theory

Continuing Education
- Use Adult Education

Continuity/Continuities/Continuous (1963-1985)
- HN DC 114420.
- Use Stability

Continuum (1963-1985)
- HN DC 114430.
- Use Rural Urban Continuum

Contraceptive/Contraceptives/Contraception (1963-1985)
- HN DC 114475.
- Use Birth Control

Contracts
- DC D171600
- HN Formerly (1963-1985) DC 114485, Contract/Contracts/Contractual/Contractor.
- UF Agreements
- RT Business
    Collective Bargaining
    Law

Contradictions
- DC D171700
- HN Formerly (1970-1985) DC 114492, Contradict/Contradicts/Contradiction/Contradictory.
- UF Paradoxes
    Social Contradictions
- RT Dialectics
    Disputes
    Dissent
    Knowledge

Contrast/Contrasts (1964-1985)
- HN DC 114500.
- Use Differences

Contribution/Contributions/Contributors (1963-1985)
- HN DC 114650, deleted 1986. See now Contributions (Donations).

Contributions (Donations)
- DC D171800
- HN Added, 1986.
- UF Charitable Contributions
    Donations
    Financial Donations
    Political Donations
- BT Financial Support
- RT Assistance
    Charities
    Gift Giving
    Philanthropy
    Social Action
    Social Interest
    Volunteers

Control
- DC D171900
- SN A context-dependent term; select a more specific entry or coordinate with other terms. Social Control is preferred unless the context is control subjects in an experiment.
- HN Formerly (1963-1985) DC 114800, Control/Controls/Controlled.

Control (cont'd)
- NT Gun Control
    Pollution Control
    Social Control
    Worker Control
- RT Coercion
    Dominance
    Influence
    Locus of Control
    Management
    Power
    Regulation
    Repression (Political)
    Security
    Stability

Control Subjects
- Use Research Subjects

Controversy/Controversies/Controversial (1963-1985)
- HN DC 114820.
- Use Disputes

Convention/Conventions/Conventional/Conventionalization (1963-1985)
- HN DC 114860, deleted 1986. See now Customs, Traditionalism, or Congresses And Conventions.

Conventions (Congresses)
- Use Congresses And Conventions

Convents
- DC D172200
- HN Formerly (1963-1985) DC 114850, Convent/Convents.
- RT Monasteries
    Monasticism
    Nuns
    Places of Worship

Convergence Theory
- DC D172350
- SN The theory that as different types of societies industrialize they become politically, socially, and culturally similar.
- HN Formerly (1966-1985) DC 114870, Convergence.
- BT Social Theories
- RT Economic Development
    Industrial Societies
    Industrialization
    Modernization
    Similarity
    Social Change
    Social Structure

Conversation
- DC D172500
- SN Informal spoken exchange of thoughts and feelings.
- HN Formerly (1967-1985) DC 114873, Converse/Conversation/Conversational.
- BT Interpersonal Communication
    Verbal Communication
- RT Conversational Analysis
    Discussion
    Ethnomethodology
    Rumors
    Self Expression
    Social Interaction
    Telephone Communications

Conversational   **Correction**

Conversational Analysis
- DC D172550
- SN Analysis of sequences of conversation for indications of how actors characterize and enforce social norms, usually utilizing transcriptions of interactions tape-recorded in fieldwork.
- HN Added, 1989.
- BT Analysis
- RT Conversation
  Ethnomethodology
  Social Interaction
  Verbal Accounts
  Verbal Communication

Convert/Converting/Conversion (1963-1985)
- HN DC 114875.
- Use Religious Conversion

Convict/Convicts (1964-1985)
- HN DC 114890.
- Use Offenders

Conviction/Convictions (1971-1985)
- HN DC 114895, deleted 1986. See now Sentencing, Verdicts, or other appropriate "Crime" and "Law" terms.

Cook Islands
- DC D172800
- HN Added, 1986.
- BT Polynesia

Cooking
- Use Food Preparation

Cooley, Charles Horton
- DC D173100
- SN Born 1864 - died 1929.
- HN Formerly (1967-1985) DC 115060.

Cooperation
- DC D173400
- HN Formerly (1963-1985) DC 115400.
- UF Collaborate/Collaboration/Collaborative (1963-1985)
  Synergy (1964-1985)
- BT Social Behavior
- NT International Cooperation
- RT Alliance
  Altruism
  Coalitions
  Competition
  Compliance
  Coordination
  Goals
  Intergroup Relations
  Interpersonal Relations
  Professional Consultation
  Reciprocity
  Sharing
  Social Interaction
  Teamwork
  Turn Taking

Cooperative Extension Services
- Use Extension Services

Cooperatives
- DC D173700
- HN Formerly (1963-1985) DC 115500, Cooperative/Cooperatives.
- UF Consumer Cooperatives
  Producer Cooperatives
- BT Organizations (Social)
- RT Common Lands
  Enterprises
  Marketing
  Purchasing

Cooptation
- DC D173800
- HN Formerly (1972-1985) DC 115540, Co-optation/Co-optive.
- BT Change
- RT Adjustment
  Assimilation
  Group Dynamics
  Group Identity
  Leadership
  Organizational Change
  Social Change
  Social Cohesion
  Stability

Coordination
- DC D174000
- HN Formerly (1963-1985) DC 115700, Coordination/Coordinating.
- RT Cooperation
  Management
  Networks
  Supervision
  Turn Taking

Copenhagen, Denmark
- DC D174300
- HN Formerly (1963-1985) DC 115729.
- BT Denmark

Copernicus, Nicolaus
- DC D174600
- SN Born 19 February 1473 - died 24 May 1543.
- HN Formerly (1965-1985) DC 115730, Copernicus.

Coping
- DC D174900
- HN Formerly (1963-1985) DC 115725.
- RT Adjustment
  Avoidance
  Behavior
  Defense Mechanisms
  Flexibility
  Life Events
  Mental Health
  Occupational Stress
  Problem Solving
  Psychological Stress
  Self Care
  Stigma
  Stress
  Well Being

Copy Editors
- Use Editors

Copyrights
- DC D175200
- SN Exclusive power to control, disseminate, or sell artistic or intellectual products for a designated length of time.
- HN Formerly (1972-1985) DC 115731, Copyright/Copyrights.
- BT Property Rights
- RT Fraud
  Publishing Industry

Core (1984-1985)
- HN DC 115732.
- Use Center And Periphery

Corn (1963-1985)
- HN DC 115733.
- Use Food

Corn Belt Farms (1981-1985)
- HN DC 115735.
- Use Farms

Coronary (1964-1985)
- HN DC 115752.
- Use Heart Diseases

Corporal Punishment
- DC D175500
- SN Infliction of physical pain on one person by another for disciplinary purposes.
- HN Formerly (1984-1985) DC 115754, Corporal.
- UF Physical Punishment
- BT Punishment
- RT Childrearing Practices

Corporate (1963-1985)
- HN DC 115760, deleted 1986. See now Corporatism, Corporations, or appropriate "Organization" or "Organizational" terms.

Corporate Directors
- Use Directors

Corporate Dissolution
- Use Organizational Dissolution

Corporate Elite
- Use Economic Elites

Corporate Networks
- Use Interlocking Directorates

Corporate Power
- Use Organizational Power

Corporations
- DC D175800
- HN Formerly (1963-1985) DC 115770, Corporation/Corporations.
- UF International Business Machines/IBM (1965-1985)
- BT Enterprises
- NT Multinational Corporations
- RT Business
  Directors
  Firms
  Institutions
  Interlocking Directorates
  Mergers

Corporatism
- DC D176100
- SN A form of government in which the major decisions are negotiated between the state and corporate bodies (eg, unions, interest groups, corporations, professional associations).
- HN Added, 1986.
- BT Political Ideologies
- RT Business Society Relationship
  Collectivism
  Interest Groups
  Labor Relations
  State Society Relationship
  Syndicalism

Correction/Corrections/Correctional/Corrective (1963-1985)
- HN DC 115850, deleted 1986.

Correctional   Counseling

Correctional Facilities
- Use Prisons

Correctional Institutions (Juvenile)
- Use Juvenile Correctional Institutions

Correctional Personnel
- DC D176400
- SN Includes prison guards, and parole and probation officers.
- HN Added, 1986.
- UF Guard/Guards/Guarding/Guarded (1972-1985)
  Probation Officers
- RT Lawyers
  Police
  Prison Culture
  Psychologists
  Public Officials
  Social Workers

Correctional Policy
- Use Criminal Justice Policy

Correctional System
- DC D176700
- SN Aspect of criminal justice concerned with the sentencing, incarceration, and rehabilitation of offenders.
- HN Added, 1986.
- UF Penal System
  Prison System
- BT Legal System
- RT Crime Prevention
  Criminal Justice
  Criminal Justice Policy
  Imprisonment
  Judiciary
  Juvenile Correctional Institutions
  Juvenile Justice
  Parole
  Penal Reform
  Penology
  Prison Culture
  Prisoners
  Prisons
  Probation
  Restitution (Corrections)

Correlates (1963-1985)
- HN DC 115950, deleted 1986.

Correlation
- DC D176800
- SN In statistics, the degree of mutual relation between two or more attributes of the subjects in a study.
- HN Formerly (1963-1985) DC 116000, Correlation/Correlations/Correlatives/Correlational.
- UF Association Measures (Statistical)
  Coefficient/Coefficients (1963-1985)
- BT Methodology (Data Analysis)
- RT Cluster Analysis
  Contingency Analysis
  Factor Analysis
  Multiple Regression Analysis
  Multivariate Analysis
  Quantitative Methods
  Regression Analysis
  Reliability
  Scores
  Statistical Significance
  Statistics
  Validity
  Variables
  Variance (Statistics)

Correspondence/Correspondent (1965-1985)
- HN DC 116050.
- Use Letters (Correspondence)

Corruption
- DC D177000
- HN Formerly (1963-1985) DC 116100.
- RT Morality
  Organized Crime
  Political Power
  Scandals
  Watergate Scandal
  White Collar Crime

Corsica
- DC D177300
- HN Formerly (1977-1985) DC 116120, Corsica/Corsican.
- BT France

Coser, Lewis Alfred
- DC D177600
- SN Born 27 November 1913 - .
- HN Formerly (1970-1985) DC 116128, Coser, L.

Cosmogeny/Cosmogenies (1983-1985)
- HN DC 116133.
- Use Cosmology

Cosmology
- DC D177900
- SN Branch of philosophy that deals with the processes, structure, and origins of the universe.
- HN Formerly (1965-1985) DC 116145, Cosmology/Cosmologies.
- UF Cosmogeny/Cosmogenies (1983-1985)
- BT Philosophy
- RT Metaphysics
  Myths
  Religious Beliefs
  Science

Cosmopolitanism
- DC D178200
- HN Formerly (1963-1985) DC 116150, Cosmopolitan/Cosmopolitans/Cosmopolitanism.
- BT Social Attitudes
- RT Localism
  Social Identity
  Urbanism

Cost Containment
- DC D178400
- HN Formerly (1966-1985) DC 114270, Containment.
- UF Containment of Costs
- RT Budgets
  Costs
  Fiscal Policy
  Inflation
  Prices
  Public Finance

Costa Rica
- DC D178500
- HN Formerly (1963-1985) DC 116225, Costa Rica/Costa Rican/Costa Ricans.
- BT Central America

Costs
- DC D178800
- HN Formerly (1963-1985) DC 116200, Cost/Costs.
- NT Housing Costs
- RT Compensation
  Cost Containment
  Expenditures
  Finance
  Inflation
  Payments
  Prices
  Value (Economics)

Costume
- Use Clothing

Cottage Industries
- DC D179000
- SN Businesses in which goods, especially crafts, are produced in the home. Do not confuse with Home Workplaces.
- HN Added, 1989.
- UF Home Industries
- BT Industry
- RT Crafts
  Home Workplaces
  Small Businesses
  Working Mothers
  Working Women

Councils
- DC D179100
- HN Formerly (1963-1985) DC 116350, Council/Councils/Councilmen.
- UF Local Councils
  Regional Councils
  World Councils
- BT Organizations (Social)
- NT Panchayats
- RT Commissions
  Governing Boards
  Policy Making

Counseling
- DC D179400
- HN Formerly (1963-1985) DC 116380, Counsel/Counseling/Counselor/Counselors.
- UF Counseling/Counselor/Counselors, Marital (1964-1985)
- BT Guidance
- RT Adjustment
  Behavior Modification
  Client Relations
  Clients
  Emergencies
  Employee Assistance Programs
  Family Therapy
  Helping Behavior
  Human Services
  Information And Referral Services
  Intervention
  Psychology
  Rehabilitation
  Role Playing
  Social Work
  Social Workers
  Telephone Communications
  Treatment

Counseling/Counselor/Counselors, Marital (1964-1985)
- HN DC 116400.
- Use Counseling

Counselor Client Relationship
 Use Client Relations

Count/Counting (1963-1985)
 HN DC 116600, deleted 1986.

Countercultures
 DC D179700
 SN Subcultures with values and goals that conflict with and contradict those of the prevailing society.
 HN Formerly (1977-1985) DC 116850, Counterculture/Countercultures.
 UF Beatnik/Beatniks (1966-1985)
    Hippie/Hippies (1968-1985)
 BT Subcultures
 RT Countermovements
    Crosscultural Analysis
    Cults
    Cultural Conflict
    Cultural Pluralism
    Cultural Values
    Dissent
    Generational Differences
    Lifestyle
    Norms
    Popular Culture
    Sects
    Social Behavior
    Youth Culture

Countermovements
 DC D180000
 SN A social movement that arises in opposition to a preexisting social movement.
 HN Formerly (1963-1985) DC 116800, Counter.
 UF Backlash (1966-1985)
 BT Movements
 RT Countercultures
    Political Movements
    Resistance
    Social Movements

Countertransference
 Use Transference (Psychology)

Counties
 DC D180300
 HN Formerly (1963-1985) DC 117350, County/Counties.
 RT Districts
    Geographic Regions
    Local Government
    States (Political Subdivisions)

Countries
 DC D180600
 SN See also specific countries by name.
 HN Formerly (1963-1985) DC 117000, Country/Countries.
 NT Arab Countries
    Developing Countries
    Mediterranean Countries
 RT Borders
    Citizens
    Foreigners
    Geographic Regions
    Geopolitics
    Government
    International Alliances
    International Relations
    National Identity
    Nationalism
    Society
    State

County Extension Services
 Use Extension Services

Couples
 DC D180900
 SN For married couples use Spouses.
 HN Formerly (1963-1985) DC 117600, Couple/Couples.
 RT Cohabitation
    Dating (Social)
    Dyads
    Opposite Sex Relations
    Sexual Behavior
    Spouses

Coups d'Etat
 DC D181200
 HN Formerly (1972-1985) DC 117590, Coup d'Etat/Coups d'Etat.
 UF Military Coups
 BT Political Violence
 RT Military Regimes
    Revolutions

Courses
 DC D181500
 HN Formerly (1972-1985) DC 117950, Course/Courses.
 BT Curriculum
 RT Educational Programs
    Seminars
    Workshops (Courses)

Court Disposition
 Use Disposition

Court Opinions
 Use Judicial Decisions

Courts
 DC D181800
 HN Formerly (1963-1985) part of DC 118000, Court/Courts/Courtly.
 UF Civil Courts
    Criminal Courts
 NT Juvenile Courts
    United States Supreme Court
 RT Institutions
    Judges
    Judiciary
    Jurisdiction
    Justice
    Law
    Legal Procedure
    Legal System
    Trials

Courts (Juvenile)
 Use Juvenile Courts

Courtship
 DC D182100
 HN Formerly (1963-1985) DC 118500, Courtship/Courting.
 NT Dating (Social)
 RT Marriage
    Mate Selection
    Sexual Behavior

Cousin Marriage
 DC D182400
 HN Added, 1986.
 UF Cross Cousin Marriage
    Matrilateral (1963-1985)
    Patrilateral (1963-1985)
 BT Marriage
 RT Consanguinity
    Endogamy
    Mate Selection

Cousin/Cousins (1964-1985)
 HN DC 118600.
 Use Relatives

Couvade
 DC D182700
 SN In certain traditional societies, the ritual simulation by males of their wives' behaviors during and after childbirth. May be applied more broadly to transvestism in certain tribal cultures.
 HN Formerly (1966-1985) DC 118660.
 RT Birth
    Customs
    Transvestism

Covariance/Covariable (1963-1985)
 HN DC 118685.
 Use Variance (Statistics)

Coverage (1964-1985)
 HN DC 118700, deleted 1986. See now News Coverage or Insurance.

Coverage (Insurance)
 Use Insurance

Coverage (News)
 Use News Coverage

Covert (1965-1985)
 HN DC 118750, deleted 1986.

Cracow, Poland (1965-1985)
 HN DC 118850, deleted 1986.

Craft Guilds
 Use Guilds

Crafts
 DC D183000
 HN Formerly (1963-1985) DC 118895, Craft/Crafts.
 UF Ceramics (1965-1985)
    Handicraft/Handicrafts/Handicraftsman (1965-1985)
    Jewel/Jewels/Jeweled/Jewelry (1971-1985)
    Pottery (1963-1985)
 BT Visual Arts
 RT Art
    Artifacts
    Artisans
    Cottage Industries
    Folk Culture
    Guilds
    Material Culture

Craftsmen (1964-1985)
 HN DC 118900.
 Use Artisans

Creationism
 DC D183200
 SN The belief or theory that the universe and all forms of life were created by a transcendent God out of nothing, instead of having gradually developed or evolved. Also, the theological doctrine that God creates a new soul for each person born.
 HN Added, 1986.
 UF Scientific Creationism
 BT Religious Beliefs
 RT Darwinism
    Evolution
    Religious Fundamentalism
    Religious Movements
    Secularization

Creative — Criminology

Creative Art
  Use Art

Creative/Creation/Created (1963-1985)
  HN DC 118945, deleted 1986.

Creativity
  DC D183300
  HN Formerly (1963-1985) DC 119000.
  UF Original/Originality (1965-1985)
  BT Personality Traits
  RT Ability
      Concept Formation
      Imagination
      Intellectuals
      Intelligence
      Inventions
      Knowledge
      Self Expression

Credentialing
  Use Certification

Credibility
  DC D183600
  HN Formerly (1967-1985) DC 119060.
  UF Authenticity (1967-1985)
      Believability
  RT Interpersonal Communication
      Persuasion
      Reputation
      Social Perception
      Trust
      Truth

Credit
  DC D183900
  HN Formerly (1963-1985) DC 119070, Credit/Credits.
  RT Banking
      Debts
      Economics
      Finance
      Loans
      Money

Creed/Creeds (1971-1985)
  HN DC 119080.
  Use Beliefs

Cremation
  DC D184200
  HN Formerly (1969-1985) DC 119085.
  BT Death Rituals
  RT Burials
      Death
      Death Attitudes

Creolized Languages
  DC D184500
  SN Languages composed of elements of different languages. Creolized languages develop in areas of intensive language contact and serve as the native languages of their speakers.
  HN Formerly (1964-1985) DC 119090, Creole/Creoles.
  UF Mixed Languages
  BT Language Varieties
      Languages
  RT Culture Contact
      Diglossia
      Language Usage

Crime
  DC D184800
  HN Formerly (1963-1985) DC 119100, Crime/Crimes.
  NT Delinquency
      Organized Crime
      Rural Crime
      Urban Crime
      White Collar Crime
  RT Aggression
      Crime Prevention
      Crime Rates
      Criminal Justice
      Decriminalization
      Deviance
      Deviant Behavior
      Fear of Crime
      Investigations (Law Enforcement)
      Law Enforcement
      Neutralization Theory
      Offenders
      Offenses
      Recidivism
      Social Disorganization
      Social Problems
      Sociopathic Personality
      Victim Offender Relations
      Victimization

Crime Fear
  Use Fear of Crime

Crime Policy
  Use Criminal Justice Policy

Crime Prevention
  DC D185100
  HN Added, 1986.
  BT Prevention
  NT Delinquency Prevention
  RT Correctional System
      Crime
      Criminal Justice Policy
      Criminology
      Detention
      Deterrence
      Fear of Crime
      Gun Control
      Law Enforcement
      Police
      Police Community Relations
      Security

Crime Rates
  DC D185400
  HN Added, 1986.
  UF Uniform Crime Reporting
  BT Rates
  RT Crime
      Mortality Rates
      Offenses

Crime Victims
  Use Victims

Crimes
  Use Offenses

Criminal Courts
  Use Courts

Criminal Justice
  DC D185700
  HN Formerly (1984-1986) DC 119130.
  UF Justice (Criminal)
  BT Legal System
  RT Correctional System
      Crime
      Criminal Justice Policy

Criminal Justice (cont'd)
  RT Forensic Psychiatry
      Judicial Decisions
      Law Enforcement
      Offenders
      Restitution (Corrections)
      Social Work
      Vigilantism

Criminal Justice Policy
  DC D186000
  HN Added, 1986.
  UF Correctional Policy
      Crime Policy
      Juvenile Justice Policy
      Penal Policy
  BT Social Policy
  RT Correctional System
      Crime Prevention
      Criminal Justice
      Decriminalization
      Juvenile Justice
      Offenders
      Penal Reform

Criminal Law
  Use Law

Criminal Procedure
  Use Legal Procedure

Criminal Proceedings
  DC D186300
  HN Added, 1986.
  UF Proceedings (Criminal)
  RT Adversary Legal System
      Defendants
      Evidence (Legal)
      Judges
      Juries
      Law Enforcement
      Lawyers
      Legal Cases
      Offenders
      Plea Bargaining
      Police
      Prosecutors
      Sentencing
      Trials
      Verdicts

Criminal/Criminals/Criminality/Criminally (1963-1985)
  HN DC 119125, deleted 1986. See now appropriate "Crime," "Offenders," and "Criminal Justice" terms.

Criminals
  Use Offenders

Criminologist/Criminologists (1968-1985)
  HN DC 119140, deleted 1986.

Criminology
  DC D186600
  HN Formerly (1963-1985) DC 119145, Criminology/Criminological.
  BT Sociology
  NT Penology
      Victimology
  RT Crime Prevention
      Delinquency Prevention
      Forensic Psychiatry
      Jurisprudence
      Social Psychology
      Sociology of Law

52

Crimogenic

Crimogenic/Crimogenesis (1966-1985)
- **HN** DC 119138, deleted 1986. See now Crime or Criminology.

Crippled
- **Use** Physically Handicapped

Crises
- **DC** D186900
- **HN** Formerly (1963-1985) DC 119160, Crisis/Crises.
- **NT** Economic Crises
- **RT** Crisis Intervention
  Disasters
  Emergencies
  Experience
  Problems
  Psychological Distress
  Shock
  Social Response
  Stress
  Tension
  Threat

Crisis Intervention
- **DC** D186925
- **SN** Brief forms of psychological treatment to aid persons in acute distress. Examples include telephone hotlines and drop-in centers staffed by paraprofessionals or volunteers.
- **HN** Added, 1989.
- **BT** Intervention
- **RT** Crises
  Treatment

Criteria
- **DC** D186950
- **HN** Formerly (1963-1985) DC 119170, Criteria/Criterion.
- **RT** Criticism
  Decision Making
  Evaluation
  Judgment
  Policy Making
  Quality
  Standards

Critic/Critics/Critical (1963-1985)
- **HN** DC 119180, deleted 1986. See now Critical Theory or Criticism and its associated terms.

Critical Theory
- **DC** D187000
- **SN** A Marxist approach to social analysis, developed by members of the Frankfurt School, that evaluates or criticizes society in addition to analyzing it. Its goal is the detection and debunking of beliefs that impede human emancipation, and it arose in reaction to institutionalized Marxism's use of criticism to legitimize Communist Party political actions.
- **HN** Formerly (1985) DC 119245.
- **BT** Social Theories
- **RT** Class Consciousness
  Dialectics
  Frankfurt School
  Freudian Psychology
  Hermeneutics
  Marxist Analysis
  Marxist Sociology
  Psychoanalytic Interpretation
  Radicalism
  Sociological Theory
  Verstehen

Criticism
- **DC** D187100
- **HN** Formerly (1963-1985) part of DC 119310, Criticism/Critique.
- **BT** Evaluation
- **NT** Literary Criticism
  Social Criticism
- **RT** Approval
  Criteria
  Judgment
  Social Influence

Criticism (Social)
- **Use** Social Criticism

Croatia, Yugoslavia
- **DC** D187200
- **HN** Formerly (1966-1985) DC 119350, Croatia/Croats.
- **BT** Yugoslavia

Croce, Benedetto
- **DC** D187500
- **SN** Born 25 February 1866 - died 20 November 1952.
- **HN** Formerly (1972-1985) DC 119353.

Crofting
- **DC** D187800
- **SN** British system of small farm tenancy.
- **HN** Formerly (1978-1985) DC 119360.
- **BT** Agrarian Structures
- **RT** Land Tenure
  Small Farms

Crop Production
- **Use** Agricultural Production

Cross- (1964-1985)
- **HN** DC 119375, deleted 1986.

Cross Cousin Marriage
- **Use** Cousin Marriage

Cross Cultural Contact
- **Use** Culture Contact

Crosscultural Analysis
- **DC** D188100
- **HN** Formerly (1963-1985) DC 119380, Cross-cultural.
- **UF** Crossnational Analysis
  Cultural Comparisons
- **BT** Comparative Analysis
- **RT** Anthropology
  Biculturalism
  Bilingualism
  Comparative Sociology
  Countercultures
  Cultural Change
  Cultural Conflict
  Cultural Universals
  Cultural Values
  Culture
  Differences
  Ethnic Groups
  Ethnic Relations
  Ethnicity
  Ethnography
  Ethnology
  Folk Culture
  Multilingualism
  Social Anthropology
  Social Integration
  Subcultures

Cults

Crossdisciplinary Approach
- **Use** Interdisciplinary Approach

Crossnational Analysis
- **Use** Crosscultural Analysis

Crowding
- **DC** D188400
- **HN** Formerly (1963-1985) part of DC 119430, Crowd/Crowds/Crowding.
- **BT** Population Density
- **RT** Environment
  Overpopulation
  Personal Space
  Space
  Stress

Crowds
- **DC** D188700
- **HN** Formerly (1963-1985) part of DC 119430, Crowd/Crowds/Crowding.
- **UF** Mob/Mobs (1964-1985)
- **BT** Groups
- **RT** Collective Behavior
  Contagion Theory
  Riots

Crow-Omaha (1969-1985)
- **HN** DC 119410, deleted 1986. See now American Indians.

Crozier, Michel
- **DC** D189000
- **SN** Born 6 November 1922 - .
- **HN** Formerly (1972-1985) DC 119435, Crozier, M.

Crude Oils
- **Use** Petroleum

Cruelty (1975-1985)
- **HN** DC 119455.
- **Use** Abuse

Cuba
- **DC** D189300
- **HN** Formerly (1963-1985) DC 119480, Cuba/Cuban/Cubans.
- **BT** Caribbean
- **NT** Havana, Cuba

Culinary (1964-1985)
- **HN** DC 119550.
- **Use** Food Preparation

Culpability (1978-1985)
- **HN** DC 119570, deleted 1986.

Cultivation (1969-1985)
- **HN** DC 119585, deleted 1986. See now Agriculture or Culture.

Cults
- **DC** D189600
- **SN** Religious groups with distinctive ideologies and rites, often considered to be extremist, and whose members live outside of conventional society under the influence of a charismatic leader.
- **HN** Formerly (1963-1985) DC 119575, Cult/Cults/Cultist/Cultists.
- **UF** New Religions
- **NT** Cargo Cults
  Unification Church
- **RT** Charisma
  Countercultures
  Devils
  Dolmen
  Ghost Dances

Cultural

Cults (cont'd)
- RT Jonestown Mass Suicide
- Millenarianism
- Mysticism
- Rastafarians
- Religions
- Religious Behavior
- Religious Rituals
- Sects
- Syncretism
- Witchcraft
- Worship

Cultural Activities
- DC D189900
- HN Added, 1986.
- UF Cultural Events
- BT Activities
- NT Festivals
- RT Culture
- Fine Arts
- Museums

Cultural Anthropology
- Use Social Anthropology

Cultural Bias
- Use Ethnocentrism

Cultural Change
- DC D190200
- SN See also Social Evolution, Social Processes, Social Change, and Sociocultural Factors.
- HN Formerly (1963-1985) DC 119610, Culture/Cultural, Change.
- UF Cultural Evolution
- BT Change
- RT Acculturation
- Assimilation
- Crosscultural Analysis
- Cultural Conflict
- Cultural Groups
- Cultural Transmission
- Culture
- Culture Contact
- Evolutionary Theories
- History
- Indigenous Populations
- Intercultural Communication
- Modernity
- Modernization
- Social Change
- Social Evolution
- Social Integration
- Social Processes
- Social Revolution
- Sociocultural Factors
- Technological Change
- Traditional Societies
- Traditionalism

Cultural Comparisons
- Use Crosscultural Analysis

Cultural Conflict
- DC D190500
- SN Discord arising from the need to adjust rapidly to an unfamiliar culture, as in the case of newly arrived immigrants, and from competition between dissimilar cultures in a common area.
- HN Added, 1986.
- UF Culture Shock
- Kulturkampf
- BT Conflict
- RT Acculturation
- Biculturalism

Cultural Conflict (cont'd)
- RT Countercultures
- Crosscultural Analysis
- Cultural Change
- Cultural Groups
- Cultural Pluralism
- Cultural Values
- Culture
- Culture Contact
- Ethnic Groups
- Ethnicity
- Ethnocentrism
- Immigrants
- Indigenous Populations
- Intercultural Communication
- Nativism
- Nativistic Movements
- Political Culture
- Shock
- Social Conflict

Cultural Events
- Use Cultural Activities

Cultural Evolution
- Use Cultural Change

Cultural Groups
- DC D190800
- SN A context-dependent term; select a more specific entry or coordinate with a geographical term for immigrant populations.
- HN Added, 1986.
- UF Nationality/Nationalities (1963-1985)
- BT Groups
- NT African Cultural Groups
- Arab Cultural Groups
- Asian Cultural Groups
- Australasian Cultural Groups
- Ethnic Groups
- European Cultural Groups
- Latin American Cultural Groups
- Middle Eastern Cultural Groups
- North American Cultural Groups
- Oceanic Cultural Groups
- Religious Cultural Groups
- Soviet Union Cultural Groups
- Subcultures
- RT Acculturation
- Assimilation
- Biculturalism
- Cultural Change
- Cultural Conflict
- Cultural Identity
- Cultural Pluralism
- Cultural Values
- Culture
- Culture Contact
- Ethnography
- Ethnolinguistic Groups
- Intercultural Communication
- National Identity
- Race
- Social Groups
- Society
- Sociocultural Factors
- Traditional Societies

Cultural Identity
- DC D191100
- HN Added, 1986.
- BT Identity
- NT National Identity
- RT Acculturation
- Biculturalism
- Bilingual Education
- Cultural Groups

Cultural Identity (cont'd)
- RT Cultural Pluralism
- Cultural Transmission
- Cultural Values
- Culture
- Ethnic Identity
- Ethnocentrism
- Ethnolinguistic Groups
- Group Identity
- Immigrants
- Language Attitudes
- Language Maintenance
- Multicultural Education
- Nativistic Movements
- Pan-Africanism
- Plural Societies
- Social Identity
- Subcultures

Cultural Pluralism
- DC D191400
- SN Refers to the existence of a number of cultures within a larger culture or society, and to the ideology that promotes this rather than homogenization into mass culture.
- HN Formerly (1963-1985) part of DC 339248, Plural/Pluralism/Pluralist/Pluralists/Pluralistic.
- UF Multiculturalism
- BT Pluralism
- NT Biculturalism
- RT Acculturation
- Anthropology
- Assimilation
- Bilingualism
- Cleavage
- Countercultures
- Cultural Conflict
- Cultural Groups
- Cultural Identity
- Culture
- Ethnic Groups
- Ethnic Minorities
- Ethnic Relations
- Ethnicity
- Ethnolinguistic Groups
- Intercultural Communication
- Language Policy
- Minority Groups
- Multicultural Education
- Multilingualism
- Plural Societies
- Political Culture
- Subcultures

Cultural Politics
- Use Political Culture

Cultural Relativism
- DC D191475
- SN An epistemological doctrine that focuses on how meaning and reality vary from culture to culture. See also Cultural Universals; compare with Positivism.
- HN Added, 1986.
- UF Cultural Relativity
- BT Relativism
- RT Cultural Universals
- Culture
- Determinism
- Ethnocentrism
- Existentialism
- Objectivity
- Positivism
- Social Anthropology
- Sociocultural Factors
- Subjectivity
- Value Neutrality
- Value Orientations

Cultural   Cybernetics

Cultural Relativity
  Use Cultural Relativism

Cultural Test Bias
  Use Test Bias

Cultural Transmission
  DC D191550
  HN Formerly (1963-1985) part of DC 471500, Transmission.
  UF Intergenerational Transmission of Culture
  RT Acculturation
    Childrearing Practices
    Cultural Change
    Cultural Identity
    Cultural Values
    Culture
    Culture Contact
    Information Dissemination
    Intergenerational Relations
    Preservation
    Social Reproduction
    Socialization
    Socialization Agents

Cultural Universals
  DC D191625
  SN Attributes found in all cultures; compare with Cultural Relativism.
  HN Formerly (1963-1985) part of DC 477400, Universal/Universalism/Universality/Universalistic.
  UF Universals of Culture
  RT Crosscultural Analysis
    Cultural Relativism
    Culture
    Norms

Cultural Values
  DC D191700
  HN Added, 1986.
  BT Values
  RT Acculturation
    Aesthetics
    Art
    Biculturalism
    Civilization
    Countercultures
    Crosscultural Analysis
    Cultural Conflict
    Cultural Groups
    Cultural Identity
    Cultural Transmission
    Culture
    Ideologies
    Norms
    Nudity
    Religious Attitudes
    Religious Cultural Groups
    Social Values
    Subcultures
    Traditional Societies
    Traditions

Culture
  DC D192000
  SN A context-dependent term encompassing the systems of shared meanings that differentiate populations. Select a more specific term or coordinate with other terms.
  HN Formerly (1963-1985) DC 119600, Culture/Cultures/Cultural/Culturally.
  NT Folk Culture
    Material Culture
    Organizational Culture
    Political Culture
    Popular Culture

Culture (cont'd)
  NT Prison Culture
    Youth Culture
  RT Acculturation
    Art
    Assimilation
    Beliefs
    Biculturalism
    Civilization
    Crosscultural Analysis
    Cultural Activities
    Cultural Change
    Cultural Conflict
    Cultural Groups
    Cultural Identity
    Cultural Pluralism
    Cultural Relativism
    Cultural Transmission
    Cultural Universals
    Cultural Values
    Culture Contact
    Customs
    Ethnic Groups
    Ethnography
    Ethnology
    Folklore
    Intellectual History
    Intercultural Communication
    Linguistics
    Race
    Religions
    Religious Cultural Groups
    Rituals
    Signs
    Social Anthropology
    Social History
    Society
    Sociocultural Factors
    Technology
    Traditional Societies
    Traditions
    Worldview

Culture Contact
  DC D192300
  HN Added, 1986.
  UF Cross Cultural Contact
  RT Acculturation
    Biculturalism
    Colonialism
    Creolized Languages
    Cultural Change
    Cultural Conflict
    Cultural Groups
    Cultural Transmission
    Culture
    Indigenous Populations
    Intercultural Communication
    Language Shift
    Social Contact
    Social Revolution

Culture Shock
  Use Cultural Conflict

Curacao
  DC D192600
  HN Formerly (1964-1985) DC 119760.
  BT Netherlands Antilles

Curiosity
  DC D192900
  HN Formerly (1965-1985) DC 119800.
  BT Personality Traits
  RT Interests
    Motivation

Currency/Currencies (1965-1985)
  HN DC 119810.
  Use Money

Current (1963-1985)
  HN DC 119815, deleted 1986.

Curriculum
  DC D193200
  HN Formerly (1963-1985) DC 119830, Curriculum/Curricula/Curricular.
  UF College Curriculum
    School Curriculum
  NT Courses
  RT Academic Departments
    Education
    Educational Programs
    Home Economics
    Marriage And Family Education
    Reading
    Schools
    Secondary Schools
    Social Science Education
    Social Studies
    Teaching
    Vocational Education

Curve/Curves (1970-1985)
  HN DC 119860.
  Use Frequency Distributions

Customer/Customers (1972-1985)
  HN DC 119883.
  Use Consumers

Customs
  DC D193500
  SN Prevailing traditions, including mores, values, and norms, in a culture or society.
  HN Formerly (1963-1985) DC 119880, Custom/Customs.
  RT Behavior
    Celebrations
    Clothing
    Couvade
    Culture
    Ethnography
    Ethnology
    Fashions
    Festivals
    Folk Culture
    Folklore
    Genital Mutilation
    Holidays
    Law
    Norms
    Rituals
    Social Anthropology
    Taboos
    Traditional Societies
    Traditions

Cybernetics
  DC D193800
  SN Science that compares the communication and control systems in electronic and mechanical systems with those present in biological organisms.
  HN Formerly (1964-1985) DC 119910, Cybernetic/Cybernetics.
  BT Technology
  RT Artificial Intelligence
    Automation
    Biotechnology
    Communication
    Computers
    Game Theory

Cyclical

Cybernetics (cont'd)
- RT High Technology Industries
- Information Processing
- Information Technology
- Information Theory
- Symbiotic Relations
- Technological Progress

Cyclical Processes
- DC D193900
- HN Formerly (1963-1985) DC 119940, Cycle/Cycles/Cyclical.
- UF Repeating Patterns
- RT Business Cycles
- Life Cycle
- Lunar Influences
- Seasonal Variations
- Time

Cyclothymia
- Use Depression (Psychology)

Cynicism
- DC D194000
- HN Formerly (1969-1985) DC 119965.
- UF Misanthropy/Misanthrope (1977-1985)
- RT Personality Traits
- Pessimism
- Philosophical Doctrines
- Skepticism
- Social Perception
- Worldview

Cyprus
- DC D194100
- HN Formerly (1968-1985) DC 119967, Cyprus/Cypriot/Cypriots.
- BT Mediterranean Countries
- Middle East
- Western Europe

Czechoslovakia
- DC D194400
- HN Formerly (1963-1985) DC 119972, Czechoslovakia/Czechoslovakian/Czech/Czechs.
- BT Eastern Europe
- NT Prague, Czechoslovakia

Dahrendorf, Ralf
- DC D194700
- SN Born 1 May 1929 - .
- HN Formerly (1963-1985) DC 119980.

Dailies (Newspapers)
- Use Newspapers

Daily Life
- Use Everyday Life

Daily/Dailies (1969-1985)
- HN DC 119982, deleted 1986.

Dairy Farms
- DC D195000
- HN Formerly (1963-1985) DC 119985, Dairy Farm/Dairy Farms/Dairy Farmer/Dairy Farmers.
- BT Farms
- RT Animal Husbandry
- Livestock

Dallas, Texas
- DC D195300
- HN Formerly (1970-1985) DC 119986, Dallas, Tex.
- BT Texas

Damascus, Syria
- DC D195400
- HN Added, 1989.
- BT Syria

Dance
- DC D195600
- HN Formerly (1966-1985) DC 119988, Dance/Dances/Dancing/Dancer/Dancers.
- UF Ballet
- Choreography
- BT Fine Arts
- RT Art
- Folk Culture
- Music
- Theater Arts

Danger (1966-1985)
- HN DC 119989.
- Use Threat

Danish (Language)
- Use Germanic Languages

Dardic Languages
- Use Indic Languages

Darwinism
- DC D195800
- SN Theory that species are derived, by varied descent, from parent forms through natural selection of those members best adapted to survive.
- HN Formerly (1963-1985) DC 120050, Darwin/Darwinism/Darwinian.
- BT Evolutionary Theories
- RT Biology
- Creationism
- Evolution
- Genetics
- Social Darwinism
- Sociobiology

Data
- DC D195900
- SN Information obtained by observation, interviews, questionnaires, tests, and experimentation, usually in numerical form.
- HN Formerly (1963-1985) DC 120075.
- UF Statistical Data
- BT Information
- NT Aggregate Data
- Categorical Data
- Data Banks
- Panel Data
- Scores
- RT Coding
- Data Collection
- Data Processing
- Graphs
- Information Sources
- Matrices
- Measurement
- Methodology (Data Analysis)
- Methodology (Data Collection)
- Phenomena
- Statistics
- Tables
- Variables

Data Analysis Methodology
- Use Methodology (Data Analysis)

Data Banks
- DC D196200
- SN Collections of data in machine-readable form, for purposes of manipulation, processing, and display by computer.

Data Banks (cont'd)
- HN Added, 1986.
- UF Databases
- Information Banks
- BT Data
- RT Archives
- Computer Assisted Research
- Computer Software
- Computers
- Data Banks
- Data Collection
- Data Processing
- Documentation
- Information Sources
- Libraries
- Methodology (Data Analysis)
- Microcomputers

Data Collection
- DC D196500
- HN Formerly (1985) DC 120090, Data Collecting.
- BT Information Processing
- RT Data
- Data Banks
- Data Processing
- Experiments
- Information Sources
- Methodology (Data Analysis)
- Methodology (Data Collection)
- Observation
- Research
- Sampling
- Secondary Analysis
- Surveys

Data Collection Methodology
- Use Methodology (Data Collection)

Data Matrices
- Use Matrices

Data Processing
- DC D196800
- HN Formerly (1964-1985) DC 120100.
- UF Automatic Data Processing
- Electronic Data Processing (1964-1985)
- BT Information Processing
- RT Automation
- Computer Assisted Research
- Computer Software
- Computers
- Data
- Data Banks
- Data Collection
- Electronic Technology
- Information Theory
- Methodology (Data Analysis)
- Microcomputers
- Research

Databases
- Use Data Banks

Dating (Social)
- DC D197100
- HN Formerly (1963-1985) part of DC 120200, Date/Dates/Dating.
- BT Courtship
- Interpersonal Relations
- RT Adolescents
- Couples
- Friendship
- Interpersonal Attraction
- Mate Selection
- Sexual Behavior
- Single Persons
- Social Behavior
- Social Life

Daughters

Daughters
- DC D197400
- HN Formerly (1963-1985) DC 120300, Daughter/Daughters.
- BT Females
- RT Children
     Child Sex Preferences
     Parent Child Relations
     Siblings
     Sons

Davis, Kingsley
- DC D197700
- SN Born 20 August 1908 - .
- HN Formerly (1963-1985) DC 120325.

Day Care
- DC D198000
- HN Formerly (1964-1985) DC 120375.
- UF Day Nurseries
- RT Caregivers
     Child Care Services
     Preschool Children

Day Nurseries
- Use Day Care

Deaconesses
- Use Deacons

Deacons
- DC D198300
- HN Formerly (1969-1985) DC 120390, Deacon/Deacons/Deaconess/Deaconesses.
- UF Deaconesses
- BT Clergy

Deaf
- DC D198600
- HN Formerly (1963-1985) DC 120400, Deaf/Deafness.
- BT Handicapped
- RT Blind
     Hearing
     Manual Communication

Deans
- DC D198900
- HN Formerly (1965-1985) DC 120600, Dean/Deans.
- UF Academic Deans
- BT Administrators
- RT College Faculty
     Educational Administration

Death
- DC D199200
- HN Formerly (1963-1985) part of DC 121000, Death/Deaths.
- BT Life Cycle
- RT Burials
     Cemeteries
     Child Mortality
     Cremation
     Death Attitudes
     Death Rituals
     Dying
     Euthanasia
     Fatalities
     Funerals
     Ghosts
     Grief
     Infant Mortality
     Mortality Rates
     Obituaries
     Physiology
     Soul
     Suicide
     Survival
     Terminal Illness
     Widowhood

Death Attitudes
- DC D199500
- HN Added, 1986.
- BT Attitudes
- RT Burials
     Cemeteries
     Cremation
     Death
     Death Rituals
     Dying
     Funerals
     Religious Beliefs
     Soul

Death Notices
- Use Obituaries

Death Penalty (1979-1985)
- HN DC 121050.
- Use Capital Punishment

Death Rates
- Use Mortality Rates

Death Rites
- Use Death Rituals

Death Rituals
- DC D199800
- HN Added, 1986.
- UF Death Rites
- BT Rites of Passage
- NT Burials
     Cremation
     Funerals
     Ghost Dances
- RT Cannibalism
     Cemeteries
     Death
     Death Attitudes
     Dolmen
     Dying
     Grief
     Obituaries
     Ossuaries
     Religious Rituals
     Soul

Debate
- DC D200100
- HN Formerly (1963-1985) DC 121150, Debate/Debates/Debating.
- UF Argument/Arguments/Argumentation (1963-1985)
     Polemic/Polemics (1969-1985)
- RT Discourse
     Discussion
     Disputes
     Language
     Persuasion
     Rhetoric
     Verbal Communication

Debility (1970-1985)
- HN DC 121200, deleted 1986.

Debts
- DC D200400
- HN Formerly (1966-1985) DC 121250, Debt/Debts.
- UF Indebtedness (1972-1985)
- NT Public Debt
- RT Bankruptcy
     Credit
     Finance
     Loans
     Money

Decisions

Debut/Debutante/Debutantes (1969-1985)
- HN DC 121253, deleted 1986.

Decadence (1963-1985)
- HN DC 121275, deleted 1986.

Decembrists (1979-1985)
- HN DC 121300, deleted 1986.

Decentralization
- DC D200700
- HN Formerly (1963-1985) DC 121400.
- BT Organizational Structure
- RT Centralization
     Organizational Change

Deception
- DC D200800
- HN Formerly (1984-1985) DC 121480, Deception/Deceptions.
- UF Falsehoods
     Hoaxes
     Lies
     Lying
- RT Cheating
     Fraud
     Lie Detection
     Morality
     Professional Ethics
     Propaganda
     Truth

Decision Making
- DC D201000
- HN Formerly (1963-1985) DC 122000.
- UF Indecision (1978-1985)
- BT Cognition
- NT Group Decision Making
     Medical Decision Making
     Participative Decision Making
- RT Ambivalence
     Choices
     Conflict Resolution
     Criteria
     Decision Models
     Decisions
     Dilemmas
     Discretion
     Discretionary Power
     Evaluation
     Forecasting
     Game Theory
     Judgment
     Management
     Policy Making
     Priorities
     Problem Solving
     Rational Choice
     Risk
     Selection Procedures

Decision Models
- DC D201100
- HN Added, 1986.
- BT Models
- NT Game Theory
- RT Decision Making
     Decisions

Decisions
- DC D201300
- SN A context-dependent term for the results of decision-making processes. Select a more specific entry or coordinate with other terms.
- HN Formerly (1963-1985) DC 121950, Decision/Decisional/Decisions.
- NT Choices

Decisions

Decisions (cont'd)
- NT Judicial Decisions
  - Verdicts
- RT Decision Making
  - Decision Models
  - Discretion
  - Discretionary Power
  - Judgment
  - Rational Choice

Decisions (Judicial)
- Use Judicial Decisions

Decline (1981-1985)
- HN DC 122145, deleted 1986.

Decolonization
- DC D201600
- HN Formerly (1965-1985) DC 122170, Decolonize/Decolonized/Decolonization.
- RT Colonization

Decriminalization
- DC D201650
- SN Elimination of criminal penalties for, or removal of legal restrictions against, a formerly illegal act.
- HN Added, 1989.
- UF Legalization
- RT Crime
  - Criminal Justice Policy
  - Offenses

Deduction
- DC D201700
- HN Formerly (1963-1985) DC 122300, Deduction/Deductive/Deductivism.
- BT Reasoning
- RT Differentiation
  - Induction
  - Inference
  - Logic
  - Principles
  - Propositions
  - Rationalism
  - Scientific Method

Defect/Defection (1963-1985)
- HN DC 123090, deleted 1986. See now Congenitally Handicapped or Political Defection.

Defective/Defects/Defectiveness (1969-1985)
- HN DC 123100, deleted 1986. See now Congenitally Handicapped or Mentally Retarded.

Defendants
- DC D201900
- HN Formerly (1965-1985) DC 123400, Defendant/Defendants.
- RT Criminal Proceedings
  - Juries
  - Litigation
  - Offenders
  - Trials
  - Witnesses

Defense Mechanisms
- DC D202200
- SN Patterns of coping behavior that protect an individual from experiencing or confronting unmanageable feelings such as anxiety, guilt, and anger.
- HN Added, 1986.
- UF Displacement (Defense Mechanism)
- NT Repression (Defense Mechanism)
- RT Coping
  - Fantasy
  - Mental Illness

Defense Spending
- DC D202300
- HN Added, 1989.
- UF Military Expenditures
- BT Government Spending
- RT Armaments
  - Armed Forces
  - Militarization
  - National Security
  - War

Defense/Defenses (1963-1985)
- HN DC 123500, deleted 1986. See now Civil Defense, Defense Mechanisms, Insanity Defense, or National Security.

Defensive/Defensiveness (1963-1985)
- HN DC 124500, deleted 1986.

Deference (1963-1985)
- HN DC 125475.
- Use Subordination

Deficiency/Deficiencies (1963-1985)
- HN DC 125500, deleted 1986. See now Malnutrition or Acquired Immune Deficiency Syndrome.

Deficits (1980-1985)
- HN DC 125525.
- Use Public Debt

Definitions
- DC D202500
- HN Formerly (1980-1985) DC 125575, Definition/Definitions/Definitional.
- UF Redefinition (1964-1985)
- RT Etymology
  - Language
  - Meaning
  - Morphology (Language)
  - Operational Definitions
  - Semantics
  - Semiotics
  - Terminology
  - Translation
  - Vocabularies
  - Words

DeGaulle, Charles Andre Joseph
- DC D202600
- SN Born 22 November 1890 - died 9 November 1970.
- HN Formerly (1964-1985) DC 125600, DeGaulle, Charles/Gaullism.

Degrees (Academic)
- Use Academic Degrees

Deindustrialization
- DC D202700
- SN In advanced industrial societies, the process of change from an economy based on manufacturing to one based on services.
- HN Added, 1989.
- BT Social Processes
- RT Economic Change
  - Employment Changes
  - Industrialization
  - Postindustrial Societies
  - Service Industries

Deinstitutionalization
- DC D202800
- SN Processes, programs, and services emphasizing out-of-hospital treatment and/or community residence of chronic psychiatric or disabled patients.

Delinquency

Deinstitutionalization (cont'd)
- HN Formerly (1984-1985) DC 125642, Deinstitutionalize/Deinstitutionalization.
- RT Adjustment
  - Community Mental Health
  - Discharge
  - Handicapped
  - Homelessness
  - Institutionalization (Persons)
  - Mental Patients
  - Mentally Retarded
  - Programs
  - Rehabilitation
  - Self Care
  - Treatment Programs

Deism (1976-1985)
- HN DC 125650, deleted 1986.

Deities
- DC D203100
- HN Formerly (1963-1985) DC 125655, Deity/Deities.
- UF God/Gods (1963-1985)
- NT God (Judeo-Christian)
- RT Atheism
  - Paganism
  - Prayer
  - Religions
  - Religious Doctrines
  - Sacrificial Rites
  - Worship

Delaware
- DC D203400
- HN Formerly (1970-1985) DC 125790.
- BT Northern States
  - United States of America

Delay of Gratification
- DC D203700
- SN Voluntary postponement of reward, need satisfaction, or fulfillment of desires.
- HN Formerly (1966-1985) DC 197310, Gratification.
- UF Gratification (Delay of)
- RT Impulsiveness
  - Locus of Control
  - Motivation
  - Needs
  - Reinforcement
  - Rewards
  - Self Concept

Delegate/Delegates/Delegation/Delegated (1972-1985)
- HN DC 125795, deleted 1986.

Delhi, India
- DC D204000
- HN Formerly (1963-1985) DC 125800.
- BT India

Delinquency
- DC D204300
- SN A context-dependent term for illegal or socially unacceptable behavior. In contexts where Delinquency is closely related to the narrower term Juvenile Delinquency, select the latter.
- HN Formerly (1963-1985) DC 126000.
- UF Delinquency, Adult (1963-1985)
- BT Crime
- NT Juvenile Delinquency
- RT Aggression
  - Delinquency Prevention
  - Etiology
  - Neutralization Theory
  - Recidivism
  - Runaways

Delinquency

Delinquency, Adult (1963-1985)
- **HN** DC 126050.
- **Use** Delinquency

Delinquency Prevention
- **DC** D204600
- **HN** Added, 1986.
- **UF** Diversion/Diversions (1982-1985)
  Juvenile Diversion Programs
  Youth Diversion Programs
- **BT** Crime Prevention
- **RT** Behavior Modification
  Community Mental Health
  Criminology
  Delinquency
  Disposition
  Juvenile Delinquency
  Juvenile Justice
  Penology
  Youth Employment

Delinquent/Delinquents (1965-1985)
- **HN** DC 126200, deleted 1986. See now Delinquency, Offenders, and other appropriate "Crime" terms.

Delivery Systems
- **DC** D204900
- **SN** Organizational or structural mechanisms for the delivery of essential services.
- **HN** Formerly (1979-1985) DC 126225, Delivery.
- **BT** Systems
- **RT** Agencies
  Health Care Utilization
  Health Planning
  Health Services
  Home Health Care
  Information And Referral Services
  Program Implementation
  Programs
  Referral
  Services

Delusion/Delusions (1963-1985)
- **HN** DC 127000.
- **Use** Irrationality

Demagogue/Demagogic/Demagogues (1972-1985)
- **HN** DC 127070, deleted 1986.

Demand/Demands (1963-1985)
- **HN** DC 127075.
- **Use** Supply And Demand

Dementia Praecox
- **Use** Schizophrenia

Democracy
- **DC** D205200
- **HN** Formerly (1963-1985) DC 127150, Democracy/Democracies/Democratic/Democrats/Democratization.
- **UF** Representative Government
- **BT** Political Systems
- **RT** Capitalism
  Civil Rights
  Elections
  Freedom
  Legislative Bodies
  Liberal Democratic Societies
  Liberalism
  Majorities (Politics)
  Political Campaigns
  Republics
  Social Democracy
  Voting

Demographic Change
- **DC** D205500
- **HN** Added, 1986.
- **UF** Depopulation (1964-1985)
  Population Change
- **BT** Change
- **NT** Population Growth
- **RT** Community Change
  Demographic Transition Theory
  Demography
  Employment Changes
  Fertility Decline
  Geographic Mobility
  Migration
  Population
  Population Distribution
  Sociodemographic Factors
  Sustenance Organization

Demographic Characteristics
- **DC** D205800
- **HN** Added, 1986.
- **UF** Population Characteristics
- **RT** Age
  Age Groups
  Cohort Analysis
  Demography
  Group Composition
  Population
  Population Distribution
  Race
  Sex
  Sociodemographic Factors
  Socioeconomic Status

Demographic Policy
- **Use** Population Policy

Demographic Transition Theory
- **DC** D206100
- **SN** A description of how birth and death rates change as a result of the transition from pre-industrial to industrial societies.
- **HN** Added, 1986.
- **UF** Transition Theory (Demographic)
- **BT** Theories
- **RT** Demographic Change
  Demography
  Developing Countries
  Fertility
  Mortality Rates
  Population Growth

Demography
- **DC** D206400
- **HN** Formerly (1963-1985) DC 127300, Demography/Demographic/Demographical.
- **BT** Sociology
- **NT** Geographic Distribution
  Population Distribution
  Residential Patterns
- **RT** Census
  Community Size
  Demographic Change
  Demographic Characteristics
  Demographic Transition Theory
  Employment
  Employment Changes
  Fertility
  Geographic Mobility
  Geography
  Land Settlement
  Life Tables
  Migration
  Migration Patterns
  Mortality Rates

Demography (cont'd)
- **RT** Nuptiality
  Overpopulation
  Population
  Population Density
  Residence
  Social Mobility
  Sociodemographic Factors
  Topography
  Unemployment Rates
  World Population

Demonic Possession
- **Use** Spirit Possession

Demons
- **DC** D206700
- **HN** Formerly (1970-1985) DC 127350, Demon/Demons.
- **BT** Spirits
- **RT** Devils
  Evil
  Spirit Possession
  Witchcraft

Demonstration/Demonstrations (1966-1985)
- **HN** DC 127355.
- **Use** Protest Movements

Denmark
- **DC** D207000
- **HN** Formerly (1963-1985) DC 127550, Denmark/Danish.
- **BT** Scandinavia
  Western Europe
- **NT** Copenhagen, Denmark
  Faeroe Islands

Denominations
- **DC** D207300
- **HN** Formerly (1963-1985) DC 127565, Denomination/Denominations/Denominational.
- **RT** Church Membership
  Churches
  Religions
  Religious Cultural Groups
  Sects

Density (1963-1985)
- **HN** DC 127600.
- **Use** Population Density

Dental (1963-1985)
- **HN** DC 127650, deleted 1986. See now specific "Dental" terms.

Dental Care
- **DC** D207600
- **HN** Added, 1986.
- **UF** Dental Health Services
- **BT** Health Care
- **RT** Dentistry
  Dentists
  Fluoridation
  Health
  Treatment

Dental Health Services
- **Use** Dental Care

Dental Sciences
- **Use** Dentistry

Dental Students
- **DC** D207900
- **HN** Added, 1986.
- **BT** Graduate Students
- **RT** Dentistry
  Medical Students
  Professional Training

Dentist | Desegregation

Dentist Patient Relationship
  Use Practitioner Patient Relationship

Dentistry
  DC D208200
  HN Formerly (1963-1985) part of DC 127665, Dentist/Dentists/Dentistry.
  UF Dental Sciences
     Oral Medicine
  BT Medicine
  RT Dental Care
     Dental Students
     Dentists

Dentists
  DC D208500
  HN Formerly (1963-1985) part of DC 127665, Dentist/Dentists/Dentistry.
  BT Professional Workers
  RT Dental Care
     Dentistry
     Health Professions
     Practitioner Patient Relationship

Denver, Colorado
  DC D208800
  HN Formerly (1963-1985) DC 127740, Denver, Colo.
  BT Colorado

Denzin, Norman K.
  DC D208900
  SN Born 24 March 1941 - .
  HN Added, 1989.

Deontology
  Use Professional Ethics

Department Stores
  Use Stores

Departments
  DC D209100
  HN Formerly (1963-1985) DC 127900, Department/Departments/Departmental/Departmentalization.
  NT Academic Departments
  RT Organizational Structure
     Organizations (Social)

Dependability
  Use Reliability

Dependency (Psychology)
  DC D209400
  HN Formerly (1964-1985) part of DC 128000, Dependence/Dependency.
  BT Personality Traits
  NT Welfare Dependency
  RT Independence
     Interpersonal Relations
     Subordination

Dependency Theory
  DC D209700
  SN Theory that perceives the social and economic development of underdeveloped countries as being conditioned by the domination of more powerful countries through the extraction of surplus value or the repatriation of profit.
  HN Formerly (1964-1985) part of DC 128000, Dependence/Dependency.
  UF Economic Dependence
  BT Economic Theories
  RT Center And Periphery
     Developing Countries
     Dual Economy
     Economic Development

Dependency Theory (cont'd)
  RT Economic Structure
     Economic Underdevelopment
     Income Inequality
     International Division of Labor
     Marxist Economics
     Modes of Production
     Multinational Corporations
     World Economy
     World System Theory

Dependent Variables
  Use Variables

Dependents
  DC D209800
  SN Persons incapable of self support due to age or disability.
  HN Formerly (1963-1985) DC 128020, Dependent/Dependents.
  RT Children
     Disability Recipients
     Elderly
     Family Size
     Financial Support
     Handicapped
     Welfare Recipients

Depersonalization
  DC D210000
  HN Formerly (1972-1985) DC 128500.
  BT Disorders
  RT Alienation
     Humanization
     Rationalization
     Schizophrenia
     Self Concept

Depolitization (1965-1985)
  HN DC 128700, deleted 1986.

Depopulation (1964-1985)
  HN DC 128800.
  Use Demographic Change

Depression (Economics)
  DC D210300
  HN Formerly (1963-1985) part of DC 129000, Depression.
  UF Economic Depression
     Recession (1964-1985)
  BT Economic Conditions
  RT Business
     Business Cycles
     Economic Change
     Economic Crises
     Economic Problems
     Plant Closure
     Unemployment

Depression (Psychology)
  DC D210600
  HN Formerly (1963-1985) part of DC 129000, Depression.
  UF Cyclothymia
     Depressive/Depressives (1963-1985)
     Manic Depressive/Manic Depression (1966-1985)
  BT Affective Illness
  RT Anxiety
     Disorders
     Emotionally Disturbed
     Emotions
     Grief
     Loneliness
     Mental Illness
     Neurosis
     Psychopathology
     Psychosis

Depressive/Depressives (1963-1985)
  HN DC 129010.
  Use Depression (Psychology)

Deprivation
  DC D210900
  HN Formerly (1963-1985) DC 129400, Deprive/Deprived/Deprivation.
  NT Relative Deprivation
  RT Disadvantaged
     Low Income Groups
     Malnutrition
     Needs
     Poverty
     Quality of Life
     Scarcity
     Social Isolation
     Social Problems
     Stimuli
     Well Being

Deprivation (Social)
  Use Social Isolation

Deprived
  Use Disadvantaged

Deprofessionalization
  Use Professionalization

Deprogramming (1981-1985)
  HN DC 129500, deleted 1986.

Derrida, Jacques
  DC D211100
  HN Added, 1986.

Descartes, Rene
  DC D211200
  SN Born 31 March 1596 - died 11 February 1650.
  HN Formerly (1967-1985) DC 129890.

Descent
  DC D211500
  HN Formerly (1963-1985) DC 129900.
  NT Cognatic Descent
     Unilineality
  RT Genealogy
     Inheritance And Succession
     Kinship
     Lineage
     Matrilineality
     Patrilineality

Description
  DC D211600
  HN Formerly (1963-1985) DC 129950, Descriptive/ Description/ Descriptions.
  UF Descriptive Methods
  RT Qualitative Methods
     Research Methodology

Descriptive Methods
  Use Description

Desegregation
  DC D211800
  HN Formerly (1963-1985) DC 130000, Desegregation/Desegregated.
  BT Segregation
  NT School Desegregation
     Tokenism
  RT Ethnic Relations
     Racial Relations
     Residential Segregation
     Social Change
     Social Integration
     Social Policy

Desertion

Desertion (Marital)
　Use　Marital Disruption

Desertion (Military)
　Use　Military Desertion

Deserts
　Use　Arid Zones

Design
　DC　D211700
　HN　Formerly (1963-1985) DC 131020, Design/Designs/Designed/Designing.
　NT　Environmental Design
　　　Research Design
　RT　Architecture
　　　Art
　　　Engineering
　　　Planning
　　　Structure

Desirability (1968-1985)
　HN　DC 131030.
　Use　Social Desirability

Desktop Computers
　Use　Microcomputers

Despotism
　DC　D212100
　HN　Formerly (1963-1985) DC 131050, Despot/Despots/Despotic/Despotism.
　UF　Tyranny (1964-1985)
　BT　Political Ideologies
　RT　Authoritarianism (Political Ideology)
　　　Dictatorship
　　　Oppression

Destiny (1969-1985)
　HN　DC 131070.
　Use　Fate

Destitution (1980-1985)
　HN　DC 131073.
　Use　Poverty

Destruction (1969-1985)
　HN　DC 131075, deleted 1986.

Detachment
　Use　Disengagement

Detective Fiction
　Use　Fiction

Detective/Detectives (1964-1985)
　HN　DC 131100, deleted 1986. See now Fiction or Police.

Detente
　Use　Peaceful Coexistence

Detention
　DC　D212400
　SN　Confinement before trial or for purposes other than serving a sentence.
　HN　Formerly (1964-1985) DC 131120.
　UF　Pretrial Detention
　　　Remand (1963-1985)
　RT　Arrests
　　　Crime Prevention
　　　Imprisonment
　　　Pretrial Release
　　　Punishment

Determinant/Determination/Determinism/Determinancy (1963-1985)
　HN　DC 131140, deleted 1986. See now Self Determination or Determinism.

Determinism
　DC　D212600
　SN　A doctrine that postulates that all events or objects are as they are because of antecedent forces that determine their nature.
　HN　Formerly (1963-1985) part of DC 131140, Determinant/Determination/Determinism/Determinancy.
　BT　Epistemological Doctrines
　RT　Causality
　　　Cultural Relativism
　　　Dialectics
　　　Idealism
　　　Indeterminism
　　　Marxism
　　　Methodological Individualism
　　　Modes of Production
　　　Positivism
　　　Reductionism
　　　Voluntarism

Deterrence
　DC　D212700
　SN　Theory of prevention in which the threat of punishment or retribution is expected to forestall some act or occurrence, eg, a criminal act.
　HN　Formerly (1963-1985) DC 131150, Deterrence/Deterrent/Deterrents.
　BT　Prevention
　RT　Capital Punishment
　　　Crime Prevention
　　　Nuclear Weapons
　　　Offenders
　　　Punishment

Detoxification
　DC　D213000
　HN　Formerly (1985) DC 131158.
　UF　Alcohol Detoxification
　　　Drug Detoxification
　BT　Treatment
　RT　Alcoholism
　　　Drug Addiction
　　　Treatment Programs

Detroit, Michigan
　DC　D213300
　HN　Formerly (1963-1985) DC 131160, Detroit, Mich.
　BT　Michigan

Develop/Developed/Developing/Developmental (1963-1985)
　HN　DC 131195.
　Use　Development

Developed Countries
　Use　Industrial Societies

Developing Countries
　DC　D213600
　HN　Formerly (1963-1985) DC 131197.
　UF　Less Developed Countries (1984-1985)
　　　Third World (1969-1985)
　　　Underdeveloped Countries (1985)
　BT　Countries
　RT　Center And Periphery
　　　Demographic Transition Theory
　　　Dependency Theory

Development

Developing Countries (cont'd)
　RT　Development
　　　Dual Economy
　　　Economic Development
　　　Economic Underdevelopment
　　　Foreign Aid
　　　Geographic Regions
　　　Industrialization
　　　International Division of Labor
　　　Poverty
　　　Technical Assistance
　　　World System Theory

Development
　DC　D213900
　SN　A context-dependent term for change over time, usually in a positive or socially desirable direction. In contexts where Development is closely related to Social Development, select the latter.
　HN　Formerly (1963-1985) DC 131200, Development/Developments.
　UF　Develop/Developed/Developing/Developmental (1963-1985)
　　　Growth (1963-1985)
　NT　Adult Development
　　　Child Development
　　　Cognitive Development
　　　Community Development
　　　Economic Development
　　　Energy Development
　　　Historical Development
　　　Improvement
　　　Moral Development
　　　Organizational Development
　　　Psychological Development
　　　Regional Development
　　　Rural Development
　　　Scientific Development
　　　Social Development
　　　Urban Development
　RT　Change
　　　Constraints
　　　Developing Countries
　　　Development Policy
　　　Development Programs
　　　Development Strategies
　　　Developmental Stages
　　　Formation
　　　Futures (of Society)
　　　History
　　　Implementation
　　　Planning
　　　Population Growth
　　　Progress
　　　Reform
　　　Research And Development
　　　Resource Allocation
　　　Resources
　　　Social Change
　　　Trends

Development Aid (Foreign)
　Use　Foreign Aid

Development Policy
　DC　D214100
　HN　Added, 1989.
　BT　Policy
　RT　Community Development
　　　Development
　　　Development Programs
　　　Development Strategies
　　　Economic Development
　　　Government Policy
　　　Regional Development
　　　Rural Development
　　　Urban Development

Development

Development Programs
- DC D214200
- HN Added, 1986.
- UF Development Projects
- BT Programs
- RT Development
  Development Policy
  Development Strategies
  Economic Development
  Economic Planning
  Economic Underdevelopment
  Energy Development
  Foreign Aid
  Low Income Areas
  Program Implementation
  Rural Development
  Urban Development

Development Projects
- Use Development Programs

Development Strategies
- DC D214275
- HN Added, 1986.
- UF Growth Strategies
- BT Strategies
- RT Community Development
  Development
  Development Policy
  Development Programs
  Economic Development
  Planning
  Priorities
  Regional Development
  Rural Development
  Urban Development

Developmental Stages
- DC D214350
- SN Phases in growth processes, including those of human beings, organizations, and economic and social systems and programs.
- HN Formerly (1963-1985) DC 443838, Stage/Stages.
- UF Stage/Stages (1963-1985)
  Stages of Development
- RT Adult Development
  Change
  Child Development
  Childhood Factors
  Cognitive Development
  Development
  Economic Development
  Life Stage Transitions
  Organizational Development
  Psychological Development
  Social Development

Deviance
- DC D214425
- HN Formerly (1963-1985) DC 131390, Deviant/Deviance/Deviates/Deviation.
- NT Deviant Behavior
  Sexual Deviation
- RT Anomie
  Conformity
  Crime
  Differences
  Disorders
  Labeling
  Offenders
  Social Disorganization
  Stigma
  Uniformity

Deviant Behavior
- DC D214500
- SN Conduct that departs from a society's established norms, rules, standards, or expectations.
- HN Formerly (1963-1985) DC 131400.
- UF Antisocial (1981-1985)
  Socially Deviant Behavior
- BT Behavior
  Deviance
- NT Cheating
- RT Abuse
  Alcoholism
  Behavior Problems
  Crime
  Discipline
  Disorders
  Drug Abuse
  Drug Addiction
  Impulsiveness
  Labeling
  Offenders
  Professional Criminals
  Promiscuity
  Public Behavior
  Recidivism
  Runaways
  Self Destructive Behavior
  Sexual Deviation
  Sociopathic Personality
  Truancy

Devils
- DC D214800
- HN Formerly (1969-1985) DC 131500, Devil.
- UF Satan (1964-1985)
- RT Bible
  Christianity
  Cults
  Demons
  Evil
  Judaism
  Spirit Possession
  Spirits
  Witchcraft

Devotion (1972-1985)
- HN DC 131540.
- Use Religiosity

Dewey, John
- DC D215100
- SN Born 20 October 1859 - died 1 June 1952.
- HN Formerly (1964-1985) DC 131600.

Dharma
- DC D215400
- SN Significant concept in Buddhism, Hinduism, and Jainism that describes the proper order of the universe and defines and enjoins the principles of conduct that maintain it.
- HN Formerly (1963-1985) DC 131770.
- BT Religious Beliefs
  Religious Rituals
- RT Buddhism
  Hinduism
  Jainism

Diabetes
- DC D215700
- HN Formerly (1965-1985) DC 131780, Diabetes/Diabetic/Diabetics.
- BT Diseases

Dialogue

Diagnosis
- DC D215850
- HN Formerly (1963-1985) DC 131800, Diagnosis/Diagnostic.
- UF Medical Diagnosis
  Psychiatric Diagnosis
- BT Medical Decision Making
- RT Diseases
  Health
  Health Care
  Mental Illness
  Primary Health Care
  Treatment

Dialectical Materialism
- DC D215900
- SN The Marxist philosophy that economic factors determine individual motivation and collective history and that human development depends on the synthesis resulting from conflicting contradictions in social systems.
- HN Formerly (1963-1985) DC 132060.
- BT Social Theories
- RT Dialectics
  Historical Materialism
  Ideologies
  Marxism
  Materialism
  Praxis

Dialectics
- DC D215950
- SN A method of argumentation in which a thesis is confronted with its antithesis and resolved through synthesis. In Marxist theory, the notion that all social and historical phenomena continuously evolve from the clash of conflicting, contradictory forces. See also Dialectical Materialism.
- HN Formerly (1963-1985) part of DC 132040, Dialectic/Dialectics/Dialectical.
- RT Contradictions
  Critical Theory
  Determinism
  Dialectical Materialism
  Epistemology
  Explanation
  Logic
  Marxism
  Marxist Analysis
  Materialism
  Ontology
  Philosophy
  Synthesis

Dialects
- DC D216000
- HN Formerly (1964-1985) DC 132020, Dialect/Dialects.
- BT Language Varieties
- RT Diglossia
  Grammar
  Language
  Language Social Class Relationship
  Language Usage
  Linguistics
  Slang
  Sociolinguistics

Dialogue (1966-1985)
- HN DC 132065.
- Use Discussion

Diary

Diary/Diaries (1972-1985)
- **HN** DC 132070.
- **Use** Autobiographical Materials

Dichotomy/Dichotomies/Dichotomous (1963-1985)
- **HN** DC 132080, deleted 1986. See now Differences or Multivariate Analysis.

Dictatorship
- **DC** D216300
- **HN** Formerly (1963-1985) DC 132100, Dictator/Dictators/Dictatorship/Dictatorships.
- **UF** Autocracy/Autocratic/Autocrat/Autocrats (1964-1985)
- **BT** Political Systems
- **RT** Authoritarianism (Political Ideology)
  Despotism
  Fascism
  Freedom
  Nazism
  Oppression
  Totalitarianism

Dictionary/Dictionaries (1963-1985)
- **HN** DC 132200.
- **Use** Reference Materials

Didactic (1964-1985)
- **HN** DC 132250, deleted 1986.

Diderot, Denis
- **DC** D216600
- **SN** Born 15 October 1713 - died 30 July 1784.
- **HN** Formerly (1964-1985) DC 132265.

Diet
- **DC** D216900
- **HN** Formerly (1963-1985) DC 132300, Diet/Diets/Dieter/Dieters/Dieting/Dietician/Dietary.
- **UF** Dietary Practices
- **RT** Feeding Practices
  Food
  Food Preparation
  Health
  Malnutrition
  Nutrition
  Obesity

Dietary Practices
- **Use** Diet

Differences
- **DC** D217200
- **SN** A context-dependent term; select a more specific entry or coordinate with other terms.
- **HN** Formerly (1963-1985) part of DC 132330, Difference/Differences/Differentials/Differentiation.
- **UF** Contrast/Contrasts (1964-1985)
  Diverge/Divergence (1971-1985)
  Variability (1963-1985)
- **NT** Age Differences
  Class Differences
  Generational Differences
  Individual Differences
  Racial Differences
  Regional Differences
  Rural Urban Differences
  Sex Differences
- **RT** Comparative Analysis
  Crosscultural Analysis
  Deviance
  Differentiation
  East And West

Differences (cont'd)
- **RT** Heterogeneity
  Language Varieties
  Seasonal Variations
  Similarity
  Specialization
  Status
  Uniformity

Differentiation
- **DC** D217300
- **SN** A context-dependent term; select a more specific entry or coordinate with other terms.
- **HN** Formerly (1963-1985) part of DC 132330, Difference/Differences/Differentials/Differentiation.
- **RT** Deduction
  Differences
  Division of Labor
  Evolution
  Social Evolution
  Social Processes
  Social Stratification
  Specialization

Difficulties (1971-1985)
- **HN** DC 132340.
- **Use** Problems

Diffusion
- **DC** D217400
- **HN** Formerly (1963-1985) DC 132360, Diffuse/Diffuseness/Diffusion.
- **RT** Adoption of Innovations
  Communication
  Information
  Information Dissemination
  Networks
  Research Applications
  Technology Transfer

Diglossia
- **DC** D217500
- **SN** Use of two languages or dialects for different functions or at different social levels within a single speech community.
- **HN** Formerly (1967-1985) DC 132400.
- **RT** Bilingualism
  Code Switching
  Creolized Languages
  Dialects
  Language Shift
  Language Social Class Relationship
  Language Usage
  Language Varieties
  Multilingualism
  Sociolinguistics

Dignity
- **Use** Human Dignity

Digraph Theory
- **Use** Graph Theory

Dilemmas
- **DC** D217800
- **SN** A context-dependent term for obstacles encountered in decision-making processes.
- **HN** Formerly (1968-1985) DC 132470, Dilemma/Dilemmas.
- **BT** Choices
- **RT** Decision Making

Disadvantaged

Dilthey, Wilhelm Christian Ludwig
- **DC** D218100
- **SN** Born 1833 - died 1911.
- **HN** Formerly (1966-1985) DC 132485, Dilthey, Wilhelm.

Dimensional Analysis
- **DC** D217900
- **SN** Statistical techniques used to measure non-quantitative aspects or attributes of social phenomena.
- **HN** Formerly (1963-1985) DC 132500, Dimension/Dimensions/Dimensional.
- **BT** Multivariate Analysis
- **RT** Cluster Analysis
  Discriminant Analysis
  Factor Analysis
  Multiple Regression Analysis
  Path Analysis

Diplomacy
- **DC** D218400
- **HN** Formerly (1963-1985) DC 132550, Diplomacy/Diplomat/Diplomats/Diplomatic.
- **RT** Foreign Policy
  International Alliances
  International Relations
  Negotiation

Diplomatic Policy
- **Use** Foreign Policy

Direct/Directed/Direction/Directive/Directness (1963-1985)
- **HN** DC 132575, deleted 1986.

Directed Graph Theory
- **Use** Graph Theory

Directors
- **DC** D218700
- **HN** Formerly (1964-1985) DC 132580, Director/Directors/Directorate/Directorates/Directorship.
- **UF** Boards of Directors
  Corporate Directors
  Organization Directors
- **BT** Administrators
- **RT** Corporations
  Executives
  Governing Boards
  Interlocking Directorates

Disabilities (Learning)
- **Use** Learning Disabilities

Disability Recipients
- **DC** D219000
- **SN** Persons receiving disability benefits due to injury or illness.
- **HN** Added, 1986.
- **RT** Benefits
  Dependents
  Handicapped
  Pensions
  Welfare Recipients
  Workers Compensation Insurance

Disable/Disabled/Disability/Disabilities (1963-1985)
- **HN** DC 132600, deleted 1986. See now Handicapped and specific "Disability" terms.

Disadvantaged
- **DC** D219300
- **HN** Formerly (1965-1985) DC 132610, Disadvantage/Disadvantages/Disadvantaged.

Disaffiliation   Discrimination

Disadvantaged (cont'd)
- UF Deprived
      Socioeconomically Disadvantaged
      Underprivileged (1963-1985)
- BT Groups
- RT Affirmative Action
      Antipoverty Programs
      Deprivation
      Dropouts
      Educational Opportunities
      Living Conditions
      Low Income Areas
      Low Income Groups
      Minority Groups
      Poverty
      Quality of Life
      Socioeconomic Status
      Welfare Recipients

Disaffiliation (1969-1985)
- HN DC 132618, deleted 1986.

Disagreement/Disagreements (1964-1985)
- HN DC 132625.
- Use Disputes

Disarmament
- DC D219600
- HN Formerly (1963-1985) DC 132650.
- UF Arms Control
      Nuclear Disarmament
- RT Antinuclear Movements
      Armaments
      International Relations
      Nuclear War
      Nuclear Weapons
      Peace
      Peaceful Coexistence
      World Problems

Disaster Relief
- DC D219900
- HN Formerly (1963-1985) part of DC 382950, Relief.
- UF Search And Rescue Operations
- RT Assistance
      Disasters
      Emergency Medical Services
      Human Services
      Natural Disasters
      Paramedical Personnel
      Survival

Disasters
- DC D220200
- HN Formerly (1963-1985) DC 132800, Disaster/Disasters.
- UF Catastrophe/Catastrophes (1966-1985)
- BT Emergencies
- NT Natural Disasters
- RT Crises
      Disaster Relief
      Emergency Medical Services
      Fire
      Social Problems
      Survival

Discharge
- DC D220500
- HN Formerly (1972-1985) DC 132983, Discharge/Discharges/Discharged/Discharging.
- UF Release (Institutional)
- RT Admissions
      After Care
      Deinstitutionalization
      Hospitalization
      Institutionalization (Persons)
      Termination of Treatment

Disciplinary (1968-1985)
- HN DC 133010, deleted 1986. See now Academic Disciplines or Interdisciplinary Approach.

Disciplinary Action
- Use Discipline

Discipline
- DC D220800
- HN Formerly (1963-1985) part of DC 133000, Discipline/Disciplines.
- UF Classroom Discipline
      Disciplinary Action
- RT Childrearing Practices
      Deviant Behavior
      Prisoners
      Punishment
      Social Control
      Student Behavior

Disciplines (Academic)
- Use Academic Disciplines

Disclosure (Individuals)
- Use Self Disclosure

Discontent
- DC D221100
- HN Formerly (1964-1985) DC 133040.
- UF Dissatisfaction
- BT Attitudes
- RT Collective Behavior
      Dissent
      Happiness
      Political Attitudes
      Resistance
      Satisfaction
      Social Conditions
      Social Unrest

Discontinuous/Discontinuance/Discontinuity (1964-1985)
- HN DC 133050.
- Use Stability

Discourse
- DC D221400
- SN Formal lengthy discussion of a topic, either written or verbal.
- HN Formerly (1967-1985) DC 133095.
- BT Rhetoric
- RT Advertising
      Debate
      Discourse Analysis
      Discussion
      Editorials
      Literature
      Propaganda
      Scholarship
      Speech
      Verbal Communication

Discourse Analysis
- DC D221450
- SN In sociolinguistics and related disciplines, analysis of passages of verbal communication as social artifacts.
- HN Added, 1986.
- BT Analysis
- RT Communication
      Communication Research
      Discourse
      Grammar
      Hermeneutics
      Language
      Language Usage
      Morphology (Language)
      Pragmatics
      Semantics

Discovery
- DC D221700
- SN A context-dependent term; select a more specific entry or coordinate with other terms.
- HN Formerly (1964-1985) DC 133100, Discovery/Discoveries.
- UF Multiple Discoveries
      Serendipity (1972-1985)
- RT Existence
      Information Sources
      Innovations
      Inventions
      Knowledge
      Learning
      Research
      Scientific Discoveries
      Theory Formation

Discrepancy (Psychology)
- Use Congruence (Psychology)

Discrepancy/Discrepancies (1972-1985)
- HN DC 133190, deleted 1986. See now Congruence (Psychology), Differences, or Errors.

Discretion
- DC D222000
- SN A context-dependent term for reasoned judgment in the process of making evaluations or decisions.
- HN Formerly (1971-1985) DC 133200.
- RT Decision Making
      Decisions
      Discretionary Power
      Law Enforcement
      Rational Choice

Discretionary Power
- DC D222100
- HN Added, 1989.
- BT Power
- RT Decision Making
      Decisions
      Discretion

Discriminant Analysis
- DC D222200
- SN A statistical technique whereby a set of predictor variables are weighted to produce the maximum difference or discrimination between two or more qualitatively different groups.
- HN Formerly (1972-1985) DC 133395, Discriminant/Discriminants.
- UF Canonical Correlation
      Multiple Discriminant Analysis
- BT Multivariate Analysis
- RT Cluster Analysis
      Dimensional Analysis
      Factor Analysis

Discrimination
- DC D222300
- HN Formerly (1963-1985) DC 133400.
- NT Ageism
      Employment Discrimination
      Racism
      Sexism
- RT Access
      Affirmative Action
      Bias
      Civil Rights
      Egalitarianism
      Inequality
      Intergroup Relations
      Nativism

Discussion

Discrimination (cont'd)
- RT Opportunities
  - Prejudice
  - Segregation
  - Social Behavior
  - Social Closure
  - Social Integration
  - Social Problems
  - Stereotypes

Discussion
- DC D222600
- SN The consideration of a subject by two or more persons.
- HN Formerly (1963-1985) DC 134200, Discussion/Discussions.
- UF Dialogue (1966-1985)
  - Discussion Groups
  - Group Discussion
- BT Interpersonal Communication
- RT Conversation
  - Debate
  - Discourse
  - Group Decision Making
  - Negotiation
  - Persuasion
  - Rhetoric
  - Verbal Communication

Discussion Groups
- Use Discussion

Disease Model
- Use Medical Model

Diseases
- DC D222900
- HN Formerly (1963-1985) DC 134400, Disease/Diseases.
- UF Cirrhosis (1964-1985)
  - Pneumonia (1965-1985)
  - Shigellosis (1964-1985)
  - Trachoma (1964-1985)
- BT Disorders
- NT Acquired Immune Deficiency Syndrome
  - Alcoholism
  - Alzheimer's Disease
  - Arthritis
  - Cancer
  - Diabetes
  - Eating Disorders
  - Epilepsy
  - Heart Diseases
  - Influenza
  - Leprosy
  - Plague
  - Poliomyelitis
  - Tuberculosis
  - Venereal Diseases
- RT Diagnosis
  - Epidemics
  - Epidemiology
  - Etiology
  - Hazards
  - Health
  - Health Care
  - Health Policy
  - Health Problems
  - Hygiene
  - Illness
  - Malnutrition
  - Morbidity
  - Obesity
  - Pollution
  - Public Health
  - Stress
  - Vaccination

Disemployment
- Use Dislocated Workers

Disengagement
- DC D223000
- SN Implies alienation from political action and decision making. Closely related to Apathy.
- HN Formerly (1964-1985) DC 134450.
- UF Detachment
- BT Social Behavior
- RT Alienation
  - Apathy
  - Dropouts
  - Elderly
  - Social Isolation
  - Social Participation

Disequilibrium (1971-1985)
- HN DC 134460.
- Use Social Equilibrium

Disintegration (1963-1985)
- HN DC 134480, deleted 1986. See now Marital Disruption or Social Disorganization.

Dislocated Workers
- DC D223100
- SN Workers who are unemployed as a result of economic change, such as industrial plant closings or changing technology.
- HN Added, 1986.
- UF Disemployment
  - Displaced Workers
  - Job Displacement
- BT Workers
- RT Dismissal
  - Employment
  - Employment Changes
  - Labor Force
  - Labor Market
  - Labor Turnover
  - Plant Closure
  - Technological Change
  - Unemployment

Dismissal
- DC D223200
- HN Formerly (1966-1985) DC 134500.
- UF Firing
  - Termination (Employees)
  - Worker Dismissal
- BT Personnel Management
- RT Dislocated Workers
  - Job Performance
  - Labor Turnover
  - Unemployment

Disobedience
- Use Obedience

Disobedience (Civil)
- Use Civil Disobedience

Disorders
- DC D223500
- SN A context-dependent term for any physical, emotional, or societal disturbance.
- HN Formerly (1963-1985) DC 134530, Disorders/Disordered.
- UF Pathology/Pathological (1963-1985)
- NT Civil Disorders
  - Depersonalization
  - Diseases
  - Language Disorders
  - Mental Illness
- RT Alienation
  - Anomie

Disputes

Disorders (cont'd)
- RT Causality
  - Depression (Psychology)
  - Deviance
  - Deviant Behavior
  - Etiology
  - Handicapped
  - Hysteria
  - Injuries
  - Marital Disruption
  - Offenses
  - Problems
  - Psychopathology
  - Sexual Dysfunction
  - Social Action
  - Sociopathic Personality
  - Violence

Disorders (Mental)
- Use Mental Illness

Disorganization (1963-1985)
- HN DC 134580.
- Use Social Disorganization

Dispersal/Dispersion (1969-1985)
- HN DC 134640.
- Use Distribution

Displaced Persons (1964-1985)
- HN DC 134680.
- Use Relocation

Displaced Workers
- Use Dislocated Workers

Displacement (1963-1985)
- HN DC 134700, deleted 1986. See now Relocation, Dislocated Workers, or Defense Mechanisms.

Displacement (Defense Mechanism)
- Use Defense Mechanisms

Displacement (Residential)
- Use Relocation

Disposition
- DC D223800
- HN Formerly (1984-1985) DC 135020.
- UF Case Disposition
  - Court Disposition
  - Intake (1964-1985)
  - Processing (Cases)
- RT Delinquency Prevention
  - Judicial Decisions
  - Legal Cases
  - Pretrial Release
  - Social Work Cases

Disposition (Personality)
- Use Personality

Dispute Settlement
- Use Conflict Resolution

Disputes
- DC D224100
- HN Formerly (1972-1985) DC 135053, Dispute/Disputes/Disputed.
- UF Controversy/Controversies/Controversial (1963-1985)
  - Disagreement/Disagreements (1964-1985)
- BT Conflict
- NT Labor Disputes
- RT Agreement
  - Consensus
  - Contradictions
  - Debate
  - Grievances
  - Mediation
  - Social Conflict

Disrupt

Disrupt/Disruption/Disruptive (1972-1985)
  HN DC 135062, deleted 1986.

Dissatisfaction
  Use Discontent

Dissent
  DC D224400
  HN Formerly (1966-1985) DC 135065, Dissent/Dissents/Dissenter/Dissenters.
  RT Civil Disobedience
      Cleavage
      Conflict
      Consensus
      Contradictions
      Countercultures
      Discontent
      Family Conflict
      Movements
      Opinions
      Partisanship
      Political Attitudes
      Political Defection
      Political Movements
      Political Violence
      Protest Movements
      Public Opinion
      Repression (Political)
      Resistance
      Social Attitudes
      Social Conflict
      Social Criticism
      Social Response
      Social Unrest

Dissertations
  DC D224700
  HN Formerly (1972-1985) DC 135067, Dissertation/Dissertations.
  RT Doctoral Degrees
      Doctoral Programs
      Graduate Students
      Scholarship

Dissociation (1970-1985)
  HN DC 135100, deleted 1986.

Dissonance (1963-1985)
  HN DC 135200, deleted 1986. See now Cognitive Dissonance, Dissent, or Conflict.

Distance (1963-1985)
  HN DC 135300.
  Use Social Distance

Distance (Social)
  Use Social Distance

Distortion/Distortions (1968-1985)
  HN DC 135470.
  Use Objectivity

Distraction/Distractions (1969-1985)
  HN DC 135500.
  Use Attention

Distress (Psychological)
  Use Psychological Distress

Distribution
  DC D225000
  HN Formerly (1963-1985) DC 135600, Distribution/Distributions.
  UF Dispersal/Dispersion (1969-1985)
      Maldistribution (1972-1985)
      Redistribution (1964-1985)
  NT Frequency Distributions
      Geographic Distribution

Distribution (cont'd)
  NT Income Distribution
      Population Distribution
  RT Allocation
      Spatial Analysis

Distributive Justice
  DC D225300
  SN Just or fair principles for distributing valued resources and allocating rights, responsibilities, and costs within a society.
  HN Added, 1986.
  BT Equity
  RT Allocation
      Commodities
      Consumption
      Income Distribution
      Income Inequality
      Social Inequality

District of Columbia
  Use Washington, D.C.

Districts
  DC D225400
  HN Formerly (1963-1985) DC 135610, District/Districts/Districting.
  UF Administrative Districts
      Prefecture/Prefectorial (1964-1985)
  NT School Districts
  RT Communities
      Counties
      Geographic Regions
      Local Government
      Zoning

Distrust (1966-1985)
  HN DC 135635.
  Use Trust

Disturb/Disturbed/Disturbing (1963-1985)
  HN DC 135655.
  Use Emotionally Disturbed

Disturbance/Disturbances (1963-1985)
  HN DC 135650, deleted 1986. See now Emotionally Disturbed, Disorders, Violence, or their respective narrower terms.

Diverge/Divergence (1971-1985)
  HN DC 135665.
  Use Differences

Diversion/Diversions (1982-1985)
  HN DC 135668.
  Use Delinquency Prevention

Diversity/Diversification (1969-1985)
  HN DC 135670, deleted 1986.

Divination
  DC D225600
  SN In traditional societies, the practice of foretelling the future by supernatural means, usually involving the observation of natural phenomena.
  HN Formerly (1964-1985) DC 135675, Divine/Divination.
  NT Astrology
  RT Extrasensory Perception
      Occultism
      Prophecy
      Shamanism
      Spiritualism
      Supernatural
      Superstitions

Doctoral

Division of Labor
  DC D225900
  SN Separation of a complex task into simpler component tasks, which are assigned to different categories of workers.
  HN Formerly (1963-1985) DC 135690.
  BT Specialization
  NT International Division of Labor
      Sexual Division of Labor
  RT Differentiation
      Labor
      Labor Process
      Occupations
      Political Economy
      Scientific Management
      Tasks
      Work Organization

Division/Divisions (1968-1985)
  HN DC 135685, deleted 1986. See now Cleavage, Polarization, or Division of Labor.

Divorce
  DC D226200
  HN Formerly (1963-1985) DC 135700, Divorce/Divorced.
  UF Marital Dissolution (1984-1985)
  BT Marital Disruption
  RT Alimony
      Annulment
      Child Custody
      Child Support
      Family Policy
      Father Absence
      Female Headed Households
      Life Stage Transitions
      Marital Satisfaction
      Marital Status
      Marriage Timing
      Mother Absence
      Remarriage
      Single Fathers
      Single Parent Family

Djibouti
  DC D226500
  HN Added, 1986.
  UF Somali/Somaliland (1963-1985)
  BT Sub Saharan Africa

Dock Workers
  Use Longshoremen

Doctor of Philosophy Degrees
  Use Doctoral Degrees

Doctor Patient Relationship
  Use Practitioner Patient Relationship

Doctor/Doctors (1963-1985)
  HN DC 135750.
  Use Physicians

Doctoral Degrees
  DC D226800
  HN Formerly (1964-1985) part of DC 135800, Doctorate/Doctorates/Doctoral.
  UF Doctor of Philosophy Degrees
      Ph.D. Degrees
  BT Academic Degrees
  RT Baccalaureate Degrees
      College Faculty
      Dissertations
      Doctoral Programs
      Graduate Students
      Masters Degrees
      Postdoctoral Programs

Doctoral Programs
- **DC** D227100
- **HN** Formerly (1965-1985) part of DC 135800, Doctorate/Doctorates/Doctoral.
- **BT** Higher Education
- **RT** Dissertations
  Doctoral Degrees
  Educational Programs
  Graduate Schools
  Graduate Students
  Medical Schools
  Postdoctoral Programs
  Professional Training
  Social Work Education
  Sociology Education
  Universities

Doctrine/Doctrines/Doctrinal (1971-1985)
- **HN** DC 135880.
- **Use** Ideologies

Doctrines (Legal)
- **Use** Law

Documentation
- **DC** D227175
- **HN** Formerly (1964-1985) part of DC 135945, Document/Documents/Documentary/Documentation.
- **RT** Archives
  Data Banks
  Documents
  Information Processing
  Research Methodology

Documents
- **DC** D227225
- **HN** Formerly (1964-1985) part of DC 135945, Document/Docments/Documentary/Documentation.
- **NT** Records (Documents)
- **RT** Documentation
  Letters (Correspondence)
  Narratives
  Publications
  Reports

Dogmatism
- **DC** D227300
- **HN** Formerly (1963-1985) DC 136200, Dogma/Dogmas/Dogmatic/Dogmatism.
- **BT** Personality Traits
- **RT** Attitudes
  Authoritarianism (Psychology)
  Beliefs
  Epistemological Doctrines
  Objectivity
  Relativism
  Skepticism

Dolmen
- **DC** D227400
- **SN** A prehistoric tomb, consisting of two or more large, upright stones capped by a horizontal one.
- **HN** Formerly (1969-1985) DC 136280.
- **RT** Cults
  Death Rituals
  Monuments
  Religious Rituals

Domestic Labor
- **Use** Housework

Domestic Science
- **Use** Home Economics

Domestic Servants
- **Use** Domestics

Domestic Violence
- **Use** Family Violence

Domestics
- **DC** D227550
- **HN** Formerly (1963-1985) part of DC 136325, Domestic/Domestics/Domestication/Domesticated.
- **UF** Domestic Servants
  Household Workers
  Housekeepers
  Maids
  Servants
- **BT** Blue Collar Workers
- **RT** Housework
  Service Industries

Domhoff, George William
- **DC** D227700
- **SN** Born 6 August 1936 - .
- **HN** Formerly (1969-1985) DC 136350, Domhoff, G. W.

Dominance
- **DC** D228000
- **HN** Formerly (1963-1985) DC 136400, Dominance/Domination/Dominant/Dominants.
- **UF** Ascendancy
  Domination
  Superiority
- **RT** Aggression
  Authoritarianism (Psychology)
  Authority
  Coercion
  Control
  Dominant Ideologies
  Elites
  Hegemony
  Power
  Subordination
  Superior Subordinate Relationship

Dominant Ideologies
- **DC** D228100
- **HN** Added, 1986.
- **UF** Ideological Hegemony
- **BT** Ideologies
- **RT** Dominance
  Hegemony
  Mass Media Effects
  Mass Society
  Political Ideologies

Domination
- **Use** Dominance

Dominica
- **DC** D228300
- **HN** Added, 1986.
- **BT** Caribbean

Dominican Republic
- **DC** D228600
- **HN** Formerly (1969-1985) DC 136412.
- **BT** Caribbean
- **NT** Santo Domingo, Dominican Republic

Dominican/Dominicans (1967-1985)
- **HN** DC 136410, deleted 1986. See now Dominican Republic or Latin American Cultural Groups.

Dominicans (Clergy)
- **DC** D228900
- **HN** Formerly (1964-1985) part of DC 136410, Dominican/Dominicans.
- **BT** Religious Orders
- **RT** Roman Catholics

Donations
- **Use** Contributions (Donations)

Dormitory/Dormitories (1964-1985)
- **HN** DC 136440, deleted 1986.

Double Meaning
- **Use** Ambiguity

Doubt (1969-1985)
- **HN** DC 136460.
- **Use** Certainty

Downs Syndrome
- **DC** D229200
- **SN** A congenital abnormal condition characterized by mental deficiency, slanting eyes, and a broad flattened skull. Synonymous with mongolism.
- **HN** Formerly (1964-1985) DC 275000, Mongoloid/Mongoloids.
- **UF** Mongoloidism
- **RT** Congenitally Handicapped
  Genetics
  Handicapped
  Mentally Retarded

Dowry
- **DC** D229500
- **HN** Formerly (1963-1985) DC 136465.
- **RT** Bridewealth
  Marriage

Draft (Military)
- **DC** D229800
- **HN** Formerly (1968-1985) DC 136469, Draft.
- **UF** Military Conscription
  Selective Service (Military)
- **RT** Conscientious Objectors
  Military Personnel
  Military Service
  War

Draftee/Draftees (1964-1985)
- **HN** DC 136470, deleted 1986. See now Draft (Military) or Military Personnel.

Drama
- **DC** D230100
- **HN** Formerly (1963-1985) part of DC 136500, Drama/Dramatic/Dramaturgy/Dramaturgical.
- **UF** Comedy (Drama)
  Plays
  Tragedy (Drama)
- **BT** Literature
  Theater Arts
- **RT** Actors
  Art
  Audiences
  Fiction
  Fictional Characters
  Folk Culture
  Passion Plays
  Poetry
  Renaissance

Dramaturgical Approach
- **DC** D230200
- **SN** Analytic approach developed by Erving Goffman using theatrical terminology to analyze and explain how individuals and teams manage social situations and personal identity.

Dramaturgical   Dual

Dramaturgical Approach (cont'd)
- HN   Formerly (1963-1985) part of DC 136500, Drama/Dramas/Dramatic/Dramaturgy/Dramaturgical.
- UF   Dramaturgical Model
- RT   Analysis
      Impression Management
      Symbolic Interactionism

Dramaturgical Model
- Use   Dramaturgical Approach

Dravidian Languages
- DC   D230400
- HN   Added, 1986.
- UF   Malayalam (Language)
      Tamil (Language)
      Telegu (Language)
- BT   Languages

Draw/Draws/Drawing/Drawings (1972-1985)
- HN   DC 137000.
- Use   Visual Arts

Dreams
- DC   D230700
- HN   Formerly (1963-1985) DC 137500, Dream/Dreams/Dreaming.
- RT   Fantasy
      Sleep

Dress/Dresses/Dressed/Dressing (1972-1985)
- HN   DC 137900.
- Use   Clothing

Drinking Behavior
- DC   D231000
- SN   Use limited to drinking alcoholic beverages.
- HN   Added, 1986.
- BT   Behavior
- RT   Alcohol Abuse
      Alcohol Use
      Alcoholism
      Drunk Driving
      Drunkenness
      Eating And Drinking Establishments
      Substance Abuse

Drinking/Drinkers (1963-1985)
- HN   DC 138500.
- Use   Alcohol Use

Drive
- Use   Motivation

Dropouts
- DC   D231300
- SN   Use limited to early withdrawl from educational or vocational training programs.
- HN   Formerly (1964-1985) DC 140000, Dropout/Dropouts.
- UF   Adult Dropouts
      School Leavers
- RT   Absenteeism
      Attendance
      Attrition
      Disadvantaged
      Disengagement
      Education
      Educational Attainment
      Enrollment
      Runaways
      School Attendance
      Schools
      Students
      Truancy

Drought/Droughts (1984-1985)
- HN   DC 140465.
- Use   Natural Disasters

Drug Abuse
- DC   D231600
- HN   Formerly (1982-1985) DC 140497, Drug Abuse/Drug Abuser/Drug Abusers.
- BT   Drug Use
      Substance Abuse
- NT   Drug Addiction
- RT   Alcohol Abuse
      Alcoholism
      Cocaine
      Deviant Behavior
      Drugs
      Drug Trafficking

Drug Addiction
- DC   D231900
- HN   Formerly (1963-1985) DC 140500, Drug Addict/Drug Addicts/Drug Addiction.
- UF   Addict/Addicts/Addicted/Addictive/Addiction (1963-1985)
- BT   Drug Abuse
- RT   Alcoholism
      Cocaine
      Detoxification
      Deviant Behavior
      Drugs
      Employee Assistance Programs
      Methadone Maintenance
      Narcotic Drugs
      Treatment Programs

Drug Consumption
- Use   Drug Use

Drug Detoxification
- Use   Detoxification

Drug Trafficking
- DC   D232100
- HN   Added, 1989.
- BT   Offenses
- RT   Drug Abuse
      Drugs
      Urban Crime

Drug Use
- DC   D232200
- HN   Formerly (1985) DC 140600.
- UF   Drug Consumption
- NT   Drug Abuse
- RT   Alcohol Use
      Behavior
      Drugs
      Health
      Marijuana
      Smoking

Drugs
- DC   D232500
- SN   Use limited to substances used illicitly or inappropriately. Do not confuse with Medications.
- HN   Formerly (1963-1985) DC 140495, Drug/Drugs.
- NT   Narcotic Drugs
      Psychedelic Drugs
      Tranquilizing Drugs
- RT   Alcoholic Beverages
      Drug Abuse
      Drug Addiction
      Drug Trafficking
      Drug Use
      Health

Drugs (cont'd)
- RT   Medical Decision Making
      Medications
      Pharmacy
      Substance Abuse

Drum Languages
- DC   D232800
- HN   Formerly (1964-1985) DC 141000, Drum/Drums.
- BT   Languages
- RT   Nonverbal Communication
      Traditional Societies

Drunk Driving
- DC   D233100
- HN   Formerly (1963-1985) DC 139000, Drive/Drives/Driving/Driver/Drivers.
- BT   Offenses
- RT   Accidents
      Alcohol Use
      Automobiles
      Drinking Behavior
      Drunkenness
      Homicide

Drunkenness
- DC   D233400
- HN   Formerly (1967-1985) DC 141050.
- UF   Alcohol Intoxication
      Intoxication (1965-1985)
- RT   Alcohol Abuse
      Alcohol Use
      Alcoholism
      Drinking Behavior
      Drunk Driving
      Temperance Movements

Du Bois, William Edward Burghardt
- DC   D233700
- SN   Born 23 February 1868 - died 27 August 1963.
- HN   Formerly (1963-1985) DC 141100, Du Bois, W. E. B.

Dual Career Family
- DC   D234000
- SN   Family in which both spouses maintain full-time employment outside the home.
- HN   Formerly (1984) DC 141097, Dual Career.
- BT   Family
- RT   Careers
      Employment
      Family Relations
      Family Structure
      Family Work Relationship
      Marital Relations
      Working Mothers
      Working Women

Dual Economy
- DC   D234300
- SN   A concept, introduced by J. H. Boeke, that refers to the co-existence in underdeveloped countries of an efficient, capitalist economy based on economic needs, and a pre-capitalist, peasant economy based on social needs.
- HN   Added, 1986.
- UF   Dualism (Economic)
      Economic Dualism
- RT   Agrarian Societies
      Center And Periphery
      Dependency Theory
      Developing Countries
      Economic Development

Dual

Dual Economy (cont'd)
- RT Economic Structure
  Economic Systems
  Economic Underdevelopment
  Economics
  Labor Market Segmentation
  Peasant Societies

Dual Labor Market Theory
- Use Labor Market Segmentation

Dual/Duality/Dualistic/Dualism/Dualist (1963-1985)
- HN DC 141095, deleted 1986. See now Dual Career Family, Dual Economy, or Dualism.

Dualism
- DC D234400
- SN The doctrine that the world is divided into two mutually irreducible elements. In philosophy, these elements are often good and evil, or mind and matter. See also Dual Economy.
- HN Formerly (1963-1985) part of DC 141095, Dual/Duality/Dualistic/Dualism/Dualist.
- BT Philosophical Doctrines
- RT Ontology
  Pluralism
  Religious Doctrines
  Soul

Dualism (Economic)
- Use Dual Economy

Due Process
- DC D234600
- HN Formerly (1969-1985) DC 141150.
- RT Civil Rights
  Juries
  Justice
  Law
  Legal Procedure
  Legal System
  Trials
  Vigilantism

Duncan, Otis Dudley
- DC D234900
- SN Born 2 December 1921 - .
- HN Formerly (1964-1985) DC 142200, Duncan, O. D.

Duolocal (1969-1985)
- HN DC 142228, deleted 1986.

Duopoly (1963-1985)
- HN DC 142300.
- Use Oligopolies

Duration
- Use Time

Durkheim, Emile
- DC D235200
- SN Born 15 April 1858 - died 15 November 1917.
- HN Formerly (1963-1985) DC 142600, Durkheim, E.

Dutch (1964-1985)
- HN DC 142650, deleted 1986. See now Netherlands or Germanic Languages.

Dutch (Language)
- Use Germanic Languages

Duty/Duties (1963-1985)
- HN DC 142710, deleted 1986. See now Obligation or Tasks.

Dwarf/Dwarfs (1969-1985)
- HN DC 142770, deleted 1986.

Dwelling/Dwellings (1965-1985)
- HN DC 142780.
- Use Housing

Dyads
- DC D235500
- SN The most elementary social units, consisting of two interacting persons.
- HN Formerly (1963-1985) DC 142800, Dyad/Dyads/Dyadic.
- BT Small Groups
- RT Couples
  Triads

Dying
- DC D235800
- HN Formerly (1984-1985) DC 142880.
- RT Death
  Death Attitudes
  Death Rituals
  Grief
  Hospices
  Life Stage Transitions
  Terminal Illness

Dynamic/Dynamics (1963-1985)
- HN DC 142900.
- Use Interaction

Dynamics (Family)
- Use Family Relations

Dynamics (Social)
- Use Social Dynamics

Dynasty/Dynasties/Dynastic (1972-1985)
- HN DC 142910, deleted 1986.

Dysfunction/Dysfunctions/Dysfunctional (1963-1985)
- HN DC 142950, deleted 1986. See now Learning Disabilities, Sexual Dysfunction, or appropriate "Family" terms.

Early Man
- Use Prehistoric Man

Earning/Earnings/Earner/Earners (1969-1985)
- HN DC 143090.
- Use Income

Earth (Planet)
- DC D236100
- HN Formerly (1969-1985) DC 143094, Earth.
- UF Planet/Planets/Planetary (1964-1985)
- RT Arctic Regions
  Arid Zones
  Ecology
  Environmental Protection
  Geography
  Islands
  Mountain Regions
  Natural Environment
  Natural Resources
  Oceans
  Pollution
  Topography
  Tropical Regions
  Weather

Eating

Earthquake/Earthquakes (1983-1985)
- HN DC 143097.
- Use Natural Disasters

East (1963-1985)
- HN DC 143100, deleted 1986.

East And West
- DC D236400
- SN Interrelations and contrasts between the Western democracies and countries in Eastern Europe and Asia.
- HN Added, 1986.
- UF Occident And Orient
  Orient And Occident
  West And East
- RT Differences
  Ideological Struggle
  International Relations
  Peaceful Coexistence
  Soviet American Relations
  Western Society

East Asia
- Use Far East

East Berlin
- Use Berlin, German Democratic Republic

East Germany
- Use German Democratic Republic

Easter Island
- DC D236700
- HN Formerly (1983-1985) DC 143600.
- BT Polynesia

Eastern (1963-1985)
- HN DC 143700, deleted 1986.

Eastern Europe
- DC D237000
- HN Formerly (1984-1985) DC 160272, Europe, East/Eastern Europe.
- BT Europe
- NT Albania
  Bulgaria
  Czechoslovakia
  German Democratic Republic
  Hungary
  Poland
  Romania
  Union of Soviet Socialist Republics
  Yugoslavia
- RT Western Europe

Eating And Drinking Establishments
- DC D237100
- HN Added, 1986.
- UF Bar/Bars (1983-1985)
  Cafe/Cafes (1964-1985)
  Coffee House (1966-1985)
  Nightclub (1965-1985)
  Restaurants
  Tavern/Taverns (1966-1985)
- RT Drinking Behavior
  Feeding Practices
  Leisure
  Popular Culture

Eating Disorders
- DC D237150
- HN Added, 1986.
- BT Diseases
- NT Anorexia Nervosa
  Bulimia
- RT Feeding Practices
  Mental Illness
  Substance Abuse

Eating

Eating Patterns
  Use Feeding Practices

Ecclesiastical (1963-1985)
  HN DC 144400, deleted 1986. See now appropriate "Ecclesiastical," "Religion," or "Church" terms.

Ecclesiastical Law
  DC D237300
  HN Added, 1986.
  BT Law
  NT Islamic Law
  RT Canons
      Church State Relationship
      Papacy
      Religious Beliefs
      Religious Doctrines

Ecological Factors
  Use Environmental Factors

Ecological Models
  DC D237500
  SN Explanatory and descriptive schemes incorporating ecological variables and conditions.
  HN Added, 1989.
  UF Environmental Models
  BT Models
  RT Ecology
      Environment
      Evolution

Ecology
  DC D237600
  HN Formerly (1963-1985) DC 144500, Ecology/Ecological/Ecologically/Ecologist/Ecologists.
  UF Ecosystem/Ecosystems (1969-1985)
  BT Biological Sciences
  NT Human Ecology
  RT Conservation
      Earth (Planet)
      Ecological Models
      Energy Conservation
      Environment
      Environmental Protection
      Ethology
      Evolution
      Natural Environment
      Natural Resources
      Noise
      Pollution
      Radiation
      Scientific Research
      Soil Conservation
      Wastes
      Water Supply
      Weather

Econometric Analysis
  DC D237800
  SN The use of statistical and mathematical methods in the analysis of economic problems and theories.
  HN Formerly (1964-1985) DC 144950, Econometric.
  UF Mathematical Economics
  BT Quantitative Methods
  RT Business Cycles
      Economic Models
      Economics
      Measurement
      Time Series Analysis

Economic Aid (Foreign)
  Use Foreign Aid

Economic Change
  DC D237900
  HN Added, 1986.
  BT Change
  RT Business Cycles
      Deindustrialization
      Depression (Economics)
      Economic Conditions
      Economic Development
      Economics
      Employment Changes
      Industrialization
      Inflation
      Labor Market
      Labor Supply
      Social Change
      Technological Change

Economic Climate
  Use Economic Conditions

Economic Conditions
  DC D238200
  HN Added, 1986.
  UF Economic Climate
  NT Affluence
      Depression (Economics)
      Poverty
      Scarcity
  RT Business Cycles
      Economic Change
      Economic Crises
      Economic Development
      Economic Factors
      Economic Policy
      Economic Structure
      Economics
      Inflation
      Labor Productivity
      Labor Supply
      Living Conditions
      Social Conditions
      Standard of Living
      World Economy

Economic Crises
  DC D238500
  HN Added, 1986.
  BT Crises
  RT Depression (Economics)
      Economic Conditions
      Economic Policy
      Economic Problems
      Economics
      Inflation
      Marxist Economics
      Public Debt

Economic Cycles
  Use Business Cycles

Economic Dependence
  Use Dependency Theory

Economic Depression
  Use Depression (Economics)

Economic Development
  DC D238800
  HN Added, 1986.
  UF Economic Growth
  BT Development
  NT Agricultural Development
      Industrial Development
  RT Community Development
      Convergence Theory

Economic

Economic Development (cont'd)
  RT Dependency Theory
      Developing Countries
      Development Policy
      Development Programs
      Development Strategies
      Developmental Stages
      Dual Economy
      Economic Change
      Economic Conditions
      Economic Planning
      Economic Policy
      Economics
      Energy Development
      Foreign Aid
      Government Spending
      Gross National Product
      Human Capital
      Industrialization
      International Economic Organizations
      Modernization
      Modes of Production
      Production
      Progress
      Regional Development
      Rural Development
      Scientific Development
      Scientific Technological Revolution
      Social Development
      Technical Assistance
      Technological Progress
      Technology Transfer
      Urban Development
      Urbanization

Economic Dualism
  Use Dual Economy

Economic Elites
  DC D239100
  HN Added, 1986.
  UF Business Elite
      Corporate Elite
      Financial Elite
  BT Elites
  RT Economics
      Interlocking Directorates
      Oligopolies
      Political Elites
      Power Elite
      Upper Class
      Wealth

Economic Factors
  DC D239400
  HN Added, 1986.
  RT Economic Conditions
      Economics
      Employment
      Environmental Factors
      Marxist Analysis
      Productivity
      Social Impact Assessment
      Socioeconomic Factors
      Supply And Demand

Economic Fluctuations
  Use Business Cycles

Economic Growth
  Use Economic Development

Economic History
  DC D239700
  HN Added, 1986.
  BT History
  RT Business Cycles
      Economic Systems

Economic

Economic History (cont'd)
- **RT** Economics
  - Imperialism
  - Marxist Analysis
  - Political Economy
  - Technological Progress

Economic Models
- **DC** D239850
- **HN** Added, 1986.
- **BT** Models
- **RT** Econometric Analysis
  - Economic Structure
  - Economics

Economic Organization
- **Use** Economic Structure

Economic Planning
- **DC** D240000
- **HN** Added, 1986.
- **BT** Planning
- **RT** Development Programs
  - Economic Development
  - Economic Policy
  - Economics
  - Government
  - Local Planning
  - Social Planning
  - State Planning
  - World Economy

Economic Policy
- **DC** D240300
- **HN** Added, 1986.
- **BT** Policy
- **NT** Agricultural Policy
  - Energy Policy
  - Fiscal Policy
  - Labor Policy
  - Protectionism
- **RT** Economic Conditions
  - Economic Crises
  - Economic Development
  - Economic Planning
  - Economics
  - European Economic Community
  - Exploitation
  - Foreign Aid
  - Government Policy
  - Government Spending
  - International Economic Organizations
  - Policy Implementation
  - Public Sector Private Sector Relations
  - Regional Development
  - Science Policy
  - Technology Transfer
  - World Economy
  - World System Theory

Economic Problems
- **DC** D240600
- **HN** Added, 1986.
- **UF** Financial Problems
- **BT** Problems
- **NT** Economic Underdevelopment
- **RT** Bankruptcy
  - Business Cycles
  - Depression (Economics)
  - Economic Crises
  - Economics
  - Inflation
  - Low Income Areas
  - Low Income Groups
  - Poverty
  - Scarcity
  - Social Problems
  - Unemployment
  - World Problems

Economic Sectors
- **DC** D240900
- **HN** Formerly (1970-1985) DC 410950, Sector/Sectors.
- **UF** Sectors (Economic)
- **NT** Informal Sector
  - Private Sector
  - Public Sector
- **RT** Agriculture
  - Business
  - Economic Structure
  - Economic Systems
  - Economics
  - Enterprises
  - Industry
  - Occupational Structure
  - Sustenance Organization

Economic Structure
- **DC** D241200
- **HN** Added, 1986.
- **UF** Economic Organization
- **BT** Structure
- **NT** Sustenance Organization
- **RT** Agrarian Structures
  - Base And Superstructure
  - Center And Periphery
  - Dependency Theory
  - Dual Economy
  - Economic Conditions
  - Economic Models
  - Economic Sectors
  - Economic Systems
  - Economics
  - Forces And Relations of Production
  - Labor Market Segmentation
  - Market Economy
  - Markets
  - Middleman Minorities
  - Modernization
  - Modes of Production
  - Monopolies
  - Occupational Segregation
  - Occupational Structure
  - Oligopolies
  - Production
  - Social Structure
  - Subsistence Economy
  - World Economy

Economic Support
- **Use** Financial Support

Economic Systems
- **DC** D241500
- **HN** Added, 1986.
- **UF** Economy/Economies (1963-1985)
- **BT** Systems
- **NT** Capitalism
  - Collectivism
  - Communism
  - Feudalism
  - Socialism
- **RT** Agrarian Structures
  - Dual Economy
  - Economic History
  - Economic Sectors
  - Economic Structure
  - Economics
  - Imperialism
  - Industrialism
  - Market Economy
  - Money
  - Oligopolies
  - Ownership
  - Political Ideologies
  - Political Systems
  - Protectionism

Economics

Economic Systems (cont'd)
- **RT** Slavery
  - Social Systems
  - Society
  - State Capitalism
  - Subsistence Economy
  - World Economy

Economic Theories
- **DC** D241800
- **HN** Added, 1986.
- **BT** Theories
- **NT** Dependency Theory
  - Labor Theory of Value
  - World System Theory
- **RT** Center And Periphery
  - Economics
  - Historical Materialism
  - Inflation
  - Keynesian Economics
  - Marxist Economics
  - Philosophical Doctrines
  - Political Economy
  - Protectionism
  - Supply And Demand
  - Value (Economics)

Economic Underdevelopment
- **DC** D242100
- **HN** Formerly (1963-1985) DC 475100, Underdevelop/Underdeveloped/Underdevelopment.
- **UF** Backwardness (Economic)
  - Underdevelopment (Economic)
- **BT** Economic Problems
- **RT** Agrarian Societies
  - Center And Periphery
  - Dependency Theory
  - Developing Countries
  - Development Programs
  - Dual Economy
  - Economics
  - International Division of Labor
  - Modes of Production
  - Subsistence Economy
  - World Economy
  - World Problems

Economics
- **DC** D242400
- **HN** Formerly (1963-1985) DC 145000, Economic/Economics/Economical.
- **BT** Social Sciences
- **NT** Agricultural Economics
  - Finance
  - Keynesian Economics
  - Marxist Economics
- **RT** Base And Superstructure
  - Business
  - Capital
  - Commodities
  - Consumption
  - Credit
  - Dual Economy
  - Econometric Analysis
  - Economic Change
  - Economic Conditions
  - Economic Crises
  - Economic Development
  - Economic Elites
  - Economic Factors
  - Economic History
  - Economic Models
  - Economic Planning
  - Economic Policy
  - Economic Problems
  - Economic Sectors
  - Economic Structure

Economists

Economics (cont'd)
- RT Economic Systems
- Economic Theories
- Economic Underdevelopment
- Employment
- Enterprises
- Exchange (Economics)
- Expenditures
- Forces And Relations of Production
- Forecasting
- Gross National Product
- Income
- Industry
- International Economic Organizations
- Labor
- Market Economy
- Marxism
- Political Economy
- Poverty
- Prices
- Production
- Production Consumption Relationship
- Productivity
- Profits
- Property
- Standard of Living
- Subsistence Economy
- Supply And Demand
- Technology
- Trade
- Value (Economics)
- Wealth
- World Economy

Economists
- DC D242700
- HN Formerly (1963-1985) DC 145010, Economist/Economists.
- BT Social Scientists
- RT Physiocrats

Economy/Economies (1963-1985)
- HN DC 145200.
- Use Economic Systems

Ecosystem/Ecosystems (1969-1985)
- HN DC 145300.
- Use Ecology

Ecuador
- DC D243000
- HN Formerly (1963-1985) DC 145475.
- BT South America

Ecumenical Christianity
- Use Ecumenicism

Ecumenical Movement
- DC D243300
- HN Formerly (1964-1985) DC 145550.
- BT Religious Movements
- RT Christianity
- Ecumenicism
- Movements

Ecumenical Organizations
- Use Ecumenicism

Ecumenicism
- DC D243600
- HN Formerly (1969-1985) DC 145545, Ecumenical/Ecumenicism.
- UF Ecumenical Christianity
- Ecumenical Organizations
- RT Christianity
- Ecumenical Movement

Editorials
- DC D243900
- HN Formerly (1965-1985) part of DC 145650, Editor/Editors/Editorial.
- BT News Media
- RT Discourse
- Editors
- Journalism
- Newspapers
- Opinions
- Periodicals
- Public Opinion
- Publications

Editors
- DC D244200
- HN Formerly (1965-1985) part of DC 145650, Editor/Editors/Editorial.
- UF Copy Editors
- RT Editorials
- Films
- Journalism
- News Media
- Publications
- Publishing Industry
- Writers

Educability (1965-1985)
- HN DC 145780.
- Use Academic Aptitude

Educate/Educates/Educated/Educating (1963-1985)
- HN DC 145800, deleted 1986. See now College Graduates, Educational Attainment, or other appropriate "Education" terms.

Education
- DC D244500
- HN Formerly (1963-1985) DC 146000, Education/Educational/Educators/Educationally.
- UF Formal Education
- BT Social Institutions
- NT Adult Education
- Bilingual Education
- Elementary Education
- Higher Education
- Marriage And Family Education
- Moral Education
- Multicultural Education
- Preschool Education
- Religious Education
- Rural Education
- Secondary Education
- Social Science Education
- Special Education
- Teacher Education
- Urban Education
- Vocational Education
- Womens Education
- RT Audiovisual Media
- Compulsory Participation
- Curriculum
- Dropouts
- Education Work Relationship
- Educational Administration
- Educational Ideologies
- Educational Opportunities
- Educational Plans
- Educational Policy
- Educational Programs
- Educational Reform
- Educational Research
- Educational Systems
- Knowledge
- Learning

Educational

Education (cont'd)
- RT Literacy Programs
- Schools
- Socialization
- Sociology of Education
- Students
- Teachers
- Teaching
- Training

Education Employment Relationship
- Use Education Work Relationship

Education Work Relationship
- DC D244800
- HN Added, 1986.
- UF Education Employment Relationship
- Occupation Education Relationship
- BT Relations
- RT Education
- Educational Attainment
- Employability
- Employment
- Human Capital
- Human Resources
- Job Performance
- Job Requirements
- Job Training
- Labor
- Occupational Aspiration
- Occupational Qualifications
- Occupational Status
- Occupations
- Opportunities
- Tracking (Education)
- Unemployment
- Work
- Work Orientations

Educational Achievement
- Use Academic Achievement

Educational Administration
- DC D245100
- HN Added, 1986.
- UF College Administration
- Educational Management
- School Administration
- BT Management
- RT Academic Departments
- College Faculty
- Deans
- Education
- Principals
- Registration
- School Boards
- Schools
- Superintendents

Educational Attainment
- DC D245400
- HN Added, 1986.
- BT Attainment
- RT Academic Achievement
- Academic Degrees
- Dropouts
- Education Work Relationship
- Educational Opportunities
- Educational Plans
- Graduates
- Intellectual Development
- Intelligentsia
- Social Mobility
- Students

Educational   Egoism

Educational Degrees
  Use Academic Degrees

Educational Ideologies
  DC   D245550
  HN   Added, 1986.
  BT   Ideologies
  RT   Education
       Educational Policy
       Educational Reform
       Educational Systems
       Sociology of Education

Educational Management
  Use Educational Administration

Educational Opportunities
  DC   D245700
  HN   Added, 1986.
  BT   Opportunities
  RT   Disadvantaged
       Education
       Educational Attainment
       Students

Educational Plans
  DC   D246000
  SN   Refers to the educational plans of individuals.
  HN   Added, 1986.
  RT   Academic Degrees
       Education
       Educational Attainment
       Life Plans
       Planning
       Students
       Youth

Educational Policy
  DC   D246300
  HN   Added, 1986.
  BT   Policy
  RT   Academic Freedom
       Affirmative Action
       Bilingual Education
       Education
       Educational Ideologies
       Educational Reform
       Educational Research
       Educational Systems
       Government Policy
       Language Planning
       Language Policy
       Multicultural Education
       Policy Implementation
       Public Schools
       School Boards
       Second Language Learning
       Social Policy

Educational Programs
  DC   D246600
  HN   Added, 1986.
  UF   Training Programs
  BT   Programs
  NT   Internship Programs
       Literacy Programs
       Project Head Start
  RT   Courses
       Curriculum
       Doctoral Programs
       Education
       Postdoctoral Programs
       Program Implementation
       Schools
       Seminars
       Tracking (Education)
       Training
       Undergraduate Programs
       Workshops (Courses)

Educational Reform
  DC   D246900
  HN   Added, 1986.
  UF   School Reform
  BT   Reform
  RT   Education
       Educational Ideologies
       Educational Policy
       Educational Systems
       Literacy Programs

Educational Research
  DC   D247000
  HN   Added, 1986.
  BT   Research
  RT   Academic Achievement
       Education
       Educational Policy
       Learning
       Social Science Research
       Sociology of Education
       Students

Educational Systems
  DC   D247200
  HN   Added, 1986.
  BT   Systems
  RT   Education
       Educational Ideologies
       Educational Policy
       Educational Reform
       Philosophical Doctrines
       Private Schools
       Public Schools
       Rural Education
       Schools
       Sociology of Education
       Urban Education

Edwards Personal Preference Scale (1966-1985)
  HN   DC 146500.
  Use Scales

Effectiveness
  DC   D247500
  HN   Formerly (1963-1985) part of DC 148425, Effect/Effects/Effectiveness.
  UF   Efficacy (1969-1985)
  BT   Performance
  NT   Organizational Effectiveness
  RT   Accountability
       Achievement
       Effects
       Efficiency
       Evaluation
       Failure
       Goals
       Morale
       Productivity
       Program Evaluation
       Redundancy
       Relevance
       Success

Effects
  DC   D247800
  HN   Formerly (1963-1985) part of DC 148425, Effect/Effects/Effectiveness.
  UF   Consequence/Consequences (1964-1985)
       Impact (1978-1985)
  NT   Altitude Effects
       Mass Media Effects
       Placebo Effect
  RT   Causality
       Effectiveness

Effects (cont'd)
  RT   Forecasting
       Goals
       Means-Ends Rationality
       Relevance

Efficacy (1969-1985)
  HN   DC 148490.
  Use Effectiveness

Efficiency
  DC   D248100
  HN   Formerly (1963-1985) DC 148500.
  RT   Effectiveness
       Organizational Effectiveness
       Performance
       Productivity
       Resource Allocation
       Time Utilization

Egalitarianism
  DC   D248400
  HN   Formerly (1963-1985) DC 148600, Egalitarian/Egalitarianism.
  UF   Equalitarian/Equalitarianism (1968-1985)
  BT   Ideologies
  RT   Authoritarianism (Psychology)
       Discrimination
       Equality
       Equity
       Philosophy
       Social Behavior
       Social Justice
       Social Values

Ego (1983-1985)
  HN   DC 149000, deleted 1986. See now Egocentrism or Self Concept.

Egocentrism
  DC   D248700
  SN   Preoccupation with one's self, with little or no regard for the desires or needs of others. Also, a stage in Jean Piaget's conception of cognitive development in which the child views, and thinks others view, the world from his own point of view.
  HN   Added, 1986.
  UF   Self Centeredness
  RT   Bias
       Child Development
       Cognitive Development
       Interpersonal Relations
       Narcissism
       Personality Traits
       Self Concept
       Social Attitudes

Egoism
  DC   D249000
  SN   Ethical doctrine or theory of motivation holding that self-interest should be, or is, the basis for morality or behavior. Also, boastfulness and an exaggerated sense of self-importance.
  HN   Formerly (1963-1985) DC 149300.
  UF   Conceit/Conceits/Conceited (1972-1985)
       Egotism
  RT   Altruism
       Anomie
       Narcissism
       Personality Traits

Egotism

Egotism
- Use Egoism

Egypt
- DC D249300
- HN Formerly (1963-1985) DC 149630, Egypt/Egyptian/Egyptians.
- UF United Arab Republic (1963-1985)
- BT Arab Countries
  Mediterranean Countries
  North Africa
- NT Cairo, Egypt

Eighteenth Century
- DC D249600
- HN Formerly (1978-1985) DC 149665.
- BT Time Periods
- RT Enlightenment

Einstein, Albert
- DC D249900
- SN Born 14 March 1879 - died 18 April 1955.
- HN Formerly (1966-1985) DC 149669.

Eire
- Use Ireland

Eisenstadt, Shmuel Noah
- DC D250200
- SN Born 10 September 1923 - .
- HN Formerly (1965-1985) DC 149675, Eisenstadt, S. N.

El Salvador
- DC D250500
- HN Formerly (1963-1985) DC 151300.
- BT Central America

Elaboration (1965-1985)
- HN DC 149720.
- Use Explanation

Elder Abuse
- DC D250800
- SN Physical or mental abuse of the elderly, especially as practiced by their children or younger caregivers.
- HN Added, 1986.
- BT Abuse
- RT Aging
  Battered Women
  Elderly
  Family Violence
  Filial Responsibility
  Spouse Abuse
  Victimization
  Victims

Elderly
- DC D251100
- SN Persons aged 65 or older.
- HN Formerly (1972-1985) DC 149733, Elder/Elders/Elderly.
- UF Aged (1963-1985)
  Older Adult (1984-1985)
  Senior Citizen/Senior Citizens (1984-1985)
- BT Adults
  Age Groups
- NT Elderly Women
- RT Ageism
  Aging
  Dependents
  Disengagement
  Elder Abuse
  Filial Responsibility
  Geriatrics
  Gerontocracy

Elderly (cont'd)
- RT Gerontology
  Grandparents
  Home Health Care
  Income Maintenance Programs
  Intergenerational Relations
  Pensions
  Retirement
  Self Care
  Social Security
  Widowhood
  Youth

Elderly Women
- DC D251200
- HN Added, 1989.
- BT Elderly
  Females
- RT Grandparents
  Mothers
  Widowhood

Elected Officials
- Use Public Officials

Election Campaigns
- Use Political Campaigns

Elections
- DC D251400
- HN Formerly (1963-1985) DC 149765, Election/Elections.
- RT Candidates
  Democracy
  Legislative Apportionment
  Political Campaigns
  Political Participation
  Political Parties
  Political Science
  Politics
  Public Officials
  Referendum
  Voters
  Voting
  Voting Behavior
  Voting Rights

Elector/Electoral (1963-1985)
- HN DC 149775, deleted 1986. See now Elections, Voting, Voting Behavior, or Voters.

Electoral Behavior
- Use Voting Behavior

Electorate (1963-1985)
- HN DC 149785.
- Use Voters

Electra Complex
- Use Oedipal Complex

Electricity
- DC D251700
- HN Formerly (1968-1985) DC 149860, Electric/Electrical/Electricity.
- RT Electronic Technology
  Energy
  Energy Policy
  Fuels
  Nuclear Reactors
  Physics
  Solar Energy

Electroencephalograph/ Electroencephalographic (1978-1985)
- HN DC 149890, deleted 1986.

Elites

Electronic Communications
- Use Telecommunications

Electronic Data Processing (1964-1985)
- HN DC 150870.
- Use Data Processing

Electronic Devices
- Use Electronic Technology

Electronic Technology
- DC D252000
- HN Formerly (1965-1985) DC 150850, Electronic.
- UF Computer Technology
  Electronic Devices
  Microelectronic Technology
- BT Technology
- RT Automation
  Computers
  Data Processing
  Electricity
  High Technology Industries
  Information Technology
  Physics
  Radio
  Telecommunications
  Television

Elementary Education
- DC D252300
- HN Added, 1986. Formerly (1971-1985) part of DC 150950, Elementary.
- UF Elementary Grades
- BT Education
- NT Primary Education
- RT Adult Education
  Elementary School Students
  Elementary Schools
  Kindergarten
  Preschool Education

Elementary Grades
- Use Elementary Education

Elementary School Students
- DC D252600
- HN Added, 1986.
- UF Primary School Students
- BT Students
- RT Children
  Elementary Education
  Elementary Schools
  Primary Education

Elementary Schools
- DC D252900
- HN Added, 1986.
- BT Schools
- RT Elementary Education
  Elementary School Students
  Primary Education
  Private Schools
  Public Schools

Elevation Effects
- Use Altitude Effects

Elias, Norbert
- DC D253100
- SN Born 22 June 1897 - .
- HN Added, 1986.

Elites
- DC D253200
- HN Formerly (1963-1985) part of DC 151100, Elite/Elites/Elitism/Elitist/Elitists.
- UF Social Elites
- NT Economic Elites
  Intelligentsia

Elitism

Elites (cont'd)
- **NT** Political Elites
  Power Elite
- **RT** Aristocracy
  Dominance
  Elitism
  Influence
  Mass Society
  Masses
  Power Structure
  Privilege
  Ruling Class
  Scientific Community
  Social Class
  Social Power
  Social Status
  Social Structure
  Upper Class
  Wealth

Elitism
- **DC** D253500
- **SN** Government by a powerful, influential, and prestigious minority. Compare with Oligarchy. Also, the awareness of or pride in belonging to a group, not necessarily political, that is recognized as superior in a specific field of endeavor (eg, scientific elite).
- **HN** Formerly (1963-1985) part of DC 151100, Elite/Elites/Elitism/Elitist/Elitists.
- **BT** Ideologies
- **RT** Aristocracy
  Elites
  Meritocracy
  Militarism
  Oligarchy
  Political Ideologies
  Privilege
  Social Attitudes
  Social Inequality
  Social Mobility
  Social Stratification

Emancipation (1964-1985)
- **HN** DC 151350, deleted 1986. See now Freedom, Feminism, or Womens Rights.

Embarrassment
- **DC** D253800
- **HN** Formerly (1968-1985) DC 151365.
- **BT** Emotions
- **RT** Guilt
  Shame

Embourgeoisement
- **DC** D254100
- **SN** Conversion from working-class to middle-class patterns of behavior and orientations as a result of improvement in the standard of living.
- **HN** Formerly (1964-1985) DC 151400.
- **BT** Social Processes
- **RT** Bourgeoisie
  Proletarianization
  Social Mobility
  Working Class

Emerge/Emergent/Emergence/Emerging (1963-1985)
- **HN** DC 151550, deleted 1986. See now Development or Formation.

Emergencies
- **DC** D254400
- **HN** Formerly (1971-1985) DC 151551, Emergency/Emergencies.
- **NT** Disasters
- **RT** Accidents
  Assistance

Emergencies (cont'd)
- **RT** Civil Disorders
  Counseling
  Crises
  Fire Fighters
  Government
  Public Services
  Social Services

Emergency Medical Services
- **DC** D254700
- **HN** Added, 1986.
- **UF** Emergency Service/Emergency Services (1980-1985)
  Medical Emergency Services
- **BT** Health Services
- **RT** Disaster Relief
  Disasters
  Hospitals
  Paramedical Personnel

Emergency Service/Emergency Services (1980-1985)
- **HN** DC 151555.
- **Use** Emergency Medical Services

Emigrant/Emigrants (1963-1985)
- **HN** DC 151650.
- **Use** Emigration

Emigration
- **DC** D255000
- **HN** Formerly (1963-1985) DC 151580.
- **UF** Emigrant/Emigrants (1963-1985)
- **BT** Migration
- **NT** Brain Drain
- **RT** Borders
  Immigration
  Overpopulation

Emotional Expression
- **Use** Self Expression

Emotional Illness
- **Use** Affective Illness

Emotionally Disturbed
- **DC** D255300
- **HN** Formerly (1964-1985) DC 151750.
- **UF** Disturb/Disturbed/Disturbing (1963-1985)
- **RT** Depression (Psychology)
  Emotions
  Handicapped
  Hysteria
  Mental Illness
  Neurosis
  Psychopathology
  Sociopathic Personality

Emotions
- **DC** D255600
- **HN** Formerly (1963-1985) DC 151700, Emotion/Emotions/Emotional/Emotionally/Emotionality.
- **UF** Affect/Affects/Affected (1963-1985)
  Affectivity/Affective (1963-1985)
  Feeling/Feelings (1963-1985)
  Mood/Moods (1971-1985)
- **NT** Alienation
  Anger
  Anxiety
  Apathy
  Boredom
  Compassion
  Embarrassment
  Fear
  Frustration
  Grief

Empiricism

Emotions (cont'd)
- **NT** Guilt
  Happiness
  Hate
  Jealousy
  Loneliness
  Love
  Shame
- **RT** Ambivalence
  Attitudes
  Depression (Psychology)
  Emotionally Disturbed
  Human Nature
  Interpersonal Relations
  Morale
  Personality Traits
  Projective Techniques
  Psychological Distress
  Psychological Factors
  Psychology
  Satisfaction
  Social Behavior
  Social Interaction
  Suffering
  Tension
  Trust

Empathy
- **DC** D255900
- **HN** Formerly (1963-1985) DC 154000, Empathy/Empathetic.
- **BT** Personality Traits
- **RT** Compassion
  Experience
  Imagination
  Interpersonal Communication
  Interpersonal Relations
  Verstehen

Empires
- **DC** D256200
- **HN** Formerly (1963-1985) DC 154070, Empire/Empires/Emperor.
- **UF** Ottoman/Ottomanism (1963-1985)
- **BT** Political Systems
- **RT** Colonialism
  Imperialism
  Monarchy

Empirical Methods
- **DC** D256250
- **SN** Techniques for accumulating knowledge through observation, experimentation, and theory formulation and revision.
- **HN** Formerly (1963-1985) DC 154075, Empirical.
- **UF** Empirical Research
- **BT** Research Methodology
- **NT** Scientific Method
- **RT** Experiments
  Measurement
  Methodology (Data Analysis)
  Methodology (Data Collection)
  Methodology (Philosophical)
  Objectivity
  Operational Definitions
  Quantitative Methods
  Value Neutrality
  Verification

Empirical Research
- **Use** Empirical Methods

Empiricism
- **DC** D256300
- **SN** An epistemological doctrine holding that the only valid source of knowledge is experience, as opposed to untested theoretical speculation. In sociology, this entails observation, experiment, and the provision of quantitative data.

Employ / Encounter

Empiricism (cont'd)
- HN Formerly (1963-1985) DC 154140, Empiricism/Empiricist.
- BT Epistemological Doctrines
- RT Behaviorism
  Experiments
  Holism
  Materialism
  Nominalism
  Observation
  Positivism
  Validity

Employ/Employed (1963-1985)
- HN DC 154170.
- Use Employment

Employability
- DC D256500
- HN Formerly (1964-1985) DC 154175.
- UF Employment Potential
- RT Education Work Relationship
  Employment
  Job Training
  Occupational Qualifications
  Professional Training
  Unemployment
  Work Experience
  Work Skills

Employee Absenteeism
- Use Absenteeism

Employee Assistance Programs
- DC D256700
- SN Social services and health care programs administered by agencies or corporations for employees and their families.
- HN Added, 1989.
- BT Programs
- RT Assistance
  Counseling
  Drug Addiction
  Human Relations Movement
  Human Services
  Information And Referral Services
  Intervention
  Job Satisfaction
  Professional Consultation
  Psychotherapy
  Quality of Working Life
  Social Support
  Treatment Programs
  Work Humanization
  Workers

Employee Benefits
- Use Benefits

Employee Ownership
- Use Worker Ownership

Employee Turnover
- Use Labor Turnover

Employee/Employees (1963-1985)
- HN DC 154200.
- Use Workers

Employers
- DC D256800
- HN Formerly (1963-1985) DC 154300, Employer/Employers.
- RT Business
  Collective Bargaining
  Employers Associations
  Employment
  Enterprises

Employers (cont'd)
- RT Labor Relations
  Management
  Managers
  Personnel Management
  Workers

Employers Associations
- DC D257100
- HN Added, 1986.
- BT Associations
- RT Collective Bargaining
  Employers
  Labor Relations
  Unions

Employment
- DC D257400
- SN A context-dependent term encompassing work for monetary gain.
- HN Formerly (1963-1985) DC 154400.
- UF Employ/Employed (1963-1985)
  Job/Jobs (1963-1985)
- NT Multiple Jobholding
  Part Time Employment
  Self Employment
  Underemployment
  Unemployment
  Youth Employment
- RT Business
  Business Society Relationship
  Careers
  Commuting (Travel)
  Demography
  Dislocated Workers
  Dual Career Family
  Economic Factors
  Economics
  Education Work Relationship
  Employability
  Employers
  Employment Changes
  Employment Discrimination
  Employment Opportunities
  Job Application
  Job Change
  Job Characteristics
  Job Performance
  Job Requirements
  Job Satisfaction
  Job Search
  Labor
  Labor Force
  Labor Market
  Labor Relations
  Occupational Choice
  Occupational Roles
  Occupational Structure
  Occupations
  Personnel Management
  Seniority
  Tenure
  Wages
  Welfare Dependency
  Work
  Work Attitudes
  Work Environment
  Work Skills
  Workers
  Working Hours
  Working Mothers
  Working Women

Employment Application
- Use Job Application

Employment Changes
- DC D257700
- SN Relatively large-scale shifts in employment patterns. Includes the growth or loss of job opportunities and changes in occupational characteristics of the employed population. Do not confuse with Job Change or Occupational Mobility.
- HN Added, 1986.
- BT Change
- RT Business Society Relationship
  Deindustrialization
  Demographic Change
  Demography
  Dislocated Workers
  Economic Change
  Employment
  Employment Opportunities
  Industrialization
  Labor Force
  Labor Market
  Labor Supply
  Occupational Classifications
  Occupational Structure
  Plant Closure
  Unemployment

Employment Discrimination
- DC D258000
- HN Added, 1986.
- UF Job Discrimination
- BT Discrimination
- RT Affirmative Action
  Employment
  Hiring Practices
  Labor Market Segmentation
  Nontraditional Occupations
  Occupational Segregation
  Personnel Management

Employment Opportunities
- DC D258300
- HN Added, 1986.
- UF Job Opportunities
  Job Vacancies
- BT Opportunities
- RT Affirmative Action
  Employment
  Employment Changes
  Job Change
  Job Requirements
  Job Search
  Labor Market
  Occupational Mobility
  Occupational Qualifications
  Personnel Management
  Promotion (Occupational)
  Recruitment

Employment Policy
- Use Labor Policy

Employment Potential
- Use Employability

Employment Preparation
- Use Job Training

Employment Qualifications
- Use Occupational Qualifications

Employment Satisfaction
- Use Job Satisfaction

Encounter/Encounters (1971-1985)
- HN DC 154580.
- Use Social Interaction

Encouragement
- **DC** D258600
- **HN** Formerly (1972-1985) DC 154581, Encourage/Encourages/ Encouraged/Encouraging/ Encouragement.
- **BT** Social Behavior
- **RT** Feedback
  Incentives
  Motivation
  Parent Child Relations
  Reinforcement
  Social Support

Encyclopedia/Encyclopedias (1963-1985)
- **HN** DC 154600.
- **Use** Reference Materials

Endocrine/Endocrines (1966-1985)
- **HN** DC 154800.
- **Use** Hormones

Endogamy
- **DC** D258900
- **SN** Marriage within the same racial, ethnic, religious, or social group.
- **HN** Formerly (1963-1985) DC 154850.
- **BT** Marriage
- **RT** Consanguinity
  Cousin Marriage
  Homogamy

Endorse/Endorsed/Endorsing/ Endorsement (1972-1985)
- **HN** DC 154860, deleted 1986.

Ends (1969-1985)
- **HN** DC 154870.
- **Use** Means-Ends Rationality

Energy
- **DC** D259200
- **HN** Formerly (1964-1985) DC 154925.
- **NT** Nuclear Energy
  Radiation
  Solar Energy
- **RT** Coal
  Electricity
  Energy Conservation
  Energy Consumption
  Energy Development
  Energy Policy
  Entropy
  Fuels
  Physics
  Resources
  Water Supply

Energy Conservation
- **DC** D259500
- **HN** Added, 1986.
- **BT** Conservation
- **RT** Ecology
  Energy
  Energy Consumption
  Energy Policy
  Fuels
  Human Ecology
  Natural Resources
  Solar Energy
  Water Supply

Energy Consumption
- **DC** D259800
- **HN** Added, 1986.
- **UF** Energy Use
- **BT** Consumption
- **RT** Conservation
  Energy
  Energy Conservation
  Energy Policy
  Fuels

Energy Development
- **DC** D260000
- **HN** Added, 1989.
- **BT** Development
- **RT** Development Programs
  Economic Development
  Energy
  Energy Policy
  Fuels
  Regional Development
  Research And Development
  Resource Allocation

Energy Policy
- **DC** D260100
- **HN** Added, 1986.
- **BT** Economic Policy
- **RT** Coal
  Electricity
  Energy
  Energy Conservation
  Energy Consumption
  Energy Development
  Fuels
  Nuclear Energy
  Petroleum
  Solar Energy

Energy Use
- **Use** Energy Consumption

Enforcement (Law)
- **Use** Law Enforcement

Engagement (1964-1985)
- **HN** DC 154960, deleted 1986.

Engels, Friedrich
- **DC** D260400
- **SN** Born 28 November 1820 - died 5 August 1895.
- **HN** Formerly (1966-1985) DC 154980.

Engineering
- **DC** D260700
- **HN** Formerly (1963-1985) part of DC 155000, Engineer/Engineers/ Engineering.
- **BT** Technology
- **RT** Biotechnology
  Construction Industry
  Design
  Engineers
  High Technology Industries
  Space Technology
  Technology Assessment

Engineers
- **DC** D261000
- **HN** Formerly (1963-1985) part of DC 155000, Engineer/Engineers/ Engineering.
- **BT** Professional Workers
- **RT** Engineering
  Scientific Community
  Scientists

England
- **DC** D261300
- **HN** Formerly (1963-1985) DC 156300, England/English.
- **BT** Great Britain
  United Kingdom
  Western Europe
- **NT** London, England

English Language
- **DC** D261600
- **HN** Added, 1986.
- **BT** Germanic Languages

Enlightenment
- **DC** D261900
- **SN** An 18th-century philosophical movement that promoted a rational and scientific approach to the world and a belief in human progress.
- **HN** Formerly (1964-1985) DC 156650.
- **BT** Time Periods
- **RT** Eighteenth Century

Enlisted Personnel
- **Use** Military Personnel

Enrollment
- **DC** D262200
- **HN** Formerly (1981-1985) DC 156675, Enrollment/Enrollments.
- **RT** Dropouts
  School Attendance
  Schools
  Students

Enterprises
- **DC** D262500
- **SN** A context-dependent term encompassing business or manufacturing organizations.
- **HN** Formerly (1963-1985) DC 156740, Enterprise/Enterprises.
- **UF** Business Enterprises
  Business Organizations
  Commercial Enterprises
- **BT** Organizations (Social)
- **NT** Agricultural Enterprises
  Corporations
  Family Businesses
  Firms
  Industrial Enterprises
  Minority Businesses
  Small Businesses
- **RT** Business
  Businessmen
  Collectives
  Cooperatives
  Economic Sectors
  Economics
  Employers
  Entrepreneurship
  Executives
  Factories
  Industry
  Labor
  Labor Productivity
  Labor Relations
  Markets
  Production
  Worker Ownership
  Workers
  Workplaces

Entertainment Industry
- **DC** D262600
- **HN** Added, 1989.
- **UF** Amusement Industry
  Film Industry
  Music Industry
  Television Industry
- **BT** Industry
- **RT** Audiences
  Mass Media
  Popular Culture
  Publishing Industry
  Recreation

Entertainment

Entertainment/Entertainer/ Entertainers (1964-1985)
- HN DC 156700.
- Use Popular Culture

Entrepreneurs
- Use Entrepreneurship

Entrepreneurship
- DC D262800
- HN Formerly (1963-1985) DC 156925, Entrepreneur/Entrepreneurs/ Entrepreneurial/Entrepreneurship.
- UF Entrepreneurs
- RT Business
  Businessmen
  Commercialization
  Enterprises
  Family Businesses
  Executives
  Finance
  Innovations
  Management
  Opportunities
  Private Sector
  Self Employment
  Small Businesses

Entropy
- DC D262900
- HN Formerly (1967-1985) DC 156950, Entropy/Entropic.
- RT Energy
  Macrosociology
  Organizational Dissolution
  Physics
  Social Change
  Systems Theory

Enumerate/Enumerates/ Enumerated/Enumeration (1971-1985)
- HN DC 157200, deleted 1986.

Environment
- DC D263100
- SN A context-dependent term; select a more specific entry or coordinate with other terms.
- HN Formerly (1963-1985) DC 157400, Environment/Environments/ Environmental/Environmentally.
- UF Circumstance/Circumstances (1971-1985)
  Context/Contexts/Contextual/ Contextualist (1963-1985)
  Milieu (1963-1985)
  Set/Sets/Settings (1963-1985)
- NT Classroom Environment
  Home Environment
  Natural Environment
  Social Environment
  Work Environment
- RT Communities
  Crowding
  Ecological Models
  Ecology
  Environmental Attitudes
  Environmental Design
  Environmental Factors
  Environmental Protection
  Environmental Sociology
  Environmentalism
  Human Ecology
  Neighborhoods
  Noise
  Pollution
  Resources
  Space
  Stress

Environmental Attitudes
- DC D263400
- HN Added, 1986.
- UF Environmental Concern
- BT Attitudes
- RT Conservation
  Environment
  Environmental Protection
  Environmentalism
  Natural Resources

Environmental Concern
- Use Environmental Attitudes

Environmental Contamination
- Use Pollution

Environmental Design
- DC D263700
- HN Added, 1986.
- BT Design
- RT Architecture
  Environment

Environmental Factors
- DC D264000
- HN Added, 1986.
- UF Ecological Factors
  Environmental Influences
- RT Altitude Effects
  Biological Factors
  Economic Factors
  Environment
  Home Environment
  Influence
  Lunar Influences
  Population Density
  Seasonal Variations
  Sociocultural Factors
  Sociodemographic Factors
  Weather

Environmental Hazards
- Use Hazards

Environmental Influences
- Use Environmental Factors

Environmental Models
- Use Ecological Models

Environmental Movements
- Use Environmentalism

Environmental Protection
- DC D264300
- HN Added, 1986.
- UF Environmental Regulation
- BT Protection
- RT Animal Human Relations
  Conservation
  Earth (Planet)
  Ecology
  Environment
  Environmental Attitudes
  Environmental Protection
  Environmentalism
  Forestry
  Land Use
  Natural Environment
  Pollution
  Pollution Control
  Quality
  Survival
  Wastes

Epistemological

Environmental Regulation
- Use Environmental Protection

Environmental Sociology
- DC D264600
- HN Added, 1986.
- BT Sociology
- RT Environment

Environmentalism
- DC D264900
- HN Added, 1986.
- UF Environmental Movements
- BT Social Movements
- RT Environment
  Environmental Attitudes
  Environmental Protection
  Natural Environment

Envy (1966-1985)
- HN DC 157500.
- Use Jealousy

Epainogamy (1964-1985)
- HN DC 157580, deleted 1986.

Epic Poetry
- Use Poetry

Epidemics
- DC D265200
- HN Formerly (1963-1985) DC 157600, Epidemic/Edpidemics.
- RT Diseases
  Epidemiology
  Plague
  Public Health

Epidemiology
- DC D265500
- HN Formerly (1963-1985) DC 157700, Epidemiology/Epidemiological.
- BT Medicine
- RT Diseases
  Epidemics
  Health Policy
  Medical Model
  Prevention
  Public Health
  Sanitation
  Vaccination

Epilepsy
- DC D265800
- HN Formerly (1965-1985) DC 158000.
- BT Diseases
- RT Brain
  Neurology

Episcopalians
- DC D266100
- HN Formerly (1963-1985) DC 158475, Episcopal/Episcopalian/ Episcopalians.
- BT Protestants
- RT Protestantism

Epistemological Doctrines
- DC D266375
- SN Any of the specific theories about the nature of knowledge and the methods for accumulating it.
- HN Added, 1986.
- BT Philosophical Doctrines
- NT Determinism
  Empiricism
  Existentialism
  Holism
  Indeterminism

Epistemology

Epistemological Doctrines (cont'd)
- NT Methodological Individualism
  - Nihilism
  - Positivism
  - Pragmatism
  - Realism (Philosophy)
  - Reductionism
  - Skepticism
  - Structuralism
- RT Beliefs
  - Cognition
  - Concept Formation
  - Dogmatism
  - Epistemology
  - Knowledge
  - Methodology (Philosophical)
  - Nominalism
  - Organicism
  - Praxis
  - Rationalism
  - Relativism
  - Science
  - Sociology of Knowledge

Epistemology
- DC D266400
- SN The study or theory of knowledge. For specific theories, see Epistemological Doctrines and its associated terms.
- HN Formerly (1963-1985) DC 158500, Epistemology/Epistemological.
- BT Philosophy
- RT Cognition
  - Cognitive Development
  - Concept Formation
  - Dialectics
  - Epistemological Doctrines
  - Intellectual History
  - Learning
  - Methodology (Philosophical)
  - Nihilism
  - Sociology of Knowledge
  - Teleology

Equal Access
- Use Access

Equal Rights Amendment/ERA (1984-1985)
- HN DC 158582.
- Use Constitutional Amendments

Equal Rights for Women
- Use Womens Rights

Equalitarian/Equalitarianism (1968-1985)
- HN DC 158575.
- Use Egalitarianism

Equality
- DC D266700
- HN Formerly (1963-1985) DC 158570, Equal/Equality/Equalization.
- RT Access
  - Egalitarianism
  - Equity
  - Freedom
  - Human Rights
  - Inequality
  - Opportunities
  - Social Justice
  - Social Structure
  - Tokenism

Equation/Equations (1963-1985)
- HN DC 158600.
- Use Mathematics

Equatorial Guinea
- DC D267000
- HN Added, 1986.
- BT Sub Saharan Africa

Equilibrium/Equilibration (1963-1985)
- HN DC 158670
- Use Social Equilibrium

Equity
- DC D267300
- HN Formerly (1967-1985) DC 158760.
- UF Fairness (1984-1985)
- NT Distributive Justice
- RT Bias
  - Egalitarianism
  - Equality
  - Justice
  - Morality

Ergonomy/Ergonomic/Ergonomics (1969-1985)
- HN DC 158820.
- Use Biotechnology

Erhard Seminar Training (EST) (1983-1985)
- HN DC 158828.
- Use Sensitivity Training

Erikson, Erik Homburger
- DC D267600
- SN Born 15 June 1902 - .
- HN Formerly (1966-1985) DC 158850, Erikson, Erik H.

Eros (1970-1985)
- HN DC 158900, deleted 1986.

Erosion (1965-1985)
- HN DC 158902.
- Use Soil Conservation

Eroticism
- DC D267900
- HN Formerly (1965-1985) DC 158920, Erotic/Eroticism.
- RT Sexual Arousal
  - Sexual Behavior

Error of Measurement
- DC D268000
- HN Added, 1986.
- UF Measurement Error
- BT Errors
- RT Measurement
  - Quantitative Methods
  - Reliability
  - Sampling
  - Scores
  - Statistical Bias

Errors
- DC D268050
- HN Formerly (1963-1985) DC 159000, Error/Errors.
- UF Mistakes
- NT Error of Measurement
  - Research Design Error
- RT Accuracy
  - Failure
  - Fallacies
  - Judgment
  - Performance
  - Reliability
  - Truth

Estimation

Escalate/Escalating/Escalation/Escalations (1971-1985)
- HN DC 159600, deleted 1986.

Escape/Escapism/Escapist (1963-1985)
- HN DC 159700, deleted 1986. See now Imprisonment, Defense Mechanisms, or Avoidance.

Eskimo Languages
- Use Oriental Languages

Eskimos
- DC D268200
- HN Formerly (1964-1985) DC 159750, Eskimo/Eskimos.
- UF Inuit
- BT North American Cultural Groups
- RT Arctic Regions
  - Indigenous Populations

ESP
- Use Extrasensory Perception

Esperanto
- DC D268500
- SN Artificial language intended for international use, invented in 1877 by L. L. Zamenhof and based primarily on modern Romance Languages.
- HN Added, 1986.
- BT Languages

Espionage
- DC D268800
- HN Formerly (1966-1985) DC 159770.
- UF Spying
- RT International Relations
  - National Security
  - Secrecy

Establishment/Establishments (1971-1985)
- HN DC 159795.
- Use Ruling Class

Estate/Estates (1963-1985)
- HN DC 159800, deleted 1986. See now appropriate "Property" or "Social Class" terms.

Esteem (1963-1985)
- HN DC 159875.
- Use Self Esteem

Esthetic/Esthetics/Estheticism/Esthete (1963-1985)
- HN DC 160000.
- Use Aesthetics

Estimation
- DC D269000
- HN Formerly (1963-1985) DC 160040, Estimate/Estimates/Estimating/Estimation/Estimator.
- UF Statistical Estimation
- NT Magnitude Estimation
- RT Computation
  - Forecasting
  - Measurement
  - Prediction
  - Probability
  - Statistical Inference
  - Statistics

Estonian

Estonian Soviet Socialist Republic
- DC D269100
- HN Formerly (1966-1985) DC 160060, Estonia/Estonian/Estonians.
- BT Baltic States
  Union of Soviet Socialist Republics

Estrangement (1965-1985)
- HN DC 160080.
- Use Alienation

Ethical Education
- Use Moral Education

Ethics
- DC D269400
- SN Science of morals.
- HN Formerly (1963-1985) DC 160100, Ethic/Ethics/Ethical.
- UF Moral Philosophy
  Moral/Morals (1963-1985)
- NT Professional Ethics
  Protestant Ethic
- RT Accountability
  Altruism
  Beliefs
  Codes of Conduct
  Ethology
  Hedonism
  Machiavellianism (Personality)
  Means-Ends Rationality
  Moral Development
  Moral Education
  Moral Judgment
  Morality
  Nihilism
  Philosophical Doctrines
  Philosophy
  Praxeology
  Principles
  Religious Doctrines
  Responsibility
  Social Responsibility
  Standards
  Technology Assessment
  Theology
  Tolerance
  Truth
  Utilitarianism
  Values

Ethiopia
- DC D269700
- HN Formerly (1963-1985) DC 160110, Ethiopia/Ethiopian/Ethiopians.
- BT Sub Saharan Africa
- NT Addis Ababa, Ethiopia

Ethnic Businesses
- Use Minority Businesses

Ethnic Communities
- Use Ethnic Groups

Ethnic Groups
- DC D270000
- HN Formerly (1963-1985) DC 160125, Ethnic/Ethnically.
- UF Ethnic Communities
  Ethnos (1972-1985)
- BT Cultural Groups
- NT Anglo Americans
  Ethnic Minorities
  Ethnolinguistic Groups
- RT Acculturation
  Assimilation
  Biculturalism
  Black Community
  Blacks

Ethnic Groups (cont'd)
- RT Caste Systems
  Crosscultural Analysis
  Cultural Conflict
  Cultural Pluralism
  Culture
  Ethnic Identity
  Ethnic Neighborhoods
  Ethnic Relations
  Ethnicity
  Ethnocentrism
  Ethnography
  Ethnology
  Indigenous Populations
  Minority Groups
  Multicultural Education
  Race
  Religious Cultural Groups
  Social Anthropology
  Social Integration
  Subcultures
  Test Bias
  Traditional Societies
  Whites

Ethnic Identity
- DC D270300
- HN Formerly (1985) DC 160130.
- UF Racial Identity
- BT Identity
- RT Black Power
  Cultural Identity
  Ethnic Groups
  Ethnicity
  Ethnocentrism
  Ethnolinguistic Groups
  Group Identity
  Minority Groups
  Multicultural Education

Ethnic Minorities
- DC D270600
- HN Added, 1986.
- BT Ethnic Groups
  Minority Groups
- RT Biculturalism
  Cultural Pluralism
  Ethnic Neighborhoods
  Ethnic Relations
  Foreigners
  Plural Societies
  Racial Relations

Ethnic Neighborhoods
- DC D270900
- HN Added, 1986.
- UF Barrio/Barrios (1964-1985)
  Chinatown/Chinatowns (1973-1985)
- BT Neighborhoods
- NT Ghettos
- RT Black Community
  Central Cities
  Ethnic Groups
  Ethnic Minorities
  Ethnic Relations
  Residential Segregation

Ethnic Relations
- DC D271200
- HN Added, 1986. Prior to 1986 use Ethnic/Ethnically (DC 160125) and Relations/Relational (DC 382485).
- UF Interethnic Relations
- BT Intergroup Relations
- RT Biculturalism
  Class Relations
  Crosscultural Analysis
  Cultural Pluralism

Ethnography

Ethnic Relations (cont'd)
- RT Desegregation
  Ethnic Groups
  Ethnic Minorities
  Ethnic Neighborhoods
  Ethnicity
  Ethnocentrism
  Indigenous Populations
  Intercultural Communication
  Middleman Minorities
  Minority Groups
  Multicultural Education
  Nativism
  Racial Relations
  Religious Cultural Groups
  Social Integration
  Subcultures

Ethnicity
- DC D271500
- HN Formerly (1963-1985) DC 160135, Ethnicity/Ethnicism.
- RT Acculturation
  Crosscultural Analysis
  Cultural Conflict
  Cultural Pluralism
  Ethnic Groups
  Ethnic Identity
  Ethnic Relations
  Ethnocentrism
  Group Composition
  Immigrants
  Nativism
  Nativistic Movements
  Race
  Social Background
  Sociocultural Factors
  Traditionalism

Ethno- (1963-1985)
- HN DC 160155, deleted 1986.

Ethnobiology (1985)
- HN DC 160160.
- Use Social Anthropology

Ethnocentrism
- DC D271800
- SN An attitude or belief that assumes the inherent superiority or importance of one's own ethnic group or culture.
- HN Formerly (1964-1985) DC 160165, Ethnocentrism/Ethnocentric/Ethnocentricity.
- UF Cultural Bias
- BT Social Attitudes
- RT Bias
  Cultural Conflict
  Cultural Identity
  Cultural Relativism
  Ethnic Groups
  Ethnic Identity
  Ethnic Relations
  Ethnicity
  Foreigners
  Intercultural Communication
  Nationalism
  Nativism
  Nativistic Movements
  Sectarianism
  Stereotypes

Ethnography
- DC D272100
- SN Direct observation and descriptive study of the culture and way of life of particular societies.
- HN Formerly (1963-1985) DC 160175, Ethnography/Ethnographic/Ethnographical.

Ethnolinguistic   European

Ethnography (cont'd)
- **BT** Anthropology
- **RT** Crosscultural Analysis
  Cultural Groups
  Culture
  Customs
  Ethnic Groups
  Ethnolinguistics
  Ethnology
  Fieldwork
  Folk Culture
  Folklore
  Kinship
  Oral History
  Social Anthropology
  Sociocultural Factors
  Traditional Societies
  Traditions

Ethnolinguistic Groups
- **DC** D272400
- **HN** Added, 1986.
- **UF** Anglophone/Anglophones (1982-1985)
  Francophone/Francophones (1982-1985)
- **BT** Ethnic Groups
- **NT** Linguistic Minorities
- **RT** Cultural Groups
  Cultural Identity
  Cultural Pluralism
  Ethnic Identity
  Intercultural Communication
  Language
  Language Usage

Ethnolinguistics
- **DC** D272700
- **SN** Study of culture and society through the intermediary of language.
- **HN** Added, 1986.
- **BT** Sociolinguistics
- **RT** Ethnography
  Ethnology
  Language
  Social Anthropology

Ethnologist/Ethnologists (1964-1985)
- **HN** DC 160188.
- **Use** Anthropologists

Ethnology
- **DC** D273000
- **SN** Scientific, historical, or comparative study of the origins, characteristics, and functioning of human cultures and societies.
- **HN** Formerly (1963-1985) DC 160200, Ethnology/Ethnologic/Ethnological.
- **BT** Anthropology
- **RT** Crosscultural Analysis
  Culture
  Customs
  Ethnic Groups
  Ethnography
  Ethnolinguistics
  Folk Culture
  Folklore
  Kinship
  Myths
  Social Anthropology
  Sociocultural Factors
  Traditional Societies
  Traditions

Ethnomethodology
- **DC** D273100
- **SN** Initiated by Harold Garfinkel and his students in the mid-1960s, systematic investigation of the methods people use in everyday life to understand and communicate socially, including those of sociologists and other scientists.
- **HN** Formerly (1977-1985) DC 160201, Ethnomethodology/Ethnomethodological.
- **BT** Social Science Research
- **RT** Conversation
  Conversational Analysis
  Everyday Life
  Fieldwork
  Participant Observation
  Phenomenology
  Reflexivity
  Social Interaction
  Sociology
  Symbolic Interactionism
  Verbal Accounts

Ethnos (1972-1985)
- **HN** DC 160205.
- **Use** Ethnic Groups

Ethology
- **DC** D273300
- **SN** Study of the causality and functions of human and animal behavior and the influence on behavior of genetic, physiological, and ecological variables.
- **HN** Formerly (1967-1985) DC 160207, Ethology/Ethologic/Ethological.
- **BT** Behavioral Sciences
  Biological Sciences
- **RT** Behavior
  Ecology
  Ethics
  Evolution
  Genetics
  Norms
  Sociobiology

Ethos (1963-1985)
- **HN** DC 160210.
- **Use** Worldview

Etiology
- **DC** D273600
- **SN** Study of causes or origins, especially of conditions considered abnormal.
- **HN** Formerly (1963-1985) DC 160237, Etiology/Etiological.
- **RT** Causality
  Delinquency
  Diseases
  Disorders
  Social Problems

Etymology
- **DC** D273900
- **HN** Formerly (1964-1985) DC 160245, Etymology/Etymological.
- **BT** Linguistics
- **RT** Definitions
  Languages
  Semantics
  Words

Etzioni, Amitai Werner
- **DC** D274200
- **SN** Born 4 January 1929 - .
- **HN** Formerly (1970-1985) DC 160247, Etzioni, A.

Eugenics
- **DC** D274500
- **SN** The study or process of improving offspring by selective breeding, especially with regard to human parents.
- **HN** Formerly (1963-1985) DC 160250, Eugenic/Eugenics.
- **BT** Genetics
- **RT** Agricultural Research
  Animal Husbandry
  Bioethics
  Biology
  Family Planning
  Health Policy
  Nazism
  Population Policy
  Race
  Reproductive Technologies
  Scientific Research
  Social Darwinism

Eurasia
- **DC** D274800
- **HN** Formerly (1963-1985) DC 160257, Eurasia/Eurasian/Eurasians.
- **NT** Asia
  Europe

Eurasian Languages
- **Use** Oriental Languages

Europe
- **DC** D275100
- **HN** Formerly (1963-1985) DC 160270.
- **BT** Eurasia
- **NT** Balkan States
  Eastern Europe
  Germany
  Prussia
  Western Europe
- **RT** European Cultural Groups
  Mediterranean Countries

European Community (1981-1985)
- **HN** DC 160288.
- **Use** European Economic Community

European Cultural Groups
- **DC** D275400
- **HN** Added, 1986. Prior to 1986, concepts representing special European cultural groups, eg, Italians, were often indexed under terms representing the geographic place name, eg, Italy/Italian/Italians.
- **BT** Cultural Groups
- **NT** Gypsies
- **RT** Europe
  Indoeuropean Languages
  Judeo-Christian Tradition
  Soviet Union Cultural Groups
  Western Civilization

European Economic Community
- **DC** D275700
- **HN** Formerly (1963-1985) DC 160292.
- **UF** Common Market (1964-1985)
  European Community (1981-1985)
- **BT** International Economic Organizations
- **RT** Economic Policy
  International Alliances
  Trade

European/Europeans/Europeanization (1963-1985)
- **HN** DC 160285, deleted 1986.

Euthanasia

Euthanasia
- **DC** D276000
- **HN** Formerly (1969-1985) DC 160296.
- **UF** Mercy Killing
- **BT** Homicide
- **RT** Death
  Terminal Illness

Evaluation
- **DC** D276140
- **SN** A context-dependent term for the process of assigning values to objects or events.
- **HN** Formerly (1963-1985) DC 160300, Evaluation/Evaluations/Evaluative.
- **UF** Appraisal/Appraisals (1965-1985)
  Assess/Assesses/Assessment/Assessments/Assessing (1964-1985)
  Performance Evaluation
- **NT** Criticism
  Needs Assessment
  Peer Review
  Program Evaluation
  Risk Assessment
  Self Evaluation
  Social Impact Assessment
  Teacher Evaluation
  Technology Assessment
- **RT** Achievement
  Analysis
  Criteria
  Decision Making
  Effectiveness
  Evaluation Research
  Failure
  Forecasting
  Goals
  Judgment
  Measures (Instruments)
  Observation
  Performance
  Qualitative Methods
  Quality
  Rational Choice
  Research
  Standards
  Success
  Tests
  Verification

Evaluation Research
- **DC** D276150
- **HN** Added, 1986.
- **BT** Action Research
- **RT** Evaluation
  Programs

Evangelism
- **DC** D276300
- **HN** Formerly (1964-1985) DC 160320, Evangelism/Evangelical.
- **UF** Televangelism
- **RT** Bible
  Proselytism
  Protestantism
  Religious Fundamentalism
  Religious Revivalism
  Sermons

Evans-Pritchard, Sir Edward Evan
- **DC** D276600
- **SN** Born 1902 - died 11 September 1973.
- **HN** Formerly (1964-1985) DC 160330, Evans-Pritchard, E. E.

Event Structure Hypothesis (1963-1985)
- **HN** DC 160340, deleted 1986.

Event/Events (1981-1985)
- **HN** DC 160339, deleted 1986. See now Life Events or Phenomena.

Events
- **Use** Phenomena

Everyday Life
- **DC** D276900
- **HN** Formerly (1965-1985) DC 160350.
- **UF** Daily Life
- **BT** Life
- **RT** Common Sense
  Communities
  Ethnomethodology
  Family Life
  Interpretive Sociology
  Lebenswelt
  Life History
  Lifestyle
  Phenomenology
  Quality of Life
  Rurality
  Social Life
  Social Reality
  Urbanism

Eviction/Evictions (1969-1985)
- **HN** DC 160360, deleted 1986. See now Housing, Landlords, or Tenants.

Evidence (Legal)
- **DC** D277200
- **HN** Formerly (1966-1985) part of DC 160364, Evidence.
- **NT** Testimony
- **RT** Criminal Proceedings
  Expert Witnesses
  Legal Procedure
  Litigation
  Trials
  Witnesses

Evil
- **DC** D277500
- **HN** Formerly (1968-1985) DC 160370.
- **RT** Demons
  Devils
  Evil Eye
  Manicheism
  Sins
  Spirit Possession
  Voodooism
  Witchcraft

Evil Eye
- **DC** D277800
- **HN** Added, 1986.
- **BT** Superstitions
- **RT** Evil
  Faith Healing
  Magic
  Supernatural
  Witchcraft

Evolution
- **DC** D278100
- **SN** A context-dependent term for gradual change in accordance with inherent natural laws. Social Evolution is preferable for nonbiological phenomena.
- **HN** Formerly (1963-1985) DC 160600, Evolution/Evolutionist/Evolutionists.
- **UF** Phylogeny (1977-1985)
- **RT** Biological Factors
  Biology

Exchange

Evolution (cont'd)
- **RT** Creationism
  Darwinism
  Differentiation
  Ecological Models
  Ecology
  Ethology
  Evolutionary Theories
  Genetics
  Physiology
  Prehistoric Man
  Social Evolution
  Sociobiology
  Time

Evolutionary Theories
- **DC** D278200
- **SN** Various doctrines concerned with how societies change. These theories are of two main types: (1) those postulating that societies change from simple to progressively more complex forms of organization; and (2) those that view societies as adapting to their environments, analogous to Charles Darwin's theory of plant and animal development.
- **HN** Formerly (1963-1985) DC 160700, Evolutionary/Evolutionism.
- **BT** Theories
- **NT** Darwinism
  Social Darwinism
- **RT** Biology
  Cultural Change
  Evolution
  Functionalism
  Progress
  Revisionism
  Social Evolution
  Social Theories
  Sociobiology
  Sociological Theory
  Utopias

Examination/Examinations (1966-1985)
- **HN** DC 160800.
- **Use** Tests

Exchange (Economics)
- **DC** D278400
- **HN** Formerly (1963-1985) part of DC 160850, Exchange/Exchanges.
- **UF** Barter
- **RT** Commodities
  Economics
  Finance
  Marxist Economics
  Money
  Purchasing
  Sales
  Supply And Demand
  Trade
  Value (Economics)

Exchange Programs (International)
- **Use** International Cooperation

Exchange Theory
- **DC** D278700
- **SN** Theory that conceptualizes social interaction and social structure in terms of individualistic or collective exchange relations—the individualistic approach is predicated on the individual's expectation that actions toward others will have some commensurate return, while the collective approach focuses on shared expectations that individuals will fulfill their obligations to society rather than pursue self-interests.

Exchange

Exchange Theory (cont'd)
- HN Formerly (1985) DC 160857. Prior to 1985 use DC 160850, Exchange/Exchanges.
- UF Social Exchange
- BT Social Theories
- RT Patronage
  Reciprocity
  Rewards
  Social Behavior
  Social Interaction
  Social Networks
  Social Power
  Social Relations
  Utilitarianism

Exchange Value
- Use Labor Theory of Value

Exchange Value Theory (1964-1985)
- HN DC 160860, deleted 1986. See now Exchange Theory or Labor Theory of Value.

Excitation (1963-1985)
- HN DC 161000.
- Use Sexual Arousal

Executive Boards
- Use Governing Boards

Executives
- DC D279000
- HN Formerly (1963-1985) DC 161890, Executive/Executives.
- BT Administrators
- RT Business
  Businessmen
  Directors
  Enterprises
  Entrepreneurship
  Management

Exercise
- Use Physical Fitness

Exhaustion
- Use Fatigue

Exhibitionism
- HN Formerly (1964-1985) part of DC 161910, Exhibition/Exhibitions/Exhibitionism.
- Use Sexual Deviation

Existence
- DC D279100
- HN Formerly (1963-1985) DC 161920.
- RT Birth
  Discovery
  Existentialism
  Experience
  Life
  Metaphysics
  Phenomena
  Reality

Existential (1963-1985)
- HN DC 161945, deleted 1986. See now Existence or Existentialism.

Existentialism
- DC D279150
- SN A modern philosophical movement that holds that individuals are responsible for how they choose to live their lives. It is a reaction to rationalistic or scientific approaches to behavior and stresses the uniqueness of individual religious and ethical experiences.

Existentialism (cont'd)
- HN Formerly (1963-1985) DC 161970, Existentialism/Existentialist.
- BT Epistemological Doctrines
  Philosophical Doctrines
- RT Alienation
  Anomie
  Cultural Relativism
  Existence
  Meaning
  Phenomenology
  Relativism
  Structuralism

Exogamous/Exogamy (1963-1985)
- HN DC 162505.
- Use Intermarriage

Expansion (1964-1985)
- HN DC 162510, deleted 1986. See now Development and its associated terms.

Expectancies
- Use Expectations

Expectations
- DC D279300
- HN Formerly (1963-1985) DC 162600, Expectations/Expectancy.
- UF Anticipation/Anticipatory (1964-1985)
  Expectancies
- RT Achievement
  Aspiration
  Attitudes
  Cognitive Mapping
  Life Plans
  Perceptions
  Performance
  Probability
  Relative Deprivation
  Salience
  Social Desirability

Expenditures
- DC D279600
- HN Formerly (1963-1985) DC 162650.
- UF Expenses
  Spending
- NT Government Spending
- RT Budgets
  Compensation
  Consumption
  Costs
  Economics
  Finance
  Fiscal Policy
  Income
  Money
  Payments
  Prices

Expenses
- Use Expenditures

Experience
- DC D279900
- SN A context-dependent term encompassing human responses to the environment.
- HN Formerly (1963-1985) DC 162700, Experience/Experiences.
- NT Work Experience
- RT Cognitive Development
  Crises
  Empathy
  Existence
  Individuals

Explanation

Experience (cont'd)
- RT Learning
  Lebenswelt
  Life
  Life Events
  Life Satisfaction
  Memory
  Participation
  Qualifications
  Salience
  Sensory Systems
  Subjectivity

Experimental Design
- Use Research Design

Experimental Replication
- Use Replication

Experimental Subjects
- Use Research Subjects

Experimentation
- Use Experiments

Experiments
- DC D280000
- HN Formerly (1963-1985) DC 163000, Experiment/Experimental/Experimentation/Experimentalism.
- UF Experimentation
- BT Methodology (Data Collection)
- RT Data Collection
  Empirical Methods
  Empiricism
  Hypotheses
  Informed Consent
  Laboratories
  Measurement
  Observation
  Replication
  Research
  Research Design
  Research Methodology
  Research Subjects
  Sampling
  Scientific Method
  Variables
  Verification

Expert Witnesses
- DC D280150
- HN Added, 1989.
- BT Experts
  Witnesses
- RT Evidence (Legal)
  Scientists
  Testimony

Experts
- DC D280200
- HN Formerly (1963-1985) DC 163600, Expert/Experts/Expertise.
- BT Specialists
- NT Expert Witnesses
- RT Advisors
  Consultants
  Intelligentsia
  Knowledge
  Scientists

Explanation
- DC D280400
- SN A context-dependent term for the process of making relatively valid accounts of human experience.
- HN Formerly (1963-1985) DC 163700, Explanation/Explanations/Explanatory.
- UF Elaboration (1965-1985)

Exploitation   Factionalism

Explanation (cont'd)
- **UF** Justify/Justified/Justifying/Justification (1972-1985)
- **RT** Causal Models
  - Causality
  - Dialectics
  - Hypotheses
  - Meaning
  - Teaching
  - Translation

Exploitation
- **DC** D280500
- **HN** Formerly (1965-1985) DC 163800, Exploitation/Exploiter/Exploiters.
- **RT** Colonialism
  - Economic Policy
  - Labor Process
  - Modes of Production
  - Oppression
  - Repression (Political)
  - Slavery
  - World System Theory

Explosion/Explosions (1964-1985)
- **HN** DC 164100, deleted 1986.

Export/Exports (1963-1985)
- **HN** DC 164295.
- **Use** Exports And Imports

Exports And Imports
- **DC** D280800
- **HN** Added, 1986.
- **UF** Export/Exports (1963-1985)
  - Import/Importing (1964-1985)
  - Tariff/Tariffs (1963-1985)
- **RT** International Division of Labor
  - Protectionism
  - Shipping Industry
  - Trade
  - World Economy

Exposure/Exposures (1964-1985)
- **HN** DC 164300, deleted 1986. See now Mass Media, Self Disclosure, or Experience.

Expressivity
- **Use** Self Expression

Expropriation
- **DC** D281100
- **HN** Formerly (1969-1985) DC 164560, Expropriation/Expropriations.
- **BT** Appropriation
- **NT** Nationalization
- **RT** Collectivization
  - Forces And Relations of Production
  - Ownership
  - Property

Extended Family
- **DC** D281400
- **HN** Formerly (1985) DC 171625, Family, Extended.
- **BT** Family
- **RT** Family Size
  - Family Structure
  - Intergenerational Relations
  - Kinship
  - Relatives

Extension Services
- **DC** D281500
- **HN** Formerly (1963-1985) part of DC 164900, Extend/Extended/Extension/Extensions.
- **UF** Agricultural Extension

Extension Services (cont'd)
- **UF** Cooperative Extension Services
  - County Extension Services
- **BT** Public Services
- **RT** Agricultural Development
  - Agricultural Technology
  - Community Development
  - Rural Areas
  - Rural Development

External Debt
- **Use** Public Debt

External/Externalization/Externals (1971-1985)
- **HN** DC 164925, deleted 1986.

Extinction (1963-1985)
- **HN** DC 165000, deleted 1986.

Extramarital Sexuality
- **DC** D281600
- **HN** Formerly (1963-1985) DC 167900, Extra/Extras.
- **UF** Adultery (1968-1985)
  - Infidelity (1964-1985)
  - Swing/Swinger/Swingers/Swinging (1970-1985)
- **BT** Sexual Behavior
- **RT** Marital Relations
  - Premarital Sex
  - Promiscuity
  - Sexual Intercourse
  - Sexual Permissiveness
  - Sexuality

Extrasensory Perception
- **DC** D281700
- **HN** Formerly (1965-1985) DC 168000.
- **UF** Clairvoyance
  - ESP
  - Mental Telepathy
  - Precognition
- **BT** Parapsychology
- **RT** Divination

Extraterrestrial Space
- **DC** D282000
- **HN** Formerly (1969-1985) DC 167990, Extraterrestrial.
- **UF** Outer Space
- **BT** Space
- **RT** Space Technology
  - Unidentified Flying Objects

Extremism
- **DC** D282300
- **HN** Formerly (1964-1985) DC 168800, Extreme/Extremes/Extremism/Extremist/Extremists.
- **UF** Fanatic/Fanatics/Fanaticism (1964-1985)
  - Political Extremism
- **BT** Political Ideologies
- **RT** Left Wing Politics
  - Polarization
  - Radicalism
  - Right Wing Politics
  - Schism
  - Vigilantism

Extroversion (1964-1985)
- **HN** DC 169000.
- **Use** Personality Traits

Exurbia/Exurbias/Exurbians (1965-1985)
- **HN** DC 169200, deleted 1986.

Eye Contact
- **DC** D282600
- **HN** Formerly (1966-1985) DC 170000, Eye/Eyes.
- **UF** Gaze
- **BT** Nonverbal Communication
- **RT** Vision

Eyewitnesses
- **Use** Witnesses

Eysenck, Hans Jurgen
- **DC** D282900
- **SN** Born 14 March 1916 - .
- **HN** Formerly (1967-1985) DC 170800, Eysenck, H. J.

F Scale
- **DC** D283000
- **HN** Formerly (1983-1985) DC 191400, F-Scale.
- **UF** California F-Scale
- **BT** Scales
- **RT** Attitude Measures
  - Authoritarianism (Psychology)
  - Fascism

Fable/Fables (1973-1985)
- **HN** DC 170860.
- **Use** Folklore

Face to Face (1963-1985)
- **HN** DC 170874.
- **Use** Social Interaction

Facial Expression/Facial Expressions (1965-1985)
- **HN** DC 170900.
- **Use** Nonverbal Communication

Facilities
- **DC** D283100
- **SN** A context-dependent term for buildings or spaces designed, built, or established to perform a specific function.
- **HN** Formerly (1968-1985) DC 170910, Facility/Facilities.
- **NT** Buildings
  - Centers
  - Clinics
  - Factories
  - Hospitals
  - Hotels
  - Laboratories
  - Museums
  - Nuclear Reactors
  - Places of Worship
  - Prisons
  - Recreational Facilities
  - Residential Institutions
  - Schools
  - Shelters
  - Stores
- **RT** Housing
  - Institutions
  - Maintenance

Fact/Facts (1963-1985)
- **HN** DC 170930.
- **Use** Phenomena

Factionalism
- **DC** D283200
- **HN** Formerly (1963-1985) DC 170940, Faction/Factions/Factional/Factionalism.
- **RT** Cleavage
  - Partisanship

Factor

Factionalism (cont'd)
- RT Polarization
  Political Parties
  Sectarianism
  Social Conflict
  Social Segmentation

Factor Analysis
- DC D283300
- SN Statistical method for identifying any underlying factors common to a large number of interrelated variables.
- HN Formerly (1963-1985) DC 171000, Factor Analysis/Factor Analytic.
- BT Multivariate Analysis
- RT Cluster Analysis
  Correlation
  Dimensional Analysis
  Discriminant Analysis
  Items (Measures)
  Latent Structure Analysis
  Path Analysis
  Statistical Inference
  Variance (Statistics)

Factor Structure
- DC D283400
- SN Internal structure of the underlying factors common to a large number of interrelated variables. See also Factor Analysis.
- HN Formerly (1963-1985) part of DC 170995, Factor/Factors/Factorial.
- UF Factorial Structure
- BT Structure
- RT Psychological Factors
  Psychosocial Factors
  Scales

Factorial Structure
- Use Factor Structure

Factories
- DC D283500
- HN Formerly (1963-1985) DC 171030, Factory/Factories.
- UF Industrial Plants
- BT Facilities
- NT Workshops (Manufacturing)
- RT Enterprises
  Industrial Enterprises
  Manufacturing Industries
  Plant Closure
  Workplaces

Factory Closure
- Use Plant Closure

Factory Workers
- Use Industrial Workers

Faculty (College)
- Use College Faculty

Faculty Evaluation
- Use Teacher Evaluation

Faculty Tenure
- Use Academic Tenure

Fads
- DC D283800
- HN Formerly (1966-1985) DC 171055, Fad/Fads.
- BT Mass Behavior
- RT Fashions

Faeroe Islands
- DC D284100
- HN Formerly (1964-1985) DC 173250, Faroe Islands.
- BT Denmark
  Scandinavia
  Western Europe

Faerose (Language)
- Use Germanic Languages

Failure
- DC D284400
- HN Formerly (1963-1985) DC 171100, Failure/Failures.
- BT Performance
- RT Achievement
  Aspiration
  Effectiveness
  Errors
  Evaluation
  Goals
  Motivation
  Quality
  Success

Fairness (1984-1985)
- HN DC 171147.
- Use Equity

Fairy Tales
- Use Folklore

Faith Healing
- DC D284700
- SN Healing through any spiritual, magical, symbolic, ritualistic, or other nonmedical means.
- HN Added, 1986. Prior to 1986 use DC 207600, Heal/Healer/Healers/Healing.
- UF Religious Healing
- BT Treatment
- RT Evil Eye
  Magic
  Religious Beliefs
  Shamanism
  Traditional Medicine

Faith/Faiths (1963-1985)
- HN DC 171165.
- Use Religions

Falkland Islands
- DC D285000
- HN Added, 1986.
- RT South America
  South Atlantic Ocean

Fallacies
- DC D285100
- HN Formerly (1969-1985) DC 171185, Fallacy/Fallacies.
- RT Errors
  Propositions
  Reasoning
  Truth
  Validity

Fallout (1964-1985)
- HN DC 171200, deleted 1986.

False/Falsity/Falsehood/Falsehoods/Falsification (1966-1985)
- HN DC 171275, deleted 1986. See now Deception or Falsification.

Family

Falsehoods
- Use Deception

Falsification
- DC D285200
- SN A criterion for scientific statements, introduced by Karl Raimund Popper, whereby hypotheses are meaningful only if they can withstand tests to empirically falsify them. If the hypotheses are proved false, they are replaced by new ones, which are in turn subjected to falsification tests.
- HN Formerly (1966-1985) part of DC 171275, False/Falsity/Falsehood/Falsehoods/Falsification.
- RT Hypotheses
  Positivism
  Research Methodology
  Verification

Familial (1963-1985)
- HN DC 171325, deleted 1986. See now appropriate "Family" terms.

Familism
- DC D285300
- SN A social system in which the family group is the basic and most important element, and in which family solidarity and obligations are greatly respected.
- HN Formerly (1963-1985) DC 171370, Familism/Familistic.
- RT Family
  Family Relations

Family
- DC D285600
- SN Social group consisting of two or more individuals related biologically or by marriage.
- HN Formerly (1963-1985) DC 171600, Family/Families.
- BT Social Institutions
- NT Black Family
  Dual Career Family
  Extended Family
  Matrifocal Family
  Nuclear Family
  Single Parent Family
  Stem Family
  Stepfamily
- RT Biological Factors
  Clans
  Familism
  Family Businesses
  Family Conflict
  Family Farms
  Family Life
  Family Planning
  Family Policy
  Family Power
  Family Relations
  Family Research
  Family Size
  Family Stability
  Family Structure
  Family Therapy
  Family Violence
  Family Work Relationship
  Genealogy
  Group Composition
  Heads of Households
  Home Environment
  Households
  Kinship
  Marriage
  Marriage And Family Education

Family

Family (cont'd)
- RT Matrilocal Residence
- Patrilocal Residence
- Primary Groups
- Relatives
- Significant Others
- Twins

Family Background
- Use Social Background

Family Businesses
- DC D285700
- HN Added, 1989.
- UF Family Firms
- BT Enterprises
- RT Entrepreneurship
- Family
- Family Farms
- Family Work Relationship
- Minority Businesses
- Small Businesses

Family Conflict
- DC D285800
- HN Added, 1989.
- BT Conflict
- RT Competition
- Dissent
- Family
- Family Power
- Family Relations
- Family Stability
- Family Violence
- Generational Differences
- Home Environment
- Intergenerational Relations
- Parent Child Relations
- Social Problems

Family Division of Labor
- Use Sexual Division of Labor

Family Dynamics
- Use Family Relations

Family Environment
- Use Home Environment

Family Farms
- DC D285900
- HN Added, 1986.
- BT Farms
- RT Family
- Family Businesses
- Part Time Farming
- Rural Population
- Small Farms

Family Firms
- Use Family Businesses

Family Income
- Use Income

Family Life
- DC D286200
- HN Formerly (1963-1985) DC 171700, Family Living/Family Life.
- BT Life
- RT Adult Children
- Adults
- Black Family
- Children
- Cohabitation
- Everyday Life
- Family
- Family Relations
- Family Role

Family Life (cont'd)
- RT Family Work Relationship
- Home Environment
- Home Workplaces
- Homemakers
- Housework
- Life Cycle
- Marital Relations
- Parent Child Relations
- Parents
- Quality of Life
- Siblings
- Social Life
- Social Reality

Family Life Education
- Use Marriage And Family Education

Family Planning
- DC D286500
- HN Formerly (1963-1985) DC 171750.
- BT Planning
- NT Birth Control
- RT Abortion
- Birth Spacing
- Childlessness
- Eugenics
- Family
- First Birth Timing
- Guidance
- Intrauterine Devices
- Population
- Social Planning

Family Policy
- DC D286800
- HN Added, 1986.
- BT Social Policy
- RT Child Custody
- Child Neglect
- Child Support
- Divorce
- Family
- Population Policy
- Welfare Policy
- Welfare Services

Family Power
- DC D287100
- HN Added, 1986.
- UF Marital Power
- Parental Power
- BT Power
- RT Family
- Family Conflict
- Family Relations
- Influence
- Marital Relations
- Parent Child Relations
- Social Power

Family Relations
- DC D287400
- HN Formerly (1963-1985) DC 382525, Relations, Family.
- UF Dynamics (Family)
- Family Dynamics
- Family Relationship
- BT Interpersonal Relations
- NT Parent Child Relations
- RT Adolescents
- Adult Children
- Attachment
- Dual Career Family
- Familism
- Family
- Family Conflict
- Family Life

Family Relations (cont'd)
- RT Family Power
- Family Role
- Family Stability
- Family Therapy
- Family Work Relationship
- Filial Responsibility
- Love
- Marital Disruption
- Marital Relations
- Nurturance
- Relatives
- Runaways
- Stepfamily
- Unwed Mothers

Family Relationship
- Use Family Relations

Family Research
- DC D287700
- HN Added, 1986.
- BT Research
- RT Family
- Social Science Research
- Sociological Research

Family Role
- DC D288000
- SN Refers to the various social roles within family structures (eg, mother, father, grandparent, child). Do not select in reference to the effects of the family as a whole on behaviors or social problems.
- HN Added, 1986.
- BT Roles
- RT Adult Children
- Children
- Family Life
- Family Relations
- Fathers
- Filial Responsibility
- Mothers
- Parent Child Relations

Family Size
- DC D288300
- HN Formerly (1985) DC 171800.
- BT Size
- RT Dependents
- Extended Family
- Family
- Family Structure
- Fertility
- Housing
- Nuclear Family
- Only Children
- Population Growth
- Single Parent Family

Family Stability
- DC D288500
- HN Added, 1989.
- BT Stability
- RT Family
- Family Conflict
- Family Relations
- Family Violence
- Father Absence
- Home Environment
- Marital Disruption
- Marital Relations
- Mother Absence
- Single Parent Family

Family

Family Structure
- DC D288600
- HN Added, 1986.
- BT Structure
- RT Base And Superstructure
  Black Family
  Childlessness
  Dual Career Family
  Extended Family
  Family
  Family Size
  Kinship
  Kinship Networks
  Matriarchy
  Nuclear Family
  Only Children
  Patriarchy
  Siblings
  Single Fathers
  Single Parent Family
  Social Structure

Family Therapy
- DC D288900
- HN Added, 1986.
- BT Treatment
- RT Behavior Modification
  Clinical Social Work
  Conjoint Therapy
  Counseling
  Family
  Family Relations
  Psychotherapy

Family Violence
- DC D289200
- HN Added, 1986.
- UF Conjugal Violence
  Domestic Violence
- BT Violence
- NT Child Abuse
  Spouse Abuse
- RT Abuse
  Assault
  Battered Women
  Child Neglect
  Elder Abuse
  Family
  Family Conflict
  Family Stability
  Home Environment
  Infanticide
  Sexual Abuse
  Social Problems
  Victimization

Family Work Relationship
- DC D289300
- SN Effects of employment on family life and reciprocal changes in work organization due, for example, to increasing numbers of dual-career families.
- HN Added, 1989.
- BT Relations
- RT Dual Career Family
  Family
  Family Businesses
  Family Life
  Family Relations
  Home Environment
  Home Workplaces
  Intergenerational Mobility
  Job Change
  Occupational Mobility
  Occupational Stress
  Parent Child Relations
  Social Class
  Work

Family Work Relationship (cont'd)
- RT Work Attitudes
  Work Leisure Relationship
  Worker Attitudes
  Working Mothers

Famine
- DC D289500
- HN Formerly (1964-1985) DC 171950, Famine/Famines.
- RT Food
  Hunger
  Malnutrition
  Natural Disasters
  Scarcity
  Starvation
  World Problems

Fanatic/Fanatics/Fanaticism (1964-1985)
- HN DC 171980.
- Use Extremism

Fanon, Frantz
- DC D289800
- SN Born 20 July 1925 - died 6 December 1961.
- HN Formerly (1966-1985) DC 171990.

Fantasy
- DC D290100
- HN Formerly (1965-1985) DC 172000, Fantasy/Fantasies.
- RT Defense Mechanisms
  Dreams
  Imagination
  Reality

Far East
- DC D290400
- HN Formerly (1963-1985) DC 172500, Far East/Far Eastern.
- UF East Asia
- BT Asia
- NT China
  Hong Kong
  Japan
  Macao
  Mongolia
  North Korea
  Peoples Republic of China
  South Korea
  Taiwan

Farm Animals
- Use Livestock

Farm Mechanization
- Use Agricultural Mechanization

Farm Production
- Use Agricultural Production

Farm Technology
- Use Agricultural Technology

Farm Tenancy
- Use Land Tenure

Farm Workers
- Use Agricultural Workers

Farm Youth
- Use Rural Youth

Farmers
- DC D290700
- HN Formerly (1963-1985) DC 173200, Farmer/Farmers.
- UF Agriculturists (1963-1985)
- BT Blue Collar Workers
- RT Agricultural Enterprises
  Agricultural Production

Fatalism

Farmers (cont'd)
- RT Agricultural Workers
  Agriculture
  Farms
  Part Time Farming
  Rural Population

Farming
- Use Agriculture

Farming Communities
- Use Rural Communities

Farming Systems
- Use Agrarian Structures

Farms
- DC D291000
- HN Formerly (1963-1985) DC 173000, Farm/Farms/Farming.
- UF Corn Belt Farms (1981-1985)
- BT Agricultural Enterprises
- NT Dairy Farms
  Family Farms
  Small Farms
- RT Agribusiness
  Agricultural Mechanization
  Agricultural Production
  Agricultural Technology
  Agricultural Workers
  Agriculture
  Farmers
  Land
  Land Tenure
  Part Time Farming

Fascism
- DC D291300
- SN Political ideology of military regimes, which glorifies state power and justifies policies on the basis of beliefs about the racial purity and superiority of the ruling group.
- HN Formerly (1963-1985) DC 173400, Fascism/Fascist.
- BT Political Ideologies
- NT Nazism
- RT Authoritarianism (Political Ideology)
  Dictatorship
  F Scale
  Militarism
  Totalitarianism

Fashion Industry
- Use Garment Industry

Fashions
- DC D291600
- HN Formerly (1965-1985) DC 173500, Fashion/Fashions/Fashionable.
- BT Mass Behavior
- RT Advertising
  Architecture
  Clothing
  Customs
  Fads
  Garment Industry
  Material Culture
  Norms
  Popular Culture

Fatalism
- DC D291900
- HN Formerly (1963-1985) part of DC 173650, Fatal/Fatalism/Fatalistic/Fatality/Fatalities.
- BT Beliefs
  Philosophical Doctrines
- RT Fate

Fatalities

Fatalities
- DC D292200
- HN Formerly (1963-1985) part of DC 173650, Fatal/Fatalism/Fatalistic/Fatality/Fatalities.
- RT Death
  Mortality Rates
  Suicide

Fatality Rates
- Use Mortality Rates

Fate
- DC D292500
- HN Formerly (1969-1985) DC 173600.
- UF Destiny (1969-1985)
  Predestination (1966-1985)
- RT Astrology
  Chance
  Fatalism
  Karma
  Religious Beliefs

Father Absence
- DC D292800
- SN Studies of the impact of missing father figures on family life and child development.
- HN Added, 1986.
- RT Divorce
  Family Stability
  Fathers
  Female Headed Households
  Males
  Marital Disruption
  Matrifocal Family
  Mother Absence
  Parent Child Relations
  Single Parent Family
  Unwed Mothers

Fathers
- DC D293100
- HN Formerly (1963-1985) DC 174000, Father/Fathers/Fatherhood/Fathering.
- UF Paternity (1967-1985)
- BT Parents
- NT Single Fathers
- RT Childrearing Practices
  Family Role
  Father Absence
  Grandparents
  Husbands
  Males
  Mothers
  Parent Child Relations
  Parental Attitudes
  Relatives
  Stepfamily

Fatigue
- DC D293400
- HN Formerly (1968-1985) DC 175000.
- UF Exhaustion
- BT Symptoms
- RT Health
  Human Body
  Sleep

Fauna
- Use Animals

Favela/Favelas (1972-1985)
- HN DC 175850.
- Use Slums

Fear
- DC D293700
- HN Formerly (1963-1985) DC 176000, Fear/Fears.
- UF Panic (1965-1985)
- BT Emotions
- NT Fear of Crime
  Phobias
- RT Anxiety
  Paranoia
  Security

Fear of Crime
- DC D294000
- HN Formerly (1984-1985) DC 176015.
- UF Crime Fear
- BT Fear
- RT Crime
  Crime Prevention
  Police Community Relations
  Victimization
  Victimology

Fecundity
- DC D294300
- SN Capacity and readiness to become pregnant. Do not confuse with Fertility.
- HN Formerly (1963-1985) DC 176100.
- RT Birth
  Birth Spacing
  Fertility
  Fertility Decline
  Pregnancy

Federal Bureau of Investigation/FBI (1984-1985)
- HN DC 176198.
- Use Government Agencies

Federal Government
- DC D294600
- HN Formerly (1963-1985) DC 176165, Federal/Federalism.
- BT Central Government
- RT Local Government
  States (Political Subdivisions)

Federal Housing Administration/FHA (1969-1985)
- HN DC 176220.
- Use Government Agencies

Federal Judiciary
- Use Judiciary

Federal Republic of Germany
- DC D294900
- HN Formerly (1963-1985) DC 193402, German/Germany/Germans/West Germany.
- UF West Germany
- BT Western Europe
- NT Berlin, Federal Republic of Germany
  Frankfurt, Federal Republic of Germany

Federations
- DC D295200
- SN Leagues formed by the union of constituent organizations.
- HN Formerly (1963-1985) DC 176250, Federation/Federations.
- UF League/Leagues (1964-1985)
- BT Organizations (Social)
- RT Coalitions
  Complex Organizations

Female

Feedback
- DC D295500
- HN Formerly (1963-1985) DC 176400.
- BT Interaction
- RT Communication
  Encouragement
  Learning
  Motivation
  Reciprocity
  Reinforcement
  Responses
  Sanctions

Feeding Practices
- DC D295800
- HN Formerly (1964-1985) DC 176450, Feeding.
- UF Eating Patterns
- BT Methods
- NT Breast Feeding
- RT Diet
  Eating And Drinking Establishments
  Eating Disorders
  Food
  Food Preparation
  Malnutrition
  Nutrition
  Obesity

Feeling/Feelings (1963-1985)
- HN DC 177000.
- Use Emotions

Fellowship (1978-1985)
- HN DC 177100, deleted 1986.

Fellowships And Scholarships
- DC D296100
- HN Formerly (1963-1985) DC 177200, Fellowships & Scholarships.
- RT Awards
  Scholarship
  Students

Female Headed Households
- DC D296300
- SN Family situations in which a single female is the primary manager and source of income.
- HN Added, 1989.
- BT Households
- RT Divorce
  Father Absence
  Heads of Households
  Single Parent Family
  Unwed Mothers
  Working Mothers
  Working Women

Female Homosexuality
- Use Lesbianism

Female Male Relations
- Use Opposite Sex Relations

Female Offenders
- DC D296400
- HN Added, 1986.
- BT Offenders
- RT Females
  Juvenile Offenders
  Prostitution

Female Roles
- Use Womens Roles

Females

Females
- **DC** D296700
- **HN** Formerly (1963-1985) DC 177300, Female/Females.
- **UF** Woman/Women (1963-1985)
- **NT** Battered Women
  Daughters
  Elderly Women
  Rural Women
  Working Women
- **RT** Affirmative Action
  Child Sex Preferences
  Female Offenders
  Femininity
  Males
  Mothers
  Opposite Sex Relations
  Sex
  Sex Role Identity
  Sex Roles
  Sex Stereotypes
  Sexual Inequality
  Womens Education
  Womens Groups
  Womens Rights
  Womens Roles

Feminine (1963-1985)
- **HN** DC 177395, deleted 1986. See now Females, Femininity, Feminism, or Sex Roles.

Femininity
- **DC** D297000
- **HN** Formerly (1964-1985) part of DC 177400, Femininity/Feminization.
- **RT** Androgyny
  Females
  Feminism
  Masculinity
  Sex Roles
  Womens Roles

Feminism
- **DC** D297300
- **HN** Formerly (1971-1985) DC 177410, Feminist/Feminists/Feminism.
- **UF** Womens Liberation Movement
- **BT** Social Movements
- **RT** Femininity
  Feminization
  Marital Relations
  Movements
  Sex Roles
  Sexism
  Sexual Inequality
  Solidarity Movements
  Womens Education
  Womens Groups
  Womens Rights
  Womens Roles
  Working Women

Feminization
- **DC** D297600
- **HN** Formerly (1971-1985) part of DC 177400, Femininity/Feminization.
- **RT** Feminism
  Sex Role Attitudes

Ferguson, Adam
- **DC** D297900
- **SN** Born 20 June 1723 - died 22 February 1816.
- **HN** Formerly (1967-1985) DC 177434.

Fertile (1963-1985)
- **HN** DC 177438, deleted 1986.

Fertility
- **DC** D298200
- **HN** Formerly (1963-1985) DC 177440.
- **UF** Natality (1968-1985)
- **BT** Rates
- **RT** Birth
  Birth Control
  Demographic Transition Theory
  Demography
  Family Size
  Fecundity
  Fertility Decline
  Nuptiality
  Population
  Population Growth
  Population Policy
  Pregnancy
  Sexual Reproduction

Fertility Decline
- **DC** D298250
- **HN** Added, 1989.
- **RT** Birth
  Birth Control
  Demographic Change
  Fecundity
  Fertility
  Population
  Population Growth

Festinger, Leon
- **DC** D298500
- **SN** Born 8 May 1919 - .
- **HN** Formerly (1963-1985) DC 177470.

Festivals
- **DC** D298800
- **HN** Formerly (1963-1985) DC 177500, Festival/Festivals.
- **UF** Carnival/Carnivals (1970-1985)
  Fiesta/Fiestas (1979-1985)
- **BT** Cultural Activities
- **RT** Celebrations
  Customs
  Holidays
  Rituals

Fetishism
- **DC** D299100
- **SN** The use of an object believed to be inhabited by a supernatural spirit, for magical purposes.
- **HN** Formerly (1970-1985) part of DC 177515, Fetish/Fetishes/Fetishism.
- **RT** Magic
  Supernatural
  Witchcraft
  Worship

Fetus
- **DC** D299400
- **HN** Formerly (1978-1985) DC 177504, Fetal/Fetus/Fetuses.
- **UF** Prenatal (1963-1985)
- **RT** Abortion
  Amniocentesis
  Personhood
  Pregnancy

Feudalism
- **DC** D299700
- **HN** Formerly (1963-1985) DC 177525, Feudal/Feudalism/Feudalist/Feudalistic.
- **BT** Economic Systems
  Political Ideologies
- **RT** Agrarian Structures
  Aristocracy

Fieldwork

Feudalism (cont'd)
- **RT** Middle Ages
  Modes of Production
  Peasant Societies
  Peasants
  Samurai

Feuds
- **DC** D300000
- **HN** Formerly (1976-1985) DC 177523, Feud/Feuds/Feuding.
- **UF** Blood Feuds
  Vendettas
- **BT** Social Conflict
- **RT** Homicide
  War

Feyerabend, Paul Karl
- **DC** D300100
- **SN** Born 13 January 1924 - .
- **HN** Added, 1989.

Fiction
- **DC** D300300
- **HN** Formerly (1963-1985) DC 177550.
- **UF** Detective Fiction
  Romances (Fiction)
  Science Fiction
- **BT** Literature
- **NT** Novels
  Short Stories
- **RT** Comics (Publications)
  Drama
  Fictional Characters
  Poetry
  Popular Culture

Fictional Characters
- **DC** D300600
- **HN** Added, 1986.
- **RT** Drama
  Fiction
  Films
  Heroes
  Literature
  Television

Fideist (1979-1985)
- **HN** DC 177570, deleted 1986.

Field (1963-1985)
- **HN** DC 177580, deleted 1986. See now Fieldwork or Academic Disciplines.

Field Research
- **Use** Fieldwork

Fieldwork
- **DC** D300700
- **SN** Empirical research involving the direct observation of subjects in their natural environment, rather than under laboratory or classroom conditions.
- **HN** Formerly (1982-1985) DC 177583, Field Work/Field Workers.
- **UF** Field Research
- **BT** Methodology (Data Collection)
- **RT** Ethnography
  Ethnomethodology
  Interviews
  Observation
  Opinion Polls
  Participant Observation
  Public Opinion Research
  Qualitative Methods
  Questionnaires
  Research
  Surveys

Fiesta　　　　　　　　　　　　　　　　　　　　　　　　　　　　　　　　　Fiscal

Fiesta/Fiestas (1979-1985)
- HN DC 177640.
- Use Festivals

Fight/Fights/Fighter/Fighters/ Fighting (1975-1985)
- HN DC 177800.
- Use Violence

Figuration Sociology
- DC D300800
- SN Introduced in 1939 by Norbert Elias, an empirical methodology for the study of historical change that integrates psychological and social-structural variables.
- HN Added, 1989.
- BT Sociology
- RT Action Theory
  Civilization
  History
  Individual Collective Relationship
  Social Change

Fiji Islands
- DC D300900
- HN Formerly (1963-1985) DC 178300, Fiji.
- BT Melanesia

Filial (1971-1985)
- HN DC 178375, deleted 1986. See now Filial Responsibility, Elder Abuse, or other appropriate "Family" terms.

Filial Responsibility
- DC D301200
- SN The obligation of adult offspring to provide economic and emotional support for elderly parents or relatives.
- HN Added, 1986.
- BT Responsibility
- RT Adult Children
  Adults
  Elder Abuse
  Elderly
  Family Relations
  Family Role
  Intergenerational Relations
  Parent Child Relations

Filipino/Filipinos (1964-1985)
- HN DC 178600, deleted 1986. See now Asian Cultural Groups or Philippines.

Film Industry
- Use Entertainment Industry

Films
- DC D301500
- HN Formerly (1963-1985) DC 179000, Film/Films.
- UF Cinema (1963-1985)
  Motion Pictures
  Movie/Movies (1963-1985)
- BT Audiovisual Media
  Mass Media
- RT Actors
  Cartoons
  Editors
  Fictional Characters
  Mass Media Effects
  Mass Media Violence
  Photographs
  Popular Culture
  Theater Arts
  Videotape Recordings
  Visual Arts

Finance
- DC D301800
- HN Formerly (1963-1985) DC 179260, Finance/Finances/Financial/Financing.
- BT Economics
- NT Public Finance
- RT Banking
  Bankruptcy
  Budgets
  Business
  Capital
  Costs
  Credit
  Debts
  Entrepreneurship
  Exchange (Economics)
  Expenditures
  Financial Support
  Income
  Industry
  Insurance
  International Economic Organizations
  Investment
  Loans
  Money
  Payments
  Prices
  Saving
  Taxation
  Trade
  Wealth

Financial Donations
- Use Contributions (Donations)

Financial Elite
- Use Economic Elites

Financial Problems
- Use Economic Problems

Financial Support
- DC D302100
- HN Added, 1986.
- UF Economic Support
  Financing
  Fund/Funds/Funding (1963-1985)
- BT Support
- NT Child Support
  Contributions (Donations)
  Foreign Aid
  Grants
  Subsidies
- RT Alimony
  Assistance
  Charities
  Dependents
  Finance
  Food Stamps
  Sponsorship
  Tithing

Financing
- Use Financial Support

Fine Arts
- DC D302400
- HN Added, 1986.
- BT Humanities
- NT Architecture
  Dance
  Music
  Theater Arts
  Visual Arts
- RT Art
  Art History
  Artists
  Cultural Activities
  Musicians

Finger Spelling
- Use Manual Communication

Finland
- DC D302700
- HN Formerly (1963-1985) DC 179530, Finland/Finnish.
- BT Baltic States
  Scandinavia
  Western Europe
- NT Helsinki, Finland

Finnish (Language)
- Use Oriental Languages

Fire
- DC D303000
- HN Formerly (1968-1985) part of DC 179600, Fire/Fires/Fireman/Firemen.
- RT Accidents
  Arson
  Disasters
  Fire Fighters
  Safety

Fire Fighters
- DC D303300
- HN Formerly (1968-1985) part of DC 179600, Fire/Fires/Fireman/Firemen.
- RT Emergencies
  Fire
  Police
  Public Officials

Firearms
- DC D303600
- HN Formerly (1984-1985) DC 179625.
- UF Gun/Guns (1969-1985)
  Handguns
  Small Arms
- BT Weapons
- RT Gun Control

Firing
- Use Dismissal

Firms
- DC D303900
- HN Formerly (1963-1985) DC 179780, Firm/Firms.
- UF Company/Companies (1963-1985)
- BT Enterprises
- RT Corporations

First Amendment (1971-1985)
- HN DC 179820.
- Use Constitutional Amendments

First Birth Timing
- DC D304200
- HN Added, 1986.
- RT Birth
  Birth Order
  Birth Spacing
  Family Planning
  Infants
  Marriage Timing

First International (1965-1985)
- HN DC 179830, deleted 1986.

Fiscal (1964-1985)
- HN DC 179910, deleted 1986. See now Fiscal Policy or Public Finance.

Fiscal

Fiscal Policy
- DC D304500
- HN Added, 1986.
- BT Economic Policy
  Government Policy
- RT Cost Containment
  Expenditures
  Government Spending
  Public Finance
  Public Policy
  Taxation

Fisheries
- Use Fishing

Fishermen
- DC D304800
- HN Formerly (1964-1985) DC 180000, Fisherman/Fishermen.
- BT Blue Collar Workers
- RT Fishing
  Fishing Communities

Fishing
- DC D305100
- HN Formerly (1963-1985) DC 180050.
- UF Fisheries
  Fishing Industry
- RT Fishermen
  Fishing Communities
  Industry
  Oceans

Fishing Communities
- DC D305400
- HN Added, 1986.
- UF Fishing Villages
- BT Communities
- RT Fishermen
  Fishing

Fishing Industry
- Use Fishing

Fishing Villages
- Use Fishing Communities

Fitness (1963-1985)
- HN DC 180075, deleted 1986.

Flag/Flags (1971-1985)
- HN DC 180450, deleted 1986.

Flanders
- DC D305600
- HN Added, 1986.
- BT Belgium

Flats (Housing)
- Use Housing

Flemish (1965-1985)
- HN DC 180690, deleted 1986. See now European Cultural Groups or Germanic Languages.

Flemish (Language)
- Use Germanic Languages

Flexibility
- DC D305700
- HN Formerly (1963-1985) DC 180800.
- UF Rigidity (1963-1985)
- RT Adjustment
  Compulsivity
  Coping
  Personality Traits
  Spontaneity

Flexible Working Hours
- Use Working Hours

Flight (1970-1985)
- HN DC 181500, deleted 1986.

Flood/Floods (1984-1985)
- HN DC 181535.
- Use Natural Disasters

Flora
- Use Plants (Botanical)

Florence, Italy (1965-1985)
- HN DC 181540, deleted 1986.

Florida
- DC D306000
- HN Formerly (1964-1985) DC 181550, Florida/Floridian/Floridians.
- BT Southern States
  United States of America
- NT Miami, Florida

Fluctuation/Fluctuations (1964-1985)
- HN DC 181560.
- Use Stability

Fluoridation
- DC D306300
- HN Formerly (1963-1985) DC 181585.
- RT Dental Care
  Public Health

Folk (1963-1985)
- HN DC 181620, deleted 1986. See now Folk Culture or Traditional Medicine.

Folk Culture
- DC D306600
- HN Added, 1986.
- BT Culture
- RT Anthropology
  Crafts
  Crosscultural Analysis
  Customs
  Dance
  Drama
  Ethnography
  Ethnology
  Folklore
  Literature
  Music
  Myths
  Nativism
  Nativistic Movements
  Peasant Societies
  Poetry
  Popular Culture
  Superstitions
  Traditional Medicine
  Traditional Societies
  Traditions

Folk Medicine
- Use Traditional Medicine

Folk Urban Continuum (1963-1985)
- HN DC 181800.
- Use Rural Urban Continuum

Folklore
- DC D306900
- HN Formerly (1963-1985) DC 181735, Folklore/Folkways/Folktales.
- UF Fable/Fables (1973-1985)
  Fairy Tales
  Legend/Legends (1963-1985)

Footnotes

Folklore (cont'd)
- UF Proverbs (1965-1985)
  Riddle/Riddles (1972-1985)
- RT Common Sense
  Culture
  Customs
  Ethnography
  Ethnology
  Folk Culture
  History
  Literature
  Myths
  Oral History
  Religions
  Traditional Medicine
  Traditions

Follower/Followers (1971-1985)
- HN DC 181970, deleted 1986.

Followup Treatment
- Use After Care

Food
- DC D307200
- HN Formerly (1963-1985) DC 182000.
- UF Cocoa (1967-1985)
  Corn (1963-1985)
  Maize (1964-1985)
  Rice (1969-1985)
  Sugar (1963-1985)
- RT Agriculture
  Diet
  Famine
  Feeding Practices
  Food Preparation
  Food Stamps
  Gardening
  Hunger
  Hunting
  Livestock
  Malnutrition
  Natural Resources
  Nutrition
  Plants (Botanical)

Food Industry
- DC D307300
- HN Added, 1989.
- BT Industry
- RT Agriculture
  Food Preparation

Food Preparation
- DC D307500
- HN Added, 1986.
- UF Cooking
  Culinary (1964-1985)
- RT Diet
  Feeding Practices
  Food
  Food Industry
  Home Economics
  Nutrition

Food Stamps
- DC D307800
- HN Formerly (1984-1985) DC 182030.
- BT Subsidies
- RT Child Welfare Services
  Financial Support
  Food
  Income Maintenance Programs

Footnotes (References)
- Use Citations (References)

Foraging

Foraging Societies
  Use Hunting And Gathering Societies

Force (1963-1985)
  HN DC 184600.
  Use Labor Force

Forced (1969-1985)
  HN DC 185000, deleted 1986.

Forces And Relations of Production
  DC D308000
  SN In Marxist analysis, determinants of the economy and all social processes. Forces of production include the means of production (eg, labor power, raw materials, tools, techniques, land); relations of production include ownership and control of the product.
  HN Added, 1986.
  UF Production Forces and Relations
   Relations of Production
   Social Relations of Production
  BT Relations
  RT Base And Superstructure
   Bourgeoisie
   Capitalism
   Class Relations
   Collectivism
   Economic Structure
   Economics
   Expropriation
   Historical Materialism
   Industrial Production
   Labor
   Labor Disputes
   Labor Process
   Management
   Marxism
   Marxist Economics
   Modes of Production
   Ownership
   Production
   Proletariat
   Property
   Reification
   Technological Progress

Forecasting
  DC D308050
  SN Scientific methods for predicting the future.
  HN Formerly (1969-1985) DC 185400, Forecast/Forecasts/Forecasting.
  UF Projections (Forecasting)
   Scenario/Scenarios (1984-1985)
  BT Prediction
  RT Decision Making
   Economics
   Effects
   Estimation
   Evaluation
   Futures (of Society)
   Reliability
   Risk Assessment
   Statistical Inference
   Time Series Analysis
   Trends

Foreign (1963-1985)
  HN DC 185500, deleted 1986.

Foreign Aid
  DC D308100
  SN Economic or other assistance, from the donating country's viewpoint.
  HN Added, 1986.
  UF Development Aid (Foreign)

Foreign Aid (cont'd)
  UF Economic Aid (Foreign)
   International Aid
  BT Assistance
   Financial Support
  RT Developing Countries
   Development Programs
   Economic Development
   Economic Policy
   Foreign Policy
   Government Spending
   International Relations
   World Economy

Foreign Debt
  Use Public Debt

Foreign Invasion
  Use Invasion

Foreign Language Learning
  Use Second Language Learning

Foreign Policy
  DC D308400
  HN Formerly (1984-1985) DC 185600.
  UF Diplomatic Policy
   International Policy
  BT Government Policy
  RT Diplomacy
   Foreign Aid
   Imperialism
   International Alliances
   International Relations
   Neutralism
   Political Science
   Protectionism
   Self Determination
   Soviet American Relations
   Treaties
   War

Foreign Workers
  DC D308700
  HN Added, 1986.
  UF Guestworker/Guestworkers (1982-1985)
  BT Workers
  RT Labor Market
   Labor Migration
   Migrant Workers
   Undocumented Immigrants

Foreigners
  DC D309000
  HN Formerly (1983-1985) DC 185800.
  UF Alien/Aliens (1984-1985)
  RT Citizenship
   Countries
   Ethnic Minorities
   Ethnocentrism
   Immigrants
   Immigration
   Indigenous Populations
   Nativism
   Nativistic Movements
   Strangers

Foremen
  DC D309300
  HN Formerly (1963-1985) DC 186000, Foreman/Foremen.
  UF Industrial Foremen
  BT Blue Collar Workers
  RT Industrial Management
   Managers

Formalization

Forensic Psychiatry
  DC D309600
  SN Psychiatry applied to the investigation of crime.
  HN Formerly (1964-1985) DC 186025, Forensic.
  BT Psychiatry
  RT Criminal Justice
   Criminology
   Legal Profession
   Penal Reform
   Social Psychiatry

Forest Management
  Use Forestry

Forestry
  DC D309900
  HN Formerly (1963-1985) part of DC 186050, Forest/Forests/Forestry.
  UF Forest Management
  RT Environmental Protection
   Industry
   Land Use
   Natural Resources
   Plants (Botanical)

Forests (Tropical)
  Use Tropical Regions

Forger/Forgers/Forgery (1964-1985)
  HN DC 186400.
  Use Fraud

Form/Forms (1972-1985)
  HN DC 186570, deleted 1986.

Formal Education
  Use Education

Formal Logic
  Use Logic

Formal Sociology
  Use Formalism

Formal Structure
  Use Structure

Formal/Formalized/Formality (1963-1985)
  HN DC 186580, deleted 1986.

Formalism
  DC D309975
  SN An approach to sociology, associated with Georg Simmel, that compares different cases of specific forms of social relationships (eg, competition examined in different societies or in different settings within the same society).
  HN Formerly (1963-1985) part of DC 186800, Formalism/Formalization.
  UF Formal Sociology
  RT Logic
   Mathematical Models
   Quantitative Methods
   Science
   Social Facts
   Social Structure
   Sociological Theory

Formalization (Theoretical)
  DC D310050
  HN Formerly (1963-1985) part of DC 186800, Formalism/Formalization.
  BT Theory Formation
  RT Operational Definitions
   Sociological Theory
   Sociology of Knowledge
   Theories

Formation

Formation
- **DC** D310125
- **SN** A context-dependent term for the process of forming, structuring, or composing.
- **HN** Formerly (1963-1985) DC 186880, Formation/Formations.
- **NT** Concept Formation
  Group Formation
  Impression Formation
  State Formation
  Theory Formation
- **RT** Development
  Social Processes

Formosa/Formosan/Formosans (1965-1985)
- **HN** DC 186900.
- **Use** Taiwan

Formula/Formulas (1963-1985)
- **HN** DC 187000, deleted 1986.

Formulation/Formulations (1964-1985)
- **HN** DC 187010, deleted 1986.

Foster Care
- **DC** D310200
- **SN** Childrearing by persons other than the natural parents, excluding adoption.
- **HN** Formerly (1984-1985) DC 187182.
- **BT** Social Services
- **RT** Caregivers
  Child Care Services
  Foster Children
  Guardianship
  Permanency Planning
  Placement
  Protection
  Surrogate Parents

Foster Children
- **DC** D310500
- **HN** Formerly (1984-1985) DC 187175, Foster/Fosters/Fosterage/Fosterhome/Fosterhomes.
- **BT** Children
- **RT** Adopted Children
  Child Welfare Services
  Foster Care
  Orphans
  Placement
  Stepfamily

Foucault, Michel
- **DC** D310800
- **SN** Born 15 October 1926 - died 25 June 1984.
- **HN** Formerly (1979-1985) DC 187185, Foucault, M.

Foundations
- **DC** D311100
- **HN** Formerly (1963-1985) DC 187200, Foundation/Foundations.
- **BT** Organizations (Social)
- **RT** Charities
  Grants
  Institutions
  Nonprofit Organizations
  Philanthropy
  Social Interest

Fractionation Methods (1965-1985)
- **HN** DC 187250, deleted 1986.

Fragmentation (1964-1985)
- **HN** DC 187400.
- **Use** Social Disorganization

Framework (1970-1985)
- **HN** DC 187480.
- **Use** Paradigms

France
- **DC** D311400
- **HN** Formerly (1963-1985) DC 187500, France/French.
- **BT** Mediterranean Countries
  Western Europe
- **NT** Corsica
  Paris, France

Franciscans
- **DC** D311700
- **HN** Formerly (1964-1985) DC 187550, Franciscan/Franciscans.
- **BT** Religious Orders
  Roman Catholics

Francophone/Francophones (1982-1985)
- **HN** DC 187560.
- **Use** Ethnolinguistic Groups

Frankfurt, Federal Republic of Germany
- **DC** D312000
- **HN** Formerly (1970-1985) DC 187600, Frankfurt, Germany.
- **BT** Federal Republic of Germany

Frankfurt Institute of Social Research
- **Use** Frankfurt School

Frankfurt School
- **DC** D312025
- **SN** A group of social scientists from the Institute of Social Research (1923-1950) of the University of Frankfurt whose ideas greatly influenced contemporary Marxism. Members of the School included Theodor W. Adorno, Erich Fromm, Max Horkheimer, and Herbert Marcuse.
- **HN** Formerly (1983-1985) DC 187650.
- **UF** Frankfurt Institute of Social Research
- **RT** Critical Theory
  Marxist Sociology
  Positivism
  Praxis
  Psychoanalytic Interpretation
  Revisionism
  Social Science Research
  Sociological Theory

Fraternal (1972-1985)
- **HN** DC 187678, deleted 1986.

Fraternities And Sororities
- **DC** D312300
- **HN** Added, 1986.
- **UF** Fraternity/Fraternities (1964-1985)
  Sorority/Sororities (1970-1985)
- **BT** Organizations (Social)
- **RT** College Students
  Professional Associations

Frequency

Fraternity/Fraternities (1964-1985)
- **HN** DC 187680.
- **Use** Fraternities And Sororities

Fratrilocal (1965-1985)
- **HN** DC 187700, deleted 1986.

Fraud
- **DC** D312600
- **HN** Formerly (1971-1985) DC 187712, Fraud/Frauds/Fraudulent/Fraudulence.
- **UF** Forger/Forgers/Forgery (1964-1985)
- **BT** Offenses
- **RT** Cheating
  Copyrights
  Deception
  White Collar Crime

Free (1966-1985)
- **HN** DC 187780, deleted 1986.

Free Market Economy
- **Use** Market Economy

Free Time (1963-1985)
- **HN** DC 187900.
- **Use** Leisure

Free Translation
- **Use** Translation

Freedom
- **DC** D312900
- **HN** Formerly (1963-1985) DC 187800.
- **UF** Liberty/Liberties (1963-1985)
- **NT** Academic Freedom
- **RT** Constraints
  Democracy
  Dictatorship
  Equality
  Human Rights
  Justice
  Repression (Political)
  Slavery
  Values

French Canada (1964-1985)
- **HN** DC 187905, deleted 1968. See now Quebec, Ethnolinguistic Groups, or other appropriate "Language" or "Culture" terms.

French Guiana
- **DC** D313200
- **HN** Formerly (1963-1985) DC 200290, Guiana/Guianan/Guianans.
- **BT** South America

French (Language)
- **Use** Romance Languages

French Polynesia
- **DC** D313500
- **HN** Added, 1986. Prior to 1986 use Polynesia (DC 340140).
- **BT** Polynesia
- **NT** Society Islands
  Tuamotu Archipelago
  Tubuai Islands

Frequency Distributions
- **DC** D313650
- **HN** Formerly (1963-1985) DC 187940, Frequency/Frequencies.
- **UF** Curve/Curves (1970-1985)
  Lorence Curves (1963-1985)
  Statistical Distributions
- **BT** Distribution
- **RT** Graphs
  Mean

Frequency Distributions (cont'd)
- RT Median
  - Parameters (Statistics)
  - Quantitative Methods
  - Reliability
  - Statistics
  - Tables
  - Variance (Statistics)

Freud, Anna
- DC D313800
- SN Born 3 December 1895 - died 8 October 1982.
- HN Formerly (1975-1985) DC 187990.

Freud, Sigmund
- DC D313810
- SN Born 6 May 1856 - died 23 September 1939.
- HN Formerly (1963-1985) part of DC 188000, Freud, Sigmund/Freudian/Freudianism.

Freudian Psychology
- DC D313850
- HN Formerly (1963-1985) part of DC 188000, Freud, Sigmund/Freudian/Freudianism.
- UF Freudianism
- BT Psychology
- RT Critical Theory
  - Mental Illness
  - Oedipal Complex
  - Personality
  - Psychoanalysis
  - Psychoanalytic Interpretation

Freudianism
- Use Freudian Psychology

Friendship
- DC D314100
- HN Formerly (1963-1985) DC 188500, Friend/Friends/Friendship.
- UF Companion/Companions/Companionship (1963-1985)
- BT Interpersonal Relations
- RT Affiliation Need
  - Cliques
  - Dating (Social)
  - Interpersonal Attraction
  - Intimacy
  - Peer Relations
  - Primary Groups
  - Rapport
  - Significant Others
  - Social Life
  - Social Support

Frigidity
- DC D314400
- HN Formerly (1964-1985) DC 188700.
- BT Sexual Behavior
- RT Orgasm
  - Sexual Dysfunction
  - Sexuality

Fromm, Erich
- DC D314700
- SN Born 23 March 1900 - died 18 March 1980.
- HN Formerly (1964-1985) DC 189900.

Frontier Areas
- Use Frontiers

Frontiers
- DC D315000
- HN Formerly (1963-1985) DC 190000, Frontier/Frontiers.
- UF Frontier Areas
- BT Geographic Regions
- RT Colonization
  - Land Settlement
  - Settlers

Frustration
- DC D315300
- HN Formerly (1963-1985) DC 191200, Frustration/Frustrations/Frustrating.
- BT Emotions
- RT Aggression
  - Anger

Fuels
- DC D315600
- HN Added, 1986.
- NT Coal
  - Petroleum
- RT Electricity
  - Energy
  - Energy Conservation
  - Energy Consumption
  - Energy Development
  - Energy Policy
  - Materials
  - Mineral Resources
  - Natural Resources

Fugitive/Fugitives (1965-1985)
- HN DC 191425, deleted 1986.

Fulfillment (1969-1985)
- HN DC 191431.
- Use Satisfaction

Function
- DC D315750
- SN A context-dependent term for the purpose or role of a phenomenon in a structure or system. In sociological analyses, the term Social Function is preferred.
- HN Formerly (1963-1985) part of DC 191500, Function/Functional/Functionalism/Functionalists.
- NT Social Function
- RT Activities
  - Behavior
  - Functionalism
  - Performance
  - Redundancy
  - Roles

Functional Analysis
- Use Functionalism

Functionalism
- DC D315800
- SN A philosophical doctrine emphasizing the adaptiveness of mental and behavioral processes to the total social environment, and the resulting systematic interdependence of all members of that environment.
- HN Formerly (1963-1985) part of DC 191500, Function/Functional/Functionalism/Functionalists.
- UF Functional Analysis
- BT Philosophical Doctrines
- RT Action Theory
  - Conflict Theory
  - Evolutionary Theories
  - Function
  - Holism

Functionalism (cont'd)
- RT Psychology
  - Religions
  - Social Equilibrium
  - Social Stratification
  - Social Structure
  - Social Theories
  - Structural-Functional Analysis
  - Systems Theory
  - Teleology

Functioning (1963-1985)
- HN DC 191540, deleted 1986. See now Coping, Deinstitutionalization, or other appropriate "Behavior" terms.

Fund/Funds/Funding (1963-1985)
- HN DC 191560.
- Use Financial Support

Fundamentalism (Religious)
- Use Religious Fundamentalism

Funerals
- DC D315900
- HN Formerly (1964-1985) DC 191580, Funeral/Funerals.
- BT Death Rituals
- RT Burials
  - Death
  - Death Attitudes
  - Religious Rituals

Further Education
- Use Adult Education

Future Orientations
- DC D316050
- HN Added, 1986.
- BT Orientation
- RT Futures (of Society)
  - Perceptions
  - Time

Futures (of Society)
- DC D316100
- HN Formerly (1964-1985) DC 191582, Future/Futurism/Futurist/Futurologist/Futurologists.
- UF Futurology
- RT Development
  - Forecasting
  - Future Orientations
  - Obsolescence
  - Planning
  - Prediction
  - Public Policy
  - Social Change
  - Social Indicators
  - Social Processes
  - Social Progress
  - Society
  - Technological Progress
  - Time

Futurology
- Use Futures (of Society)

Gabon
- DC D316200
- HN Added, 1986.
- BT Sub Saharan Africa

Gadamer, Hans Georg
- DC D316500
- SN Born 11 February 1900 - .
- HN Formerly (1980-1985) DC 191582c, Gadamer, H.

Galbraith　　　　　　　　　　　　　　　　　　　　　　　Generalization

Galbraith, John Kenneth
- DC D316800
- SN Born 15 October 1908 - .
- HN Formerly (1973-1985) DC 191582a, Galbraith, J. K.

Gallup Poll (1963-1985)
- HN DC 191585.
- Use Opinion Polls

Gambia
- DC D317100
- HN Formerly (1974-1985) DC 191640.
- BT Sub Saharan Africa

Gambling
- DC D317400
- HN Formerly (1963-1985) DC 191650, Gamble/Gambling/Gambler/Gamblers.
- UF Bet/Bets/Bettor/Betting (1964-1985)
  Compulsive Gambling
  Gaming
- RT Chance
  Offenses
  Organized Crime

Game Hunting
- Use Hunting

Game Theory
- DC D317650
- SN A set of mathematical theories that analyze and model the rational, strategic choices available to individuals or groups in conflict or competition with each other.
- HN Formerly (1963-1985) DC 192000.
- UF Gaming Models
- BT Decision Models
- RT Choices
  Competition
  Cybernetics
  Decision Making
  Probability
  Risk
  Simulation
  Theories

Games
- DC D317700
- HN Formerly (1963-1985) DC 191800, Game/Games/Gaming.
- BT Activities
- RT Play
  Recreation
  Sports

Gaming
- Use Gambling

Gaming Models
- Use Game Theory

Gandhi, Mohandas Karamchand
- DC D318000
- SN Born 2 October 1869 - died 30 January 1948.
- HN Formerly (1963-1985) DC 193890, Gandhi, Mahatma.

Gangs
- DC D318300
- HN Formerly (1963-1985) DC 192150, Gang/Gangs.
- BT Peer Groups
- RT Juvenile Offenders
  Youth Organizations

Gardening
- DC D318600
- HN Formerly (1971-1985) DC 192170.
- RT Agriculture
  Food
  Plants (Botanical)

Garfinkel, Harold
- DC D318900
- SN Born 29 October 1917 - .
- HN Formerly (1972-1985) DC 192182, Garfinkel, H.

Garment Industry
- DC D319200
- HN Added, 1986.
- UF Apparel Industry
  Clothing Industry
  Fashion Industry
- BT Manufacturing Industries
- RT Clothing
  Fashions
  Textile Industry

Garvey, Marcus Moziah
- DC D319500
- SN Born 17 August 1887 - died 10 June 1940.
- HN Formerly (1972-1985) DC 192185, Garvey, Marcus.

Gay (1984-1985)
- HN DC 192200.
- Use Homosexuality

Gay Relationships
- Use Homosexual Relationships

Gaze
- Use Eye Contact

Gehlen, Arnold
- DC D319800
- SN Born 29 January 1904 - died 30 January 1976.
- HN Formerly (1967-1985) DC 192240.

Gemeinschaft And Gesellschaft
- DC D319950
- SN Contrasting ideal types of Social Order, the first referring to small communal groups characterized by a sense of shared beliefs or Social Identity, the second referring to large groups characterized by impersonal or contractual relationships. Often associated with Rural Urban Differences and used in contrasting Traditional Society with Modern Society.
- HN Added, 1986.
- UF Gemeinschaft/Gemeinschafts (1963-1985)
  Gesellschaft (1963-1985)
- RT Communities
  Industrial Societies
  Industrialization
  Modern Society
  Rural Urban Differences
  Social Relations
  Sociological Theory
  Traditional Societies

Gemeinschaft/Gemeinschafts (1963-1985)
- HN DC 192300.
- Use Gemeinschaft And Gesellschaft

Gender Differences (1984-1985)
- HN DC 192374.
- Use Sex Differences

Gender Identity
- Use Sex Role Identity

Gender Inequality (1985)
- HN DC 192377.
- Use Sexual Inequality

Gender Stereotypes
- Use Sex Stereotypes

Gender/Genders (1972-1985)
- HN DC 192370.
- Use Sex

Genealogy
- DC D320100
- SN A detailed account of the ancestry of an individual or group
- HN Formerly (1963-1985) DC 192380, Genealogy/Genealogies/Genealogical.
- RT Chronologies
  Descent
  Family
  History
  Kinship
  Life History
  Lineage

General (1963-1985)
- HN DC 192390, deleted 1986.

General Medicine
- Use Medicine

General Public
- DC D320400
- HN Added, 1986.
- UF Mass Public
  Public (General)
- RT Citizens
  Civil Society
  Consumers
  Masses
  Public Opinion
  Public Policy
  Public Support
  State Society Relationship

General Systems Theory
- Use Systems Theory

General Theory of Action
- Use Action Theory

Generalization
- DC D320500
- HN Formerly (1963-1985) DC 192500, Generalization/Generalizations.
- BT Reasoning
- RT Abstraction
  Concept Formation
  Constructs
  Induction
  Inference
  Learning
  Propositions
  Research Methodology
  Scientific Method
  Specificity
  Statistical Inference
  Synthesis
  Theories
  Theory Formation
  Validity

Generation

Generation Gap
- **Use** Generational Differences

Generational Differences
- **DC** D320700
- **SN** Used in analyses in which a social problem or phenomenon is explained as a consequence or correlate of differences in similar populations from adjacent generations.
- **HN** Formerly (1963-1985) DC 193050, Generation/Generations/Generational.
- **UF** Generation Gap
- **BT** Differences
- **RT** Age Differences
  Age Groups
  Countercultures
  Family Conflict
  Intergenerational Mobility
  Intergenerational Relations
  Parent Child Relations
  Social Mobility

Generational Occupational Mobility (1975-1985)
- **HN** DC 193052.
- **Use** Intergenerational Mobility

Genetics
- **DC** D321000
- **HN** Formerly (1963-1985) DC 193065, Genetic/Genetically/Genetics.
- **UF** Heredity/Hereditary (1963-1985)
- **BT** Biological Sciences
- **NT** Eugenics
- **RT** Biological Factors
  Biology
  Blood Groups
  Congenitally Handicapped
  Darwinism
  Downs Syndrome
  Ethology
  Evolution
  Medical Technology
  Medicine
  Race
  Reproductive Technologies
  Social Darwinism
  Sociobiology

Geneva, Switzerland
- **DC** D321300
- **HN** Formerly (1963-1985) DC 193090.
- **BT** Switzerland

Genital Mutilation
- **DC** D321600
- **SN** Used in anthropological discussions of ritual surgical procedures performed on male and female genitalia.
- **HN** Added, 1986.
- **BT** Surgery
- **RT** Circumcision
  Customs
  Genitals
  Initiation Rites
  Rites of Passage

Genitalia
- **Use** Genitals

Genitals
- **DC** D321900
- **HN** Formerly (1964-1985) DC 193095, Genital/Genitals.
- **UF** Genitalia
- **RT** Castration
  Circumcision
  Genital Mutilation
  Human Body
  Venereal Diseases

Genius
- **DC** D322200
- **HN** Formerly (1982-1985) DC 193096, Genius/Geniuses.
- **BT** Intelligence
- **RT** Ability
  Achievement
  Gifted

Genocide
- **DC** D322500
- **HN** Formerly (1964-1985) DC 193100.
- **BT** Homicide
- **RT** Holocaust
  Nazism
  Political Violence
  Survival
  World War II

Genotype/Genotypic (1963-1985)
- **HN** DC 193110, deleted 1986.

Gens (1972-1985)
- **HN** DC 193112.
- **Use** Clans

Gentiles
- **DC** D322800
- **HN** Formerly (1964-1985) DC 193117, Gentile/Gentiles.
- **BT** Religious Cultural Groups
- **RT** Christians
  Jews
  Judaism

Geographer/Geographers (1967-1985)
- **HN** DC 193128.
- **Use** Social Scientists

Geographic Distribution
- **DC** D323100
- **HN** Formerly (1963-1985) part of DC 193130, Geographic/Geographical.
- **BT** Demography
  Distribution
- **RT** Geographic Mobility
  Geographic Regions
  Geography
  Migration Patterns
  Population Distribution
  Spatial Analysis

Geographic Mobility
- **DC** D323400
- **SN** Tendency or capacity of individuals to move from one geographic region to another, as distinguished from nomadism, relatively permanent migration, or widespread population shifts.
- **HN** Added, 1986. Prior to 1986 use Geographic/Geographical (DC 193130) and Mobility (DC 274000).
- **BT** Mobility
- **RT** Demographic Change
  Demography
  Geographic Distribution
  Geographic Regions
  Geography
  Internal Migration
  Migration
  Population
  Relocation
  Residential Mobility
  Social Mobility
  Travel

Geopolitics

Geographic Regions
- **DC** D323700
- **SN** See also specific geographic regions by name, eg, Middle East.
- **HN** Formerly (1963-1985) part of DC 377800, Region/Regions/Regional/Regionalism/Regionalization.
- **UF** Area/Areas (1963-1985)
  Regions (Geographic)
  Territories (Geographic)
- **NT** Arctic Regions
  Arid Zones
  Frontiers
  Mountain Regions
  Tropical Regions
- **RT** Borders
  Counties
  Countries
  Developing Countries
  Districts
  Geographic Distribution
  Geographic Mobility
  Geography
  Islands
  Low Income Areas
  Metropolitan Areas
  Nonmetropolitan Areas
  North And South
  Population
  Provinces
  Regional Development
  Regional Differences
  Regional Movements
  Regional Sociology
  Regionalism
  Rural Areas
  School Districts
  States (Political Subdivisions)
  Suburbs
  Urban Areas
  Weather

Geographic/Geographical (1963-1985)
- **HN** DC 193130, deleted 1986. See now specific "Geographic," "Regional," or "Area" terms.

Geography
- **DC** D324000
- **HN** Formerly (1963-1985) DC 193150.
- **UF** Social Geography
- **BT** Social Sciences
- **RT** Demography
  Earth (Planet)
  Geographic Distribution
  Geographic Mobility
  Geographic Regions
  Sociodemographic Factors
  Topography

Geology
- **DC** D324300
- **HN** Formerly (1977-1985) DC 193165.
- **UF** Mineralogy
  Paleontology (1969-1985)
- **BT** Physical Sciences
- **RT** Coal
  Mineral Resources
  Natural Resources
  Scientific Research

Geopolitics
- **DC** D324600
- **SN** Political analysis that emphasizes the importance of geographic factors for international relations.
- **HN** Formerly (1963-1985) DC 193175, Geopolitical/Geopolitics.

Georgia

Geopolitics (cont'd)
- **BT** Politics
- **RT** Countries
  Ideological Struggle
  International Alliances
  International Conflict
  Pan-Africanism

Georgia
- **DC** D324900
- **HN** Formerly (1964-1985) DC 193185, Georgia/Georgian/Georgians.
- **BT** Southern States
  United States of America
- **NT** Atlanta, Georgia
- **RT** Appalachia

Geriatrics
- **DC** D325200
- **HN** Formerly (1964-1985) DC 193200, Geriatric/Geriatrics.
- **BT** Medicine
- **RT** Elderly
  Gerontology

German Democratic Republic
- **DC** D325500
- **HN** Formerly (1963-1985) DC 193401, German/Germany/Germans/East Germany.
- **UF** East Germany
- **BT** Eastern Europe
- **NT** Berlin, German Democratic Republic

German (Language)
- **Use** Germanic Languages

Germanic Languages
- **DC** D325800
- **HN** Added, 1986.
- **UF** Afrikaans
  Danish (Language)
  Dutch (Language)
  Faerose (Language)
  Flemish (Language)
  German (Language)
  Icelandic (Language)
  Norwegian (Language)
  Swedish (Language)
- **BT** Indoeuropean Languages
- **NT** English Language

Germany
- **DC** D326100
- **SN** Use limited to Germany prior to 1945. See also Federal Republic of Germany or German Democratic Republic.
- **HN** Formerly (1963-1985) DC 193400, German/Germany/Germans.
- **BT** Europe
  Western Europe
- **NT** Berlin, Germany
- **RT** Prussia

Gerontocracy
- **DC** D326400
- **SN** Form of social organization in which the elderly or a council of elders dominate or excercise control by virtue of the wisdom associated with their age status.
- **HN** Formerly (1983-1985) DC 193580.
- **BT** Political Systems
- **RT** Elderly

Gerontology
- **DC** D326700
- **SN** Study of aging and the concerns of the elderly.
- **HN** Formerly (1963-1985) DC 193600.
- **BT** Social Sciences
- **RT** Aging
  Elderly
  Geriatrics
  Life Cycle
  Life Stage Transitions
  Psychology

Gesellschaft (1963-1985)
- **HN** DC 193750.
- **Use** Gemeinschaft And Gesellschaft

Gestalt Psychology
- **DC** D327000
- **HN** Formerly (1965-1985) DC 193800.
- **BT** Psychology
- **RT** Holism

Gesture/Gestures/Gestural (1963-1985)
- **HN** DC 193840.
- **Use** Nonverbal Communication

Ghana
- **DC** D327300
- **HN** Formerly (1963-1985) DC 193870, Ghana/Ghanaian/Ghanaians.
- **BT** Sub Saharan Africa

Ghettos
- **DC** D327600
- **HN** Formerly (1965-1985) DC 193895, Ghetto/Ghettos.
- **BT** Ethnic Neighborhoods
- **RT** Central Cities
  Community Structure
  Residential Segregation
  Slums

Ghost Dances
- **DC** D327900
- **HN** Formerly (1963-1985) DC 193897, Ghost Dance.
- **BT** Death Rituals
- **RT** Cults
  Ghosts
  Religious Beliefs
  Religious Rituals
  Spirits
  Supernatural

Ghosts
- **DC** D328200
- **HN** Formerly (1964-1985) DC 193896, Ghost/Ghosts.
- **BT** Spirits
- **RT** Ancestor Worship
  Death
  Ghost Dances
  Soul
  Spiritualism
  Supernatural
  Superstitions

Gibraltar
- **DC** D328500
- **HN** Added, 1986.
- **BT** Western Europe

Giddens, Anthony
- **DC** D328600
- **SN** Born 1939-.
- **HN** Added, 1989.

Gift Giving
- **DC** D328700
- **HN** Formerly (1963-1985) DC 193900, Gift/Gifts/Gifting.
- **RT** Altruism
  Celebrations
  Charities
  Christmas
  Contributions (Donations)
  Loans
  Philanthropy
  Potlatches
  Rituals
  Social Interaction

Gift of Tongues
- **Use** Glossolalia

Gifted
- **DC** D328800
- **SN** Especially intelligent or creative people.
- **HN** Formerly (1973-1985) DC 194500.
- **RT** Ability
  Academic Aptitude
  Genius
  Individuals
  Intelligence
  Skills
  Special Education

Gilbert And Ellice Islands
- **DC** D329100
- **HN** Formerly (1965-1985) DC 194800, Gilbert Islands.
- **BT** Micronesia

Gini, Corrado
- **DC** D329400
- **SN** Born 1884 - died 1965.
- **HN** Formerly (1963-1985) DC 195100.

Girl/Girls (1963-1985)
- **HN** DC 195200.
- **Use** Children

Given Names
- **Use** Naming Practices

Giving Help
- **Use** Helping Behavior

Glaser, Daniel
- **DC** D329700
- **SN** Born 23 December 1918 - .
- **HN** Formerly (1974-1985) DC 195490.

Glasgow, Scotland
- **DC** D330000
- **HN** Formerly (1965-1985) DC 195500.
- **BT** Scotland

Glazer, Nathan
- **DC** D330300
- **SN** Born 25 February 1923 - .
- **HN** Formerly (1968-1985) DC 195540, Glazer, N.

Global (1964-1985)
- **HN** DC 195575, deleted 1986. See now appropriate "International" or "World" terms.

Global Problems
- **Use** World Problems

Glossolalia
- **DC** D330600
- **SN** Spontaneous, often bizarre, speech during episodes of extreme religious fervor.

Glossolalia (cont'd)
- HN Formerly (1969-1985) DC 195650.
- UF Gift of Tongues
  Speaking in Tongues
- BT Religious Behavior
- RT Pentacostalists
  Religious Beliefs

Glueck Social Prediction Table (1964-1985)
- HN DC 195700, deleted 1986.

Goals
- DC D330900
- HN Formerly (1963-1985) DC 196000, Goal/Goals.
- UF Aims (1968-1985)
  Objectives
- NT Social Goals
- RT Achievement
  Anomie
  Aspiration
  Commitment
  Competition
  Cooperation
  Effectiveness
  Effects
  Evaluation
  Failure
  Intentionality
  Life Plans
  Means-Ends Rationality
  Motivation
  Needs
  Performance
  Planning
  Policy
  Priorities
  Quotas
  Relevance
  Resource Allocation
  Success

God (Judeo-Christian)
- DC D331200
- HN Added, 1986.
- BT Deities
- RT Bible
  Christianity
  Jesus Christ
  Judaism
  Judeo-Christian Tradition
  Rabbinical Literature
  Theology

God/Gods (1963-1985)
- HN DC 196150.
- Use Deities

Godparenthood
- DC D331500
- HN Formerly (1971-1985) DC 196250, Godparent/Godparents/Godparenthood.
- RT Compadrazgo
  Kinship
  Parents

Goethe, Johann Wolfgang von
- DC D331800
- SN Born 28 August 1749 - died 22 March 1832.
- HN Formerly (1963-1985) DC 196253, Goethe, Johann.

Goffman, Erving
- DC D332100
- SN Born 11 June 1911 - died November 1982.
- HN Formerly (1968-1985) DC 196254.

Goldmann, Lucien
- DC D332400
- SN Born 20 July 1913 - died 4 October 1970.
- HN Formerly (1969-1985) DC 196257, Goldmann, L.

Gompertz Curve (1969-1985)
- HN DC 196263, deleted 1986.

Gonorrhea
- Use Venereal Diseases

Good/Goods/Goodness (1964-1985)
- HN DC 196300, deleted 1986. See now Commodities, Public Goods, or Morality.

Goodman, Leo A.
- DC D332700
- SN Born 7 August 1928 - .
- HN Formerly (1976-1985) DC 196310.

Goodness
- Use Morality

Goods (Public)
- Use Public Goods

Gospel/Gospels (1967-1985)
- HN DC 196400.
- Use Bible

Gossip (1978-1985)
- HN DC 196460, deleted 1986. See now Conversation or Rumors.

Gouldner, Alvin Ward
- DC D333000
- SN Born 29 July 1920 - died 1982.
- HN Formerly (1964-1985) DC 196490, Gouldner, Alvin W.

Governing Boards
- DC D333200
- HN Formerly (1964-1985) part of DC 058508, Board/Boards.
- UF Boards of Trustees
  Executive Boards
- BT Organizations (Social)
- NT School Boards
- RT Advisory Committees
  Commissions
  Committees
  Councils
  Directors
  Management
  Policy Making

Government
- DC D333300
- HN Formerly (1963-1985) DC 196500, Govern/Governing/Government/Governmental/Governments.
- BT Social Institutions
- NT Central Government
  Local Government
- RT Commissions
  Constitutions
  Countries
  Economic Planning
  Emergencies
  Government Agencies
  Government Policy
  Government Regulation
  Governors
  Judiciary
  Law
  Legal System
  Legislation

Government (cont'd)
- RT Legislative Bodies
  Legislators
  Legitimacy
  Legitimation
  Military Regimes
  Political Ideologies
  Political Philosophy
  Political Power
  Political Systems
  Politics
  Presidents
  Public Administration
  Public Finance
  Public Officials
  Public Policy
  Public Sector
  Public Services
  Ruling Class
  State
  State Society Relationship
  Taxation

Government Agencies
- DC D333600
- HN Added, 1986.
- UF Bureau of Indian Affairs (1963-1985)
  Federal Bureau of Investigation/FBI (1984-1985)
  Federal Housing Administration/FHA (1969-1985)
  National Science Foundation/NSF (1970-1985)
  Veterans Administration (1963-1985)
- BT Agencies
- RT Government
  Government Policy
  Government Regulation
  Human Services
  Institutions
  International Organizations
  Law Enforcement
  Legislative Bodies
  Public Administration
  Public Officials
  Public Services

Government Finance
- Use Public Finance

Government Intervention
- Use State Intervention

Government Officials
- Use Public Officials

Government Planning
- Use State Planning

Government Policy
- DC D333900
- HN Added, 1986.
- BT Policy
- NT Fiscal Policy
  Foreign Policy
  Language Policy
- RT Agricultural Policy
  Antipoverty Programs
  Apartheid
  City Planning
  Development Policy
  Economic Policy
  Educational Policy
  Government
  Government Agencies
  Housing Policy
  Legislation
  Policy Implementation
  Political Science

Government Great

Government Policy (cont'd)
- RT Population Policy
  Presidents
  Protest Movements
  Public Policy
  Public Sector Private Sector Relations
  Social Policy
  Social Problems
  Social Programs
  Technological Change
  Welfare Policy

Government Regulation
- DC D334200
- SN Regulation by government, particularly in the private sector.
- HN Added, 1986.
- BT Regulation
- RT Government
  Government Agencies
  Land Use
  Legislation
  Patents
  Pollution Control
  Public Sector Private Sector Relations
  Social Control
  State Intervention
  State Society Relationship

Government Spending
- DC D334300
- HN Added, 1989.
- UF Public Spending
- BT Expenditures
- NT Defense Spending
- RT Economic Development
  Economic Policy
  Fiscal Policy
  Foreign Aid
  Public Debt
  Public Finance
  Subsidies

Government Sponsored Housing
- Use Public Housing

Governors
- DC D334500
- HN Formerly (1966-1985) DC 196700, Governor/Governors.
- BT Public Officials
- RT Government
  Provinces
  States (Political Subdivisions)

Grades (Scholastic)
- DC D334800
- HN Formerly (1963-1985) DC 197000, Grade/Grades.
- UF Grading/Gradings (1963-1985)
- RT Academic Achievement
  Scores
  Student Teacher Relationship

Grading/Gradings (1963-1985)
- HN DC 197020.
- Use Grades (Scholastic)

Graduate Schools
- DC D335000
- HN Added, 1989.
- BT Colleges
- NT Medical Schools
- RT Doctoral Programs
  Graduate Students
  Higher Education
  Postdoctoral Programs
  Teacher Education

Graduate Students
- DC D335100
- HN Formerly (1985) DC 448500, Student, Graduate.
- UF Student, Graduate (1985)
- BT College Students
- NT Dental Students
  Medical Students
- RT College Graduates
  Dissertations
  Doctoral Degrees
  Doctoral Programs
  Graduate Schools
  Higher Education
  Masters Degrees
  Postdoctoral Programs
  Professional Training

Graduates
- DC D335400
- HN Formerly (1963-1985) DC 197100, Graduate/Graduates/Graduation.
- NT College Graduates
- RT Educational Attainment
  High Schools
  Students

Graffiti
- DC D335700
- HN Formerly (1978-1985), DC 197110.
- RT Audiovisual Media
  Nonverbal Communication

Grammar
- DC D336000
- HN Formerly (1964-1985) DC 197150, Grammar/Grammatical.
- UF Syntax (1978-1985)
- BT Linguistics
- NT Morphology (Language)
- RT Dialects
  Discourse Analysis
  Language Attitudes
  Language Usage
  Pragmatics
  Psycholinguistics
  Semantics
  Sociolinguistics

Gramsci, Antonio
- DC D336300
- SN Born 1891 - died 1937.
- HN Formerly (1969-1985) DC 197160, Gramsci, A.

Grandchildren
- DC D336600
- HN Formerly (1969-1985) DC 197180, Grandchild/Grandchildren.
- BT Children
- RT Grandparents

Grandparents
- DC D336900
- HN Formerly (1963-1985) DC 197185, Grandparent/Grandparents.
- BT Parents
- RT Elderly
  Elderly Women
  Fathers
  Grandchildren
  Intergenerational Relations
  Kinship
  Mothers
  Relatives

Grants
- DC D337200
- HN Formerly (1963-1985) DC 197215, Grant/Grants.
- BT Financial Support
- RT Foundations
  Philanthropy
  Sponsorship
  Subsidies

Graph Theory
- DC D337450
- SN A branch of mathematics that deals with a special type of graph, which uses a set of points joined by lines to show the relationships among pairs of abstract elements. In sociology, the points usually represent individuals or groups, and the lines represent the social networks among them.
- HN Added, 1986.
- UF Digraph Theory
  Directed Graph Theory
- BT Mathematics
  Theories
- RT Graphs
  Models
  Network Analysis
  Sociometric Analysis

Graphology
- DC D337500
- SN Methods for making inferences about personality traits from samples of handwriting.
- HN Formerly (1964-1985) DC 197300.
- UF Handwriting Analysis
- RT Personality Traits
  Psychology

Graphs
- DC D337550
- HN Formerly (1964-1985) DC 197250, Graph/Graphs/Graphic.
- UF Charts
- RT Data
  Frequency Distributions
  Graph Theory
  Statistics
  Structural Models
  Tables

Grass Roots (1969-1985)
- HN DC 197305, deleted 1986. See now Social Action, Social Movements, or appropriate "Community" terms.

Gratification (Delay of)
- Use Delay of Gratification

Gratitude (1966-1985)
- HN DC 197400, deleted 1986.

Graveyards
- Use Cemeteries

Gravity (1964-1985)
- HN DC 197500, deleted 1986.

Great Britain
- DC D337800
- SN England, Scotland, and Wales.
- HN Formerly (1963-1985) DC 197530.
- BT United Kingdom
  Western Europe
- NT England
  Scotland
  Wales

Greater Antilles
  Use Caribbean

Greece
  DC D338100
  HN Formerly (1963-1985) DC 197550, Greece/Greek.
  BT Balkan States
       Mediterranean Countries
       Western Europe
  NT Athens, Greece

Greek Philosophy
  Use Ancient Greek Philosophy

Greenland
  DC D338400
  HN Formerly (1964-1985) DC 197555, Greenland/Greenlander/Greenlanders.
  BT North America
       Scandinavia
  RT Arctic Regions

Greeting Cards
  Use Letters (Correspondence)

Grenada
  DC D338700
  HN Formerly (1985) DC 197555c.
  BT Caribbean

Grid/Grids (1969-1985)
  HN DC 197556, deleted 1986.

Grief
  DC D339000
  HN Formerly (1964-1985) DC 197557.
  UF Bereavement
  BT Emotions
  RT Death
       Death Rituals
       Depression (Psychology)
       Dying
       Suffering

Grievances
  DC D339300
  HN Formerly (1969-1985) DC 197560, Grievance/Grievances.
  UF Complaint/Complaints (1966-1985)
  RT Disputes
       Mediation

Gross National Product
  DC D339600
  HN Formerly (1968-1985) DC 197620.
  RT Economic Development
       Economics
       Income
       Standard of Living
       Wealth

Ground Rents
  Use Rents

Group Cohesion
  Use Social Cohesion

Group Composition
  DC D339850
  HN Added, 1986.
  RT Communities
       Demographic Characteristics
       Ethnicity
       Family
       Group Dynamics
       Group Formation
       Group Size
       Groups

Group Composition (cont'd)
  RT Heterogeneity
       Homogeneity
       Households
       Race
       Sex
       Social Groups
       Social Interaction

Group Decision Making
  DC D339900
  HN Added, 1986.
  UF Group Problem Solving
  BT Decision Making
  RT Choices
       Consensus
       Discussion
       Group Dynamics
       Groups
       Participative Decision Making
       Problem Solving
       Teamwork

Group Discussion
  Use Discussion

Group Dynamics
  DC D340200
  HN Formerly (1964-1985) DC 198300.
  UF Group Relations (1964-1985)
       Intragroup (1964-1985)
  BT Social Dynamics
       Social Interaction
  RT Balance Theory
       Centrality
       Consensus
       Cooptation
       Group Composition
       Group Decision Making
       Group Norms
       Group Research
       Group Therapy
       Groups
       Individual Collective Relationship
       Interpersonal Communication
       Interpersonal Relations
       Macrosociology
       Microsociology
       Organizational Behavior
       Psychodynamics
       Sensitivity Training
       Small Groups
       Social Behavior
       Social Cohesion
       Social Psychology
       Sociometric Analysis
       Work Groups

Group Formation
  DC D340500
  HN Added, 1986.
  BT Formation
       Social Processes
  NT Class Formation
       Coalition Formation
  RT Group Composition
       Groups
       Social Segmentation

Group Health Organizations
  Use Health Maintenance Organizations

Group Identification
  Use Group Identity

Group Identity
  DC D340800
  HN Added, 1986.
  UF Collective Identity

Group Identity (cont'd)
  UF Group Identification
  BT Identity
  NT Class Identity
       Professional Identity
  RT Black Community
       Cooptation
       Cultural Identity
       Ethnic Identity
       Group Norms
       Groups
       Individual Collective Relationship
       Membership
       Organizational Commitment
       Social Identity
       Socialization

Group Individual Relationship
  Use Individual Collective Relationship

Group Membership
  Use Membership

Group Norms
  DC D341100
  HN Formerly (1964-1985) DC 198850, Group Norm.
  BT Norms
  RT Codes of Conduct
       Group Dynamics
       Group Identity
       Groups
       Small Groups
       Social Behavior
       Social Cohesion
       Social Groups

Group Problem Solving
  Use Group Decision Making

Group Relations (1964-1985)
  HN DC 199475.
  Use Group Dynamics

Group Research
  DC D341350
  HN Added, 1986. Prior to 1986 use Group/Groups/Grouping/Groupism (DC 197700) and Research/Researcher/Researchers (DC 385000).
  UF Small Group Research
  BT Research
  RT Group Dynamics
       Groups
       Social Science Research
       Sociometric Analysis

Group Size
  DC D341400
  HN Added, 1986.
  BT Size
  RT Community Size
       Group Composition
       Groups
       Organization Size
       Small Groups

Group Therapy
  DC D341700
  HN Formerly (1964-1985) DC 200070.
  BT Treatment
  RT Clinical Social Work
       Conjoint Therapy
       Group Dynamics
       Groups
       Psychotherapy
       Self Help
       Self Help Groups
       Sensitivity Training
       Support Groups

Group

Group Work
- DC D342000
- SN Group therapy techniques applied by Social Workers.
- HN Formerly (1985) DC 200125.
- UF Social Group Work
- BT Social Work

Groups
- DC D342300
- SN A context-dependent term for any identifiable aggregate; select a more specific entry or coordinate with other terms. In sociological contexts, Social Groups is the preferred term.
- HN Formerly (1963-1985) DC 197700, Group/Groups/Grouping/Groupism.
- NT Age Groups
  Audiences
  Cadres
  Coalitions
  Communities
  Crowds
  Cultural Groups
  Disadvantaged
  Interest Groups
  Low Income Groups
  Majority Groups
  Minority Groups
  Organizations (Social)
  Reference Groups
  Self Help Groups
  Small Groups
  Social Class
  Social Groups
  Spectators
  Support Groups
  Task Oriented Groups
  Teams
  Womens Groups
  Work Groups
- RT Group Composition
  Group Decision Making
  Group Dynamics
  Group Formation
  Group Identity
  Group Norms
  Group Research
  Group Size
  Group Therapy
  Heterogeneity
  Homogeneity
  Individual Collective Relationship
  Intergroup Relations
  Membership
  Social Cohesion
  Society
  Stratification

Growing-up (1963-1985)
- HN DC 200185, deleted 1986.

Growth (1963-1985)
- HN DC 200200.
- Use Development

Growth Strategies
- Use Development Strategies

Guadeloupe
- DC D342600
- HN Added, 1986.
- BT Caribbean

Guam
- DC D342900
- HN Added, 1986.
- BT Mariana Islands

Guard/Guards/Guarding/Guarded (1972-1985)
- HN DC 200238.
- Use Correctional Personnel

Guardianship
- DC D343200
- HN Formerly (1971-1985), DC 200240.
- RT Child Custody
  Foster Care
  Representation

Guatemala
- DC D343500
- HN Formerly (1963-1985) DC 200260, Guatemala/Guatemalan/Guatemalans.
- BT Central America

Guerrillas
- DC D343800
- HN Formerly (1964-1985) DC 200270, Guerrilla.
- RT Civil War
  Maoism
  Paramilitary Forces
  Political Violence
  Rebellions
  Revolutions
  Terrorism

Guestworker/Guestworkers (1982-1985)
- HN DC 200273.
- Use Foreign Workers

Guidance
- DC D344100
- HN Formerly (1963-1985) DC 200300.
- UF Child Guidance
  School Guidance
  Vocational Guidance
- NT Counseling
- RT Assistance
  Childrearing Practices
  Family Planning
  Occupational Choice
  Student Teacher Relationship
  Vocational Education

Guide/Guiding (1963-1985)
- HN DC 200650.
- Use Reference Materials

Guilds
- DC D344400
- HN Formerly (1965-1985) DC 200700, Guild/Guilds.
- UF Craft Guilds
- BT Organizations (Social)
- RT Artisans
  Crafts
  Unions

Guilt
- DC D344700
- HN Formerly (1964-1985) DC 201000.
- BT Emotions
- RT Anxiety
  Confession
  Conscience
  Embarrassment
  Morality
  Sexual Behavior
  Shame

Gynecology

Guinea
- DC D345000
- HN Formerly (1968-1985) DC 201050, Guinea/Guinean/Guineans.
- BT Sub Saharan Africa

Guinea Bissau
- DC D345300
- HN Added, 1986.
- BT Sub Saharan Africa

Gujarat, India
- DC D345600
- HN Formerly (1966-1985) DC 201100.
- BT India

Gun Control
- DC D345900
- HN Added, 1986.
- BT Control
- RT Crime Prevention
  Firearms

Gun/Guns (1969-1985)
- HN DC 201350.
- Use Firearms

Gurvitch, Georges
- DC D346200
- SN Born 2 November 1894 - died 12 December 1965.
- HN Formerly (1963-1985) DC 201500.

Gusfield, Joseph Robert
- DC D346400
- SN Born 6 September 1923 - .
- HN Added, 1989.

Guttman, Louis
- DC D346500
- SN Born 10 February 1916 - died 25 October 1987.
- HN Formerly (1968-1985) DC 201515.

Guttman Scales
- DC D346525
- HN Formerly (1964-1985) DC 201520, Guttman Scale/Guttman Scales.
- UF Scalogram (1964-1985)
- BT Scales
- RT Attitude Measures
  Latent Structure Analysis

Guyana
- DC D346800
- HN Formerly (1978-1985) DC 201550, Guyana/Guyanan/Guyanans.
- BT South America

Gymnasium (1963-1985)
- HN DC 201600, deleted 1986. See now Recreational Facilities or Secondary Education.

Gynecology
- DC D347100
- HN Formerly (1965-1985) DC 201620, Gynecology/Gynecological.
- UF Obstetrics
- BT Medicine
- RT Birth
  Childlessness
  Midwifery
  Pregnancy
  Reproductive Technologies
  Sex Information
  Sexual Reproduction

Gypsies
- **DC** D347400
- **HN** Formerly (1964-1985) DC 201640, Gypsy/Gypsies.
- **UF** Romani
- **BT** European Cultural Groups
- **RT** Migrants
  Nomadic Societies
  Traditional Societies

Habeas Corpus
- **HN** DC 201647, deleted 1986.

Habermas, Jurgen
- **DC** D347700
- **SN** Born 18 June 1926 - .
- **HN** Formerly (1969-1985) DC 201678.

Habitat/Habitats/Habitation (1964-1985)
- **SN** The concept of critical developmental periods, developed by Eric Homburger Erikson, during which an individual passes between one of the eight life stages to the next, characterized by attitude or behavioral choices that affect one's ability to adjust to subsequent stages. May refer broadly to any life stage development scheme.
- **HN** DC 201690.
- **Use** Housing

Habits
- **DC** D348000
- **HN** Formerly (1964-1985) DC 201700, Habit/Habits/Habitual.
- **BT** Behavior
- **RT** Interests
  Personality
  Smoking

Hacienda/Haciendas (1963-1985)
- **HN** DC 201725.
- **Use** Plantations

Hagiography (1978-1985)
- **HN** DC 202800.
- **Use** Saints

Haiti
- **DC** D348300
- **HN** Formerly (1963-1985) DC 202820, Haiti/Haitian/Haitians.
- **BT** Caribbean

Hallucinations
- **DC** D348450
- **HN** Formerly (1966-1985) DC 203000, Hallucination/Hallucinations.
- **RT** Psychedelic Drugs
  Psychopathology
  Sensory Systems
  Supernatural

Hallucinogenic Drugs
- **Use** Psychedelic Drugs

Handguns
- **Use** Firearms

Handicap, Occupational (1965-1985)
- **HN** DC 206400, deleted 1986.

Handicapped
- **DC** D348600
- **HN** Formerly (1963-1985) DC 206300, Handicap/Handicapped.
- **NT** Blind
  Congenitally Handicapped

Handicapped (cont'd)
- **NT** Deaf
  Mentally Retarded
  Physically Handicapped
- **RT** Cerebral Palsy
  Deinstitutionalization
  Dependents
  Disability Recipients
  Disorders
  Downs Syndrome
  Emotionally Disturbed
  Health
  Individuals
  Language Disorders
  Learning Disabilities
  Rehabilitation
  Special Education

Handicraft/Handicrafts/Handicraftsman (1965-1985)
- **HN** DC 206500.
- **Use** Crafts

Hands
- **DC** D348900
- **HN** Formerly (1976-1985) DC 203700, Hand/Hands.
- **RT** Human Body

Handwriting Analysis
- **Use** Graphology

Hanoi, Vietnam
- **DC** D349000
- **HN** Added, 1989.
- **BT** Vietnam

Happiness
- **DC** D349200
- **HN** Formerly (1966-1985) DC 207125.
- **UF** Joy
- **BT** Emotions
- **RT** Discontent
  Life Satisfaction
  Love
  Optimism
  Satisfaction
  Self Esteem
  Well Being

Harass/Harassment (1981-1985)
- **HN** DC 207135.
- **Use** Sexual Harassment

Harlem (1965-1985)
- **HN** DC 207160.
- **Use** New York City, New York

Hartford, Connecticut
- **DC** D349500
- **HN** Added, 1986.
- **BT** Connecticut

Harvard University (1964-1985)
- **HN** DC 207175.
- **Use** Universities

Hashish (1971-1985)
- **HN** DC 207178.
- **Use** Marijuana

Hassidim
- **DC** D349800
- **HN** Formerly (1963-1985) part of DC 207180, Hassid/Hassidim/Hassidic/Hassidism.
- **UF** Chassidim
- **BT** Jews
- **RT** Hassidism

Hassidism
- **DC** D350100
- **HN** Formerly (1963-1985) part of DC 207180, Hassid/Hassidim/Hassidic/Hassidism.
- **UF** Chassidism
- **BT** Judaism
- **RT** Hassidim
  Mysticism

Hate
- **DC** D350400
- **HN** Formerly (1969-1985) DC 207182.
- **UF** Contempt (1969-1985)
  Malevolence/Malevolent (1971-1985)
- **BT** Emotions
- **RT** Anger
  Hostility
  Interpersonal Conflict
  Interpersonal Relations

Hauser, Robert Mason
- **DC** D350500
- **SN** Born 3 September 1942 - .
- **HN** Added, 1989.

Havana, Cuba
- **DC** D350600
- **HN** Added, 1989.
- **BT** Cuba

Hawaii
- **DC** D350700
- **HN** Formerly (1963-1985) DC 207250, Hawaii/Hawaiian/Hawaiians.
- **BT** Polynesia
  United States of America

Hazards
- **DC** D350850
- **HN** Formerly (1965-1985) DC 207259, Hazard/Hazards.
- **UF** Environmental Hazards
- **RT** Accidents
  Diseases
  Living Conditions
  Natural Disasters
  Occupational Safety And Health
  Poisoning
  Risk
  Safety
  Social Problems
  Survival
  Threat
  Toxic Substances

Head Start (1971-1985)
- **HN** DC 207510.
- **Use** Project Head Start

Heads of Households
- **DC** D350900
- **HN** Added, 1989.
- **RT** Family
  Female Headed Households
  Households
  Parents

Heal/Healer/Healers/Healing (1965-1985)
- **HN** DC 207600, deleted 1986. See now Faith Healing or Traditional Medicine.

Healing (Traditional)
- **Use** Traditional Medicine

Health

Health
- DC D351000
- HN Formerly (1963-1985) DC 208000, Health/Healthy.
- UF Health Status
    Physical Health
    Wellness
- NT Mental Health
    Occupational Safety And Health
    Public Health
- RT Accidents
    Alcohol Use
    Blood Pressure
    Dental Care
    Diagnosis
    Diet
    Diseases
    Drug Use
    Drugs
    Fatigue
    Handicapped
    Health Behavior
    Health Care
    Health Insurance
    Health Planning
    Health Policy
    Health Problems
    Health Professions
    Health Services
    Human Body
    Hygiene
    Illness
    Injuries
    Longevity
    Medical Sociology
    Medicine
    Nutrition
    Obesity
    Physical Fitness
    Poisoning
    Pollution
    Safety
    Sanitation
    Sleep
    Smoking
    Stress
    Toxic Substances
    Vaccination
    Well Being

Health Attitudes
- Use Health Behavior

Health Behavior
- DC D351200
- HN Added, 1989.
- UF Health Attitudes
    Health Beliefs
- BT Behavior
- RT Health
    Health Care Utilization
    Illness Behavior
    Treatment Compliance

Health Beliefs
- Use Health Behavior

Health Care
- DC D351300
- HN Formerly (1977-1985) DC 208100.
- UF Medical Care
- NT Dental Care
    Home Health Care
    Primary Health Care
- RT After Care
    Caregivers
    Clinics
    Diagnosis

Health Care (cont'd)
- RT Diseases
    Health
    Health Care Utilization
    Health Insurance
    Health Maintenance Organizations
    Health Planning
    Health Policy
    Health Professions
    Hospices
    Hospitals
    Illness
    Informed Consent
    Medical Model
    Medications
    Medicine
    Mental Health Services
    Nursing Homes
    Patients
    Placebo Effect
    Practitioner Patient Relationship
    Rehabilitation
    Self Care
    Socialized Medicine
    Surgery
    Treatment Compliance

Health Care Planning
- Use Health Planning

Health Care Providers
- Use Health Professions

Health Care Technology
- Use Medical Technology

Health Care Utilization
- DC D351600
- HN Added, 1986.
- UF Medical Care Utilization
    Visits (Medical)
- BT Utilization
- RT Behavior
    Delivery Systems
    Health Behavior
    Health Care
    Health Services
    Help Seeking Behavior
    Medical Decision Making
    Mental Health
    Mental Health Services
    Patients
    Professional Consultation
    Termination of Treatment

Health Insurance
- DC D351900
- HN Added, 1986.
- BT Insurance
- RT Health
    Health Care
    Medicare
    Socialized Medicine
    Workers Compensation Insurance

Health Maintenance Organizations
- DC D352200
- HN Formerly (1984-1985) DC 208175.
- UF Group Health Organizations
    HMOs
- RT Health Care

Health Personnel
- Use Health Professions

Health Planning
- DC D352500
- HN Added, 1986.
- UF Health Care Planning
- BT Planning
- RT Delivery Systems
    Health

Health Planning (cont'd)
- RT Health Care
    Health Policy
    Health Services
    Local Planning
    Medical Decision Making
    Socialized Medicine

Health Policy
- DC D352800
- HN Added, 1986.
- BT Social Policy
- RT Child Mortality
    Diseases
    Epidemiology
    Eugenics
    Health
    Health Care
    Health Planning
    Health Services
    Infant Mortality
    Morbidity
    Pollution Control
    Public Health
    Socialized Medicine
    Survival

Health Problems
- DC D353100
- HN Formerly (1985) DC 208200.
- BT Problems
- RT Acquired Immune Deficiency Syndrome
    Diseases
    Health
    Illness
    Lead Poisoning

Health Professions
- DC D353400
- HN Added, 1986.
- UF Health Personnel
    Medical Professions
- BT Professions
- RT Caregivers
    Chiropractors
    Dentists
    Health
    Health Care
    Medical Decision Making
    Medical Sociology
    Medicine
    Nurses
    Optometry
    Paramedical Personnel
    Pharmacists
    Physicians
    Practitioner Patient Relationship
    Psychiatrists
    Psychologists
    Therapists

Health Services
- DC D353700
- HN Formerly (1984-1985) DC 208300.
- UF Community Health Services
    Public Health Services
- BT Human Services
- NT Emergency Medical Services
    Mental Health Services
- RT Delivery Systems
    Health
    Health Care Utilization
    Health Planning
    Health Policy
    Medicaid
    Medicare
    Optometry

Health

Health Services (cont'd)
- RT Public Health
- Socialized Medicine
- Treatment
- Vaccination

Health Status
- Use Health

Hearing
- DC D354000
- HN Formerly (1964-1985) DC 208900.
- UF Audition
- BT Sensory Systems
- RT Deaf
- Vision

Heart
- DC D354300
- HN Formerly (1963-1985) DC 209000.
- RT Blood
- Heart Diseases
- Human Body

Heart Diseases
- DC D354600
- HN Added, 1986. Prior to 1986 use Heart (DC 209000) or Coronary (DC 115752).
- UF Cardiovascular Diseases
- Coronary (1964-1985)
- BT Diseases
- RT Heart

Heathenism
- Use Paganism

Hebrew Language
- Use Semitic Languages

Hebrew/Hebrews/Hebraic (1964-1985)
- HN DC 212100, deleted 1986. See now Semitic Languages or Jews.

Hedonism
- DC D354725
- SN The doctrine that the seeking of pleasure and avoidance of pain are the ultimate aims and motivating forces of human action.
- HN Formerly (1965-1985) DC 212325, Hedonism/Hedonistic.
- BT Philosophical Doctrines
- RT Ethics
- Utilitarianism

Hegel, Georg Wilhelm Friedrich
- DC D354850
- SN Born 27 August 1770 - died 14 November 1831.
- HN Formerly (1963-1985) DC 212350, Hegel, G. W. F./Hegelian/Hegelianism.

Hegemony
- DC D354900
- SN Dominance of one group or class over others in social, political, economic, and ideological spheres. Introduced by Antonio Gramsci.
- HN Formerly (1971-1985) DC 212360, Hegemony/Hegemonies.
- RT Coercion
- Dominance
- Dominant Ideologies
- State
- State Power

Heidegger, Martin
- DC D355200
- SN Born 26 September 1889 - died 26 May 1976.
- HN Formerly (1963-1985) DC 212440.

Height (1963-1985)
- HN DC 212550.
- Use Body Height

Help Giving
- Use Helping Behavior

Help Seeking Behavior
- DC D355500
- SN Searching for and requesting assistance from others. For the use of professional health services, see Health Care Utilization.
- HN Added, 1986.
- UF Seeking Help
- BT Social Behavior
- RT Assistance
- Health Care Utilization
- Problem Solving
- Professional Consultation
- Self Actualization
- Self Help
- Self Help Groups

Helping Behavior
- DC D355800
- HN Formerly (1964-1985) part of DC 212570, Help/Helping/Helper/Helpers.
- UF Giving Help
- Help Giving
- BT Behavior
- RT Altruism
- Assistance
- Client Relations
- Counseling
- Interpersonal Relations
- Intervention
- Paramedical Personnel
- Practitioner Patient Relationship
- Self Help Groups
- Social Interest
- Social Responsibility
- Social Work
- Student Teacher Relationship
- Treatment

Helsinki, Finland
- DC D356100
- HN Formerly (1966-1985) DC 212580.
- BT Finland

Herbs
- Use Plants (Botanical)

Herding Societies
- Use Pastoral Societies

Heredity/Hereditary (1963-1985)
- HN DC 213000.
- Use Genetics

Heresy
- DC D356400
- HN Formerly (1963-1985) DC 213025, Heretic/Heretics/Heresy.
- UF Heretics
- BT Religious Beliefs
- RT Agnosticism
- Apostasy
- Atheism
- Manicheism
- Photian Schism
- Religions
- Religious Orthodoxy
- Schism

Heteronomy

Heretics
- Use Heresy

Heritage (1964-1985)
- HN DC 213050, deleted 1986. See now Social Background or Culture.

Hermeneutics
- DC D356600
- SN The philosophical position, developed by Wilhelm Christian Ludwig Dilthey, based on the subjective interpretation of human acts and creations in terms of the total context of a creator's Worldview. Contrast with Positivism, which emphasizes objective observation.
- HN Formerly (1979-1985) DC 213075, Hermeneutic/Hermeneutics.
- BT Philosophy
- RT Action Theory
- Analysis
- Bible
- Critical Theory
- Discourse Analysis
- Interpretive Sociology
- Marxist Aesthetics
- Methodology (Philosophical)
- Phenomenology
- Positivism
- Semiotics
- Sociolinguistics
- Verstehen
- Worldview

Heroes
- DC D356700
- HN Formerly (1963-1985) DC 213100, Hero/Heros/Heroism/Heroine/Heroines.
- UF Heroines
- Literary Heroes
- Protagonists
- Superheroes
- RT Fictional Characters
- Literature

Heroin
- DC D357000
- HN Formerly (1964-1985) DC 213115.
- BT Opiates
- RT Methadone Maintenance

Heroines
- Use Heroes

Herpes Simplex Genitalis
- Use Venereal Diseases

Heterogamy (1969-1985)
- HN DC 213136.
- Use Intermarriage

Heterogeneity
- DC D357300
- SN Diversity of traits in a population or group. Opposite of Homogeneity.
- HN Formerly (1963-1985) DC 213140, Heterogeneity/Heterogeneous.
- RT Differences
- Group Composition
- Groups
- Homogeneity
- Population

Heteronomy (1983-1985)
- HN DC 213200.
- Use Autonomy

Heteroscedastic

Heteroscedastic/Heteroscedasity (1969-1985)
- **HN** DC 213235.
- **Use** Quantitative Methods

Heterosexuality
- **DC** D357600
- **HN** Formerly (1964-1985) DC 213240, Heterosexual/Heterosexuality.
- **BT** Sexuality
- **RT** Bisexuality
  Homosexual Relationships
  Homosexuality
  Sexual Behavior
  Sexual Preferences

Heuristic Methods
- **Use** Heuristics

Heuristics
- **DC** D357700
- **SN** The study or practice of using scientifically unproved assumptions, concepts, or constructs to aid in analyzing observed phenomena.
- **HN** Formerly (1971-1985) DC 213250, Heuristic.
- **UF** Heuristic Methods
- **RT** Constructs
  Hypotheses
  Ideal Types
  Methods
  Postulates
  Research Methodology
  Theory Formation

Hierarchy
- **DC** D357800
- **HN** Formerly (1963-1985) DC 213270, Hierarchy/Hierarchal/Hierarchies.
- **BT** Structure
- **RT** Bureaucracy
  Classification
  Ranking
  Status
  Stratification

High School Students
- **DC** D357900
- **HN** Formerly (1985) DC 448600, Student, High School.
- **UF** Student, High School (1985)
- **BT** Students
- **RT** Adolescents
  High Schools
  Secondary Education
  Secondary Schools

High Schools
- **DC** D358200
- **HN** Formerly (1963-1985) DC 213500, High School/High Schools.
- **BT** Secondary Schools
- **RT** Graduates
  High School Students
  Private Schools
  Public Schools
  Secondary Education

High Technology Industries
- **DC** D358300
- **HN** Added, 1989.
- **BT** Industry
- **RT** Adoption of Innovations
  Appropriate Technologies
  Computer Software
  Computers
  Cybernetics
  Electronic Technology

High Technology Industries (cont'd)
- **RT** Engineering
  Industrial Automation
  Industrial Development
  Information Technology
  Inventions
  Manufacturing Industries
  Medical Technology
  Metallurgical Technology
  Research Applications
  Technological Change
  Technological Innovations
  Technology
  Technology Transfer

Higher Education
- **DC** D358500
- **HN** Formerly (1963-1985) DC 213530.
- **UF** Postsecondary Education
- **BT** Education
- **NT** Doctoral Programs
  Postdoctoral Programs
  Undergraduate Programs
- **RT** Academic Degrees
  Academic Disciplines
  Adult Education
  College Faculty
  College Majors
  College Students
  Colleges
  Community Colleges
  Graduate Schools
  Graduate Students
  Knowledge
  Polytechnic Schools
  Professional Training
  Universities

Highways
- **DC** D358800
- **HN** Formerly (1972-1985) DC 213550, Highway/Highways/Highwayman/Highwaymen.
- **UF** Roads
- **RT** Automobiles
  Traffic
  Transportation

Himalayan States
- **DC** D359100
- **HN** Formerly (1967-1985) DC 213615, Himalayas/Himalayan/Himalayans.
- **BT** South Asia
- **NT** Bhutan
  Nepal
- **RT** Mountain Regions

Hindi (1969-1985)
- **HN** DC 213650.
- **Use** Indic Languages

Hinduism
- **DC** D359400
- **HN** Formerly (1963-1985) part of DC 213700, Hindu/Hindus/Hinduism.
- **BT** Religions
- **RT** Brahmins
  Caste Systems
  Dharma
  Hindus
  Karma
  Purdah
  Sadhus
  Yoga

Historical

Hindus
- **DC** D359700
- **HN** Formerly (1963-1985) part of DC 213700, Hindu/Hindus/Hinduism.
- **BT** Religious Cultural Groups
- **NT** Brahmins
  Sadhus
- **RT** Hinduism
  Purdah

Hindustani
- **Use** Indic Languages

Hippie/Hippies (1968-1985)
- **HN** DC 213716.
- **Use** Countercultures

Hippocrates/Hippocratic (1965-1985)
- **HN** DC 213800, deleted 1986.

Hiring Practices
- **DC** D360000
- **HN** Formerly (1966-1985) DC 213950, Hire/Hiring/Hired.
- **UF** Nepotism (1967-1985)
- **BT** Personnel Management
- **RT** Affirmative Action
  Employment Discrimination
  Job Requirements
  Job Search
  Occupational Segregation
  Personnel Policy
  Recruitment

Hiroshima, Japan
- **DC** D360300
- **HN** Formerly (1965-1985) DC 213965.
- **BT** Japan

Hispanic Americans
- **DC** D360600
- **HN** Formerly (1965-1985) DC 214100, Hispanic.
- **UF** Spanish Americans
- **BT** North American Cultural Groups
- **NT** Mexican Americans

Historians
- **DC** D360900
- **HN** Formerly (1963-1985) DC 214125, Historian/Historians.
- **BT** Social Scientists
- **RT** History

Historic Preservation
- **Use** Preservation

Historical Development
- **DC** D360925
- **SN** Changes over long time spans, particularly from points in the past to modern times and viewed in the broad context of historical events.
- **HN** Added, 1989.
- **BT** Change
  Development
- **RT** Historicism
  History
  Political Movements
  Progress
  Social Evolution
  Trends

Historical Materialism
- **DC** D360950
- **SN** The Marxist theory that all forms of social thought and institutions are determined by economic relations.
- **HN** Added, 1986.

Historicism

Historical Materialism (cont'd)
- RT Dialectical Materialism
- Economic Theories
- Forces And Relations of Production
- History
- Marxism
- Marxist Sociology
- Materialism
- Modes of Production
- Social Evolution
- Utopias

Historicism
- DC D361000
- SN Theory that social and cultural phenomena are determined by historical developments and that each historical period can only be understood in its own terms. Also, the theory that historical development is determined by fixed laws.
- HN Formerly (1963-1985) DC 214225, Historicism/Historicity.
- BT Philosophical Doctrines
- RT Historical Development
  - History
  - Materialism
  - Relativism
  - Social Evolution
  - Social History
  - Sociology of Knowledge
  - Verstehen

Historiography
- DC D361200
- SN The study, criticism, principles, and methodology of historical writing.
- HN Formerly (1963-1985) DC 214275.
- BT Research Methodology
- RT History
  - Intellectual History
  - Marxist Analysis
  - Psychohistory
  - Scholarship
  - Social Science Research

History
- DC D361500
- HN Formerly (1963-1985) DC 214300, History/Historic/Historical.
- BT Social Sciences
- NT Art History
  - Chronologies
  - Economic History
  - History of Sociology
  - Intellectual History
  - Oral History
  - Psychohistory
  - Social History
- RT Antiquity
  - Archaeology
  - Change
  - Civilization
  - Cultural Change
  - Development
  - Figuration Sociology
  - Folklore
  - Genealogy
  - Historians
  - Historical Development
  - Historical Materialism
  - Historicism
  - Historiography
  - Life History
  - Political Movements
  - Prehistory
  - Revolutions
  - Social Evolution
  - Social Progress
  - Time Periods
  - War

History of Ideas
- Use Intellectual History

History of Sociology
- DC D361800
- HN Added, 1986.
- UF Sociological History
- BT History
- RT Chicago School of Sociology
  - Metasociology
  - Social Theories
  - Sociology

Hitler, Adolph
- DC D362100
- SN Born 20 April 1889 - died 30 April 1945.
- HN Formerly (1964-1985) DC 214350.

HMOs
- Use Health Maintenance Organizations

Ho Chi Minh City, Vietnam
- DC D362150
- HN Added, 1989.
- BT Vietnam

Hoaxes
- Use Deception

Hobbes, Thomas
- DC D362250
- SN Born 5 April 1588 - died 4 December 1679.
- HN Formerly (1963-1985) DC 214372, Hobbes, T./Hobbesian.

Hobbies (1978-1985)
- HN DC 214375.
- Use Leisure

Hobo/Hobos (1984-1985)
- HN DC 214360.
- Use Homelessness

Holidays
- DC D362400
- HN Formerly (1965-1985) DC 214380, Holiday/Holidays.
- UF Holy Days
  - Religious Holidays
- NT Christmas
- RT Calendars
  - Celebrations
  - Customs
  - Festivals
  - Rituals

Holism
- DC D362500
- SN The theory that individuals and societies have properties as totalities that are not simply the sum of their parts, and thus should be studied as wholes or as systems of interacting parts.
- HN Formerly (1971-1985) DC 214385, Holistic.
- BT Epistemological Doctrines
  - Philosophical Doctrines
- NT Holistic Medicine
- RT Action Theory
  - Empiricism
  - Functionalism
  - Gestalt Psychology
  - Methodological Individualism
  - Ontology
  - Reductionism
  - Social Systems
  - Systems Theory

Home

Holistic Medicine
- DC D362550
- HN Added, 1986.
- BT Holism
  - Medicine

Holland (1963-1985)
- HN DC 214390.
- Use Netherlands

Hollingshead, August deBelmont
- DC D362700
- SN Born 15 April 1907 - died 28 October 1980.
- HN Formerly (1968-1985) DC 214393, Hollingshead, A. B.

Holocaust
- DC D363000
- SN Use restricted to the attempted genocide of the Jews by the Nazis during World War II.
- HN Formerly (1982-1985) DC 214393a.
- UF Jewish Holocaust
- RT Anti-Semitism
  - Concentration Camps
  - Genocide
  - Jews
  - Nazism
  - Survival
  - World War II

Holy (1969-1985)
- HN DC 214394, deleted 1986. See now Saints, Sacredness, or other appropriate "Religion" terms.

Holy Days
- Use Holidays

Holy See
- Use Vatican

Homans, George Caspar
- DC D363300
- SN Born 11 August 1910 - .
- HN Formerly (1964-1985) DC 214395, Homans, George C.

Home Economics
- DC D363600
- HN Formerly (1964-1985) DC 214410.
- UF Domestic Science
- RT Curriculum
  - Food Preparation
  - Marriage And Family Education

Home Environment
- DC D363900
- HN Added, 1986.
- UF Family Environment
- BT Environment
- RT Childhood Factors
  - Children
  - Environmental Factors
  - Family
  - Family Conflict
  - Family Life
  - Family Stability
  - Family Violence
  - Family Work Relationship
  - Home Workplaces
  - Housing
  - Living Conditions
  - Marital Relations
  - Parent Child Relations

Home Health Care
- **DC** D364000
- **SN** Skilled and supportive services to promote, maintain, or restore health or to minimize the effects of illness or disability for aged, disabled, sick, or convalescing individuals at home or in the homes of caregivers.
- **HN** Added, 1989.
- **BT** Health Care
- **RT** After Care
  Caregivers
  Delivery Systems
  Elderly
  Outpatients

Home Industries
- **Use** Cottage Industries

Home Ownership
- **DC** D364200
- **HN** Added, 1986.
- **UF** Homeowners
  House Purchase
- **BT** Ownership
- **RT** Homesteading
  Housing
  Housing Costs
  Land Ownership
  Landlords
  Real Estate Industry

Home Workplaces
- **DC** D364400
- **SN** Situations in which professionals work at home or in which wage earners have work stations at home connected to corporate offices via computer and telecommunications systems. Do not confuse with Cottage Industries.
- **HN** Added, 1989.
- **BT** Workplaces
- **RT** Cottage Industries
  Family Life
  Family Work Relationship
  Home Environment
  Self Employment
  Small Businesses
  Work Environment
  Working Mothers
  Working Women

Home/Homes (1963-1985)
- **HN** DC 214400.
- **Use** Housing

Homelessness
- **DC** D364500
- **HN** Formerly (1984-1985) DC 214422.
- **UF** Hobo/Hobos (1984-1985)
- **RT** Deinstitutionalization
  Housing
  Poverty
  Refugees
  Skid Row
  Social Problems
  Squatters
  Urban Poverty

Homemakers
- **DC** D364800
- **HN** Formerly (1964-1985) DC 214425, Homemaker/Homemakers.
- **UF** Homemaking (1965-1985)
  Housewife/Housewives (1963-1985)
- **RT** Family Life
  Housework
  Sexual Division of Labor
  Wives
  Workers

Homemaking (1965-1985)
- **HN** DC 214435.
- **Use** Homemakers

Homeostasis/Homeostatic (1966-1985)
- **HN** DC 214450.
- **Use** Social Equilibrium

Homeowners
- **Use** Home Ownership

Homesteading
- **DC** D365100
- **HN** Formerly (1966-1985) DC 214480, Homestead/Homesteader/Homesteaders.
- **BT** Agrarian Structures
- **RT** Agricultural Enterprises
  Home Ownership
  Land Settlement
  Land Tenure
  Settlers

Homicide
- **DC** D365400
- **SN** Killing of one person by another, whether unlawful or legally justifiable.
- **HN** Formerly (1963-1985) DC 214500.
- **UF** Manslaughter
  Mass Murder
  Murder/Murders/Murderer/Murderers (1963-1985)
  Serial Murder
- **BT** Offenses
- **NT** Assassination
  Euthanasia
  Genocide
  Infanticide
- **RT** Assault
  Drunk Driving
  Feuds
  Lynching

Homilies
- **Use** Sermons

Hominid (1967-1985)
- **HN** DC 214550.
- **Use** Prehistoric Man

Homo Faber (1965-1985)
- **HN** DC 214725, deleted 1986.

Homogamy
- **DC** D365700
- **SN** Marriage between persons having similar physical or psychological traits.
- **HN** Formerly (1966-1985) DC 214740.
- **UF** Assortative (1964-1985)
- **BT** Marriage
- **RT** Complementary Needs
  Endogamy
  Marital Satisfaction
  Mate Selection

Homogeneity
- **DC** D366000
- **SN** Uniformity or close similarity of traits in a population or group. Opposite of Heterogeneity.
- **HN** Formerly (1963-1985) DC 214750.
- **RT** Group Composition
  Groups
  Heterogeneity
  Population

Homosexual Relationships
- **DC** D366200
- **SN** Includes relationships among male homosexuals and among lesbians.
- **HN** Added, 1989.
- **UF** Gay Relationships
- **BT** Interpersonal Relations
- **RT** Heterosexuality
  Homosexuality
  Lesbianism
  Sexual Behavior
  Sexual Preferences

Homosexuality
- **DC** D366300
- **SN** Use limited to male homosexuality; for female homosexuality use Lesbianism.
- **HN** Formerly (1963-1985) DC 215000 Homosexual/Homosexuality.
- **UF** Gay (1984-1985)
- **BT** Sexuality
- **NT** Lesbianism
- **RT** Bisexuality
  Heterosexuality
  Homosexual Relationships
  Sexual Behavior
  Sexual Preferences
  Sodomy
  Transsexualism

Honduras
- **DC** D366600
- **HN** Formerly (1964-1985) DC 215135, Honduras/Honduran/Hondurans.
- **BT** Central America

Honest/Honesty (1963-1985)
- **HN** DC 215140.
- **Use** Morality

Honeymoon (1964-1985)
- **HN** DC 215150, deleted 1986.

Hong Kong
- **DC** D366900
- **HN** Formerly (1963-1985) DC 215250.
- **BT** Far East
- **RT** China

Honolulu, Hawaii (1963-1985)
- **HN** DC 215300, deleted 1986.

Honor
- **DC** D367200
- **HN** Formerly (1963-1985) DC 215310.
- **RT** Human Dignity
  Morality
  Reputation
  Respect
  Self Concept
  Shame

Hoodoo (1964-1985)
- **HN** DC 215350.
- **Use** Voodooism

Hope Chest (1969-1985)
- **HN** DC 215400, deleted 1986.

Hopefulness
- **Use** Optimism

Hopelessness
- **Use** Pessimism

Horkheimer, Max
- **DC** D367500
- **SN** Born 14 February 1895 - died 7 July 1973.
- **HN** Formerly (1984-1985) DC 215432.

Hormones

Hormones
- DC D367800
- HN Formerly (1965-1985) DC 215500, Hormone/Hormones/Hormonal.
- UF Endocrine/Endocrines (1966-1985)
- RT Human Body

Horoscope (1983-1985)
- HN DC 215700.
- Use Astrology

Horowitz, Irving Louis
- DC D368100
- SN Born 25 September 1929 - .
- HN Formerly (1971-1985) DC 215710, Horowitz, I. L.

Hospices
- DC D368400
- SN Facilities that provide palliative and supportive care to dying patients and their families.
- HN Formerly (1982-1985) DC 215730.
- UF Terminal Care Facilities
- RT Dying
  Health Care
  Hospitals
  Terminal Illness

Hospital Wards
- DC D368700
- HN Formerly (1963-1985) DC 483875, Ward.
- UF Wards (Hospital)
- RT Hospitals

Hospitalization
- DC D369000
- HN Formerly (1963-1985) DC 216150.
- UF Mental Hospitalization
  Psychiatric Hospitalization
- BT Institutionalization (Persons)
- RT Admissions
  Discharge
  Hospitals
  Medical Decision Making
  Patients
  Treatment

Hospitals
- DC D369300
- HN Formerly (1963-1965) DC 216000, Hospital/Hospitals.
- BT Facilities
- NT Mental Hospitals
- RT Emergency Medical Services
  Health Care
  Hospices
  Hospital Wards
  Hospitalization
  Institutions
  Nursing Homes

Hostages
- DC D369600
- HN Formerly (1981-1985) DC 216242, Hostage/Hostages.
- RT Terrorism
  Victims

Hostels
- DC D369900
- SN Supervised lodgings for traveling young people.
- HN Formerly (1964-1985) DC 216250, Hostel.
- RT Buildings
  Hotels
  Housing

Hostility
- DC D370200
- HN Formerly (1963-1985) DC 216300, Hostility/Hostilities.
- UF Antagonism/Antagonize/Antagonist/Antagonists (1971-1985)
  Resentment
- BT Anger
- RT Aggression
  Alienation
  Conflict
  Hate
  Interpersonal Conflict
  Interpersonal Relations
  Prejudice
  Scapegoating
  Social Behavior
  Tension
  Threat
  Violence

Hotels
- DC D370500
- HN Formerly (1964-1985) DC 216320, Hotel/Hotels.
- UF Motels
- BT Facilities
- RT Buildings
  Hostels
  Housing
  Tourism

Hours of Work
- Use Working Hours

House Purchase
- Use Home Ownership

House/Houses (1963-1985)
- HN DC 216380.
- Use Housing

Household Tasks
- Use Housework

Household Workers
- Use Domestics

Households
- DC D370800
- HN Formerly (1963-1985) DC 216382, Household/Households.
- RT Family
  Female Headed Households
  Group Composition
  Heads of Households
  Housing
  Residence

Housekeepers
- Use Domestics

Housewife/Housewives (1963-1985)
- HN DC 216392.
- Use Homemakers

Housework
- DC D371100
- HN Formerly (1983-1985) DC 216395.
- UF Domestic Labor
  Household Tasks
- BT Work
- RT Domestics
  Family Life
  Homemakers
  Sexual Division of Labor

Housing

Housing
- DC D371400
- HN Formerly (1963-1985) DC 216400.
- UF Apartment/Apartments (1963-1985)
  Dwelling/Dwellings (1965-1985)
  Flats (Housing)
  Habitat/Habitats/Habitation (1964-1985)
  Home/Homes (1963-1985)
  House/Houses (1963-1985)
  Residences
- NT Public Housing
  Rental Housing
- RT Buildings
  City Planning
  Community Satisfaction
  Facilities
  Family Size
  Home Environment
  Home Ownership
  Homelessness
  Hostels
  Hotels
  Households
  Housing Costs
  Housing Market
  Housing Policy
  Living Conditions
  Low Income Areas
  Neighborhoods
  Real Estate Industry
  Relocation
  Residence
  Residential Institutions
  Residential Mobility
  Residential Patterns
  Residential Preferences
  Residential Segregation
  Shelters
  Slums
  Squatters
  Tenants
  Tenure

Housing Costs
- DC D371500
- HN Added, 1989.
- BT Costs
- NT Rents
- RT Home Ownership
  Housing
  Housing Market

Housing Market
- DC D371700
- HN Added, 1986.
- BT Markets
- RT Housing
  Housing Costs
  Real Estate Industry
  Residential Patterns
  Residential Segregation

Housing Patterns
- Use Residential Patterns

Housing Policy
- DC D372000
- HN Added, 1986.
- BT Social Policy
- RT Government Policy
  Housing
  Public Housing
  Urban Policy
  Welfare Policy

Housing

Housing Preferences
  Use Residential Preferences

Housing Segregation
  Use Residential Segregation

Houston, Texas
- **DC** D372300
- **HN** Added, 1986.
- **BT** Texas

Human Actions
  Use Behavior

Human Body
- **DC** D372600
- **HN** Added, 1986.
- **UF** Body/Bodies (1963-1985)
  Physiognomy/Physiognomies (1975-1985)
- **RT** Attractiveness
  Biological Sciences
  Biology
  Blood
  Blood Pressure
  Body Height
  Body Weight
  Brain
  Fatigue
  Genitals
  Hands
  Health
  Heart
  Hormones
  Hygiene
  Medicine
  Nudity
  Physical Characteristics
  Physical Contact
  Physically Handicapped
  Physiology
  Sensory Systems
  Skin

Human Capital
- **DC** D372900
- **SN** Education and training expenditures considered as an investment that can yield future benefits and profits. Do not confuse with Human Resources.
- **HN** Added, 1986.
- **BT** Investment
- **RT** Economic Development
  Education Work Relationship
  Human Resources
  Job Training
  Labor Productivity
  Labor Supply

Human Dignity
- **DC** D373050
- **HN** Formerly (1971-1985) DC 132425, Dignity.
- **UF** Dignity
  Individual Dignity
- **RT** Attitudes
  Honor
  Humanism
  Humanitarianism
  Respect
  Self Esteem
  Social Values

Human Ecology
- **DC** D373200
- **SN** Study of the adaptation of human organization to the environment. Specifically, the influence of competition and cooperation on the spatial and temporal organization and distribution of the physical environment (eg, streets, neighborhoods).

Human Ecology (cont'd)
- **HN** Added, 1986.
- **UF** Man Environment Relationship
  Man Nature Relationship
  Social Ecology
- **BT** Ecology
- **RT** Air Pollution
  Communities
  Conservation
  Energy Conservation
  Environment
  Natural Resources
  Pollution
  Pollution Control
  Social Area Analysis
  Sociology
  Soil Conservation
  Sustenance Organization
  Wastes

Human Factors Engineering
  Use Biotechnology

Human Nature
- **DC** D373500
- **HN** Added, 1986.
- **RT** Behavior
  Emotions
  Interaction
  Mind
  Needs
  Personality

Human Relations Movement
- **DC** D373800
- **SN** Approach to industrial sociology that emphasizes the importance of understanding and improving interpersonal relations among employees to job satisfaction and improved performance.
- **HN** Formerly (1963-1985) DC 217000, Human Relations.
- **RT** Employee Assistance Programs
  Industrial Management
  Industrial Sociology
  Interpersonal Relations
  Labor
  Labor Productivity
  Labor Relations
  Work Groups
  Work Humanization

Human Relations Training
  Use Sensitivity Training

Human Resources
- **DC** D374100
- **SN** A source of supply of people available for employment. Do not confuse with Human Capital.
- **HN** Added, 1986.
- **BT** Resources
- **NT** Labor
- **RT** Education Work Relationship
  Human Capital
  Intelligentsia
  Labor Force
  Occupations
  Skills
  Technical Assistance
  Workers

Human Rights
- **DC** D374400
- **HN** Formerly (1981-1985) DC 217100.
- **UF** Civil Liberties (1965-1985)
  Individual Rights
  Natural Rights
- **BT** Rights
- **NT** Civil Rights
  Womens Rights
- **RT** Equality
  Freedom

Humanism

Human Rights (cont'd)
- **RT** Individuals
  Liberal Democratic Societies
  Oppression
  Personhood
  Religious Beliefs
  Slavery
  Social Inequality
  Social Justice
  Social Movements
  Torture
  World Problems

Human Sacrifices
  Use Sacrificial Rites

Human Sciences
  Use Social Sciences

Human Service Organizations
- **DC** D374700
- **HN** Added, 1986.
- **BT** Social Agencies
- **RT** Charities
  Human Services
  Social Services

Human Services
- **DC** D375000
- **HN** Formerly (1983-1985) DC 217120.
- **BT** Services
- **NT** Child Care Services
  Health Services
  Social Services
- **RT** Assistance
  Counseling
  Disaster Relief
  Employee Assistance Programs
  Government Agencies
  Human Service Organizations
  Law Enforcement
  Needs
  Public Services
  Social Support
  Volunteers

Human Settlement
  Use Land Settlement

Human Sexuality
  Use Sexuality

Human Subjects (Research)
  Use Research Subjects

Human/Humans/Humanity (1963-1985)
- **HN** DC 216470, deleted 1986. See now specific "Human" terms.

Humanism
- **DC** D375300
- **SN** The cultivation of human rather than supernatural concerns and values. Originally, the revival of classical literature and ideals during the Renaissance.
- **HN** Formerly (1963-1985) DC 216750.
- **UF** Humanist/Humanists (1963-1985)
- **BT** Philosophical Doctrines
- **RT** Agnosticism
  Atheism
  Human Dignity
  Individualism
  Renaissance

Humanist　　　Ideal

Humanist/Humanists (1963-1985)
- HN　DC 216830.
- Use　Humanism

Humanistic Sociology
- DC　D375600
- HN　Formerly (1963-1985) DC 216800, Humanistic.
- BT　Sociology

Humanitarianism
- DC　D375900
- HN　Formerly (1964-1985) DC 216880, Humanitarian/Humanitarianism.
- RT　Altruism
　　Charities
　　Human Dignity
　　Social Values

Humanities
- DC　D376200
- HN　Formerly (1963-1985) DC 216850.
- UF　Arts
- NT　Fine Arts
　　Literature
　　Philosophy
- RT　Academic Disciplines
　　Art

Humanization
- DC　D376500
- HN　Formerly (1963-1985) DC 216900.
- NT　Work Humanization
- RT　Depersonalization
　　Life Satisfaction
　　Lifestyle
　　Needs
　　Quality of Life

Hume, David
- DC　D376800
- SN　Born 26 April 1711 - died 25 August 1776.
- HN　Formerly (1972-1985) DC 217300.

Humor
- DC　D377100
- HN　Formerly (1965-1985) DC 218000, Humor/Humorous.
- NT　Jokes
- RT　Cartoons
　　Comics (Publications)
　　Laughter

Hungarian (Language)
- Use　Oriental Languages

Hungary
- DC　D377400
- HN　Formerly (1963-1985) DC 218400, Hungary/Hungarian/Hungarians.
- BT　Eastern Europe

Hunger
- DC　D377700
- HN　Formerly (1964-1985) DC 218500.
- RT　Famine
　　Food
　　Instinct
　　Malnutrition
　　Nutrition
　　Poverty
　　Starvation
　　World Problems

Hunting
- DC　D378000
- HN　Formerly (1964-1985) DC 218520.
- UF　Game Hunting
　　Shooting
　　Trapping
- RT　Agricultural Policy
　　Animals
　　Food
　　Hunting And Gathering Societies

Hunting And Gathering Societies
- DC　D378300
- HN　Formerly (1985) DC 218517, Hunter-gatherers.
- UF　Foraging Societies
- BT　Traditional Societies
- RT　Hunting
　　Nomadic Societies
　　Prehistoric Man
　　Prehistory

Hurricane/Hurricanes (1984-1985)
- HN　DC 218580.
- Use　Natural Disasters

Husbands
- DC　D378600
- HN　Formerly (1963-1985) DC 218600, Husband/Husbands.
- UF　Married Men
- BT　Spouses
- RT　Fathers
　　Marital Relations
　　Spouse Abuse
　　Wives

Husserl, Edmund
- DC　D378900
- SN　Born 8 April 1859 - died 27 April 1938.
- HN　Formerly (1967-1985) DC 218620, Husserl, E.

Hutterite Brethren
- Use　Hutterites

Hutterites
- DC　D379200
- HN　Formerly (1966-1985) DC 218700, Hutterite/Hutterites.
- UF　Hutterite Brethren
- BT　Mennonites
- RT　Protestantism

Hydraulic (1977-1985)
- HN　DC 218760.
- Use　Technology

Hygiene
- DC　D379500
- HN　Formerly (1963-1985) DC 218770.
- UF　Body Care
　　Personal Hygiene
- RT　Diseases
　　Health
　　Human Body
　　Sanitation

Hypergamy (1970-1985)
- HN　DC 218900, deleted 1986.

Hypertension
- Use　Blood Pressure

Hypnosis
- DC　D379800
- HN　Formerly (1964-1985) DC 220000, Hypnosis/Hypnotic.
- UF　Hypnotherapy
- RT　Psychotherapy

Hypnotherapy
- Use　Hypnosis

Hypogamy (1970-1985)
- HN　DC 221010, deleted 1986.

Hypotheses
- DC　D379950
- HN　Formerly (1963-1985) DC 221100, Hypothesis/Hypotheses/Hypothetic/Hypothetical.
- BT　Propositions
- RT　Experiments
　　Explanation
　　Falsification
　　Heuristics
　　Operational Definitions
　　Prediction
　　Research Design
　　Research Methodology
　　Statistical Inference
　　Statistical Significance
　　Verification

Hysteria
- DC　D380100
- HN　Formerly (1965-1985) DC 222000, Hysteria/Hysterical.
- UF　Mass Hysteria
- RT　Disorders
　　Emotionally Disturbed

I And R Services
- Use　Information And Referral Services

Iatmul Culture (1977-1985)
- HN　DC 222100, deleted 1986. See now Oceanic Cultural Groups.

Iceland
- DC　D380400
- HN　Formerly (1963-1985) DC 222175, Iceland/Icelandic.
- BT　Scandinavia
　　Western Europe
- RT　North Atlantic Ocean

Icelandic (Language)
- Use　Germanic Languages

Idaho
- DC　D380700
- HN　Formerly (1967-1985) DC 222188.
- BT　United States of America
　　Western States

Idea/Ideas/Ideational (1963-1985)
- HN　DC 222195.
- Use　Concepts

Ideal Types
- DC　D380800
- SN　Abstract conceptualizations of social phenomena (eg, "marginal man," "perfectly competitive market," "church," "state") based on the most prominent characteristics of these phenomena. Ideal types are used as provisional aids in constructing hypotheses of empirical reality and imply a logical, not moral, conception of the ideal.
- HN　Added, 1986.
- UF　Constructed Types
- BT　Types
- RT　Analysis
　　Constructs
　　Heuristics
　　Models
　　Social Types
　　Stereotypes
　　Theories
　　Verstehen

Idealism

Idealism
- DC D380850
- SN The philosophical position that objects of the external world are representations of the mind or consciousness.
- HN Formerly (1963-1985) part of DC 222200, Ideal/Ideals/Idealism/Idealistic/Idealize/Idealization.
- BT Philosophical Doctrines
- RT Determinism
    Materialism
    Nominalism
    Phenomenology
    Realism (Philosophy)
    Symbolic Interactionism

Ideals
- Use Values

Ideation
- Use Concept Formation

Identification (1963-1985)
- HN DC 223002.
- Use Identity

Identity
- DC D381000
- SN A context-dependent term; select a more specific entry or coordinate with other terms. In contexts where Identity is closely related to Social Identity, select the latter.
- HN Formerly (1963-1985) DC 223300, Identity/Identities.
- UF Identification (1963-1985)
- NT Cultural Identity
    Ethnic Identity
    Group Identity
    Self Concept
    Sex Role Identity
    Social Identity
- RT Naming Practices
    Orientation
    Stereotypes

Ideological Conflict
- Use Ideological Struggle

Ideological Hegemony
- Use Dominant Ideologies

Ideological Struggle
- DC D381075
- HN Added, 1986.
- UF Ideological Conflict
- BT Conflict
- RT Class Struggle
    East And West
    Geopolitics
    Political Ideologies
    Politics
    Revolutions

Ideologies
- DC D381100
- SN Belief systems with emotional and utopian components, often seen as a source of distortion or bias.
- HN Formerly (1963-1985) DC 223500, Ideology/Ideologies/Ideological.
- UF Doctrine/Doctrines/Doctrinal (1971-1985)
- NT Bourgeois Ideologies
    Dominant Ideologies
    Educational Ideologies
    Egalitarianism
    Elitism
    Philosophical Doctrines

Ideologies (cont'd)
- NT Political Ideologies
    Religious Doctrines
- RT Base And Superstructure
    Beliefs
    Cultural Values
    Dialectical Materialism
    Leninism
    Marxism
    Marxist Sociology
    Methodology (Philosophical)
    Norms
    Political Systems
    Principles
    Social Values
    Sociology of Knowledge
    Theories
    Values
    Worldview

Igbo
- Use African Languages

Ignorance
- DC D381300
- HN Formerly (1963-1985) DC 223550.
- RT Knowledge
    Literacy

Illegal (1963-1985)
- HN DC 223570, deleted 1986.

Illegal Alien/Illegal Aliens (1985)
- HN DC 223572.
- Use Undocumented Immigrants

Illegal/Unethical Conduct (1985)
- HN DC 223574, deleted 1986.

Illegitimacy
- DC D381600
- HN Formerly (1963-1985) DC 223580, Illegitimacy/Illegitimate.
- UF Children (Illegitimate)
- RT Birth
    Unwanted Pregnancy

Illinois
- DC D381900
- HN Formerly (1963-1985) DC 223620.
- BT Midwestern States
    United States of America
- NT Chicago, Illinois

Illiterate/Illiterates/Illiteracy (1963-1985)
- HN DC 223635.
- Use Literacy

Illness
- DC D382200
- SN State or condition of being ill.
- HN Formerly (1963-1985) DC 223700, Illness/Illnesses.
- UF Sickness (1963-1985)
- NT Chronic Illness
    Terminal Illness
- RT Diseases
    Health
    Health Care
    Health Problems
    Illness Behavior
    Medicine
    Morbidity
    Patients
    Practitioner Patient Relationship
    Primary Health Care
    Self Care
    Sick Role
    Symptoms

Immigration

Illness Behavior
- DC D382500
- HN Added, 1986.
- BT Behavior
- RT Health Behavior
    Illness
    Patients
    Sick Role
    Treatment Compliance

Imagery (1963-1985)
- HN DC 226000.
- Use Images

Images
- DC D382800
- HN Formerly (1963-1985) DC 225000, Image/Images.
- UF Imagery (1963-1985)
- RT Art
    Audiovisual Media
    Concepts
    Mind
    Perceptions
    Self Concept
    Symbolism

Imagination
- DC D383100
- HN Formerly (1964-1985) DC 226300.
- BT Cognition
- RT Creativity
    Empathy
    Fantasy
    Intuition
    Play
    Reality
    Thinking

Imitation
- DC D383400
- HN Formerly (1963-1985) DC 226500.
- BT Behavior
- RT Learning
    Role Models

Immaturity/Immature (1975-1985)
- HN DC 226525, deleted 1986.

Immigrants
- DC D383700
- HN Formerly (1963-1985) DC 226540, Immigrant/Immigrants.
- NT Undocumented Immigrants
- RT Assimilation
    Biculturalism
    Borders
    Cultural Conflict
    Cultural Identity
    Ethnicity
    Foreigners
    Immigration
    Migrants
    Migration
    Nativism
    Newcomers
    Refugees
    Settlement Patterns
    Settlers
    Social Integration

Immigration
- DC D384000
- HN Formerly (1963-1985) DC 226565.
- BT Migration
- RT Borders
    Colonization
    Emigration
    Foreigners
    Immigrants
    Sponsorship

Immunization

Immunization
- **Use** Vaccination

Impact (1978-1985)
- **HN** DC 226620.
- **Use** Effects

Imperialism
- **DC** D384300
- **SN** Policy of extending the rule of one nation over foreign countries, often for economic gain.
- **HN** Formerly (1963-1985) DC 226630, Imperialism/Imperialist/Imperialists.
- **BT** Political Ideologies
- **NT** Colonialism
- **RT** Capitalism
  Center And Periphery
  Economic History
  Economic Systems
  Empires
  Foreign Policy
  Invasion
  Militarism
  Modes of Production
  State Power
  War

Implementation
- **DC** D384450
- **HN** Formerly (1984-1985) DC 226641.
- **NT** Policy Implementation
  Program Implementation
- **RT** Activities
  Development
  Management
  Performance
  Planning
  Praxis

Implication/Implications (1971-1985)
- **HN** DC 226643, deleted 1986. See now Meaning, Effects, or Influence.

Import/Importing (1964-1985)
- **HN** DC 226650.
- **Use** Exports And Imports

Impression Formation
- **DC** D384600
- **HN** Formerly (1963-1985) part of DC 22680, Impression/Impressions.
- **BT** Formation
  Social Perception
- **RT** Attribution
  Impression Management
  Situation
  Social Attitudes
  Social Interaction

Impression Management
- **DC** D384900
- **SN** In symbolic interactionism, the capacity to play normative roles adroitly, successfully controlling the course of social encounters by interpreting and sending appropriate verbal and nonverbal cues.
- **HN** Formerly (1963-1985) part of DC 226680, Impression/Impressions.
- **UF** Altercasting (1964-1985)
  Ingratiation
- **BT** Management
- **RT** Dramaturgical Approach
  Impression Formation
  Self Presentation
  Situation
  Social Behavior
  Social Interaction
  Social Perception

Impressionism
- **Use** Artistic Styles

Impressionist/Impressionists/Impressionism (1964-1985)
- **HN** DC 226685, deleted 1986. See now Artists or Artistic Styles.

Imprisonment
- **DC** D385200
- **HN** Formerly (1966-1985) DC 226700.
- **UF** Incarceration (1984-1985)
- **RT** Correctional System
  Detention
  Institutionalization (Persons)
  Juvenile Offenders
  Offenders
  Parole
  Penal Reform
  Pretrial Release
  Prisoners
  Prisonization
  Prisons
  Probation
  Recidivism
  Sentencing

Improvement
- **DC** D385300
- **HN** Formerly (1970-1985) DC 226800, Improvement/Improvements.
- **BT** Development
- **RT** Achievement
  Antipoverty Programs
  Change
  Innovations
  Progress
  Reform
  Rehabilitation
  Satisfaction
  Urban Renewal

Impulsiveness
- **DC** D385350
- **HN** Formerly (1964-1985) DC 226900, Impulse/Impulsiveness/Impulsivity.
- **UF** Reflective/Reflection (1969-1985)
- **BT** Personality Traits
- **RT** Behavior
  Compulsivity
  Delay of Gratification
  Deviant Behavior
  Spontaneity

In Vitro Fertilization
- **Use** Artificial Insemination

Inanimate Objects
- **DC** D385425
- **HN** Added, 1986.
- **UF** Objects (Things)
  Physical Objects
  Things
- **RT** Interpretive Sociology
  Material Culture
  Materials

Inbreeding
- **DC** D385500
- **SN** Use for human inbreeding only. For the breeding of animals use Animal Husbandry.
- **HN** Formerly (1963-1985) DC 226990, Inbreed/Inbreeding.
- **RT** Birth
  Consanguinity
  Incest

Income

Incarceration (1984-1985)
- **HN** DC 226995.
- **Use** Imprisonment

Incentives
- **DC** D385800
- **HN** Formerly (1963-1985) DC 227000, Incentive/Incentives.
- **NT** Profit Motive
- **RT** Awards
  Encouragement
  Motivation
  Recognition (Achievement)
  Rewards

Incest
- **DC** D386100
- **HN** Formerly (1963-1985) DC 227500.
- **BT** Sexual Behavior
- **RT** Child Sexual Abuse
  Consanguinity
  Inbreeding
  Oedipal Complex
  Rape
  Sexual Deviation
  Sexual Intercourse
  Taboos
  Unwanted Pregnancy

Income
- **DC** D386400
- **HN** Formerly (1963-1985) DC 227600, Income/Incomes.
- **UF** Earning/Earnings/Earner/Earners (1969-1985)
  Family Income
  Revenue (1985)
- **NT** Profits
- **RT** Budgets
  Capital
  Compensation
  Economics
  Expenditures
  Finance
  Gross National Product
  Income Distribution
  Income Inequality
  Informal Sector
  Low Income Areas
  Low Income Groups
  Money
  Pensions
  Rents
  Salaries
  Saving
  Standard of Living
  Taxation
  Wages
  Wealth

Income Distribution
- **DC** D386700
- **SN** Income patterns by social factors such as class, gender, age, and ethnicity.
- **HN** Added, 1986.
- **UF** Income Redistribution
- **BT** Distribution
- **RT** Distributive Justice
  Income
  Income Inequality
  Salaries
  Standard of Living
  Wages
  Wealth

Income

Income Inequality
- **DC** D387000
- **HN** Added, 1986.
- **BT** Inequality
- **RT** Dependency Theory
  Distributive Justice
  Income
  Income Distribution
  Labor Market Segmentation
  Occupational Segregation
  Sexual Division of Labor
  Social Class
  Social Stratification
  Socioeconomic Status
  Wages
  Wealth

Income Maintenance Programs
- **DC** D387300
- **HN** Added, 1986.
- **BT** Programs
- **RT** Antipoverty Programs
  Elderly
  Food Stamps
  Low Income Groups

Income Redistribution
- **Use** Income Distribution

Incongruity/Incongruities/Incongruence (1963-1985)
- **HN** DC 227620, deleted 1986. See now Status Inconsistency or Congruence (Psychology).

Inconsistency (Status)
- **Use** Status Inconsistency

Indebtedness (1972-1985)
- **HN** DC 227637.
- **Use** Debts

Indecision (1978-1985)
- **HN** DC 227640.
- **Use** Decision Making

Independence
- **DC** D387600
- **HN** Formerly (1963-1985) DC 227660, Independent/Independence/Independency.
- **RT** Autonomy
  Dependency (Psychology)

Independent Schools
- **Use** Private Schools

Independent Variables
- **Use** Variables

Indeterminism
- **DC** D387650
- **SN** The doctrine that some events and behaviors may not entirely be governed by cause and effect but may also be the result of free will or chance.
- **HN** Formerly (1963-1985) DC 227680, Indeterminism/Indeterminacy.
- **BT** Epistemological Doctrines
- **RT** Determinism
  Psychology
  Voluntarism
  Will

Indexes (Measures)
- **DC** D387700
- **HN** Formerly (1963-1985) DC 227700, Index/Indexes/Indexing.
- **UF** Composite Indexes

Indexes (Measures) (cont'd)
- **UF** Indicators (1969-1985)
- **BT** Measures (Instruments)
- **NT** Social Indicators
- **RT** Operational Definitions
  Scales
  Trends

India
- **DC** D387900
- **HN** Formerly (1963-1985) DC 228000, India/Indian/Indians.
- **BT** South Asia
- **NT** Andhra Pradesh, India
  Bengal
  Bihar, India
  Bombay, India
  Calcutta, India
  Delhi, India
  Gujarat, India
  Kerala, India
  Madras, India
  Punjab, India
  Rajasthan, India
  Uttar Pradesh, India
  West Bengal, India

Indian/Indians (1964-1985)
- **HN** DC 228500.
- **Use** American Indians

Indiana
- **DC** D388200
- **HN** Formerly (1963-1985) DC 228675.
- **BT** Midwestern States
  United States of America
- **NT** Indianapolis, Indiana

Indianapolis, Indiana
- **DC** D388500
- **HN** Formerly (1963-1985) DC 228700, Indianapolis, Ind.
- **BT** Indiana

Indic Languages
- **DC** D388800
- **HN** Added, 1986.
- **UF** Assamese (Language)
  Bengali (Language)
  Dardic Languages
  Hindi (1969-1985)
  Hindustani
  Marathi (Language)
  Nepali (Language)
  Oriya (Language)
  Panjabi (Language)
  Sanskrit
  Sindi (Language)
  Sinhala (Language)
- **BT** Indoeuropean Languages

Indicators (1969-1985)
- **HN** DC 228759.
- **Use** Indexes (Measures)

Indies, East/Indian, East/Indians, East (1964-1985)
- **HN** DC 228765, deleted 1986. See now Southeast Asia, Indonesia, or Malaysia.

Indies, West/Indian, West/Indians, West (1964-1985)
- **HN** DC 228767.
- **Use** Caribbean

Individual

Indifference (1971-1985)
- **HN** DC 228775.
- **Use** Apathy

Indigenous Populations
- **DC** D389100
- **HN** Formerly (1976-1985) DC 228776, Indigenous.
- **UF** Native/Natives (1967-1985)
- **RT** Aboriginal Australians
  Acculturation
  American Indians
  Assimilation
  Colonialism
  Cultural Change
  Cultural Conflict
  Culture Contact
  Eskimos
  Ethnic Groups
  Ethnic Relations
  Foreigners
  Intercultural Communication
  Mayans
  Mestizos
  Nativism
  Nativistic Movements
  Population
  Race
  Social Integration
  Social Isolation
  Traditional Societies

Indigent/Indigence (1969-1985)
- **HN** DC 228777.
- **Use** Poverty

Individual Collective Relationship
- **DC** D389200
- **SN** Studies of social and cultural identity dealing with both individual and shared aspects and the processes through which people affiliate with social groups.
- **HN** Added, 1986.
- **UF** Collective Individual Relationship
  Group Individual Relationship
  Society Individual Relationship
- **BT** Relations
- **RT** Alienation
  Collective Behavior
  Figuration Sociology
  Group Dynamics
  Group Identity
  Groups
  Individuals
  Intergroup Relations
  Interpersonal Relations
  Membership
  Peer Relations
  Social Acceptance
  Social Dynamics
  Social Groups
  Social Interaction
  Social Isolation
  Society

Individual Differences
- **DC** D389225
- **SN** Qualitative or quantitative differences in specific characteristics (eg, personality, learning ability) that explain variations in the behavior, attitudes, or performance of individuals.
- **HN** Added, 1986.
- **BT** Differences
- **RT** Age Differences
  Behavior
  Child Development
  Personality
  Physical Characteristics
  Sex Differences
  Social Background

Individual

Individual Dignity
  Use Human Dignity

Individual Rights
  Use Human Rights

Individualism
  DC D389275
  SN Any doctrine that advocates the interests, liberty, and independent action of the individual.
  HN Formerly (1963-1985) part of DC 229000, Individual/Individualism/ Individuality/Individualistic/ Individualization.
  UF Self Interest
  BT Political Ideologies
  RT Collectivism
      Humanism
      Individuals
      Liberalism
      Philosophical Doctrines
      Self Actualization

Individualization (1975-1985)
  HN DC 230050, deleted 1986. See now Anomie or Differentiation.

Individuals
  DC D389300
  HN Formerly (1963-1985) part of DC 229000, Individual/Individualism/ Individuality/Individualization.
  UF Person/Persons (1963-1985)
  RT Adult Development
      Age Groups
      Child Development
      Conscience
      Experience
      Gifted
      Handicapped
      Human Rights
      Individual Collective Relationship
      Individualism
      Life Satisfaction
      Moral Development
      Personality
      Personhood
      Roles
      Self Actualization
      Self Concept
      Self Disclosure
      Self Esteem
      Self Help
      Socialization
      Subjectivity

Indochina
  DC D389400
  SN Use limited to Indochina prior to 1954. See also Vietnam, Laos, and Kampuchea.
  HN Formerly (1966-1985) DC 230200.
  BT Southeast Asia
  RT Kampuchea
      Laos
      Vietnam

Indoctrination
  DC D389700
  HN Formerly (1963-1985) DC 230430.
  NT Brainwashing
  RT Attitude Change
      Political Socialization
      Propaganda

Indoeuropean Languages
  DC D390000
  HN Formerly (1963-1985) DC 230270, Indoeuropean.
  BT Languages
  NT Germanic Languages
      Indic Languages
      Romance Languages
      Slavic Languages
  RT European Cultural Groups

Indonesia
  DC D390300
  HN Formerly (1963-1985) DC 230460, Indonesia/Indonesian/Indonesians.
  UF Borneo (1963-1985)
      Sumatra, Indonesia (1963-1985)
  BT Southeast Asia
  NT Bali
      Jakarta, Indonesia

Indo-Pakistan (1964-1985)
  HN DC 230375, deleted 1986.

Induction
  DC D390450
  SN Inference about the whole based on assessment of facts about representative cases.
  HN Formerly (1963-1985) DC 230500, Induction/Inductive/Inductivism.
  BT Reasoning
  RT Deduction
      Generalization
      Inference
      Logic
      Scientific Method

Industrial (1963-1985)
  HN DC 230575, deleted 1986. See now specific "Industrial" or "Labor" terms.

Industrial Automation
  DC D390600
  HN Added, 1986.
  UF Robotization in Industry
  BT Automation
  RT Biotechnology
      Computers
      High Technology Industries
      Industrial Production
      Industry
      Machinery
      Technological Change
      Work Humanization
      Worker Machine Relationship

Industrial Collectives
  DC D390900
  HN Added, 1986.
  BT Collectives
      Industrial Enterprises

Industrial Conflict
  Use Labor Disputes

Industrial Countries (1985)
  HN DC 230585.
  Use Industrial Societies

Industrial Democracy
  DC D391200
  SN Industrial workers' participation in management decisions that concern working conditions.
  HN Added, 1986.
  BT Industrial Management
  NT Worker Control
      Worker Participation
  RT Collective Bargaining
      Labor

Industrial

Industrial Democracy (cont'd)
  RT Labor Relations
      Management
      Unions
      Worker Ownership

Industrial Development
  DC D391500
  HN Added, 1986.
  BT Economic Development
  RT High Technology Industries
      Industrial Production
      Industrialization
      Industry
      Public Sector Private Sector Relations
      Research And Development
      Technological Innovations
      Urban Development

Industrial Enterprises
  DC D391800
  HN Added, 1986.
  UF Industrial Firms
      Industrial Organizations
  BT Enterprises
  NT Industrial Collectives
  RT Factories
      Industrial Management
      Industrial Production
      Industrial Workers
      Industry
      Manufacturing Industries
      Nationalization
      Privatization
      Work Organization

Industrial Firms
  Use Industrial Enterprises

Industrial Foremen
  Use Foremen

Industrial Management
  DC D392100
  HN Added, 1986.
  BT Management
  NT Industrial Democracy
  RT Foremen
      Human Relations Movement
      Industrial Enterprises
      Industrial Sociology
      Industrial Workers
      Industry
      Labor Productivity
      Labor Relations
      Organizational Effectiveness
      Personnel Management
      Work Organization

Industrial Organizations
  Use Industrial Enterprises

Industrial Plants
  Use Factories

Industrial Production
  DC D392250
  HN Added, 1986.
  UF Mass Production (1963-1985)
  BT Production
  RT Forces And Relations of Production
      Industrial Automation
      Industrial Development
      Industrial Enterprises
      Industrialization
      Industry
      Labor Process
      Manufacturing Industries
      Modes of Production

Industrial

Industrial Relations
  Use Labor Relations

Industrial Research
  Use Research And Development

Industrial Revolution
  Use Industrialization

Industrial Safety
  Use Occupational Safety And Health

Industrial Sanitation
  Use Sanitation

Industrial Sectors
  Use Industry

Industrial Self Management
  Use Worker Control

Industrial Societies
  DC D392400
  HN Added, 1986.
  UF Developed Countries
     Industrial Countries (1985)
  BT Society
  RT Capitalist Societies
     Civilization
     Complex Societies
     Convergence Theory
     Gemeinschaft And Gesellschaft
     Industrial Sociology
     Industrialism
     Industrialization
     Industry
     International Division of Labor
     Mass Society
     Modern Society
     Modernization
     Postindustrial Societies
     Rationalization
     Urbanization
     Western Civilization

Industrial Sociology
  DC D392700
  HN Formerly (1985) DC 230610.
  BT Sociology
  RT Human Relations Movement
     Industrial Management
     Industrial Societies
     Industry
     Sociology of Work

Industrial Workers
  DC D393000
  HN Added, 1986.
  UF Factory Workers
  BT Blue Collar Workers
  RT Industrial Enterprises
     Industrial Management
     Industry
     Manufacturing Industries
     Worker Machine Relationship
     Working Class

Industrialism
  DC D393300
  HN Formerly (1963-1985) DC 230650.
  RT Economic Systems
     Industrial Societies
     Industrialization
     Industry
     Pollution
     Western Society

Industrialization
  DC D393600
  HN Formerly (1963-1985) DC 230800, Industrialization/Industrializing.
  UF Industrial Revolution
  BT Social Processes
  RT Convergence Theory
     Deindustrialization
     Developing Countries
     Economic Change
     Economic Development
     Employment Changes
     Gemeinschaft And Gesellschaft
     Industrial Development
     Industrial Production
     Industrial Societies
     Industrialism
     Industry
     Labor Process
     Modernization
     Occupational Structure
     Social Change
     Technological Change
     Technology Transfer
     Unionization
     Urbanization

Industrialized (1970-1985)
  HN DC 232308, deleted 1986.

Industry
  DC D393900
  HN Formerly (1963-1985) DC 232000, Industry/Industries.
  UF Industrial Sectors
  NT Construction Industry
     Cottage Industries
     Entertainment Industry
     Food Industry
     High Technology Industries
     Manufacturing Industries
     Mining Industry
     Petroleum Industry
     Public Sector Private Sector Relations
     Publishing Industry
     Retail Industry
     Service Industries
     Shipping Industry
  RT Agriculture
     Business
     Commodities
     Economic Sectors
     Economics
     Enterprises
     Finance
     Fishing
     Food Industry
     Forestry
     Industrial Automation
     Industrial Development
     Industrial Enterprises
     Industrial Management
     Industrial Production
     Industrial Societies
     Industrial Sociology
     Industrial Workers
     Industrialism
     Industrialization
     Labor
     Labor Relations
     Machinery
     Markets
     Materials
     Oligopolies
     Plant Closure
     Postindustrial Societies
     Production

Infants

Industry (cont'd)
  RT Products
     Raw Materials
     Technology
     Transportation

Inequality
  DC D394200
  SN A context-dependent term; select a more specific entry or coordinate with other terms. In contexts where Inequality is closely related to Social Inequality, select the latter.
  HN Formerly (1963-1985) DC 232150, Inequality/Inequalities.
  UF Inequity/Inequities (1972-1985)
  NT High Technology Industry
     Income Inequality
     Sexual Inequality
     Social Inequality
  RT Discrimination
     Equality
     Oppression
     Prejudice
     Segregation
     Social Justice
     Stratification

Inequity/Inequities (1972-1985)
  HN DC 232180.
  Use Inequality

Infant Mortality
  DC D394500
  HN Added, 1986.
  UF Perinatal Mortality
     Stillbirth/Stillbirths/Stillborn (1974-1985)
  BT Child Mortality
  RT Birth
     Death
     Health Policy
     Infanticide
     Mortality Rates
     Pediatrics
     Premature Infants
     Survival

Infanticide
  DC D394800
  SN Killing a child aged 24 months or younger.
  HN Formerly (1963-1985) DC 232400.
  BT Homicide
  RT Abortion
     Family Violence
     Infant Mortality

Infantile Autism
  Use Autism

Infantile Paralysis
  Use Poliomyelitis

Infants
  DC D395100
  SN Persons aged 0 to 24 months.
  HN Formerly (1963-1985) DC 232300, Infant/Infants/Infancy.
  UF Baby/Babies (1984-1985)
     Neonate/Neonatal (1963-1985)
     Newborn/Newborns (1964-1985)
  BT Age Groups
     Children
  NT Premature Infants
  RT Birth
     Child Development
     First Birth Timing
     Parent Child Relations
     Pediatrics

Inference

Inference
- DC D395200
- HN Formerly (1963-1985) DC 232465, Inference/Inferences/Inferential.
- BT Reasoning
- RT Analogy
  Constructs
  Deduction
  Generalization
  Induction
  Logic
  Propositions
  Statistical Inference
  Validity

Inferential Statistics
- Use Statistical Inference

Inferiority (1964-1985)
- HN DC 232500.
- Use Subordination

Infertility (1966-1985)
- HN DC 232525.
- Use Childlessness

Infidelity (1964-1985)
- HN DC 232600.
- Use Extramarital Sexuality

Inflation
- DC D395400
- HN Formerly (1964-1985) DC 232660.
- RT Business Cycles
  Cost Containment
  Costs
  Economic Change
  Economic Conditions
  Economic Crises
  Economic Problems
  Economic Theories
  Prices
  Supply And Demand

Influence
- DC D395600
- SN A context-dependent term encompassing the ability to effect change through indirect means. In contexts where Influence is closely related to the narrower term Social Influence, select the latter.
- HN Formerly (1963-1985) DC 232700, Influence/Influences/Influencer/Influencers.
- NT Social Influence
- RT Authority
  Biological Factors
  Causality
  Control
  Elites
  Environmental Factors
  Family Power
  Interest Groups
  Power
  Pressure
  Primary Groups
  Reference Groups
  Relevance
  Salience
  Significant Others
  Sociocultural Factors
  Socioeconomic Factors

Influentials/Influentiality (1964-1985)
- HN DC 232780, deleted 1986. See now Influence or Opinion Leaders.

Influenza
- DC D395700
- HN Formerly (1965-1985) DC 232810.
- BT Diseases

Informal Economies (1985)
- HN DC 232898.
- Use Informal Sector

Informal Sector
- DC D396000
- SN The area of a nation's economy derived from self-employed trade or labor.
- HN Added, 1986.
- UF Informal Economies (1985)
  Underground Economy
- BT Economic Sectors
- RT Income
  Nonprofit Organizations

Informal Structure
- Use Structure

Informal/Informality (1963-1985)
- HN DC 232890, deleted 1986. See now Informal Sector or Structure.

Informant/Informants (1963-1985)
- HN DC 232930.
- Use Respondents

Information
- DC D396300
- HN Formerly (1963-1985) DC 233000, Information/Informational.
- NT Data
- RT Communication
  Diffusion
  Information And Referral Services
  Information Dissemination
  Information Processing
  Information Sources
  Information Technology
  Information Theory
  Knowledge
  Scientific Technological Revolution
  Technological Change

Information And Referral Services
- DC D396350
- HN Added, 1986.
- UF I And R Services
- BT Community Services
- RT Community Organizations
  Counseling
  Delivery Systems
  Employee Assistance Programs
  Information
  Information Dissemination
  Libraries
  Referral
  Social Agencies
  Social Response
  Social Work

Information Banks
- Use Data Banks

Information Dissemination
- DC D396600
- HN Added, 1986.
- RT Academic Freedom
  Censorship
  Cultural Transmission
  Diffusion
  Information
  Information And Referral Services
  Information Processing

Informed

Information Dissemination (cont'd)
- RT Information Sources
  Information Theory
  Libraries
  Mass Media
  Propaganda
  Publicity
  Publishing Industry
  Referral
  Technology Transfer

Information Processing
- DC D396900
- HN Formerly (1985) DC 233300.
- NT Coding
  Data Collection
  Data Processing
- RT Cognition
  Communication
  Cybernetics
  Documentation
  Information
  Information Dissemination
  Information Technology
  Information Theory

Information Sources
- DC D397100
- HN Added, 1986.
- UF Sources of Information
- RT Archives
  Data
  Data Banks
  Data Collection
  Discovery
  Information
  Information Dissemination
  Knowledge
  Libraries
  Mass Media
  Reference Materials

Information Technology
- DC D397175
- HN Added, 1989.
- BT Technology
- RT Communication
  Computers
  Cybernetics
  Electronic Technology
  High Technology Industries
  Information
  Information Processing
  Telecommunications

Information Theory
- DC D397200
- SN Mathematical theories dealing with the efficiency, accuracy, and encoding effectiveness of communication and signal transmission.
- HN Formerly (1964-1985) DC 233400.
- BT Theories
- RT Communication
  Cybernetics
  Data Processing
  Information
  Information Dissemination
  Information Processing
  Telecommunications

Informed Consent
- DC D397300
- SN Agreement to an experimental or therapeutic procedure on the basis of the subject fully understanding its nature and possible risks.
- HN Formerly (1971-1985) DC 112480, Consent.
- UF Consent (Informed)
- RT Agreement
  Experiments

Ingratiation

Informed Consent (cont'd)
- RT Health Care
- Medical Decision Making
- Research Subjects
- Treatment

Ingratiation
- Use Impression Management

Inheritance And Succession
- DC D397500
- HN Formerly (1963-1985), DC 233700, Inheritance.
- UF Patrimony/Patrimonial (1972-1985)
- Succession (1963-1985)
- RT Ascription
- Birth Order
- Descent
- Kinship
- Property

Inhibit/Inhibition/Inhibitions/Inhibiting (1965-1985)
- HN DC 234000, deleted 1986.

Initiation Rites
- DC D397800
- HN Formerly (1963-1985) DC 234628, Initiation/Initiations.
- BT Rites of Passage
- RT Genital Mutilation
- Life Stage Transitions
- Puberty
- Social Status
- Traditional Societies

Initiative (1963-1985)
- HN DC 234630, deleted 1986.

Injuries
- DC D398100
- HN Formerly (1963-1985) DC 234635, Injury/Injuries.
- RT Accidents
- Disorders
- Health
- Occupational Safety And Health
- Rehabilitation
- Safety
- Shock
- Workers Compensation Insurance

In-Law/In-Laws (1964-1985)
- HN DC 234638.
- Use Relatives

Inmate/Inmates (1963-1985)
- HN DC 234640.
- Use Prisoners

Inner And Other Directedness
- DC D398400
- SN In social psychology, the degree of personal autonomy, with total independence on one extreme and conformism and psychological dependency on the other.
- HN Added, 1986.
- UF Inner Directed (1969-1985)
- Other Directed (1969-1985)
- BT Orientation
- RT Locus of Control
- Reference Groups

Inner City
- Use Central Cities

Inner City Poverty
- Use Urban Poverty

Inner Directed (1969-1985)
- HN DC 234641.
- Use Inner And Other Directedness

Innovations
- DC D398700
- HN Formerly (1963-1985) DC 234645, Innovation/Innovations/Innovative/Innovativeness/Innovators.
- NT Technological Innovations
- RT Adoption of Innovations
- Agricultural Mechanization
- Alternative Approaches
- Discovery
- Entrepreneurship
- Improvement
- Inventions
- Patents
- Science And Technology
- Scientific Discoveries
- Technology Transfer

Inorganic Chemistry
- Use Chemistry

Input (1964-1985)
- HN DC 234665, deleted 1986.

Inquiry/Inquiries (1963-1985)
- HN DC 234670.
- Use Research

Insanity
- Use Psychosis

Insanity Defense
- DC D399000
- HN Formerly (1963-1985) DC 234680, Insane/Insanity.
- UF Plea (Insanity)
- BT Legal Procedure
- RT Mental Illness
- Offenders
- Trials

Insecurity (1966-1985)
- HN DC 234800.
- Use Security

Insemination (1968-1985)
- HN DC 234850.
- Use Artificial Insemination

Insight (1965-1985)
- HN DC 234900.
- Use Intuition

Insolvency
- Use Bankruptcy

Instability (1963-1985)
- HN DC 234976.
- Use Stability

Instinct
- DC D399300
- HN Formerly (1963-1985) DC 234980, Instinct/Instincts.
- BT Behavior
- RT Hunger
- Knowledge
- Motivation
- Sexual Behavior
- Spontaneity

Instruct

Institutes
- DC D399500
- HN Formerly (1963-1985) DC 235300, Institute/Institutes.
- UF Research Institutes
- BT Organizations (Social)
- RT Congresses And Conventions
- Symposia

Institutional/Institutionalism (1963-1985)
- HN DC 235580, deleted 1986. See now appropriate "Organizational" terms.

Institutionalization (Persons)
- DC D399600
- SN Placement or confinement of an individual in a mental hospital, correctional facility, or other such institution.
- HN Formerly (1963-1985) part of DC 235630, Institutionalize/Institutionalized/Institutionalization.
- UF Commitment (Civil)
- NT Hospitalization
- RT Admissions
- After Care
- Deinstitutionalization
- Discharge
- Imprisonment
- Prisoners
- Recidivism
- Residential Institutions

Institutionalization (Social)
- DC D399900
- SN The growth and crystallization of norms, values, and laws governing social behavior.
- HN Formerly (1963-1985) part of DC 235630, Institutionalize/Institutionalized/Institutionalization.
- RT Social Behavior
- Social Institutions
- Social Processes

Institutions
- DC D400000
- SN A context-dependent term for formally structured social organizations. Select a more specific entry or coordinate with other terms. In sociological contexts where Institutions is closely related to Social Institutions, the latter is preferred.
- HN Formerly (1963-1985) DC 235500, Institution/Institutions.
- NT Social Institutions
- RT Associations
- Churches
- Corporations
- Courts
- Facilities
- Foundations
- Government Agencies
- Hospitals
- Libraries
- Museums
- Prisons
- Residential Institutions
- Schools

Instruct/Instruction/Instructions/Instructors (1964-1985)
- HN DC 235635, deleted 1986. See now Teachers or Teaching.

Instruction   Intercultural

Instruction
- **Use** Teaching

Instructional Methods
- **Use** Teaching Methods

Instructor Attitudes
- **Use** Teacher Attitudes

Instructors
- **Use** Teachers

Instrument/Instruments/Instrumental (1963-1985)
- **HN** DC 235640.
- **Use** Measures (Instruments)

Insurance
- **DC** D400200
- **HN** Formerly (1963-1985) DC 236085.
- **UF** Actuary/Actuarial (1968-1985)
  Coverage (Insurance)
- **NT** Health Insurance
  Workers Compensation Insurance
- **RT** Benefits
  Finance
  Risk
  Service Industries

Insurgence/Insurgency (1969-1985)
- **HN** DC 236090.
- **Use** Rebellions

Insurrections
- **Use** Rebellions

Intake (1964-1985)
- **HN** DC 236100.
- **Use** Disposition

Integral/Integrals/Integralism (1972-1985)
- **HN** DC 236108, deleted 1986.

Integrate/Integrated/Integration/Integrative (1963-1985)
- **HN** DC 236110.
- **Use** Social Integration

Integration of Innovations
- **Use** Adoption of Innovations

Integration (Social)
- **Use** Social Integration

Integrity (1972-1985)
- **HN** DC 236150.
- **Use** Morality

Intellect/Intellects (1969-1985)
- **HN** DC 236425.
- **Use** Mind

Intellectual Development
- **DC** D400500
- **HN** Added, 1986.
- **BT** Cognitive Development
- **RT** Educational Attainment
  Intelligence
  Knowledge
  Moral Development
  Self Actualization

Intellectual Disciplines
- **Use** Academic Disciplines

Intellectual History
- **DC** D400800
- **HN** Added, 1986.
- **UF** History of Ideas
- **BT** History
- **RT** Culture
  Epistemology

Intellectual History (cont'd)
- **RT** Historiography
  Knowledge
  Science And Technology
  Social History
  Sociology of Knowledge

Intellectuals
- **DC** D401100
- **HN** Formerly (1963-1985) part of DC 236500, Intellectual/Intellectuals/Intellectualism.
- **BT** Intelligentsia
- **RT** Creativity
  Knowledge
  Scholarship

Intelligence
- **DC** D401400
- **HN** Formerly (1963-1985) DC 237500, Intelligence/IQ.
- **UF** Intelligence Quotient
- **NT** Genius
- **RT** Ability
  Academic Aptitude
  Artificial Intelligence
  Cognition
  Comprehension
  Creativity
  Gifted
  Intellectual Development
  Intelligence Tests
  Mentally Retarded
  Reasoning

Intelligence Measures
- **Use** Intelligence Tests

Intelligence Quotient
- **Use** Intelligence

Intelligence Tests
- **DC** D401550
- **HN** Formerly (1964-1985) DC 237505, Intelligence Test/Intelligence Tests/Intelligence Testing.
- **UF** Intelligence Measures
- **BT** Tests
- **RT** Academic Aptitude
  Cognition
  Intelligence
  Psychometric Analysis

Intelligentsia
- **DC** D401700
- **SN** Self-identified intellectuals who form an artistic, social, or political vanguard or elite.
- **HN** Formerly (1963-1985) DC 238300.
- **BT** Elites
- **NT** Intellectuals
- **RT** Educational Attainment
  Experts
  Human Resources
  Scientific Community
  Social Power
  Upper Class

Intensivity/Intensification (1963-1985)
- **HN** DC 238700, deleted 1986.

Intentionality
- **DC** D402000
- **SN** In phenomenology and interpretive sociology, action initiated and shaped to fulfill imagined outcomes.
- **HN** Formerly (1967-1985) DC 238704, Intent/Intention/Intentions/Intentional.

Intentionality (cont'd)
- **UF** Purposiveness
- **RT** Action
  Action Theory
  Commitment
  Consciousness
  Goals
  Motivation
  Phenomenology
  Rationality
  Will

Inter- (1965-1985)
- **HN** DC 238712, deleted 1986. See now specific terms.

Interaction
- **DC** D402300
- **SN** A context-dependent term; select a more specific entry or coordinate with other terms. In contexts where Interaction is closely related to Social Interaction, select the latter.
- **HN** Formerly (1963-1985) part of DC 238715, Interaction/Interactions/Interactional/Interactionalism.
- **UF** Dynamic/Dynamics (1963-1985)
- **NT** Alliance
  Conflict
  Feedback
  Manipulation
  Negotiation
  Reciprocity
  Social Interaction
- **RT** Balance Theory
  Behavior
  Causality
  Communication
  Human Nature
  Participation
  Responses
  Spatial Behavior
  Symbiotic Relations
  Violence

Interactionism
- **DC** D402600
- **HN** Formerly (1963-1985) part of DC 238715, Interaction/Interactions/Interactional/Interactionalism.
- **NT** Symbolic Interactionism
- **RT** Social Interaction
  Social Psychology

Intercollegiate Sports
- **Use** College Sports

Intercorporate Networks
- **Use** Interlocking Directorates

Intercourse (1963-1985)
- **HN** DC 238850.
- **Use** Sexual Intercourse

Intercultural Communication
- **DC** D402900
- **HN** Formerly (1963-1985) DC 238862, Intercultural.
- **BT** Communication
- **RT** Acculturation
  Bilingualism
  Cultural Change
  Cultural Conflict
  Cultural Groups
  Cultural Pluralism
  Culture
  Culture Contact
  Ethnic Relations
  Ethnocentrism

Intercultural Communication (cont'd)
- **RT** Ethnolinguistic Groups
  Indigenous Populations
  International Cooperation
  Multicultural Education
  Racial Relations
  Social Integration
  Subcultures

Interdependence (1963-1985)
- **HN** DC 238870.
- **Use** Interpersonal Relations

Interdisciplinary (1963-1985)
- **HN** DC 238880.
- **Use** Interdisciplinary Approach

Interdisciplinary Approach
- **DC** D403200
- **HN** Added, 1986.
- **UF** Crossdisciplinary Approach
  Interdisciplinary (1963-1985)
  Interprofessional (1969-1985)
  Multidisciplinary Approach
- **BT** Methods
- **RT** Academic Disciplines
  Social Science Research
  Social Services
  Teamwork

Interest Groups
- **DC** D403500
- **HN** Formerly (1984-1985) DC 239005, Interest Group/Interest Groups. Prior to 1984 use Group/Groups/Grouping/Groupism (DC 197700) and Interest/Interests (DC 239000).
- **UF** Pressure Groups
  Special Interest Groups
- **BT** Groups
- **RT** Activism
  Civil Rights Organizations
  Corporatism
  Influence
  Legislation
  Lobbying
  Political Action
  Political Action Committees
  Political Behavior
  Political Power
  Professional Associations
  Public Policy
  Religion Politics Relationship
  Social Movements

Interests
- **DC** D403800
- **HN** Formerly (1963-1985) DC 239000, Interest/Interests.
- **NT** Social Interest
- **RT** Amateurs
  Attitudes
  Curiosity
  Habits

Interethnic Relations
- **Use** Ethnic Relations

Interfaith (1963-1985)
- **HN** DC 239600.
- **Use** Intermarriage

Interference (1963-1985)
- **HN** DC 239700, deleted 1986.

Intergenerational Mobility
- **DC** D404100
- **SN** The socioeconomic status of individuals compared with that of their parents.
- **HN** Formerly (1963-1985) part of DC 239715, Intergeneration/Intergenerational.
- **UF** Generational Occupational Mobility (1975-1985)
  Occupational Mobility (Intergenerational)
- **BT** Social Mobility
- **RT** Children
  Family Work Relationship
  Generational Differences
  Occupational Mobility
  Parents

Intergenerational Relations
- **DC** D404400
- **HN** Formerly (1963-1985) part of DC 239715, Intergeneration/Intergenerational.
- **BT** Interpersonal Relations
- **RT** Adult Children
  Age Groups
  Cultural Transmission
  Elderly
  Extended Family
  Family Conflict
  Filial Responsibility
  Generational Differences
  Grandparents
  Parent Child Relations

Intergenerational Transmission of Culture
- **Use** Cultural Transmission

Intergovernmental Organizations
- **Use** International Organizations

Intergroup Conflict
- **Use** Intergroup Relations

Intergroup Contact
- **Use** Social Contact

Intergroup Interaction
- **Use** Intergroup Relations

Intergroup Relations
- **DC** D404700
- **HN** Formerly (1963-1985) DC 239722, Intergroup.
- **UF** Intergroup Conflict
  Intergroup Interaction
- **BT** Social Relations
- **NT** Class Relations
  Ethnic Relations
  Interorganizational Relations
  Labor Relations
  Racial Relations
- **RT** Alliance
  Center And Periphery
  Coalitions
  Competition
  Conflict
  Conflict Resolution
  Cooperation
  Discrimination
  Family Conflict
  Groups
  Individual Collective Relationship
  Intermarriage
  Majority Groups
  Nativism
  Prejudice

Intergroup Relations (cont'd)
- **RT** Social Conflict
  Social Contact
  Social Distance
  Social Integration
  Social Segmentation
  Social Unrest
  Tension

Interlocking Directorates
- **DC** D405000
- **SN** Interorganizational relations in which individuals serve on the boards of directors of more than one corporation at the same time.
- **HN** Formerly (1964-1985) part of DC 132580, Director/Directors/Directorate/Directorates/Directorship.
- **UF** Corporate Networks
  Intercorporate Networks
- **BT** Interorganizational Networks
- **RT** Corporations
  Directors
  Economic Elites

Interloper (1969-1985)
- **HN** DC 239735, deleted 1986.

Intermarriage
- **DC** D405300
- **SN** Marriage between different racial, religious, and social group members.
- **HN** Formerly (1963-1985) DC 239740.
- **UF** Exogamous/Exogamy (1963-1985)
  Heterogamy (1969-1985)
  Interfaith (1963-1985)
  Interreligious (1963-1985)
  Miscegenation (1964-1985)
  Mixed Marriage
- **BT** Marriage
- **RT** Clans
  Intergroup Relations
  Mestizos
  Social Integration
  Taboos

Interments
- **Use** Burials

Internal External Locus of Control
- **Use** Locus of Control

Internal Labor Market Theory
- **Use** Labor Market Segmentation

Internal Migration
- **DC** D405600
- **SN** Permanent or semi-permanent change of residence within the boundaries of a nation.
- **HN** Formerly (1985) DC 239780.
- **UF** Population Redistribution
- **BT** Migration
- **RT** Geographic Mobility
  Population Distribution
  Residential Mobility
  Rural Population
  Rural to Urban Migration
  Urban Population
  Urban to Rural Migration

Internal/Internalize/Internalized/Internalist (1963-1985)
- **HN** DC 239775, deleted 1986.

Internalization

Internalization
- DC D405900
- HN Formerly (1965-1985) DC 239785.
- BT Socialization
- RT Behavior
  Norms
  Social Values

International (1963-1985)
- HN DC 239800, deleted 1986. See now specific "International" terms.

International Agencies
- Use International Organizations

International Aid
- Use Foreign Aid

International Alliances
- DC D406200
- HN Added, 1986.
- UF Allied Countries
  North Atlantic Treaty Organization/ NATO (1967-1985)
- BT Coalitions
- RT Alliance
  Countries
  Diplomacy
  European Economic Community
  Foreign Policy
  Geopolitics
  International Cooperation
  International Economic Organizations
  International Relations
  Treaties
  United Nations

International Business Machines/IBM (1965-1985)
- HN DC 239802.
- Use Corporations

International Conflict
- DC D406500
- HN Added, 1986.
- BT Conflict
  International Relations
- RT Borders
  Geopolitics
  Invasion
  War

International Congresses And Conventions
- Use Congresses And Conventions

International Cooperation
- DC D406800
- HN Added, 1986.
- UF Exchange Programs (International)
  International Exchange Programs
- BT Cooperation
- RT Intercultural Communication
  International Alliances
  International Relations
  Olympic Games
  Technical Assistance
  Technology Transfer

International Division of Labor
- DC D407100
- HN Added, 1986.
- BT Division of Labor
- RT Center And Periphery
  Dependency Theory
  Developing Countries
  Economic Underdevelopment
  Exports And Imports
  Industrial Societies
  Labor Migration
  World Economy

International Economic Organizations
- DC D407400
- HN Added, 1986.
- UF International Monetary Fund
  OPEC (1983-1985)
  Organization for Economic Coop & Development (1984-1985)
  World Bank
- BT International Organizations
- NT European Economic Community
- RT Banking
  Economic Development
  Economic Policy
  Economics
  Finance
  International Alliances
  Trade
  World Economy

International Economy
- Use World Economy

International Exchange Programs
- Use International Cooperation

International Ladies' Garment Workers Union (1970-1985)
- HN DC 239804.
- Use Unions

International Law
- DC D407700
- HN Added, 1986.
- BT Law
- RT International Relations
  Political Science
  Treaties

International Monetary Fund
- Use International Economic Organizations

International Organizations
- DC D408000
- HN Added, 1986.
- UF Intergovernmental Organizations
  International Agencies
  Red Cross (1970-1985)
- BT Organizations (Social)
- NT International Economic Organizations
  United Nations
- RT Government Agencies
  International Relations

International Policy
- Use Foreign Policy

International Problems
- Use World Problems

International Relations
- DC D408300
- HN Formerly (1963-1985) DC 239805.
- BT Relations
- NT International Conflict
  Peaceful Coexistence
  Soviet American Relations
- RT Alliance
  Borders
  Cold War
  Countries
  Diplomacy
  Disarmament
  East And West
  Espionage
  Foreign Aid
  Foreign Policy
  International Alliances
  International Cooperation

Interpersonal

International Relations (cont'd)
- RT International Law
  International Organizations
  International Studies
  Internationalism
  National Security
  Peace
  Political Defection
  Political Science
  Technical Assistance
  Treaties
  United Nations
  War
  World Economy
  World Problems

International Studies
- DC D408600
- HN Added, 1986.
- BT Social Science Education
- RT International Relations
  Political Science

International War
- Use War

Internationalism
- DC D408900
- HN Formerly (1966-1985) DC 239860.
- BT Political Ideologies
- RT International Relations
  Nationalism

Internment Camps
- Use Concentration Camps

Internship Programs
- DC D409200
- HN Formerly (1965-1985) DC 239770, Intern/Interns/Internship.
- BT Educational Programs
  Programs
- RT Job Training
  Undergraduate Programs

Interorganizational Networks
- DC D409500
- HN Added, 1986.
- BT Networks
- NT Interlocking Directorates
- RT Interorganizational Relations
  Organizations (Social)

Interorganizational Relations
- DC D409800
- HN Added, 1986.
- BT Intergroup Relations
- RT Complex Organizations
  Interorganizational Networks
  Organizations (Social)

Interpersonal Attraction
- DC D410100
- HN Added, 1986.
- UF Affinity (Attraction)
- BT Interpersonal Relations
- RT Attachment
  Attractiveness
  Dating (Social)
  Friendship
  Love
  Opposite Sex Relations
  Physical Characteristics
  Rapport
  Social Interaction

Interpersonal　　　　　　　　　　　　　　　　　　　　　　　　　　　　Interviewee

Interpersonal Communication
- DC D410400
- HN Added, 1986.
- UF Communication Style
- BT Communication
- NT Conversation
  Discussion
- RT Agreement
  Assertiveness
  Confidentiality
  Credibility
  Empathy
  Group Dynamics
  Interpersonal Relations
  Interviews
  Intimacy
  Laughter
  Letters (Correspondence)
  Nonverbal Communication
  Persuasion
  Rapport
  Rumors
  Self Disclosure
  Self Expression
  Small Groups
  Social Behavior
  Telephone Communications
  Verbal Communication

Interpersonal Conflict
- DC D410500
- HN Added, 1989.
- BT Conflict
  Interpersonal Relations
- RT Aggression
  Conflict Resolution
  Hate
  Hostility

Interpersonal Contact
- Use Social Contact

Interpersonal Interaction
- Use Social Interaction

Interpersonal Perception
- Use Social Perception

Interpersonal Relations
- DC D410700
- HN Formerly (1963-1985) DC 382534, Relations, Interpersonal.
- UF Interdependence (1963-1985)
  Intrapersonal (1964-1985)
- BT Relations
- NT Client Relations
  Dating (Social)
  Family Relations
  Friendship
  Homosexual Relationships
  Intergenerational Relations
  Interpersonal Attraction
  Interpersonal Conflict
  Intimacy
  Marital Relations
  Opposite Sex Relations
  Peer Relations
  Rapport
  Researcher Subject Relations
  Student Teacher Relationship
  Superior Subordinate Relationship
  Victim Offender Relations
- RT Acceptance
  Altruism
  Assertiveness
  Attachment
  Balance Theory
  Compassion

Interpersonal Relations (cont'd)
- RT Competition
  Cooperation
  Dependency (Psychology)
  Egocentrism
  Emotions
  Empathy
  Group Dynamics
  Hate
  Helping Behavior
  Hostility
  Human Relations Movement
  Individual Collective Relationship
  Interpersonal Communication
  Jealousy
  Love
  Manipulation
  Primary Groups
  Privacy
  Psychodynamics
  Rejection
  Respect
  Self Esteem
  Sensitivity Training
  Small Groups
  Sociability
  Social Acceptance
  Social Contact
  Social Groups
  Social Identity
  Social Interaction
  Social Networks
  Symbiotic Relations
  Tension
  Trust

Interpersonal/Interpersonalism (1963-1985)
- HN DC 240000, deleted 1986. See now appropriate "Interpersonal," "Interaction," or "Relations" terms.

Interpretation/Interpretations/Interpretative (1963-1985)
- HN DC 240500, deleted 1986. See now Hermeneutics, Verstehen, or appropriate "Analysis" terms.

Interpretive Method
- Use Verstehen

Interpretive Sociology
- DC D410710
- SN Perspectives in sociology that reject Positivism and focus on how individuals make sense of, while participating in, the social world.
- HN Added, 1989.
- UF Constructivism
  Phenomenological Sociology
- BT Sociology
- RT Action Theory
  Everyday Life
  Hermeneutics
  Phenomenology
  Sociology of Knowledge
  Structuration
  Verstehen
  Worldview

Interprofessional (1969-1985)
- HN DC 240530.
- Use Interdisciplinary Approach

Interracial (1963-1985)
- HN DC 240565, deleted 1986. See now Intermarriage or Racial Relations.

Interrelation/Interrelations/Interrelationship (1963-1985)
- HN DC 240571.
- Use Relations

Interreligious (1963-1985)
- HN DC 240575.
- Use Intermarriage

Interrogation (1965-1985)
- HN DC 240583.
- Use Investigations (Law Enforcement)

Intersexual/Intersexuality (1965-1985)
- HN DC 240590, deleted 1986.

Interstate (1963-1985)
- HN DC 240600, deleted 1986.

Interval Measurement
- DC D410725
- SN Method of determining the range of numerical values that constitute various segments or classes in a frequency distribution or in a quantitative series, such as a scale.
- HN Formerly (1964-1985) DC 240950, Interval/Intervals.
- BT Measurement
- RT Nominal Measurement
  Ordinal Measurement
  Scales

Intervention
- DC D410750
- SN Activity undertaken to prevent or cope with social problems, usually by local or governmental welfare agencies and workers in helping professions.
- HN Formerly (1963-1985) DC 240965.
- NT Crisis Intervention
  State Intervention
- RT Assistance
  Behavior Modification
  Child Welfare Services
  Clinical Social Work
  Counseling
  Employee Assistance Programs
  Helping Behavior
  Mediation
  Protection
  Psychotherapy
  Rehabilitation
  Social Action
  Social Work
  Treatment Methods
  Treatment Programs

Interview Schedules
- DC D410775
- SN Precoded questionnaires for gathering sociological data, which are administered and filled out during face-to-face interviews with respondents.
- HN Formerly (1963-1985) part of DC 404100, Schedule.
- UF Schedules (Interview)
- BT Questionnaires
- RT Interviews

Interviewee (1965-1985)
- HN DC 241160.
- Use Respondents

Interviewer

Interviewer Characteristics
- DC D410800
- HN Formerly (1963-1985) DC 241185, Interviewer.
- RT Interviews
  Researchers
  Respondents

Interviewing
- Use Interviews

Interviews
- DC D410850
- SN Data collection method in which information is elicited through verbal interaction with respondents. For employment interviews, coordinate with Job Search, for newsmaker interviews, coordinate with News Coverage.
- HN Formerly (1963-1985) DC 241000, Interview/Interviews/Interviewing.
- UF Interviewing
- BT Methodology (Data Collection)
- RT Fieldwork
  Interpersonal Communication
  Interview Schedules
  Interviewer Characteristics
  Measures (Instruments)
  Questionnaires
  Research Design
  Research Methodology
  Respondents
  Surveys
  Telephone Surveys

Intimacy
- DC D411000
- HN Formerly (1963-1985) DC 241215, Intimacy/Intimacies.
- BT Interpersonal Relations
- RT Attachment
  Friendship
  Interpersonal Communication
  Love
  Physical Contact
  Rapport
  Self Disclosure

Intolerance (1971-1985)
- HN DC 241220.
- Use Prejudice

Intonation (1964-1985)
- HN DC 241225.
- Use Speech

Intoxication (1965-1985)
- HN DC 241235.
- Use Drunkenness

Intragenerational Mobility
- Use Social Mobility

Intragroup (1964-1985)
- HN DC 241265.
- Use Group Dynamics

Intrapersonal (1964-1985)
- HN DC 241270.
- Use Interpersonal Relations

Intrauterine Devices
- DC D411300
- HN Formerly (1972-1985) DC 241276, Intrauterine Device/IUD/IUD'S.
- UF IUD
- BT Birth Control
- RT Family Planning
  Sterilization
  Vasectomy

Intravenous (1969-1985)
- HN DC 241277, deleted 1986.

Introversion (1964-1985)
- HN DC 241300.
- Use Personality Traits

Intuition
- DC D411600
- HN Formerly (1966-1985) DC 241330.
- UF Insight (1965-1985)
- BT Cognition
- RT Comprehension
  Consciousness
  Imagination
  Reasoning

Inuit
- Use Eskimos

Invasion
- DC D411800
- HN Formerly (1967-1985) DC 241375.
- UF Foreign Invasion
  Land Invasion
- RT Aggression
  Borders
  Colonization
  Combat
  Imperialism
  International Conflict
  Militarism
  War

Inventions
- DC D411900
- HN Formerly (1964-1985) DC 241500, Invention/Inventions/Inventive.
- RT Creativity
  Discovery
  High Technology Industries
  Innovations
  Patents
  Products
  Research
  Research And Development
  Scientific Discoveries
  Technological Change
  Technological Innovations
  Technological Progress
  Technology
  Technology Transfer

Inventories (Personality)
- Use Personality Measures

Inventory/Inventories/Inventorying (1963-1985)
- HN DC 241700.
- Use Measures (Instruments)

Investigations (Law Enforcement)
- DC D412100
- HN Formerly (1963-1985) DC 241800, Investigation/Investigations/Investigators.
- UF Interrogation (1965-1985)
  Police Investigations
- BT Research
- RT Crime
  Law Enforcement
  Offenses
  Police

Investment
- DC D412200
- HN Formerly (1963-1985) DC 241815, Invest/Invested/Investment/Investor/Investors.
- NT Human Capital
- RT Banking
  Business

Investment (cont'd)
- RT Capital
  Finance
  Money
  Profits
  Wealth

Involuntary Relocation
- Use Relocation

Involvement (1963-1985)
- HN DC 241890.
- Use Participation

Involvement (Social)
- Use Social Participation

Iowa
- DC D412500
- HN Formerly (1963-1985) DC 242000.
- BT Midwestern States
  United States of America

Iran
- DC D412800
- HN Formerly (1963-1985) DC 242200, Iran/Iranian/Iranians.
- UF Persia/Persian/Persians (1963-1985)
- BT Middle East
- NT Teheran, Iran

Iraq
- DC D413100
- HN Formerly (1963-1985) DC 242210, Iraq/Iraqi/Iraqis.
- BT Arab Countries
  Middle East
- NT Baghdad, Iraq

Ireland
- DC D413400
- HN Formerly (1963-1985) DC 242300, Ireland/Irish.
- UF Eire
- BT Western Europe

Ireland (Northern)
- Use Northern Ireland

Iron Age (1964-1985)
- HN DC 242375.
- Use Prehistory

Iron Curtain (1965-1985)
- HN DC 242377, deleted 1986.

Irrationality
- DC D413700
- HN Formerly (1963-1985) DC 242385, Irrational/Irrationalism/Irrationality.
- UF Delusion/Delusions (1963-1985)
- RT Beliefs
  Mental Illness
  Rationality
  Reasoning

Irrigation
- DC D414000
- HN Formerly (1963-1985) DC 242390.
- UF Watering
- BT Agricultural Technology
- RT Soil Conservation
  Water Supply

Islam
- DC D414300
- HN Formerly (1963-1985) part of DC 242400, Islam/Islamic.
- UF Mohammedanism
- BT Religions
- RT Arab Cultural Groups
  Black Muslims

Islam (cont'd)
- RT Islamic Law
  - Koran
  - Mahdis
  - Muslims
  - Purdah
  - Religious Fundamentalism
  - Religious Revivalism

Islamic Law
- DC D414600
- HN Formerly (1963-1985) part of DC 242400, Islam/Islamic.
- BT Ecclesiastical Law
- RT Arab Cultural Groups
  - Isiam
  - Koran
  - Muslims
  - Purdah

Islanders
- Use Islands

Islands
- DC D414900
- HN Formerly (1963-1985) DC 242550, Island/Islands/Islanders.
- UF Archipelago (1969-1985)
  - Islanders
- RT Earth (Planet)
  - Geographic Regions
  - Oceans
  - Topography

Isolate/Isolates (1964-1985)
- HN DC 242900.
- Use Social Isolation

Isolation/Isolationism/Isolationist (1963-1985)
- HN DC 243000.
- Use Social Isolation

Isomorph/Isomorphic/Isomorphism (1970-1985)
- HN DC 243030, deleted 1986.

Israel
- DC D415200
- HN Formerly (1963-1985) DC 243300, Israel/Israeli/Israelis.
- BT Mediterranean Countries
  - Middle East
- NT Jerusalem, Israel
  - Tel Aviv, Israel
- RT Kibbutz
  - Palestine

Issue/Issues (1963-1985)
- HN DC 243365.
- Use Problems

Istanbul, Turkey
- DC D415500
- HN Formerly (1963-1985) DC 243370.
- BT Turkey

Italian (Language)
- Use Romance Languages

Italy
- DC D415800
- HN Formerly (1963-1985) DC 243400, Italy/Italian/Italians.
- BT Mediterranean Countries
  - Western Europe
- NT Milan, Italy
  - Naples, Italy
  - Rome, Italy

Italy (cont'd)
- NT Sardinia
  - Sicily
- RT San Marino
  - Vatican

Items (Measures)
- DC D415900
- SN Parts of a scale of observed characteristics considered as discrete units for purposes of quantitative measurement.
- HN Formerly (1964-1985) DC 243500, Item.
- UF Scale Items
  - Test Items
- RT Coding
  - Factor Analysis
  - Measures (Instruments)
  - Questionnaires
  - Scales
  - Scores
  - Tests
  - Weighting

IUD
- Use Intrauterine Devices

Ivory Coast
- DC D416100
- HN Formerly (1963-1985) DC 243520.
- BT Sub Saharan Africa

Jail (1964-1985)
- HN DC 243650.
- Use Prisons

Jaina
- Use Jainism

Jainism
- DC D416400
- SN Religion in India dating from the sixth century BC, which emerged along with Buddhism as a protest against Hinduism.
- HN Formerly (1965-1985) DC 243666, Jain/Jaina.
- UF Jaina
- BT Religions
- RT Dharma
  - Karma

Jajmani System (1964-1985)
- HN DC 243680.
- Use Caste Systems

Jakarta, Indonesia
- DC D416500
- HN Added, 1989.
- BT Indonesia

Jamaica
- DC D416700
- HN Formerly (1963-1985) DC 243700, Jamaica/Jamaican/Jamaicans.
- BT Caribbean

Janowitz, Morris
- DC D416800
- SN Born 22 October 1919 - died 6 November 1988.
- HN Added, 1989.

Japan
- DC D417000
- HN Formerly (1963-1985) DC 243800, Japan/Japanese.
- BT Far East
- NT Hiroshima, Japan
  - Tokyo, Japan

Japanese (Language)
- Use Oriental Languages

Java/Javanese (1963-1985)
- HN DC 243870, deleted 1986. See now Indonesia or Austronesian Languages.

Jazz (1963-1985)
- HN DC 243874.
- Use Music

Jealousy
- DC D417300
- HN Formerly (1970-1985) DC 243876.
- UF Envy (1966-1985)
- BT Emotions
- RT Interpersonal Relations
  - Personality Traits

Jefferson, Thomas/Jeffersonian (1967-1985)
- HN DC 243878.
- Use Presidents

Jehovah's Witnesses
- DC D417600
- HN Formerly (1963-1985) DC 243880.
- BT Protestants
- RT Millenarianism
  - Protestantism

Jensen, Arthur Robert
- DC D417900
- SN Born 24 August 1923 - .
- HN Formerly (1973-1985) DC 243905, Jensen, A. R.

Jerusalem, Israel
- DC D418200
- HN Formerly (1963-1985) DC 243930.
- BT Israel

Jesuits
- DC D418500
- HN Formerly (1966-1985) DC 243975, Jesuit/Jesuits.
- UF Society of Jesus
- BT Religious Orders
  - Roman Catholics

Jesus Christ
- DC D418800
- HN Added, 1986. Prior to 1986 use Jesus (DC 243990) or Christ (DC 090500).
- UF Christ (1964-1985)
- BT Messianic Figures
- RT Bible
  - Christianity
  - Christmas
  - God (Judeo-Christian)
  - Passion Plays

Jesus Movement
- DC D419100
- HN Added, 1986.
- BT Religious Movements
- RT Christianity
  - Movements
  - Religious Fundamentalism

Jewel/Jewels/Jeweled/Jewelry (1971-1985)
- HN DC 244050.
- Use Crafts

Jewish

Jewish Community
  Use Jews

Jewish Cultural Groups
  DC D419350
  SN Groups within Jewry distinguished by particular cultural, linguistic, or religious traditions.
  HN Added, 1986.
  UF Ashkenazic Jews
      Sephardic Jews
  BT Religious Cultural Groups
  RT Jews
      Semitic Languages

Jewish Faith
  Use Judaism

Jewish Holocaust
  Use Holocaust

Jewry
  Use Jews

Jews
  DC D419400
  HN Formerly (1963-1985) DC 244000, Jew/Jews/Jewry/Jewish.
  UF Jewish Community
      Jewry
  BT Religious Cultural Groups
  NT Hassidim
      Rabbis
  RT Aliyah
      Anti-Semitism
      Gentiles
      Holocaust
      Jewish Cultural Groups
      Judaism
      Judeo-Christian Tradition
      Synagogues
      Zionism

Job Application
  DC D419600
  HN Added, 1986.
  UF Employment Application
  RT Employment
      Job Change
      Job Search
      Occupational Choice
      Occupational Qualifications

Job Attitudes
  Use Work Attitudes

Job Change
  DC D419700
  SN Change of employer without change of occupation. Do not confuse with Employment Changes or Occupational Mobility.
  HN Added, 1986.
  UF Job Mobility
      Worker Mobility
  BT Change
  RT Employment
      Employment Opportunities
      Family Work Relationship
      Job Application
      Job Satisfaction
      Job Search
      Labor Market
      Labor Turnover
      Occupational Mobility
      Recruitment
      Seniority

Job Characteristics
  DC D420000
  HN Added, 1986.
  UF Job Scope
      Work Characteristics
  RT Employment
      Job Requirements
      Job Satisfaction
      Nontraditional Occupations
      Occupational Classifications
      Occupational Qualifications
      Occupational Roles
      Occupational Stress
      Occupations
      Tasks
      Work
      Work Environment
      Work Skills
      Working Hours

Job Classifications
  Use Occupational Classifications

Job Discrimination
  Use Employment Discrimination

Job Displacement
  Use Dislocated Workers

Job Hunting
  Use Job Search

Job Market
  Use Labor Market

Job Mobility
  Use Job Change

Job Opportunities
  Use Employment Opportunities

Job Performance
  DC D420300
  HN Added, 1986.
  BT Performance
  RT Dismissal
      Education Work Relationship
      Employment
      Job Training
      Labor Productivity
      Morale
      Motivation
      Occupational Achievement
      Peer Review
      Promotion (Occupational)
      Supervision
      Task Performance
      Work
      Work Environment
      Workers

Job Promotion
  Use Promotion (Occupational)

Job Qualifications
  Use Occupational Qualifications

Job Requirements
  DC D420600
  HN Added, 1986.
  UF Work Requirements
  BT Qualifications
  RT Education Work Relationship
      Employment
      Employment Opportunities
      Hiring Practices
      Job Characteristics
      Labor Market
      Occupational Classifications

Job

Job Requirements (cont'd)
  RT Occupational Qualifications
      Occupational Status
      Personnel Policy
      Recruitment
      Work
      Work Experience
      Work Skills

Job Roles
  Use Occupational Roles

Job Satisfaction
  DC D420900
  HN Formerly (1984-1985) DC 247000, Job Satisfaction/Job Dissatisfaction.
  UF Employment Satisfaction
      Occupational Satisfaction
      Work Satisfaction
  BT Satisfaction
  RT Employee Assistance Programs
      Employment
      Job Change
      Job Characteristics
      Life Satisfaction
      Morale
      Occupational Roles
      Occupational Status
      Organizational Development
      Quality of Working Life
      Role Satisfaction
      Work Attitudes
      Work Environment
      Work Humanization
      Work Orientations
      Work Values
      Workers

Job Scope
  Use Job Characteristics

Job Search
  DC D421200
  HN Added, 1986.
  UF Job Hunting
  RT Employment
      Employment Opportunities
      Hiring Practices
      Job Application
      Job Change
      Job Training
      Labor Market
      Occupational Qualifications
      Unemployment

Job Selection
  Use Occupational Choice

Job Skills
  Use Work Skills

Job Status
  Use Occupational Status

Job Stress
  Use Occupational Stress

Job Training
  DC D421500
  HN Added, 1986.
  UF Employment Preparation
      Occupational Training
      Off the Job Training
      On the Job Training
  BT Training
  NT Apprenticeships
  RT Education Work Relationship
      Employability
      Human Capital

Job Training (cont'd)
- **RT** Internship Programs
  Job Performance
  Job Search
  Occupational Qualifications
  Professional Training
  Vocational Education
  Work Skills
  Workshops (Manufacturing)

Job Vacancies
- **Use** Employment Opportunities

Job/Jobs (1963-1985)
- **HN** DC 245000.
- **Use** Employment

Johannesburg, South Africa
- **DC** D421800
- **HN** Formerly (1963-1985) DC 247030.
- **BT** South Africa

Joint Custody
- **Use** Child Custody

Jokes
- **DC** D422100
- **HN** Formerly (1963-1985) DC 247055, Joke/Jokes/Joking.
- **BT** Humor

Jonestown Mass Suicide
- **DC** D422400
- **HN** Formerly (1981-1985) DC 247062, Jonestown.
- **UF** Peoples Temple
- **BT** Suicide
- **RT** Cults
  Messianic Figures

Jordan
- **DC** D422700
- **HN** Formerly (1964-1985) DC 247075, Jordan/Jordanian/Jordanians.
- **BT** Arab Countries
  Middle East
- **RT** Palestine

Journal Articles
- **Use** Articles

Journalism
- **DC** D423000
- **HN** Formerly (1963-1985) DC 247105, Journalism/Journalistic.
- **RT** Editorials
  Editors
  Journalists
  Literature
  Mass Media
  News Coverage
  News Media
  Newspapers
  Periodicals
  Photographs
  Publications
  Radio
  Reports
  Television
  Writing for Publication

Journalists
- **DC** D423300
- **HN** Formerly (1964-1985) DC 247110, Journalist/Journalists.
- **UF** Columnists
  Newsmen (1965-1985)
  Newswriters (1964-1985)
  Reporters
- **BT** Professional Workers
- **RT** Journalism
  News Media
  Newspapers
  Writers

Journals
- **DC** D423600
- **SN** Use limited to scholarly publications.
- **HN** Formerly (1963-1985) DC 247100, Journal/Journals.
- **UF** Professional Journals
  Scholarly Journals
- **BT** Periodicals
- **RT** Scholarship
  Writing for Publication

Joy
- **Use** Happiness

Judaism
- **DC** D423900
- **HN** Formerly (1963-1985) DC 247140, Judaism/Judaic.
- **UF** Jewish Faith
  Judezmo
- **BT** Religions
- **NT** Hassidism
- **RT** Bible
  Cabala
  Devils
  Gentiles
  God (Judeo-Christian)
  Jews
  Judeo-Christian Tradition
  Rabbinical Literature
  Rabbis
  Religious Orthodoxy
  Synagogues
  Western Civilization

Judeo- (1963-1985)
- **HN** DC 247160, deleted 1986. See now specific terms.

Judeo-Christian Tradition
- **DC** D424200
- **HN** Added, 1986.
- **RT** Bible
  Christianity
  Christians
  European Cultural Groups
  God (Judeo-Christian)
  Jews
  Judaism
  Religious Beliefs
  Traditionalism
  Western Civilization

Judezmo
- **Use** Judaism

Judges
- **DC** D424500
- **HN** Formerly (1963-1985) DC 247190, Judge/Judges.
- **BT** Professional Workers
  Public Officials
- **RT** Courts
  Criminal Proceedings
  Judicial Decisions
  Judiciary
  Jurisprudence
  Lawyers
  Legal Profession
  Litigation
  Prosecutors
  Trials

Judgment
- **DC** D424650
- **HN** Formerly (1963-1985) DC 247200, Judgment/Judgments.
- **BT** Cognition
- **NT** Moral Judgment
- **RT** Accuracy
  Attitudes

Judgment (cont'd)
- **RT** Choices
  Cognitive Development
  Criteria
  Criticism
  Decision Making
  Decisions
  Errors
  Evaluation
  Rating
  Rational Choice
  Reasoning
  Values

Judgments (Judicial)
- **Use** Judicial Decisions

Judicial Decisions
- **DC** D424800
- **HN** Added, 1986.
- **UF** Court Opinions
  Decisions (Judicial)
  Judgments (Judicial)
  Opinions (Judicial)
- **BT** Decisions
- **NT** Sentencing
- **RT** Criminal Justice
  Disposition
  Judges
  Jurisprudence
  Legal Cases
  Legal Procedure
  United States Supreme Court
  Verdicts

Judicial System
- **Use** Legal System

Judiciary
- **DC** D425100
- **HN** Formerly (1963-1985) part of DC 247230, Judicial/Judiciary.
- **UF** Federal Judiciary
- **RT** Correctional System
  Courts
  Government
  Judges
  Jurisprudence
  Law
  Legal Profession
  Legal System

Jung, Carl Gustav
- **DC** D425400
- **SN** Born 26 July 1875 - died 6 June 1961.
- **HN** Formerly (1964-1985) DC 247370, Jung, C. G.

Junior Colleges
- **Use** Community Colleges

Junior High Schools
- **DC** D425700
- **HN** Formerly (1964-1985) DC 247400, Junior High School.
- **UF** Middle Schools
- **BT** Secondary Schools
- **RT** Secondary Education

Juridic/Juridical (1963-1985)
- **HN** DC 247408, deleted 1986. See now Sociology of Law, Jurisprudence, or Criminology.

Juries
- **DC** D426000
- **HN** Formerly (1963-1985) DC 247422, Jury/Juries/Juror/Jurors.
- **RT** Criminal Proceedings

Jurisdiction

Juries (cont'd)
- RT Defendants
  - Due Process
  - Litigation
  - Trials
  - Verdicts

Jurisdiction
- DC D426300
- HN Formerly (1964-1985) DC 247414.
- RT Courts

Jurisprudence
- DC D426600
- HN Formerly (1963-1985) DC 247418, Jurisprudence/Jurisprudential.
- UF Legal Theory
- RT Criminology
  - Judges
  - Judicial Decisions
  - Judiciary
  - Law
  - Sociology of Law

Jurist/Jurists (1963-1985)
- HN DC 247420, deleted 1986. See now Judges, Jurisprudence, or Judiciary.

Jury Decisions
- Use Verdicts

Justice
- DC D426900
- HN Formerly (1963-1985) DC 247427.
- NT Social Justice
- RT Courts
  - Due Process
  - Equity
  - Freedom
  - Law
  - Legal System
  - Rights
  - Treatment
  - Truth
  - Values

Justice (Criminal)
- Use Criminal Justice

Justice (Juvenile)
- Use Juvenile Justice

Justify/Justified/Justifying/ Justification (1972-1985)
- HN DC 247428.
- Use Explanation

Juvenile Correctional Institutions
- DC D427200
- SN Confinement facilities for delinquents and offenders for periods less than or exceeding one year.
- HN Added, 1986.
- UF Correctional Institutions (Juvenile)
  - Reformatory/Reform School (1964-1985)
- BT Residential Institutions
- RT Borstal
  - Correctional System
  - Prisons

Juvenile Courts
- DC D427500
- HN Added, 1986.
- UF Courts (Juvenile)
- BT Courts
- RT Juvenile Delinquency
  - Juvenile Justice
  - Juvenile Offenders

Juvenile Delinquency
- DC D427800
- HN Formerly (1963-1985) DC 126140, Delinquency, Juvenile.
- UF Adolescent Delinquency
- BT Delinquency
- RT Adolescents
  - Child Neglect
  - Delinquency Prevention
  - Juvenile Courts
  - Juvenile Justice
  - Juvenile Offenders
  - Offenses
  - Parent Child Relations
  - Shoplifting
  - Sociopathic Personality
  - Youth

Juvenile Diversion Programs
- Use Delinquency Prevention

Juvenile Justice
- DC D428100
- HN Added, 1986.
- UF Justice (Juvenile)
- BT Legal System
- RT Correctional System
  - Criminal Justice Policy
  - Delinquency Prevention
  - Juvenile Courts
  - Juvenile Delinquency
  - Prosecutors

Juvenile Justice Policy
- Use Criminal Justice Policy

Juvenile Offenders
- DC D428400
- HN Added, 1986.
- BT Offenders
- RT Adolescents
  - Female Offenders
  - Gangs
  - Imprisonment
  - Juvenile Courts
  - Juvenile Delinquency
  - Penal Reform

Juvenile Runaways
- Use Runaways

Juvenile/Juveniles (1963-1985)
- HN DC 247435, deleted 1986. See now Children, Adolescents, Youth, or Juvenile Delinquency.

Kabul, Afghanistan
- DC D428600
- HN Added, 1989.
- BT Afghanistan

Kampala, Uganda
- DC D428650
- HN Added, 1989.
- BT Uganda

Kampuchea
- DC D428700
- HN Added, 1986. Prior to 1986 use Cambodia/Cambodian/Cambodians (DC 069143).
- UF Cambodia/Cambodian/Cambodians (1963-1985)
- BT Southeast Asia
- RT Indochina

Kansas
- DC D429000
- HN Formerly (1964-1985) DC 247456.
- BT Midwestern States
  - United States of America

Kansas City, Missouri
- DC D429300
- HN Added, 1986. Prior to 1986 use Kansas City/Kan. Mo. (DC 247460).
- BT Missouri

Kansas City/Kan. Mo. (1964-1985)
- HN DC 247460, deleted 1986.

Kant, Immanuel
- DC D429600
- SN Born 22 April 1724 - died 12 February 1804.
- HN Formerly (1966-1985) DC 247462.

Karachi, Pakistan
- DC D429800
- HN Added, 1989.
- BT Pakistan

Karma
- DC D429900
- SN In Eastern religions such as Hinduism and Buddhism, action seen as bringing inevitable results to the agent, both good and bad, in the current lifetime or in a reincarnation.
- HN Formerly (1983-1985) DC 247469.
- BT Religious Beliefs
- RT Buddhism
  - Fate
  - Hinduism
  - Jainism

Kentucky
- DC D430200
- HN Formerly (1979-1985) DC 247493.
- BT Southern States
  - United States of America
- RT Appalachia

Kenya
- DC D430500
- HN Formerly (1979-1985) DC 247494, Kenya/Kenyan/Kenyans.
- BT Sub Saharan Africa

Kerala, India
- DC D430800
- HN Formerly (1964-1985) DC 247496.
- BT India

Keynesian Economics
- DC D431100
- HN Formerly (1979-1985) DC 247500, Keynes, John M./Keynesian.
- UF Keynesianism
- BT Economics
- RT Economic Theories

Keynesianism
- Use Keynesian Economics

Khaldoun, Ibn
- DC D431400
- SN Born 27 May 1332 - died 16 March 1406.
- HN Formerly (1965-1985) DC 247510.

Khoin Languages
- Use African Languages

Kibbutz

Kibbutz
- DC D431700
- SN Type of collective, agriculture-based community originating in Israel.
- HN Formerly (1963-1985) DC 247600, Kibbutz/Kibbutzim.
- BT Communes
- RT Agricultural Collectives
    Israel

Kidney Transplantation
- Use Organ Transplantation

Kierkegaard, Soren Aabye
- DC D432000
- SN Born 5 May 1813 - died 11 November 1855.
- HN Formerly (1966-1985) DC 247640, Kierkegaard, Soren.

Kiev, Union of Soviet Socialist Republics
- DC D432100
- HN Added, 1989.
- BT Union of Soviet Socialist Republics

Kin Terms
- Use Kinship Terminology

Kindergarten
- DC D432300
- HN Formerly (1964-1985) DC 247700.
- RT Elementary Education
    Preschool Children
    Preschool Education
    Primary Education

Kindred (1963-1985)
- HN DC 247710.
- Use Relatives

King, Martin Luther
- DC D432600
- SN Born 15 January 1929 - died 4 April 1968.
- HN Formerly (1967-1985) DC 247810.

King/Kings/Kingdom/Kingship (1963-1985)
- HN DC 247800.
- Use Monarchy

Kinsey, Alfred Charles
- DC D432900
- SN Born 23 June 1894 - died 25 August 1956.
- HN Formerly (1966-1985) DC 247835, Kinsey, Alfred C.

Kinshasa, Zaire
- DC D433100
- HN Added, 1989.
- BT Zaire

Kinship
- DC D433200
- HN Formerly (1963-1985) DC 247675, Kin/Kinship.
- BT Social Relations
- RT Affinity (Kinship)
    Clans
    Cognatic Descent
    Compadrazgo
    Consanguinity
    Descent
    Ethnography
    Ethnology
    Extended Family
    Family

Kinship (cont'd)
- RT Family Structure
    Genealogy
    Godparenthood
    Grandparents
    Inheritance And Succession
    Kinship Networks
    Kinship Terminology
    Lineage
    Marriage
    Matriarchy
    Matrilocal Residence
    Naming Practices
    Nuclear Family
    Parents
    Patriarchy
    Patrilocal Residence
    Relatives
    Siblings
    Social Structure
    Traditional Societies
    Unilineality

Kinship Networks
- DC D433500
- HN Added, 1986.
- BT Social Networks
- RT Family Structure
    Kinship
    Relatives

Kinship Terminology
- DC D433800
- HN Added, 1986.
- UF Kin Terms
    Vocabulary of Kinship
- BT Terminology
- RT Kinship
    Sociolinguistics

Knowledge
- DC D434100
- HN Formerly (1963-1985) DC 247900.
- NT Common Sense
    Scientific Knowledge
- RT Academic Disciplines
    Cognition
    Comprehension
    Contradictions
    Creativity
    Discovery
    Education
    Epistemological Doctrines
    Experts
    Higher Education
    Ignorance
    Information
    Information Sources
    Instinct
    Intellectual Development
    Intellectual History
    Intellectuals
    Learning
    Postulates
    Praxis
    Rationalism
    Relativism
    Research
    Scholarship
    Science And Technology
    Skepticism
    Sociology of Knowledge
    Synthesis
    Theories

König, René
- DC D434200
- SN Born 5 July 1906 - .
- HN Added, 1989.

Kolkhoz/Kolkhozes (1965-1985)
- HN DC 248100.
- Use Agricultural Collectives

Koran
- DC D434400
- HN Formerly (1967-1985) DC 248190.
- BT Religious Literature
- RT Islam
    Islamic Law
    Muslims

Korea/Korean/Koreans (1963-1985)
- HN DC 248200, deleted 1986. See now North Korea or South Korea.

Korean (Language)
- Use Oriental Languages

Ku Klux Klan (1964-1985)
- HN DC 248530.
- Use Secret Societies

Kuala Lumpur, Malaysia
- DC D434500
- HN Added, 1989.
- BT Malaysia

Kuhn, Manford H.
- DC D434700
- HN Formerly (1967-1985) DC 248460, Kuhn, Manford.

Kuhn, Thomas Samuel
- DC D435000
- SN Born 18 July 1922 - .
- HN Formerly (1979-1985) DC 248475, Kuhn, Thomas S.

Kula (1963-1985)
- HN DC 248532, deleted 1986.

Kulturkampf
- Use Cultural Conflict

Kuwait
- DC D435300
- HN Formerly (1967-1985) DC 248537.
- BT Arab Countries
    Middle East

Labeling
- DC D435600
- SN The stereotypic designation or definition of a person by a word or phrase that connotes stigma, status, or other characteristics.
- HN Formerly (1969-1985) DC 248550, Label/Labels/Labeling.
- RT Classification
    Deviance
    Deviant Behavior
    Scapegoating
    Social Perception
    Social Response
    Social Types
    Stereotypes
    Stigma
    Symbolic Interactionism

Labor
- DC D435900
- SN A context-dependent term; select a more specific entry or coordinate with other terms.
- HN Formerly (1963-1985) DC 248600, Labor/Labors.

Labor

Labor (cont'd)
- BT Human Resources
- RT Business
  - Business Society Relationship
  - Capital
  - Capitalism
  - Collective Bargaining
  - Division of Labor
  - Economics
  - Education Work Relationship
  - Employment
  - Enterprises
  - Forces And Relations of Production
  - Human Relations Movement
  - Industrial Democracy
  - Industry
  - Labor Disputes
  - Labor Force
  - Labor Force Participation
  - Labor Market
  - Labor Market Segmentation
  - Labor Migration
  - Labor Movements
  - Labor Parties
  - Labor Policy
  - Labor Process
  - Labor Productivity
  - Labor Relations
  - Labor Supply
  - Labor Turnover
  - Occupations
  - Production
  - Unions
  - Work
  - Work Humanization
  - Workers
  - Workplaces

Labor Collectives
- Use Collectives

Labor Disputes
- DC D436200
- HN Added, 1986.
- UF Industrial Conflict
- BT Disputes
- NT Strikes
- RT Collective Bargaining
  - Forces And Relations of Production
  - Labor
  - Labor Relations
  - Social Problems
  - Unions
  - Workers

Labor Efficiency
- Use Labor Productivity

Labor Force
- DC D436500
- HN Formerly (1984-1985) DC 248690. Prior to 1984 use Labor/Labors (DC 248600) and Force (DC 184600).
- UF Force (1963-1985)
  - Work Force
- RT Dislocated Workers
  - Employment
  - Employment Changes
  - Human Resources
  - Labor
  - Labor Force Participation
  - Labor Market
  - Labor Supply
  - Labor Turnover
  - Occupational Classifications
  - Occupational Structure
  - Occupations
  - Unions

Labor Force (cont'd)
- RT Work
  - Workers
  - Working Class
  - Working Women

Labor Force Participation
- DC D436800
- HN Added, 1986.
- BT Participation
- RT Labor
  - Labor Force
  - Unemployment
  - Work Orientations
  - Working Women

Labor Humanization
- Use Work Humanization

Labor Market
- DC D437100
- HN Formerly (1984-1985) DC 248693.
- UF Job Market
- BT Markets
- RT Dislocated Workers
  - Economic Change
  - Employment
  - Employment Changes
  - Employment Opportunities
  - Foreign Workers
  - Job Change
  - Job Requirements
  - Job Search
  - Labor
  - Labor Force
  - Labor Market Segmentation
  - Labor Process
  - Labor Supply
  - Labor Turnover
  - Underemployment
  - Work Skills
  - Workers

Labor Market Segmentation
- DC D437400
- SN Theories that view labor markets as divided into two or more sub-markets. Dual labor market theory suggests a division between large firms offering high wages and stable employment, primarily to white males; and small firms offering low wages and unstable employment, primarily to disadvantaged groups such as ethnic minorities and women. Internal labor market theory emphasizes varying patterns of reward and status within firms.
- HN Added, 1986.
- UF Dual Labor Market Theory
  - Internal Labor Market Theory
  - Split Labor Market Theory
- RT Center And Periphery
  - Dual Economy
  - Economic Structure
  - Employment Discrimination
  - Income Inequality
  - Labor
  - Labor Market
  - Manual Workers
  - Occupational Segregation
  - Occupational Structure
  - Sexual Division of Labor
  - Social Closure
  - Social Segmentation
  - Working Women

Labor Migration
- DC D437700
- HN Added, 1986.
- BT Migration
- RT Foreign Workers
  - International Division of Labor
  - Labor
  - Migrant Workers
  - Undocumented Immigrants

Labor Movements
- DC D438000
- HN Added, 1986.
- UF Labor Organization
  - Workers Movements
- BT Movements
- RT Class Politics
  - Labor
  - Labor Parties
  - Political Movements
  - Political Power
  - Solidarity Movements
  - Syndicalism
  - Unionization
  - Unions
  - Worker Consciousness
  - Workers
  - Working Class

Labor Organization
- Use Labor Movements

Labor Parties
- DC D438300
- HN Formerly (1964-1985) DC 248695, Labor Party.
- BT Political Parties
- RT Labor
  - Labor Movements
  - Left Wing Politics
  - Socialist Parties
  - Unions

Labor Policy
- DC D438600
- HN Added, 1986.
- UF Employment Policy
- BT Economic Policy
- RT Labor
  - Unemployment
  - Workers

Labor Process
- DC D438800
- SN An organized system in which people work to produce useful products or services. In Marxist analysis, the labor process comprises physical work, raw materials, and tools and equipment, and creates all value.
- HN Added, 1986.
- UF Production Process
- RT Capitalism
  - Division of Labor
  - Exploitation
  - Forces And Relations of Production
  - Industrial Production
  - Industrialization
  - Labor
  - Labor Market
  - Labor Relations
  - Production
  - Rationalization
  - Raw Materials
  - Scientific Management
  - Technology
  - Tools
  - Value (Economics)
  - Work
  - Work Humanization

Labor

Labor Productivity
- DC D438900
- HN Added, 1986.
- UF Labor Efficiency
- BT Productivity
- RT Economic Conditions
  Enterprises
  Human Capital
  Human Relations Movement
  Industrial Management
  Job Performance
  Labor
  Organizational Effectiveness
  Production
  Work
  Workers
  Working Hours

Labor Relations
- DC D439200
- HN Formerly (1963-1985) DC 248700.
- UF Industrial Relations
  Relations, Industrial (1963-1985)
  Union Management Relations (1963-1985)
- BT Intergroup Relations
- RT Collective Bargaining
  Corporatism
  Employers
  Employers Associations
  Employment
  Enterprises
  Human Relations Movement
  Industrial Democracy
  Industrial Management
  Industry
  Labor
  Labor Disputes
  Labor Process
  Paternalism
  Personnel Management
  Personnel Policy
  Scientific Management
  Strikes
  Unions
  Work Environment
  Workers

Labor Shortage
- Use Labor Supply

Labor Supply
- DC D439500
- HN Added, 1986.
- UF Labor Shortage
  Labor Surplus
  Manpower (1963-1985)
  Supply of Labor
  Surplus Labor
- RT Economic Change
  Economic Conditions
  Employment Changes
  Human Capital
  Labor
  Labor Force
  Labor Market
  Labor Turnover
  Supply And Demand
  Underemployment
  Workers

Labor Surplus
- Use Labor Supply

Labor Theory of Value
- DC D439800
- SN In Marxist analysis, the theory that the economic value of commodities is determined by the labor time spent in their production. Although workers are entitled to the value they create, they are paid only enough for subsistence, the remainder, or surplus value, being appropriated by the capitalist.

Labor Theory of Value (cont'd)
- HN Added, 1986.
- UF Exchange Value
  Surplus Value
- BT Economic Theories
- RT Base And Superstructure
  Marxism
  Marxist Economics
  Political Economy
  Value (Economics)

Labor Turnover
- DC D440100
- HN Formerly (1982-1985) DC 472900, Turnover.
- UF Employee Turnover
  Resignation (1964-1985)
  Turnover
- RT Attrition
  Dislocated Workers
  Dismissal
  Job Change
  Labor
  Labor Force
  Labor Market
  Labor Supply
  Personnel Management
  Retirement

Labor Unions
- Use Unions

Laboratories
- DC D440200
- HN Formerly (1963-1985) DC 248650, Laboratory/Laboratories.
- BT Facilities
- RT Experiments
  Medical Research
  Scientific Research

Laborer/Laborers (1963-1985)
- HN DC 248685.
- Use Manual Workers

Lacan, Jacques Marie Emile
- DC D440250
- SN Born 13 April 1901 - died 9 September 1981.
- HN Added, 1986.

Lactation
- DC D440400
- HN Formerly (1965-1985) DC 248775.
- RT Birth Spacing
  Breast Feeding

Lagos, Nigeria
- DC D440600
- HN Added, 1989.
- BT Nigeria

Lahore, Pakistan
- DC D440700
- HN Formerly (1963-1985) DC 248800.
- BT Pakistan

Laicism
- Use Laity (Religious)

Laissez-faire (1963-1985)
- HN DC 248820.
- Use Market Economy

Laity (Religious)
- DC D441000
- HN Formerly (1963-1985) DC 248825, Laity/Laicism. For nonprofessionals, see Laymen.
- UF Laicism
- NT Congregations
- RT Church Membership
  Clergy
  Parishioners

Land

Lamaism
- DC D441300
- HN Formerly (1964-1985) DC 248850, Lama/Lamaism.
- BT Zen Buddhism
- RT Buddhists

Land
- DC D441600
- HN Formerly (1963-1985) DC 248875, Land/Lands.
- BT Natural Resources
- NT Common Lands
- RT Farms
  Land Ownership
  Land Reform
  Land Settlement
  Land Tenure
  Land Use
  Mineral Resources
  Parks
  Production
  Property
  Real Estate Industry
  Rents
  Soil Conservation

Land Invasion
- Use Invasion

Land Ownership
- DC D441900
- HN Added, 1986.
- BT Land Tenure
  Ownership
- RT Common Lands
  Home Ownership
  Land
  Rents

Land Reform
- DC D442200
- HN Added, 1986.
- UF Agrarian Reform
- BT Reform
- RT Agrarian Structures
  Agricultural Policy
  Land
  Land Tenure
  Maoism
  Plantations
  Relocation
  Rural Development
  Social Reform

Land Settlement
- DC D442500
- HN Formerly (1963-1985) part of DC 418800, Settlement/Settler/Settlers.
- UF Human Settlement
- NT Colonization
- RT Communities
  Demography
  Frontiers
  Homesteading
  Land
  Land Tenure
  Migration
  Population Distribution
  Relocation
  Residential Patterns
  Settlement Patterns
  Settlers
  Squatters

Land

Land Tenancy
  Use Land Tenure

Land Tenure
- **DC** D442800
- **HN** Added, 1986.
- **UF** Farm Tenancy
  Land Tenancy
  Tenancy (1964-1985)
  Tenure (Land)
- **BT** Tenure
- **NT** Land Ownership
- **RT** Agrarian Structures
  Agricultural Economics
  Agricultural Enterprises
  Crofting
  Farms
  Homesteading
  Land
  Land Reform
  Land Settlement
  Rents
  Sharecropping

Land Use
- **DC** D443100
- **SN** Purpose for which real property is utilized, eg, agricultural, forestry, or residential use.
- **HN** Formerly (1985) DC 248875c, Land Use Management.
- **BT** Utilization
- **RT** Agrarian Structures
  Agricultural Development
  Agricultural Policy
  Agricultural Technology
  Agriculture
  Common Lands
  Conservation
  Environmental Protection
  Forestry
  Government Regulation
  Land
  Natural Resources
  Parks
  Pollution
  Recreational Facilities
  Resource Management
  Rural Development
  Soil Conservation
  Urban Development
  Zoning

Landforms
  Use Topography

Landlord Tenant Relations
- **DC** D443300
- **HN** Added, 1989.
- **RT** Landlords
  Rental Housing
  Rents
  Tenants

Landlords
- **DC** D443400
- **HN** Formerly (1963-1985) DC 248878, Landlord/Landlords.
- **RT** Home Ownership
  Landlord Tenant Relations
  Real Estate Industry
  Rental Housing
  Tenants

Language
- **DC** D443700
- **SN** Aspect of human behavior involving the use of vocal sounds, and, often, corresponding written symbols to form, express, and communicate thoughts and feelings.

Language

Language (cont'd)
- **HN** Formerly (1963-1985) part of DC 249000, Language/Languages.
- **RT** Behavior
  Code Switching
  Debate
  Definitions
  Dialects
  Discourse Analysis
  Ethnolinguistic Groups
  Ethnolinguistics
  Language Acquisition
  Language Attitudes
  Language Disorders
  Language Maintenance
  Language Planning
  Language Policy
  Language Shift
  Language Usage
  Language Varieties
  Languages
  Linguistics
  Manual Communication
  Metaphors
  Morphology (Language)
  Pragmatics
  Rhetoric
  Second Language Learning
  Semiotics
  Speech
  Symbolism
  Terminology
  Verbal Communication
  Words
  Writing

Language Acquisition
- **DC** D444000
- **SN** Process of developing native language skills.
- **HN** Formerly (1963-1985) DC 010900, Acquisition/Acquisitions/Acquisitive/Acquisitiveness.
- **BT** Cognitive Development
- **RT** Language
  Psycholinguistics
  Speech

Language Attitudes
- **DC** D444300
- **HN** Added, 1986.
- **UF** Linguistic Attitudes
- **BT** Attitudes
- **RT** Cultural Identity
  Grammar
  Language
  Language Planning
  Language Social Class Relationship
  Language Usage
  Psycholinguistics
  Social Attitudes
  Sociolinguistics

Language Disorders
- **DC** D444600
- **HN** Added, 1986.
- **UF** Language Handicaps
- **BT** Disorders
- **NT** Aphasia
- **RT** Handicapped
  Language
  Learning Disabilities
  Psycholinguistics
  Speech

Language Families
  Use Languages

Language Handicaps
  Use Language Disorders

Language Maintenance
- **DC** D444900
- **HN** Added, 1986.
- **BT** Maintenance
- **RT** Biculturalism
  Bilingual Education
  Bilingualism
  Cultural Identity
  Language
  Language Planning
  Language Policy
  Language Shift
  Language Usage
  Languages
  Linguistic Minorities
  Multilingualism
  Sociolinguistics

Language Minority Groups
  Use Linguistic Minorities

Language Planning
- **DC** D445200
- **HN** Added, 1986.
- **BT** Planning
  Sociolinguistics
- **RT** Bilingual Education
  Bilingualism
  Educational Policy
  Language
  Language Attitudes
  Language Maintenance
  Language Policy
  Language Usage
  Languages
  Multilingualism

Language Policy
- **DC** D445500
- **HN** Added, 1986.
- **UF** Linguistic Policy
- **BT** Government Policy
- **RT** Biculturalism
  Bilingual Education
  Bilingualism
  Cultural Pluralism
  Educational Policy
  Language
  Language Maintenance
  Language Planning
  Language Usage
  Languages
  Plural Societies
  Political Culture
  Sociolinguistics

Language Shift
- **DC** D445800
- **SN** Change from the use of one language as the principal medium of everyday communication to another language.
- **HN** Added, 1986.
- **UF** Linguistic Shift
  Shift (Language)
- **BT** Change
- **RT** Acculturation
  Culture Contact
  Diglossia
  Language
  Language Maintenance
  Linguistics
  Minority Groups
  Sociolinguistics

Language

Language Social Class Relationship
- DC D446000
- SN In sociolinguistics, the correlates of social class in spoken language and the impact of language on social stratification and mobility.
- HN Added, 1989.
- BT Relations
- RT Bilingualism
    Class Differences
    Class Relations
    Code Switching
    Dialects
    Diglossia
    Language Attitudes
    Language Usage
    Language Varieties
    Monolingualism
    Multilingualism
    Social Class
    Sociocultural Factors
    Sociolinguistics

Language Usage
- DC D446100
- HN Added, 1986.
- RT Code Switching
    Communicative Action
    Creolized Languages
    Dialects
    Diglossia
    Discourse Analysis
    Ethnolinguistic Groups
    Grammar
    Language
    Language Attitudes
    Language Maintenance
    Language Planning
    Language Policy
    Language Social Class Relationship
    Language Varieties
    Languages
    Linguistic Minorities
    Linguistics
    Obscenity
    Pragmatics
    Slang
    Sociolinguistics
    Speech

Language Varieties
- DC D446400
- HN Formerly (1966-1985) DC 479750, Variety/Varieties.
- UF Linguistic Variants
    Varieties (Language)
- BT Languages
- NT Creolized Languages
    Dialects
- RT Code Switching
    Differences
    Diglossia
    Language
    Language Social Class Relationship
    Language Usage
    Linguistics
    Slang
    Sociolinguistics

Languages
- DC D446700
- HN Formerly (1963-1985) part of DC 249000, Language/Languages.
- UF Language Families
- NT African Languages
    Amerindian Languages
    Austronesian Languages
    Creolized Languages

Languages (cont'd)
- NT Dravidian Languages
    Drum Languages
    Esperanto
    Indoeuropean Languages
    Language Varieties
    Oriental Languages
    Semitic Languages
- RT Bilingualism
    Etymology
    Language
    Language Maintenance
    Language Planning
    Language Policy
    Language Usage
    Linguistics
    Monolingualism
    Multilingualism
    Translation

Laos
- DC D447000
- HN Formerly (1963-1985) DC 249050, Laos/Laotian/Laotians.
- BT Southeast Asia
- RT Indochina

Lapland
- DC D447300
- HN Formerly (1965-1985) DC 249100, Lapland/Lapp/Lapps.
- BT Scandinavia
    Western Europe
- RT Arctic Regions

Larceny
- DC D447600
- SN The wrongful taking of another's personal property for purposes of gain.
- HN Formerly (1982-1985) DC 249130.
- UF Stealing (1964-1985)
    Theft (Larceny)
- BT Offenses
- NT Robbery
    Shoplifting
- RT Burglary

Latency Period
- Use Childhood

Latent Class Analysis
- Use Latent Structure Analysis

Latent Structure Analysis
- DC D447800
- SN The examination of a range of data, especially in a scale, in order to determine the categories assumed to be intrinsic.
- HN Formerly (1964-1985) part of DC 249170, Latent/Latency.
- UF Latent Class Analysis
- BT Analysis
- RT Attitude Measures
    Attitudes
    Factor Analysis
    Guttman Scales

Latifundium/Latifundia/Latifundismo/Latifundists (1970-1985)
- HN DC 249300.
- Use Plantations

Latin
- DC D447900
- HN Formerly (1963-1985) DC 249325.
- BT Romance Languages

Law

Latin America
- DC D448200
- HN Formerly (1963-1985) DC 249345, Latin America/Latin American/Latin Americans.
- NT Caribbean
    Central America
    Mexico
    South America
- RT Latin American Cultural Groups
    North America

Latin American Cultural Groups
- DC D448500
- HN Added, 1986. Prior to 1986, concepts representing specific Latin American cultural groups, eg, Mexicans, were often indexed under terms representing the geographic place name, eg, Mexico/Mexican/Mexicans.
- UF Mesoamerican/Mesoamericans (1963-1985)
    South American Cultural Groups
- BT Cultural Groups
- NT American Indians
    Caribbean Cultural Groups
- RT Latin America
    North American Cultural Groups

Latter-Day Saints
- Use Mormons

Latvian Soviet Socialist Republic
- DC D448800
- HN Formerly (1964-1985) DC 249382, Latvia/Latvian/Latvians.
- BT Baltic States
    Union of Soviet Socialist Republics

Laughter
- DC D449100
- HN Formerly (1965-1985) DC 249390.
- RT Humor
    Interpersonal Communication

Law
- DC D449400
- HN Formerly (1963-1985) DC 249400, Law/Laws.
- UF Civil Law
    Criminal Law
    Doctrines (Legal)
    Legal Doctrines
- BT Social Institutions
    Social Sciences
- NT Ecclesiastical Law
    International Law
- RT Civil Rights
    Constitutions
    Contracts
    Courts
    Customs
    Due Process
    Government
    Judiciary
    Jurisprudence
    Justice
    Law Enforcement
    Legal Procedure
    Legal Profession
    Legal System
    Legislation
    Norms
    Patents
    Policy
    Political Science
    Regulation
    Rights

131

Law

Law (cont'd)
- RT Sanctions
- Social Policy
- Sociology of Law
- Traditions

Law Enforcement
- DC D449700
- HN Added, 1986. Prior to 1986 use Enforcement (DC 154945).
- UF Enforcement (Law)
- RT Compliance
- Crime
- Crime Prevention
- Criminal Justice
- Criminal Proceedings
- Discretion
- Government Agencies
- Human Services
- Investigations (Law Enforcement)
- Law
- Legal System
- Offenses
- Police
- Police Community Relations
- Prosecutors
- Protection
- Public Services
- Security
- Social Control
- Social Order
- Vigilantism

Law Enforcement Officers
- Use Police

Lawlessness (1963-1985)
- HN DC 249440, deleted 1986.

Laws (Statutes)
- Use Statutes

Lawsuits
- Use Litigation

Lawyer Client Relationship
- Use Client Relations

Lawyers
- DC D450000
- HN Formerly (1963-1985) DC 249460, Lawyer/Lawyers.
- UF Attorneys
- BT Professional Workers
- NT Prosecutors
- RT Clients
- Correctional Personnel
- Criminal Proceedings
- Judges
- Legal Profession
- Litigation

Laymen
- DC D450300
- SN Persons lacking expertise in relation to some profession or specialized area of knowledge. For non-clergy, see Laity (Religious).
- HN Formerly (1963-1985) DC 249470, Layman/Laymen.
- RT Amateurs
- Professions

Lazarsfeld, Paul Felix
- DC D450600
- SN Born 13 February 1901 - .
- HN Formerly (1969-1985) DC 249484, Lazarsfeld, Paul F.

Le Play, Pierre Guillaume Frederic
- DC D450900
- SN Born 11 April 1806 - died 5 April 1882.
- HN Formerly (1963-1985) DC 251770, Le Play, F.

Lead Poisoning
- DC D451050
- HN Formerly (1977-1986) DC 249485, Lead.
- BT Poisoning
- RT Health Problems
- Living Conditions
- Toxic Substances

Leadership
- DC D451200
- HN Formerly (1963-1985) DC 249500, Leader/Leaders/Leadership.
- RT Ability
- Administrators
- Authority
- Cadres
- Charisma
- Cooptation
- Legislators
- Opinion Leaders
- Politicians
- Power Elite
- Prestige
- Responsibility
- Social Power
- Superior Subordinate Relationship

League/Leagues (1964-1985)
- HN DC 249850.
- Use Federations

Learning
- DC D451500
- HN Formerly (1963-1985) DC 250000, Learning/Learned.
- NT Second Language Learning
- RT Ability
- Academic Achievement
- Academic Aptitude
- Cognition
- Cognitive Mapping
- Conditioning
- Discovery
- Education
- Educational Research
- Epistemology
- Experience
- Feedback
- Generalization
- Imitation
- Knowledge
- Learning Disabilities
- Mass Media Effects
- Memory
- Recognition (Psychology)
- Scholarship
- Socialization
- Teaching
- Teaching Methods

Learning Disabilities
- DC D451800
- HN Added, 1986.
- UF Disabilities (Learning)
- RT Aphasia
- Cognition
- Handicapped
- Language Disorders
- Learning
- Neurology

Legal

Lease (1966-1985)
- HN DC 251150, deleted 1986. See now Land Tenure or Rents.

Lebanon
- DC D452100
- HN Formerly (1963-1985) DC 251200, Lebanon/Lebanese.
- BT Arab Countries
- Mediterranean Countries
- Middle East
- NT Beirut, Lebanon

Lebenswelt
- DC D452200
- SN German for life-world, everyday life as experienced subjectively by members of society.
- HN Formerly (1973-1985) DC 251250.
- UF Life World
- RT Common Sense
- Everyday Life
- Experience

Lecture/Lectures/Lectured/ Lecturer/Lecturing (1963-1985)
- HN DC 251290, deleted 1986. See now Teachers or Teaching.

Lee, Alfred McClung
- DC D452300
- SN Born 23 August 1906 - .
- HN Added, 1989.

Leeward Islands
- Use Caribbean

Lefebvre, Henri
- DC D452400
- SN Born 16 June 1901 - .
- HN Formerly (1972-1985) DC 251320, Lefebvre, H.

Left Wing Politics
- DC D452700
- HN Formerly (1964-1985) DC 251330, Left-Wing.
- UF New Left (1970-1985)
- BT Politics
- RT Communist Parties
- Extremism
- Labor Parties
- Radicalism
- Socialist Parties

Legal Cases
- DC D453000
- HN Formerly (1963-1985) part of DC 070000, Case.
- UF Cases (Legal)
- RT Criminal Proceedings
- Disposition
- Judicial Decisions
- Legal Procedure
- Legal System
- Litigation

Legal Doctrines
- Use Law

Legal Liability
- Use Liability

Legal Procedure
- DC D453300
- HN Added, 1986.
- UF Civil Procedure
- Criminal Procedure
- Practice (Legal)
- NT Insanity Defense
- Plea Bargaining

Legal

Legal Procedure (cont'd)
- **NT** Trials
- **RT** Courts
  Due Process
  Evidence (Legal)
  Judicial Decisions
  Law
  Legal Cases
  Litigation
  United States Supreme Court

Legal Profession
- **DC** D453600
- **HN** Added, 1986.
- **BT** Professions
- **RT** Advocacy
  Client Relations
  Forensic Psychiatry
  Judges
  Judiciary
  Law
  Lawyers
  Legal System
  Prosecutors
  Representation
  Sociology of Law

Legal Sociology
- **Use** Sociology of Law

Legal System
- **DC** D453900
- **HN** Added, 1986.
- **UF** Judicial System
- **BT** Systems
- **NT** Adversary Legal System
  Correctional System
  Criminal Justice
  Juvenile Justice
- **RT** Courts
  Due Process
  Government
  Judiciary
  Justice
  Law
  Law Enforcement
  Legal Cases
  Legal Profession
  Litigation
  Sociology of Law
  Vigilantism

Legal Theory
- **Use** Jurisprudence

Legal/Legalism/Legality (1963-1985)
- **HN** DC 251360, deleted 1986. See now Law, Legal Profession, or Legal System.

Legalization
- **Use** Decriminalization

Legend/Legends (1963-1985)
- **HN** DC 251400.
- **Use** Folklore

Legislation
- **DC** D454200
- **HN** Formerly (1963-1985) DC 251575.
- **UF** Social Legislation (1963-1985)
- **NT** Statutes
- **RT** Compliance
  Constitutional Amendments
  Government
  Government Policy
  Government Regulation
  Interest Groups
  Law

Legislation (cont'd)
- **RT** Legislative Bodies
  Legislators
  Lobbying
  Policy Implementation
  Policy Making
  Politics
  Public Policy
  Referendum

Legislative Apportionment
- **DC** D454500
- **HN** Formerly (1965-1985) DC 035170, Apportionment.
- **UF** Apportionment (Legislative)
  Reapportionment (1965-1985)
- **RT** Elections
  Legislative Bodies

Legislative Bodies
- **DC** D454800
- **HN** Formerly (1963-1985) DC 251590, Legislative/Legislature/Legislatures.
- **UF** Congress (Legislative Body)
  Legislatures
  Parliament/Parliamentary/
    Parliamentarianism (1963-1985)
  Senate/Senates (1964-1985)
- **RT** Democracy
  Government
  Government Agencies
  Legislation
  Legislative Apportionment
  Legislators
  Political Power
  Political Representation
  Political Systems

Legislators
- **DC** D455100
- **HN** Formerly (1963-1985) DC 251600, Legislator/Legislators.
- **UF** Congressmen/Congressman (1963-1985)
  Senator/Senators/Senatorial (1963-1985)
- **BT** Public Officials
- **RT** Government
  Leadership
  Legislation
  Legislative Bodies
  Political Representation
  Politicians

Legislatures
- **Use** Legislative Bodies

Legitimacy
- **DC** D455400
- **SN** The quality of being morally justified, especially with reference to political Authority.
- **HN** Formerly (1963-1985) DC 251640.
- **RT** Authority
  Government
  Legitimation
  State

Legitimation
- **DC** D455700
- **SN** The process or means by which political Authority is considered to possess Legitimacy.
- **HN** Formerly (1963-1985) DC 251650, Legitimate/Legitimation.
- **RT** Government
  Legitimacy
  State

Lesbianism

Leibnitz, Gottfried Wilhelm
- **DC** D456000
- **SN** Born 1 July 1646 - died 14 November 1716.
- **HN** Formerly (1968-1985) DC 251675, Leibnitz, G. W.

Leisure
- **DC** D456300
- **HN** Formerly (1963-1985) DC 251700.
- **UF** Free Time (1963-1985)
  Hobbies (1978-1985)
  Leisure Time
  Leisure Utilization
  Pastime/Pastimes (1963-1985)
- **RT** Activities
  Amateurs
  Clubs
  Eating And Drinking Establishments
  Recreation
  Retirement
  Sociology of Leisure
  Sports
  Television Viewing
  Time Utilization
  Work Leisure Relationship

Leisure Time
- **Use** Leisure

Leisure Utilization
- **Use** Leisure

Length (1963-1985)
- **HN** DC 251750, deleted 1986.

Leningrad, Union of Soviet Socialist Republics
- **DC** D456425
- **HN** Added, 1989.
- **BT** Union of Soviet Socialist Republics

Leninism
- **DC** D456500
- **HN** Formerly (1966-1985) DC 251760, Lenin, V. I. (N.)/Leninism/Leninist.
- **BT** Marxism
- **RT** Bolshevism
  Class Consciousness
  Communism
  Ideologies
  Revolutions
  Scientific Management
  Stalinism

Lenski, Gerhard Emmanuel
- **DC** D456600
- **SN** Born 13 August 1924 - .
- **HN** Formerly (1966-1985) DC 251767, Lenski, G.

Leprosy
- **DC** D456900
- **HN** Formerly (1963-1985) DC 251775.
- **BT** Diseases

Lesbianism
- **DC** D457200
- **HN** Formerly (1968-1985) DC 251782 Lesbian/Lesbians/Lesbianism.
- **UF** Female Homosexuality
- **BT** Homosexuality
- **RT** Bisexuality
  Homosexual Relationships
  Transsexualism

Lesotho

Lesotho
- DC D457500
- HN Formerly (1985) DC 251785.
- BT Sub Saharan Africa

Less Developed Countries (1984-1985)
- HN DC 251787.
- Use Developing Countries

Lesser Antilles
- Use Caribbean

Letters (Correspondence)
- DC D457800
- HN Formerly (1963-1985) DC 251792, Letter/Letters.
- UF Correspondence/Correspondent (1965-1985)
  Greeting Cards
  Postcards
- BT Verbal Communication
- RT Autobiographical Materials
  Documents
  Interpersonal Communication
  Literature
  Writing

Leukemia
- DC D458100
- HN Formerly (1964-1985) DC 251800.
- BT Cancer
- RT Blood

Level/Levels (1963-1985)
- HN DC 251805, deleted 1986.

Levi-Strauss, Claude
- DC D458400
- SN Born 28 November 1908 - .
- HN Formerly (1964-1985) DC 251820, Levi-Strauss, C.

Levy-Bruhl, Lucien
- DC D458700
- SN Born 10 April 1857 - died 13 March 1939.
- HN Formerly (1964-1985) DC 251823, Levy-Bruhl, L.

Lewin, Kurt
- DC D459000
- SN Born 9 September 1890 - died 2 December 1947.
- HN Formerly (1964-1985) DC 251825.

Lexicon/Lexicons/Lexical (1963-1985)
- HN DC 251830, deleted 1986. See now Reference Materials or Vocabularies.

Lexicostatistics (1969-1985)
- HN DC 251833.
- Use Linguistics

Liability
- DC D459300
- HN Formerly (1967-1985) DC 251842.
- UF Legal Liability
- RT Litigation
  Professional Malpractice
  Responsibility

Liberal Democratic Countries
- Use Liberal Democratic Societies

Liberal Democratic Societies
- DC D459600
- HN Added, 1986.

Liberal Democratic Societies (cont'd)
- UF Liberal Democratic Countries
- BT Society
- RT Capitalist Societies
  Communist Societies
  Democracy
  Human Rights
  Liberalism
  Political Ideologies
  Socialist Societies
  Welfare State
  Western Society

Liberal/Liberals/Liberality/Liberalization (1963-1985)
- HN DC 251850, deleted 1986.

Liberalism
- DC D459900
- HN Formerly (1963-1985) DC 251880.
- BT Political Ideologies
- RT Civil Rights
  Conservatism
  Democracy
  Individualism
  Liberal Democratic Societies
  New Deal
  Utilitarianism
  Welfare State

Liberate/Liberation (1968-1985)
- HN DC 251887, deleted 1986. See now Political Movements or Social Movements.

Liberia
- DC D460200
- HN Formerly (1963-1985) DC 251900, Liberia/Liberian/Liberians.
- BT Sub Saharan Africa

Libertarians
- DC D460500
- HN Formerly (1969-1985) DC 251907.
- RT Political Ideologies

Liberty/Liberties (1963-1985)
- HN DC 251915.
- Use Freedom

Libido/Libidinal (1963-1985)
- HN DC 251919.
- Use Sexuality

Libraries
- DC D460800
- HN Formerly (1963-1985) DC 251930, Library/Libraries/Librarian/Librarians.
- UF Public Libraries
- RT Archives
  Data Banks
  Information And Referral Services
  Information Dissemination
  Information Sources
  Institutions
  Reference Materials

Libya
- DC D461100
- HN Formerly (1963-1985) DC 251945, Libya/Libyan/Libyans.
- BT Arab Countries
  Mediterranean Countries
  North Africa

Life

Licenses
- DC D461400
- HN Formerly (1964-1985) DC 251950, License/Licensing.
- UF Licensure (1975-1985)
- RT Certification
  Occupational Qualifications

Licensure (1975-1985)
- HN DC 251955.
- Use Licenses

Lie Detection
- DC D461700
- HN Formerly (1975-1985) DC 251965.
- UF Polygraph
- RT Deception
  Offenses
  Testimony

Liechtenstein
- DC D462000
- HN Added, 1986.
- BT Western Europe

Lies
- Use Deception

Life
- DC D462300
- SN A context-dependent term; select a more specific entry or coordinate with other terms.
- HN Formerly (1963-1985) DC 251975.
- NT Everyday Life
  Family Life
  Social Life
- RT Biology
  Existence
  Experience
  Life Cycle
  Life Events
  Life History
  Life Plans
  Life Stage Transitions
  Life Tables
  Lifestyle
  Living Conditions
  Quality of Life
  Rites of Passage

Life Course (1985)
- HN DC 251977, deleted 1986.

Life Cycle
- DC D462600
- HN Formerly (1979-1985) DC 251980, Life Cycle/Life Cycles.
- NT Aging
  Birth
  Death
  Puberty
- RT Child Development
  Cyclical Processes
  Family Life
  Gerontology
  Life
  Life Events
  Life Stage Transitions
  Menarche
  Menopause

Life Events
- DC D462900
- SN Significant or unusual experiences that signify or bring about changes in life circumstances, such as marriage, divorce, bereavement, or unemployment.
- HN Formerly (1985) DC 251981.

Life　　　　　　　　　　　　　　　　　　　　　　　　　　　　Linguistic

Life Events (cont'd)
- **BT** Phenomena
- **RT** Adjustment
  - Celebrations
  - Coping
  - Experience
  - Life
  - Life Cycle
  - Life Stage Transitions
  - Stress

Life Expectancy
- **Use** Longevity

Life History
- **DC** D463200
- **SN** Research technique in which the subject gives an accurate and detailed account of life experiences, including significant emotions, observations, and internal and environmental events.
- **HN** Formerly (1965-1985) DC 251982.
- **BT** Methodology (Data Collection)
- **RT** Chicago School of Sociology
  - Everyday Life
  - Genealogy
  - History
  - Life
  - Oral History
  - Psychohistory
  - Social Science Research

Life Plans
- **DC** D463500
- **HN** Added, 1986.
- **UF** Career Plans
- **RT** Aspiration
  - Careers
  - Educational Plans
  - Expectations
  - Goals
  - Life
  - Life Satisfaction
  - Occupational Achievement
  - Occupational Mobility
  - Planning

Life Quality
- **Use** Quality of Life

Life Satisfaction
- **DC** D463800
- **HN** Formerly (1985) DC 251983.
- **BT** Satisfaction
- **RT** Experience
  - Happiness
  - Humanization
  - Individuals
  - Job Satisfaction
  - Life Plans
  - Lifestyle
  - Marital Satisfaction
  - Mental Health
  - Quality of Life
  - Role Satisfaction
  - Self Actualization
  - Social Conditions
  - Social Indicators
  - Social Life
  - Social Status
  - Standard of Living
  - Well Being

Life Sciences
- **Use** Biological Sciences

Life Span
- **Use** Longevity

Life Stage Transitions
- **DC** D464100
- **SN** Processes of change from one stage of life to the next, for example, from adolescent to adult and from older adult to elderly.
- **HN** Added, 1986.
- **UF** Lifecourse Transition
  - Lifecycle Transition
  - Midlife Transition
  - Role Transition
  - Transition (Life)
- **RT** Adjustment
  - Adult Development
  - Aging
  - Behavior
  - Childhood
  - Developmental Stages
  - Divorce
  - Dying
  - Gerontology
  - Initiation Rites
  - Life
  - Life Cycle
  - Life Events
  - Marital Disruption
  - Marriage
  - Middle Aged Adults
  - Parenthood
  - Puberty
  - Retirement
  - Rites of Passage
  - Roles
  - Widowhood

Life Tables
- **DC** D464400
- **SN** Statistical tables that show the average lifespan of specific age groups.
- **HN** Formerly (1963-1985) DC 251985, Life Table.
- **UF** Cohort Life Tables (1965-1985)
  - Tables (Life)
- **BT** Tables
- **RT** Demography
  - Life
  - Longevity
  - Mortality Rates
  - Social Science Research

Life World
- **Use** Lebenswelt

Lifecourse Transition
- **Use** Life Stage Transitions

Lifecycle Transition
- **Use** Life Stage Transitions

Lifestyle
- **DC** D464700
- **SN** The way of life that characterizes a specific individual or group.
- **HN** Formerly (1981-1985) DC 251984, Lifestyle/Lifestyles.
- **UF** Alternative Lifestyle
  - Way of Life (1985)
- **BT** Styles
- **RT** Behavior
  - Countercultures
  - Everyday Life
  - Humanization
  - Life
  - Life Satisfaction
  - Living Conditions
  - Personality

Lifestyle (cont'd)
- **RT** Rural Urban Continuum
  - Rural Urban Differences
  - Rurality
  - Social Life
  - Urbanism
  - Worldview

Likert, Rensis
- **DC** D465000
- **SN** Born 5 August 1903 - died 3 September 1981.
- **HN** Formerly (1964-1985) DC 252600, Likert, R.

Lima, Peru
- **DC** D465300
- **HN** Formerly (1965-1985) DC 252700.
- **BT** Peru

Limit/Limits/Limited (1963-1985)
- **HN** DC 252747.
- **Use** Limitations

Limitations
- **DC** D465400
- **HN** Formerly (1963-1985) DC 252750, Limitation/Limitations.
- **UF** Limit/Limits/Limited (1963-1985)
- **RT** Constraints
  - Problems
  - Time

Line Islands
- **DC** D465600
- **HN** Added, 1986.
- **BT** Polynesia

Lineage
- **DC** D465900
- **HN** Formerly (1963-1985) DC 252770.
- **RT** Clans
  - Descent
  - Genealogy
  - Kinship
  - Naming Practices

Linear Analysis
- **DC** D466050
- **HN** Formerly (1964-1985) DC 252775, Linear/Linearity/Linearal.
- **UF** Linear Models
- **BT** Methodology (Data Analysis)
  - Quantitative Methods
- **NT** Loglinear Analysis
- **RT** Models

Linear Models
- **Use** Linear Analysis

Linear Regression
- **Use** Regression Analysis

Lingualism (1969-1985)
- **HN** DC 252801.
- **Use** Multilingualism

Linguistic Attitudes
- **Use** Language Attitudes

Linguistic Minorities
- **DC** D466200
- **SN** Ethnic groups in a culturally pluralistic society that use a language different from that of the majority.
- **HN** Added, 1986.
- **UF** Language Minority Groups
- **BT** Ethnolinguistic Groups
  - Minority Groups
- **RT** Language Maintenance
  - Language Usage
  - Plural Societies

Linguistic   Living

Linguistic Policy
  Use Language Policy

Linguistic Shift
  Use Language Shift

Linguistic Variants
  Use Language Varieties

Linguistics
- DC D466500
- SN The systematic study and description of language, primarily in its spoken form, and involving observation of either individual speakers or entire linguistic groups.
- HN Formerly (1963-1985) DC 252810, Linguistic/Linguistics.
- UF Lexicostatistics (1969-1985)
- NT Etymology
    Grammar
    Phonetics
    Psycholinguistics
    Semantics
    Semiotics
    Sociolinguistics
- RT Communication
    Culture
    Dialects
    Language
    Language Shift
    Language Usage
    Language Varieties
    Languages
    Signs
    Social Anthropology
    Speech
    Structuralism
    Translation
    Verbal Communication

Linkage (1963-1985)
- HN DC 252875.
- Use Relations

Lipset, Seymour Martin
- DC D466800
- SN Born 18 March 1922 - .
- HN Formerly (1963-1985) DC 252900, Lipset, Seymour M.

Liquor (1966-1985)
- HN DC 252930.
- Use Alcoholic Beverages

Listener (1965-1985)
- HN DC 252980.
- Use Audiences

Literacy
- DC D467100
- HN Formerly (1963-1985) DC 253400, Literacy/Literate/Literates.
- UF Illiterate/Illiterates/Illiteracy (1963-1985)
- NT Writing
- RT Ignorance
    Literacy Programs
    Reading
    Vocabularies

Literacy Campaigns
  Use Literacy Programs

Literacy Education
  Use Literacy Programs

Literacy Programs
- DC D467400
- HN Added, 1986.
- UF Literacy Campaigns
    Literacy Education
    Universal Primary Education Programs
    UPE Campaigns
- BT Educational Programs
    Programs
- RT Adult Education
    Education
    Educational Reform
    Literacy
    Writing

Literary (1964-1985)
- HN DC 253440, deleted 1986. See now Literary Criticism or Literature.

Literary Criticism
- DC D467700
- SN Discussions of literary criticism as a form of sociological analysis.
- HN Formerly (1985) DC 253450.
- BT Criticism
- RT Aesthetics
    Book Reviews
    Content Analysis
    Literature
    Sociology of Literature

Literary Heroes
  Use Heroes

Literary Texts
  Use Literature

Literature
- DC D468000
- HN Formerly (1963-1985) DC 253500.
- UF Classical Literature
    Literary Texts
- BT Humanities
- NT Biographies
    Drama
    Fiction
    Poetry
- RT Art
    Authorship
    Autobiographical Materials
    Books
    Content Analysis
    Discourse
    Fictional Characters
    Folk Culture
    Folklore
    Heroes
    Journalism
    Letters (Correspondence)
    Literary Criticism
    Literature Reviews
    Marxist Aesthetics
    Metaphors
    Myths
    Narratives
    Naturalism
    Poets
    Postmodernism
    Publishing Industry
    Renaissance
    Romanticism
    Satire
    Sociology of Literature
    Symbolism
    Utopias
    Writers

Literature Reviews
- DC D468300
- SN Discussions of literature reviews as tools in social science research.
- HN Added, 1986.
- UF Research Reviews
    Reviews of the Literature
- BT Publications
- RT Bibliographies
    Book Reviews
    Citations (References)
    Literature

Litigation
- DC D468600
- HN Formerly (1969-1985) DC 253525.
- UF Civil Proceedings
    Lawsuits
- RT Adversary Legal System
    Arbitration
    Defendants
    Evidence (Legal)
    Judges
    Juries
    Lawyers
    Legal Cases
    Legal Procedure
    Legal System
    Liability
    Trials
    Verdicts

Littering
- DC D468900
- HN Formerly (1971-1985) DC 253534, Litter/Littering.
- BT Offenses

Liturgy
- DC D469200
- HN Formerly (1963-1985) DC 253530, Liturgy/Liturgical.
- BT Religious Rituals
- RT Christianity
    Worship

Livelihood (1979-1985)
- HN DC 253540, deleted 1986.

Livestock
- DC D469500
- HN Formerly (1983-1985) DC 253549.
- UF Cattle/Cattlebreeding (1964-1985)
    Farm Animals
    Poultry
- BT Animals
- RT Agricultural Development
    Agricultural Production
    Animal Husbandry
    Dairy Farms
    Food
    Pastoral Societies

Living Conditions
- DC D469800
- HN Formerly (1963-1985) DC 253555, Living.
- RT Affluence
    Communities
    Community Satisfaction
    Disadvantaged
    Economic Conditions
    Hazards
    Home Environment
    Housing
    Lead Poisoning
    Life
    Lifestyle
    Quality of Life

Living / Longitudinal

Living Conditions (cont'd)
- **RT** Social Conditions
    Standard of Living
    Work Environment

Living Standard
- **Use** Standard of Living

Loans
- **DC** D470100
- **HN** Formerly (1963-1985) DC 253560, Loan/Loans/Loansharking.
- **RT** Banking
    Credit
    Debts
    Finance
    Gift Giving
    Money
    Subsidies

Lobbying
- **DC** D470400
- **HN** Formerly (1964-1985) DC 253565, Lobby/Lobbying/Lobbyist/Lobbyists.
- **RT** Activism
    Interest Groups
    Legislation
    Lobbying
    Political Action
    Political Action Committees
    Political Power
    Representation

Local Communities
- **Use** Communities

Local Councils
- **Use** Councils

Local Education Agencies
- **Use** School Districts

Local Government
- **DC** D470700
- **HN** Added, 1986.
- **BT** Government
- **RT** Central Government
    Cities
    City Planning
    Communities
    Community Services
    Counties
    Districts
    Federal Government
    Local Planning
    Local Politics
    Mayors
    Panchayats
    School Districts

Local Organizations
- **Use** Community Organizations

Local Planning
- **DC** D471000
- **HN** Formerly (1985) DC 253600.
- **UF** Community Planning
- **BT** Planning
- **NT** City Planning
- **RT** Communities
    Community Development
    Economic Planning
    Health Planning
    Local Government
    Local Politics
    New Towns
    Social Planning
    State Planning

Local Politics
- **DC** D471300
- **HN** Added, 1986.
- **UF** Community Politics
    Municipal Politics
- **BT** Politics
- **RT** Cities
    Communities
    Community Power
    Local Government
    Local Planning
    Mayors
    Political Participation

Local Residents
- **Use** Residents

Local/Locals/Localism/Locality/Localization (1963-1985)
- **HN** DC 253575, deleted 1986. See now Localism and appropriate "Community," "Local," "Rural," or "Urban" terms.

Localism
- **DC** D471600
- **HN** Formerly (1963-1985) part of DC 253575, Local/Locals/Localism/Locality/Localization.
- **BT** Social Attitudes
- **RT** Communities
    Cosmopolitanism
    Regionalism
    Rurality
    Social Identity

Location/Locations/Locational (1964-1985)
- **HN** DC 253640, deleted 1986. See now Residence, Community, and their associated terms.

Locke, John
- **DC** D471900
- **SN** Born 29 August 1632 - died 28 October 1704.
- **HN** Formerly (1963-1985) DC 253670.

Locus of Control
- **DC** D472200
- **SN** Center of responsibility for the control of an individual's behavior: internal, which entails the conviction that one can use one's own behavior to achieve desired goals; or external, which entails the belief that real power lies outside of the individual.
- **HN** Added, 1986.
- **UF** Internal External Locus of Control
- **BT** Personality Traits
- **RT** Attribution
    Control
    Delay of Gratification
    Inner And Other Directedness
    Self Concept

Lodz, Poland
- **DC** D472500
- **HN** Formerly (1966-1985) DC 253684.
- **BT** Poland

Logarithmic (1975-1985)
- **HN** DC 253690, deleted 1986.

Logic
- **DC** D472600
- **HN** Formerly (1963-1985) DC 253700, Logic/Logical/Logicians.
- **UF** Formal Logic

Logic (cont'd)
- **UF** Mathematical Logic
    Symbolic Logic
- **BT** Philosophy
- **RT** Analogy
    Deduction
    Dialectics
    Formalism
    Induction
    Inference
    Mathematics
    Rationalism
    Reasoning
    Validity

Logical Positivism
- **Use** Positivism

Loglinear Analysis
- **DC** D472665
- **HN** Formerly (1979-1985) DC 253720, Log-Linear.
- **BT** Linear Analysis
- **RT** Causal Models
    Contingency Analysis
    Models
    Multivariate Analysis

Lombardy, Italy (1966-1985)
- **HN** DC 253750, deleted 1986.

Lombroso, Cesare
- **DC** D472800
- **SN** Born 6 November 1835 - died 9 October 1909.
- **HN** Formerly (1963-1985) DC 253752.

London, England
- **DC** D473100
- **HN** Formerly (1963-1985) DC 253758.
- **BT** England

Loneliness
- **DC** D473400
- **HN** Formerly (1963-1985) DC 253785.
- **BT** Emotions
- **RT** Alienation
    Depression (Psychology)
    Social Contact
    Social Interaction
    Social Isolation

Longevity
- **DC** D473700
- **HN** Formerly (1963-1985) DC 253795.
- **UF** Life Expectancy
    Life Span
- **RT** Health
    Life Tables
    Mortality Rates
    Survival

Longitudinal Studies
- **DC** D473800
- **SN** Methods of Data Collection in which the same persons or groups are observed over a period of time.
- **HN** Formerly (1963-1985) DC 253810, Longitudinal Study/Longitudinal Studies.
- **BT** Methodology (Data Collection)
- **RT** Attrition
    Case Studies
    Cohort Analysis
    Panel Data
    Research

Longshoremen

Longshoremen
- DC D474000
- HN Formerly (1983-1985) DC 253825.
- UF Dock Workers
- BT Blue Collar Workers
- RT Shipping Industry

Looting (1968-1985)
- HN DC 253870, deleted 1986. See now Riots, Offenses, Larceny, or other appropriate "Crime" terms.

Lorence Curves (1963-1985)
- HN DC 253900.
- Use Frequency Distributions

Los Angeles, California
- DC D474300
- HN Formerly (1963-1985) DC 253950, Los Angeles, Calif.
- UF Watts, Los Angeles (1968-1985)
- BT California

Louisiana
- DC D474600
- HN Formerly (1963-1985) DC 254100.
- BT Southern States
  United States of America
- NT New Orleans, Louisiana

Louisville, Ky. (1980-1985)
- HN DC 254150, deleted 1986.

Love
- DC D474900
- HN Formerly (1963-1985) DC 254500.
- UF Affection (1964-1985)
  Romance/Romances/Romantic (1968-1985)
- BT Emotions
- NT Narcissism
- RT Attachment
  Family Relations
  Happiness
  Interpersonal Attraction
  Interpersonal Relations
  Intimacy
  Marital Relations
  Needs

Low Income Areas
- DC D475200
- HN Formerly (1963-1985) part of DC 254690, Low Income.
- UF Low Income Counties
  Low Income Countries
  Poverty Areas
- NT Slums
- RT Development Programs
  Disadvantaged
  Economic Problems
  Geographic Regions
  Housing
  Income
  Low Income Groups
  Poverty
  Rural Poverty
  Skid Row

Low Income Counties
- Use Low Income Areas

Low Income Countries
- Use Low Income Areas

Low Income Groups
- DC D475500
- HN Formerly (1963-1985) part of DC 254690, Low Income.
- BT Groups
- RT Antipoverty Programs
  Deprivation

Low Income Groups (cont'd)
- RT Disadvantaged
  Economic Problems
  Income
  Income Maintenance Programs
  Low Income Areas
  Lower Class
  Minority Groups
  Peasants
  Poverty
  Slums
  Welfare Policy
  Welfare Recipients
  Welfare Services
  Working Class

Low Income Housing
- Use Public Housing

Lowenthal, Leo
- DC D475700
- SN Born 3 November 1900 - .
- HN Added, 1989.

Lower Class
- DC D475800
- HN Added, 1986.
- BT Social Class
- RT Blue Collar Workers
  Low Income Groups
  Peasants
  Proletariat
  Working Class

Loyalty
- DC D476100
- HN Formerly (1963-1985) DC 254725, Loyalty/Loyalties.
- NT Commitment
- RT Patriotism
  Personality Traits
  Political Defection

LSD
- Use Lysergic Acid Diethylamide

Luck (1969-1985)
- HN DC 254778.
- Use Chance

Luhmann, Niklas
- DC D476400
- SN Born 1927 - .
- HN Formerly (1973-1985) DC 254830.

Lukacs, Georg
- DC D476700
- SN Born 13 April 1885 - died 4 June 1971.
- HN Formerly (1963-1985) DC 254840.

Lunar Influences
- DC D477000
- HN Formerly (1984-1985) DC 254872, Lunar.
- UF Moon Influences
- RT Cyclical Processes
  Environmental Factors

Luther, Martin
- DC D477300
- SN Born 10 November 1483 - died 18 February 1546.
- HN Formerly (1964-1985) DC 255200.

Lutheran Churches
- Use Lutherans

Machinery

Lutherans
- DC D477600
- HN Formerly (1963-1985) DC 255225, Lutheran/Lutherans.
- UF Lutheran Churches
- BT Protestants
- RT Protestantism

Luxembourg
- DC D477900
- HN Added, 1986.
- BT Western Europe

Luxemburg, Rosa
- DC D478200
- SN Born 5 March 1870 - died 15 January 1919.
- HN Formerly (1967-1985) DC 255300.

Lying
- Use Deception

Lynching
- DC D478500
- HN Formerly (1964-1985) DC 255400.
- RT Assault
  Homicide

Lynd, Robert Staughton
- DC D478800
- SN Born 26 September 1892 - died 1 November 1970.
- HN Formerly (1964-1985) DC 255410, Lynd, Robert.

Lyric Poetry
- Use Poetry

Lysergic Acid Diethylamide
- DC D479100
- HN Formerly (1966-1985) DC 254750, LSD/Lysergic Acid Diethylamide.
- UF LSD
- BT Psychedelic Drugs

Macao
- DC D479400
- HN Added, 1986.
- BT Far East
- RT China

Machiavellianism (Personality)
- DC D479600
- SN Being or acting in accordance with the principle that any means, no matter how unscrupulous, deceptive, or dishonest, are justified to achieve power or manipulate others.
- HN Formerly (1965-1985) DC 255900, Machiavelli/Machiavellian/Machiavellianism.
- BT Personality Traits
- RT Ethics
  Manipulation
  Morality
  Social Behavior
  Value Orientations

Machine Translation
- Use Translation

Machinery
- DC D479700
- HN Formerly (1963-1985) DC 256000, Machine/Machinery.
- UF Machines
- RT Agricultural Mechanization
  Agricultural Technology
  Automation
  Automobiles

Machines

Machinery (cont'd)
- **RT** Computers
  - Industrial Automation
  - Industry
  - Maintenance
  - Material Culture
  - Nuclear Reactors
  - Tools
  - Worker Machine Relationship

Machines
- **Use** Machinery

Macrosociology
- **DC** D480000
- **SN** The study of large collectivities (eg, nations, the city) and their interrelationships. Compare with Microsociology.
- **HN** Formerly (1971-1985) DC 256090, Macrosociology/Macrosociological.
- **BT** Sociology
- **RT** Conflict Theory
  - Entropy
  - Group Dynamics
  - Marxist Sociology
  - Society
  - Sociological Research

Madagascar
- **DC** D480300
- **HN** Formerly (1963-1985) DC 256100, Madagascar/Madagascan/Madagascans.
- **UF** Malagasy Republic
- **BT** Sub Saharan Africa

Madeira
- **DC** D480600
- **HN** Added, 1986.
- **BT** Western Europe
- **RT** North Africa
  - North Atlantic Ocean

Madison, Wisc. (1981-1985)
- **HN** DC 256125, deleted 1986.

Madras, India
- **DC** D480900
- **HN** Formerly (1964-1985) DC 256150.
- **BT** India

Madrid, Spain
- **DC** D481200
- **HN** Formerly (1964-1985) DC 256165.
- **BT** Spain

Mafia (1966-1985)
- **HN** DC 256180.
- **Use** Organized Crime

Magazines
- **DC** D481500
- **HN** Formerly (1963-1985) DC 256200, Magazine/Magazines.
- **UF** Popular Magazines
  - Teen Magazines
- **BT** Periodicals
- **RT** Popular Culture

Maghreb
- **DC** D481800
- **SN** A region including northwest Africa, especially Morocco, Algeria, and Tunisia.
- **HN** Formerly (1969-1985) DC 256400.
- **RT** North Africa

Magic
- **DC** D482100
- **HN** Formerly (1963-1985) DC 256275, Magic/Magical/Magicians.
- **RT** Beliefs
  - Evil Eye
  - Faith Healing
  - Fetishism
  - Occultism
  - Shamanism
  - Supernatural
  - Superstitions
  - Voodooism
  - Witchcraft

Magnitude Estimation
- **DC** D482200
- **HN** Formerly (1972-1985) DC 256475, Magnitude/Magnitudes.
- **BT** Estimation
- **RT** Scales

Mahdis
- **DC** D482400
- **SN** Islamic religious leaders with messianic status.
- **HN** Formerly (1969-1985) DC 256545, Mahdi/Mahdis.
- **BT** Messianic Figures
  - Muslims
- **RT** Islam
  - Salvation

Maids
- **Use** Domestics

Mail Surveys
- **DC** D482600
- **SN** Research in which self-administered questionnaires are sent to and returned by samples of respondents through the mail.
- **HN** Added, 1986. Prior to 1986 use Mail/Mailed (DC 256565) and Survey/Surveys (DC 453200).
- **BT** Surveys
- **RT** Questionnaires
  - Research Responses

Maine
- **DC** D482700
- **HN** Formerly (1968-1985) DC 256575.
- **BT** Northern States
  - United States of America

Maintenance
- **DC** D482800
- **HN** Formerly (1969-1985) DC 256579.
- **NT** Language Maintenance
  - Preservation
- **RT** Facilities
  - Machinery
  - Obsolescence
  - Property

Maize (1964-1985)
- **HN** DC 256584.
- **Use** Food

Majorities (Politics)
- **DC** D483000
- **HN** Formerly (1963-1985) part of DC 256590, Majority/Majorities.
- **UF** Plurality (1965-1985)
- **RT** Democracy
  - Majority Groups
  - Political Parties
  - Politics
  - Voters

Males

Majority Groups
- **DC** D483300
- **HN** Formerly (1963-1985) part of DC 256590, Majority/Majorities.
- **BT** Groups
- **RT** Black White Relations
  - Center And Periphery
  - Intergroup Relations
  - Majorities (Politics)
  - Minority Groups
  - Race
  - Social Control
  - Social Structure

Majors (Students)
- **Use** College Majors

Maladjustment/Maladjusted (1964-1985)
- **HN** DC 256610.
- **Use** Adjustment

Malagasy Republic
- **Use** Madagascar

Malawi
- **DC** D483600
- **HN** Formerly (1969-1985) DC 256619.
- **UF** Nyasaland, Africa (1963-1985)
- **BT** Sub Saharan Africa

Malay (1971-1985)
- **HN** DC 256672, deleted 1986. See now Asian Cultural Groups or Austronesian And Oceanic Languages.

Malaya/Malayan/Malayans (1963-1985)
- **HN** DC 256620.
- **Use** Malaysia

Malayalam (Language)
- **Use** Dravidian Languages

Malayo Polynesian Languages
- **Use** Austronesian Languages

Malaysia
- **DC** D483900
- **HN** Formerly (1964-1985) DC 256629, Malaysia/Malaysian/Malaysians.
- **UF** Malaya/Malayan/Malayans (1963-1985)
- **BT** Southeast Asia
- **NT** Kuala Lumpur, Malaysia

Maldistribution (1972-1985)
- **HN** DC 256633.
- **Use** Distribution

Male Child Preference
- **Use** Child Sex Preferences

Male Female Relations
- **Use** Opposite Sex Relations

Male Roles
- **Use** Sex Roles

Males
- **DC** D484200
- **HN** Formerly (1963-1985) DC 256635, Male/Males.
- **UF** Man/Men (1963-1985)
- **NT** Sons
- **RT** Child Sex Preferences
  - Father Absence
  - Fathers
  - Females
  - Masculinity

Malevolence

Males (cont'd)
- RT Opposite Sex Relations
  - Sex
  - Sex Role Identity
  - Sex Roles
  - Sex Stereotypes

Malevolence/Malevolent (1971-1985)
- HN DC 256660.
- Use Hate

Mali
- DC D484500
- HN Formerly (1968-1985) DC 256662, Mali, Republic of.
- BT Sub Saharan Africa

Malinowski, Bronislaw Kaspar
- DC D484800
- SN Born 7 April 1884 - died 16 May 1942.
- HN Formerly (1964-1985) DC 256663, Malinowski, Bronislaw.

Malnutrition
- DC D485100
- HN Formerly (1969-1985) DC 256665.
- UF Nutritional Deficiencies
  - Undernourishment (1965-1985)
- BT Nutrition
- RT Anorexia Nervosa
  - Body Weight
  - Deprivation
  - Diet
  - Diseases
  - Famine
  - Feeding Practices
  - Food
  - Hunger
  - Starvation

Malpractice (Professional)
- Use Professional Malpractice

Malta
- DC D485400
- HN Formerly (1965-1985) DC 256675, Malta/Maltese.
- BT Mediterranean Countries
  - Western Europe

Malthus, Thomas Robert
- DC D485500
- SN Born 17 February 1766 - died 23 December 1834.
- HN Formerly (1963-1985) DC 256685, Malthus, T. R./Malthusian.

Man Environment Relationship
- Use Human Ecology

Man Machine Relationship
- Use Worker Machine Relationship

Man Nature Relationship
- Use Human Ecology

Man/Men (1963-1985)
- HN DC 256700.
- Use Males

Mana
- DC D485700
- SN In the native religions of Oceania, an impersonal supernatural force or power inherent in certain places, sacred objects, or persons. Mana can be inherited, acquired, or conferred.
- HN Formerly (1966-1985) DC 256900.

Mana (cont'd)
- RT Oceanic Cultural Groups
  - Power
  - Sacredness
  - Supernatural
  - Traditional Societies

Management
- DC D486000
- HN Formerly (1963-1985) DC 257000, Manage/Managed/Manages/Managing/Management.
- UF Administration
- NT Educational Administration
  - Impression Management
  - Industrial Management
  - Personnel Management
  - Public Administration
  - Resource Management
  - Scientific Management
- RT Accounting
  - Administrators
  - Budgets
  - Cadres
  - Control
  - Coordination
  - Decision Making
  - Employers
  - Entrepreneurship
  - Executives
  - Forces And Relations of Production
  - Governing Boards
  - Implementation
  - Industrial Democracy
  - Management Styles
  - Managers
  - Organizational Behavior
  - Organizational Development
  - Organizational Effectiveness
  - Organizational Structure
  - Planning
  - Strategies
  - Supervision
  - Time Utilization
  - Worker Participation

Management of Time
- Use Time Utilization

Management Styles
- DC D486300
- HN Added, 1986.
- UF Supervisory Styles
- BT Styles
- RT Management
  - Managers
  - Organizational Effectiveness
  - Personnel Management
  - Superior Subordinate Relationship
  - Supervision
  - Work Environment

Managerial Personnel
- Use Managers

Managers
- DC D486600
- HN Formerly (1963-1985) DC 257500, Managers/Managerial.
- UF Managerial Personnel
  - Supervisor/Supervisors/Supervisory (1963-1985)
- BT Administrators
- RT Cadres
  - Employers
  - Foremen
  - Management
  - Management Styles
  - Planners
  - Superior Subordinate Relationship

Manpower

Managua, Nicaragua
- DC D486700
- HN Added, 1989.
- BT Nicaragua

Mandate/Mandates (1977-1985)
- HN DC 257600, deleted 1986.

Manhood (1969-1985)
- HN DC 257700, deleted 1986.

Manic Depressive/Manic Depression (1966-1985)
- HN DC 258000.
- Use Depression (Psychology)

Manicheism
- DC D486900
- SN A dualistic, syncretistic religion, founded by the third century Persian, Manes, which combines doctrines from Gnostic Christianity, Buddhism, Zoroastrianism, and other religions.
- HN Formerly (1969-1985) DC 258030, Manichean/Manicheism.
- BT Religions
- RT Asceticism
  - Cathari
  - Evil
  - Heresy
  - Syncretism

Manifesto (1963-1985)
- HN DC 258085, deleted 1986.

Manila, Philippines
- DC D487200
- HN Formerly (1964-1985) DC 258088.
- BT Philippines

Manipulation
- DC D487500
- HN Formerly (1965-1985) DC 258090, Manipulate/Manipulative/Manipulation.
- BT Interaction
- RT Interpersonal Relations
  - Machiavellianism (Personality)
  - Social Behavior

Manitoba
- DC D487800
- HN Formerly (1984-1985) DC 258110, Manitoba Northwest Territories, Canada.
- BT Canada

Manners (1965-1985)
- HN DC 258175.
- Use Norms

Mannheim, Karl
- DC D488100
- SN Born 27 March 1893 - died 9 January 1947.
- HN Formerly (1963-1985) DC 258200.

Manpower (1963-1985)
- HN DC 258300.
- Use Labor Supply

Manpower Development & Training Act (1965-1985)
- HN DC 258305.
- Use Statutes

Manslaughter — Market

Manslaughter
  Use Homicide

Manual Communication
  DC D488400
  HN Added, 1986.
  UF Finger Spelling
      Sign Language
  BT Communication
  RT Deaf
      Language
      Nonverbal Communication

Manual Workers
  DC D488700
  HN Formerly (1963-1985) part of DC 258325, Manual/Manuals.
  UF Laborer/Laborers (1963-1985)
      Unskilled (1963-1985)
  BT Blue Collar Workers
  RT Labor Market Segmentation
      Work Skills

Manual/Manuals (1963-1985)
  HN DC 258325, deleted 1986. See now Manual Communication, Manual Workers, or Reference Materials.

Manufacturer/Manufacturers (1963-1985)
  HN DC 258338.
  Use Manufacturing Industries

Manufacturing Industries
  DC D489000
  HN Formerly (1963-1985) DC 258340, Manufacturing.
  UF Manufacturer/Manufacturers (1963-1985)
  BT Industry
  NT Automobile Industry
      Chemical Industry
      Garment Industry
      Metal Industry
      Textile Industry
  RT Factories
      High Technology Industries
      Industrial Enterprises
      Industrial Production
      Industrial Workers
      Materials
      Worker Machine Relationship
      Workshops (Manufacturing)

Mao Tse-tung
  DC D489100
  SN Born 26 December 1893 - died 9 September 1976.
  HN Formerly (1964-1985) part of DC 258385, Mao Tse-tung/Maoism/Maoist.
  UF Mao Zedong

Mao Zedong
  Use Mao Tse-tung

Maoism
  DC D489125
  HN Formerly (1964-1985) part of DC 258385, Mao Tse-tung/Maoism/Maoist.
  BT Marxism
  RT Agricultural Collectives
      Collectivism
      Communism
      Guerrillas
      Land Reform
      Peasant Rebellions
      Revolutions
      Totalitarianism

Map/Maps/Mapped/Mapping (1963-1985)
  HN DC 258400, deleted 1986. See now Cognitive Mapping or Geographic Distribution.

Marathi (Language)
  Use Indic Languages

Marcuse, Herbert
  DC D489300
  SN Born 19 July 1898 - died 29 July 1979.
  HN Formerly (1968-1985) DC 258428, Marcuse, H.

Marginality
  DC D489500
  SN The quality by which a person or group possesses traits intermediate between, or peripheral to, other larger groups. Such a person or group may, as a result, experience internalized Alienation or externalized Segregation.
  HN Formerly (1963-1985) DC 258455, Marginal/Marginality/Marginalist.
  UF Social Marginality
  RT Alienation
      Center And Periphery
      Centrality
      Minority Groups
      Segregation
      Social Distance
      Social Isolation
      Social Status
      Social Structure

Mariana Islands
  DC D489600
  HN Added, 1986.
  BT Micronesia
  NT Guam

Marijuana
  DC D489900
  HN Formerly (1968-1985) DC 258465.
  UF Cannabis
      Hashish (1971-1985)
  RT Drug Use
      Narcotic Drugs
      Psychedelic Drugs

Marital Adjustment
  DC D490200
  HN Added, 1986.
  BT Adjustment
  RT Marital Relations
      Marital Satisfaction
      Marriage

Marital Disruption
  DC D490500
  SN The psychological and socioeconomic effects of separation and divorce.
  HN Added, 1986.
  UF Desertion (Marital)
      Separation (Marital)
  NT Annulment
      Divorce
  RT Disorders
      Family Relations
      Family Stability
      Father Absence
      Life Stage Transitions
      Marital Satisfaction
      Marital Status
      Mother Absence
      Parent Child Relations
      Widowhood

Marital Dissolution (1984-1985)
  HN DC 258471.
  Use Divorce

Marital Power
  Use Family Power

Marital Relations
  DC D490800
  HN Added, 1986. Prior to 1986 use DC 382565, Relations, Marriage.
  UF Conjugal Relations
  BT Interpersonal Relations
  RT Dual Career Family
      Extramarital Sexuality
      Family Life
      Family Power
      Family Relations
      Family Stability
      Feminism
      Home Environment
      Husbands
      Love
      Marital Adjustment
      Marital Satisfaction
      Marriage
      Opposite Sex Relations
      Premarital Sex
      Spouses
      Wives

Marital Satisfaction
  DC D491100
  HN Added, 1986.
  BT Satisfaction
  RT Annulment
      Complementary Needs
      Divorce
      Homogamy
      Life Satisfaction
      Marital Adjustment
      Marital Disruption
      Marital Relations
      Marriage

Marital Status
  DC D491150
  HN Added, 1989.
  BT Status
  RT Divorce
      Marital Disruption
      Marriage
      Single Persons
      Social Status
      Widowhood

Maritime (1965-1985)
  HN DC 258475.
  Use Shipping Industry

Market Economy
  DC D491400
  SN System of economic organization in which private persons or corporations control the production, distribution, and exchange of most goods and services, according to the laws of supply and demand and with minimal government regulation.
  HN Added, 1986.
  UF Free Market Economy
      Laissez-faire (1963-1985)
  RT Business Cycles
      Capitalism
      Economic Structure
      Economic Systems
      Economics
      Markets
      Political Economy

Market   Marxism

Market Economy (cont'd)
- RT Private Sector
     Production Consumption Relationship
     Protectionism
     Supply And Demand
     Trade

Market Research
- DC D491700
- HN Formerly (1964-1985) DC 258800.
- BT Social Science Research
- RT Consumers
     Marketing
     Markets
     Retail Industry
     Surveys

Market Structure
- Use Markets

Marketing
- DC D492000
- HN Formerly (1963-1985) part of DC 258500, Market/Markets/Marketing.
- UF Merchandising (1965-1985)
- RT Advertising
     Consumerism
     Consumers
     Cooperatives
     Market Research
     Markets
     Merchants
     Products
     Purchasing
     Retail Industry
     Sales
     Trade

Marketplace
- Use Markets

Markets
- DC D492300
- HN Formerly (1963-1985) part of DC 258500, Market/Markets/Marketing.
- UF Market Structure
     Marketplace
- NT Housing Market
     Labor Market
- RT Business
     Economic Structure
     Enterprises
     Industry
     Market Economy
     Market Research
     Marketing
     Protectionism
     Supply And Demand
     Trade

Markov Chains
- Use Markov Process

Markov Process
- DC D492400
- SN A statistical model that determines the probability of the occurrence of an event based on the probabilities of its present and immediately preceding states, ignoring all other time periods. See also Stochastic Models.
- HN Formerly (1968-1985) DC 258840.
- UF Chains (Markov)
     Markov Chains
- BT Stochastic Models
- RT Probability

Marquesas Islands
- DC D492600
- HN Formerly (1964-1985) DC 258900, Marquesan Island/Marquesan Islanders.
- BT Polynesia

Marriage
- DC D492900
- HN Formerly (1963-1985) DC 259000, Marriage/Marriages/Marital.
- UF Matrimony/Matrimonial (1968-1985)
     Newlywed/Newlyweds (1969-1985)
- BT Social Institutions
- NT Cousin Marriage
     Endogamy
     Homogamy
     Intermarriage
     Monogamy
     Polygamy
     Remarriage
- RT Affinity (Kinship)
     Bridewealth
     Cohabitation
     Consanguinity
     Courtship
     Dowry
     Family
     Kinship
     Life Stage Transitions
     Marital Adjustment
     Marital Relations
     Marital Satisfaction
     Marital Status
     Marriage And Family Education
     Marriage Patterns
     Marriage Timing
     Married Students
     Mate Selection
     Nuptiality
     Single Persons
     Spouse Abuse
     Spouses
     Stepfamily
     Unwed Mothers
     Virginity
     Weddings
     Widowhood

Marriage & Family (1963-1985)
- HN DC 259400, deleted 1986. See now appropriate "Marriage" or "Family" terms.

Marriage And Family Education
- DC D493200
- HN Added, 1986.
- UF Family Life Education
- BT Education
- NT Sex Education
- RT Curriculum
     Family
     Home Economics
     Marriage

Marriage Counseling (1964-1985)
- HN DC 259410, deleted 1986. See now Family Therapy or Conjoint Therapy.

Marriage Partners
- Use Spouses

Marriage Patterns
- DC D493500
- HN Added, 1986.
- RT Marriage

Marriage Rates
- Use Nuptiality

Marriage Rites
- Use Weddings

Marriage Timing
- DC D493800
- HN Added, 1986.
- UF Remarriage Timing
- RT Divorce
     First Birth Timing
     Marriage
     Remarriage
     Young Adults

Married (1963-1985)
- HN DC 259465, deleted 1986. See now specific "Marriage," "Marital," or "Spouse" terms.

Married Couples
- Use Spouses

Married Men
- Use Husbands

Married Students
- DC D494100
- HN Added, 1986.
- BT Students
- RT College Students
     Marriage
     Young Adults

Married Women
- Use Wives

Marshall Islands
- DC D494400
- HN Added, 1986.
- BT Micronesia

Martindale, Donald Albert
- DC D494700
- SN Born 9 February 1915 - died 17 May 1985.
- HN Added, 1986.

Martinique
- DC D495000
- HN Formerly (1964-1985) DC 259475.
- BT Caribbean

Marx, Karl
- DC D495150
- SN Born 15 May 1818 - died 14 March 1883.
- HN Formerly (1963-1985) part of DC 259480, Marx, Karl/Marxist/Marxism.

Marxism
- DC D495175
- SN Social philosophy of Karl Marx applied as a political ideology or form of government. Do not confuse with Marxist Analysis.
- HN Formerly (1963-1985) part of DC 259480, Marx, Karl/Marxist/Marxism.
- BT Philosophical Doctrines
- NT Bolshevism
     Communism
     Leninism
     Maoism
     Revisionism
     Stalinism
- RT Base And Superstructure
     Bourgeois Societies

Marxism (cont'd)
- **RT** Capitalism
  - Class Analysis
  - Class Consciousness
  - Class Struggle
  - Collectives
  - Determinism
  - Dialectical Materialism
  - Dialectics
  - Economics
  - Forces And Relations of Production
  - Historical Materialism
  - Ideologies
  - Labor Theory of Value
  - Marxist Aesthetics
  - Marxist Analysis
  - Marxist Economics
  - Marxist Sociology
  - Materialism
  - Modes of Production
  - Political Economy
  - Political Ideologies
  - Political Power
  - Praxis
  - Proletariat
  - Realism (Philosophy)
  - Reification
  - Revolutions
  - Social Criticism
  - Socialism
  - Socialist Societies
  - Utopias

Marxist Aesthetics
- **DC** D495185
- **HN** Added, 1986.
- **BT** Aesthetics
- **RT** Art
  - Hermeneutics
  - Literature
  - Marxism
  - Marxist Analysis
  - Marxist Sociology
  - Reification
  - Semiotics
  - Structuralism

Marxist Analysis
- **DC** D495200
- **SN** Theories, concepts, and body of knowledge established by Karl Marx applied as a method of scientific investigation. Do not confuse with Marxism.
- **HN** Added, 1986.
- **BT** Analysis
- **RT** Alienation
  - Class Analysis
  - Critical Theory
  - Dialectics
  - Economic Factors
  - Economic History
  - Historiography
  - Marxism
  - Marxist Aesthetics
  - Marxist Economics
  - Marxist Sociology
  - Social Change
  - Social Science Research
  - Social Theories
  - Sociological Theory

Marxist Economics
- **DC** D495225
- **HN** Added, 1986.
- **BT** Economics
- **RT** Accumulation
  - Capital

Marxist Economics (cont'd)
- **RT** Capitalism
  - Communism
  - Dependency Theory
  - Economic Crises
  - Economic Theories
  - Exchange (Economics)
  - Forces And Relations of Production
  - Labor Theory of Value
  - Marxism
  - Marxist Analysis
  - Marxist Sociology
  - Modes of Production
  - Political Economy
  - Production
  - Socialism
  - Value (Economics)

Marxist Revisionism
- **Use** Revisionism

Marxist Sociology
- **DC** D495300
- **HN** Formerly (1985) DC 259483.
- **BT** Sociology
- **RT** Base And Superstructure
  - Bourgeois Sociology
  - Capitalism
  - Class Consciousness
  - Class Struggle
  - Conflict Theory
  - Critical Theory
  - Frankfurt School
  - Historical Materialism
  - Ideologies
  - Macrosociology
  - Marxism
  - Marxist Aesthetics
  - Marxist Analysis
  - Marxist Economics
  - Materialism
  - Political Economy
  - Social Reproduction
  - Socialist Societies
  - Sociological Theory
  - Structuralism

Maryland
- **DC** D495600
- **HN** Formerly (1964-1985) DC 259485.
- **BT** Northern States
  - United States of America
- **NT** Baltimore, Maryland

Masculinity
- **DC** D495900
- **HN** Formerly (1963-1985) DC 259500, Masculine/Masculinity.
- **RT** Androgyny
  - Femininity
  - Males
  - Personality Traits
  - Sex Roles

Masks
- **DC** D496200
- **HN** Formerly (1963-1985) DC 260000, Mask/Masks.
- **RT** Artifacts
  - Clothing
  - Rituals
  - Traditional Societies

Maslow, Abraham Harold
- **DC** D496500
- **SN** Born 1 April 1908 - died 8 June 1970.
- **HN** Formerly (1969-1985) DC 260050, Maslow, A. H.

Masochism (1984-1985)
- **HN** DC 260062.
- **Use** Sexual Deviation

Mass Behavior
- **DC** D496800
- **SN** Collective behavior induced by both indirect and impersonal mass communication. Compare with Collective Behavior.
- **HN** Formerly (1985) DC 260166.
- **BT** Collective Behavior
- **NT** Fads
  - Fashions
- **RT** Mass Media
  - Mass Society
  - Popular Culture

Mass Communication (1963-1985)
- **HN** DC 260175.
- **Use** Mass Media

Mass Communication Research
- **Use** Communication Research

Mass Culture (1963-1985)
- **HN** DC 260180.
- **Use** Popular Culture

Mass Hysteria
- **Use** Hysteria

Mass Media
- **DC** D497100
- **HN** Formerly (1963-1985) DC 260300.
- **UF** Broadcast/Broadcasts/Broadcasting/Broadcasters (1963-1985)
  - Communications Media
  - Mass Communication (1963-1985)
- **NT** Films
  - News Media
  - Radio
  - Television
- **RT** Advertising
  - Audiences
  - Audiovisual Media
  - Communication Research
  - Communicative Action
  - Content Analysis
  - Entertainment Industry
  - Information Dissemination
  - Information Sources
  - Journalism
  - Mass Behavior
  - Mass Media Effects
  - Mass Media Violence
  - Mass Society
  - Messages
  - News Coverage
  - Popular Culture
  - Propaganda
  - Publications
  - Public Relations
  - Publicity
  - Publishing Industry
  - Telecommunications

Mass Media Effects
- **DC** D497400
- **HN** Added, 1986.
- **UF** Media Influences
- **BT** Effects
- **RT** Advertising
  - Audiences
  - Cartoons
  - Dominant Ideologies
  - Films
  - Learning

Mass / Mathematician

Mass Media Effects (cont'd)
- RT Mass Media
  - Mass Media Violence
  - News Media
  - Newspapers
  - Popular Culture
  - Propaganda
  - Public Opinion
  - Radio
  - Television
  - Television Viewing

Mass Media Violence
- DC D497700
- SN Violence portrayed on television or in other forms of mass media, usually for purposes of commercial exploitation.
- HN Added, 1986.
- UF Television Violence
- BT Violence
- RT Cartoons
  - Films
  - Mass Media
  - Mass Media Effects
  - News Coverage
  - News Media
  - Sports Violence
  - Television

Mass Murder
- Use Homicide

Mass Production (1963-1985)
- HN DC 260320.
- Use Industrial Production

Mass Public
- Use General Public

Mass Society
- DC D498000
- SN A large form of Social Structure that combines the characteristics of Industrial Societies, Urbanization, and bureaucratic Civil Society, and is often characterized as leaving the individual without a sense of Identity and contributing to Alienation.
- HN Formerly (1963-1985) DC 260340.
- BT Society
- RT Alienation
  - Anomie
  - Civil Society
  - Dominant Ideologies
  - Elites
  - Industrial Societies
  - Mass Behavior
  - Mass Media
  - Masses
  - Modern Society
  - Popular Culture
  - Urbanization

Massachusetts
- DC D498300
- HN Formerly (1964-1985) DC 260150.
- BT Northern States
  - United States of America
- NT Boston, Massachusetts

Massacre/Massacres (1969-1985)
- HN DC 260160, deleted 1986.

Masses
- DC D498600
- SN A context-dependent term denoting large numbers of people, often considered as reacting similarly to common cultural stimuli.

Masses (cont'd)
- HN Formerly (1963-1985) DC 260100, Mass/Masses.
- RT Elites
  - General Public
  - Mass Society
  - Peasants
  - Working Class

Masters Degrees
- DC D498900
- HN Added, 1986.
- BT Academic Degrees
- RT Baccalaureate Degrees
  - Doctoral Degrees
  - Graduate Students

Masturbation
- DC D499200
- HN Formerly (1964-1985) DC 260380, Masturbation/Masturbating.
- UF Autoeroticism
- BT Sexual Behavior
- RT Orgasm
  - Sexual Arousal

Match/Matching/Matched/ Matchmaking (1972-1985)
- HN DC 260400, deleted 1986.

Matchmaking
- Use Mate Selection

Mate Selection
- DC D499500
- HN Added, 1986.
- UF Matchmaking
  - Partner Selection
- RT Choices
  - Complementary Needs
  - Courtship
  - Cousin Marriage
  - Dating (Social)
  - Homogamy
  - Marriage
  - Selection Procedures
  - Spouses

Mate/Mates/Mating/Matings (1963-1985)
- HN DC 260430, deleted 1986. See now Mate Selection, Spouses, or appropriate "Sex" terms.

Material Culture
- DC D500100
- SN Refers to the physical objects or artifacts of human activity and the ideas behind them, how they are made and used, and their place in society.
- HN Added, 1986.
- BT Culture
- NT Artifacts
- RT Art
  - Clothing
  - Crafts
  - Fashions
  - Inanimate Objects
  - Machinery
  - Materials
  - Monuments
  - Museums
  - Tools
  - Traditional Societies

Materialism
- DC D500250
- SN The doctrine that all phenomena, including mental processes, are made of physical matter. Also, the theory that all social phenomena are caused by economic relations.
- HN Formerly (1963-1985) DC 260445, Materialism/Materialistic.
- BT Philosophical Doctrines
- RT Atheism
  - Dialectical Materialism
  - Dialectics
  - Empiricism
  - Historical Materialism
  - Historicism
  - Idealism
  - Marxism
  - Marxist Sociology
  - Nominalism
  - Ontology
  - Praxis
  - Realism (Philosophy)
  - Social Theories

Materials
- DC D500400
- SN A context-dependent term; select a more specific entry or coordinate with other terms.
- HN Formerly (1966-1985) DC 260440, Material/Materials.
- NT Raw Materials
- RT Fuels
  - Inanimate Objects
  - Industry
  - Manufacturing Industries
  - Material Culture
  - Resources
  - Tools

Maternal Attitudes (1966-1985)
- HN DC 260700.
- Use Parental Attitudes

Maternal Employment
- Use Working Mothers

Maternal/Maternity (1963-1985)
- HN DC 260500, deleted 1986. See now Mothers, Parental Attitudes, or Working Women.

Mathematical Economics
- Use Econometric Analysis

Mathematical Logic
- Use Logic

Mathematical Models
- DC D500650
- HN Added, 1986.
- BT Models
- RT Formalism
  - Mathematics

Mathematical Sociology
- DC D500700
- HN Formerly (1985) DC 261100.
- BT Sociology
- RT Mathematics

Mathematician/Mathematicians (1965-1985)
- HN DC 260995, deleted 1986.

Mathematics

Mathematics
- **DC** D501000
- **HN** Formerly (1963-1985) DC 261000, Mathematics/Mathematical.
- **UF** Algebra/Algebraic (1964-1985)
  Equation/Equations (1963-1985)
- **NT** Graph Theory
  Matrices
  Statistics
- **RT** Academic Disciplines
  Algorithms
  Computation
  Logic
  Mathematical Models
  Mathematical Sociology
  Probability
  Ratios
  Social Science Research
  Sociology of Science

Matriarchy
- **DC** D501300
- **HN** Formerly (1964-1985) DC 261280, Matriarch/Matriarchy/Matriarchial.
- **RT** Family Structure
  Kinship
  Patriarchy

Matricentric (1971-1985)
- **HN** DC 261283.
- **Use** Matrifocal Family

Matrices
- **DC** D501450
- **HN** Formerly (1964-1985) DC 261500, Matrix/Matrices.
- **UF** Data Matrices
- **BT** Mathematics
- **RT** Data
  Quantitative Methods
  Statistics
  Tables

Matrifocal Family
- **DC** D501600
- **SN** A family structure centered on a female and mother-child relations, without a male regularly playing the husband-father role.
- **HN** Formerly (1963-1985) DC 261285, Matrifocal.
- **UF** Matricentric (1971-1985)
- **BT** Family
- **RT** Father Absence
  Mothers

Matrilateral (1963-1985)
- **HN** DC 261290.
- **Use** Cousin Marriage

Matrilineality
- **DC** D501900
- **SN** Cultural identity pattern in which descent is traced through the female ancestors.
- **HN** Formerly (1963-1985) DC 261300, Matrilineal/Matrilineality.
- **BT** Unilineality
- **RT** Descent
  Patrilineality

Matrilocal Residence
- **DC** D502200
- **SN** Cultural settings in which the norm is for newly married couples to reside with or near the bride's relatives.
- **HN** Formerly (1963-1985) DC 261400, Matrilocal.
- **UF** Uxorilocal (1977-1985)
- **BT** Residence
- **RT** Family
  Kinship

Matrimony/Matrimonial (1968-1985)
- **HN** DC 261450.
- **Use** Marriage

Mature/Maturation/Maturity (1963-1985)
- **HN** DC 261700, deleted 1986.

Matza, David
- **DC** D502450
- **SN** Born 1 May 1930 - .
- **HN** Added, 1989.

Mau Mau Rebellion
- **DC** D502500
- **HN** Formerly (1963-1985) DC 261735, Mau Mau.
- **BT** Rebellions
- **RT** Political Movements
  Political Violence
  Terrorism

Mauritania
- **DC** D502800
- **HN** Formerly (1973-1985) DC 261755, Mauritania/Mauritanian.
- **BT** Sub Saharan Africa

Mauritius
- **DC** D503100
- **HN** Formerly (1963-1985) DC 261760.
- **BT** Sub Saharan Africa

Mauss, Marcel
- **DC** D503400
- **SN** Born 1872 - died 1950.
- **HN** Formerly (1971-1985) DC 261765.

Maximize/Maximizing (1964-1985)
- **HN** DC 261775, deleted 1986.

Mayans
- **DC** D503700
- **HN** Formerly (1963-1985) DC 261785, Maya/Mayan/Mayans.
- **BT** American Indians
- **RT** Indigenous Populations

Mayors
- **DC** D504000
- **HN** Formerly (1963-1985) DC 261825, Mayor/Mayors/Mayoral.
- **BT** Public Officials
- **RT** Cities
  Local Government
  Local Politics

Mazdaism
- **Use** Zoroastrianism

McCarthyism
- **DC** D504100
- **SN** A political attitude and investigative technique in the U.S. during the mid-20th century that consisted of unsubstantiated public accusations of persons thought to be disloyal, especially through alleged communist activity. These tactics are associated with U.S. Senator Joseph R. McCarthy.
- **HN** Formerly (1968-1985) DC 261887, McCarthy, J./McCarthyism.
- **RT** Communism
  Conservatism
  Political Attitudes
  Repression (Political)
  Right Wing Politics

Measurement

McLuhan, Herbert Marshall
- **DC** D504300
- **SN** Born 21 July 1911 - died 31 December 1980.
- **HN** Formerly (1967-1985) DC 261968, McLuhan, Marshall.

Mead, George Herbert
- **DC** D504600
- **SN** Born 27 February 1863 - died 26 April 1931.
- **HN** Formerly (1963-1985) DC 261975.

Mead, Margaret
- **DC** D504900
- **SN** Born 16 December 1901 - died 15 November 1978.
- **HN** Formerly (1965-1985) DC 261980.

Mean
- **DC** D504925
- **SN** In statistics, the simple average of repeated observations in a sample. Do not confuse with Median.
- **HN** Formerly (1963-1985) DC 262495, Mean/Means.
- **RT** Frequency Distributions
  Median
  Parameters (Statistics)
  Quantitative Methods
  Statistics

Meaning
- **DC** D504950
- **HN** Formerly (1963-1985) DC 262500, Meaning/Meanings/Meaningful.
- **RT** Ambiguity
  Collective Representation
  Communication
  Comprehension
  Definitions
  Existentialism
  Explanation
  Messages
  Naming Practices
  Nonverbal Communication
  Pragmatism
  Signs
  Social Determination of Meaning
  Symbolism
  Translation
  Verstehen

Meaninglessness
- **Use** Alienation

Means-Ends Rationality
- **DC** D504975
- **SN** Predisposition to judge or choose actions or prefer certain behavior, based on the pursuit of a specific goal.
- **HN** Formerly (1969-1985) DC 263100, Means-End Complex.
- **UF** Ends (1969-1985)
- **RT** Change
  Effects
  Ethics
  Goals
  Methods

Measurement
- **DC** D505000
- **HN** Formerly (1963-1985) part of DC 264000, Measure/Measures/Measuring/Measurement.
- **NT** Interval Measurement
  Nominal Measurement
  Ordinal Measurement
- **RT** Accuracy
  Computation

Measurement / Medical

Measurement (cont'd)
- RT Data
  - Econometric Analysis
  - Empirical Methods
  - Error of Measurement
  - Estimation
  - Experiments
  - Measures (Instruments)
  - Methodology (Data Collection)
  - Observation
  - Operational Definitions
  - Prediction
  - Profiles
  - Quantitative Methods
  - Ranking
  - Rating
  - Ratios
  - Reliability
  - Research
  - Research Methodology
  - Scores
  - Standards
  - Statistics
  - Tests
  - Validity
  - Variables

Measurement Error
- Use Error of Measurement

Measures (Instruments)
- DC D505050
- HN Formerly (1963-1985) part of DC 264000, Measure/Measures/Measuring/Measurement.
- UF Instrument/Instruments/Instrumental (1963-1985)
  - Inventory/Inventories/Inventorying (1963-1985)
- BT Methodology (Data Collection)
- NT Attitude Measures
  - Indexes (Measures)
  - Personality Measures
  - Questionnaires
  - Scales
  - Tests
- RT Evaluation
  - Interviews
  - Items (Measures)
  - Measurement
  - Profiles
  - Research
  - Research Methodology
  - Scores
  - Surveys
  - Validity
  - Weighting

Mechanic/Mechanics/Mechanical/Mechanize/Mechanization (1963-1985)
- HN DC 264100, deleted 1986. See now Automation or Agricultural Mechanization.

Mechanism/Mechanisms (1963-1985)
- HN DC 264110, deleted 1986.

Mechanistic (1964-1985)
- HN DC 264120, deleted 1986.

Mechanization
- Use Automation

Media Coverage
- Use News Coverage

Media Influences
- Use Mass Media Effects

Media/Medium (1963-1985)
- HN DC 264200, deleted 1986. See now Mass Media, News Media, or Mass Media Effects.

Median
- DC D505150
- SN In statistics, the measure of the central element in a group of observations, the score or frequency that divides a distribution in half. Do not confuse with Mean.
- HN Formerly (1963-1985) DC 264400, Median/Medians.
- RT Frequency Distributions
  - Mean
  - Parameters (Statistics)
  - Quantitative Methods
  - Statistics

Mediation
- DC D505200
- HN Formerly (1964-1985) DC 264800, Mediator/Mediators/Mediating.
- UF Conciliation (1976-1985)
  - Mediator Role
- BT Conflict Resolution
- RT Disputes
  - Grievances
  - Intervention
  - Negotiation

Mediator Role
- Use Mediation

Medicaid
- DC D505500
- HN Formerly (1972-1985) DC 264990.
- UF Medical Assistance Program
- BT Socialized Medicine
- RT Health Services
  - Medicare
  - Welfare Services

Medical (1963-1985)
- HN DC 265000, deleted 1986. See now specific "Health" or "Medical" terms.

Medical Assistance Program
- Use Medicaid

Medical Care
- Use Health Care

Medical Care Utilization
- Use Health Care Utilization

Medical Compliance
- Use Treatment Compliance

Medical Decision Making
- DC D505600
- HN Added, 1989.
- BT Decision Making
- NT Diagnosis
- RT Drugs
  - Health Care Utilization
  - Health Planning
  - Health Professions
  - Hospitalization
  - Informed Consent
  - Medical Research
  - Medications
  - Medicine
  - Surgery
  - Treatment
  - Treatment Compliance

Medical Diagnosis
- Use Diagnosis

Medical Emergency Services
- Use Emergency Medical Services

Medical Malpractice
- Use Professional Malpractice

Medical Model
- DC D505700
- SN Theory and practice of scientific medicine extended to problems that are not diseases in the literal sense, such as crime, deviance, and mental illness. In feminist analyses, the medical model is associated with male hegemony.
- HN Added, 1989.
- UF Disease Model
- BT Models
- RT Epidemiology
  - Health Care
  - Medical Research
  - Medical Sociology
  - Medical Technology
  - Medicine

Medical Patients
- Use Patients

Medical Pluralism
- DC D505800
- HN Formerly (1963-1985) part of DC 339248, Plural/Pluralism/Pluralist/Pluralists/Pluralistic.
- BT Pluralism
- RT Medical Technology
  - Medicine
  - Traditional Medicine

Medical Practice
- Use Medicine

Medical Professions
- Use Health Professions

Medical Research
- DC D506000
- HN Added, 1986.
- UF Biomedical Research
- BT Scientific Research
- RT Bioethics
  - Laboratories
  - Medical Decision Making
  - Medical Model
  - Medical Schools
  - Medical Technology
  - Medicine

Medical Schools
- DC D506100
- HN Added, 1986. Prior to 1986 use Medical (DC 265000) and Schools (DC 405000).
- BT Graduate Schools
- RT Doctoral Programs
  - Medical Research
  - Medical Students
  - Medicine
  - Professional Training
  - Universities

Medical Sciences
- Use Medicine

Medical Sociology
- DC D506400
- HN Added, 1986.
- UF Sociology of Medicine
- BT Sociology
- RT Health
  - Health Professions
  - Medical Model
  - Medical Technology
  - Medicine

Medical

Medical Students
- DC D506700
- HN Added, 1986. Formerly (1985) DC 448700, Student, Medical.
- UF Student, Medical (1985)
- BT Graduate Students
- RT Dental Students
  Medical Schools
  Medicine
  Professional Training

Medical Technology
- DC D507000
- HN Added, 1986.
- UF Health Care Technology
  Nursing Technology
- BT Technology
- NT Reproductive Technologies
- RT Bioethics
  Genetics
  High Technology Industries
  Medical Model
  Medical Pluralism
  Medical Research
  Medical Sociology
  Medicine
  Radiation
  Traditional Medicine

Medicare
- DC D507300
- HN Formerly (1963-1985) DC 265100.
- BT Socialized Medicine
- RT Health Insurance
  Health Services
  Medicaid
  Social Security

Medications
- DC D507600
- HN Added, 1986.
- UF Medicines
  Pharmaceutical Drugs
- RT Drugs
  Health Care
  Medical Decision Making
  Pharmacy
  Treatment

Medicine
- DC D507900
- HN Formerly (1963-1985) DC 265500, Medicine/Medicinal.
- UF General Medicine
  Medical Practice
  Medical Sciences
  Scientific Medicine
- NT Biomedicine
  Dentistry
  Epidemiology
  Geriatrics
  Gynecology
  Holistic Medicine
  Medical Model
  Neurology
  Pediatrics
  Pharmacy
  Psychiatry
  Socialized Medicine
  Traditional Medicine
- RT Academic Disciplines
  Bioethics
  Genetics
  Health
  Health Care
  Health Professions
  Human Body
  Illness

Medicine (cont'd)
- RT Medical Decision Making
  Medical Model
  Medical Pluralism
  Medical Research
  Medical Schools
  Medical Sociology
  Medical Students
  Medical Technology
  Optometry
  Physiology
  Practitioner Patient Relationship
  Primary Health Care
  Scientific Research
  Social Sciences
  Surgery
  Treatment

Medicines
  Use Medications

Medieval (1963-1985)
- HN DC 265600.
- Use Middle Ages

Meditation (Transcendental)
  Use Transcendental Meditation

Mediterranean Countries
- DC D508200
- HN Formerly (1967-1985) DC 265670, Mediterranean.
- BT Countries
- NT Algeria
  Cyprus
  Egypt
  France
  Greece
  Israel
  Italy
  Lebanon
  Libya
  Malta
  Monaco
  Morocco
  Palestine
  Spain
  Syria
  Tunisia
  Turkey
- RT Arab Countries
  Europe
  Middle East
  North Africa

Meetings
- DC D508500
- HN Formerly (1963-1985) DC 265690, Meeting/Meetings.
- NT Congresses And Conventions
- RT Seminars
  Symposia

Megalopolis (1964-1985)
- HN DC 265725, deleted 1986.

Melanesia
- DC D508800
- SN One of the three principal divisions of Oceania, comprising the island groups in the South Pacific Ocean northeast of Australia.
- HN Formerly (1963-1985) DC 265750, Melanesia/Melanesian/Melanesians.
- BT Oceania
- NT Fiji Islands
  New Caledonia
  Santa Cruz Islands
  Solomon Islands

Melanesian (Language)
  Use Austronesian Languages

Melbourne, Australia
- DC D508900
- HN Added, 1989.
- BT Australia

Membership
- DC D509100
- HN Formerly (1963-1985) DC 265860, Member/Members/Membership.
- UF Affiliation
  Group Membership
- BT Participation
- NT Church Membership
- RT Acceptance
  Affiliation Need
  Associations
  Group Identity
  Groups
  Individual Collective Relationship
  Organizational Commitment
  Organizations (Social)
  Political Affiliation
  Recruitment
  Social Contact

Memoir/Memoirs (1969-1985)
- HN DC 265980.
- Use Autobiographical Materials

Memory
- DC D509400
- HN Formerly (1963-1985) DC 266000, Memory/Memories/Memorization.
- UF Recall (1963-1985)
- BT Cognition
- NT Recognition (Psychology)
- RT Experience
  Learning

Menarche
- DC D509700
- HN Formerly (1964-1985) DC 266520, Menarche/Menarcheal.
- BT Menstruation
- RT Life Cycle
  Puberty

Mennonites
- DC D510000
- HN Formerly (1963-1985) DC 266600, Mennonite/Mennonites.
- BT Protestants
- NT Hutterites
- RT Amish
  Protestantism

Menopause
- DC D510300
- HN Formerly (1972-1985) DC 266610, Menopause/Menopausal.
- RT Life Cycle
  Menstruation
  Middle Aged Adults

Mens Roles
  Use Sex Roles

Menstruation
- DC D510600
- HN Formerly (1964-1985) DC 266650, Menstrual/Menstruation.
- NT Menarche
- RT Menopause

Mental — Messianic

Mental Development
- Use Cognitive Development

Mental Health
- DC D510900
- HN Formerly (1963-1985) DC 267000.
- BT Health
- NT Community Mental Health
- RT Adjustment
  Coping
  Health Care Utilization
  Life Satisfaction
  Mental Health Services
  Mental Illness
  Morale
  Neurology
  Self Actualization
  Well Being

Mental Health Services
- DC D510925
- HN Added, 1989.
- BT Health Services
- RT Community Mental Health
  Health Care
  Health Care Utilization
  Mental Health
  Mental Illness

Mental Hospitalization
- Use Hospitalization

Mental Hospitals
- DC D511200
- HN Formerly (1963-1985) DC 267100, Mental Hospital/Mental Hospitals.
- UF Asylum/Asylums (1969-1985)
  Psychiatric Hospitals
  State Mental Hospitals
- BT Hospitals
- RT Mental Illness
  Mental Patients

Mental Illness
- DC D511500
- HN Formerly (1963-1985) DC 267175, Mental Illness/Mentally Ill.
- UF Disorders (Mental)
  Mentally Ill
- BT Disorders
- NT Psychosis
- RT Affective Illness
  Alcoholism
  Anorexia Nervosa
  Autism
  Behavior
  Bulimia
  Defense Mechanisms
  Depression (Psychology)
  Diagnosis
  Eating Disorders
  Emotionally Disturbed
  Freudian Psychology
  Insanity Defense
  Irrationality
  Mental Health
  Mental Health Services
  Mental Hospitals
  Mental Patients
  Neurosis
  Paranoia
  Phobias
  Psychiatric Research
  Psychiatry
  Psychoanalysis
  Psychopathology
  Psychotherapy
  Schizophrenia
  Senility

Mental Patients
- DC D511800
- SN Includes persons formerly institutionalized or hospitalized for mental or emotional problems, as well as those currently under treatment.
- HN Formerly (1963-1985) DC 271460, Mental Patient/Mental Patients.
- UF Psychiatric Patients
- BT Patients
- RT Community Mental Health Centers
  Deinstitutionalization
  Mental Hospitals
  Mental Illness
  Psychiatric Research
  Psychiatry
  Schizophrenia

Mental Telepathy
- Use Extrasensory Perception

Mental/Mentally (1963-1985)
- HN DC 266700, deleted 1986. See now Intelligence, Mentally Retarded, or specific "Mental" terms.

Mentality/Mentalities (1963-1985)
- HN DC 270000.
- Use Mind

Mentally Ill
- Use Mental Illness

Mentally Retarded
- DC D512100
- HN Formerly (1982-1985) DC 271468, Mental Retardation/Mentally Retarded.
- UF Retarded/Retardation/Retardates (1963-1985)
  Subnormality (1965-1985)
- BT Handicapped
- RT Cerebral Palsy
  Deinstitutionalization
  Downs Syndrome
  Intelligence

Menticide
- Use Brainwashing

Merchandising (1965-1985)
- HN DC 271500.
- Use Marketing

Merchant Marines (1985)
- HN DC 271511.
- Use Shipping Industry

Merchants
- DC D512400
- HN Formerly (1963-1985) DC 271510, Merchant/Merchants.
- BT Businessmen
- RT Consumers
  Marketing
  Retail Industry
  Sales Workers
  Stores

Mercy Killing
- Use Euthanasia

Mergers
- DC D512700
- HN Formerly (1963-1985) DC 271512, Merger/Mergers.
- UF Acquisitions And Mergers
  Consolidate/Consolidating/Consolidation (1972-1985)
  Takeovers (Corporate)
- RT Corporations

Merit/Merits (1963-1985)
- HN DC 271513.
- Use Achievement

Meritocracy
- DC D513000
- SN A form of political ideology or Social Order in which leadership or occupational positions are determined on the basis of merit, in terms of objective achievement criteria.
- HN Formerly (1968-1985) DC 271514.
- RT Elitism
  Political Ideologies
  Technocracy

Merleau-Ponty, Maurice
- DC D513100
- SN Born 1908 - died 1961.
- HN Added, 1989.

Merton, Robert King
- DC D513150
- SN Born 5 July 1910 - .
- HN Formerly (1964-1985) DC 271518, Merton, Robert K./Mertonian.

Mescal/Mescaline (1963-1985)
- HN DC 271522.
- Use Psychedelic Drugs

Mesoamerican/Mesoamericans (1963-1985)
- HN DC 271525.
- Use Latin American Cultural Groups

Mesopotamia/Mesopotamian/Mesopotamians (1963-1985)
- HN DC 271536.
- Use Antiquity

Messages
- DC D513300
- HN Formerly (1963-1985) DC 271545, Message/Messages.
- RT Audiences
  Communication
  Content Analysis
  Mass Media
  Meaning
  Rumors
  Signs

Messiahs
- Use Messianic Figures

Messianic Figures
- DC D513600
- HN Formerly (1963-1985) part of DC 271560, Messiah/Messiahs/Messianism/Messianic/Messianist.
- UF Messiahs
- NT Jesus Christ
  Mahdis
- RT Charisma
  Jonestown Mass Suicide
  Messianic Movements
  Mysticism
  Prophecy
  Salvation

Messianic Movements
- DC D513900
- SN Religious movements centering around a highly charismatic leader and marked by an eschatological, utopian, or revolutionary ideology.
- HN Formerly (1963-1985) part of DC 271560, Messiah/Messiahs/Messianism/Messianic/Messianist.

Messianism / Methodology

Messianic Movements (cont'd)
- UF Messianism
- BT Religious Movements
- RT Cargo Cults
  Messianic Figures
  Movements
  Religious Revivalism
  Salvation

Messianism
- Use Messianic Movements

Mestizos
- DC D514200
- HN Formerly (1969-1985) DC 271575.
- RT Acculturation
  American Indians
  Indigenous Populations
  Intermarriage

Metabolism (1969-1985)
- HN DC 271600, deleted 1986.

Metal Industry
- DC D514500
- HN Added, 1986.
- UF Steel Industry
- BT Manufacturing Industries
- RT Metallurgical Technology

Metallurgical Technology
- DC D514800
- HN Formerly (1964-1985) DC 271650, Metallurgy/Metallurgical.
- UF Metallurgy
  Steel Making
- BT Technology
- RT Automation
  Chemistry
  High Technology Industries
  Metal Industry
  Physics

Metallurgy
- Use Metallurgical Technology

Metaphors
- DC D515100
- HN Formerly (1963-1985) DC 271655, Metaphor/Metaphors/Metaphorical.
- RT Language
  Literature
  Symbolism

Metaphysics
- DC D515400
- SN Branch of philosophy that systematically investigates the nature of first principles and problems of ultimate reality.
- HN Formerly (1963-1985) DC 271660, Metaphysics/Metaphysical.
- BT Philosophy
- NT Ontology
- RT Cosmology
  Existence
  Nihilism
  Nominalism
  Reality
  Teleology
  Theology

Metasociology
- DC D515700
- HN Formerly (1963-1985) DC 271670, Metasociology/Metasociological.
- RT History of Sociology
  Sociological Research
  Sociological Theory

Metasociology (cont'd)
- RT Sociology

Meteorology
- DC D516000
- HN Formerly (1963-1985) DC 271690, Meteorology/Meteorological.
- BT Physical Sciences
- RT Weather

Methadone Maintenance
- DC D516300
- HN Formerly (1972-1985) DC 271780, Methadone.
- RT Drug Addiction
  Heroin
  Treatment Programs

Methodists
- DC D516600
- HN Formerly (1963-1985) DC 271810, Methodist/Methodists.
- BT Protestants
- RT Protestantism

Methodological Individualism
- DC D516700
- SN An epistemological doctrine which holds that sociological explanations can be reduced analytically to psychological variables. See also Methodology (Philosophical) and Social Facts.
- HN Added, 1986.
- BT Epistemological Doctrines
- RT Determinism
  Holism
  Methodology (Philosophical)
  Phenomenology
  Positivism
  Reductionism
  Social Facts
  Social Theories
  Sociological Theory
  Verstehen

Methodological Issues
- Use Methodological Problems

Methodological Problems
- DC D516750
- HN Added, 1986.
- UF Methodological Issues
- BT Problems
- RT Methodology (Data Analysis)
  Methodology (Data Collection)
  Methodology (Philosophical)
  Methods
  Qualitative Methods
  Quantitative Methods
  Research
  Research Design
  Research Methodology
  Theoretical Problems

Methodology (Data Analysis)
- DC D516763
- SN Includes studies of how to process and interpret existing sociological data. Do not confuse with Methodology (Data Collection).
- HN Added, 1986.
- UF Data Analysis Methodology
- BT Research Methodology
- NT Contingency Analysis
  Correlation
  Linear Analysis
  Multivariate Analysis
  Regression Analysis

Methodology (Data Analysis) (cont'd)
- NT Statistical Inference
  Statistical Significance
  Variance (Statistics)
- RT Analysis
  Data
  Data Banks
  Data Collection
  Data Processing
  Empirical Methods
  Methodological Problems
  Ranking
  Rating
  Statistical Bias
  Statistics

Methodology (Data Collection)
- DC D516776
- SN Encompasses studies of how to collect sociological data, given the specifics of the research problem and available resources. Do not confuse with Methodology (Data Analysis).
- HN Added, 1986.
- UF Data Collection Methodology
- BT Research Methodology
- NT Case Studies
  Census
  Content Analysis
  Experiments
  Fieldwork
  Interviews
  Life History
  Longitudinal Studies
  Measures (Instruments)
  Observation
  Surveys
  Videotape Recordings
- RT Archival Research
  Data
  Data Collection
  Empirical Methods
  Measurement
  Methodological Problems
  Qualitative Methods
  Quantitative Methods
  Research Design
  Research Subjects
  Researcher Subject Relations
  Respondents
  Sampling

Methodology (Philosophical)
- DC D516789
- SN Analyses of concepts, theories of truth and meaning (ie, epistemology), and arguments about how best to approach the study of social phenomena.
- HN Added, 1986.
- BT Research Methodology
- NT Theory Formation
- RT Analysis
  Causal Models
  Causality
  Concept Formation
  Concepts
  Empirical Methods
  Epistemological Doctrines
  Epistemology
  Hermeneutics
  Ideologies
  Methodological Individualism
  Methodological Problems
  Models
  Objectivity
  Paradigms

Methodology   Middle

Methodology (Philosophical) (cont'd)
- RT Phenomena
- Philosophical Doctrines
- Philosophy
- Positivism
- Postulates
- Reflexivity
- Theories
- Verstehen
- Worldview

Methodology/Methodologies/ Methodological (1963-1985)
- HN DC 271830.
- Use Methods

Methods
- DC D516800
- SN A context-dependent term; select a more specific entry or coordinate with other terms.
- HN Formerly (1963-1985) DC 271800, Method/Methods.
- UF Approach/Approaches (1964-1985)
  Methodology/Methodologies/ Methodological (1963-1985)
  Practice/Practices (1963-1985)
  Technique/Techniques (1963-1985)
- NT Childrearing Practices
  Feeding Practices
  Interdisciplinary Approach
  Naming Practices
  Projective Techniques
  Research Methodology
  Selection Procedures
  Simulation
  Strategies
  Teaching Methods
  Treatment Methods
- RT Algorithms
  Alternative Approaches
  Change Agents
  Heuristics
  Means-Ends Rationality
  Methodological Problems
  Theory Practice Relationship

Metric (1963-1985)
- HN DC 271850, deleted 1986.

Metropolitan Areas
- DC D516900
- HN Formerly (1963-1985) DC 271860, Metropolis/Metropolitan/ Metropolises.
- BT Urban Areas
- RT Center And Periphery
  Central Cities
  Cities
  Geographic Regions
  Nonmetropolitan Areas
  Suburbs

Mexican Americans
- DC D517200
- SN Use limited to United States citizens from Mexican families.
- HN Formerly (1983-1985) DC 271875, Mexican American/Mexican Americans.
- UF Chicano/Chicanos (1972-1985)
- BT Hispanic Americans

Mexico
- DC D517500
- HN Formerly (1963-1985) DC 271900, Mexico/Mexican/Mexicans.
- BT Latin America

Mexico (cont'd)
- BT North America
- NT Mexico City, Mexico
- RT Central America

Mexico City, Mexico
- DC D517800
- HN Formerly (1965-1985) DC 271905, Mexico City.
- BT Mexico

Miami, Florida
- DC D518100
- HN Formerly (1963-1985) DC 271908, Miami, Fla.
- BT Florida

Michels, Robert
- DC D518400
- SN Born 9 January 1876 - died 3 May 1936.
- HN Formerly (1966-1985) DC 271909.

Michigan
- DC D518700
- HN Formerly (1963-1985) DC 271910.
- BT Midwestern States
  United States of America
- NT Detroit, Michigan

Microcomputers
- DC D519000
- SN Compact, relatively inexpensive computers, consisting of a microprocessor and other miniaturized components.
- HN Added, 1986.
- UF Desktop Computers
  Microprocessors
  Personal Computers
- BT Computers
- RT Data Banks
  Data Processing
  Office Automation
  Scientific Technological Revolution

Microelectronic Technology
- Use Electronic Technology

Micronesia
- DC D519300
- SN One of the three principal divisions of Oceania, comprising the small Pacific islands north of the equator and east of the Philippines, whose main groups are the Mariana Islands, the Caroline Islands, and the Marshall Islands.
- HN Formerly (1963-1985) DC 271926, Micronesia/Micronesian/ Micronesians.
- BT Oceania
- NT Caroline Islands
  Gilbert And Ellice Islands
  Mariana Islands
  Marshall Islands
  Wake Island

Micronesian (Language)
- Use Austronesian Languages

Micropolitics (1977-1985)
- HN DC 271928, deleted 1986.

Microprocessors
- Use Microcomputers

Microsociology
- DC D519600
- SN The study of interpersonal behavior and everyday social encounters in small groups and communities. Compare with Macrosociology.
- HN Formerly (1970-1985) DC 271934, Microsociological/Microsociology.
- BT Sociology
- RT Conflict Theory
  Group Dynamics
  Small Groups
  Sociological Research

Middle Aged Adults
- DC D520200
- SN Persons aged 45 to 64.
- HN Formerly (1963-1985) DC 271940, Middle Age/Middle Aged.
- BT Adults
  Age Groups
- RT Aging
  Life Stage Transitions
  Menopause

Middle Ages
- DC D520500
- HN Formerly (1963-1985) DC 271942.
- UF Byzantium/Byzantine (1967-1985)
  Medieval (1963-1985)
- BT Time Periods
- RT Feudalism
  Monasticism
  Papacy
  Peasant Societies

Middle Class
- DC D520800
- HN Added, 1986.
- BT Social Class
- NT New Middle Class
- RT Bourgeoisie
  Proletarianization

Middle East
- DC D521100
- HN Formerly (1963-1985) DC 271975, Middle East/Middle Eastern.
- UF Near East (1963-1985)
- BT Asia
- NT Afghanistan
  Bahrain
  Cyprus
  Iran
  Iraq
  Israel
  Jordan
  Kuwait
  Lebanon
  Oman
  Palestine
  Qatar
  Saudi Arabia
  Syria
  Turkey
  United Arab Emirates
  Yemen Arab Republic
  Yemen (Peoples Democratic Republic)
- RT Arab Countries
  Arab Cultural Groups
  Mediterranean Countries
  Middle Eastern Cultural Groups

Middle Eastern Cultural Groups
- DC D521150
- HN Added, 1989.
- BT Cultural Groups
- RT Arab Cultural Groups
  Middle East

Middle

Middle Range Theories
- **DC** D521200
- **HN** Added, 1986.
- **UF** Miniature Theories
  Partial Theories
  Theories of the Middle Range
- **BT** Social Theories
- **RT** Social Science Research
  Sociological Theory

Middle Schools
- **Use** Junior High Schools

Middleman Minorities
- **DC** D521225
- **SN** A concept dealing with minority groups that have overcome the discrimination and economic barriers encountered in host countries by occupying a middle-rank position in the stratification system and serving as intermediaries or middlemen in the movement of goods and services.
- **HN** Formerly (1972-1985) DC 271985, Middleman/Middlemen.
- **RT** Economic Structure
  Ethnic Relations
  Minority Businesses
  Minority Groups

Middletown Studies
- **DC** D521250
- **SN** Studies modeled after Robert Staughton Lynd's and Helen Merrell Lynd's analysis of Muncie, Indiana, published in 1929 as *Middletown: A Study in Contemporary American Culture.*
- **HN** Formerly (1981-1985) DC 271989, Middletown.
- **RT** Community Research
  Social Change

Midget/Midgets (1969-1985)
- **HN** DC 271990, deleted 1969.

Midlife Transition
- **Use** Life Stage Transitions

Midrash
- **Use** Rabbinical Literature

Midway Islands
- **DC** D521400
- **HN** Added, 1986.
- **BT** Polynesia

Midwestern States
- **DC** D521700
- **HN** Formerly (1965-1985) part of DC 271991, Midwest/Midwestern.
- **BT** States (Political Subdivisions)
- **NT** Illinois
  Indiana
  Iowa
  Kansas
  Michigan
  Minnesota
  Missouri
  Nebraska
  North Dakota
  Ohio
  South Dakota
  Wisconsin
- **RT** North And South
  United States of America

Midwifery
- **DC** D522000
- **HN** Formerly (1975-1985) DC 271993, Midwife/Midwifery.
- **RT** Birth
  Gynecology
  Nurses
  Paramedical Personnel

Migrant Population
- **Use** Migrants

Migrant Workers
- **DC** D522300
- **HN** Added, 1986.
- **BT** Workers
- **RT** Agricultural Workers
  Foreign Workers
  Labor Migration

Migrants
- **DC** D522600
- **HN** Formerly (1963-1985) DC 271998, Migrant/Migrants/Migratory.
- **UF** Migrant Population
- **RT** Gypsies
  Immigrants
  Migration
  Migration Patterns
  Refugees

Migration
- **DC** D522900
- **HN** Formerly (1963-1985) DC 272000.
- **UF** Population Mobility
  Population Movements
- **BT** Mobility
- **NT** Emigration
  Immigration
  Internal Migration
  Labor Migration
  Return Migration
  Rural to Urban Migration
  Urban to Rural Migration
- **RT** Colonization
  Demographic Change
  Demography
  Geographic Mobility
  Immigrants
  Land Settlement
  Migrants
  Migration Patterns
  Nomadic Societies
  Population
  Population Distribution
  Population Policy
  Refugees
  Relocation
  Residence
  Residential Mobility
  Settlement Patterns
  Undocumented Immigrants

Migration Patterns
- **DC** D523200
- **HN** Added, 1986.
- **UF** Migration Trends
- **RT** Demography
  Geographic Distribution
  Migrants
  Migration
  Population Distribution
  Relocation
  Residential Patterns
  Settlement Patterns

Military

Migration Trends
- **Use** Migration Patterns

Milan, Italy
- **DC** D523400
- **HN** Added, 1989.
- **BT** Italy

Milieu (1963-1985)
- **HN** DC 272300.
- **Use** Environment

Militant/Militants/Militancy (1968-1985)
- **HN** DC 272380.
- **Use** Activism

Militarism
- **DC** D523500
- **HN** Formerly (1963-1985) part of DC 272400, Military/Militarism/Militarization/Militarist/Militarists.
- **BT** Political Ideologies
- **RT** Armaments
  Armed Forces
  Elitism
  Fascism
  Imperialism
  Invasion
  Militarization
  Military Regimes
  Military Sociology
  Nationalism
  Pacifism
  Samurai
  War

Militarization
- **DC** D523600
- **HN** Reinstated, 1989. Formerly (1963-1985) included in DC 272400, Military/Militarism/Militarization/Militarist/Militarists.
- **BT** Social Processes
- **RT** Armed Forces
  Defense Spending
  Militarism
  Military Civilian Relations
  War

Military Civilian Relations
- **DC** D523800
- **HN** Added, 1986.
- **UF** Civilian Military Relations
- **BT** Social Relations
- **RT** Armed Forces
  Citizens
  Civil Defense
  Militarization
  Military Regimes
  Police
  Police Community Relations
  Repression (Political)
  State Society Relationship

Military Conscription
- **Use** Draft (Military)

Military Coups
- **Use** Coups d'Etat

Military Desertion
- **DC** D524100
- **HN** Formerly (1964-1985) part of DC 130015, Desertion/Deserter/Deserters.
- **UF** Absent Without Leave
  Desertion (Military)
- **RT** Combat
  Military Personnel

Military   Minor

Military Expenditures
　Use　Defense Spending

Military Experience
　Use　Military Service

Military Forces
　Use　Armed Forces

Military Governments
　Use　Military Regimes

Military Officers
　DC　D524400
　HN　Added, 1986.
　UF　Officers (Military)
　BT　Military Personnel
　RT　Military Regimes
　　　Veterans

Military Participation
　Use　Military Service

Military Personnel
　DC　D524700
　HN　Added, 1986.
　UF　Enlisted Personnel
　　　Recruits (Military)
　　　Servicemen
　　　Soldier/Soldiers (1963-1985)
　NT　Military Officers
　RT　Armaments
　　　Armed Forces
　　　Draft (Military)
　　　Military Desertion
　　　Military Service
　　　Military Sociology
　　　Veterans
　　　War

Military Regimes
　DC　D525000
　HN　Formerly (1963-1985) DC 377760, Regime/Regimes.
　UF　Military Governments
　　　Regimes (Military)
　RT　Coups d'Etat
　　　Government
　　　Militarism
　　　Military Civilian Relations
　　　Military Officers

Military Service
　DC　D525300
　HN　Added, 1986.
　UF　Military Experience
　　　Military Participation
　RT　Armed Forces
　　　Citizenship
　　　Conscientious Objectors
　　　Draft (Military)
　　　Military Personnel
　　　Participation
　　　Veterans
　　　War

Military Sociology
　DC　D525600
　HN　Added, 1986.
　BT　Sociology
　RT　Armed Forces
　　　Militarism
　　　Military Personnel

Military/Militarism/Militarization/ Militarists (1963-1985)
　HN　DC 272400, deleted 1986. See now Militarism and specific "Military" terms.

Mill, John Stuart
　DC　D525900
　SN　Born 20 May 1806 - died 8 May 1873.
　HN　Formerly (1966-1985) DC 272605.

Millenarianism
　DC　D526200
　SN　Pertains to any religious social movement based on belief in total social change brought about by supernatural means for the benefit of the faithful.
　HN　Formerly (1963-1985) DC 272600, Millennium/Millenarian/ Millenarianism.
　UF　Millennialism/Millennialistic (1963-1985)
　　　Millennium
　BT　Religious Beliefs
　RT　Anabaptists
　　　Bible
　　　Cargo Cults
　　　Christianity
　　　Cults
　　　Jehovah's Witnesses
　　　Prophecy
　　　Religious Movements
　　　Social Movements
　　　Utopias

Millennialism/Millennialistic (1963-1985)
　HN　DC 272596.
　Use　Millenarianism

Millennium
　Use　Millenarianism

Mills, Charles Wright
　DC　D526500
　SN　Born 1916 - died 20 March 1962.
　HN　Formerly (1963-1985) DC 272652, Mills, C. Wright.

Mind
　DC　D526800
　HN　Formerly (1963-1985) DC 272700.
　UF　Intellect/Intellects (1969-1985)
　　　Mentality/Mentalities (1963-1985)
　　　Psyche
　RT　Cognition
　　　Concept Formation
　　　Concepts
　　　Conscience
　　　Consciousness
　　　Human Nature
　　　Images
　　　Soul
　　　Thinking
　　　Unconscious (Psychology)
　　　Will

Mindanao, Philippines (1966-1985)
　HN　DC 272710.
　Use　Philippines

Mine Workers
　Use　Miners

Mineral Oils
　Use　Petroleum

Mineral Resources
　DC　D527100
　HN　Formerly (1964-1985) DC 272785, Mineral/Minerals/Mineralogy.
　BT　Natural Resources
　RT　Fuels
　　　Geology
　　　Land
　　　Mining Industry

Mineralogy
　Use　Geology

Miners
　DC　D527400
　HN　Formerly (1963-1985) part of DC 272800, Miners/Mining.
　UF　Coal Miners
　　　Mine Workers
　BT　Blue Collar Workers
　RT　Mining Industry

Miniature Theories
　Use　Middle Range Theories

Minifundia/Minifundismo (1971-1985)
　HN　DC 272825.
　Use　Small Farms

Minimum Wage
　DC　D527700
　HN　Formerly (1963-1985) DC 272835, Minimum Wage/Minimum Wages.
　BT　Wages

Mining Industry
　DC　D528000
　HN　Formerly (1963-1985) part of DC 272800, Miners/Mining.
　BT　Industry
　RT　Coal
　　　Mineral Resources
　　　Miners

Ministers (Clergy)
　DC　D528300
　HN　Formerly (1963-1985) part of DC 272850, Minister/Ministers/ Ministerial.
　BT　Clergy

Ministry (Religion)
　Use　Clergy

Ministry/Ministries (1964-1985)
　HN　DC 272900, deleted 1986. See now Clergy or Government Agencies.

Minneapolis, Minnesota
　DC　D528600
　HN　Formerly (1965-1985) DC 272950, Minneapolis, Minn.
　BT　Minnesota

Minnesingers
　Use　Poets

Minnesota
　DC　D528900
　HN　Formerly (1964-1985) DC 272970.
　BT　Midwestern States
　　　United States of America
　NT　Minneapolis, Minnesota

Minnesota Multiphasic Personality Inventory
　DC　D528950
　HN　Formerly (1966-1985) DC 272980, Minnesota Multiphasic Personality Inventory/MMPI.
　UF　MMPI
　BT　Personality Measures

Minor/Minors (1965-1985)
　HN　DC 273400, deleted 1986. See now Children, Adolescents, or Youth.

Minority

Minority Businesses
- DC D529200
- HN Added, 1986.
- UF Ethnic Businesses
- BT Enterprises
- RT Business
  Family Businesses
  Middleman Minorities
  Minority Groups
  Small Businesses

Minority Groups
- DC D529500
- HN Formerly (1963-1985) DC 273500, Minority/Minorities.
- BT Groups
- NT Ethnic Minorities
  Linguistic Minorities
- RT Affirmative Action
  Assimilation
  Black White Relations
  Biculturalism
  Center And Periphery
  Class Differences
  Cultural Pluralism
  Disadvantaged
  Ethnic Groups
  Ethnic Identity
  Ethnic Relations
  Language Shift
  Low Income Groups
  Majority Groups
  Marginality
  Middleman Minorities
  Minority Businesses
  Multicultural Education
  Plural Societies
  Prejudice
  Race
  Racial Relations
  Religious Cultural Groups
  Self Determination
  Social Inequality
  Social Structure

Misanthropy/Misanthrope (1977-1985)
- HN DC 273540.
- Use Cynicism

Misbehavior
- Use Behavior Problems

Miscarriage
- DC D529800
- HN Formerly (1972-1985) DC 273547, Miscarriage/Miscarriages.
- UF Spontaneous Abortion
- RT Abortion
  Pregnancy

Miscegenation (1964-1985)
- HN DC 273550.
- Use Intermarriage

Misconduct
- Use Behavior Problems

Missile/Missiles (1963-1985)
- HN DC 273690, deleted 1986.

Mission/Missions (1963-1985)
- HN DC 273770, deleted 1986. See now Missionaries or Human Service Organizations.

Missionaries
- DC D530100
- HN Formerly (1963-1985) DC 273780, Missionary/Missionaries.
- BT Clergy
- RT Proselytism
  Religious Conversion

Mississippi
- DC D530400
- HN Formerly (1963-1985) DC 273830.
- BT Southern States
  United States of America

Missouri
- DC D530700
- HN Formerly (1964-1985) DC 273860.
- BT Midwestern States
  United States of America
- NT Kansas City, Missouri
  St. Louis, Missouri
- RT Ozark Mountains

Mistakes
- Use Errors

Mixed Languages
- Use Creolized Languages

Mixed Marriage
- Use Intermarriage

MMPI
- Use Minnesota Multiphasic Personality Inventory

Mob/Mobs (1964-1985)
- HN DC 273990.
- Use Crowds

Mobility
- DC D531000
- SN A context-dependent term for individual or group movement; select a more specific entry or coordinate with other terms.
- HN Formerly (1963-1985) DC 274000.
- NT Geographic Mobility
  Migration
  Residential Mobility
  Social Mobility
- RT Change

Mobilization
- DC D531300
- HN Formerly (1963-1985) DC 274175.
- NT Resource Mobilization
- RT Agitation
  Political Action

Mode/Modes/Modalic (1969-1985)
- HN DC 274375, deleted 1986.

Modeling Methods
- Use Models

Models
- DC D531500
- SN A context-dependent term for heuristic constructs used to explore or predict phenomena.
- HN Formerly (1963-1985) DC 274400, Model/Modeling/Models.
- UF Modeling Methods
- NT Causal Models
  Decision Models
  Ecological Models
  Economic Models
  Mathematical Models
  Medical Models

Modernization

Models (cont'd)
- NT Paradigms
  Prediction Models
  Stochastic Models
  Structural Models
- RT Computer Assisted Research
  Constructs
  Graph Theory
  Ideal Types
  Linear Analysis
  Loglinear Analysis
  Methodology (Philosophical)
  Quantitative Methods
  Research
  Research Design
  Research Methodology
  Role Models
  Simulation
  Theories
  Typology

Models (Role)
- Use Role Models

Modern Society
- DC D531600
- HN Added, 1986.
- UF Contemporary Society
- BT Society
- RT Civil Society
  Complex Societies
  Gemeinschaft And Gesellschaft
  Industrial Societies
  Mass Society
  Modernity
  Modernization
  Popular Culture
  Postindustrial Societies
  Twentieth Century
  Urbanization
  Western Society

Modernity
- DC D531900
- HN Formerly (1963-1985) DC 274480, Modern/Modernity/Modernism/Modernist/Modernists/Modernizing.
- RT Cultural Change
  Modern Society
  Postmodernism
  Social Attitudes
  Time Periods
  Traditionalism

Modernization
- DC D532200
- HN Formerly (1963-1985) DC 274540.
- BT Social Processes
- RT Convergence Theory
  Cultural Change
  Economic Development
  Economic Structure
  Industrial Societies
  Industrialization
  Modern Society
  Preservation
  Progress
  Rationalization
  Scientific Technological Revolution
  Secularization
  Social Change
  Social Revolution
  Technological Change
  Technology Transfer
  Traditional Societies
  Urbanization

Modes of Production
- **DC** D532300
- **SN** A concept developed by Karl Marx to describe relationships between the forces of production (ie, labor power, raw materials, tools, techniques, land) and the relations of production (ie, ownership and control of the product). Different relationships between the forces and relations of production result in different modes of production (eg, the feudal, capitalist, Asiatic, and slave modes of production).
- **HN** Added, 1986.
- **UF** Production Modes
- **RT** Base And Superstructure
  Capitalism
  Communism
  Dependency Theory
  Determinism
  Economic Development
  Economic Structure
  Economic Underdevelopment
  Exploitation
  Feudalism
  Forces And Relations of Production
  Historical Materialism
  Imperialism
  Industrial Production
  Marxism
  Marxist Economics
  Political Economy
  Production
  Slavery
  Structuralism

Modification (Behavior)
Use Behavior Modification

Mohammed/Mohammedans/Mohammedanism (1963-1985)
- **HN** DC 274550, deleted 1986. See now Muslims, Islam, or Mohammed.

Mohammedanism
Use Islam

Mohammedanists
Use Muslims

Moiety/Moieties (1976-1985)
- **HN** DC 274560.
- **Use** Clans

Monaco
- **DC** D532500
- **HN** Formerly (1964-1985) DC 274590, Monaco/Monacan/Monacans.
- **BT** Mediterranean Countries
  Western Europe

Monarchy
- **DC** D532800
- **HN** Formerly (1963-1985) DC 274600, Monarchy/Monarchies/Monarchial.
- **UF** King/Kings/Kingdom/Kingship (1963-1985)
- **BT** Political Systems
- **RT** Aristocracy
  Empires
  Royalty

Monasteries
- **DC** D533100
- **HN** Formerly (1963-1985) part of DC 274650, Monastery/Monastic/Monasticism.
- **RT** Convents
  Monasticism

Monasteries (cont'd)
- **RT** Monks
  Places of Worship

Monastic Life
Use Monasticism

Monasticism
- **DC** D533400
- **HN** Formerly (1963-1985) part of DC 274650, Monastery/Monastic/Monasticism.
- **UF** Monastic Life
- **RT** Asceticism
  Convents
  Middle Ages
  Monasteries
  Monks
  Nuns
  Religious Orders

Money
- **DC** D533700
- **HN** Formerly (1964-1985) DC 274700, Money/Monetary.
- **UF** Currency/Currencies (1965-1985)
- **RT** Capital
  Credit
  Debts
  Economic Systems
  Exchange (Economics)
  Expenditures
  Finance
  Income
  Investment
  Loans
  Payments
  Profits
  Saving
  Value (Economics)
  Wealth

Mongolia
- **DC** D534000
- **HN** Formerly (1971-1985) DC 274950, Mongolia/Mongolian/Mongols.
- **BT** Far East
- **RT** China

Mongoloidism
Use Downs Syndrome

Monitoring (1984-1985)
- **HN** DC 275150, deleted 1986. See now Observation or Evaluation.

Monkeys (1964-1985)
- **HN** DC 276000.
- **Use** Primates

Mon-Khmer Languages
Use Oriental Languages

Monks
- **DC** D534300
- **HN** Formerly (1963-1985) DC 275950, Monk/Monks.
- **BT** Clergy
- **RT** Asceticism
  Monasteries
  Monasticism
  Religious Orders

Monogamy
- **DC** D534600
- **HN** Formerly (1963-1985) DC 276175.
- **BT** Marriage
- **RT** Polygamy

Monograph/Monographs/Monographic (1964-1985)
- **HN** DC 276180.
- **Use** Books

Monolingualism
- **DC** D534900
- **HN** Formerly (1966-1985) DC 276190, Monolingual.
- **RT** Bilingualism
  Language Social Class Relationship
  Languages
  Multilingualism
  Second Language Learning
  Sociolinguistics

Monopolies
- **DC** D535200
- **HN** Formerly (1963-1985) part of DC 276250, Monopoly/Monopolies/Monopolization.
- **UF** Monopolization
- **RT** Competition
  Economic Structure
  Monopoly Capitalism
  Oligopolies

Monopolization
Use Monopolies

Monopoly Capitalism
- **DC** D535500
- **SN** In Marxist theory, a stage in capitalist development in which a small number of people control the means of production (eg, labor power, raw materials, tools, techniques, land) and distribution.
- **HN** Formerly (1963-1985) part of DC 276250, Monopoly/Monopolies/Monopolization.
- **BT** Capitalism
- **RT** Monopolies
  Oligopolies

Montana
- **DC** D535800
- **HN** Formerly (1966-1985) DC 276400.
- **BT** United States of America
  Western States

Montenegro, Yugoslavia
- **DC** D536100
- **HN** Formerly (1968-1985) DC 276569, Montenegro.
- **BT** Yugoslavia

Montesquieu, Charles Louis de Secondat
- **DC** D536400
- **SN** Born 18 January 1689 - died 10 February 1755.
- **HN** Formerly (1966-1985) DC 276570, Montesquieu, Charles Louis de.

Montevideo, Uruguay
- **DC** D536700
- **HN** Formerly (1964-1985) DC 276576.
- **BT** Uruguay

Montreal, Quebec
- **DC** D537000
- **HN** Formerly (1963-1985) DC 276580.
- **BT** Quebec

Montserrat
- **DC** D537300
- **HN** Added, 1986.
- **BT** Caribbean

Monuments
- **DC** D537600
- **HN** Formerly (1964-1985) DC 276615, Monument/Monuments.
- **RT** Art
  Dolmen
  Material Culture

Mood/Moods (1971-1985)
- **HN** DC 276617.
- **Use** Emotions

Moon Influences
- **Use** Lunar Influences

Moonies
- **Use** Unification Church

Moonlighting/Moonlighters (1964-1985)
- **HN** DC 276620.
- **Use** Multiple Jobholding

Moore, Barrington
- **DC** D537900
- **SN** Born 12 May 1913 - .
- **HN** Formerly (1972-1985) DC 276626.

Moore, Wilbert Ellis
- **DC** D538200
- **SN** Born 26 October 1914 - .
- **HN** Formerly (1968-1985) DC 276630, Moore, W. E.

Moral Behavior
- **Use** Morality

Moral Development
- **DC** D538500
- **SN** Acquisition and integration of moral principles into one's life, particularly in the course of child maturation and cognitive development.
- **HN** Added, 1986.
- **UF** Conscience Development
  Moral Maturity
- **BT** Development
- **RT** Adult Development
  Ethics
  Individuals
  Intellectual Development
  Moral Education
  Moral Judgment
  Morality
  Psychological Development

Moral Education
- **DC** D538800
- **HN** Added, 1986.
- **UF** Ethical Education
- **BT** Education
- **RT** Ethics
  Moral Development
  Morality
  Religious Education

Moral Judgment
- **DC** D539100
- **HN** Formerly (1985) DC 276650.
- **UF** Moral Reasoning (1985)
- **BT** Judgment
- **RT** Conscience
  Ethics
  Moral Development
  Morality

Moral Maturity
- **Use** Moral Development

Moral Philosophy
- **Use** Ethics

Moral Reasoning (1985)
- **HN** DC 276740.
- **Use** Moral Judgment

Moral Values
- **Use** Morality

Moral/Morals (1963-1985)
- **HN** DC 276640.
- **Use** Ethics

Morale
- **DC** D539400
- **HN** Formerly (1963-1985) DC 277000.
- **RT** Certainty
  Effectiveness
  Emotions
  Job Performance
  Job Satisfaction
  Mental Health
  Motivation
  Occupational Stress
  Organizational Development
  Well Being
  Work Attitudes

Morality
- **DC** D539700
- **HN** Formerly (1963-1985) DC 278000, Morality/Moralist.
- **UF** Goodness
  Honest/Honesty (1963-1985)
  Integrity (1972-1985)
  Moral Behavior
  Moral Values
  Purity (1965-1985)
  Virtue (1963-1985)
- **RT** Bioethics
  Censorship
  Conscience
  Corruption
  Deception
  Equity
  Ethics
  Guilt
  Honor
  Machiavellianism (Personality)
  Moral Development
  Moral Education
  Moral Judgment
  Obligation
  Religious Beliefs
  Reputation
  Shame
  Sins
  Social Values
  Truth
  Utilitarianism
  Value Orientations
  Values

Morbidity
- **DC** D540000
- **SN** The incidence of illness and disease in a given population.
- **HN** Formerly (1963-1985) DC 278015.
- **RT** Diseases
  Health Policy
  Illness
  Mortality Rates
  Public Health

Mores (1963-1985)
- **HN** DC 278100.
- **Use** Norms

Morgan, Lewis Henry
- **DC** D540300
- **SN** Born 1818 - died 1881.
- **HN** Formerly (1964-1985) DC 278115.

Mormon Church
- **Use** Mormons

Mormons
- **DC** D540600
- **HN** Formerly (1963-1986) DC 278250, Mormon/Mormons.
- **UF** Latter-Day Saints
  Mormon Church
- **BT** Protestants
- **RT** Protestantism

Morocco
- **DC** D540900
- **HN** Formerly (1963-1985) DC 278270, Morocco/Moroccan/Moroccans.
- **BT** Arab Countries
  Mediterranean Countries
  North Africa

Morphemes (1979-1985)
- **HN** DC 278290.
- **Use** Morphology (Language)

Morphology (Language)
- **DC** D541200
- **HN** Added, 1986.
- **UF** Morphemes (1979-1985)
- **BT** Grammar
- **RT** Code Switching
  Definitions
  Discourse Analysis
  Language
  Phonetics
  Speech
  Structure
  Words

Morphology/Morphological (1963-1985)
- **HN** DC 278315, deleted 1986. See now Social Structure or Morphology (Language).

Mortality Rates
- **DC** D541500
- **HN** Formerly (1963-1985) DC 278400, Mortality.
- **UF** Death Rates
  Fatality Rates
- **BT** Rates
- **RT** Child Mortality
  Crime Rates
  Death
  Demographic Transition Theory
  Demography
  Fatalities
  Health
  Infant Mortality
  Life Tables
  Longevity
  Morbidity
  Mortality Rates
  Suicide

Mortuary Rites
- **Use** Burials

Mosca, Gaetano
- **DC** D541800
- **SN** Born 1 April 1858 - died 8 November 1941.
- **HN** Formerly (1966-1985) DC 278600.

Moscow, Union of Soviet Socialist Republics
- **DC** D542100
- **HN** Formerly (1963-1985) DC 278650, Moscow, USSR.
- **BT** Union of Soviet Socialist Republics

Moshav (1964-1985)
- **HN** DC 278775.
- **Use** Agricultural Collectives

Moslem (1963-1985)
- **HN** DC 278800.
- **Use** Muslims

Motels
- **Use** Hotels

Mother Absence
- **DC** D542300
- **HN** Added, 1989.
- **RT** Child Custody
  Divorce
  Family Stability
  Father Absence
  Marital Disruption
  Mothers
  Parent Child Relations
  Single Fathers
  Single Parent Family

Mother Complex
- **Use** Oedipal Complex

Mothers
- **DC** D542400
- **HN** Formerly (1963-1985) DC 279000, Mother/Mothers/Motherhood/Mothering.
- **BT** Parents
- **NT** Unwed Mothers
  Working Mothers
- **RT** Childrearing Practices
  Elderly Women
  Family Role
  Fathers
  Females
  Grandparents
  Matrifocal Family
  Mother Absence
  Oedipal Complex
  Parent Child Relations
  Parental Attitudes
  Relatives
  Stepfamily
  Wives

Motion Pictures
- **Use** Films

Motivation
- **DC** D542700
- **HN** Formerly (1963-1985) DC 282000, Motive/Motives/Motivation/Motivational.
- **UF** Drive
- **RT** Achievement
  Approval
  Aspiration
  Commitment
  Curiosity
  Delay of Gratification
  Encouragement

Motivation (cont'd)
- **RT** Failure
  Feedback
  Goals
  Incentives
  Instinct
  Intentionality
  Job Performance
  Morale
  Needs
  Organizational Effectiveness
  Performance
  Profit Motive
  Psychodynamics
  Reinforcement
  Rewards
  Success
  Welfare Dependency
  Work Attitudes

Motor Vehicles
- **Use** Automobiles

Motorcycles
- **Use** Automobiles

Mountain Regions
- **DC** D543000
- **HN** Formerly (1965-1985) DC 284500, Mountain.
- **UF** Alpine (1964-1985)
- **BT** Geographic Regions
- **RT** Altitude Effects
  Andes
  Arctic Regions
  Arid Zones
  Earth (Planet)
  Himalayan States
  Ozark Mountains
  Topography
  Tropical Regions

Mourning (1964-1985)
- **HN** DC 284700, deleted 1986. See now Death Rituals or Grief.

Movements
- **DC** D543100
- **SN** A context-dependent term encompassing mass behaviors; select a more specific entry or coordinate with other terms. In sociological contexts where Movements is closely related to Social Movements, select the latter.
- **HN** Formerly (1963-1985) DC 285000, Movement/Movements.
- **NT** Countermovements
  Labor Movements
  Peace Movements
  Political Movements
  Regional Movements
  Religious Movements
  Social Movements
  Temperance Movements
  Youth Movements
- **RT** Activism
  Antinuclear Movements
  Black Power
  Civil Disorders
  Dissent
  Ecumenical Movement
  Feminism
  Jesus Movement
  Messianic Movements
  Political Action
  Protest Movements
  Reform
  Schism

Movements (cont'd)
- **RT** Social Action
  Social Change
  Underground Movements
  Zionism

Movements (Solidarity)
- **Use** Solidarity Movements

Movie/Movies (1963-1985)
- **HN** DC 285450.
- **Use** Films

Moving (1966-1985)
- **HN** DC 285520.
- **Use** Residential Mobility

Moynihan, Daniel Patrick
- **DC** D543300
- **SN** Born 16 March 1927 - .
- **HN** Formerly (1967-1985) DC 285540, Moynihan, Daniel P.

Mozambique
- **DC** D543600
- **HN** Formerly (1985) DC 285565.
- **BT** Sub Saharan Africa

Mt. Sinai Hospital, N.Y. (1966-1985)
- **HN** DC 284600, deleted 1986.

Muckraker/Muckrakers/Muckraking (1963-1985)
- **HN** DC 285600, deleted 1986.

Mugging
- **Use** Robbery

Multi-/Multiple (1964-1985)
- **HN** DC 285750, deleted 1986.

Multicultural Education
- **DC** D543750
- **HN** Added, 1986.
- **BT** Education
- **RT** Biculturalism
  Bilingual Education
  Cultural Identity
  Cultural Pluralism
  Educational Policy
  Ethnic Groups
  Ethnic Identity
  Ethnic Relations
  Intercultural Communication
  Minority Groups

Multiculturalism
- **Use** Cultural Pluralism

Multidimensional Scaling
- **Use** Scales

Multidisciplinary Approach
- **Use** Interdisciplinary Approach

Multilingualism
- **DC** D543900
- **HN** Added, 1986.
- **UF** Lingualism (1969-1985)
  Pluralingualism
- **RT** Bilingual Education
  Bilingualism
  Code Switching
  Crosscultural Analysis
  Cultural Pluralism
  Diglossia
  Language Maintenance
  Language Planning
  Language Social Class Relationship
  Languages

Multilingualism (cont'd)
- **RT** Monolingualism
  Plural Societies
  Psycholinguistics
  Second Language Learning
  Sociolinguistics

Multinational Corporations
- **DC** D544200
- **HN** Formerly (1983-1985) DC 285755, Multinational Corporation.
- **UF** Transnational Corporation (1985)
  Transnational Groups (1972-1985)
- **BT** Corporations
- **RT** Dependency Theory
  Oligopolies
  World Economy

Multiple Authorship
- **Use** Authorship

Multiple Discoveries
- **Use** Discovery

Multiple Discriminant Analysis
- **Use** Discriminant Analysis

Multiple Jobholding
- **DC** D544500
- **HN** Added, 1986.
- **UF** Moonlighting/Moonlighters (1964-1985)
- **BT** Employment
- **RT** Part Time Employment

Multiple Regression Analysis
- **DC** D544600
- **HN** Added, 1986.
- **BT** Regression Analysis
- **RT** Correlation
  Dimensional Analysis
  Path Analysis
  Prediction

Multiplier (1971-1985)
- **HN** DC 285760, deleted 1986.

Multivariate Analysis
- **DC** D544650
- **SN** Statistical techniques used to analyze and interpret the interrelationships among several variables.
- **HN** Formerly (1983-1985) DC 285815.
- **BT** Methodology (Data Analysis)
  Quantitative Methods
- **NT** Cluster Analysis
  Dimensional Analysis
  Discriminant Analysis
  Factor Analysis
  Path Analysis
- **RT** Correlation
  Loglinear Analysis
  Regression Analysis
  Sampling
  Statistical Inference
  Variables
  Variance (Statistics)

Munda Languages
- **Use** Oriental Languages

Municipal Annexation
- **Use** Annexation

Municipal Politics
- **Use** Local Politics

Municipal/Municipality/Municipalities (1963-1985)
- **HN** DC 285880.
- **Use** Cities

Munitions
- **Use** Armaments

Murder/Murders/Murderer/Murderers (1963-1985)
- **HN** DC 286000.
- **Use** Homicide

Murdock, George Peter
- **DC** D544800
- **SN** Born 11 May 1897 - died 29 March 1985.
- **HN** Formerly (1964-1985) DC 286700, Murdock, George P.

Museums
- **DC** D545100
- **HN** Formerly (1964-1985) DC 287200, Museum/Museums.
- **BT** Facilities
- **RT** Anthropology
  Art
  Cultural Activities
  Institutions
  Material Culture
  Visual Arts

Music
- **DC** D545400
- **HN** Formerly (1963-1985) DC 288000, Music/Musical.
- **UF** Concert/Concerts (1972-1985)
  Jazz (1963-1985)
  Popular Songs (1966-1985)
  Song/Songs (1964-1985)
  Vocal Music
- **BT** Fine Arts
- **RT** Art
  Artistic Styles
  Dance
  Folk Culture
  Musicians
  Popular Culture
  Recordings
  Renaissance
  Romanticism
  Videotape Recordings

Music Industry
- **Use** Entertainment Industry

Musicians
- **DC** D545700
- **HN** Formerly (1963-1985) DC 288180, Musician/Musicians.
- **BT** Artists
  Professional Workers
- **RT** Fine Arts
  Music

Muslims
- **DC** D546000
- **HN** Formerly (1964-1985) DC 288600, Muslim/Muslims.
- **UF** Mohammedanists
  Moslem (1963-1985)
- **BT** Religious Cultural Groups
- **NT** Black Muslims
  Mahdis
- **RT** Arab Cultural Groups
  Islam
  Islamic Law
  Koran
  Purdah

Mutation/Mutations (1963-1985)
- **HN** DC 288800, deleted 1986.

Mutual Help
- **Use** Self Help

Myrdal, Karl Gunnar
- **DC** D546300
- **SN** Born 6 December 1898 - died 17 May 1987.
- **HN** Formerly (1963-1985) DC 288900, Myrdal, Gunnar.

Mysticism
- **DC** D546600
- **HN** Formerly (1963-1985) DC 289000, Mystic/Mysticism/Mystical.
- **BT** Philosophical Doctrines
- **RT** Asceticism
  Beliefs
  Cabala
  Cults
  Hassidism
  Messianic Figures
  Philosophy
  Religions
  Religious Beliefs

Mystification (1964-1985)
- **HN** DC 289200, deleted 1986.

Mythology (1963-1985)
- **HN** DC 289625.
- **Use** Myths

Myths
- **DC** D546900
- **SN** Narrative tales explaining the cosmological and supernatural traditions, gods, heroes, cultural traits, religious beliefs, worldview, and value system of a social group.
- **HN** Formerly (1963-1985) DC 289500, Myth/Myths/Mythical/Mythification.
- **UF** Mythology (1963-1985)
- **RT** Animism
  Cannibalism
  Cosmology
  Ethnology
  Folk Culture
  Folklore
  Literature
  Religions
  Rituals
  Structuralism

Myths (Oedipal)
- **Use** Oedipal Complex

NAACP/National Assn Advancement Colored People (1966-1985)
- **HN** DC 290400. Abbreviated here due to character restrictions. Formerly used in indexing under its full name NAACP/National Association for the Advancement of Colored People.
- **Use** Civil Rights Organizations

Namibia
- **DC** D547200
- **HN** Formerly (1984-1985) DC 289940, Namibia (South West Africa).
- **UF** South West Africa
- **BT** Sub Saharan Africa

Naming Practices
- **DC** D547300
- **HN** Formerly (1966-1985) DC 289930, Name/Names/Naming.
- **UF** Given Names

Naples

Naming Practices (cont'd)
- UF   Nicknames
    Personal Names
    Surnames
- BT   Methods
- RT   Identity
    Kinship
    Lineage
    Meaning
    Rituals
    Sociolinguistics

Naples, Italy
- DC   D547400
- HN   Added, 1989.
- BT   Italy

Napoleon Bonaparte
- DC   D547500
- SN   Born 15 August 1769 - died 5 May 1821.
- HN   Formerly (1969-1985) DC 289965.

Narcissism
- DC   D547800
- HN   Formerly (1981-1985) DC 290225, Narcissism/Narcissistic.
- UF   Self Love
- BT   Love
- RT   Egocentrism
    Egoism
    Neurosis
    Personality Traits
    Self Esteem

Narcotic Drugs
- DC   D548100
- HN   Formerly (1966-1985) DC 290250, Narcotic/Narcotics.
- BT   Drugs
- NT   Opiates
- RT   Cocaine
    Drug Addiction
    Marijuana
    Psychedelic Drugs

Narratives
- DC   D548400
- HN   Formerly (1972-1985) DC 290270, Narrate/Narrator/Narration/Narrative.
- UF   Personal Narratives
- BT   Reports
- RT   Autobiographical Materials
    Biographies
    Documents
    Literature
    Records (Documents)
    Storytelling
    Verbal Accounts
    Verbal Communication

Nasser, Gamal Abdal
- DC   D548700
- SN   Born 15 January 1918 - died 28 September 1970.
- HN   Formerly (1968-1985) DC 290300, Nasser, G. A./Nasserism.

Natality (1968-1985)
- HN   DC 290315.
- Use   Fertility

Nation of Islam
- Use   Black Muslims

Nation State
- Use   State

Nation/Nations (1963-1985)
- HN   DC 290330, deleted 1986. See now Countries or appropriate "State" or "Society" terms.

National Debt
- Use   Public Debt

National Government
- Use   Central Government

National Health Service
- Use   Socialized Medicine

National Identity
- DC   D549000
- HN   Added, 1986.
- BT   Cultural Identity
- RT   Civil Religion
    Countries
    Cultural Groups
    Nationalism

National Organization for Women/NOW (1977-1985)
- HN   DC 290432.
- Use   Womens Groups

National Parks
- Use   Parks

National Reconstruction
- Use   Reconstruction

National Science Foundation/NSF (1970-1985)
- HN   DC 290440.
- Use   Government Agencies

National Security
- DC   D549300
- HN   Formerly (1985) DC 290445.
- UF   State Security
- BT   Security
- RT   Armaments
    Defense Spending
    Espionage
    International Relations
    Secrecy
    State
    Survival
    War

Nationalism
- DC   D549600
- HN   Formerly (1963-1985) DC 290395, National/Nationalism/Nationalist/Nationalists/Nationalistic.
- BT   Political Ideologies
- RT   Black Power
    Countries
    Ethnocentrism
    Internationalism
    Militarism
    National Identity
    Nazism
    Patriotism
    Regionalism
    Self Determination
    State Formation

Nationality/Nationalities (1963-1985)
- HN   DC 290450.
- Use   Cultural Groups

Natural

Nationalization
- DC   D549900
- HN   Formerly (1963-1985) DC 290455, Nationalize/Nationalized/Nationalization.
- BT   Expropriation
- RT   Industrial Enterprises
    Ownership
    Privatization
    Public Sector
    Public Sector Private Sector Relations
    State Power

Native American/Native Americans (1979-1985)
- HN   DC 290495.
- Use   American Indians

Native/Natives (1967-1985)
- HN   DC 290490.
- Use   Indigenous Populations

Nativism
- DC   D550200
- SN   Ideology or policy of favoring the native-born people of a country over immigrants in matters such as education, political eligibility, social status, and economic opportunity.
- HN   Formerly (1963-1985) part of DC 290500, Nativism/Nativistic.
- BT   Social Attitudes
- RT   Assimilation
    Cultural Conflict
    Discrimination
    Ethnic Relations
    Ethnicity
    Ethnocentrism
    Folk Culture
    Foreigners
    Immigrants
    Indigenous Populations
    Intergroup Relations
    Social Integration

Nativistic Movements
- DC   D550300
- SN   Movements advocating the perpetuation or reestablishment of native culture and a concomitant restriction or removal of foreign cultural elements.
- HN   Formerly (1963-1985) part of DC 290500, Nativism/Nativistic.
- BT   Social Movements
- RT   Colonialism
    Cultural Conflict
    Cultural Identity
    Ethnicity
    Ethnocentrism
    Folk Culture
    Foreigners
    Indigenous Populations

Natural Disasters
- DC   D550500
- HN   Added, 1986.
- UF   Drought/Droughts (1984-1985)
    Earthquake/Earthquakes (1983-1985)
    Flood/Floods (1984-1985)
    Hurricane/Hurricanes (1984-1985)
    Tornado (1978-1985)
- BT   Disasters
- RT   Civil Defense
    Disaster Relief
    Famine
    Hazards
    Reconstruction
    Scarcity
    Survival
    Weather

Natural

Natural Environment
- **DC** D550800
- **HN** Formerly (1963-1985) part of DC 290550, Nature/Natural/Naturalism/Naturalistic.
- **UF** Nature
  Wilderness
- **BT** Environment
- **RT** Animal Human Relations
  Conservation
  Earth (Planet)
  Ecology
  Environmental Protection
  Environmentalism
  Parks
  Pollution
  Preservation

Natural Resources
- **DC** D551100
- **HN** Formerly (1985) DC 290574.
- **BT** Resources
- **NT** Coal
  Land
  Mineral Resources
  Water Supply
- **RT** Agricultural Development
  Animals
  Conservation
  Earth (Planet)
  Ecology
  Energy Conservation
  Environmental Attitudes
  Food
  Forestry
  Fuels
  Geology
  Human Ecology
  Land Use
  Oceans
  Parks
  Petroleum
  Plants (Botanical)
  Pollution
  Raw Materials
  Soil Conservation

Natural Rights
- **Use** Human Rights

Natural Sciences
- **DC** D551400
- **HN** Added, 1986.
- **NT** Biological Sciences
  Physical Sciences
- **RT** Academic Disciplines
  Science
  Scientists

Naturalism
- **DC** D551700
- **SN** In theology and philosophy, the doctrine that natural laws and causes provide an explanation for all phenomena and are the basis for all religious and ethical truths; in art and literature, a movement characterized by the refusal to idealize experience and a scrupulous care for authenticity and accuracy of detail.
- **HN** Formerly (1963-1985) part of DC 290550, Nature/Natural/Naturalism/Naturalistic.
- **BT** Philosophical Doctrines
- **RT** Art
  Artistic Styles
  Literature
  Philosophy
  Positivism
  Realism (Philosophy)
  Verstehen

Nature
- **Use** Natural Environment

Navy (1965-1985)
- **HN** DC 290600.
- **Use** Armed Forces

Nazism
- **DC** D552000
- **HN** Formerly (1963-1985) DC 290800, Nazi/Nazis/Nazism.
- **BT** Fascism
- **RT** Anti-Semitism
  Dictatorship
  Eugenics
  Genocide
  Holocaust
  Nationalism

Near East (1963-1985)
- **HN** DC 290900.
- **Use** Middle East

Nebraska
- **DC** D552300
- **HN** Formerly (1964-1985) DC 290960, Nebraska/Nebraskan/Nebraskans.
- **BT** Midwestern States
  United States of America

Necessity (1971-1985)
- **HN** DC 290970.
- **Use** Needs

Needs
- **DC** D552600
- **SN** A context-dependent term; select a more specific entry or coordinate with other terms.
- **HN** Formerly (1963-1985) DC 291000, Need/Needs.
- **UF** Necessity (1971-1985)
- **NT** Affiliation Need
  Complementary Needs
- **RT** Assistance
  Constraints
  Delay of Gratification
  Deprivation
  Goals
  Human Nature
  Human Services
  Humanization
  Love
  Motivation
  Needs Assessment
  Nurturance
  Priorities
  Relevance
  Resources
  Satisfaction
  Security
  Social Acceptance
  Well Being

Needs Assessment
- **DC** D552900
- **SN** Identification of community or group needs, through household surveys or case studies.
- **HN** Added, 1986.
- **BT** Evaluation
- **RT** Needs
  Planning
  Priorities

Neighborhoods

Negative/Negativity (1972-1985)
- **HN** DC 291315, deleted 1986.

Negotiated Pleas
- **Use** Plea Bargaining

Negotiation
- **DC** D553200
- **HN** Formerly (1963-1985) DC 291400, Negotiation/Negotiations.
- **UF** Bargain/Bargains/Bargaining (1963-1985)
  Compromise/Compromises (1964-1985)
  Concession/Concessions (1970-1985)
- **BT** Interaction
- **NT** Collective Bargaining
  Plea Bargaining
- **RT** Arbitration
  Conflict Resolution
  Diplomacy
  Discussion
  Mediation
  Ombudsmen
  Persuasion
  Social Behavior
  Symbolic Interactionism

Negritude (1967-1985)
- **HN** DC 291800, deleted 1986.

Negro/Negroes (1963-1985)
- **HN** DC 292000.
- **Use** Blacks

Nehru, Jawaharlal
- **DC** D553500
- **SN** Born 14 November 1889 - died 27 May 1964.
- **HN** Formerly (1966-1985) DC 292300.

Neighborhood Change
- **DC** D553800
- **HN** Added, 1986.
- **UF** Neighborhood Decline
  Neighborhood Redevelopment
- **BT** Community Change
- **RT** City Planning
  Community Development
  Neighborhoods
  Urban Development

Neighborhood Decline
- **Use** Neighborhood Change

Neighborhood Organizations
- **Use** Community Organizations

Neighborhood Redevelopment
- **Use** Neighborhood Change

Neighborhood Satisfaction
- **Use** Community Satisfaction

Neighborhood Segregation
- **Use** Residential Segregation

Neighborhoods
- **DC** D554100
- **HN** Formerly (1963-1985) DC 292525, Neighborhood/Neighborhoods.
- **UF** Urban Neighborhoods
- **BT** Communities
- **NT** Ethnic Neighborhoods
- **RT** Cities
  Environment
  Housing
  Neighborhood Change
  Neighbors

Neighborhoods (cont'd)
- **RT** Residence
  Residential Mobility
  Residents
  Urban Areas

Neighbors
- **DC** D554400
- **HN** Formerly (1965-1985) DC 292500, Neighbors/Neighborliness/Neighboring.
- **RT** Communities
  Neighborhoods
  Residents
  Social Contact
  Social Groups

Neolithic (1964-1985)
- **HN** DC 292665.
- **Use** Prehistory

Neologism/Neologisms (1970-1985)
- **HN** DC 292690.
- **Use** Words

Neonate/Neonatal (1963-1985)
- **HN** DC 292730.
- **Use** Infants

Neoplasms
- **Use** Cancer

Nepal
- **DC** D554700
- **HN** Formerly (1963-1985) DC 292760, Nepal/Nepalese.
- **BT** Himalayan States
  South Asia

Nepali (Language)
- **Use** Indic Languages

Nepotism (1967-1985)
- **HN** DC 292850.
- **Use** Hiring Practices

Nervous System (1963-1985)
- **HN** DC 294000, deleted 1986.

Netherlands
- **DC** D555000
- **HN** Formerly (1963-1985) DC 297550.
- **UF** Holland (1963-1985)
- **BT** Western Europe
- **NT** Amsterdam, Netherlands

Netherlands Antilles
- **DC** D555300
- **HN** Added, 1986.
- **BT** Caribbean
- **NT** Aruba
  Curacao

Network Analysis
- **DC** D555600
- **HN** Added, 1986.
- **BT** Analysis
- **RT** Graph Theory
  Networks
  Social Networks
  Sociometric Analysis

Networks
- **DC** D555900
- **SN** A context-dependent term; select a more specific entry or coordinate with other terms. In contexts where Networks is closely related to the narrower term Social Networks, select the latter.
- **HN** Formerly (1963-1985) DC 297620, Network/Networks.

Networks (cont'd)
- **BT** Relations
- **NT** Interorganizational Networks
  Social Networks
- **RT** Coordination
  Diffusion
  Network Analysis
  Organizational Structure

Neurology
- **DC** D556200
- **HN** Formerly (1972-1985) DC 297700, Neurology/Neurological.
- **UF** Neurophysiology/Neurophysiological (1963-1985)
- **BT** Medicine
- **RT** Alzheimer's Disease
  Brain
  Cerebral Palsy
  Epilepsy
  Learning Disabilities
  Mental Health
  Psychiatry

Neurophysiology/Neurophysiological (1963-1985)
- **HN** DC 298200.
- **Use** Neurology

Neuropsychiatry/Neuropsychiatric (1967-1985)
- **HN** DC 298300.
- **Use** Psychiatry

Neuropsychology/Neuropsychological (1972-1985)
- **HN** DC 298303.
- **Use** Psychology

Neurosis
- **DC** D556500
- **HN** Formerly (1963-1985) DC 298400, Neurosis/Neuroses.
- **UF** Neurotic/Neurotics (1963-1985)
  Psychoneurotic/Psychoneurotics (1984-1985)
- **RT** Depression (Psychology)
  Emotionally Disturbed
  Mental Illness
  Narcissism
  Neuroticism
  Phobias

Neurotic/Neurotics (1963-1985)
- **HN** DC 298460.
- **Use** Neurosis

Neuroticism
- **DC** D556800
- **HN** Formerly (1967-1985) DC 298464.
- **RT** Neurosis
  Personality Traits

Neutralism
- **DC** D557100
- **SN** Political policy of nonalignment with conflicting parties or alliances.
- **HN** Formerly (1964-1985) part of DC 298475, Neutralism/Neutrality/Neutralist/Neutralists.
- **UF** Nonalignment
- **BT** Political Ideologies
- **RT** Foreign Policy
  Pacifism

Neutralization Theory
- **DC** D557400
- **SN** The view that delinquents often use linguistic constructions to neutralize (ie, excuse or rationalize) the guilt resulting from their delinquent behavior (eg, denial of responsibility or injury, blaming the victim or the accusers).
- **HN** Formerly (1964-1985) part of DC 298475, Neutralism/Neutrality/Neutralist/Neutralists.
- **RT** Crime
  Delinquency

Nevada
- **DC** D557700
- **HN** Formerly (1972-1985) DC 298482.
- **BT** United States of America
  Western States

New Brunswick
- **DC** D558000
- **HN** Added, 1986.
- **BT** Canada

New Caledonia
- **DC** D558300
- **HN** Formerly (1971-1985) DC 298514, New Caledonia/New Caledonian/New Caledonians.
- **BT** Melanesia

New Deal
- **DC** D558600
- **HN** Formerly (1964-1985) DC 298550.
- **RT** Liberalism
  Social Reform
  Social Security

New England (1963-1985)
- **HN** DC 298570.
- **Use** Northern States

New Guinea/New Guinean/New Guineans (1963-1985)
- **HN** DC 298585, deleted 1986. See now Indonesia or Papua New Guinea.

New Hampshire
- **DC** D559200
- **HN** Formerly (1969-1985) DC 298595.
- **BT** Northern States
  United States of America

New Haven, Conn. (1963-1985)
- **HN** DC 298600, deleted 1986.

New Jersey
- **DC** D559500
- **HN** Formerly (1963-1985) DC 298625.
- **BT** Northern States
  United States of America

New Left (1970-1985)
- **HN** DC 298630.
- **Use** Left Wing Politics

New Mexico
- **DC** D559800
- **HN** Formerly (1963-1985) DC 298650, New Mexico/New Mexican/New Mexicans.
- **BT** United States of America
  Western States

New

New Middle Class
- **DC** D560100
- **SN** Salaried employees in clerical, administrative, sales, and technical occupations who have relatively low social status and little social power. Sometimes synonymous with White Collar Workers. Contrasted with Blue Collar Workers, Entrepreneurs, Managers, and Professional Workers.
- **HN** Added, 1986.
- **BT** Middle Class
- **RT** White Collar Workers

New Orleans, Louisiana
- **DC** D560400
- **HN** Formerly (1963-1985) DC 298660, New Orleans, La.
- **BT** Louisiana

New Religions
- **Use** Cults

New Right (1982-1985)
- **HN** DC 298675.
- **Use** Right Wing Politics

New South Wales, Australia (1965-1985)
- **HN** DC 298680, deleted 1986.

New Testament
- **Use** Bible

New Towns
- **DC** D560700
- **SN** Comprehensively planned, self-sufficient urban communities that provide extensive social facilities and often absorb residents from nearby, overcrowded metropolises.
- **HN** Formerly (1971-1985) DC 298810, New Town/New Towns.
- **BT** Towns
- **RT** Community Development
  Local Planning
  Retirement Communities
  Suburbs

New World (1963-1985)
- **HN** DC 298820, deleted 1986. See now North America, Latin America, South America, Central America, or United States of America.

New York
- **DC** D561000
- **HN** Formerly (1963-1985) DC 298825.
- **BT** Northern States
  United States of America
- **NT** Buffalo, New York
  New York City, New York

New York City, New York
- **DC** D561300
- **HN** Formerly (1963-1985) DC 298860, New York City.
- **UF** Brooklyn, N.Y. (1969-1985)
  Harlem (1965-1985)
- **BT** New York

New York Herald Tribune (1985)
- **HN** DC 298900.
- **Use** Newspapers

New York Times (1964-1985)
- **HN** DC 298890.
- **Use** Newspapers

New Zealand
- **DC** D561600
- **HN** Formerly (1963-1985) DC 298910, New Zealand/New Zealander/New Zealanders.
- **BT** Australasia

Newborn/Newborns (1964-1985)
- **HN** DC 298500.
- **Use** Infants

Newcomb, Theodore Mead
- **DC** D561900
- **SN** Born 24 July 1903 - died 28 December 1984.
- **HN** Formerly (1965-1985) DC 298530, Newcomb, Theodore.

Newcomers
- **DC** D562200
- **HN** Formerly (1963-1985) DC 298540, Newcomer/Newcomers.
- **RT** Assimilation
  Communities
  Immigrants
  Strangers

Newfoundland
- **DC** D562500
- **HN** Formerly (1964-1985) DC 298580.
- **BT** Canada

Newlywed/Newlyweds (1969-1985)
- **HN** DC 298632.
- **Use** Marriage

News Coverage
- **DC** D562800
- **HN** Added, 1986. Formerly (1964-1985) part of DC 118700, Coverage.
- **UF** Coverage (News)
  Media Coverage
  Newsworthiness (1969-1985)
  Press Coverage
  Television Coverage
- **RT** Journalism
  Mass Media
  Mass Media Violence
  News Media

News Media
- **DC** D563100
- **HN** Formerly (1963-1985) DC 298700, News.
- **UF** Press, The (1963-1985)
- **BT** Mass Media
- **NT** Editorials
  Newspapers
- **RT** Editors
  Journalism
  Journalists
  Mass Media Effects
  Mass Media Violence
  News Coverage
  Radio
  Reports
  Television

Newsmen (1965-1985)
- **HN** DC 298725.
- **Use** Journalists

Newspaper Articles
- **Use** Articles

Newspapers
- **DC** D563400
- **HN** Formerly (1963-1985) DC 298750, Newspaper/Newspapers.
- **UF** Dailies (Newspapers)

Nihilism

Newspapers (cont'd)
- **UF** New York Herald Tribune (1985)
  New York Times (1964-1985)
  Weeklies (Newspapers)
- **BT** News Media
  Publications
- **RT** Comics (Publications)
  Editorials
  Journalism
  Journalists
  Mass Media Effects
  Periodicals
  Popular Culture
  Readership

Newsworthiness (1969-1985)
- **HN** DC 298760.
- **Use** News Coverage

Newswriters (1964-1985)
- **HN** DC 298800.
- **Use** Journalists

Nicaragua
- **DC** D563700
- **HN** Formerly (1971-1985) DC 298917, Nicaragua/Nicaraguans.
- **BT** Central America
- **NT** Managua, Nicaragua

Nicknames
- **Use** Naming Practices

Niebuhr, Reinhold H.
- **DC** D564000
- **SN** Born 21 June 1892 - died 1 June 1971.
- **HN** Formerly (1963-1985) DC 298920, Niebuhr, R.

Nietzsche, Friedrich Wilhelm
- **DC** D564300
- **SN** Born 15 October 1844 - died 25 August 1900.
- **HN** Formerly (1963-1985) DC 298923, Nietzsche, Friedrich.

Niger
- **DC** D564600
- **HN** Formerly (1968-1985) DC 298924, Niger, Republic of.
- **BT** Sub Saharan Africa

Nigeria
- **DC** D564900
- **HN** Formerly (1963-1985) DC 298925, Nigeria/Nigerian/Nigerians.
- **BT** Sub Saharan Africa
- **NT** Lagos, Nigeria

Nightclub (1965-1985)
- **HN** DC 298930.
- **Use** Eating And Drinking Establishments

Nihilism
- **DC** D565000
- **SN** An extreme form of skepticism that denies the objective reality of all values, beliefs, and truths. Also, the political doctrine that conditions are bad enough to make violent destruction of social structures a good in itself, without a constructive, alternative program in mind.
- **HN** Formerly (1969-1985) DC 298935, Nihilism/Nihilist/Nihilistic.
- **BT** Epistemological Doctrines
  Philosophical Doctrines
- **RT** Anarchism
  Epistemology

Nineteenth

Nihilism (cont'd)
- RT Ethics
- Metaphysics
- Political Ideologies
- Terrorism

Nineteenth Century
- DC D565200
- HN Formerly (1985) DC 298945.
- BT Time Periods
- RT Victorian Period

Nisbet, Robert Alexander
- DC D565500
- SN Born 30 September 1913 - .
- HN Formerly (1964-1985) DC 298950, Nisbet, Robert F.

Nixon, Richard Milhous
- DC D565800
- SN Born 9 January 1913 - .
- HN Formerly (1964-1985) DC 298965, Nixon, Richard.

Nobel Prize (1963-1985)
- HN DC 298975.
- Use Awards

Nobility (1963-1985)
- HN DC 298985.
- Use Aristocracy

Noise
- DC D566100
- HN Formerly (1963-1985) DC 299000.
- UF Volume (Sound)
- RT Communication
- Ecology
- Environment
- Pollution
- Silence

Nomadic Societies
- DC D566400
- HN Formerly (1963-1985) DC 299040, Nomad/Nomads/Nomadic.
- UF Nomadism (1963-1985)
- BT Traditional Societies
- RT Arab Cultural Groups
- Arid Zones
- Gypsies
- Hunting And Gathering Societies
- Migration
- Pastoral Societies
- Prehistory

Nomadism (1963-1985)
- HN DC 299055.
- Use Nomadic Societies

Nomenclature (1964-1985)
- HN DC 299065.
- Use Terminology

Nominal Measurement
- DC D566500
- HN Formerly (1965-1985) DC 299080, Nominal.
- UF Nominal Scales
- BT Measurement
- RT Interval Measurement
- Ordinal Measurement
- Scales

Nominal Scales
- Use Nominal Measurement

Nominalism
- DC D566550
- SN The doctrine that words denoting concepts, abstractions, and universals (eg, society, goodness) are conventional names for classifications of objects, and that only individual objects and events are real.
- HN Formerly (1964-1985) DC 299090.
- BT Philosophical Doctrines
- RT Concepts
- Empiricism
- Epistemological Doctrines
- Idealism
- Materialism
- Metaphysics
- Positivism
- Realism (Philosophy)

Nomothesis/Nomothetic (1963-1985)
- HN DC 299110, deleted 1986.

Nonalignment
- Use Neutralism

Nonbook Materials
- Use Audiovisual Media

Nonconformity
- Use Conformity

Nonindustrial Societies
- Use Traditional Societies

Nonmetropolitan Areas
- DC D566700
- HN Formerly (1963-1985) DC 299280, Nonmetropolitan.
- RT Geographic Regions
- Metropolitan Areas
- Rural Areas

Nonpartisan/Nonpartisanship (1972-1985)
- HN DC 299300.
- Use Partisanship

Nonprint Media
- Use Audiovisual Media

Nonprofit Organizations
- DC D566800
- HN Added, 1989.
- BT Organizations (Social)
- RT Agencies
- Associations
- Charities
- Churches
- Foundations
- Informal Sector
- Social Interest
- Volunteers

Nonpublic Schools
- Use Private Schools

Nonresponse (Research)
- Use Research Responses

Nontraditional Approaches
- Use Alternative Approaches

Nontraditional Careers
- Use Nontraditional Occupations

Nontraditional Occupations
- DC D567000
- HN Formerly (1984-1985) DC 299340, Nontraditional.
- UF Nontraditional Careers
- BT Occupations
- RT Employment Discrimination
- Job Characteristics

Norms

Nontraditional Occupations (cont'd)
- RT Occupational Roles
- Occupational Segregation
- Professional Women
- Sex Stereotypes
- Sexual Division of Labor
- Working Women

Nonverbal Behavior
- Use Nonverbal Communication

Nonverbal Communication
- DC D567300
- SN Conveyance of meaning through nonverbal behavior, eg, body movement, facial expression, spatial relationships, etc.
- HN Formerly (1982-1985) part of DC 299350, Nonverbal.
- UF Body Language
- Communication (Nonverbal)
- Facial Expression/Facial Expressions (1965-1985)
- Gesture/Gestures/Gestural (1963-1985)
- Nonverbal Behavior
- Smiling (1965-1985)
- BT Communication
- NT Eye Contact
- RT Clothing
- Drum Languages
- Graffiti
- Interpersonal Communication
- Manual Communication
- Meaning
- Personal Space
- Self Expression
- Signs
- Silence
- Symbolic Interactionism
- Verbal Communication

Nonviolence
- DC D567600
- HN Formerly (1969-1985) DC 299360, Nonviolent/Nonviolence.
- RT Civil Disobedience
- Conscientious Objectors
- Pacifism
- Violence

Non-Western (1963-1985)
- HN DC 299370, deleted 1986.

Nonwhite/Nonwhites (1969-1985)
- HN DC 299375, deleted 1986. See now Blacks or Minority Groups.

Nordic Countries (1964-1985)
- HN DC 299455.
- Use Scandinavia

Normal/Normality (1963-1985)
- HN DC 299575, deleted 1986.

Normative (1963-1985)
- HN DC 299580.
- Use Norms

Normless/Normlessness (1971-1985)
- HN DC 299600.
- Use Anomie

Norms
- DC D567900
- SN Rules that govern social activities and define social roles, role relations, and standards of appropriate conduct.

North

Norms (cont'd)
- HN Formerly (1963-1985) DC 299500, Norm/Norms.
- UF Manners (1965-1985)
  Mores (1963-1985)
  Normative (1963-1985)
  Social Norms (1985)
- NT Group Norms
  Taboos
- RT Action
  Behavior
  Beliefs
  Conformity
  Countercultures
  Cultural Universals
  Cultural Values
  Customs
  Ethology
  Fashions
  Ideologies
  Internalization
  Law
  Praxis
  Reference Groups
  Roles
  Sanctions
  Social Behavior
  Social Control
  Social Disorganization
  Social Institutions
  Social Values
  Standards
  Traditions
  Uniformity
  Utilitarianism

North Africa
- DC D568200
- HN Formerly (1963-1985) DC 299607.
- BT Africa
- NT Algeria
  Egypt
  Libya
  Morocco
  Sudan
  Tunisia
- RT Arab Countries
  Canary Islands
  Madeira
  Maghreb
  Mediterranean Countries
  Sub Saharan Africa

North African Cultural Groups
- DC D568300
- HN Added, 1989.
- BT African Cultural Groups
- RT Arab Cultural Groups
  Southern African Cultural Groups

North America
- DC D568500
- HN Formerly (1963-1985) DC 299613.
- NT Bermuda
  Canada
  Greenland
  Mexico
  United States of America
- RT Latin America
  North American Cultural Groups

North American Cultural Groups
- DC D568800
- HN Added, 1986. Prior to 1986, concepts representing specific North American cultural groups, eg, Canadians, were often indexed under terms representing the geographic place name, eg, Canada/Canadian/Canadians.

North American Cultural Groups (cont'd)
- BT Cultural Groups
- NT American Indians
  Eskimos
  Hispanic Americans
- RT Anglo Americans
  Caribbean Cultural Groups
  Latin American Cultural Groups
  North America

North American Indian Languages
- Use Amerindian Languages

North And South
- DC D569100
- HN Added, 1986.
- RT Geographic Regions
  Midwestern States
  Northern States
  Regional Differences
  Southern States

North Atlantic Ocean
- DC D569400
- HN Added, 1986. Prior to 1986 use Atlantic (DC 043565).
- BT Atlantic Ocean
- RT Azores
  Bermuda
  Canary Islands
  Cape Verde Islands
  Iceland
  Madeira
  South Atlantic Ocean

North Atlantic Treaty Organization/ NATO (1967-1985)
- HN DC 299618.
- Use International Alliances

North Carolina
- DC D569700
- HN Formerly (1964-1985) DC 299628.
- BT Southern States
  United States of America

North Dakota
- DC D570000
- HN Formerly (1971-1985) DC 299634.
- BT Midwestern States
  United States of America

North Korea
- DC D570300
- HN Added, 1986. Prior to 1986 use Korea/Korean/Koreans (DC 248200).
- BT Far East

North Pacific Ocean
- DC D570600
- HN Formerly (1969-1985) DC 299670, North Pacific.
- BT Pacific Ocean
- RT South Pacific Ocean

North Vietnam
- Use Vietnam

North/Northern/Northerner/ Northerners (1975-1985)
- HN DC 299615, deleted 1986.

Northern Ireland
- DC D570900
- HN Formerly (1982-1985) DC 299644.
- UF Ireland (Northern)
  Ulster
- BT United Kingdom
  Western Europe

Nuclear

Northern Rhodesia
- Use Zambia

Northern States
- DC D571000
- HN Formerly (1975-1985) part of DC 299615, North/Northern/Northerner/Northerners.
- UF New England (1963-1985)
- BT States (Political Subdivisions)
- NT Connecticut
  Delaware
  Maine
  Maryland
  Massachusetts
  New Hampshire
  New Jersey
  New York
  Pennsylvania
  Rhode Island
  Vermont
- RT North And South
  United States of America

Northwest Territories
- DC D571200
- HN Added, 1986.
- BT Canada
- RT Arctic Regions

Norway
- DC D571800
- HN Formerly (1963-1985) DC 299700, Norway/Norwegian/Norwegians.
- BT Scandinavia
  Western Europe
- NT Oslo, Norway

Norwegian (Language)
- Use Germanic Languages

Notation (1982-1985)
- HN DC 299735.
- Use Coding

Nova Scotia
- DC D572100
- HN Formerly (1966-1985) DC 299760, Nova Scotia, Canada.
- BT Canada

Novellas
- Use Novels

Novels
- DC D572400
- HN Formerly (1963-1985) DC 299775, Novel/Novels/Novelist/Novelists.
- UF Novellas
- BT Fiction
- RT Books

Nuclear (1963-1985)
- HN DC 299865, deleted 1986. See now specific "Nuclear" terms.

Nuclear Disarmament
- Use Disarmament

Nuclear Energy
- DC D572700
- HN Formerly (1985) DC 299869, Nuclear Energy/Nuclear Power.
- UF Atomic Power
  Nuclear Power
  Thermonuclear Energy
- BT Energy
- RT Antinuclear Movements
  Energy Policy
  Nuclear Reactors

Nuclear

Nuclear Energy (cont'd)
- RT Nuclear War
- Nuclear Weapons
- Physical Sciences
- Physics
- Radiation

Nuclear Energy Agency (1967-1985)
- HN DC 299870, deleted 1986.

Nuclear Family
- DC D573000
- HN Formerly (1985) DC 171675, Family, Nuclear.
- UF Conjugal Family
- BT Family
- RT Family Size
- Family Structure
- Kinship
- Parent Child Relations

Nuclear Freeze Movement
- Use Antinuclear Movements

Nuclear Power
- Use Nuclear Energy

Nuclear Power Plants
- Use Nuclear Reactors

Nuclear Reactors
- DC D573300
- HN Formerly (1985) DC 299885.
- UF Nuclear Power Plants
- BT Facilities
- RT Electricity
- Machinery
- Nuclear Energy

Nuclear War
- DC D573600
- HN Formerly (1985) DC 299890, Nuclear War/Nuclear Warfare.
- UF Atomic War
- BT War
- RT Antinuclear Movements
- Armaments
- Disarmament
- Nuclear Energy
- Nuclear Weapons

Nuclear Weapons
- DC D573900
- HN Formerly (1985) DC 299895, Nuclear Weapons/Nuclear Weaponry.
- UF Atomic Weapons
- BT Weapons
- RT Antinuclear Movements
- Deterrence
- Disarmament
- Nuclear Energy
- Nuclear War

Nudity
- DC D574200
- HN Formerly (1966-1985) DC 300000, Nudism/Nudist/Nudity.
- RT Cultural Values
- Human Body

Number/Numbers (1963-1985)
- HN DC 300160, deleted 1986.

Nuns
- DC D574500
- HN Formerly (1964-1985) DC 300170, Nun/Nuns.
- UF Sisters (Clergy)
- BT Clergy
- RT Convents
- Monasticism
- Religious Orders

Nuptiality
- DC D574800
- SN Frequency of marriages within a given population.
- HN Formerly (1963-1985) DC 300200.
- UF Marriage Rates
- BT Rates
- RT Demography
- Fertility
- Marriage

Nuremberg Tribunal (1976-1985)
- HN DC 300300.
- Use World War II

Nurse Patient Relationship
- Use Practitioner Patient Relationship

Nursery School Children
- Use Preschool Children

Nursery School Education
- Use Preschool Education

Nursery/Nurseries (1982-1985)
- HN DC 301030, deleted 1986.

Nurses
- DC D575100
- HN Formerly (1963-1985) DC 301000, Nurse/Nurses/Nursing.
- RT Health Professions
- Midwifery
- Physicians
- Practitioner Patient Relationship

Nursing Homes
- DC D575400
- HN Formerly (1984-1985) DC 301115, Nursing Home/Nursing Homes.
- BT Residential Institutions
- RT Health Care
- Hospitals

Nursing Technology
- Use Medical Technology

Nurturance
- DC D575700
- HN Formerly (1963-1985) DC 301200, Nurture/Nurturance.
- RT Childrearing Practices
- Family Relations
- Needs

Nutrition
- DC D576000
- HN Formerly (1963-1985) DC 301400, Nutrition/Nutritional.
- NT Malnutrition
- RT Diet
- Feeding Practices
- Food
- Food Preparation
- Health
- Hunger

Nutritional Deficiencies
- Use Malnutrition

Nyasaland, Africa (1963-1985)
- HN DC 301500.
- Use Malawi

Nymphomania/Nymphomaniac/Nymphomaniacs (1965-1985)
- HN DC 301600.
- Use Sexual Deviation

Obligation

Oath/Oaths (1969-1985)
- HN DC 301869, deleted 1986.

Obedience
- DC D576300
- HN Formerly (1965-1985) DC 301910.
- UF Disobedience
- BT Social Behavior
- RT Authoritarianism (Psychology)
- Authority
- Behavior Problems
- Coercion
- Compliance
- Passiveness
- Superior Subordinate Relationship

Obesity
- DC D576600
- HN Formerly (1964-1985) DC 302000.
- RT Body Weight
- Diet
- Diseases
- Feeding Practices
- Health

Obituaries
- DC D576900
- HN Formerly (1963-1985) DC 302400, Obituary/Obituaries.
- UF Death Notices
- BT Articles
- RT Death
- Death Rituals

Object/Objects (1963-1985)
- HN DC 302415, deleted 1986. See now Goals, Inanimate Objects, or Objectivity.

Objectives
- Use Goals

Objectivity
- DC D577200
- HN Formerly (1963-1985) DC 302425, Objective/Objectives/Objectivity/Objectivism.
- UF Distortion/Distortions (1968-1985)
- NT Value Neutrality
- RT Cultural Relativism
- Dogmatism
- Empirical Methods
- Methodology (Philosophical)
- Professional Ethics
- Rational Choice
- Rationality
- Scholarship
- Scientific Method
- Subjectivity
- Truth
- Values

Objects (Things)
- Use Inanimate Objects

Obligation
- DC D577500
- HN Formerly (1965-1985) DC 302430, Obligation/Obligations.
- RT Commitment
- Conscience
- Morality
- Responsibility
- Rights

Obscenity

Obscenity
- DC D577800
- HN Formerly (1964-1985) DC 302475.
- UF Profane/Profanity (1963-1985)
- RT Language Usage
  Offenses
  Pornography

Observation
- DC D577900
- HN Formerly (1963-1985) DC 302500, Observation/Observations/Observational/Observability.
- UF Observer (1964-1985)
- BT Methodology (Data Collection)
- NT Participant Observation
- RT Data Collection
  Empiricism
  Evaluation
  Experiments
  Fieldwork
  Measurement
  Performance
  Research Methodology

Observer (1964-1985)
- HN DC 302550.
- Use Observation

Obsolescence
- DC D577950
- HN Formerly (1968-1985) DC 302660, Obsolete/Obsolescence.
- UF Technological Obsolescence
- RT Futures (of Society)
  Maintenance
  Preservation
  Technological Change
  Technological Progress
  Time

Obstacle/Obstacles (1967-1985)
- HN DC 302700.
- Use Problems

Obstetrics
- Use Gynecology

Occident And Orient
- Use East And West

Occident/Occidental (1966-1985)
- HN DC 302900, deleted 1986.

Occidental Civilization
- Use Western Civilization

Occultism
- DC D578100
- HN Formerly (1971-1985) DC 303800, Occult/Occultism.
- UF Paranormal Beliefs
- NT Cabala
- RT Astrology
  Beliefs
  Divination
  Magic
  Parapsychology
  Spiritualism
  Supernatural
  Voodooism
  Witchcraft

Occupancy (1969-1985)
- HN DC 303980, deleted 1986.

Occupation Education Relationship
- Use Education Work Relationship

Occupational Achievement
- DC D578400
- HN Added, 1986.
- UF Occupational Success
  Professional Achievement
- BT Achievement
- RT Careers
  Job Performance
  Life Plans
  Occupational Mobility
  Occupational Status
  Occupations
  Promotion (Occupational)

Occupational Aspiration
- DC D578700
- HN Added, 1986.
- UF Career Goals
- BT Aspiration
- RT Careers
  Education Work Relationship
  Occupational Choice
  Occupational Mobility
  Occupational Qualifications
  Occupations
  Work
  Work Orientations
  Work Values

Occupational Attainment
- Use Occupational Status

Occupational Choice
- DC D579000
- HN Formerly (1985) DC 304400.
- UF Career Choice
  Career Decisions
  Job Selection
  Occupational Choice
  Vocational Choice
  Work Choice
- BT Choices
- RT Careers
  Employment
  Guidance
  Job Application
  Occupational Aspiration
  Occupations
  Tracking (Education)

Occupational Classifications
- DC D579300
- HN Added, 1986.
- UF Job Classifications
- BT Classification
- RT Blue Collar Workers
  Employment Changes
  Job Characteristics
  Job Requirements
  Labor Force
  Occupational Qualifications
  Occupational Segregation
  Occupational Structure
  Occupations
  Professional Workers
  Professions
  White Collar Workers
  Work
  Work Skills

Occupational Diseases
- Use Occupational Safety And Health

Occupational

Occupational Mobility
- DC D579600
- SN The degree or frequency of change from one occupation to another.
- HN Added, 1986.
- UF Career Mobility
- BT Social Mobility
- RT Career Patterns
  Careers
  Employment Opportunities
  Family Work Relationship
  Intergenerational Mobility
  Job Change
  Life Plans
  Occupational Achievement
  Occupational Aspiration
  Occupational Status
  Occupations
  Promotion (Occupational)

Occupational Mobility (Intergenerational)
- Use Intergenerational Mobility

Occupational Promotion
- Use Promotion (Occupational)

Occupational Qualifications
- DC D579900
- HN Added, 1986.
- UF Employment Qualifications
  Job Qualifications
  Work Qualifications
- BT Qualifications
- RT Academic Degrees
  Certification
  Education Work Relationship
  Employability
  Employment Opportunities
  Job Application
  Job Characteristics
  Job Requirements
  Job Search
  Job Training
  Licenses
  Occupational Aspiration
  Occupational Classifications
  Occupational Status
  Occupations
  Unemployment
  Vocational Education
  Work Experience
  Work Skills

Occupational Roles
- DC D580200
- HN Added, 1986.
- UF Job Roles
  Professional Roles
  Work Roles
- BT Roles
- RT Employment
  Job Characteristics
  Job Satisfaction
  Nontraditional Occupations
  Occupational Status
  Occupations
  Role Ambiguity
  Role Models
  Sexual Division of Labor
  Tasks
  Workers
  Working Women

Occupational   Offenders

Occupational Safety And Health
- DC D580500
- HN Added, 1986.
- UF Industrial Safety
  Occupational Diseases
  Work Safety
- BT Health
  Safety
- RT Accidents
  Hazards
  Injuries
  Occupations
  Public Health
  Sanitation
  Work Environment
  Workers Compensation Insurance
  Workplaces

Occupational Satisfaction
- Use Job Satisfaction

Occupational Segregation
- DC D580800
- SN Prevalence of people with similar characteristics, ie, sex or race, in certain job categories.
- HN Added, 1986.
- UF Race Segregated Occupations
  Sex Segregated Occupations
- BT Segregation
- RT Affirmative Action
  Economic Structure
  Employment Discrimination
  Hiring Practices
  Income Inequality
  Labor Market Segmentation
  Nontraditional Occupations
  Occupational Classifications
  Occupational Structure
  Occupations
  Racial Segregation
  Sex Differences
  Sex Stereotypes
  Sexism
  Sexual Division of Labor
  Working Women

Occupational Status
- DC D581100
- SN The actual or perceived importance or rank of a particular job to a society or organization.
- HN Added, 1986.
- UF Job Status
  Occupational Attainment
  Prestige (Occupational)
  Professional Status
- BT Social Status
- RT Careers
  Education Work Relationship
  Job Requirements
  Job Satisfaction
  Occupational Achievement
  Occupational Mobility
  Occupational Qualifications
  Occupational Roles
  Occupational Structure
  Occupations
  Prestige
  Privilege
  Professional Workers
  Professions
  Work Skills
  Working Women

Occupational Stratification
- Use Occupational Structure

Occupational Stress
- DC D581400
- HN Added, 1986.
- UF Burnout (1983-1985)
  Job Stress
  Overwork (1970-1985)
- BT Stress
- RT Coping
  Family Work Relationship
  Job Characteristics
  Morale
  Occupations
  Psychological Stress
  Work Environment

Occupational Structure
- DC D581700
- SN The job or skill categories found in an industry, service, firm, or society.
- HN Added, 1986.
- UF Occupational Stratification
- BT Structure
- RT Business Society Relationship
  Economic Sectors
  Economic Structure
  Employment
  Employment Changes
  Industrialization
  Labor Force
  Labor Market Segmentation
  Occupational Classifications
  Occupational Segregation
  Occupational Status
  Occupations
  Situses
  Tasks
  Work
  Workers

Occupational Success
- Use Occupational Achievement

Occupational Training
- Use Job Training

Occupations
- DC D582000
- HN Formerly (1963-1985) DC 304000, Occupation/Occupations/Occupational.
- UF Vocation/Vocations (1963-1985)
- NT Nontraditional Occupations
  Professions
- RT Blue Collar Workers
  Careers
  Division of Labor
  Education Work Relationship
  Employment
  Human Resources
  Job Characteristics
  Labor
  Labor Force
  Occupational Achievement
  Occupational Aspiration
  Occupational Choice
  Occupational Classifications
  Occupational Mobility
  Occupational Qualifications
  Occupational Roles
  Occupational Safety And Health
  Occupational Segregation
  Occupational Status
  Occupational Stress
  Occupational Structure
  Professionalization
  Situses

Occupations (cont'd)
- RT Sociology of Work
  Specialists
  Specialization
  Vocational Education
  White Collar Workers
  Workers

Oceania
- DC D582300
- SN Islands of the central and south Pacific regions.
- HN Formerly (1974-1985) DC 305005.
- NT Melanesia
  Micronesia
  Polynesia
- RT Oceanic Cultural Groups

Oceanic Cultural Groups
- DC D582600
- HN Added, 1986. Prior to 1986, concepts representing specific Oceanic cultural groups, eg, Melanesians, were often indexed under terms representing the geographic place name, eg, Melanesia/Melanesian/Melanesians.
- UF Pacific Island Cultural Groups
- BT Cultural Groups
- RT Austronesian Languages
  Cargo Cults
  Mana
  Oceania

Oceans
- DC D582900
- HN Formerly (1969-1985) part of DC 305000, Ocean/Oceans/Oceanic.
- NT Atlantic Ocean
  Pacific Ocean
- RT Earth (Planet)
  Fishing
  Islands
  Natural Resources
  Shipping Industry
  Topography

Oedipal Complex
- DC D583200
- HN Formerly (1966-1985) DC 307000, Oedipus/Oedipal.
- UF Electra Complex
  Mother Complex
  Myths (Oedipal)
- RT Child Development
  Freudian Psychology
  Incest
  Mothers
  Psychoanalysis
  Sexual Deviation

Off the Job Training
- Use Job Training

Offender Victim Relations
- Use Victim Offender Relations

Offenders
- DC D583500
- HN Formerly (1963-1985) DC 308200, Offender/Offenders.
- UF Convict/Convicts (1964-1985)
  Criminals
- NT Career Criminals
  Female Offenders
  Juvenile Offenders
- RT Arrests
  Crime
  Criminal Justice

Offenses

Offenders (cont'd)
- RT Criminal Justice Policy
  - Criminal Proceedings
  - Defendants
  - Deterrence
  - Deviance
  - Deviant Behavior
  - Imprisonment
  - Insanity Defense
  - Offenses
  - Parole
  - Pretrial Release
  - Prisoners
  - Recidivism
  - Restitution (Corrections)
  - Sentencing
  - Victim Offender Relations

Offenses
- DC D583800
- HN Formerly (1963-1985) DC 308210, Offense/Offenses/Offensive.
- UF Blackmail/Blackmailing (1964-1985)
  - Bribery (1964-1985)
  - Crimes
- NT Arson
  - Assault
  - Burglary
  - Drug Trafficking
  - Drunk Driving
  - Fraud
  - Homicide
  - Larceny
  - Littering
  - Prostitution
  - Vandalism
- RT Abuse
  - Arrests
  - Assassination
  - Banditry
  - Cheating
  - Crime
  - Crime Rates
  - Decriminalization
  - Disorders
  - Gambling
  - Investigations (Law Enforcement)
  - Juvenile Delinquency
  - Law Enforcement
  - Lie Detection
  - Obscenity
  - Offenders
  - Rape
  - Robbery
  - Scandals
  - Sexual Harassment
  - Violence

Office (1971-1985)
- HN DC 308500, deleted 1986. See now Clerical Workers or Office Automation.

Office Automation
- DC D584100
- HN Added, 1986.
- BT Automation
- RT Clerical Workers
  - Microcomputers
  - Worker Machine Relationship

Office Workers
- Use Clerical Workers

Officer/Officers (1963-1985)
- HN DC 309000, deleted 1986. See now appropriate "Personnel" or "Officer" terms, eg, Correctional Personnel, Military Officers.

Officers (Military)
- Use Military Officers

Official/Officials (1963-1985)
- HN DC 309800, deleted 1986. See now Administrators or Public Officials.

Offspring (1969-1985)
- HN DC 309850, deleted 1986. See now Filial Responsibility, Parent Child Relations, or other appropriate "Children" terms.

Ohio
- DC D584400
- HN Formerly (1963-1985) DC 309880.
- BT Midwestern States
  - United States of America
- NT Cincinnati, Ohio
  - Cleveland, Ohio

Oil (1982-1985)
- HN DC 309887.
- Use Petroleum

Oil Industry
- Use Petroleum Industry

Okinawa, Japan (1965-1985)
- HN DC 309910, deleted 1986.

Oklahoma
- DC D584700
- HN Formerly (1969-1985) DC 309920.
- BT United States of America
  - Western States
- RT Ozark Mountains

Old Age (1963-1985)
- HN DC 310000.
- Use Aging

Old Order Amish
- Use Amish

Old Testament
- Use Bible

Older Adult (1984-1985)
- HN DC 310100.
- Use Elderly

Oligarchy
- DC D585000
- SN Government of a state or organization by a small group. The term often connotes corruption and lack of responsibility to the ruled majority. Compare with Elitism.
- HN Formerly (1963-1985) DC 310400, Oligarchy/Oligarchies/Oligarchic/Oligarchical.
- BT Political Systems
- RT Aristocracy
  - Elitism
  - Political Elites
  - Ruling Class
  - Technocracy

Oligopolies
- DC D585300
- SN Market conditions in which a small number of firms control a large proportion of production, with the potential for restricting price competition and otherwise limiting the market.
- HN Formerly (1966-1985) DC 310410, Oligopoly/Oligopolistic/Oligopolies.
- UF Duopoly (1963-1985)
- RT Business
  - Competition

Opera

Oligopolies (cont'd)
- RT Economic Elites
  - Economic Structure
  - Economic Systems
  - Industry
  - Monopolies
  - Monopoly Capitalism
  - Multinational Corporations
  - Prices

Olympic Games
- DC D585600
- HN Formerly (1967-1985) DC 310500.
- RT Athletes
  - International Cooperation
  - Sports

Oman
- DC D585900
- HN Added, 1986.
- BT Middle East

Ombudsmen
- DC D586200
- HN Formerly (1964-1985) DC 310615, Ombudsman.
- RT Negotiation
  - Public Officials

On the Job Training
- Use Job Training

One Parent Family
- Use Single Parent Family

Only Children
- DC D586500
- SN Children with no living siblings and the effects of that circumstance on later life.
- HN Formerly (1981-1985) DC 310675, Only Child.
- BT Children
- RT Birth Order
  - Family Size
  - Family Structure

Ontario
- DC D586800
- HN Formerly (1964-1985) DC 310700, Ontario, Canada.
- BT Canada
- NT Ottawa, Ontario
  - Toronto, Ontario

Ontology
- DC D587100
- SN Branch of metaphysics concerned with the nature and relations of existence.
- HN Formerly (1968-1985) DC 311025, Ontology/Ontological.
- BT Metaphysics
- RT Dialectics
  - Dualism
  - Holism
  - Materialism
  - Reality

OPEC (1983-1985)
- HN DC 311032.
- Use International Economic Organizations

Opera/Operatic (1973-1985)
- HN DC 311040.
- Use Theater Arts

Operant

Operant (1971-1985)
- HN DC 311045.
- Use Conditioning

Operational Definitions
- DC D587300
- SN Explanations of abstract concepts in terms of empirically observed and measured phenomena (eg, intelligence defined as an I.Q. score).
- HN Formerly (1963-1985) part of DC 311075, Operational/Operationalizing/Operationalization.
- UF Operationalization
- RT Classification
  Concepts
  Definitions
  Empirical Methods
  Formalization (Theoretical)
  Hypotheses
  Indexes (Measures)
  Measurement
  Research Design
  Research Methodology

Operationalization
- Use Operational Definitions

Operations (1963-1985)
- HN DC 311175, deleted 1986.

Operator/Operators/Operative/Operatives (1970-1985)
- HN DC 311500, deleted 1986. See now Industrial Workers or Farmers.

Opiates
- DC D587400
- HN Formerly (1968-1985) DC 311750, Opiate/Opiates.
- BT Narcotic Drugs
- NT Heroin

Opinion Leaders
- DC D587700
- HN Added, 1986.
- RT Leadership
  Opinions
  Power Elite
  Social Influence

Opinion Polls
- DC D588000
- HN Formerly (1963-1985) DC 340080, Poll/Polls.
- UF Gallup Poll (1963-1985)
  Polls (Opinion)
- BT Surveys
- RT Fieldwork
  Opinions
  Political Attitudes
  Public Opinion
  Public Opinion Research
  Questionnaires
  Voting Behavior

Opinion Scales
- Use Attitude Measures

Opinions
- DC D588300
- HN Formerly (1963-1985) DC 312000, Opinion/Opinions.
- BT Attitudes
- NT Public Opinion
- RT Attitude Measures
  Beliefs
  Dissent
  Editorials

Opinions (cont'd)
- RT Opinion Leaders
  Opinion Polls
  Perceptions
  Questionnaires
  Reputation

Opinions (Judicial)
- Use Judicial Decisions

Opportunities
- DC D588600
- HN Formerly (1963-1985) DC 312300, Opportunity/Opportunities.
- NT Educational Opportunities
  Employment Opportunities
- RT Access
  Affirmative Action
  Constraints
  Discrimination
  Education Work Relationship
  Entrepreneurship
  Equality
  Self Determination
  Social Closure

Opposite Sex Relations
- DC D588700
- HN Added, 1986.
- UF Female Male Relations
  Male Female Relations
- BT Interpersonal Relations
- RT Couples
  Females
  Interpersonal Attraction
  Males
  Marital Relations
  Peer Relations
  Sex Roles
  Sexual Harassment
  Sexual Inequality

Opposite/Opposites (1964-1985)
- HN DC 312315, deleted 1986.

Opposition/Oppositions (1964-1985)
- HN DC 312320.
- Use Resistance

Oppression
- DC D588900
- HN Formerly (1971-1985) DC 312325, Oppress/Oppressive/Oppression/Oppressors/Oppressed.
- UF Persecution
- RT Coercion
  Despotism
  Dictatorship
  Exploitation
  Human Rights
  Inequality
  Repression (Political)
  Slavery
  Totalitarianism

Optic/Optics/Optical (1963-1985)
- HN DC 312350, deleted 1986.

Optimism
- DC D589100
- HN Formerly (1972-1985) DC 312365, Optimism/Optimist/Optimists/Optimistic.
- UF Hopefulness
- RT Happiness
  Personality Traits
  Pessimism
  Social Attitudes
  Trust
  Worldview

Organic

Optometrists
- Use Optometry

Optometry
- DC D589200
- HN Formerly (1963-1985) DC 312390.
- UF Optometrists
- RT Health Professions
  Health Services
  Medicine
  Vision

Oral History
- DC D589500
- HN Added, 1986.
- BT History
- RT Ethnography
  Folklore
  Life History
  Recordings
  Verbal Accounts

Oral Medicine
- Use Dentistry

Oral/Orality (1963-1985)
- HN DC 312780, deleted 1986. See now Birth Control, Oral History, or Sexual Behavior.

Oratory
- Use Rhetoric

Order (Social)
- Use Social Order

Order/Orders/Ordered/Ordering (1963-1985)
- HN DC 312820, deleted 1986. See now Birth Order, Social Order, or Religious Orders.

Ordinal Measurement
- DC D589700
- HN Formerly (1963-1985) DC 312880, Ordinal/Ordinality.
- UF Rank Order Measurement
- BT Measurement
- RT Interval Measurement
  Nominal Measurement
  Ranking
  Scales

Oregon
- DC D589800
- HN Formerly (1963-1985) DC 312900.
- BT United States of America
  Western States
- NT Portland, Oregon

Organ Transplantation
- DC D590100
- HN Added, 1986.
- UF Kidney Transplantation
  Transplant/Transplants/Transplanted (1972-1985)
- BT Surgery

Organ/Organs/Organism/Organisms (1964-1985)
- HN DC 312950, deleted 1986. See now Organ Transplantation or Sociobiology.

Organic Chemistry
- Use Chemistry

Organicism

Organicism
- DC D590250
- SN The concept that society is structurally and developmentally analogous to a biological organism.
- HN Formerly (1964-1985) DC 312960, Organic/Organist.
- BT Social Theories
- RT Epistemological Doctrines

Organization Directors
- Use Directors

Organization for Economic Coop & Development (1984-1985)
- HN DC 313175. Abbreviated here due to character restrictions. Formerly used in indexing under its full name Organization for Economic Cooperation & Development (OECD).
- Use International Economic Organizations

Organization Size
- DC D590400
- HN Formerly (1972-1985) DC 425400, Size, Organizational.
- BT Size
- RT Complex Organizations
  Group Size
  Organizations (Social)
  Small Businesses

Organization, Social (1964-1985)
- HN DC 313600.
- Use Social Structure

Organization (Structure)
- Use Structure

Organization Theory
- DC D590700
- HN Added, 1986.
- UF Contingency Theory
  Organizational Theory
- BT Theories
- RT Organizational Research
  Organizational Sociology
  Organizational Structure
  Organizations (Social)

Organizational Behavior
- DC D591000
- HN Added, 1986.
- BT Behavior
- RT Group Dynamics
  Management
  Organizational Culture
  Organizational Effectiveness
  Organizations (Social)
  Social Behavior

Organizational Change
- DC D591300
- HN Added, 1986.
- UF Reorganization (1964-1985)
- BT Change
- RT Centralization
  Change Agents
  Cooptation
  Decentralization
  Organizational Development
  Organizational Dissolution
  Organizational Structure
  Organizations (Social)

Organizational Climate
- Use Work Environment

Organizational Commitment
- DC D591600
- HN Added, 1986.
- BT Commitment
- RT Group Identity
  Membership
  Organizations (Social)
  Work Attitudes

Organizational Culture
- DC D591900
- HN Added, 1986.
- BT Culture
- RT Complex Organizations
  Organizational Behavior
  Organizations (Social)

Organizational Death
- Use Organizational Dissolution

Organizational Decline
- Use Organizational Dissolution

Organizational Development
- DC D592200
- SN The use of behavioral, management, or other methods in an organization to incorporate the growth needs of individual members into the objectives of the organization. See also Organizations (Social) and Social Processes.
- HN Added, 1986.
- BT Development
- RT Developmental Stages
  Job Satisfaction
  Management
  Morale
  Organizational Change
  Organizational Dissolution
  Organizations (Social)
  Participative Decision Making
  Work Orientations

Organizational Dissolution
- DC D592300
- SN Process in which a previously viable social organization or business deteriorates and ceases to function.
- HN Added, 1989.
- UF Corporate Dissolution
  Organizational Death
  Organizational Decline
- RT Bankruptcy
  Entropy
  Organizational Change
  Organizational Development
  Organizational Power
  Organizations (Social)
  Plant Closure
  Social Cohesion
  Social Conflict
  Social Disorganization

Organizational Effectiveness
- DC D592500
- SN Degree to which an organization satisfactorily accomplishes its goals or purposes.
- HN Added, 1986.
- UF Organizational Performance
- BT Effectiveness
- RT Efficiency
  Industrial Management
  Labor Productivity
  Management

Organizations

Organizational Effectiveness (cont'd)
- RT Management Styles
  Motivation
  Organizational Behavior
  Organizations (Social)
  Success

Organizational Performance
- Use Organizational Effectiveness

Organizational Power
- DC D592800
- HN Added, 1986.
- UF Corporate Power
- BT Power
- RT Organizational Dissolution
  Organizations (Social)

Organizational Research
- DC D593100
- HN Added, 1986.
- BT Research
- RT Organization Theory
  Organizational Sociology
  Organizations (Social)
  Social Science Research
  Sociological Research

Organizational Sociology
- DC D593400
- HN Added, 1986.
- UF Sociology of Organizations
- BT Sociology
- RT Organization Theory
  Organizational Research
  Organizations (Social)
  Sociology of Work

Organizational Structure
- DC D593450
- SN Framework of normative relations and practices prevailing in any social organization that maintains stability and coherence and gives the organization its unique identity.
- HN Added, 1986.
- BT Structure
- NT Bureaucracy
  Centralization
  Decentralization
- RT Balance Theory
  Centrality
  Departments
  Management
  Networks
  Organization Theory
  Organizational Change
  Organizations (Social)
  Social Structure
  Superior Subordinate Relationship
  Work Organization

Organizational Theory
- Use Organization Theory

Organizations (Social)
- DC D593700
- HN Formerly (1963-1985) DC 313000, Organization/Organizations/Organizational/Organizing.
- BT Groups
- NT Agencies
  Associations
  Charities
  Churches
  Civil Rights Organizations
  Clubs
  Collectives
  Commissions

Organized   Overpopulation

Organizations (Social) (cont'd)
- NT   Committees
       Community Organizations
       Complex Organizations
       Cooperatives
       Councils
       Enterprises
       Federations
       Foundations
       Fraternities And Sororities
       Governing Boards
       Guilds
       Institutes
       International Organizations
       Nonprofit Organizations
       Political Parties
       Religious Brotherhoods
       Unions
       Youth Organizations
- RT   Bureaucracy
       Departments
       Interorganizational Networks
       Interorganizational Relations
       Membership
       Organization Size
       Organization Theory
       Organizational Behavior
       Organizational Change
       Organizational Commitment
       Organizational Culture
       Organizational Development
       Organizational Dissolution
       Organizational Effectiveness
       Organizational Power
       Organizational Research
       Organizational Sociology
       Organizational Structure
       Social Groups
       Social Institutions
       Social Structure
       Work Groups

Organized Crime
- DC   D594000
- HN   Added, 1986.
- UF   Mafia (1966-1985)
       Racket/Rackets/Racketeering (1964-1985)
- BT   Crime
- RT   Career Criminals
       Corruption
       Gambling
       Prostitution

Orgasm
- DC   D594300
- HN   Formerly (1966-1985) DC 313850, Orgasm/Orgasmic.
- BT   Sexual Behavior
- RT   Frigidity
       Masturbation
       Sexual Arousal
       Sexual Intercourse

Orient And Occident
- Use   East And West

Orient/Orientalism (1963-1985)
- HN   DC 313900, deleted 1986.

Oriental Cultural Groups
- Use   Asian Cultural Groups

Oriental Languages
- DC   D594600
- HN   Added, 1986.
- UF   Altaic Language (1965-1985)
       Asian Languages
       Eskimo Languages

Oriental Languages (cont'd)
- UF   Eurasian Languages
       Finnish (Language)
       Hungarian (Language)
       Japanese (Language)
       Korean (Language)
       Mon-Khmer Languages
       Munda Languages
       Sinotibetan Languages
       Thai Languages
       Uralic Language (1965-1985)
       Vietnamese (Language)
- BT   Languages
- RT   Asian Cultural Groups

Oriental/Orientals (1963-1985)
- HN   DC 314100, deleted 1986. See now Oriental Languages or Asian Cultural Groups.

Orientation
- DC   D594900
- SN   A context-dependent term; select a more specific entry or coordinate with other terms.
- HN   Formerly (1963-1985) DC 314200, Orientation/Orientations.
- NT   Future Orientations
       Inner And Other Directedness
       Religious Orientations
       Sex Role Orientations
       Universalism-Particularism
       Value Orientations
       Work Orientations
- RT   Adjustment
       Attitudes
       Identity
       Perceptions

Origin/Origins (1963-1985)
- HN   DC 314220, deleted 1986. See now Causality, Etiology, or Formation and its associated terms.

Original/Originality (1965-1985)
- HN   DC 314240.
- Use   Creativity

Oriya (Language)
- Use   Indic Languages

Orphans
- DC   D595200
- HN   Formerly (1984-1985) DC 314246, Orphan/Orphans/Orphanage.
- RT   Adopted Children
       Children
       Foster Children

Ortega y Gasset, Jose
- DC   D595500
- SN   Born 9 May 1883 - died 18 October 1955.
- HN   Formerly (1964-1985) DC 314250, Ortega y Gasset, J.

Orthodoxy (Religious)
- Use   Religious Orthodoxy

Orthopedic (1964-1985)
- HN   DC 314280.
- Use   Physically Handicapped

Orwell, George
- DC   D595600
- SN   Born 25 June 1903 - died 21 January 1950.
- HN   Formerly (1963-1985) DC 314300, Orwell, G.

Osgood, Charles Egerton
- DC   D595800
- SN   Born 20 November 1916 - .
- HN   Formerly (1963-1985) DC 314320, Osgood, C. E.

Oslo, Norway
- DC   D596100
- HN   Formerly (1966-1985) DC 314330.
- BT   Norway

Ossowski, Stanislav
- DC   D596400
- SN   Born 1897 - died 7 November 1963.
- HN   Formerly (1966-1985) DC 314358, Ossowski, Stanislaw.

Ossuaries
- DC   D596700
- HN   Formerly (1963-1985) DC 314365, Ossuary/Ossuaries.
- BT   Cemeteries
- RT   Death Rituals

Ostracism (1963-1985)
- HN   DC 314380, deleted 1986. See now Rejection or Social Isolation.

Other Directed (1969-1985)
- HN   DC 314404.
- Use   Inner And Other Directedness

Ottawa, Ontario
- DC   D597000
- HN   Formerly (1968-1985) DC 314420, Ottawa, Canada.
- BT   Ontario

Ottoman/Ottomanism (1963-1985)
- HN   DC 314425.
- Use   Empires

Outcaste/Outcastes (1963-1985)
- HN   DC 314469, deleted 1986. See now Caste Systems or Social Isolation.

Outcome/Outcomes (1984-1985)
- HN   DC 314469a, deleted 1986. See now Effects or Evaluation.

Outer Space
- Use   Extraterrestrial Space

Outpatients
- DC   D597300
- HN   Formerly (1963-1985) DC 314470, Outpatient/Outpatients.
- BT   Patients
- RT   After Care
       Clinics
       Home Health Care

Output/Outputs (1963-1985)
- HN   DC 314480.
- Use   Productivity

Outsider/Outsiders (1969-1985)
- HN   DC 314490, deleted 1986.

Overlap/Overlaps/Overlapped/Overlapping (1972-1985)
- HN   DC 314540, deleted 1986.

Overpopulation
- DC   D597600
- HN   Formerly (1963-1985) DC 314550.
- BT   Population
- RT   Crowding
       Demography
       Emigration

Overview

Overpopulation (cont'd)
- RT Population Density
  - Population Growth
  - Population Policy
  - Social Problems
  - Survival
  - World Population
  - World Problems

Overview (1968-1985)
- HN DC 314611, deleted 1986.

Overwork (1970-1985)
- HN DC 314615.
- Use Occupational Stress

Ownership
- DC D597900
- HN Formerly (1964-1985) DC 314700.
- NT Home Ownership
  - Land Ownership
  - Worker Ownership
- RT Economic Systems
  - Expropriation
  - Forces And Relations of Production
  - Nationalization
  - Property
  - Property Rights
  - Slavery
  - Wealth

Ozark Mountains
- DC D598200
- HN Formerly (1969-1985) DC 314725.
- RT Arkansas
  - Missouri
  - Mountain Regions
  - Oklahoma

Pacific Island Cultural Groups
- Use Oceanic Cultural Groups

Pacific Ocean
- DC D598500
- HN Formerly (1963-1985) DC 314800, Pacific.
- BT Oceans
- NT North Pacific Ocean
  - South Pacific Ocean
- RT Atlantic Ocean

Pacification (1973-1985)
- HN DC 314810, deleted 1986.

Pacifism
- DC D598800
- HN Formerly (1964-1985) DC 314875, Pacificism/Pacifist.
- BT Political Ideologies
- RT Conscientious Objectors
  - Militarism
  - Neutralism
  - Nonviolence
  - Peace
  - Peace Movements

Paganism
- DC D599100
- HN Formerly (1964-1985) DC 314940, Pagan/Pagans/Paganize/Paganization.
- UF Heathenism
  - Polytheistic Religions
- BT Religions
- RT Animism
  - Christianity
  - Deities
  - Sacrificial Rites
  - Syncretism
  - Traditional Societies

Paganization
- Use Religious Conversion

Pain
- DC D599400
- HN Formerly (1963-1985) DC 317075, Pain/Pains.
- BT Symptoms
- RT Chronic Illness
  - Psychological Distress
  - Sensory Systems
  - Suffering

Painting/Paintings (1963-1985)
- HN DC 317078.
- Use Visual Arts

Pair/Pairs (1969-1985)
- HN DC 317105, deleted 1986.

Pakistan
- DC D599700
- HN Formerly (1963-1985) DC 317150, Pakistan/Pakistani/Pakistanis.
- BT South Asia
- NT Karachi, Pakistan
  - Lahore, Pakistan

Paleontology (1969-1985)
- HN DC 317200.
- Use Geology

Palestine
- DC D600000
- SN Use limited to Palestine prior to 1948. See also Israel or Jordan.
- HN Formerly (1970-1985) DC 317250.
- BT Arab Countries
  - Mediterranean Countries
  - Middle East
- RT Israel
  - Jordan
  - Palestinians

Palestinians
- DC D600300
- HN Formerly (1970-1985) part of DC 317250, Palestine.
- BT Arab Cultural Groups
- RT Palestine
  - Refugees

Pan-Africanism
- DC D600600
- HN Formerly (1963-1985) DC 317350, Pan-Africa/Pan-African/Pan-Africanism.
- RT Africa
  - Black Power
  - Cultural Identity
  - Geopolitics
  - Regional Movements

Panama
- DC D600900
- HN Formerly (1963-1985) DC 317375.
- BT Central America

Pan-American (1963-1985)
- HN DC 317385, deleted 1986.

Panchayats
- DC D601200
- SN Village councils in India—historically, mechanisms of caste government.
- HN Formerly (1963-1985) DC 317425, Panchayat/Panchayats.
- BT Councils
- RT Caste Systems
  - Local Government

Paradoxes

Pandering
- Use Prostitution

Panel Data
- DC D601350
- HN Formerly (1963-1985) DC 317450, Panel.
- BT Data
- RT Attrition
  - Cohort Analysis
  - Longitudinal Studies
  - Time Series Analysis

Panic (1965-1985)
- HN DC 317475.
- Use Fear

Panjabi (Language)
- Use Indic Languages

Papacy
- DC D601500
- HN Formerly (1966-1985) DC 340176, Pope/Popes/Papal.
- UF Papal Encyclicals
  - Popes
- RT Clergy
  - Ecclesiastical Law
  - Middle Ages
  - Roman Catholicism
  - Roman Catholics
  - Vatican

Papal Encyclicals
- Use Papacy

Papal State
- Use Vatican

Papua New Guinea
- DC D601800
- HN Formerly (1963-1985) DC 317600.
- BT Southeast Asia
- NT Trobriand Islands

Papuan Languages
- Use Austronesian Languages

Paradigmatic Techniques (Psychotherapy)
- Use Psychotherapy

Paradigms
- DC D602000
- SN Sets of concepts, assumptions, propositions, and procedures used as models to guide scientific research.
- HN Formerly (1963-1985) DC 317660, Paradigm/Paradigms.
- UF Framework (1970-1985)
- BT Models
- RT Constructs
  - Methodology (Philosophical)
  - Propositions
  - Qualitative Methods
  - Revolutions
  - Social Science Research
  - Sociological Theory

Paradox/Paradoxes/Paradoxical (1971-1985)
- HN DC 317680, deleted 1986. See now Psychotherapy or Contradictions.

Paradoxes
- Use Contradictions

Paradoxical

Paradoxical Techniques (Psychotherapy)
  Use Psychotherapy

Paraguay
  DC D602100
  HN Formerly (1966-1985) DC 317760, Paraguay/Paraguayan/Paraguayans.
  BT South America

Parallel/Parallelism (1964-1985)
  HN DC 317800, deleted 1986.

Paralysis (1979-1985)
  HN DC 318000, deleted 1986.

Paramedical Personnel
  DC D602400
  HN Formerly (1969-1985) DC 318020, Paramedical.
  UF Allied Health Personnel
  BT Paraprofessional Workers
  RT Disaster Relief
      Emergency Medical Services
      Health Professions
      Helping Behavior
      Midwifery

Parameters (Statistics)
  DC D602500
  SN Measurements that describe characteristics of a statistical population or universe.
  HN Formerly (1963-1985) DC 318200, Parameter/Parameters/Parametric/Parametrical.
  UF Population Parameters
  RT Frequency Distributions
      Mean
      Median
      Quantitative Methods
      Sampling
      Statistical Inference
      Statistics

Paramilitary Forces
  DC D602700
  HN Formerly (1980-1985) DC 319000, Paramilitary.
  RT Armed Forces
      Guerrillas
      Police

Paranoia
  DC D603000
  HN Formerly (1963-1985) DC 320000, Paranoia/Paranoid.
  BT Psychosis
  RT Fear
      Mental Illness
      Schizophrenia

Paranormal (1984-1985)
  HN DC 320080.
  Use Parapsychology

Paranormal Beliefs
  Use Occultism

Parapolitical (1963-1985)
  HN DC 320900, deleted 1986.

Paraprofessional Workers
  DC D603300
  HN Formerly (1982-1985) DC 320925, Paraprofessional/Paraprofessionals.
  BT White Collar Workers
  NT Paramedical Personnel
      Technicians
  RT Professional Workers

Parapsychology
  DC D603600
  HN Formerly (1964-1985) DC 321000.
  UF Paranormal (1984-1985)
  NT Extrasensory Perception
  RT Occultism
      Psychology
      Spiritualism
      Supernatural
      Witchcraft

Parent Child Relations
  DC D603900
  HN Added, 1986.
  BT Family Relations
  RT Adolescents
      Adopted Children
      Adult Children
      Attachment
      Child Abuse
      Child Custody
      Child Development
      Child Sexual Abuse
      Childhood Factors
      Childrearing Practices
      Children
      Daughters
      Encouragement
      Family Conflict
      Family Life
      Family Power
      Family Role
      Family Work Relationship
      Father Absence
      Fathers
      Filial Responsibility
      Generational Differences
      Home Environment
      Infants
      Intergenerational Relations
      Juvenile Delinquency
      Marital Disruption
      Mother Absence
      Mothers
      Nuclear Family
      Parents
      Runaways
      Siblings
      Sons
      Stepfamily
      Unwed Mothers
      Working Mothers
      Youth

Parental Attitudes
  DC D604200
  SN Attitudes and values of, not toward, parents.
  HN Added, 1986.
  UF Childrearing Attitudes
      Maternal Attitudes (1966-1985)
      Paternal Attitudes
  BT Attitudes
  RT Child Sex Preferences
      Childhood Factors
      Childrearing Practices
      Fathers
      Mothers
      Parental Attitudes
      Parenthood
      Parents
      Sex Role Attitudes
      Working Mothers

Parental Power
  Use Family Power

Parental Sex Preferences
  Use Child Sex Preferences

Parenthood
  DC D604500
  HN Formerly (1963-1985) DC 323030.
  RT Childlessness
      Life Stage Transitions
      Parental Attitudes
      Roles
      Single Parent Family
      Surrogate Parents

Parenting Methods
  Use Childrearing Practices

Parents
  DC D604800
  HN Formerly (1963-1985) DC 322000, Parent/Parents/Parental.
  NT Fathers
      Grandparents
      Mothers
      Surrogate Parents
  RT Adult Children
      Adults
      Childrearing Practices
      Family Life
      Godparenthood
      Heads of Households
      Intergenerational Mobility
      Kinship
      Parent Child Relations
      Parental Attitudes
      Spouses
      Stepfamily
      Unwed Mothers

Pareto, Vilfredo
  DC D605100
  SN Born 15 July 1848 - died 19 August 1923.
  HN Formerly (1964-1985) DC 323045.

Paris, France
  DC D605400
  HN Formerly (1964-1985) DC 323073, Paris, France/Parisian/Parisians.
  BT France

Parishioners
  DC D605700
  HN Formerly (1963-1985) DC 323075, Parish/Parishes/Parishioners.
  RT Churches
      Congregations
      Laity (Religious)

Park, Robert Ezra
  DC D606000
  SN Born 1864 - died 1944.
  HN Formerly (1964-1985) DC 323125, Park, R.

Parks
  DC D606300
  HN Formerly (1965-1985) DC 323110, Park/Parks.
  UF National Parks
  BT Recreational Facilities
  RT Common Lands
      Land
      Land Use
      Natural Environment
      Natural Resources
      Recreation

Parliament

Parliament/Parliamentary/
Parliamentarianism (1963-1985)
- HN DC 323170.
- Use Legislative Bodies

Parochial Schools
- Use Private Schools

Parochial/Parochialism (1963-1985)
- HN DC 323225, deleted 1986. See now Localism or Private Schools.

Parole
- DC D606600
- HN Formerly (1963-1985) DC 323250, Parole/Paroled/Parolee/Parolees.
- RT Correctional System
  Imprisonment
  Offenders
  Penal Reform
  Prisoners
  Probation

Parsons, Talcott
- DC D606800
- SN Born 13 December 1902 - died 8 May 1979.
- HN Formerly (1963-1985) DC 323300, Parsons, T./Parsonian.

Part Time Employment
- DC D606900
- HN Formerly (1963-1985) DC 323700, Part Time.
- UF Part Time Jobs
- BT Employment
- RT Multiple Jobholding
  Part Time Farming
  Underemployment
  Working Hours
  Youth Employment

Part Time Farming
- DC D607200
- HN Added, 1986.
- BT Agriculture
- RT Agricultural Economics
  Family Farms
  Farmers
  Farms
  Part Time Employment
  Small Farms

Part Time Jobs
- Use Part Time Employment

Partial Theories
- Use Middle Range Theories

Participant Observation
- DC D607400
- SN Research method in which data are gathered by researchers serving or posing as members of a group or organization. The researchers' scientific motives may be concealed from subjects or revealed depending on circumstances.
- HN Formerly (1964-1985) DC 323379, Participant-Observer/Participant-Observation.
- BT Observation
- RT Ethnomethodology
  Fieldwork
  Research Design
  Research Methodology
  Researchers

Participant/Participants (1963-1985)
- HN DC 323375.
- Use Participation

Participation
- DC D607500
- HN Formerly (1963-1985) DC 323400, Participate/Participatory/Participation/Participative.
- UF Involvement (1963-1985)
  Participant/Participants (1963-1985)
- BT Behavior
- NT Activism
  Citizen Participation
  Community Involvement
  Compulsory Participation
  Labor Force Participation
  Membership
  Political Participation
  Social Participation
  Sports Participation
  Worker Participation
- RT Activities
  Experience
  Interaction
  Military Service
  Participative Decision Making
  Performance
  Programs
  Recruitment
  Social Behavior
  Volunteers

Participation, Social (1964-1985)
- HN DC 323450.
- Use Social Participation

Participative Decision Making
- DC D607800
- HN Added, 1986.
- BT Decision Making
- RT Group Decision Making
  Organizational Development
  Participation
  Worker Participation

Participative Management
- Use Worker Participation

Particularism/Particularistic (1965-1985)
- HN DC 323475.
- Use Universalism-Particularism

Partisanship
- DC D608100
- HN Formerly (1963-1985) DC 323625, Partisan/Partisans/Partisanship.
- UF Nonpartisan/Nonpartisanship (1972-1985)
- RT Dissent
  Factionalism
  Polarization
  Political Parties
  Propaganda
  Schism
  Sectarianism

Partner Selection
- Use Mate Selection

Partner/Partners/Partnership (1963-1985)
- HN DC 323675, deleted 1986.

Parturition
- Use Birth

Party Affiliation
- Use Political Affiliation

Party/Parties (1963-1985)
- HN DC 323730.
- Use Political Parties

Passion Plays
- DC D608400
- SN Traditional, dramatic representations of the suffering and death of Jesus.
- HN Formerly (1969-1985) DC 323830, Passion Play.
- BT Religious Rituals
- RT Christianity
  Drama
  Jesus Christ

Passiveness
- DC D608700
- HN Formerly (1965-1985) DC 323850, Passive/Passivity.
- BT Personality Traits
- RT Apathy
  Obedience
  Subordination

Pastime/Pastimes (1963-1985)
- HN DC 323900.
- Use Leisure

Pastoral Societies
- DC D609000
- HN Formerly (1963-1985) part of DC 324045, Pastor/Pastors/Pastoralism.
- UF Herding Societies
  Pastoralism
- BT Traditional Societies
- RT Livestock
  Nomadic Societies
  Peasant Societies

Pastoralism
- Use Pastoral Societies

Pastorate (1969-1985)
- HN DC 324080.
- Use Clergy

Pastors
- DC D609300
- HN Formerly (1963-1985) part of DC 324045, Pastor/Pastors/Pastoralism.
- BT Clergy

Patents
- DC D609600
- HN Formerly (1964-1985) DC 324088, Patent/Patents.
- RT Government Regulation
  Innovations
  Inventions
  Law
  Products
  Property Rights
  Scientific Discoveries
  Technological Innovations
  Technology Transfer

Paternal Attitudes
- Use Parental Attitudes

Paternalism

Paternalism
- **DC** D609900
- **HN** Formerly (1964-1985) DC 324090, Paternal/Paternalism/Paternalist/Paternalistic.
- **RT** Labor Relations
  Patronage
  Social Relations
  Superior Subordinate Relationship

Paternity (1967-1985)
- **HN** DC 324093.
- **Use** Fathers

Path Analysis
- **DC** D610100
- **SN** A method of multivariate analysis that permits the quantification of causal relationships among several variables.
- **HN** Formerly (1969-1985) DC 324098, Path.
- **BT** Multivariate Analysis
- **RT** Causal Models
  Causality
  Dimensional Analysis
  Factor Analysis
  Multiple Regression Analysis
  Variables

Pathogenesis/Pathogenic (1967-1985)
- **HN** DC 324100, deleted 1986.

Pathology/Pathological (1963-1985)
- **HN** DC 324140.
- **Use** Disorders

Patients
- **DC** D610200
- **HN** Formerly (1963-1985) DC 324200, Patient/Patients.
- **UF** Medical Patients
- **NT** Mental Patients
  Outpatients
- **RT** Admissions
  Client Characteristics
  Clients
  Health Care
  Health Care Utilization
  Hospitalization
  Illness
  Illness Behavior
  Practitioner Patient Relationship
  Sick Role

Patriarchy
- **DC** D610500
- **HN** Formerly (1963-1985) DC 324240, Patriarch/Patriarchal/Patriarchalism.
- **RT** Family Structure
  Kinship
  Matriarchy

Patrilateral (1963-1985)
- **HN** DC 324280.
- **Use** Cousin Marriage

Patrilineality
- **DC** D610800
- **SN** Cultural identity pattern in which descent is traced through the male ancestors.
- **HN** Formerly (1963-1985) DC 324300, Patrilineage/Patrilineal/Patrilineality.
- **UF** Agnate/Agnation (1967-1985)
- **BT** Unilineality
- **RT** Descent
  Matrilineality

Patrilocal Residence
- **DC** D611100
- **SN** The residence of a married couple in the husband's house or that of his family.
- **HN** Formerly (1963-1985) DC 324320, Patrilocal.
- **UF** Virilocal Residence
- **BT** Residence
- **RT** Family
  Kinship

Patrimony/Patrimonial (1972-1985)
- **HN** DC 324330.
- **Use** Inheritance And Succession

Patriotism
- **DC** D611400
- **HN** Formerly (1964-1985) DC 324350, Patriot/Patriotism.
- **BT** Political Ideologies
- **RT** Loyalty
  Nationalism
  War

Patronage
- **DC** D611700
- **HN** Formerly (1964-1985) DC 324360, Patron/Patronage.
- **RT** Exchange Theory
  Paternalism
  Social Relations
  Sponsorship
  Superior Subordinate Relationship

Pattern/Patterns/Patterning (1963-1985)
- **HN** DC 324375, deleted 1986. See now Career Patterns, Marriage Patterns, Migration Patterns, Residential Patterns, Settlement Patterns, or appropriate "Structure" terms.

Pauling, Linus Carl
- **DC** D612000
- **SN** Born 28 February 1901 - .
- **HN** Formerly (1963-1985) DC 324388, Pauling, Linus.

Pay Off (1964-1985)
- **HN** DC 324460, deleted 1986. See now Game Theory or Effects.

Pay (Wages)
- **Use** Wages

Payments
- **DC** D612300
- **HN** Formerly (1963-1985) DC 324450, Payment/Payments.
- **RT** Child Support
  Compensation
  Costs
  Expenditures
  Finance
  Money
  Prices
  Rents
  Subsidies

Peace
- **DC** D612600
- **HN** Formerly (1963-1985) DC 324480.
- **RT** Conflict Resolution
  Disarmament
  International Relations
  Pacifism
  Peace Movements
  Peaceful Coexistence

Peace (cont'd)
- **RT** War

Peace Corps (1964-1985)
- **HN** DC 324484.
- **Use** Technical Assistance

Peace Movements
- **DC** D612900
- **HN** Added, 1986.
- **BT** Movements
- **NT** Antinuclear Movements
- **RT** Pacifism
  Peace
  Political Movements
  War

Peaceful Coexistence
- **DC** D613000
- **HN** Formerly (1963-1985) DC 094900, Coexistence.
- **UF** Coexistence (International Relations)
  Detente
- **BT** International Relations
- **RT** Cold War
  Disarmament
  East And West
  Peace
  Soviet American Relations

Peasant Rebellions
- **DC** D613200
- **HN** Added, 1986.
- **UF** Peasant Revolts
- **BT** Rebellions
- **RT** Maoism
  Peasants

Peasant Revolts
- **Use** Peasant Rebellions

Peasant Societies
- **DC** D613500
- **HN** Added, 1986.
- **BT** Traditional Societies
- **RT** Agrarian Societies
  Agrarian Structures
  Dual Economy
  Feudalism
  Folk Culture
  Middle Ages
  Pastoral Societies
  Peasants

Peasant Youth
- **Use** Rural Youth

Peasantry
- **Use** Peasants

Peasants
- **DC** D613800
- **HN** Formerly (1963-1985) DC 324580, Peasant/Peasants/Peasantry.
- **UF** Peasantry
  Serf/Serfs/Serfdom (1970-1985)
- **BT** Agricultural Workers
- **RT** Aristocracy
  Feudalism
  Low Income Groups
  Lower Class
  Masses
  Peasant Rebellions
  Peasant Societies
  Plantations
  Rural Communities
  Working Class

174

Pedagogy

Pedagogy/Pedagogic/Pedagogical (1964-1985)
- HN DC 324625.
- Use Teaching

Pediatrics
- DC D614100
- HN Formerly (1963-1985) DC 324640, Pediatric/Pediatrics.
- BT Medicine
- RT Child Development
  Children
  Infant Mortality
  Infants

Peer Evaluation
- Use Peer Review

Peer Groups
- DC D614400
- HN Formerly (1985) DC 324750, Peer Group.
- BT Primary Groups
- NT Gangs
- RT Affiliation Need
  Age Groups
  Cliques
  Conformity
  Peer Relations
  Peers
  Reference Groups
  Social Status

Peer Influence
- DC D614700
- HN Added, 1986.
- BT Social Influence
- RT Conformity
  Peers
  Reference Groups
  Social Behavior
  Social Pressure
  Socialization

Peer Relations
- DC D615000
- HN Added, 1986.
- BT Interpersonal Relations
- RT Acceptance
  Friendship
  Individual Collective Relationship
  Opposite Sex Relations
  Peer Groups
  Peer Review
  Peers
  Sociability
  Teamwork

Peer Review
- DC D615300
- HN Added, 1986.
- UF Peer Evaluation
- BT Evaluation
- RT Job Performance
  Peer Relations
  Peers
  Performance
  Personnel Management
  Self Evaluation

Peers
- DC D615600
- HN Formerly (1963-1985) DC 324700, Peer/Peers.
- RT Age Groups
  Peer Groups
  Peer Influence
  Peer Relations
  Peer Review

Peers (cont'd)
- RT Significant Others
  Social Status
  Socialization Agents

Peking, Peoples Republic of China
- DC D615900
- HN Formerly (1965-1985) DC 326050, Peking, China.
- BT Peoples Republic of China

Peloponnesia/Peloponnesian/Peloponnesians (1964-1985)
- HN DC 326100.
- Use Antiquity

Penal Policy
- Use Criminal Justice Policy

Penal Reform
- DC D616200
- HN Added, 1986.
- BT Reform
- RT Correctional System
  Criminal Justice Policy
  Forensic Psychiatry
  Imprisonment
  Juvenile Offenders
  Parole
  Penology
  Prisoners
  Prisons

Penal System
- Use Correctional System

Penalty/Penalties (1969-1985)
- HN DC 326210, deleted 1986. See now Deterrence, Prevention, or Punishment.

Penitentiary/Penitentiaries (1964-1985)
- HN DC 326220.
- Use Prisons

Pennsylvania
- DC D616500
- HN Formerly (1963-1985) DC 326250, Pennsylvania/Pennsylvanian/Pennsylvanians.
- BT Northern States
  United States of America
- NT Philadelphia, Pennsylvania
  Pittsburgh, Pennsylvania
- RT Appalachia

Penologist/Penologists (1963-1985)
- HN DC 326295, deleted 1986.

Penology
- DC D616800
- SN Theory and practice of prison administration and offender rehabilitation.
- HN Formerly (1964-1985) DC 326300.
- BT Criminology
- RT Correctional System
  Delinquency Prevention
  Penal Reform
  Prisons
  Rehabilitation

Pensions
- DC D617100
- HN Formerly (1964-1985) DC 326375, Pension/Pensions/Pensioner/Pensioners.
- UF Retirement Benefits
- BT Compensation
- RT Benefits
  Disability Recipients

Performance

Pensions (cont'd)
- RT Elderly
  Income
  Retirement
  Social Security
  Workers

Pentecostal Assemblies
- Use Pentecostalists

Pentecostal Churches
- Use Pentecostalists

Pentecostalists
- DC D617400
- HN Formerly (1964-1985) DC 326425, Pentacostal.
- UF Pentecostal Assemblies
  Pentecostal Churches
- BT Protestants
- RT Glossolalia
  Protestantism

People/Peoples (1963-1985)
- HN DC 326600, deleted 1986. See now specific "Group," "Society," or "Individual" terms.

Peoples Republic of China
- DC D617700
- HN Formerly (1977-1985) DC 326640, People's Republic of China.
- BT Far East
- NT Peking, Peoples Republic of China
  Tibet

Peoples Temple
- Use Jonestown Mass Suicide

Per Capita (1966-1985)
- HN DC 326800, deleted 1986.

Perceptions
- DC D618000
- SN Use limited to socially defined viewpoints held by research subjects or members of target populations.
- HN Formerly (1963-1985) DC 327000, Perception/Perceptions/Perceptual/Perceptivity.
- BT Consciousness
- NT Worldview
- RT Attitudes
  Beliefs
  Expectations
  Future Orientations
  Images
  Opinions
  Orientation
  Relative Deprivation
  Salience
  Social Perception

Perceptual Systems
- Use Sensory Systems

Perfection/Perfectionism (1966-1985)
- HN DC 328390, deleted 1986.

Performance
- DC D618300
- HN Formerly (1963-1985) DC 328400.
- BT Behavior
- NT Effectiveness
  Failure
  Job Performance
  Success
  Task Performance
- RT Ability
  Accountability

Performance

Performance (cont'd)
- RT Achievement
- Aspiration
- Awards
- Competence
- Competition
- Efficiency
- Errors
- Evaluation
- Expectations
- Function
- Goals
- Implementation
- Motivation
- Observation
- Participation
- Peer Review
- Productivity
- Qualifications
- Quality
- Recognition (Achievement)
- Reliability
- Skills
- Standards

Performance Evaluation
- Use Evaluation

Performing Arts
- Use Theater Arts

Perinatal Mortality
- Use Infant Mortality

Periodicals
- DC D618600
- HN Formerly (1964-1985) DC 328575, Periodical/Periodicals.
- UF Weekly Periodicals
- BT Publications
- NT Journals
- Magazines
- RT Articles
- Editorials
- Journalism
- Newspapers
- Writing for Publication

Periods (Time)
- Use Time Periods

Peripheral/Periphery (1983-1985)
- HN DC 328582.
- Use Center And Periphery

Perjury (1964-1985)
- HN DC 328600, deleted 1986.

Permanency Planning
- DC D618800
- SN In social work, seeking adoptive families for orphaned children and permanent homes for wards of the court and previously institutionalized clients.
- HN Formerly (1984-1985) DC 328646, Permanency.
- BT Planning
- RT Adopted Children
- Child Welfare Services
- Foster Care
- Placement
- Social Work
- Stability

Permissiveness (Sexual)
- Use Sexual Permissiveness

Peronism
- DC D618900
- HN Formerly (1972-1985) DC 328670, Peron, Juan/Peronism/Peronists.
- RT Populism

Persecution
- Use Oppression

Persia/Persian/Persians (1963-1985)
- HN DC 328800.
- Use Iran

Person Perception
- Use Social Perception

Person/Persons (1963-1985)
- HN DC 328840.
- Use Individuals

Personal Computers
- Use Microcomputers

Personal Hygiene
- Use Hygiene

Personal Identity
- Use Self Concept

Personal Names
- Use Naming Practices

Personal Narratives
- Use Narratives

Personal Property
- Use Property

Personal Rejection
- Use Rejection

Personal Space
- DC D619200
- HN Added, 1986.
- UF Proxemic (1964-1985)
- BT Space
- RT Crowding
- Nonverbal Communication
- Privacy
- Social Interaction
- Spatial Behavior
- Territoriality

Personal/Personalization (1963-1985)
- HN DC 328850, deleted 1986.

Personality
- DC D619500
- SN Attributes of individual identity. The term usually implies a continuum including inherited traits and aptitudes, relatively more socialized characteristics such as intelligence, attitudes, and language, and highly socialized individual factors, such as social values, roles, normative expectations, and many aspects of social identity.
- HN Formerly (1963-1985) Personality/Personalities.
- UF Character
- Disposition (Personality)
- Temperament (1968-1985)
- NT Sociopathic Personality
- RT Attribution
- Behavior
- Client Characteristics
- Freudian Psychology
- Habits

Personality

Personality (cont'd)
- RT Human Nature
- Individual Differences
- Individuals
- Lifestyle
- Personality Measures
- Personality Traits
- Psychodynamics
- Psychological Factors
- Psychological Research
- Psychology
- Self Actualization
- Self Concept
- Socialization
- Subjectivity

Personality Measures
- DC D619650
- HN Added, 1986.
- UF Inventories (Personality)
- Personality Tests
- BT Measures (Instruments)
- NT Minnesota Multiphasic Personality Inventory
- RT Attitude Measures
- Personality
- Personality Traits
- Projective Techniques
- Psychological Research
- Psychometric Analysis
- Semantic Differential

Personality Tests
- Use Personality Measures

Personality Traits
- DC D619800
- HN Formerly (1963-1985) DC 470000, Trait/Traits.
- UF Extroversion (1964-1985)
- Introversion (1964-1985)
- Traits (Personality)
- NT Authoritarianism (Psychology)
- Charisma
- Compulsivity
- Creativity
- Curiosity
- Dependency (Psychology)
- Dogmatism
- Empathy
- Impulsiveness
- Locus of Control
- Machiavellianism (Personality)
- Passiveness
- RT Androgyny
- Anxiety
- Assertiveness
- Complementary Needs
- Conformity
- Cynicism
- Egocentrism
- Egoism
- Emotions
- Flexibility
- Graphology
- Jealousy
- Loyalty
- Masculinity
- Narcissism
- Neuroticism
- Optimism
- Personality
- Personality Measures
- Pessimism
- Self Esteem
- Sexuality
- Sociability
- Social Desirability
- Tolerance

Personhood
- **DC** D619900
- **HN** Added, 1986.
- **RT** Bioethics
  Fetus
  Human Rights
  Individuals

Personnel (1963-1985)
- **HN** DC 331700, deleted 1986. See now Occupations, Workers, and specific "Personnel" terms.

Personnel Management
- **DC** D620100
- **HN** Added, 1986.
- **BT** Management
- **NT** Dismissal
  Hiring Practices
  Promotion (Occupational)
- **RT** Absenteeism
  Employers
  Employment
  Employment Discrimination
  Employment Opportunities
  Industrial Management
  Labor Relations
  Labor Turnover
  Management Styles
  Peer Review
  Placement
  Recruitment
  Superior Subordinate Relationship
  Supervision
  Work Environment
  Workers

Personnel Policy
- **DC** D620400
- **HN** Added, 1986.
- **BT** Policy
- **RT** Academic Tenure
  Affirmative Action
  Hiring Practices
  Job Requirements
  Labor Relations
  Retirement
  Seniority
  Work Environment
  Working Hours

Perspective/Perspectives (1963-1985)
- **HN** DC 333340, deleted 1986. See now Attitudes, Orientation, or Perceptions.

Persuasibility (1963-1985)
- **HN** DC 333360.
- **Use** Persuasion

Persuasion
- **DC** D620700
- **HN** Formerly (1963-1985) DC 333400, Persuasion/Persuasive.
- **UF** Persuasibility (1963-1985)
  Persuasive Communication
- **BT** Communication
- **RT** Agitation
  Agreement
  Conflict Resolution
  Credibility
  Debate
  Discussion
  Interpersonal Communication
  Negotiation
  Propaganda

Persuasive Communication
- **Use** Persuasion

Peru
- **DC** D621000
- **HN** Formerly (1963-1985) DC 333425, Peru/Peruvian/Peruvians.
- **BT** South America
- **NT** Lima, Peru

Pessimism
- **DC** D621200
- **HN** Formerly (1963-1985) DC 333450.
- **UF** Hopelessness
- **RT** Alienation
  Cynicism
  Optimism
  Personality Traits
  Psychological Distress
  Social Attitudes
  Worldview

Pesticides
- **DC** D621300
- **HN** Formerly (1964-1985) DC 333452, Pesticide/Pesticides.
- **BT** Toxic Substances
- **RT** Agricultural Technology

Petite Bourgeoisie
- **Use** Bourgeoisie

Petition/Petitions (1967-1985)
- **HN** DC 333453, deleted 1986.

Petroleum
- **DC** D621600
- **HN** Formerly (1979-1985) DC 333453b.
- **UF** Crude Oils
  Mineral Oils
  Oil (1982-1985)
- **BT** Fuels
- **RT** Energy Policy
  Natural Resources
  Petroleum Industry

Petroleum Industry
- **DC** D621900
- **HN** Added, 1986.
- **UF** Oil Industry
- **BT** Industry
- **RT** Chemical Industry
  Petroleum

Pets
- **DC** D622200
- **HN** Formerly (1984-1985) DC 333452a.
- **BT** Animals
- **RT** Animal Human Relations

Peyote (1963-1985)
- **HN** DC 333454.
- **Use** Psychedelic Drugs

Ph.D. Degrees
- **Use** Doctoral Degrees

Phallus/Phallic (1967-1985)
- **HN** DC 333465, deleted 1986.

Pharmaceutical Drugs
- **Use** Medications

Pharmacists
- **DC** D622500
- **HN** Formerly (1964-1985) part of DC 333470, Pharmacy/Pharmaceutical.
- **BT** Professional Workers
- **RT** Health Professions
  Pharmacy

Pharmacy
- **DC** D622800
- **HN** Formerly (1964-1985) part of DC 333470, Pharmacy/Pharmaceutical.
- **BT** Medicine
- **RT** Drugs
  Medications
  Pharmacists

Phase (1964-1985)
- **HN** DC 333480, deleted 1986. See now Business Cycles, Cyclical Processes, Developmental Stages, or Life Cycle.

Phenomena
- **DC** D622900
- **SN** A context-dependent term describing events or patterns in the most general way possible. Select a more specific entry or coordinate with other terms.
- **HN** Formerly (1963-1985) DC 333520, Phenomena/Phenomenon/Phenomenalists/Phenomenalistic.
- **UF** Events
  Fact/Facts (1963-1985)
- **NT** Life Events
  Social Facts
- **RT** Concepts
  Data
  Existence
  Methodology (Philosophical)
  Phenomenology
  Reality
  Theories
  Theory Formation
  Truth

Phenomenological Sociology
- **Use** Interpretive Sociology

Phenomenology
- **DC** D622950
- **SN** The study of the various forms of consciousness, intentionality, and experience of everyday life, focusing on explaining the meaning of phenomena through intuition.
- **HN** Formerly (1979-1985) DC 333522, Phenomenology/Phenomenological.
- **BT** Philosophical Doctrines
- **RT** Action Theory
  Cognition
  Consciousness
  Ethnomethodology
  Everyday Life
  Existentialism
  Hermeneutics
  Idealism
  Intentionality
  Interpretive Sociology
  Methodological Individualism
  Phenomena
  Psychology
  Reflexivity
  Sociology of Knowledge
  Symbolic Interactionism
  Verstehen

Phenotype/Phenotypic (1963-1985)
- **HN** DC 333530, deleted 1986.

Philadelphia, Pennsylvania
- **DC** D623100
- **HN** Formerly (1964-1985) DC 333545, Philadelphia, Pa.
- **BT** Pennsylvania

Philanthropy

Philanthropy
- DC D623400
- HN Formerly (1963-1985) DC 333560, Philanthropy/Philanthropic.
- RT Altruism
  Charities
  Contributions (Donations)
  Foundations
  Gift Giving
  Grants

Philippines
- DC D623700
- HN Formerly (1963-1985) DC 333585, Philippine/Philippines.
- UF Mindanao, Philippines (1966-1985)
- BT Southeast Asia
- NT Manila, Philippines

Philology/Philologist/Philologists/Philological (1966-1985)
- HN DC 333588, deleted 1986. See now Linguistics or Literature.

Philosophers
- DC D624000
- HN Formerly (1964-1985) DC 333590, Philosopher/Philosophers.
- RT Ancient Greek Philosophy
  Philosophy

Philosophical Doctrines
- DC D624150
- HN Added, 1986.
- UF Philosophical Systems
  Schools of Philosophy
- BT Ideologies
- NT Agnosticism
  Atheism
  Behaviorism
  Dualism
  Epistemological Doctrines
  Existentialism
  Fatalism
  Functionalism
  Hedonism
  Historicism
  Holism
  Humanism
  Idealism
  Marxism
  Materialism
  Mysticism
  Naturalism
  Nihilism
  Nominalism
  Phenomenology
  Pluralism
  Rationalism
  Relativism
  Spiritualism
  Teleology
  Utilitarianism
  Voluntarism
- RT Beliefs
  Cynicism
  Economic Theories
  Educational Systems
  Ethics
  Individualism
  Methodology (Philosophical)
  Philosophy
  Political Philosophy
  Psychology
  Religious Beliefs
  Religious Doctrines
  Social Relations
  Systems

Philosophical Systems
- Use Philosophical Doctrines

Philosophy
- DC D624300
- SN A context-dependent term covering disciplined thinking that rationally analyzes the nature and foundations of being, knowledge, truth, meaning, ethics, conduct, aesthetics, and ultimate reality.
- HN Formerly (1963-1985) DC 333600, Philosophy/Philosophies/Philosophical.
- BT Humanities
- NT Ancient Greek Philosophy
  Cosmology
  Epistemology
  Hermeneutics
  Logic
  Metaphysics
  Political Philosophy
  Semiotics
  Social Philosophy
  Theology
- RT Dialectics
  Egalitarianism
  Ethics
  Methodology (Philosophical)
  Mysticism
  Naturalism
  Philosophers
  Philosophical Doctrines
  Political Ideologies
  Reality
  Religions

Phobias
- DC D624600
- HN Formerly (1967-1985) DC 333900, Phobia/Phobias.
- UF Xenophile/Xenophobic/Xenophobia (1978-1985)
- BT Fear
- RT Mental Illness
  Neurosis

Phoenix, Arizona
- DC D624900
- HN Added, 1986.
- BT Arizona

Phoenix Islands
- DC D625200
- HN Added, 1986.
- BT Polynesia

Phoneme/Phonemic (1979-1985)
- HN DC 334000.
- Use Phonetics

Phonetics
- DC D625500
- HN Formerly (1964-1985) DC 334050, Phonetic/Phonetics.
- UF Phoneme/Phonemic (1979-1985)
  Phonology (1965-1985)
- BT Linguistics
- RT Code Switching
  Morphology (Language)
  Speech

Phonograph Records
- Use Recordings

Phonology (1965-1985)
- HN DC 334075.
- Use Phonetics

Physical

Photian Schism
- DC D625800
- HN Formerly (1965-1985) DC 334250.
- BT Religious Movements
  Schism
- RT Heresy

Photographs
- DC D626100
- HN Formerly (1963-1985) part of DC 334255, Photography/Photographic.
- UF Camera/Cameras (1972-1985)
- BT Audiovisual Media
- RT Films
  Journalism
  Visual Arts

Photography/Photographic (1963-1985)
- HN DC 334255, deleted 1986. See now Visual Arts or Photographs.

Phratries
- Use Clans

Phylogeny (1977-1985)
- HN DC 334280.
- Use Evolution

Physical Anthropology
- Use Anthropology

Physical Attractiveness
- Use Attractiveness

Physical Characteristics
- DC D626300
- HN Formerly (1963-1985) DC 334325, Physical.
- UF Physique (1976-1985)
- NT Age
  Body Height
  Body Weight
  Race
  Sex
- RT Age Differences
  Attractiveness
  Human Body
  Individual Differences
  Interpersonal Attraction
  Sex Differences
  Symptoms

Physical Contact
- DC D626400
- HN Added, 1986.
- UF Bodily Contact
  Touching
- RT Childrearing Practices
  Human Body
  Intimacy
  Sensory Systems
  Sexuality
  Social Contact
  Spatial Behavior
  Sports

Physical Fitness
- DC D626500
- HN Added, 1986.
- UF Exercise
- BT Activities
- RT Health

Physical Health
- Use Health

Physical

Physical Objects
  Use Inanimate Objects

Physical Punishment
  Use Corporal Punishment

Physical Sciences
  DC D626700
  HN Added, 1986.
  BT Natural Sciences
  NT Astronomy
      Chemistry
      Geology
      Meteorology
      Physics
  RT Nuclear Energy
      Radiation
      Science
      Scientists
      Space Technology

Physically Handicapped
  DC D627000
  HN Formerly (1963-1985) DC 334400, Physical Handicap/Physically Handicapped.
  UF Crippled
      Orthopedic (1964-1985)
  BT Handicapped
  RT Chronic Illness
      Human Body

Physician Patient Relationship
  Use Practitioner Patient Relationship

Physicians
  DC D627300
  HN Formerly (1963-1985) DC 334500, Physician/Physicians.
  UF Doctor/Doctors (1963-1985)
      Residents (Medical)
  BT Professional Workers
  RT Health Professions
      Nurses
      Practitioner Patient Relationship
      Primary Health Care
      Psychiatrists

Physicist/Physicists (1963-1985)
  HN DC 334510, deleted 1986. See now Scientists and Physics.

Physics
  DC D627600
  HN Formerly (1963-1985) DC 334600.
  BT Physical Sciences
  RT Electricity
      Electronic Technology
      Energy
      Entropy
      Metallurgical Technology
      Nuclear Energy
      Radiation
      Scientific Research
      Space Technology

Physiocrats
  DC D627900
  SN Group of 18th-century French economists, led by Francois Quesnay, who argued against political interference in the natural economic order, contending that agriculture was the only source of wealth and only proper source of public revenue.
  HN Formerly (1972-1985) DC 334640, Physiocrat/Physiocrats.
  RT Economists
      Political Ideologies

Physiognomy/Physiognomies (1975-1985)
  HN DC 334650.
  Use Human Body

Physiology
  DC D628200
  HN Formerly (1963-1985) DC 335000, Physiology/Physiological/Physiologist/Physiologists.
  BT Biological Sciences
  RT Biology
      Birth
      Blood
      Death
      Evolution
      Human Body
      Medicine
      Scientific Research
      Stress

Physique (1976-1985)
  HN DC 335600.
  Use Physical Characteristics

Piaget, Jean
  DC D628800
  SN Born 9 August 1896 - died 16 September 1980.
  HN Formerly (1963-1985) DC 335700.

Piecework
  DC D629100
  HN Formerly (1965-1985) DC 335760.
  BT Work
  RT Wages

Piety (1964-1985)
  HN DC 335800.
  Use Religiosity

Pilgrimages
  DC D629400
  HN Formerly (1965-1985) DC 336900, Pilgrim/Pilgrims/Pilgrimage.
  BT Religious Rituals
  RT Shrines
      Travel

Pilot/Pilots (1963-1985)
  HN DC 337000, deleted 1986.

Pimp/Pimps/Pimping (1973-1985)
  HN DC 337600.
  Use Prostitution

Pioneer/Pioneers (1965-1985)
  HN DC 338000.
  Use Settlers

Pittsburgh, Pennsylvania
  DC D629700
  HN Added, 1986.
  BT Pennsylvania

Place (1966-1985)
  HN DC 339065, deleted 1986. See now Workplaces or appropriate "Community," "Space," or "Environment" terms.

Place of Residence
  Use Residence

Placebo Effect
  DC D629900
  HN Formerly (1964-1985) DC 339066.
  UF Placebo Therapy
  BT Effects
  RT Health Care
      Treatment Programs

Placebo Therapy
  Use Placebo Effect

Placement
  DC D630000
  SN A context-dependent term; select a more specific entry or coordinate with other terms. In the context of social work, coordinate Placement with Foster Care.
  HN Formerly (1963-1985) DC 339068.
  RT Achievement Tests
      Adopted Children
      Child Custody
      Child Neglect
      Foster Care
      Foster Children
      Permanency Planning
      Personnel Management
      Students
      Tracking (Education)

Places of Worship
  DC D630300
  HN Added, 1986.
  UF Chapel/Chapels (1964-1985)
      Church Buildings
      Temple/Temples (1970-1985)
  BT Facilities
  NT Synagogues
  RT Church Attendance
      Churches
      Convents
      Monasteries
      Religions
      Religious Cultural Groups
      Religious Rituals
      Sacredness
      Shrines
      Worship

Plagiarize/Plagiarism/Plagiarists (1967-1985)
  HN DC 339085.
  Use Authorship

Plague
  DC D630600
  HN Formerly (1972-1985) DC 339090, Plague/Plagues.
  UF Black Death
  BT Diseases
  RT Epidemics

Plains (1963-1985)
  HN DC 339100, deleted 1986.

Planet/Planets/Planetary (1964-1985)
  HN DC 339146.
  Use Earth (Planet)

Planners
  DC D630900
  HN Formerly (1963-1985) part of DC 339140, Plan/Plans/Planning/Planned/Planners.
  UF City Planners
      Planning Commissions
  BT Professional Workers
  RT Administrators
      Commissions
      Managers
      Planning

Planning
- **DC** D631200
- **HN** Formerly (1963-1985) part of DC 339140, Plan/Plans/Planning/Planned/Planners.
- **NT** Economic Planning
  Family Planning
  Health Planning
  Language Planning
  Local Planning
  Permanency Planning
  Social Planning
  State Planning
- **RT** Design
  Development
  Development Strategies
  Educational Plans
  Futures (of Society)
  Goals
  Implementation
  Life Plans
  Management
  Needs Assessment
  Planners
  Policy Making
  Prediction
  Priorities
  Strategies

Planning Commissions
Use Planners

Plant Closure
- **DC** D631500
- **HN** Added, 1986.
- **UF** Factory Closure
  Plant Shutdown
  Shutdowns (Industrial)
- **BT** Closure
- **RT** Depression (Economics)
  Dislocated Workers
  Employment Changes
  Factories
  Industry
  Organizational Dissolution

Plant Shutdown
Use Plant Closure

Plant/Plants (1963-1985)
- **HN** DC 339155, deleted 1986. See now Plants (Botanical), Plant Closure, or Factories.

Plantations
- **DC** D631800
- **HN** Formerly (1964-1985) DC 339165, Plantation.
- **UF** Hacienda/Haciendas (1963-1985)
  Latifundium/Latifundia/Latifundismo/Latifundists (1970-1985)
- **BT** Agricultural Enterprises
- **RT** Agrarian Structures
  Agricultural Workers
  Land Reform
  Peasants
  Sharecropping

Plants (Botanical)
- **DC** D632100
- **HN** Formerly (1963-1985) part of DC 339155, Plant/Plants.
- **UF** Flora
  Herbs
  Vegetation
- **RT** Agriculture
  Biology
  Food

Plants (Botanical) (cont'd)
- **RT** Forestry
  Gardening
  Natural Resources
  Raw Materials
  Traditional Medicine

Plato/Platonic (1964-1985)
- **HN** DC 339175.
- **Use** Ancient Greek Philosophy

Play
- **DC** D632400
- **HN** Formerly (1963-1985) DC 339200, Play/Playful/Playing.
- **BT** Activities
- **RT** Behavior
  Children
  Games
  Imagination

Plays
Use Drama

Plea Bargaining
- **DC** D632700
- **SN** In criminal proceedings, an agreement in which a guilty plea is obtained in exchange for a reduction in the seriousness of the charges. The judicial system benefits by saving the expense of a trial by jury, and the guilty offender benefits by receiving a less severe punishment than might result from a jury trial.
- **HN** Formerly (1984-1985) DC 339204.
- **UF** Negotiated Pleas
  Plea Negotiations
- **BT** Legal Procedure
  Negotiation
- **RT** Criminal Proceedings
  Prosecutors
  Sentencing

Plea (Insanity)
Use Insanity Defense

Plea Negotiations
Use Plea Bargaining

Pleistocene Period (1977-1985)
- **HN** DC 339218.
- **Use** Prehistory

Plural Societies
- **DC** D633000
- **HN** Formerly (1963-1985) part of DC 339248, Plural/Pluralism/Pluralist/Pluralists/Pluralistic.
- **BT** Society
- **RT** Biculturalism
  Cultural Identity
  Cultural Pluralism
  Ethnic Minorities
  Language Policy
  Linguistic Minorities
  Minority Groups
  Multilingualism
  Pluralism
  Separatism

Pluralingualism
Use Multilingualism

Pluralism
- **DC** D633300
- **HN** Formerly (1963-1985) part of DC 339248, Plural/Pluralism/Pluralist/Pluralists/Pluralistic.
- **BT** Philosophical Doctrines
- **NT** Cultural Pluralism
  Medical Pluralism
- **RT** Dualism
  Plural Societies
  Political Power

Plurality (1965-1985)
- **HN** DC 339255
- **Use** Majorities (Politics)

Pneumonia (1965-1985)
- **HN** DC 339259.
- **Use** Diseases

Poetry
- **DC** D633600
- **HN** Formerly (1964-1985) DC 339266, Poem/Poems/Poetry/Poetic/Poetics.
- **UF** Epic Poetry
  Lyric Poetry
  Verse (1967-1985)
- **BT** Literature
- **RT** Drama
  Fiction
  Folk Culture
  Poets

Poets
- **DC** D633900
- **HN** Formerly (1966-1985) DC 339272, Poet/Poets.
- **UF** Bards
  Minnesingers
  Troubadors
- **BT** Writers
- **RT** Literature
  Poetry

Poggi, Gianfranco
- **DC** D634200
- **SN** Born 28 February 1934 - .
- **HN** Formerly (1966-1985) DC 339276.

Pogroms (1982-1985)
- **HN** DC 339280, deleted 1986.

Poisoning
- **DC** D634500
- **HN** Formerly (1972-1985) DC 339300, Poison/Poisons/Poisoner/Poisoners.
- **NT** Lead Poisoning
- **RT** Hazards
  Health
  Pollution
  Pollution Control
  Toxic Substances
  Wastes

Poisons
Use Toxic Substances

Poland
- **DC** D634800
- **HN** Formerly (1963-1985) DC 339350, Poland/Poles/Polish.
- **BT** Eastern Europe
- **NT** Lodz, Poland
  Warsaw, Poland

Polanyi, Karl Paul
- **DC** D635100
- **SN** Born 25 October 1886 - died 23 April 1964.
- **HN** Formerly (1970-1985) DC 339368, Polanyi, K.

Polanyi, Michael
- **DC** D635400
- **SN** Born 11 March 1891 - died 22 February 1976.
- **HN** Formerly (1967-1985) DC 339370.

Polarization

Polarization
- DC D635700
- HN Formerly (1969-1985) DC 339400, Polar/Polarity/Polarities/ Polarization/Polarizations.
- BT Social Processes
- RT Cleavage
  Extremism
  Factionalism
  Partisanship
  Political Parties
  Public Opinion
  Schism
  Social Conflict
  Social Segmentation

Polemic/Polemics (1969-1985)
- HN DC 339412.
- Use Debate

Police
- DC D636000
- HN Formerly (1963-1985) DC 339425, Police/Policing/Policemen.
- UF Law Enforcement Officers
- RT Correctional Personnel
  Crime Prevention
  Criminal Proceedings
  Fire Fighters
  Investigations (Law Enforcement)
  Law Enforcement
  Military Civilian Relations
  Paramilitary Forces
  Police Community Relations
  Public Officials

Police Citizen Relations
- Use Police Community Relations

Police Community Relations
- DC D636100
- HN Added, 1989.
- UF Police Citizen Relations
- BT Social Relations
- RT Citizen Participation
  Communities
  Community Satisfaction
  Crime Prevention
  Fear of Crime
  Law Enforcement
  Military Civilian Relations
  Police
  Public Support
  State Society Relationship

Police Investigations
- Use Investigations (Law Enforcement)

Policy
- DC D636300
- SN Explicit plan or set of guidelines adopted by the members of a group or their leaders to solve a problem or bring about a desired state of affairs.
- HN Formerly (1963-1985) DC 339500, Policy/Policies.
- NT Development Policy
  Economic Policy
  Educational Policy
  Government Policy
  Personnel Policy
  Public Policy
  Science Policy
  Social Policy
  Urban Policy
- RT Goals
  Law
  Policy Analysis

Policy (cont'd)
- RT Policy Implementation
  Policy Making
  Policy Research
  Policy Science
  Reform

Policy Analysis
- DC D636400
- HN Formerly (1985) DC 339533.
- BT Analysis
- RT Policy
  Policy Making
  Policy Research
  Policy Science

Policy Formation
- Use Policy Making

Policy Implementation
- DC D636500
- HN Added, 1986.
- BT Implementation
- RT Economic Policy
  Educational Policy
  Government Policy
  Legislation
  Policy
  Policy Making
  Policy Research
  Public Officials
  Public Policy
  Social Policy

Policy Making
- DC D636600
- HN Formerly (1983-1985) DC 339527, Policymaker/Policy Making.
- UF Policy Formation
  Policy Planning
- RT Administrators
  Councils
  Criteria
  Decision Making
  Governing Boards
  Legislation
  Planning
  Policy
  Policy Analysis
  Policy Implementation
  Policy Research
  Policy Science
  Priorities
  Public Officials
  Social Policy
  Strategies

Policy Planning
- Use Policy Making

Policy Research
- DC D636800
- HN Added, 1986.
- BT Research
- RT Policy
  Policy Analysis
  Policy Implementation
  Policy Making
  Policy Science
  Social Science Research

Policy Science
- DC D636900
- HN Formerly (1977-1985) DC 339540.
- BT Social Sciences
- RT Policy
  Policy Analysis
  Policy Making
  Policy Research
  Political Science

Political

Poliomyelitis
- DC D637200
- HN Formerly (1963-1985) DC 339600.
- UF Infantile Paralysis
- BT Diseases

Polish Solidarity Movement
- Use Solidarity Movements

Political Action
- DC D637500
- HN Added, 1986.
- BT Action
- RT Activism
  Agitation
  Civil Disobedience
  Civil Rights Organizations
  Coalitions
  Collective Action
  Interest Groups
  Lobbying
  Mobilization
  Movements
  Political Action Committees
  Political Attitudes
  Political Behavior
  Political Movements
  Politics
  Progressivism
  Protest Movements
  Social Action
  Voting

Political Action Committees
- DC D637550
- HN Added, 1989.
- BT Committees
- RT Interest Groups
  Lobbying
  Political Action
  Political Campaigns

Political Affiliation
- DC D637800
- HN Added, 1986.
- UF Party Affiliation
- RT Membership
  Political Attitudes
  Political Parties
  Politics
  Sectarianism

Political Agitation
- Use Agitation

Political Attitudes
- DC D638100
- HN Added, 1986.
- UF Political Opinions
- BT Attitudes
- RT Apathy
  Discontent
  Dissent
  McCarthyism
  Opinion Polls
  Political Action
  Political Affiliation
  Political Factors
  Political Parties
  Political Philosophy
  Political Socialization
  Politics
  Progressivism
  Public Opinion
  Public Support
  Religion Politics Relationship
  Social Attitudes
  Tolerance
  Traditionalism
  Voters
  Voting Behavior

181

Political

Political Behavior
- **DC** D638400
- **HN** Formerly (1985) DC 339700.
- **BT** Behavior
- **NT** Civil Disobedience
  Political Participation
  Voting Behavior
- **RT** Interest Groups
  Political Action
  Political Factors
  Political Movements
  Political Science
  Political Sociology
  Political Violence
  Politics
  Social Consciousness
  Voters

Political Campaigns
- **DC** D638700
- **HN** Formerly (1963-1985) DC 069167, Campaign/Campaigns.
- **UF** Campaigns (Political)
  Election Campaigns
- **RT** Candidates
  Democracy
  Elections
  Political Action Committees
  Political Parties
  Politicians
  Politics

Political Candidates
- **Use** Candidates

Political Censorship
- **Use** Censorship

Political Culture
- **DC** D639000
- **HN** Added, 1986.
- **UF** Cultural Politics
- **BT** Culture
- **RT** Cultural Conflict
  Cultural Pluralism
  Language Policy
  Political Socialization
  Politics

Political Defection
- **DC** D639300
- **HN** Added, 1986.
- **RT** Apostasy
  Citizenship
  Dissent
  International Relations
  Loyalty
  Politics
  Refugees
  Schism

Political Donations
- **Use** Contributions (Donations)

Political Economy
- **DC** D639500
- **SN** A social science dealing with political policy, aggregate economic activity, and resource allocation. In the 18th and 19th centuries, it dealt chiefly with governmental production and management of wealth. It later developed into pure economic theory and Marxist economics.
- **HN** Added, 1986.
- **RT** Accumulation
  Capitalism
  Division of Labor
  Economic History

Political Economy (cont'd)
- **RT** Economic Theories
  Economics
  Labor Theory of Value
  Market Economy
  Marxism
  Marxist Economics
  Marxist Sociology
  Modes of Production
  Politics
  Value (Economics)

Political Elites
- **DC** D639600
- **HN** Added, 1986.
- **BT** Elites
- **RT** Authoritarianism (Political Ideology)
  Economic Elites
  Oligarchy
  Political Power
  Politics
  Polyarchy
  Power Elite
  Ruling Class

Political Extremism
- **Use** Extremism

Political Factors
- **DC** D639650
- **HN** Added, 1989.
- **RT** Political Attitudes
  Political Behavior
  Political Power
  Politics

Political Ideologies
- **DC** D639900
- **HN** Added, 1986.
- **BT** Ideologies
- **NT** Anarchism
  Authoritarianism (Political Ideology)
  Capitalism
  Communism
  Conservatism
  Corporatism
  Despotism
  Extremism
  Fascism
  Feudalism
  Imperialism
  Individualism
  Internationalism
  Liberalism
  Militarism
  Nationalism
  Neutralism
  Pacifism
  Patriotism
  Populism
  Radicalism
  Separatism
  Socialism
  Syndicalism
  Totalitarianism
- **RT** Bourgeois Ideologies
  Capitalist Societies
  Civil Religion
  Communist Societies
  Dominant Ideologies
  Economic Systems
  Elitism
  Government
  Ideological Struggle
  Liberal Democratic Societies
  Libertarians
  Marxism
  Meritocracy

Political Ideologies (cont'd)
- **RT** Nihilism
  Philosophy
  Physiocrats
  Political Parties
  Political Philosophy
  Political Science
  Political Socialization
  Political Systems
  Politics
  Praxis
  Progressivism
  Regionalism
  Revolutions
  Schism
  Sectarianism
  Social Democracy
  Social Reform
  Social Systems
  Social Values
  Socialist Societies
  State

Political Movements
- **DC** D640200
- **HN** Added, 1986.
- **BT** Movements
- **NT** Underground Movements
- **RT** Activism
  Black Power
  Civil Disobedience
  Countermovements
  Dissent
  Historical Development
  History
  Labor Movements
  Mau Mau Rebellion
  Peace Movements
  Political Action
  Political Behavior
  Politics
  Protest Movements
  Rebellions
  Reform
  Regional Movements
  Revolutions
  Self Determination
  Social Change
  Social Movements
  Youth Movements

Political Opinions
- **Use** Political Attitudes

Political Participation
- **DC** D640500
- **HN** Added, 1986.
- **BT** Participation
  Political Behavior
- **RT** Citizen Participation
  Citizens
  Elections
  Local Politics
  Political Parties
  Politics
  Protest Movements
  Public Policy
  Self Determination
  Voting

Political Parties
- **DC** D640800
- **HN** Formerly (1985) DC 339720, Political Party.
- **UF** Party/Parties (1963-1985)
  Two Party System (1963-1985)
- **BT** Organizations (Social)
- **NT** Communist Parties
  Labor Parties

Political

Political Parties (cont'd)
- NT Socialist Parties
- RT Candidates
  - Elections
  - Factionalism
  - Majorities (Politics)
  - Partisanship
  - Polarization
  - Political Affiliation
  - Political Attitudes
  - Political Campaigns
  - Political Ideologies
  - Political Participation
  - Political Power
  - Politicians
  - Politics
  - Schism
  - Social Democracy

Political Philosophy
- DC D641100
- HN Formerly (1971-1985) DC 339725.
- BT Philosophy
- RT Government
  - Philosophical Doctrines
  - Political Attitudes
  - Political Ideologies
  - Political Systems
  - Politics
  - State

Political Power
- DC D641400
- HN Formerly (1985) DC 339727.
- BT Power
- RT Black Power
  - Candidates
  - Civil Disobedience
  - Corruption
  - Government
  - Interest Groups
  - Labor Movements
  - Legislative Bodies
  - Lobbying
  - Marxism
  - Pluralism
  - Political Elites
  - Political Factors
  - Political Parties
  - Political Sociology
  - Political Violence
  - Politicians
  - Politics
  - Power Elite
  - Religion Politics Relationship
  - Ruling Class
  - Sovereignty
  - State Power
  - Voters

Political Representation
- DC D641550
- HN Added, 1986.
- BT Representation
- RT Legislative Bodies
  - Legislators
  - Politics
  - Voting

Political Repression
- Use Repression (Political)

Political Science
- DC D641700
- HN Formerly (1963-1985) DC 339730.
- BT Social Sciences
- RT Elections
  - Foreign Policy

Political Science (cont'd)
- RT Government Policy
  - International Law
  - International Relations
  - International Studies
  - Law
  - Policy Science
  - Political Behavior
  - Political Ideologies
  - Political Systems
  - Politics
  - Public Administration
  - State

Political Socialization
- DC D642000
- HN Added, 1986.
- BT Socialization
- RT Indoctrination
  - Political Attitudes
  - Political Culture
  - Political Ideologies
  - Politics
  - Social Attitudes

Political Sociology
- DC D642300
- HN Formerly (1963-1985) DC 339740.
- BT Sociology
- RT Conflict Theory
  - Political Behavior
  - Political Power
  - Politics
  - Sociology of Law

Political Systems
- DC D642600
- HN Added, 1986.
- UF Polity/Polities (1963-1985)
- BT Systems
- NT Chieftaincies
  - Democracy
  - Dictatorship
  - Empires
  - Gerontocracy
  - Monarchy
  - Oligarchy
  - Polyarchy
  - Republics
  - Technocracy
- RT Aristocracy
  - Constitutions
  - Economic Systems
  - Government
  - Ideologies
  - Legislative Bodies
  - Political Ideologies
  - Political Philosophy
  - Political Science
  - Politics
  - Social Systems
  - Society
  - State

Political Violence
- DC D642900
- HN Added, 1986.
- BT Violence
- NT Assassination
  - Coups d'Etat
  - Rebellions
  - Terrorism
- RT Civil Disorders
  - Civil War
  - Dissent
  - Genocide
  - Guerrillas
  - Mau Mau Rebellion

Politics

Political Violence (cont'd)
- RT Political Behavior
  - Political Power
  - Politics
  - Protest Movements
  - Repression (Political)
  - Revolutions
  - Riots
  - Torture

Political/Politically/Politicalization (1963-1985)
- HN DC 339690, deleted 1986. See now specific "Political" terms.

Politicians
- DC D643200
- HN Formerly (1963-1985) DC 339800, Politician/Politicians.
- RT Candidates
  - Leadership
  - Legislators
  - Political Campaigns
  - Political Parties
  - Political Power
  - Politics
  - Public Officials

Politico (1963-1985)
- HN DC 339900, deleted 1986.

Politics
- DC D643500
- HN Formerly (1963-1985) DC 340000.
- NT Class Politics
  - Geopolitics
  - Left Wing Politics
  - Local Politics
  - Right Wing Politics
- RT Candidates
  - Elections
  - Government
  - Ideological Struggle
  - Legislation
  - Majorities (Politics)
  - Political Action
  - Political Affiliation
  - Political Attitudes
  - Political Behavior
  - Political Campaigns
  - Political Culture
  - Political Defection
  - Political Economy
  - Political Elites
  - Political Factors
  - Political Ideologies
  - Political Movements
  - Political Participation
  - Political Parties
  - Political Philosophy
  - Political Power
  - Political Representation
  - Political Science
  - Political Socialization
  - Political Sociology
  - Political Systems
  - Political Violence
  - Politicians
  - Power Structure
  - Religion Politics Relationship
  - State

Politics Religion Relationship
- Use Religion Politics Relationship

Polity

Polity/Polities (1963-1985)
  HN DC 340050.
  Use Political Systems

Polls (Opinion)
  Use Opinion Polls

Pollution
  DC D643800
  HN Formerly (1969-1985) DC 340095.
  UF Environmental Contamination
  NT Air Pollution
  RT Conservation
      Diseases
      Earth (Planet)
      Ecology
      Environment
      Environmental Protection
      Health
      Human Ecology
      Industrialism
      Land Use
      Natural Environment
      Natural Resources
      Noise
      Poisoning
      Pollution Control
      Public Health
      Radiation
      Toxic Substances
      Wastes
      Water Supply
      World Problems

Pollution Control
  DC D644100
  HN Added, 1986.
  BT Control
  RT Air Pollution
      Environmental Protection
      Government Regulation
      Health Policy
      Human Ecology
      Poisoning
      Pollution
      Resource Management
      Wastes

Polyandry
  DC D644400
  HN Formerly (1963-1985) DC 340100.
  BT Polygamy
  RT Polygyny

Polyarchy
  DC D644700
  SN Government characterized by a balance of power between leaders and active participants outside of the leadership.
  HN Formerly (1964-1985) DC 340110, Polyarchy/Polyarchical.
  BT Political Systems
  RT Political Elites

Polygamy
  DC D645000
  HN Formerly (1963-1985) DC 340120.
  BT Marriage
  NT Polyandry
      Polygyny
  RT Monogamy

Polygraph
  Use Lie Detection

Polygyny
  DC D645300
  SN The concurrent marriage of one man to more than one woman.
  HN Formerly (1963-1985) DC 340125.
  BT Polygamy
  RT Polyandry

Polynesia
  DC D645600
  SN One of the three principal divisions of Oceania, comprising those island groups in the Pacific Ocean lying east of Melanesia and Micronesia and extending from Hawaii south to New Zealand.
  HN Formerly (1963-1985) DC 340140, Polynesia/Polynesian/Polynesians.
  BT Oceania
  NT American Samoa
      Cook Islands
      Easter Island
      French Polynesia
      Hawaii
      Line Islands
      Marquesas Islands
      Midway Islands
      Phoenix Islands
      Tokelau Islands
      Tonga
      Western Samoa

Polytechnic Schools
  DC D645900
  HN Formerly (1977-1985) DC 340155, Polytechnic.
  BT Colleges
  RT College Students
      Higher Education
      Vocational Education

Polytheistic Religions
  Use Paganism

Poor (1965-1985)
  HN DC 340174, deleted 1986. See now Disadvantaged, Low Income Groups, or Poverty.

Popes
  Use Papacy

Popper, Karl Raimund
  DC D646200
  SN Born 28 July 1902 - .
  HN Formerly (1964-1985) DC 340177, Popper, Karl R.

Popular Culture
  DC D646500
  SN Culture of the masses, often considered as a unique characteristic of modern urban society and dependent on commercialism or mass media, and having a diversity reflecting the various segments of a given population.
  HN Formerly (1963-1985) DC 340180, Popular/Popularity/Popularization.
  UF Entertainment/Entertainer/ Entertainers (1964-1985)
      Mass Culture (1963-1985)
  BT Culture
  RT Comics (Publications)
      Countercultures
      Eating And Drinking Establishments
      Entertainment Industry
      Fashions
      Fiction
      Films

Population

Popular Culture (cont'd)
  RT Folk Culture
      Magazines
      Mass Behavior
      Mass Media
      Mass Media Effects
      Mass Society
      Modern Society
      Music
      Newspapers
      Radio
      Television
      Western Society
      Youth Culture

Popular Magazines
  Use Magazines

Popular Songs (1966-1985)
  HN DC 340188.
  Use Music

Popularity
  Use Approval

Population
  DC D646800
  HN Formerly (1963-1985) DC 340200, Population/Populations/ Populationists.
  NT Overpopulation
      Rural Population
      Urban Population
      World Population
  RT Birth Control
      Census
      Demographic Change
      Demographic Characteristics
      Demography
      Family Planning
      Fertility
      Fertility Decline
      Geographic Mobility
      Geographic Regions
      Heterogeneity
      Homogeneity
      Indigenous Populations
      Migration
      Population Density
      Population Distribution
      Population Growth
      Population Policy

Population Change
  Use Demographic Change

Population Characteristics
  Use Demographic Characteristics

Population Density
  DC D647100
  HN Added, 1986.
  UF Density (1963-1985)
  NT Crowding
  RT Community Size
      Demography
      Environmental Factors
      Overpopulation
      Population
      Privacy
      Space
      Urban Areas

Population Distribution
  DC D647400
  HN Added, 1986.
  BT Demography
      Distribution
  RT Demographic Change
      Demographic Characteristics

Population

Population Distribution (cont'd)
- RT Geographic Distribution
    Internal Migration
    Land Settlement
    Migration
    Migration Patterns
    Population
    Relocation
    Residential Patterns
    Rural Population
    Settlement Patterns
    Urban Population
    World Population

Population Growth
- DC D647700
- HN Added, 1986.
- BT Demographic Change
- RT Demographic Transition Theory
    Development
    Family Size
    Fertility
    Fertility Decline
    Overpopulation
    Population
    Rural Population
    Urban Population
    World Population

Population Mobility
- Use Migration

Population Movements
- Use Migration

Population Parameters
- Use Parameters (Statistics)

Population Policy
- DC D648000
- HN Added, 1986.
- UF Demographic Policy
- BT Social Policy
- RT Abortion
    Birth Control
    Eugenics
    Family Policy
    Fertility
    Government Policy
    Migration
    Overpopulation
    Population

Population Redistribution
- Use Internal Migration

Population Statistics
- Use Census

Population Turnaround
- Use Return Migration

Populism
- DC D648300
- HN Formerly (1964-1985) DC 340300, Populism/Populist.
- BT Political Ideologies
- RT Peronism

Pornography
- DC D648600
- HN Formerly (1965-1985) DC 340335, Pornography/Pornographic.
- RT Obscenity
    Publications
    Sexuality

Portland, Oregon
- DC D648900
- HN Added, 1986.
- BT Oregon

Porto Alegre, Brazil
- DC D649000
- HN Added, 1989.
- BT Brazil

Portugal
- DC D649200
- HN Formerly (1963-1985) DC 340450, Portugal/Portuguese.
- BT Western Europe

Portuguese (Language)
- Use Romance Languages

Position/Positions/Positional (1964-1985)
- HN DC 340470, deleted 1986. See now Status, Attitudes, or Orientation.

Positivism
- DC D649350
- SN The philosophical position, developed by Auguste Comte, that scientific knowledge can come only from direct observation, experimentation, and the provision of quantitative data.
- HN Formerly (1963-1985) DC 340490, Positivism/Positivist/Positivistic.
- UF Logical Positivism
- BT Epistemological Doctrines
- RT Behaviorism
    Cultural Relativism
    Determinism
    Empiricism
    Falsification
    Frankfurt School
    Hermeneutics
    Methodological Individualism
    Methodology (Philosophical)
    Naturalism
    Nominalism
    Rationalism
    Reductionism
    Sociological Theory
    Verstehen

Postcards
- Use Letters (Correspondence)

Postdoctoral Programs
- DC D649500
- HN Formerly (1965-1985) DC 340540, Postdoctoral.
- BT Higher Education
- RT Doctoral Degrees
    Doctoral Programs
    Educational Programs
    Graduate Schools
    Graduate Students
    Universities

Postindustrial Societies
- DC D649800
- SN Term introduced by Daniel Bell describing the decline in manufacturing industries and the ascendancy of service industries and technological production in the late 20th century.
- HN Formerly (1979-1985) DC 340555, Postindustrial.
- BT Society
- RT Complex Societies
    Deindustrialization

Poverty

Postindustrial Societies (cont'd)
- RT Industrial Societies
    Industry
    Modern Society
    Service Industries
    Urbanization
    Western Society

Postmodernism
- DC D649850
- HN Added, 1989.
- BT Artistic Styles
- RT Architecture
    Art History
    Literature
    Modernity
    Traditionalism

Postsecondary Education
- Use Higher Education

Postulates
- DC D649900
- HN Formerly (1963-1985) DC 340625, Postulate/Postulates.
- UF Assumption/Assumptions (1984-1985)
    Presuppose/Presupposes/Presuppositions (1972-1985)
    Supposition (1964-1985)
- BT Propositions
- RT Heuristics
    Knowledge
    Methodology (Philosophical)
    Reasoning
    Science
    Theories

Postwar Reconstruction
- Use Reconstruction

Potential (1963-1985)
- HN DC 340700, deleted 1986.

Potlatches
- DC D650100
- SN Ceremonies practiced by certain American Indian tribes of the Pacific Northwest, in which property is distributed or destroyed as a demonstration of generosity and power.
- HN Formerly (1963-1985) DC 340730, Potlatch.
- BT Rituals
- RT American Indians
    Gift Giving

Pottery (1963-1985)
- HN DC 340745.
- Use Crafts

Poultry
- Use Livestock

Poverty
- DC D650400
- HN Formerly (1963-1985) DC 340800.
- UF Destitution (1980-1985)
    Indigent/Indigence (1969-1985)
- BT Economic Conditions
- NT Rural Poverty
    Urban Poverty
- RT Affluence
    Antipoverty Programs
    Beggary
    Deprivation
    Developing Countries
    Disadvantaged
    Economic Problems

Poverty

Poverty (cont'd)
- RT Economics
- Homelessness
- Hunger
- Low Income Areas
- Low Income Groups
- Skid Row
- Slums
- Social Class
- Social Inequality
- Social Problems
- Standard of Living
- Unemployment
- Wealth
- Welfare Services
- World Problems

Poverty Areas
- Use Low Income Areas

Poverty Programs
- Use Antipoverty Programs

Power
- DC D650700
- HN Formerly (1963-1985) DC 341000.
- UF Power Relations
- NT Authority
  - Community Power
  - Discretionary Power
  - Family Power
  - Organizational Power
  - Political Power
  - Social Power
  - State Power
- RT Balance Theory
  - Coercion
  - Conflict
  - Control
  - Dominance
  - Influence
  - Mana
  - Power Elite
  - Power Structure

Power Elite
- DC D651000
- SN Closely knit alliance of military, government, and corporate leaders, perceived as the center of financial and political power.
- HN Added, 1986.
- BT Elites
- RT Economic Elites
  - Leadership
  - Opinion Leaders
  - Political Elites
  - Political Power
  - Power
  - Ruling Class
  - Social Control
  - Social Influence

Power Relations
- Use Power

Power Structure
- DC D651300
- HN Formerly (1985) DC 341010.
- BT Structure
- RT Elites
  - Politics
  - Power
  - Privilege
  - Social Control
  - Social Structure

Powerless/Powerlessness (1970-1985)
- HN DC 341005.
- Use Alienation

Practice (Legal)
- Use Legal Procedure

Practice Theory Relationship
- Use Theory Practice Relationship

Practice/Practices (1963-1985)
- HN DC 342000.
- Use Methods

Practitioner Patient Relationship
- DC D651600
- HN Added, 1986.
- UF Dentist Patient Relationship
  - Doctor Patient Relationship
  - Nurse Patient Relationship
  - Physician Patient Relationship
- BT Client Relations
- RT Client Characteristics
  - Confidentiality
  - Dentists
  - Health Care
  - Health Professions
  - Helping Behavior
  - Illness
  - Medicine
  - Nurses
  - Patients
  - Physicians
  - Sick Role
  - Treatment
  - Treatment Methods

Practitioner/Practitioners (1963-1985)
- HN DC 342200, deleted 1986. See now Health Professions and its associated terms.

Pragmatics
- DC D651900
- HN Formerly (1963-1985) part of DC 342350, Pragmatism/Pragmatic/Pragmatist.
- UF Universal Pragmatics
- BT Semiotics
- RT Discourse Analysis
  - Grammar
  - Language
  - Language Usage
  - Semantics
  - Sociolinguistics
  - Speech

Pragmatism
- DC D652000
- SN A philosophical method that measures the truth, meaning, or value of a proposition by its practical usefulness.
- HN Formerly (1963-1985) part of DC 342350, Pragmatism/Pragmatic/Pragmatist.
- BT Epistemological Doctrines
- RT Achievement
  - Meaning
  - Symbolic Interactionism
  - Truth

Prague, Czechoslovakia
- DC D652200
- HN Formerly (1970-1985) DC 342355.
- BT Czechoslovakia

Prediction

Praxeology
- DC D652500
- SN Study of human action, behavior, and conduct, often in relation to moral, religious, social, logical, and aesthetic values.
- HN Formerly (1968-1985) DC 342390, Praxeology/Praxeological.
- BT Psychology
- RT Behaviorism
  - Ethics
  - Social Behavior
  - Values

Praxis
- DC D652600
- SN In Marxian theory, the concept of Action or material production as opposed to speculation or thought.
- HN Formerly (1979-1985) DC 342395.
- RT Action
  - Activities
  - Dialectical Materialism
  - Epistemological Doctrines
  - Frankfurt School
  - Implementation
  - Knowledge
  - Marxism
  - Materialism
  - Norms
  - Political Ideologies
  - Theory Practice Relationship

Prayer
- DC D652800
- HN Formerly (1964-1985) DC 342400.
- BT Religious Behavior
- RT Deities
  - Religious Rituals
  - Saints
  - Worship

Preachers
- DC D653100
- HN Formerly (1967-1985) part of DC 342450, Preacher/Preachers/Preaching.
- BT Clergy

Preaching
- Use Sermons

Precapitalist Societies
- Use Traditional Societies

Precognition
- Use Extrasensory Perception

Predators
- Use Animals

Predestination (1966-1985)
- HN DC 342900.
- Use Fate

Prediction
- DC D653300
- SN A context-dependent term; select a more specific entry or coordinate with other terms.
- HN Formerly (1963-1985) DC 343000, Prediction/Predictions/Predictive/Predictors/Predictability.
- UF Prognosis/Prognostication (1965-1985)
- NT Forecasting
- RT Estimation
  - Futures (of Society)
  - Hypotheses
  - Measurement

Prediction

Prediction (cont'd)
- RT Multiple Regression Analysis
  - Planning
  - Prediction Models
  - Probability
  - Prophecy
  - Reliability
  - Social Indicators
  - Statistics

Prediction Models
- DC D653325
- HN Added, 1986.
- BT Models
- RT Prediction

Predictor Variables
- Use Variables

Predispositions (1967-1985)
- HN DC 343300.
- Use Attitudes

Prefecture/Prefectorial (1964-1985)
- HN DC 343450.
- Use Districts

Preferences
- DC D653400
- HN Formerly (1963-1985) DC 343500, Preference/Preferences.
- UF Taste (1965-1985)
- NT Child Sex Preferences
  - Residential Preferences
  - Sexual Preferences
- RT Attitudes
  - Choices

Pregnancy
- DC D653700
- HN Formerly (1963-1985) DC 344000, Pregnancy/Pregnancies/Pregnant.
- UF Conceive (1965-1985)
  - Conception (Biology)
- NT Unwanted Pregnancy
- RT Abortion
  - Amniocentesis
  - Artificial Insemination
  - Birth
  - Fecundity
  - Fertility
  - Fetus
  - Gynecology
  - Miscarriage
  - Premature Infants
  - Reproductive Technologies
  - Sexual Reproduction

Prehistoric Man
- DC D654000
- HN Added, 1986.
- UF Early Man
  - Hominid (1967-1985)
  - Primitive Man
  - Telanthropus (1969-1985)
- RT Archaeology
  - Evolution
  - Hunting And Gathering Societies
  - Prehistory
  - Primates

Prehistory
- DC D654300
- HN Formerly (1972-1985) DC 344500, Prehistory/Prehistoric.
- UF Bronze Age (1971-1985)
  - Iron Age (1964-1985)
  - Neolithic (1964-1985)
  - Pleistocene Period (1977-1985)

Prehistory (cont'd)
- UF Stone Age
  - Upper Paleolithic (1963-1985)
- BT Time Periods
- RT Anthropology
  - Archaeology
  - History
  - Hunting And Gathering Societies
  - Nomadic Societies
  - Prehistoric Man
  - Traditional Societies

Prejudice
- DC D654600
- HN Formerly (1963-1985) DC 345000, Prejudice/Prejudices/Prejudiced.
- UF Bigotry (1965-1985)
  - Intolerance (1971-1985)
  - Social Bias
- BT Attitudes
  - Bias
- NT Anti-Semitism
- RT Ageism
  - Discrimination
  - Hostility
  - Inequality
  - Intergroup Relations
  - Minority Groups
  - Racism
  - Religious Attitudes
  - Sexism
  - Social Attitudes
  - Social Distance
  - Social Problems
  - Stereotypes
  - Tolerance

Prekindergarten
- Use Preschool Education

Premarital Sex
- DC D654900
- HN Formerly (1964-1985) DC 345100, Premarital.
- BT Sexual Behavior
- RT Adolescents
  - Birth Control
  - Cohabitation
  - Extramarital Sexuality
  - Marital Relations
  - Promiscuity
  - Sexual Intercourse
  - Sexual Permissiveness
  - Single Persons
  - Unwed Mothers

Premature Infants
- DC D655200
- HN Formerly (1964-1985) DC 345180, Prematurity.
- BT Infants
- RT Infant Mortality
  - Pregnancy

Prenatal (1963-1985)
- HN DC 345200.
- Use Fetus

Preparation (1963-1985)
- HN DC 345265, deleted 1986. See now Education, Job Training, or Food Preparation.

Prerogative/Prerogatives (1982-1985)
- HN DC 345295.
- Use Privilege

Presidents

Presbyterian Churches
- Use Presbyterians

Presbyterians
- DC D655500
- HN Formerly (1963-1985) DC 345310, Presbyterian.
- UF Presbyterian Churches
- BT Protestants
- RT Protestantism

Preschool Children
- DC D655800
- HN Formerly (1981-1985) part of DC 345320, Preschool.
- UF Nursery School Children
  - Preschoolers
- BT Children
- RT Day Care
  - Kindergarten
  - Preschool Education
  - Project Head Start

Preschool Education
- DC D656100
- HN Formerly (1981-1985) part of DC 345320, Preschool.
- UF Nursery School Education
  - Prekindergarten
  - Preschool Programs
- BT Education
- RT Elementary Education
  - Kindergarten
  - Preschool Children
  - Project Head Start

Preschool Programs
- Use Preschool Education

Preschoolers
- Use Preschool Children

Preservation
- DC D656200
- HN Formerly (1969-1985) DC 345330.
- UF Historic Preservation
- BT Maintenance
- RT Change
  - Conservation
  - Cultural Transmission
  - Modernization
  - Natural Environment
  - Obsolescence
  - Prevention
  - Protection
  - Survival

Presidency
- Use Presidents

Presidents
- DC D656400
- HN Formerly (1963-1985) DC 345350, Presidency/Presidential/President.
- UF Jefferson, Thomas/Jeffersonian (1967-1985)
  - Presidency
- BT Public Officials
- RT Carter Administration
  - Central Government
  - Government
  - Government Policy
  - Reagan Administration
  - Watergate Scandal

Press

Press Coverage
- Use News Coverage

Press, The (1963-1985)
- HN DC 345425.
- Use News Media

Pressure
- DC D656600
- HN Formerly (1963-1985) DC 345470, Pressure/Pressures.
- NT Blood Pressure
  Social Pressure
- RT Influence
  Stress

Pressure Groups
- Use Interest Groups

Prestige
- DC D656700
- HN Formerly (1963-1985) DC 345500.
- RT Awards
  Leadership
  Occupational Status
  Privilege
  Recognition (Achievement)
  Reputation
  Social Influence
  Social Status
  Social Values
  Success

Prestige (Occupational)
- Use Occupational Status

Presuppose/Presupposes/ Presuppositions (1972-1985)
- HN DC 345550.
- Use Postulates

Pretoria, South Africa
- DC D656900
- HN Added, 1989.
- BT South Africa

Pretrial Detention
- Use Detention

Pretrial Release
- DC D657000
- SN Allowing accused juveniles or adults to remain free before and during their trial.
- HN Added, 1986.
- UF Bail Decisions
- RT Arrests
  Detention
  Disposition
  Imprisonment
  Offenders
  Trials

Prevention
- DC D657300
- HN Formerly (1963-1985) DC 345600, Prevention/Preventive.
- NT Crime Prevention
  Deterrence
- RT Epidemiology
  Preservation
  Recidivism
  Treatment Compliance

Prices
- DC D657600
- HN Formerly (1963-1985) DC 345675, Price/Prices.
- RT Consumption

Prices (cont'd)
- RT Cost Containment
  Costs
  Economics
  Expenditures
  Finance
  Inflation
  Oligopolies
  Payments
  Production Consumption Relationship
  Products
  Purchasing
  Standard of Living
  Supply And Demand
  Value (Economics)

Pride (1968-1985)
- HN DC 345700.
- Use Self Esteem

Priesthood
- Use Priests

Priests
- DC D657900
- HN Formerly (1963-1985) DC 345740, Priest/Priests/Priesthood.
- UF Priesthood
- BT Clergy
- RT Religious Orders
  Shamanism

Primary Education
- DC D658200
- SN Children's first formal educational experience, usually consisting of kindergarten and the first three grades of elementary school.
- HN Added, 1986.
- BT Elementary Education
- RT Elementary School Students
  Elementary Schools
  Kindergarten

Primary Groups
- DC D658500
- SN A term introduced by Charles Horton Cooley to describe small, intimate social groups whose members have frequent, face-to-face interaction (eg, family, friends, certain work groups).
- HN Added, 1986.
- BT Social Groups
- NT Cliques
  Peer Groups
- RT Family
  Friendship
  Influence
  Interpersonal Relations
  Sociability
  Social Cohesion
  Social Contact
  Social Interaction
  Social Space
  Social Support

Primary Health Care
- DC D658550
- HN Added, 1989.
- BT Health Care
- RT Diagnosis
  Illness
  Medicine
  Physicians

Priorities

Primary School Students
- Use Elementary School Students

Primary/Primacy (1963-1985)
- HN DC 345780, deleted 1986.

Primates
- DC D658600
- HN Formerly (1969-1985) DC 345785, Primate/Primates.
- UF Monkeys (1964-1985)
- BT Animals
- RT Prehistoric Man

Primitive Man
- Use Prehistoric Man

Primitive/Primitives/Primitivism (1963-1985)
- HN DC 345815.
- Use Traditional Societies

Primogeniture (1972-1985)
- HN DC 345870.
- Use Birth Order

Prince Edward Island
- DC D658800
- HN Added, 1986.
- BT Canada

Principal Components Analysis
- DC D659000
- HN Added, 1986.
- BT Analysis
- RT Quantitative Methods

Principals
- DC D659100
- HN Formerly (1969-1985) DC 345878, Principal/Principals.
- BT Administrators
- RT Educational Administration
  Schools
  Teachers

Principles
- DC D659200
- SN A context-dependent term for basic rules or assumptions. Select a more specific entry or coordinate with other terms.
- HN Formerly (1963-1985) DC 345880, Principle/Principles.
- NT Propositions
- RT Deduction
  Ethics
  Ideologies
  Standards
  Synthesis
  Theories
  Values

Printing
- DC D659400
- HN Formerly (1964-1985) DC 345925.
- UF Printing Trades
  Typography
- RT Publications
  Publishing Industry
  Visual Arts

Printing Trades
- Use Printing

Priorities
- DC D659500
- HN Formerly (1966-1985) DC 345960, Priority/Priorities.
- RT Decision Making

Prison   Problems

Priorities (cont'd)
- RT Development Strategies
  Goals
  Needs
  Needs Assessment
  Planning
  Policy Making
  Resource Allocation
  Social Values

Prison Culture
- DC D659600
- HN Added, 1986.
- BT Culture
- RT Correctional Personnel
  Correctional System
  Prisoners
  Prisonization
  Prisons
  Subcultures

Prison System
- Use Correctional System

Prisoners
- DC D659700
- HN Formerly (1963-1985) part of DC 346000, Prison/Prisons/Prisoner/Prisoners.
- UF Inmate/Inmates (1963-1985)
- NT Prisoners of War
- RT Correctional System
  Discipline
  Imprisonment
  Institutionalization (Persons)
  Offenders
  Parole
  Penal Reform
  Prison Culture
  Prisonization
  Prisons

Prisoners of War
- DC D660000
- HN Added, 1986.
- UF Captivity (1966-1985)
  War Prisoners
- BT Prisoners
- RT War

Prisonization
- DC D660300
- SN Adjustment to prison life and prisoner identity, especially overadjustment and dependency on prison structure.
- HN Formerly (1966-1985) DC 347100.
- BT Socialization
- RT Imprisonment
  Prison Culture
  Prisoners
  Prisons

Prisons
- DC D660600
- HN Formerly (1963-1985) part of DC 346000, Prison/Prisons/Prisoner/Prisoners.
- UF Correctional Facilities
  Jail (1964-1985)
  Penitentiary/Penitentiaries (1964-1985)
- BT Facilities
- NT Concentration Camps
- RT Correctional System
  Imprisonment
  Institutions
  Juvenile Correctional Institutions
  Penal Reform

Prisons (cont'd)
- RT Penology
  Prison Culture
  Prisoners
  Prisonization

Privacy
- DC D660900
- HN Formerly (1963-1985) DC 347200, Privacy/Private.
- NT Confidentiality
- RT Anonymity
  Civil Rights
  Interpersonal Relations
  Personal Space
  Population Density
  Social Behavior

Private Enterprise
- Use Private Sector

Private Schools
- DC D661200
- HN Added, 1986.
- UF Independent Schools
  Nonpublic Schools
  Parochial Schools
  Proprietary Schools
- BT Schools
- RT Colleges
  Educational Systems
  Elementary Schools
  High Schools
  Public Schools
  Religious Education
  Students

Private Sector
- DC D661500
- SN The area of a nation's economy under private, rather than governmental, control.
- HN Added, 1986.
- UF Private Enterprise
- BT Economic Sectors
- RT Business
  Entrepreneurship
  Market Economy
  Privatization
  Public Sector
  Public Sector Private Sector Relations

Privatization
- DC D661600
- SN Transfer of assets or service functions under governmental control or ownership to the private sector.
- HN Added, 1989.
- RT Industrial Enterprises
  Nationalization
  Private Sector
  Public Sector
  Public Sector Private Sector Relations

Privilege
- DC D661800
- HN Formerly (1970-1985) DC 347400, Privilege/Privileges.
- UF Advantage/Advantages/Advantaged (1969-1985)
  Prerogative/Prerogatives (1982-1985)
- RT Elites
  Elitism
  Occupational Status
  Power Structure
  Prestige

Privilege (cont'd)
- RT Recognition (Achievement)
  Ruling Class
  Social Inequality
  Social Power
  Social Status

Privileged Communications
- Use Confidentiality

Prize/Prizes (1963-1985)
- HN DC 347500.
- Use Awards

Probabilism/Probabilistic (1963-1985)
- HN DC 347900.
- Use Probability

Probability
- DC D662000
- HN Formerly (1963-1985) DC 348000, Probability/Probabilities.
- UF Probabilism/Probabilistic (1963-1985)
- RT Chance
  Estimation
  Expectations
  Game Theory
  Markov Process
  Mathematics
  Prediction
  Quantitative Methods
  Reliability
  Risk
  Sampling
  Statistical Inference
  Statistical Significance
  Statistics
  Stochastic Models
  Variance (Statistics)

Probation
- DC D662100
- SN Criminal sentence in which the offender is allowed to remain out of prison under the supervision of an officer appointed by the court.
- HN Formerly (1963-1985) DC 348060, Probation/Probationer/Probationers.
- RT Correctional System
  Imprisonment
  Parole
  Sentencing

Probation Officers
- Use Correctional Personnel

Problem Solving
- DC D662400
- HN Formerly (1983-1985) DC 348135.
- BT Cognition
- RT Coping
  Decision Making
  Group Decision Making
  Help Seeking Behavior
  Problems
  Reasoning

Problems
- DC D662700
- SN A context-dependent term; select a more specific entry or coordinate with other terms. In sociological contexts where Problems is closely related to Social Problems, select the latter.
- HN Formerly (1963-1985) DC 348100, Problem/Problematic/Problems.

Procedure

Problems (cont'd)
- UF Difficulties (1971-1985)
  - Issue/Issues (1963-1985)
  - Obstacle/Obstacles (1967-1985)
- NT Behavior Problems
  - Economic Problems
  - Health Problems
  - Methodological Problems
  - Social Problems
  - Theoretical Problems
  - World Problems
- RT Adjustment
  - Conflict
  - Constraints
  - Crises
  - Disorders
  - Limitations
  - Problem Solving

Procedure/Procedures/Procedural (1964-1985)
- HN DC 348200, deleted 1986. See now Legal Procedure or Methods.

Proceedings (Criminal)
- Use Criminal Proceedings

Process Models (Stochastic)
- Use Stochastic Models

Process/Processes (1963-1985)
- HN DC 348235, deleted 1986.

Processing (1963-1985)
- HN DC 348260, deleted 1986. See now Disposition, Data Processing, or Information Processing.

Processing (Cases)
- Use Disposition

Procreation (1966-1985)
- HN DC 348270, deleted 1986.

Producer Cooperatives
- Use Cooperatives

Production
- DC D662900
- HN Formerly (1963-1985) part of DC 348300, Production/Productivity/Producer/Producers.
- NT Agricultural Production
  - Industrial Production
- RT Capital
  - Consumption
  - Economic Development
  - Economic Structure
  - Economics
  - Enterprises
  - Forces And Relations of Production
  - Industry
  - Labor
  - Labor Process
  - Labor Productivity
  - Land
  - Marxist Economics
  - Modes of Production
  - Production Consumption Relationship
  - Productivity
  - Sustenance Organization

Production Consumption Relationship
- DC D662925
- HN Added, 1986.
- UF Consumption Production Relationship
- BT Relations
- RT Commodities
  - Economics

Production Consumption Relationship (cont'd)
- RT Market Economy
  - Prices
  - Production
  - Supply And Demand

Production Forces and Relations
- Use Forces And Relations of Production

Production Modes
- Use Modes of Production

Production Process
- Use Labor Process

Productivity
- DC D663000
- HN Formerly (1963-1985) part of DC 348300, Production/Productivity/Producer/Producers.
- UF Output/Outputs (1963-1985)
- NT Labor Productivity
- RT Accountability
  - Economic Factors
  - Economics
  - Effectiveness
  - Efficiency
  - Performance
  - Production
  - Quotas
  - Scientific Management
  - Time Utilization

Products
- DC D663300
- HN Formerly (1963-1985) DC 348275, Product/Products/Productive/Productiveness.
- UF Consumer Products
- RT Business
  - Commodities
  - Consumers
  - Industry
  - Inventions
  - Marketing
  - Patents
  - Prices
  - Research And Development
  - Sales
  - Trade

Profane/Profanity (1963-1985)
- HN DC 348380.
- Use Obscenity

Professional Achievement
- Use Occupational Achievement

Professional Associations
- DC D663600
- SN Organizations formed to advance the interests of the various professions, eg, engineering, law, medicine. Includes learned and scholarly societies.
- HN Added, 1986.
- UF American Anthropological Association (1969-1985)
  - American Psychological Association (1965-1985)
  - American Statistical Association (1966-1985)
  - Scholarly Societies
  - Society for Psych Study of Social Issues/SPSSI (1970-1985)
- BT Associations
- NT Sociological Associations
- RT Fraternities And Sororities
  - Interest Groups
  - Professions

Professional

Professional Athletes
- Use Athletes

Professional Certification
- Use Certification

Professional Consultation
- DC D663900
- HN Formerly (1963-1985) part of DC 113410, Consult/Consults/Consultation/Consultant/Consulting.
- UF Consultation (Professional)
- RT Advisors
  - Assistance
  - Consultants
  - Cooperation
  - Employee Assistance Programs
  - Health Care Utilization
  - Help Seeking Behavior
  - Professions
  - Referral

Professional Criminals
- Use Career Criminals

Professional Ethics
- DC D664200
- HN Added, 1986.
- UF Deontology
- BT Ethics
- NT Research Ethics
- RT Codes of Conduct
  - Deception
  - Objectivity
  - Professional Orientations
  - Professions

Professional Identity
- DC D664500
- HN Added, 1986.
- BT Group Identity
- RT Professional Orientations
  - Professional Socialization
  - Professional Workers
  - Professions
  - Social Identity

Professional Journals
- Use Journals

Professional Malpractice
- DC D664800
- HN Formerly (1972-1985) DC 256668, Malpractice/Malpractices.
- UF Malpractice (Professional)
  - Medical Malpractice
- RT Accountability
  - Client Relations
  - Liability
  - Professions
  - Treatment

Professional Occupations
- Use Professions

Professional Orientations
- DC D665100
- HN Added, 1986.
- UF Socioprofessional Orientations
- BT Work Orientations
- RT Professional Ethics
  - Professional Identity
  - Professionalism
  - Professions
  - Work Values

Professional

Professional Personnel
- Use Professional Workers

Professional Roles
- Use Occupational Roles

Professional Socialization
- DC D665400
- SN Socialization of practitioners, eg, teachers, lawyers, physicians, military officers.
- HN Added, 1986.
- BT Socialization
- RT Professional Identity
  Professional Training
  Professional Workers
  Professions

Professional Sports
- DC D665700
- HN Added, 1986.
- BT Sports
- RT Sports Violence

Professional Status
- Use Occupational Status

Professional Training
- DC D666000
- HN Added, 1986.
- BT Training
- RT Academic Degrees
  Dental Students
  Doctoral Programs
  Employability
  Graduate Students
  Higher Education
  Job Training
  Medical Schools
  Medical Students
  Professional Socialization
  Professional Workers
  Professions

Professional Women
- DC D666300
- HN Added, 1986.
- BT Working Women
- RT Nontraditional Occupations
  Professional Workers
  Professions
  Womens Roles

Professional Workers
- DC D666600
- HN Added, 1986.
- UF Professional Personnel
- BT Workers
- NT Accountants
  Administrators
  Architects
  Artists
  Chiropractors
  Clergy
  Dentists
  Engineers
  Journalists
  Judges
  Lawyers
  Musicians
  Pharmacists
  Physicians
  Planners
  Psychiatrists
  Psychologists
  Researchers
  Scientists
  Social Scientists
  Social Workers

Professional Workers (cont'd)
- NT Statisticians
  Teachers
  Therapists
  Writers
- RT Blue Collar Workers
  Businessmen
  Consultants
  Occupational Classifications
  Occupational Status
  Paraprofessional Workers
  Professional Identity
  Professional Socialization
  Professional Training
  Professional Women
  Professions
  Referral
  Salaries
  Specialists
  White Collar Workers

Professionalism
- DC D666900
- HN Formerly (1963-1985) part of DC 348400, Profession/Professions/Professional/Professionalism.
- BT Work Attitudes
- RT Professional Orientations
  Professions
  Work Values

Professionalization
- DC D667200
- HN Formerly (1963-1985) DC 348480.
- UF Deprofessionalization
- BT Social Processes
- RT Occupations
  Professions

Professions
- DC D667500
- HN Formerly (1963-1985) part of DC 348400, Profession/Professions/Professional/Professionalism.
- UF Professional Occupations
- BT Occupations
- NT Health Professions
  Legal Profession
- RT Brain Drain
  Careers
  Laymen
  Occupational Classifications
  Occupational Status
  Professional Associations
  Professional Consultation
  Professional Ethics
  Professional Identity
  Professional Malpractice
  Professional Orientations
  Professional Socialization
  Professional Training
  Professional Women
  Professional Workers
  Professionalism
  Professionalization

Professor/Professors/Professorial (1963-1985)
- HN DC 348482.
- Use College Faculty

Proficiency (1978-1985)
- HN DC 348500.
- Use Competence

Profiles
- DC D667700
- SN A context-dependent term for biographical sketches or general descriptions of social phenomena based on statistical data.

Programming

Profiles (cont'd)
- HN Formerly (1963-1985) DC 348600, Profile/Profiles.
- RT Aggregate Data
  Analysis
  Measurement
  Measures (Instruments)

Profit Motive
- DC D667800
- HN Formerly (1977-1985) DC 348636.
- BT Incentives
- RT Businessmen
  Capitalism
  Motivation
  Profits

Profitability (1963-1985)
- HN DC 348630.
- Use Profits

Profits
- DC D668100
- HN Formerly (1964-1985) DC 348615, Profit/Profits.
- UF Profitability (1963-1985)
- BT Income
- RT Business
  Capital
  Economics
  Investment
  Money
  Profit Motive
  Wealth

Prognosis/Prognostication (1965-1985)
- HN DC 348650.
- Use Prediction

Program Evaluation
- DC D668300
- HN Formerly (1984-1985) DC 348670.
- BT Evaluation
- RT Effectiveness
  Programs
  Treatment Programs

Program Implementation
- DC D668350
- HN Added, 1986.
- BT Implementation
- RT Delivery Systems
  Development Programs
  Educational Programs
  Programs
  Services
  Social Programs
  Treatment Programs

Programmed Learning (1963-1985)
- HN DC 348740.
- Use Computer Assisted Instruction

Programming (Broadcast)
- DC D668400
- SN Selection and scheduling of television or radio programs for a station or network. Includes analyses of the contents of broadcast programs.
- HN Formerly (1963-1985) DC 348800, Programming.
- UF Broadcast Scheduling
  Radio Programming
  Television Programming
- RT Radio
  Recordings
  Television
  Television Viewing
  Videotape Recordings

Programming

Programming (Computers)
  Use Computer Software

Programs
- DC D668450
- SN Activities organized to accomplish specific goals or to provide controlled flows of information.
- HN Formerly (1963-1985) DC 348660, Program/Programs/Programmer/Programmers.
- UF Project/Projects (1963-1985)
- NT Antipoverty Programs
      Development Programs
      Educational Programs
      Employee Assistance Programs
      Income Maintenance Programs
      Internship Programs
      Literacy Programs
      Social Programs
      Treatment Programs
- RT Deinstitutionalization
      Delivery Systems
      Evaluation Research
      Participation
      Program Evaluation
      Program Implementation
      Services

Progress
- DC D668550
- HN Formerly (1963-1985) DC 348875.
- NT Social Progress
      Technological Progress
- RT Development
      Economic Development
      Evolutionary Theories
      Historical Development
      Improvement
      Modernization
      Progressivism
      Reform
      Scientific Development
      Scientific Technological Revolution

Progressivism
- DC D668600
- SN The belief in improving political, economic, or educational conditions through moderate change, using governmental power if necessary.
- HN Formerly (1964-1985) DC 348960, Progressive/Progressives/Progressivism/Progressiveness.
- RT Activism
      Political Action
      Political Attitudes
      Political Ideologies
      Progress
      Social Attitudes
      Social Criticism
      Social Theories

Prohibition (1964-1985)
- HN DC 349175, deleted 1986. See now Legislation or Taboos.

Project Head Start
- DC D668700
- HN Added, 1986.
- UF Head Start (1971-1985)
- BT Educational Programs
- RT Academic Achievement
      Preschool Children
      Preschool Education

Project/Projects (1963-1985)
- HN DC 349300.
- Use Programs

Projection/Projections/Projecting/Projective (1963-1985)
- HN DC 350000, deleted 1986. See now Forecasting, Prediction, or Projective Techniques.

Projections (Forecasting)
  Use Forecasting

Projective Techniques
- DC D668800
- SN Psychological testing in which the subject verbalizes reactions to sets of pictures or objects.
- HN Formerly (1963-1985) DC 351000.
- UF Rorschach Test (1963-1985)
- BT Methods
- RT Attitude Measures
      Emotions
      Personality Measures

Proletarianization
- DC D669000
- SN In Marxist analysis, the process precursing revolution in which the Middle Class realigns its interests with those of the Working Class.
- HN Formerly (1963-1985) part of DC 351080, Proletariat/Proletarian/Proletarianization.
- BT Social Processes
- RT Embourgeoisement
      Middle Class
      Proletariat
      Social Mobility
      Working Class

Proletariat
- DC D669300
- SN The working class, as conceived in Marxian analyses, especially manual workers not owning property. Contrast with Bourgeoisie.
- HN Formerly (1963-1985) part of DC 351080, Proletariat/Proletarian/Proletarianization.
- RT Class Struggle
      Forces And Relations of Production
      Lower Class
      Marxism
      Proletarianization
      Working Class

Promiscuity
- DC D669600
- HN Formerly (1964-1985) DC 351120, Promiscuous/Promiscuity.
- BT Sexual Behavior
- RT Deviant Behavior
      Extramarital Sexuality
      Premarital Sex
      Sexual Permissiveness

Promotion (Occupational)
- DC D669900
- HN Formerly (1963-1985) DC 351150, Promotion/Promotions.
- UF Job Promotion
      Occupational Promotion
- BT Personnel Management
- RT Careers
      Employment Opportunities
      Job Performance
      Occupational Achievement
      Occupational Mobility
      Recognition (Achievement)
      Seniority

Propositions

Propaganda
- DC D670200
- HN Formerly (1963-1985) DC 351200, Propaganda/Propagandist/Propagandistic.
- BT Communication
- RT Agitation
      Deception
      Discourse
      Indoctrination
      Information Dissemination
      Mass Media
      Mass Media Effects
      Partisanship
      Persuasion
      Public Opinion
      Public Relations

Propensity (1964-1985)
- HN DC 351280, deleted 1986.

Property
- DC D670500
- HN Formerly (1963-1985) DC 351300, Property/Properties.
- UF Personal Property
      Real Property
- RT Accumulation
      Capital
      Economics
      Expropriation
      Forces And Relations of Production
      Inheritance And Succession
      Land
      Maintenance
      Ownership
      Property Rights
      Tenure
      Value (Economics)
      Wealth

Property Rights
- DC D670800
- HN Added, 1986.
- BT Civil Rights
- NT Copyrights
- RT Ownership
      Patents
      Property

Prophecy
- DC D671100
- SN Inspired revelation, often concerning the future, imparted under the influence of a religious or psychic experience.
- HN Formerly (1963-1985) DC 351340.
- RT Apocalypse
      Divination
      Messianic Figures
      Millenarianism
      Prediction
      Religious Beliefs

Propinquity (1963-1985)
- HN DC 351350, deleted 1986.

Propositions
- DC D671250
- HN Formerly (1971-1985) DC 351351, Proposition/Propositions/Propositional.
- BT Principles
- NT Hypotheses
      Postulates
- RT Deduction
      Fallacies
      Generalization
      Inference
      Paradigms
      Science
      Theories

Proprietary / Psychedelic

Proprietary Schools
- **Use** Private Schools

Proprietor/Proprietors/Propriety (1979-1985)
- **HN** DC 351352, deleted 1986.

Prosecute/Prosecution/Prosecuting/Prosecutors (1963-1985)
- **HN** DC 351353, deleted 1986. See now Criminal Proceedings, Litigation, or Prosecutors.

Prosecutors
- **DC** D671400
- **HN** Formerly (1963-1985) part of DC 351353, Prosecute/Prosecution/Prosecuting/Prosecuted/Prosecutor.
- **UF** Attorneys (Prosecuting)
- **BT** Lawyers
- **RT** Criminal Proceedings
  Judges
  Juvenile Justice
  Law Enforcement
  Legal Profession
  Plea Bargaining
  Trials

Proselytism
- **DC** D671700
- **HN** Formerly (1969-1986) DC 351354, Proselytize/Proselytizing.
- **BT** Religious Behavior
- **RT** Evangelism
  Missionaries
  Religious Conversion

Prosperity (1964-1985)
- **HN** DC 351355.
- **Use** Affluence

Prostitution
- **DC** D672000
- **HN** Formerly (1963-1985) DC 351362, Prostitute/Prostitutes/Prostitution.
- **UF** Pandering
  Pimp/Pimps/Pimping (1973-1985)
- **BT** Offenses
- **RT** Female Offenders
  Organized Crime
  Sexual Behavior

Protagonists
- **Use** Heroes

Protection
- **DC** D672200
- **HN** Formerly (1964-1985) DC 351395, Protection/Protective.
- **NT** Consumerism
  Environmental Protection
- **RT** Foster Care
  Intervention
  Law Enforcement
  Preservation
  Safety
  Security

Protectionism
- **DC** D672250
- **HN** Added, 1989.
- **BT** Economic Policy
- **RT** Economic Systems
  Economic Theories
  Exports and Imports
  Foreign Policy
  Market Economy
  Markets
  Trade
  World Economy

Protest Movements
- **DC** D672300
- **HN** Formerly (1963-1985) DC 351398, Protest/Protesters.
- **UF** Demonstration/Demonstrations (1966-1985)
  Sit-In/Sit-Ins (1963-1985)
- **BT** Social Movements
- **NT** Boycotts
- **RT** Activism
  Antinuclear Movements
  Civil Disobedience
  Civil Disorders
  Civil Rights Organizations
  Dissent
  Government Policy
  Movements
  Political Action
  Political Movements
  Political Participation
  Political Violence
  Social Action
  Social Conflict
  Social Criticism
  Social Unrest

Protestant Ethic
- **DC** D672600
- **SN** Values attached to hard work, thrift, and efficiency, deemed in certain Protestant theological teachings as signs of eternal salvation.
- **HN** Added, 1986.
- **UF** Puritan Ethic
  Work Ethic
- **BT** Ethics
- **RT** Protestantism
  Work Orientations
  Work Values

Protestant Reformation
- **DC** D672900
- **HN** Added, 1986.
- **UF** Reformation (1964-1985)
- **BT** Religious Movements
- **RT** Protestantism
  Roman Catholicism

Protestantism
- **DC** D673200
- **HN** Formerly (1963-1985) part of DC 351400, Prostestant/Protestants/Protestantism.
- **BT** Christianity
- **NT** Calvinism
- **RT** Amish
  Anabaptists
  Anglicans
  Baptists
  Episcopalians
  Evangelism
  Hutterites
  Jehovah's Witnesses
  Lutherans
  Mennonites
  Methodists
  Mormons
  Pentacostalists
  Presbyterians
  Protestant Ethic
  Protestant Reformation
  Protestants
  Puritans
  Quakers
  Religious Fundamentalism
  Unitarians

Protestants
- **DC** D673500
- **HN** Formerly (1963-1985) part of DC 351400, Protestant/Protestants/Protestantism.
- **BT** Christians
- **NT** Amish
  Anabaptists
  Anglicans
  Baptists
  Calvinists
  Episcopalians
  Jehovah's Witnesses
  Lutherans
  Mennonites
  Methodists
  Mormons
  Pentacostalists
  Presbyterians
  Puritans
  Quakers
  Unitarians
- **RT** Protestantism
  Religious Fundamentalism

Proudhon, Pierre-Joseph
- **DC** D673800
- **SN** Born 15 January 1809 - died 19 January 1865.
- **HN** Formerly (1966-1985) DC 351490, Proudhon, J. J.

Proverbs (1965-1985)
- **HN** DC 351500.
- **Use** Folklore

Provinces
- **DC** D674100
- **HN** Formerly (1966-1985) DC 351510, Province/Provinces.
- **UF** Provincial (1964-1985)
- **RT** Central Government
  Geographic Regions
  Governors
  Regional Movements
  States (Political Subdivisions)

Provincial (1964-1985)
- **HN** DC 351560.
- **Use** Provinces

Proxemic (1964-1985)
- **HN** DC 351570.
- **Use** Personal Space

Prussia
- **DC** D674400
- **HN** Formerly (1968-1985) DC 351573, Prussia/Prussian/Prussians.
- **BT** Europe
- **RT** Germany

Pseudonyms (1964-1985)
- **HN** DC 351600.
- **Use** Authorship

Psyche
- **Use** Mind

Psychedelic Drugs
- **DC** D674700
- **HN** Formerly (1966-1985) DC 351900, Psychedelic.
- **UF** Hallucinogenic Drugs
  Mescal/Mescaline (1963-1985)
  Peyote (1963-1985)
- **BT** Drugs
- **NT** Lysergic Acid Diethylamide
- **RT** Cocaine
  Hallucinations
  Marijuana
  Narcotic Drugs

Psychiatric

Psychiatric Diagnosis
  Use Diagnosis

Psychiatric Hospitalization
  Use Hospitalization

Psychiatric Hospitals
  Use Mental Hospitals

Psychiatric Patients
  Use Mental Patients

Psychiatric Research
  DC D674900
  HN Added, 1986.
  BT Research
  RT Mental Illness
     Mental Patients
     Psychiatry
     Psychological Research

Psychiatric Social Work
  Use Clinical Social Work

Psychiatric Social Workers
  Use Social Workers

Psychiatrists
  DC D675000
  HN Formerly (1963-1985) DC 352000, Psychiatrist/Psychiatrists.
  BT Professional Workers
  RT Health Professions
     Physicians
     Psychiatry
     Psychoanalysis
     Psychologists
     Therapists

Psychiatry
  DC D675300
  HN Formerly (1963-1985) DC 353000, Psychiatry/Psychiatric.
  UF Neuropsychiatry/Neuropsychiatric (1967-1985)
  BT Medicine
  NT Forensic Psychiatry
     Social Psychiatry
  RT Behavioral Sciences
     Mental Illness
     Mental Patients
     Neurology
     Psychiatric Research
     Psychiatrists
     Psychoanalysis
     Psychology
     Psychopathology
     Psychotherapy

Psychic (1963-1985)
  HN DC 353200, deleted 1986.

Psycho (1963-1985)
  HN DC 353500, deleted 1986.

Psychoanalysis
  DC D675600
  HN Formerly (1963-1985) DC 354000, Psychoanalysis/Psychoanalytic/Psychoanalyst/Psychoanalysts.
  UF Psychoanalytic Therapy
  BT Psychotherapy
  RT Freudian Psychology
     Mental Illness
     Oedipal Complex
     Psychiatrists
     Psychiatry

Psychoanalytic Interpretation
  DC D675900
  HN Added, 1986.
  UF Theory (Psychoanalytic)
  RT Critical Theory
     Frankfurt School
     Freudian Psychology
     Psychohistory
     Sociological Theory
     Unconscious (Psychology)

Psychoanalytic Therapy
  Use Psychoanalysis

Psychobiology (1964-1985)
  HN DC 356340, deleted 1986.

Psychodynamics
  DC D676200
  SN Psychological theories and systems that emphasize processes of mental or emotional development and/or analyze behavior in terms of motivation or drive.
  HN Added, 1986.
  RT Cognitive Development
     Group Dynamics
     Interpersonal Relations
     Motivation
     Personality
     Psychological Factors
     Social Interaction
     Symbiotic Relations

Psychohistory
  DC D676500
  SN Method of qualitative historical investigation that focuses on individual and group Freudian psychodynamics.
  HN Added, 1986.
  BT History
  RT Biographies
     Historiography
     Life History
     Psychoanalytic Interpretation
     Psychological Factors
     Psychology
     Social Science Research

Psycholinguistics
  DC D676800
  SN Interdisciplinary study of language within the context of general human behavior, especially concerning the observation of linguistic processes, eg, language acquisition, and how they relate to psychological studies of perception, memory, intelligence, etc.
  HN Formerly (1964-1985) DC 357580.
  BT Linguistics
  RT Bilingualism
     Grammar
     Language Acquisition
     Language Attitudes
     Language Disorders
     Multilingualism
     Psychology
     Sociolinguistics

Psychological Adjustment
  Use Adjustment

Psychological Development
  DC D677000
  HN Added, 1989.
  BT Development
  NT Cognitive Development
  RT Adult Development
     Child Development
     Developmental Stages
     Moral Development
     Psychosocial Factors

Psychology

Psychological Distress
  DC D677100
  HN Formerly (1984-1985) DC 135550, Distress.
  UF Anguish
     Distress (Psychological)
  RT Crises
     Emotions
     Pain
     Pessimism
     Psychological Factors
     Psychological Stress
     Suffering

Psychological Factors
  DC D677200
  HN Added, 1989.
  RT Behavior
     Childhood Factors
     Conditioning
     Emotions
     Personality
     Psychodynamics
     Psychohistory
     Psychological Distress
     Psychological Stress
     Psychology
     Psychosocial Factors

Psychological Research
  DC D677300
  HN Added, 1986.
  BT Social Science Research
  RT Behavior
     Personality
     Personality Measures
     Psychiatric Research
     Psychology
     Psychometric Analysis

Psychological Stress
  DC D677400
  HN Formerly (1985) DC 358010.
  BT Stress
  RT Anxiety
     Cognitive Dissonance
     Coping
     Occupational Stress
     Psychological Distress
     Psychological Factors
     Tension

Psychologists
  DC D677700
  HN Formerly (1963-1985) DC 357700, Psychologist/Psychologists.
  BT Professional Workers
  RT Correctional Personnel
     Health Professions
     Psychiatrists
     Psychology
     Researchers
     Social Scientists
     Social Workers
     Therapists

Psychology
  DC D678000
  HN Formerly (1963-1985) part of DC 358000, Psychology/Psychological/Psychologically/Psychologism.
  UF Neuropsychology/Neuropsychological (1972-1985)
  BT Behavioral Sciences
  NT Behaviorism
     Freudian Psychology
     Gestalt Psychology
     Praxeology

Psychology (cont'd)
- NT Psychopathology
  - Social Psychology
- RT Behavior
  - Cognition
  - Conditioning
  - Counseling
  - Emotions
  - Functionalism
  - Gerontology
  - Graphology
  - Indeterminism
  - Parapsychology
  - Personality
  - Phenomenology
  - Philosophical Doctrines
  - Psychiatry
  - Psychohistory
  - Psycholinguistics
  - Psychological Factors
  - Psychological Research
  - Psychologists
  - Psychometric Analysis
  - Psychotherapy
  - Social Work
  - Structuralism

Psychometric Analysis
- DC D678150
- SN The measurement of psychological traits, abilities, and processes using standardized devices such as intelligence and personality tests.
- HN Formerly (1963-1985) DC 358020, Psychometry/Psychometric.
- UF Psychometry
- BT Quantitative Methods
- RT Clinical Social Work
  - Intelligence Tests
  - Personality Measures
  - Psychological Research
  - Psychology

Psychometry
- Use Psychometric Analysis

Psychoneurotic/Psychoneurotics (1984-1985)
- HN DC 359500.
- Use Neurosis

Psychopathic Personality
- Use Sociopathic Personality

Psychopathology
- DC D678300
- HN Formerly (1963-1985) DC 360000, Psychopath/Psychopathic/ Psychopathy/Psychopathology.
- UF Abnormal Psychology
- BT Psychology
- RT Depression (Psychology)
  - Disorders
  - Emotionally Disturbed
  - Hallucinations
  - Mental Illness
  - Psychiatry
  - Social Psychology

Psychosis
- DC D678600
- HN Formerly (1963-1985) DC 361300, Psychosis/Psychoses/Psychotic/ Psychotics.
- UF Insanity
- BT Mental Illness
- NT Paranoia
  - Schizophrenia
- RT Depression (Psychology)

Psychosocial (1963-1985)
- HN DC 361600, deleted 1986.

Psychosocial Factors
- DC D678800
- SN A context-dependent term encompassing both psychological and social variables used together to explain specific social problems.
- HN Reinstated 1989. Formerly (1963-1985) DC 361600, Psychosocial.
- RT Psychological Development
  - Psychological Factors
  - Social Factors

Psychosomatic (1963-1985)
- HN DC 361700, deleted 1986.

Psychotherapeutic Transference
- Use Transference (Psychology)

Psychotherapist/Psychotherapists (1966-1985)
- HN DC 362190.
- Use Therapists

Psychotherapy
- DC D678900
- HN Formerly (1963-1985) DC 362200, Psychotherapy/Psychotherapeutic.
- UF Paradigmatic Techniques (Psychotherapy)
  - Paradoxical Techniques (Psychotherapy)
  - Reality Therapy
- BT Treatment
- NT Psychoanalysis
- RT Behavior Modification
  - Clinical Social Work
  - Client Relations
  - Clients
  - Conjoint Therapy
  - Employee Assistance Programs
  - Family Therapy
  - Group Therapy
  - Hypnosis
  - Intervention
  - Mental Illness
  - Psychiatry
  - Psychology
  - Role Playing
  - Self Disclosure
  - Social Workers
  - Transference (Psychology)

Puberty
- DC D679200
- HN Formerly (1963-1985) DC 362940.
- BT Life Cycle
- RT Adolescents
  - Childhood
  - Initiation Rites
  - Life Stage Transitions
  - Menarche
  - Rites of Passage

Public (1963-1985)
- HN DC 362970, deleted 1986. See now specific "Public" terms.

Public Administration
- DC D679500
- SN Study and practice of management of governmental functions and agencies.
- HN Formerly (1963-1985) DC 362975.
- BT Management
- RT Bureaucracy
  - Cities

Public Administration (cont'd)
- RT Civil Service
  - Government
  - Government Agencies
  - Political Science
  - Public Officials
  - Public Sector
  - Public Services
  - Registration

Public Attitudes
- Use Public Opinion

Public Behavior
- DC D679800
- SN Behavior in public places.
- HN Added, 1986.
- BT Behavior
- RT Anonymity
  - Deviant Behavior
  - Sociability
  - Social Behavior

Public Confidence
- Use Public Support

Public Debt
- DC D680100
- SN Internal or external public debt.
- HN Added, 1986.
- UF Deficits (1980-1985)
  - External Debt
  - Foreign Debt
  - National Debt
- BT Debts
- RT Budgets
  - Economic Crises
  - Government Spending
  - Public Finance
  - World Economy

Public Enterprises
- Use Public Sector

Public Finance
- DC D680400
- HN Added, 1986.
- UF Government Finance
  - State Finance
- BT Finance
- RT Cost Containment
  - Fiscal Policy
  - Government
  - Government Spending
  - Public Debt
  - Taxation

Public (General)
- Use General Public

Public Goods
- DC D680700
- HN Added, 1986.
- UF Goods (Public)
- RT Public Services

Public Health
- DC D681000
- HN Formerly (1963-1985) DC 362980.
- BT Health
- RT Diseases
  - Epidemics
  - Epidemiology
  - Fluoridation
  - Health Policy
  - Health Services
  - Morbidity
  - Occupational Safety And Health
  - Pollution

Public

Public Health (cont'd)
- RT Sanitation
- Socialized Medicine
- Toxic Substances
- Vaccination
- Wastes

Public Health Services
- Use Health Services

Public Housing
- DC D681300
- HN Added, 1986.
- UF Government Sponsored Housing
- Low Income Housing
- BT Housing
- RT Housing Policy
- Public Services
- Rental Housing
- Tenants
- Welfare Services

Public Libraries
- Use Libraries

Public Officials
- DC D681600
- HN Added, 1986.
- UF Elected Officials
- Government Officials
- State Officials
- NT Governors
- Judges
- Legislators
- Mayors
- Presidents
- RT Administrators
- Candidates
- Civil Service
- Correctional Personnel
- Elections
- Fire Fighters
- Government
- Government Agencies
- Ombudsmen
- Police
- Policy Implementation
- Policy Making
- Politicians
- Public Administration
- Public Services
- Superintendents

Public Opinion
- DC D681900
- HN Formerly (1963-1985) DC 363000.
- UF Public Attitudes
- Public Perceptions
- BT Opinions
- RT Citizens
- Consensus
- Dissent
- Editorials
- General Public
- Mass Media Effects
- Opinion Polls
- Polarization
- Political Attitudes
- Propaganda
- Public Opinion Research
- Public Policy
- Public Relations
- Public Support
- Scandals
- Social Attitudes

Public Opinion Research
- DC D681950
- HN Added, 1986.
- BT Social Science Research
- RT Fieldwork
- Opinion Polls
- Public Opinion
- Surveys

Public Opposition
- Use Public Support

Public Participation
- Use Citizen Participation

Public Perceptions
- Use Public Opinion

Public Policy
- DC D682200
- HN Formerly (1984-1985) DC 363050.
- BT Policy
- RT Agricultural Policy
- Fiscal Policy
- Futures (of Society)
- General Public
- Government
- Government Policy
- Interest Groups
- Legislation
- Policy Implementation
- Political Participation
- Public Opinion
- Social Goals
- Social Policy

Public Relations
- DC D682300
- SN Use of publicity to create favorable public opinion for a business, government, etc. Do not confuse with Advertising, whose principal goal is the sale of a product or service.
- HN Added, 1989.
- BT Relations
- RT Advertising
- Business Society Relationship
- Mass Media
- Propaganda
- Public Opinion
- Publicity

Public Response
- Use Social Response

Public Schools
- DC D682500
- HN Formerly (1963-1985) DC 363100, Public School/Public Schools.
- BT Schools
- RT Colleges
- Community Colleges
- Educational Policy
- Educational Systems
- Elementary Schools
- High Schools
- Private Schools
- School Districts
- Students

Public Sector
- DC D682800
- SN The area of a nation's economy under governmental, rather than private, control.
- HN Added, 1986.
- UF Public Enterprises
- BT Economic Sectors
- RT Government
- Nationalization

Public Sector (cont'd)
- RT Private Sector
- Privatization
- Public Administration
- Public Sector Private Sector Relations
- Public Services
- State

Public Sector Private Sector Relations
- DC D682900
- SN Interactions and reciprocal effects among social institutions and agencies administered by federal, state, and local governments, and those owned and operated by private parties.
- HN Added, 1989.
- BT Industry
- Social Relations
- RT Business Society Relationship
- Economic Policy
- Government Policy
- Government Regulation
- Industrial Development
- Nationalization
- Private Sector
- Privatization
- Public Sector
- State Society Relationship

Public Services
- DC D683100
- HN Formerly (1979-1985) DC 363150, Public Service/Public Services.
- BT Services
- NT Extension Services
- RT Community Services
- Emergencies
- Government
- Government Agencies
- Human Services
- Law Enforcement
- Public Administration
- Public Goods
- Public Housing
- Public Officials
- Public Sector
- Public Transportation
- Social Policy
- Welfare State

Public Spending
- Use Government Spending

Public Support
- DC D683400
- HN Added, 1986.
- UF Public Confidence
- Public Opposition
- BT Support
- RT General Public
- Police Community Relations
- Political Attitudes
- Public Opinion
- Resistance
- Social Response

Public Transportation
- DC D683500
- HN Added, 1989.
- BT Transportation
- RT Air Transportation
- Automobiles
- City Planning
- Commuting (Travel)
- Public Services
- Railroads
- Traffic
- Urban Development

Publication

Publication Productivity
  Use Writing for Publication

Publications
  DC D683700
  HN Formerly (1963-1985) part of DC 363200, Publication/Publications.
  NT Articles
      Book Reviews
      Books
      Comics (Publications)
      Literature Reviews
      Newspapers
      Periodicals
      Reference Materials
      Reports
  RT Audiovisual Media
      Authorship
      Censorship
      Documents
      Editorials
      Editors
      Journalism
      Mass Media
      Pornography
      Printing
      Publishing Industry
      Readership
      Records (Documents)
      Writers
      Writing for Publication

Publicity
  DC D684000
  HN Formerly (1964-1985) DC 363500.
  BT Communication
  NT Advertising
  RT Information Dissemination
      Mass Media
      Public Relations
      Telecommunications

Publishing Houses
  Use Publishing Industry

Publishing Industry
  DC D684300
  HN Formerly (1964-1985) DC 363700, Publish/Publisher/Publishers/Published/Publishing.
  UF Book Industry
      Publishing Houses
  BT Industry
  RT Copyrights
      Editors
      Entertainment Industry
      Information Dissemination
      Literature
      Mass Media
      Printing
      Publications
      Writers
      Writing for Publication

Pueblo (1969-1985)
  HN DC 363800, deleted 1986.

Puerto Rico
  DC D684600
  HN Formerly (1963-1985) DC 363850, Puerto Rico/Puerto Rican/Puerto Ricans.
  BT Caribbean
  NT San Juan, Puerto Rico

Punishment
  DC D684900
  SN Confinement, restriction of activities, infliction of pain, or other measures taken for retribution, to force compliance, or invoke behavioral changes.
  HN Formerly (1963-1985) DC 364000.
  UF Punitive/Punitiveness (1964-1985)
      Retributive/Retribution (1969-1985)
  BT Sanctions
  NT Capital Punishment
      Corporal Punishment
  RT Coercion
      Detention
      Deterrence
      Discipline
      Reinforcement
      Repression (Political)
      Social Control
      Torture
      Vigilantism

Punitive/Punitiveness (1964-1985)
  HN DC 364100.
  Use Punishment

Punjab, India
  DC D685200
  HN Added, 1986. Prior to 1986 use Punjab, India/Punjabi/Punjabis (DC 364110).
  BT India

Punjab, India/Punjabi/Punjabis (1963-1985)
  HN DC 364110, deleted 1986. See now Punjab, India, or Indic Languages.

Punk (1985)
  HN DC 364120.
  Use Youth Culture

Pupil Teacher Relationship
  Use Student Teacher Relationship

Pupils
  Use Students

Purchasing
  DC D685500
  HN Formerly (1963-1985) DC 364240, Purchase/Purchasing.
  UF Buying
  RT Advertising
      Brand Names
      Business
      Consumerism
      Consumers
      Consumption
      Cooperatives
      Exchange (Economics)
      Marketing
      Prices
      Retail Industry
      Sales
      Trade

Purdah
  DC D685800
  SN Islamic institution involving the seclusion of women from public observation by means of concealing clothing (eg, veils), screens, and curtains.
  HN Formerly (1965-1985) DC 364290.
  UF Purdah Societies
  RT Hinduism
      Hindus
      Islam
      Islamic Law
      Muslims

Purdah Societies
  Use Purdah

Purge/Purges (1973-1985)
  HN DC 364310, deleted 1986.

Purification (1971-1985)
  HN DC 364330, deleted 1986.

Puritan Ethic
  Use Protestant Ethic

Puritans
  DC D686100
  HN Formerly (1963-1985) DC 364345, Puritan/Puritans/Puritanism.
  BT Protestants
  RT Protestantism

Purity (1965-1985)
  HN DC 364355.
  Use Morality

Purpose/Purposes/Purposeful/Purposefulness (1963-1985)
  HN DC 364365, deleted 1986. See now Function, Goals, or Intentionality.

Purposiveness
  Use Intentionality

Qatar
  DC D686400
  HN Added, 1986.
  BT Arab Countries
      Middle East

Quakers
  DC D686700
  HN Formerly (1965-1985) DC 364410, Quaker/Quakers.
  UF Society of Friends
  BT Protestants
  RT Protestantism

Qualifications
  DC D687000
  HN Formerly (1971-1985) DC 364411, Qualify/Qualification/Qualifications.
  UF Requirements (1964-1985)
  NT Job Requirements
      Occupational Qualifications
  RT Ability
      Certification
      Experience
      Performance
      Reputation
      Skills

Qualitative Analysis
  Use Qualitative Methods

Qualitative Methods
  DC D687200
  SN A context-dependent term encompassing techniques for collection and analysis of non-numerical data.
  HN Formerly (1963-1985) part of DC 364413, Quality/Qualities/Qualitative.
  UF Qualitative Analysis
      Qualitative Research
      Qualitative Studies
  BT Research Methodology
  RT Analysis
      Case Studies
      Categorical Data
      Description
      Evaluation
      Fieldwork

Qualitative / Race

Qualitative Methods (cont'd)
- RT Methodological Problems
  Methodology (Data Collection)
  Paradigms
  Quantitative Methods
  Research Design
  Verstehen

Qualitative Research
- Use Qualitative Methods

Qualitative Studies
- Use Qualitative Methods

Quality
- DC D687250
- HN Formerly (1963-1985) part of DC 364413, Quality/Qualities/Qualitative.
- NT Quality of Life
- RT Accuracy
  Achievement
  Criteria
  Environmental Protection
  Evaluation
  Failure
  Performance
  Satisfaction
  Standards
  Success

Quality of Life
- DC D687300
- SN Subjective evaluation of an individual's or group's way of life, lifestyle, or living conditions, usually using an explicit inventory of factors.
- HN Formerly (1979-1985) DC 364414.
- UF Life Quality
- BT Quality
- NT Quality of Working Life
- RT Affluence
  Deprivation
  Disadvantaged
  Everyday Life
  Family Life
  Humanization
  Life
  Life Satisfaction
  Living Conditions
  Social Conditions
  Social Environment
  Social Impact Assessment
  Social Indicators
  Social Status
  Social Values
  Socioeconomic Status
  Standard of Living
  Technological Progress
  Well Being

Quality of Working Life
- DC D687600
- SN Subjective evaluation of an occupational environment, based on factors such as degree of boredom and stress, personal development, and interpersonal relationships.
- HN Formerly (1984-1985) DC 364414a.
- UF Work Life Quality
- BT Quality of Life
- RT Employee Assistance Programs
  Job Satisfaction
  Work
  Work Environment
  Work Humanization
  Worker Machine Relationship
  Workers

Quantify/Quantifying/Quantification (1966-1985)
- HN DC 364417, deleted 1986.

Quantitative Analysis
- Use Quantitative Methods

Quantitative Methods
- DC D687700
- SN A context-dependent term covering techniques for collection and analysis of numerical data.
- HN Formerly (1963-1985) DC 364418, Quantitative.
- UF Heteroscedastic/Heteroscedasity (1969-1985)
  Quantitative Analysis
  Quantitative Research
  Quantitative Studies
  Statistical Analysis
- BT Research Methodology
- NT Contingency Analysis
  Econometric Analysis
  Linear Analysis
  Multivariate Analysis
  Psychometric Analysis
  Regression Analysis
  Sociometric Analysis
  Statistical Inference
- RT Aggregate Data
  Analysis
  Chi Square Test
  Componential Analysis
  Correlation
  Empirical Methods
  Error of Measurement
  Formalism
  Frequency Distributions
  Matrices
  Mean
  Measurement
  Median
  Methodological Problems
  Methodology (Data Collection)
  Models
  Parameters (Statistics)
  Principal Components Analysis
  Probability
  Qualitative Methods
  Reliability
  Research Design
  Sampling
  Scientific Research
  Statistical Bias
  Statistical Significance
  Statistics
  Trends
  Validity
  Variables
  Variance (Statistics)

Quantitative Research
- Use Quantitative Methods

Quantitative Studies
- Use Quantitative Methods

Quantity/Quantities (1971-1985)
- HN DC 364425, deleted 1986.

Quebec
- DC D687900
- HN Formerly (1963-1985) DC 364445, Quebec/Quebecois/Quebec City/Quebec Province.
- BT Canada
- NT Montreal, Quebec

Question/Questions/Questioning (1963-1985)
- HN DC 364460, deleted 1986. See now Research Methodology, Questionnaires, Surveys, Interviews, Items (Measures), or their associated terms.

Questionnaires
- DC D688000
- HN Formerly (1963-1985) DC 364600, Questionnaire/Questionnaires.
- BT Measures (Instruments)
- NT Interview Schedules
- RT Attitude Measures
  Fieldwork
  Interviews
  Items (Measures)
  Mail Surveys
  Opinion Polls
  Opinions
  Research
  Research Responses
  Respondents
  Surveys

Quiet (1980-1985)
- HN DC 364900.
- Use Silence

Quotas
- DC D688200
- HN Formerly (1965-1985) Quota/Quotas.
- RT Affirmative Action
  Goals
  Productivity
  Ratios

Rabbinate
- Use Rabbis

Rabbinical Literature
- DC D688500
- HN Formerly (1970-1985) part of DC 364980, Rabbinical/Rabbinate.
- UF Midrash
  Talmud
- BT Religious Literature
- RT Bible
  God (Judeo-Christian)
  Judaism
  Rabbis

Rabbinical/Rabbinate (1970-1985)
- HN DC 364980.
- Use Rabbis

Rabbis
- DC D688800
- HN Formerly (1964-1985) DC 364925, Rabbi/Rabbis.
- UF Rabbinate
  Rabbinical/Rabbinate (1970-1985)
- BT Clergy
  Jews
- RT Judaism
  Rabbinical Literature

Race
- DC D689100
- HN Formerly (1963-1985) DC 366000, Race/Races/Racial/Racially.
- BT Physical Characteristics
- RT Anthropology
  Biology
  Blacks
  Cultural Groups
  Culture

Race

Race (cont'd)
- RT Demographic Characteristics
  - Ethnic Groups
  - Ethnicity
  - Eugenics
  - Genetics
  - Group Composition
  - Indigenous Populations
  - Majority Groups
  - Minority Groups
  - Racial Differences
  - Racial Relations
  - Racism
  - Whites

Race Segregated Occupations
- Use Occupational Segregation

Racial Differences
- DC D689350
- HN Added, 1989.
- BT Differences
- NT Black White Differences
- RT Race
  - Racial Relations
  - Social Attitudes

Racial Discrimination
- Use Racism

Racial Identity
- Use Ethnic Identity

Racial Relations
- DC D689400
- HN Formerly (1963-1985) DC 382585, Relations, Race/Relations, Racial.
- BT Intergroup Relations
- NT Black White Relations
- RT Blacks
  - Civil Rights Organizations
  - Class Relations
  - Desegregation
  - Ethnic Minorities
  - Ethnic Relations
  - Intercultural Communication
  - Minority Groups
  - Race
  - Racial Differences
  - Racial Segregation
  - Racism
  - Social Darwinism

Racial Segregation
- DC D689700
- HN Added, 1986.
- BT Segregation
- RT Apartheid
  - Civil Rights
  - Occupational Segregation
  - Racial Relations
  - Racism
  - Residential Segregation

Racism
- DC D690000
- HN Formerly (1963-1985) DC 366250, Racism/Racist/Racists.
- UF Racial Discrimination
- BT Discrimination
- RT Anti-Semitism
  - Apartheid
  - Bias
  - Prejudice
  - Race
  - Racial Relations
  - Racial Segregation
  - Residential Segregation
  - Segregation
  - Social Attitudes

Racket/Rackets/Racketeering (1964-1985)
- HN DC 366400.
- Use Organized Crime

Radcliffe-Brown, Alfred Reginald
- DC D690300
- SN Born 17 January 1881 - died 24 October 1955.
- HN Formerly (1964-1985) DC 367400, Radcliffe-Brown, A. R.

Radiation
- DC D690600
- HN Formerly (1981-1985) DC 367500, Radiation/Radiations.
- BT Energy
- RT Chemistry
  - Ecology
  - Medical Technology
  - Nuclear Energy
  - Physical Sciences
  - Physics
  - Pollution
  - Solar Energy
  - Wastes

Radical Sociology
- DC D690850
- HN Added, 1986.
- BT Sociology
- RT Bourgeois Sociology
  - Radicalism

Radical/Radicals/Radicalization/Radicalizing (1963-1985)
- HN DC 367800, deleted 1986. See now Radical Sociology or Radicalism.

Radicalism
- DC D690900
- HN Formerly (1963-1985) DC 367900.
- BT Political Ideologies
- RT Critical Theory
  - Extremism
  - Left Wing Politics
  - Radical Sociology

Radio
- DC D691200
- HN Formerly (1963-1985) DC 368000.
- BT Mass Media
  - Telecommunications
- RT Audiences
  - Electronic Technology
  - Journalism
  - Mass Media Effects
  - News Media
  - Popular Culture
  - Programming (Broadcast)
  - Recordings
  - Television

Radio Programming
- Use Programming (Broadcast)

Railroads
- DC D691500
- HN Formerly (1963-1985) DC 368200, Railroad.
- UF Railwaymen (1976-1985)
  - Trains
- RT Public Transportation
  - Transportation

Railwaymen (1976-1985)
- HN DC 368215.
- Use Railroads

Rain/Rainfall (1983-1985)
- HN DC 368219.
- Use Weather

Raise/Raised/Raising (1977-1985)
- HN DC 368225, deleted 1986.

Rajasthan, India
- DC D691800
- HN Formerly (1963-1985) DC 368280.
- BT India

Rancherio (1968-1985)
- HN DC 368320.
- Use Slums

Random Samples
- DC D691900
- HN Formerly (1963-1985) DC 368330, Random/Randomization.
- BT Sampling

Randomness
- DC D691950
- HN Formerly (1963-1985) DC 368375.
- RT Causality
  - Chance

Rangoon, Burma
- DC D692000
- HN Added, 1989.
- BT Burma

Rank Order Measurement
- Use Ordinal Measurement

Ranking
- DC D692025
- HN Formerly (1963-1985) DC 368425, Rank/Ranks/Ranking.
- RT Hierarchy
  - Measurement
  - Methodology (Data Analysis)
  - Ordinal Measurement
  - Rating
  - Scales
  - Status

Ranking (Social)
- Use Social Stratification

Rape
- DC D692100
- HN Formerly (1968-1985) DC 368685, Rape/Raped/Rapist/Rapists.
- BT Sexual Assault
- RT Incest
  - Offenses
  - Sexual Abuse
  - Sexual Intercourse
  - Unwanted Pregnancy
  - Victim Offender Relations
  - Victims

Rapport
- DC D692400
- HN Formerly (1968-1985) DC 368775.
- BT Interpersonal Relations
- RT Agreement
  - Friendship
  - Interpersonal Attraction
  - Interpersonal Communication
  - Intimacy

Rastafarians

Rastafarians
- DC D692600
- HN Added, 1989.
- BT Religious Cultural Groups
- RT Cults

Rates
- DC D692700
- SN Measures of a phenomenon proportional to known units of a separate phenomenon; for example, the crime rate is the number of crimes per 1,000 population in a given year.
- HN Formerly (1963-1985) DC 369940, Rate/Rates.
- NT Crime Rates
  Fertility
  Mortality Rates
  Nuptiality
  Unemployment Rates
- RT Statistics

Rating
- DC D692750
- HN Formerly (1963-1985) DC 370000, Rating/Ratings.
- RT Judgment
  Measurement
  Methodology (Data Analysis)
  Ranking
  Scales

Rating Scales
- Use Scales

Rational Choice
- DC D692900
- HN Added, 1989.
- BT Choices
- RT Decision Making
  Discretion
  Evaluation
  Judgment
  Objectivity
  Rationality
  Reasoning

Rationalism
- DC D692950
- SN A doctrine stressing reason, logic, and systematic thinking as the only valid bases for truth and knowledge.
- HN Formerly (1963-1985) part of DC 370240, Rational/Rationalist/Rationalistic/Rationalism.
- BT Philosophical Doctrines
- RT Agnosticism
  Atheism
  Cognition
  Deduction
  Epistemological Doctrines
  Knowledge
  Logic
  Positivism
  Rationality
  Realism (Philosophy)
  Reality
  Romanticism
  Science

Rationality
- DC D693000
- HN Formerly (1963-1985) DC 370275.
- UF Reasonable/Reasonability/Reasonableness (1969-1985)
- RT Beliefs
  Intentionality
  Irrationality
  Objectivity

Rationality (cont'd)
- RT Rational Choice
  Rationalism
  Rationalization
  Reasoning

Rationalization
- DC D693300
- SN Variety of related processes by which ever-greater aspects of social life are subjected to precise means-end calculations, measurement, and rational-legal domination.
- HN Formerly (1969-1985) DC 370300.
- BT Social Processes
- RT Bureaucratization
  Capitalist Societies
  Depersonalization
  Industrial Societies
  Labor Process
  Modernization
  Rationality
  Scientific Management
  Secularization

Ratios
- DC D693400
- HN Formerly (1963-1985) DC 370235, Ratio/Ratios.
- RT Computation
  Mathematics
  Measurement
  Quotas
  Relations

Raw Materials
- DC D693600
- HN Formerly (1977-1985) DC 370425, Raw Material.
- BT Materials
- RT Coal
  Commodities
  Industry
  Labor Process
  Natural Resources
  Plants (Botanical)
  Resources

Reaction/Reactionary/Reactions/Reactive (1963-1985)
- HN DC 370500.
- Use Responses

Readability
- DC D693900
- HN Formerly (1964-1985) DC 370800.
- UF Readability Formulas
- RT Reading
  Textbooks

Readability Formulas
- Use Readability

Readers (Texts)
- Use Textbooks

Readership
- DC D694200
- HN Formerly (1963-1985) part of DC 370880, Reader/Readers/Readership.
- UF Reading Habits
  Reading Patterns
- RT Newspapers
  Publications
  Reading
  Textbooks

Reading
- DC D694500
- HN Formerly (1963-1985) DC 371000.
- RT Curriculum
  Literacy
  Readability
  Readership
  Storytelling
  Teaching
  Textbooks
  Verbal Communication
  Vocabularies

Reading Habits
- Use Readership

Reading Patterns
- Use Readership

Readjustments (1967-1985)
- HN DC 371600.
- Use Adjustment

Readmissions
- Use Admissions

Reagan Administration
- DC D694800
- HN Formerly (1983-1985) DC 371660, Reagan, Ronald/Reaganomics.
- RT Presidents

Real Estate Industry
- DC D695100
- HN Formerly (1963-1985) DC 371775, Real Estate.
- BT Service Industries
- RT Home Ownership
  Housing
  Housing Market
  Land
  Landlords

Real Property
- Use Property

Realism (Art)
- Use Artistic Styles

Realism (Philosophy)
- DC D695150
- SN The doctrine that universals, abstract concepts (eg, society, culture), and objects of sense perception exist independently of the human mind. Also, the view that the purpose of natural and social science is to discover the often unobservable, underlying causes of phenomena.
- HN Formerly (1963-1985) DC 371800, Realism/Realist/Realistic.
- BT Epistemological Doctrines
- RT Idealism
  Marxism
  Materialism
  Naturalism
  Nominalism
  Rationalism
  Reality
  Sociological Theory
  Structuralism

Reality
- DC D695200
- HN Formerly (1963-1985) DC 372000.
- RT Abstraction
  Beliefs
  Existence
  Fantasy

200

Reality

Reality (cont'd)
- **RT** Imagination
  - Metaphysics
  - Ontology
  - Phenomena
  - Philosophy
  - Rationalism
  - Realism (Philosophy)
  - Social Reality
  - Truth

Reality Therapy
- **Use** Psychotherapy

Realpolitik (1978-1985)
- **HN** DC 372100, deleted 1986.

Reapportionment (1965-1985)
- **HN** DC 372400.
- **Use** Legislative Apportionment

Rearing/Reared (1966-1985)
- **HN** DC 372600.
- **Use** Childrearing Practices

Rearmament
- **Use** Armaments

Reasonable/Reasonability/ Reasonableness (1969-1985)
- **HN** DC 373600.
- **Use** Rationality

Reasoning
- **DC** D695400
- **HN** Formerly (1963-1985) DC 373000, Reason/Reasoning.
- **BT** Thinking
- **NT** Deduction
  - Generalization
  - Induction
  - Inference
- **RT** Abstraction
  - Analogy
  - Concept Formation
  - Fallacies
  - Intelligence
  - Intuition
  - Irrationality
  - Judgment
  - Logic
  - Postulates
  - Problem Solving
  - Rational Choice
  - Rationality

Rebellions
- **DC** D695700
- **HN** Formerly (1963-1985) DC 373850, Rebel/Rebellion/Rebellions/ Rebellious/Rebelliousness/Rebels.
- **UF** Insurgence/Insurgency (1969-1985)
  - Insurrections
  - Revolt/Revolts (1963-1985)
- **BT** Political Violence
- **NT** Mau Mau Rebellion
  - Peasant Rebellions
- **RT** Civil War
  - Guerrillas
  - Political Movements
  - Revolutions
  - Riots

Recall (1963-1985)
- **HN** DC 374000.
- **Use** Memory

Receivership
- **Use** Bankruptcy

Recession (1964-1985)
- **HN** DC 374230.
- **Use** Depression (Economics)

Recidivism
- **DC** D696000
- **SN** Repetition or recurrence of delinquent or criminal behavior or a behavior disorder, especially following punishment or rehabilitation.
- **HN** Formerly (1963-1985) DC 374350, Recidivism/Recidivists.
- **UF** Relapse (1964-1985)
- **RT** Crime
  - Delinquency
  - Deviant Behavior
  - Imprisonment
  - Institutionalization (Persons)
  - Offenders
  - Prevention
  - Professional Criminals

Recipients (1971-1985)
- **HN** DC 374400, deleted 1986. See now Disability Recipients or Welfare Recipients.

Reciprocity
- **DC** D696300
- **HN** Formerly (1963-1985) DC 374500, Reciprocity/Reciprocal.
- **BT** Interaction
- **RT** Cooperation
  - Exchange Theory
  - Feedback
  - Sharing
  - Social Behavior
  - Symbiotic Relations
  - Turn Taking

Recognition (Achievement)
- **DC** D696600
- **HN** Formerly (1965-1985) part of DC 375000, Recognition.
- **NT** Awards
- **RT** Achievement
  - Incentives
  - Performance
  - Prestige
  - Privilege
  - Promotion (Occupational)
  - Rewards
  - Self Esteem

Recognition (Psychology)
- **DC** D696900
- **HN** Formerly (1965-1985) part of DC 375000, Recognition.
- **BT** Memory
- **RT** Learning

Reconcile/Reconciliation (1972-1985)
- **HN** DC 375250.
- **Use** Conflict Resolution

Reconstruction
- **DC** D697050
- **SN** Restoration of economic and social structures following war, natural disaster, or other periods of social upheaval or calamity.
- **HN** Formerly (1963-1985) DC 375300.
- **UF** National Reconstruction
  - Postwar Reconstruction
- **RT** Natural Disasters
  - Social Disorganization
  - War

Recruitment

Recordings
- **DC** D697200
- **HN** Formerly (1964-1985) part of DC 375500, Record.
- **UF** Audio Recordings
  - Phonograph Records
  - Sound Image Recordings
  - Tape Recordings
- **BT** Audiovisual Media
- **NT** Videotape Recordings
- **RT** Music
  - Oral History
  - Programming (Broadcast)
  - Radio

Records (Documents)
- **DC** D697500
- **HN** Formerly (1964-1985) part of DC 375500, Record.
- **UF** Annals (1969-1985)
- **BT** Documents
- **RT** Archival Research
  - Chronologies
  - Narratives
  - Publications
  - Registration
  - Reports

Recovery (1981-1985)
- **HN** DC 375580.
- **Use** Rehabilitation

Recreation
- **DC** D697800
- **HN** Formerly (1964-1985) DC 376000, Recreation/Recreational.
- **RT** Activities
  - Entertainment Industry
  - Games
  - Leisure
  - Parks
  - Recreational Facilities
  - Sociology of Leisure
  - Tourism

Recreational Areas
- **Use** Recreational Facilities

Recreational Facilities
- **DC** D698100
- **HN** Added, 1986.
- **UF** Amusement/Amusements (1967-1985)
  - Recreational Areas
  - Resort/Resorts (1972-1985)
- **BT** Facilities
- **NT** Parks
- **RT** Camping
  - Common Lands
  - Land Use
  - Recreation
  - Tourism

Recreational Vehicles
- **Use** Automobiles

Recruitment
- **DC** D698400
- **HN** Formerly (1963-1985) DC 376200, Recruits/Recruitment.
- **RT** Employment Opportunities
  - Hiring Practices
  - Job Change
  - Job Requirements
  - Membership
  - Participation
  - Personnel Management

Recruits

Recruits (Military)
  Use Military Personnel

Red Cross (1970-1985)
  HN DC 376275.
  Use International Organizations

Redefinition (1964-1985)
  HN DC 376425.
  Use Definitions

Redevelopment (1965-1985)
  HN DC 376515, deleted 1986. See now Community Change, Neighborhood Change, Urban Renewal, or appropriate "Development" terms.

Redistribution (1964-1985)
  HN DC 376600.
  Use Distribution

Reductionism
  DC D698550
  SN Application of specific theories or levels of analysis to any and all phenomena, particularly when forced or inappropriate.
  HN Formerly (1963-1985) DC 376750, Reduction/Reductive/Reductivism.
  BT Epistemological Doctrines
  RT Behaviorism
      Determinism
      Holism
      Methodological Individualism
      Positivism

Redundancy
  DC D698600
  HN Formerly (1969-1985) DC 376760.
  RT Attention
      Effectiveness
      Function

Reeducation (1965-1985)
  HN DC 376800.
  Use Rehabilitation

Reexamination (1969-1985)
  HN DC 376825, deleted 1986.

Reference Groups
  DC D698700
  SN Groups of persons used as standards for evaluation of one's own status, or groups incorporated in an individual's self-concept.
  HN Formerly (1985) DC 377000, Reference Group.
  UF Reference/References/Referent/Referents (1963-1985)
  BT Groups
  RT Influence
      Inner And Other Directedness
      Norms
      Peer Groups
      Peer Influence
      Relative Deprivation
      Self Concept
      Significant Others
      Social Identity
      Social Space
      Social Values
      Socialization

Reference Materials
  DC D699000
  HN Added, 1986.
  UF Atlas/Atlases (1972-1985)
      Dictionary/Dictionaries (1963-1985)
      Encyclopedia/Encyclopedias (1963-1985)

Reference Materials (cont'd)
  UF Guide/Guiding (1963-1985)
  BT Publications
  NT Bibliographies
      Citations (References)
  RT Information Sources
      Libraries

Reference/References/Referent/Referents (1963-1985)
  HN DC 376850.
  Use Reference Groups

Referendum
  DC D699300
  HN Formerly (1963-1985) DC 377200.
  RT Elections
      Legislation
      Voting

Referral
  DC D699400
  HN Formerly (1983-1985) DC 377230.
  RT Delivery Systems
      Information And Referral Services
      Information Dissemination
      Professional Consultation
      Professional Workers

Reflective/Reflection (1969-1985)
  HN DC 377390.
  Use Impulsiveness

Reflex/Reflexes (1964-1985)
  HN DC 377500, deleted 1986.

Reflexivity
  DC D699500
  SN Breakdown of the subject-object distinction in which the observer's perceptions contaminate the field of vision. Also, the attribute of descriptions that they may convey information about the describer and the described simultaneously.
  HN Formerly (1984-1985) DC 377510, Reflexive.
  RT Ethnomethodology
      Methodology (Philosophical)
      Phenomenology
      Subjectivity

Reform
  DC D699600
  HN Formerly (1963-1985) DC 377600, Reform/Reformed/Reformers/Reformism/Reformists/Reforms.
  BT Change
  NT Educational Reform
      Land Reform
      Penal Reform
      Social Reform
      Welfare Reform
  RT Development
      Improvement
      Movements
      Policy
      Political Movements
      Progress
      Strategies

Reformation (1964-1985)
  HN DC 377620.
  Use Protestant Reformation

Reformatory/Reform School (1964-1985)
  HN DC 377650.
  Use Juvenile Correctional Institutions

Regional

Refuge (1979-1985)
  HN DC 377695.
  Use Shelters

Refugees
  DC D699900
  HN Formerly (1963-1985) DC 377700, Refugee/Refugees.
  RT Acculturation
      Homelessness
      Immigrants
      Migrants
      Migration
      Palestinians
      Political Defection
      Relocation
      Social Problems
      Undocumented Immigrants
      War
      World Problems

Refuse
  Use Wastes

Refutation (1971-1985)
  HN DC 377740, deleted 1986.

Regimentation (1964-1985)
  HN DC 377770, deleted 1986.

Regimes (Military)
  Use Military Regimes

Regional Councils
  Use Councils

Regional Development
  DC D700200
  HN Added, 1986.
  BT Development
  RT Development Policy
      Development Strategies
      Economic Development
      Economic Policy
      Energy Development
      Geographic Regions
      Rural Development
      Urban Development

Regional Differences
  DC D700500
  SN Used in analyses in which a phenomenon or problem is explained as a consequence or correlate of differences in the region of residence of a similar population.
  HN Added, 1986.
  BT Differences
  RT Black White Differences
      Borders
      Comparative Sociology
      Geographic Regions
      North And South
      Regional Sociology
      Rural Urban Differences

Regional Movements
  DC D700800
  HN Added, 1986.
  BT Movements
  RT Geographic Regions
      Pan-Africanism
      Political Movements
      Provinces
      Regionalism
      States (Political Subdivisions)

Regional

Regional Sociology
- DC D701100
- HN Added, 1986.
- BT Sociology
- RT Geographic Regions
  Regional Differences

Regionalism
- DC D701400
- HN Formerly (1963-1985) part of DC 377800, Region/Regions/Regional/Regionalism/Regionalization.
- BT Social Attitudes
- RT Geographic Regions
  Localism
  Nationalism
  Political Ideologies
  Regional Movements
  Separatism

Regions (Geographic)
- Use Geographic Regions

Registration
- DC D701500
- HN Formerly (1972-1985) DC 377820.
- RT Educational Administration
  Public Administration
  Records (Documents)

Regression Analysis
- DC D701600
- HN Formerly (1963-1985) DC 377900, Regression.
- UF Linear Regression
- BT Methodology (Data Analysis)
  Quantitative Methods
- NT Multiple Regression Analysis
- RT Causal Models
  Correlation
  Multivariate Analysis
  Time Series Analysis
  Validity
  Variance (Statistics)

Regularity/Regularities (1964-1985)
- HN DC 379000, deleted 1986.

Regulation
- DC D701700
- HN Formerly (1964-1985) DC 379500, Regulation/Regulations.
- NT Government Regulation
- RT Control
  Law
  Uniformity

Rehabilitation
- DC D701850
- HN Formerly (1963-1985) DC 380000.
- UF Recovery (1981-1985)
  Reeducation (1965-1985)
  Reintegration (1971-1985)
- NT Vocational Rehabilitation
- RT Adjustment
  Counseling
  Deinstitutionalization
  Handicapped
  Health Care
  Improvement
  Injuries
  Intervention
  Penology
  Self Care
  Social Work
  Treatment
  Treatment Methods
  Treatment Programs

Rehabilitation Programs
- Use Treatment Programs

Reich, Wilhelm
- DC D702000
- SN Born 24 March 1897 - died 3 November 1957.
- HN Formerly (1973-1985) DC 380604, Reich, Wilhelm A.

Reification
- DC D702300
- SN The process by which ideas are given substance and reinforced as an indirect consequence of their uses in social relations and interactions.
- HN Formerly (1971-1985) DC 380790, Reify/Reification/Reifications.
- UF Commodity Fetishism
- RT Alienation
  Forces And Relations of Production
  Marxism
  Marxist Aesthetics
  Social Relations

Reign (1977-1985)
- HN DC 380800, deleted 1986.

Reinforcement
- DC D702600
- HN Formerly (1963-1985) DC 381000, Reinforcement/Reinforcements.
- UF Social Reinforcement
  Verbal Reinforcement
- NT Rewards
- RT Behavior Modification
  Conditioning
  Delay of Gratification
  Encouragement
  Feedback
  Motivation
  Punishment

Reinstate/Reinstatement (1972-1985)
- HN DC 382400, deleted 1986.

Reintegration (1971-1985)
- HN DC 382425.
- Use Rehabilitation

Rejection
- DC D702900
- HN Formerly (1963-1985) DC 382435, Reject/Rejects/Rejecting/Rejection/Rejections.
- UF Personal Rejection
  Social Rejection
- BT Social Behavior
- RT Acceptance
  Interpersonal Relations
  Resistance
  Social Acceptance
  Social Attitudes
  Social Response
  Stigma

Relapse (1964-1985)
- HN DC 382470.
- Use Recidivism

Relate/Related (1971-1982)
- HN DC 382480, deleted 1986.

Relations
- DC D703200
- SN A context-dependent term; select a more specific entry or coordinate with other terms. In sociological contexts where Relations is closely related to Social Relations, select the latter.

Relatives

Relations (cont'd)
- HN Formerly (1963-1985) DC 382485, Relations/Relational.
- UF Interrelation/Interrelations/Interrelationship (1963-1985)
  Linkage (1963-1985)
  Relationship/Relationships (1963-1985)
- NT Animal Human Relations
  Education Work Relationship
  Family Work Relationship
  Forces And Relations of Production
  Individual Collective Relationship
  International Relations
  Interpersonal Relations
  Language Social Class Relationship
  Networks
  Production Consumption Relationship
  Public Relations
  Social Relations
  Symbiotic Relations
  Theory Practice Relationship
  Work Leisure Relationship
  Worker Machine Relationship
- RT Classification
  Ratios
  Stability

Relations, Industrial (1963-1985)
- HN DC 382530.
- Use Labor Relations

Relations of Production
- Use Forces And Relations of Production

Relationship/Relationships (1963-1985)
- HN DC 382600.
- Use Relations

Relative Deprivation
- DC D703500
- SN A concept, introduced by Samuel A. Stouffer et al and developed by Robert K. Merton, that describes the deprivation people feel when they compare their circumstances unfavorably to those of a reference group of like status (eg, a millionaire feeling deprived because his friends are billionaires).
- HN Added, 1986.
- BT Deprivation
- RT Expectations
  Perceptions
  Reference Groups
  Self Concept
  Socioeconomic Status

Relatives
- DC D703800
- SN Persons related by blood or marriage.
- HN Formerly (1970-1985) DC 382625.
- UF Cousin/Cousins (1964-1985)
  In-Law/In-Laws (1964-1985)
  Kindred (1963-1985)
- RT Affinity (Kinship)
  Children
  Extended Family
  Family
  Family Relations
  Fathers
  Grandparents
  Kinship
  Kinship Networks
  Mothers
  Siblings

Relativism   Religious

Relativism
- **DC** D703900
- **SN** The doctrine that the criteria for truth, knowledge, right, and wrong are not absolute, but vary according to the different sense perceptions of individuals and their environments.
- **HN** Formerly (1963-1985) DC 382675, Relative/Relativism/Relativist/Relativistic.
- **UF** Relativity of Knowledge
- **BT** Philosophical Doctrines
- **NT** Cultural Relativism
- **RT** Dogmatism
  Epistemological Doctrines
  Existentialism
  Historicism
  Knowledge
  Social Determination of Meaning
  Sociology of Knowledge

Relativity (1963-1985)
- **HN** DC 382677, deleted 1986. See now Physics or Relativism.

Relativity of Knowledge
- **Use** Relativism

Release (Institutional)
- **Use** Discharge

Relevance
- **DC** D703975
- **HN** Formerly (1966-1985) DC 382685.
- **UF** Applicability
- **RT** Effectiveness
  Effects
  Goals
  Influence
  Needs
  Values

Reliability
- **DC** D704025
- **SN** In statistics, the extent to which data accurately represent the phenomena under investigation.
- **HN** Formerly (1963-1985) DC 382700.
- **UF** Dependability
- **RT** Accuracy
  Correlation
  Error of Measurement
  Errors
  Forecasting
  Frequency Distributions
  Measurement
  Performance
  Prediction
  Probability
  Quantitative Methods
  Replication
  Research Methodology
  Sampling
  Validity

Reliance (1971-1985)
- **HN** DC 382725, deleted 1986.

Relief Services
- **Use** Welfare Services

Religiocentrism/Religiocentric (1972-1985)
- **HN** DC 382990, deleted 1986.

Religion Politics Relationship
- **DC** D704050
- **SN** Influence of religion or religious groups in political life and vice versa. For relations between political and religious institutions, see Church State Relationship.
- **HN** Added, 1989.
- **UF** Politics Religion Relationship
- **BT** Social Relations
- **RT** Church State Relationship
  Interest Groups
  Political Attitudes
  Political Power
  Politics
  Religions
  Religious Fundamentalism
  Religious Movements
  Secularization

Religions
- **DC** D704100
- **HN** Formerly (1963-1985) DC 383000, Religion/Religions/Religious.
- **UF** Faith/Faiths (1963-1985)
- **BT** Social Institutions
- **NT** Bahaism
  Buddhism
  Christianity
  Confucianism
  Hinduism
  Islam
  Jainism
  Judaism
  Manicheism
  Paganism
  Shintoism
  Sikhism
  Taoism
  Zoroastrianism
- **RT** Ancestor Worship
  Animism
  Apostasy
  Beliefs
  Churches
  Church State Relationship
  Civil Religion
  Clergy
  Cults
  Culture
  Deities
  Denominations
  Folklore
  Functionalism
  Heresy
  Mysticism
  Myths
  Philosophy
  Places of Worship
  Religion Politics Relationship
  Religiosity
  Religious Attitudes
  Religious Behavior
  Religious Beliefs
  Religious Conversion
  Religious Cultural Groups
  Religious Doctrines
  Religious Education
  Religious Fundamentalism
  Religious Literature
  Religious Movements
  Religious Orientations
  Religious Orthodoxy
  Religious Revivalism
  Religious Rituals
  Sacredness
  Schism
  Sects

Religions (cont'd)
- **RT** Secularization
  Sociology of Religion
  Syncretism
  Theology
  Totemism
  Traditionalism
  Worship

Religiosity
- **DC** D704400
- **SN** The extent of a person's participation in and commitment to religious beliefs and practices.
- **HN** Formerly (1963-1985) DC 383175.
- **UF** Devotion (1972-1985)
  Piety (1964-1985)
- **RT** Church Attendance
  Religions
  Religious Behavior
  Religious Beliefs
  Religious Fundamentalism
  Religious Orientations
  Religious Orthodoxy
  Secularization

Religious Affiliation
- **Use** Church Membership

Religious Attitudes
- **DC** D704550
- **HN** Added, 1986.
- **BT** Attitudes
- **RT** Cultural Values
  Prejudice
  Religions
  Religious Orientations
  Tolerance

Religious Behavior
- **DC** D704700
- **HN** Added, 1986.
- **NT** Asceticism
  Church Attendance
  Glossolalia
  Prayer
  Proselytism
  Religious Conversion
- **RT** Church Membership
  Cults
  Religions
  Religiosity
  Religious Beliefs
  Religious Rituals

Religious Beliefs
- **DC** D705000
- **HN** Added, 1986.
- **BT** Beliefs
- **NT** Agnosticism
  Atheism
  Creationism
  Dharma
  Heresy
  Karma
  Millenarianism
  Religious Orthodoxy
  Syncretism
- **RT** Apocalypse
  Asceticism
  Canons
  Church Membership
  Cosmology
  Death Attitudes
  Ecclesiastical Law
  Faith Healing
  Fate
  Ghost Dances

Religious Beliefs (cont'd)
- RT Glossolalia
- Human Rights
- Judeo-Christian Tradition
- Morality
- Mysticism
- Philosophical Doctrines
- Prophecy
- Religions
- Religiosity
- Religious Behavior
- Religious Conversion
- Religious Cultural Groups
- Religious Doctrines
- Religious Education
- Religious Literature
- Religious Movements
- Religious Orientations
- Sacredness
- Salvation
- Schism
- Secularization
- Shamanism
- Sins
- Sociology of Religion
- Soul
- Superstitions
- Theology
- Tolerance
- Worship

Religious Brotherhoods
- DC D705100
- HN Formerly (1969-1985) DC 067350, Brotherhood.
- UF Brotherhoods (Religious)
- BT Organizations (Social)
- RT Religious Cultural Groups
- Religious Movements
- Religious Orders
- Religious Revivalism
- Secret Societies
- Subcultures

Religious Ceremonies
Use Religious Rituals

Religious Communities
Use Religious Cultural Groups

Religious Conversion
- DC D705300
- HN Added, 1986.
- UF Christianization
- Convert/Converting/Conversion (1963-1985)
- Paganization
- BT Religious Behavior
- RT Apostasy
- Missionaries
- Proselytism
- Religions
- Religious Beliefs
- Salvation
- Syncretism

Religious Cultural Groups
- DC D705600
- HN Added, 1986.
- UF Religious Communities
- Religious Groups
- BT Cultural Groups
- NT Buddhists
- Cathari
- Christians
- Gentiles
- Hindus
- Jewish Cultural Groups

Religious Cultural Groups (cont'd)
- NT Jews
- Muslims
- Rastafarians
- Sikhs
- RT Cultural Values
- Culture
- Denominations
- Ethnic Groups
- Ethnic Relations
- Minority Groups
- Places of Worship
- Religions
- Religious Beliefs
- Religious Brotherhoods
- Religious Movements
- Religious Revivalism
- Religious Rituals
- Secularization
- Sociology of Religion
- Subcultures

Religious Doctrines
- DC D705750
- HN Added, 1986.
- UF Church Doctrines
- BT Ideologies
- NT Canons
- RT Deities
- Dualism
- Ecclesiastical Law
- Ethics
- Philosophical Doctrines
- Religions
- Religious Beliefs
- Religious Literature
- Schism
- Theology

Religious Education
- DC D705900
- HN Added, 1986.
- BT Education
- RT Church State Relationship
- Moral Education
- Private Schools
- Religions
- Religious Beliefs
- Religious Literature
- Seminarians

Religious Fundamentalism
- DC D706000
- HN Formerly (1963-1985) DC 191550, Fundamental/Fundamentals/ Fundamentalism/Fundamentalists.
- UF Fundamentalism (Religious)
- RT Conservatism
- Creationism
- Evangelism
- Islam
- Jesus Movement
- Protestantism
- Protestants
- Religion Politics Relationship
- Religions
- Religiosity
- Religious Orthodoxy
- Sects

Religious Groups
Use Religious Cultural Groups

Religious Healing
Use Faith Healing

Religious Holidays
Use Holidays

Religious Literature
- DC D706200
- HN Added, 1986.
- UF Sacred Literature
- NT Bible
- Koran
- Rabbinical Literature
- RT Canons
- Religions
- Religious Beliefs
- Religious Doctrines
- Religious Education
- Sacredness
- Sermons
- Theology

Religious Movements
- DC D706500
- HN Added, 1986.
- BT Movements
- NT Ecumenical Movement
- Jesus Movement
- Messianic Movements
- Photian Schism
- Protestant Reformation
- Religious Revivalism
- Social Gospel Movement
- Zionism
- RT Bahaism
- Charisma
- Creationism
- Millenarianism
- Religion Politics Relationship
- Religions
- Religious Beliefs
- Religious Brotherhoods
- Religious Cultural Groups
- Secularization
- Social Movements

Religious Orders
- DC D706800
- HN Added, 1986.
- NT Dominicans (Clergy)
- Franciscans
- Jesuits
- RT Clergy
- Monasticism
- Monks
- Nuns
- Priests
- Religious Brotherhoods

Religious Orientations
- DC D707100
- HN Added, 1986.
- BT Orientation
- RT Religions
- Religiosity
- Religious Attitudes
- Religious Beliefs
- Sectarianism
- Socialization
- Value Orientations

Religious Orthodoxy
- DC D707400
- HN Formerly (1963-1985) Orthodox/ Orthodoxy.
- UF Orthodoxy (Religious)
- BT Religious Beliefs
- RT Catholicism
- Heresy
- Judaism
- Religions

Religious — Repression

Religious Orthodoxy (cont'd)
- **RT** Religiosity
  Religious Fundamentalism
  Religious Rituals
  Schism
  Secularization

Religious Revivalism
- **DC** D707700
- **SN** Renewed attention to or restoration of religious faith and practice.
- **HN** Formerly (1969-1985) DC 390783, Revival/Revivalism/Revivalist/Revivalists.
- **UF** Revivalism (Religious)
- **BT** Religious Movements
- **RT** Evangelism
  Islam
  Messianic Movements
  Religions
  Religious Brotherhoods
  Religious Cultural Groups

Religious Rites
- **Use** Religious Rituals

Religious Rituals
- **DC** D708000
- **HN** Added, 1986.
- **UF** Religious Ceremonies
  Religious Rites
  Sacraments (1978-1985)
- **BT** Rituals
- **NT** Baptism
  Dharma
  Liturgy
  Passion Plays
  Pilgrimages
  Sacrificial Rites
  Sermons
  Tithing
- **RT** Burials
  Christmas
  Church Attendance
  Confession
  Cults
  Death Rituals
  Dolmen
  Funerals
  Ghost Dances
  Places of Worship
  Prayer
  Religions
  Religious Behavior
  Religious Cultural Groups
  Religious Orthodoxy
  Rites of Passage
  Secret Societies
  Shamanism
  Shrines
  Syncretism
  Worship
  Yoga

Relocation
- **DC** D708300
- **HN** Formerly (1964-1985) DC 383184.
- **UF** Displaced Persons (1964-1985)
  Displacement (Residential)
  Involuntary Relocation
  Resettlement (1964-1985)
  Residential Displacement
- **RT** American Indian Reservations
  Geographic Mobility
  Housing
  Land Reform
  Land Settlement
  Migration

Relocation (cont'd)
- **RT** Migration Patterns
  Population Distribution
  Refugees
  Residence
  Residential Mobility
  Urban Renewal

Remand (1963-1985)
- **HN** DC 383200.
- **Use** Detention

Remarriage
- **DC** D708600
- **HN** Formerly (1964-1985) DC 383225, Remarriage/Remarriages.
- **BT** Marriage
- **RT** Annulment
  Divorce
  Marriage Timing
  Stepfamily
  Widowhood

Remarriage Timing
- **Use** Marriage Timing

Remuneration (1964-1985)
- **HN** DC 383300.
- **Use** Compensation

Renaissance
- **DC** D708900
- **SN** The humanistic revival of classical influence in European art and literature extending from the 14th through the 17th century.
- **HN** Formerly (1963-1985) DC 383550.
- **BT** Time Periods
- **RT** Architecture
  Art History
  Drama
  Humanism
  Literature
  Music
  Seventeenth Century
  Sixteenth Century

Rental Housing
- **DC** D709200
- **HN** Added, 1986. Prior to 1986 use DC 383590, Rent/Rents.
- **BT** Housing
- **RT** Landlord Tenant Relations
  Landlords
  Public Housing
  Rents
  Tenants

Renters
- **Use** Tenants

Rents
- **DC** D709500
- **HN** Formerly (1968-1985) DC 383590, Rent/Rents.
- **UF** Ground Rents
- **BT** Housing Costs
- **RT** Income
  Land
  Land Ownership
  Land Tenure
  Landlord Tenant Relations
  Payments
  Rental Housing
  Tenants

Reorganization (1964-1985)
- **HN** DC 383600.
- **Use** Organizational Change

Reparations (1972-1985)
- **HN** DC 383620.
- **Use** Compensation

Repatriation/Repatriated (1965-1985)
- **HN** DC 383630.
- **Use** Return Migration

Repeal (1963-1985)
- **HN** DC 383640, deleted 1986.

Repeating Patterns
- **Use** Cyclical Processes

Repentant (1971-1985)
- **HN** DC 383645, deleted 1986.

Replication
- **DC** D709700
- **HN** Formerly (1964-1985) DC 383660, Replicate/Replication.
- **UF** Experimental Replication
  Research Replication
- **RT** Experiments
  Reliability
  Research Methodology
  Verification

Reporters
- **HN** Formerly (1963-1985) part of DC 383700, Report/Reportage/Reporter/Reporters.
- **Use** Journalists

Reports
- **DC** D709800
- **HN** Formerly (1963-1985) part of DC 383700, Report/Reportage/Reporter/Reporters.
- **BT** Publications
- **NT** Narratives
  Verbal Accounts
- **RT** Documents
  Journalism
  News Media
  Records (Documents)

Representation
- **DC** D710000
- **SN** State or process of acting on behalf of another or of being represented by another.
- **HN** Formerly (1963-1985) DC 383900, Representation/Representative/Representativeness.
- **NT** Political Representation
- **RT** Advocacy
  Citizen Participation
  Guardianship
  Legal Profession
  Lobbying
  Worker Participation

Representation (Collective)
- **Use** Collective Representation

Representative Government
- **Use** Democracy

Repression (Defense Mechanism)
- **DC** D710100
- **HN** Formerly (1964-1985) part of DC 384000, Repression/Repressions.
- **BT** Defense Mechanisms
- **RT** Avoidance

Repression (Political)
- **DC** D710400
- **SN** Subjection, pressure, or forcible restraint exercised by political or military forces. Do not confuse with Repression (Defense Mechanism).
- **HN** Formerly (1964-1985) part of DC 384000, Repression/Repressions.
- **UF** Political Repression
  Suppression (1969-1985)
- **RT** Authoritarianism (Political Ideology)
  Censorship
  Civil Disorders
  Conflict
  Control
  Dissent
  Exploitation
  Freedom
  McCarthyism
  Military Civilian Relations
  Oppression
  Political Violence
  Punishment
  State Power

Reproduction/Reproductive (1963-1985)
- **HN** DC 384300, deleted 1986. See now Sexual Reproduction or Social Reproduction.

Reproductive Technologies
- **DC** D710500
- **SN** Advances in medical technology applied to enhancing fertility, conception, and the birth process.
- **HN** Added, 1989.
- **BT** Medical Technology
- **NT** Artificial Insemination
- **RT** Amniocentesis
  Birth
  Eugenics
  Genetics
  Gynecology
  Pregnancy
  Sexual Reproduction

Republic of South Africa
- **Use** South Africa

Republican/Republicans/Republicanism (1963-1985)
- **HN** DC 384700, deleted 1986. See now Republics or Political Parties.

Republics
- **DC** D710700
- **HN** Formerly (1963-1985) DC 384450, Republic.
- **BT** Political Systems
- **RT** Democracy

Reputation
- **DC** D711000
- **HN** Formerly (1963-1985) DC 384715, Reputation/Reputations/Reputational.
- **RT** Credibility
  Honor
  Morality
  Opinions
  Prestige
  Qualifications
  Social Influence
  Social Status

Requirements (1964-1985)
- **HN** DC 384850.
- **Use** Qualifications

Rescue (1975-1985)
- **HN** DC 384950, deleted 1986. See now Disasters, Homelessness, or Shelters.

Research
- **DC** D711200
- **HN** Formerly (1963-1985) part of DC 385000, Research/Researcher/Researchers.
- **UF** Applied Research
  Basic Research
  Inquiry/Inquiries (1963-1985)
- **NT** Action Research
  Agricultural Research
  Archival Research
  Communication Research
  Community Research
  Computer Assisted Research
  Educational Research
  Family Research
  Group Research
  Investigations (Law Enforcement)
  Organizational Research
  Policy Research
  Psychiatric Research
  Research And Development
  Scientific Research
  Social Science Research
- **RT** Academic Disciplines
  Analysis
  Case Studies
  Constructs
  Data Collection
  Data Processing
  Discovery
  Evaluation
  Experiments
  Fieldwork
  Inventions
  Knowledge
  Longitudinal Studies
  Measurement
  Measures (Instruments)
  Methodological Problems
  Models
  Questionnaires
  Research Applications
  Research Design
  Research Ethics
  Research Methodology
  Researchers
  Scholarship
  Secondary Analysis
  Statistics
  Surveys
  Theories

Research And Development
- **DC** D711220
- **HN** Formerly (1984-1985) DC 385100, Research & Development/R&D.
- **UF** Industrial Research
- **BT** Research
- **RT** Development
  Energy Development
  Industrial Development
  Inventions
  Products
  Research Applications
  Scientific Discoveries
  Scientific Research
  Technological Innovations

Research Applications
- **DC** D711235
- **HN** Added, 1986.
- **UF** Applications of Research
- **RT** Adoption of Innovations
  Applied Sociology
  Diffusion
  High Technology Industries
  Research
  Research And Development
  Technology
  Technology Transfer
  Theory Practice Relationship

Research Design
- **DC** D711265
- **HN** Added, 1986.
- **UF** Experimental Design
  Research Planning
- **BT** Design
- **RT** Experiments
  Hypotheses
  Interviews
  Methodological Problems
  Methodology (Data Collection)
  Models
  Operational Definitions
  Participant Observation
  Qualitative Methods
  Quantitative Methods
  Research
  Research Design Error
  Research Methodology
  Sampling
  Surveys
  Theoretical Problems
  Variables
  Verification

Research Design Error
- **DC** D711275
- **HN** Added, 1986.
- **BT** Errors
- **RT** Research Design
  Statistical Bias
  Validity

Research Ethics
- **DC** D711300
- **HN** Added, 1986.
- **BT** Professional Ethics
- **NT** Bioethics
- **RT** Research
  Research Subjects
  Researchers
  Scientific Research
  Value Neutrality

Research Institutes
- **Use** Institutes

Research Methodology
- **DC** D711400
- **SN** Interrelated techniques for formulating research problems, and collecting, analyzing, and presenting findings.
- **HN** Formerly (1985) DC 385400, Research Methods.
- **BT** Methods
- **NT** Empirical Methods
  Historiography
  Methodology (Data Analysis)
  Methodology (Data Collection)
  Methodology (Philosophical)
  Qualitative Methods
  Quantitative Methods
- **RT** Description
  Documentation

Research

Research Methodology (cont'd)
- RT Experiments
  - Falsification
  - Generalization
  - Heuristics
  - Hypotheses
  - Interviews
  - Measurement
  - Measures (Instruments)
  - Methodological Problems
  - Models
  - Observation
  - Operational Definitions
  - Participant Observation
  - Reliability
  - Replication
  - Research
  - Research Design
  - Research Subjects
  - Sampling
  - Social Science Research
  - Statistics
  - Surveys
  - Theory Formation
  - Validity
  - Value Neutrality
  - Verification

Research Planning
- Use Research Design

Research Replication
- Use Replication

Research Responses
- DC D711450
- HN Added, 1986.
- UF Nonresponse (Research)
  - Response Rates
  - Survey Responses
- BT Responses
- RT Mail Surveys
  - Questionnaires
  - Respondents
  - Statistical Bias
  - Surveys

Research Reviews
- Use Literature Reviews

Research Subjects
- DC D711475
- HN Added, 1986.
- UF Control Subjects
  - Experimental Subjects
  - Human Subjects (Research)
- RT Experiments
  - Informed Consent
  - Methodology (Data Collection)
  - Research Ethics
  - Research Methodology
  - Researcher Subject Relations

Researcher Subject Relations
- DC D711500
- HN Added, 1986.
- BT Interpersonal Relations
- RT Methodology (Data Collection)
  - Research Subjects
  - Researchers

Researchers
- DC D711525
- HN Formerly (1963-1985) part of DC 385000, Research/Researcher/Researchers.
- BT Professional Workers
- RT Academic Careers
  - Interviewer Characteristics

Researchers (cont'd)
- RT Participant Observation
  - Psychologists
  - Research
  - Research Ethics
  - Researcher Subject Relations
  - Scientists
  - Social Scientists
  - Sociologists

Resentment
- Use Hostility

Reservations (American Indian)
- Use American Indian Reservations

Resettlement (1964-1985)
- HN DC 385740.
- Use Relocation

Residence
- DC D711600
- HN Formerly (1963-1985) part of DC 385760, Residence/Residences/Residential/Resident/Residents.
- UF Place of Residence
  - Residential Location
- NT Matrilocal Residence
  - Patrilocal Residence
- RT Communities
  - Demography
  - Households
  - Housing
  - Migration
  - Neighborhoods
  - Relocation
  - Residential Mobility
  - Residential Patterns
  - Residential Preferences
  - Residential Segregation
  - Workplaces

Residences
- Use Housing

Resident Satisfaction
- Use Community Satisfaction

Residential Change
- Use Residential Mobility

Residential Displacement
- Use Relocation

Residential Institutions
- DC D711900
- SN Alternatives to closed institutions such as prisons and mental hospitals, residential institutions include close supervision and structured expectations for resident clients, with a more home-like environment and the opportunity for exposure to the surrounding community through work and social activities.
- HN Added, 1986.
- UF Residential Treatment Facilities
- BT Facilities
- NT Juvenile Correctional Institutions
  - Nursing Homes
- RT Housing
  - Institutionalization (Persons)
  - Institutions
  - Treatment Programs

Residential Location
- Use Residence

Residents

Residential Mobility
- DC D712200
- SN Movement from residence to residence within the same community or geographic area. Do not confuse with Geographic Mobility.
- HN Added, 1986. Prior to 1986 use Residence/Residences/Residential/Resident/Residents (DC 385760) and Mobility (DC 274000).
- UF Moving (1966-1985)
  - Residential Change
- BT Mobility
- RT Communities
  - Geographic Mobility
  - Housing
  - Internal Migration
  - Migration
  - Neighborhoods
  - Relocation
  - Residence
  - Residential Patterns

Residential Patterns
- DC D712500
- HN Added, 1986.
- UF Housing Patterns
- BT Demography
- RT Commuting (Travel)
  - Housing
  - Housing Market
  - Land Settlement
  - Migration Patterns
  - Population Distribution
  - Residence
  - Residential Mobility
  - Settlement Patterns

Residential Preferences
- DC D712800
- HN Added, 1986.
- UF Housing Preferences
- BT Preferences
- RT Cohabitation
  - Community Satisfaction
  - Housing
  - Residence
  - Residential Segregation

Residential Segregation
- DC D713100
- HN Added, 1986.
- UF Housing Segregation
  - Neighborhood Segregation
- BT Segregation
- RT Desegregation
  - Ethnic Neighborhoods
  - Ghettos
  - Housing
  - Housing Market
  - Racial Segregation
  - Racism
  - Residence
  - Residential Preferences

Residential Treatment Facilities
- Use Residential Institutions

Residents
- DC D713400
- HN Formerly (1963-1985) part of DC 385760, Residence/Residences/Residential/Resident/Residents.
- UF Community Residents
  - Local Residents
- RT Communities
  - Neighborhoods
  - Neighbors
  - Rural Population
  - Urban Population

Residents

Residents (Medical)
  Use Physicians

Resignation (1964-1985)
  HN DC 385770.
  Use Labor Turnover

Resistance
  DC D713700
  HN Formerly (1963-1985) DC 385785.
  UF Opposition/Oppositions (1964-1985)
  BT Social Behavior
  RT Acceptance
     Approval
     Change
     Conflict
     Countermovements
     Discontent
     Dissent
     Public Support
     Rejection

Resolution/Resolutions (1963-1985)
  HN DC 385795.
  Use Conflict Resolution

Resort/Resorts (1972-1985)
  HN DC 385798.
  Use Recreational Facilities

Resource Allocation
  DC D714000
  HN Added, 1986.
  UF Allocation of Resources
  BT Allocation
  RT Appropriation
     Budgets
     Development
     Efficiency
     Energy Development
     Goals
     Priorities
     Resource Management
     Resource Mobilization
     Resources

Resource Management
  DC D714300
  HN Added, 1986.
  BT Management
  NT Conservation
  RT Land Use
     Pollution Control
     Resource Allocation
     Resources

Resource Mobilization
  DC D714400
  HN Added, 1989.
  BT Mobilization
  RT Resource Allocation
     Resources

Resources
  DC D714600
  HN Formerly (1963-1985) DC 385800, Resource/Resources.
  NT Human Resources
     Natural Resources
  RT Constraints
     Development
     Energy
     Energy Development
     Environment
     Materials
     Needs
     Raw Materials
     Resource Allocation
     Resource Management

Resources (cont'd)
  RT Resource Mobilization
     Scarcity
     Services
     Technology
     Tools

Respect
  DC D714900
  HN Formerly (1966-1985) DC 385970, Respect/Respectability.
  BT Social Behavior
  RT Honor
     Human Dignity
     Interpersonal Relations
     Self Esteem

Respondents
  DC D715100
  HN Formerly (1964-1985) DC 386300, Respondent/Respondents.
  UF Informant/Informants (1963-1985)
     Interviewee (1965-1985)
  RT Interviewer Characteristics
     Interviews
     Methodology (Data Collection)
     Questionnaires
     Research Responses
     Surveys

Response Rates
  Use Research Responses

Responses
  DC D715200
  HN Formerly (1963-1985) DC 386500, Response/Responsive/Responsiveness/Responses.
  UF Reaction/Reactionary/Reactions/Reactive (1963-1985)
     Responsiveness
  BT Behavior
  NT Research Responses
     Social Response
  RT Conditioning
     Feedback
     Interaction
     Shock
     Stimuli

Responsibility
  DC D715500
  HN Formerly (1963-1985) DC 387200, Responsibility/Responsibilities.
  NT Accountability
     Filial Responsibility
     Social Responsibility
  RT Authority
     Ethics
     Leadership
     Liability
     Obligation
     Social Behavior

Responsiveness
  Use Responses

Rest/Resting (1971-1985)
  HN DC 387400, deleted 1986.

Restaurants
  Use Eating And Drinking Establishments

Restitution (Corrections)
  DC D715800
  SN A criminal justice program under which an offender is required to repay the victim or society in money or services, as a condition of the sentence.

Retirement

Restitution (Corrections) (cont'd)
  HN Formerly (1969-1985) DC 387500, Restitution.
  UF Victim Compensation
  BT Compensation
  RT Correctional System
     Criminal Justice
     Offenders
     Sentencing
     Victim Offender Relations
     Victims

Restoration (1965-1985)
  HN DC 387590, deleted 1986.

Restraint/Restraints (1964-1985)
  HN DC 387700.
  Use Constraints

Restriction/Restrictions (1963-1985)
  HN DC 387715.
  Use Constraints

Result/Results (1964-1985)
  HN DC 387720, deleted 1986. See now Effects or Evaluation.

Resurrection (1963-1985)
  HN DC 387740, deleted 1986.

Retail Industry
  DC D716100
  HN Formerly (1963-1985) DC 387760, Retail/Retailing/Retailer/Retailers.
  UF Retailing
  BT Industry
  RT Advertising
     Brand Names
     Business
     Consumerism
     Consumers
     Market Research
     Marketing
     Merchants
     Purchasing
     Sales
     Sales Workers
     Stores
     Trade

Retail Stores
  Use Stores

Retailing
  Use Retail Industry

Retarded/Retardation/Retardates (1963-1985)
  HN DC 387900.
  Use Mentally Retarded

Retention (1964-1985)
  HN DC 388000, deleted 1986.

Retirement
  DC D716400
  HN Formerly (1963-1985) DC 390100, Retire/Retired/Retirement.
  RT Ageism
     Elderly
     Labor Turnover
     Leisure
     Life Stage Transitions
     Pensions
     Personnel Policy
     Retirement Communities
     Social Security
     Workers

Retirement

Retirement Benefits
- Use Pensions

Retirement Communities
- DC D716700
- HN Added, 1986.
- BT Communities
- RT New Towns
  Retirement

Retributive/Retribution (1969-1985)
- HN DC 390350.
- Use Punishment

Return Migration
- DC D717000
- SN Permanent or semi-permanent change of residence back to a place where one had formerly resided.
- HN Added, 1986.
- UF Population Turnaround
  Repatriation/Repatriated (1965-1985)
  Reverse Migration
- BT Migration
- RT Urban to Rural Migration

Reunion
- DC D717300
- HN Added, 1986.
- BT Sub Saharan Africa

Revenge/Revenges/Revenging (1971-1985)
- HN DC 390450, deleted 1986.

Revenue (1985)
- HN DC 390470.
- Use Income

Reverse Migration
- Use Return Migration

Review/Reviews (1963-1985)
- HN DC 390500, deleted 1986. See now Book Reviews, Literature Reviews, or Peer Review.

Reviews of the Literature
- Use Literature Reviews

Revisionism
- DC D717450
- HN Formerly (1964-1985) DC 390775, Revisionism/Revisionist/Revisionists.
- UF Communist Revisionism
  Marxist Revisionism
- BT Marxism
- RT Communism
  Evolutionary Theories
  Frankfurt School
  Socialism

Revitalization (1984-1985)
- HN DC 390780, deleted 1986. See now Community Change, Neighborhood Change, or Urban Renewal.

Revivalism (Religious)
- Use Religious Revivalism

Revolt/Revolts (1963-1985)
- HN DC 390900.
- Use Rebellions

Revolution (Scientific Technological)
- Use Scientific Technological Revolution

Revolutionary Movements
- Use Revolutions

Revolutions
- DC D717600
- SN Sweeping changes associated with the downfall and replacement of a previously stable social order.
- HN Formerly (1963-1985) part of DC 390800, Revolution/Revolutions/Revolutionary.
- UF Revolutionary Movements
- BT Change
- NT Scientific Technological Revolution
  Social Revolution
- RT Civil War
  Coups d'Etat
  Guerrillas
  History
  Ideological Struggle
  Leninism
  Maoism
  Marxism
  Paradigms
  Political Ideologies
  Political Movements
  Political Violence
  Rebellions
  Scientific Development
  Social Change
  Social Reform
  Sociology of Science
  State
  Theory Formation
  Underground Movements

Reward Distribution
- Use Rewards

Reward Systems
- Use Rewards

Rewards
- DC D717900
- HN Formerly (1963-1985) DC 391000, Reward/Rewards/Rewarding.
- UF Reward Distribution
  Reward Systems
- BT Reinforcement
  Sanctions
- RT Awards
  Delay of Gratification
  Exchange Theory
  Incentives
  Motivation
  Recognition (Achievement)
  Social Closure
  Social Control

Rhetoric
- DC D718200
- SN Art of speaking or writing effectively.
- HN Formerly (1969-1985) DC 391800, Rhetoric/Rhetorics/Rhetorical.
- UF Oratory
- NT Discourse
- RT Debate
  Discussion
  Language
  Speech

Rheumatic (1964-1985)
- HN DC 391940, deleted 1986.

Rheumatism
- Use Arthritis

Risk

Rhode Island
- DC D718500
- HN Formerly (1963-1985) DC 391980, Rhode Island/Rhode Islander/Rhode Islanders.
- BT Northern States
  United States of America

Rhodesia/Rhodesian/Rhodesians (1963-1985)
- HN DC 391985, deleted 1986. See now Zambia or Zimbabwe.

Rice (1969-1985)
- HN DC 392200.
- Use Food

Riddle/Riddles (1972-1985)
- HN DC 392475.
- Use Folklore

Riesman, David
- DC D718800
- SN Born 22 September 1909 - .
- HN Formerly (1963-1985) DC 392495.

Right Wing Politics
- DC D719100
- HN Formerly (1964-1985) DC 392800, Right-Wing.
- UF New Right (1982-1985)
- BT Politics
- RT Conservatism
  Extremism
  McCarthyism
  Vigilantism

Rights
- DC D719400
- SN A context-dependent term; select a more specific entry or coordinate with other terms.
- HN Formerly (1963-1985) DC 392600, Right/Rights.
- NT Human Rights
- RT Access
  Justice
  Law
  Obligation

Rigidity (1963-1985)
- HN DC 393000.
- Use Flexibility

Rio de Janeiro, Brazil
- DC D719600
- HN Added, 1989.
- BT Brazil

Riots
- DC D719700
- HN Formerly (1964-1985) DC 393150, Riot/Riots/Rioting.
- BT Collective Behavior
- RT Civil Disorders
  Crowds
  Political Violence
  Rebellions

Risk
- DC D720000
- HN Formerly (1963-1985) DC 393250, Risk/Risks.
- UF Risky Shift
- RT Chance
  Decision Making
  Game Theory
  Hazards
  Insurance

Risk

Risk (cont'd)
- RT Probability
- Risk Assessment
- Security
- Social Behavior
- Threat
- Vulnerability

Risk Assessment
- DC D720100
- HN Added, 1989.
- BT Evaluation
- RT Forecasting
- Risk

Risky Shift
- Use Risk

Rite/Rites (1963-1985)
- HN DC 393280.
- Use Rituals

Rites of Passage
- DC D720300
- HN Added, 1986.
- BT Rituals
- NT Death Rituals
- Initiation Rites
- RT Genital Mutilation
- Life
- Life Stage Transitions
- Puberty
- Religious Rituals
- Traditions

Ritual Circumcision
- Use Circumcision

Rituals
- DC D720600
- HN Formerly (1963-1985) DC 393320, Ritual/Rituals/Ritualism/Ritualization.
- UF Ceremony/Ceremonial/Ceremonialism (1963-1985)
- Rite/Rites (1963-1985)
- NT Potlatches
- Religious Rituals
- Rites of Passage
- Weddings
- RT Cannibalism
- Celebrations
- Culture
- Customs
- Festivals
- Gift Giving
- Holidays
- Masks
- Myths
- Naming Practices
- Symbolism
- Traditional Societies
- Traditions

Rivalry (1964-1985)
- HN DC 393330.
- Use Conflict

Roads
- Use Highways

Robbery
- DC D720900
- HN Formerly (1969-1985) DC 393425, Robbery/Robberies.
- UF Mugging
- BT Larceny
- RT Assault
- Banditry
- Burglary
- Offenses

Robotization in Industry
- Use Industrial Automation

Rochester, N.Y. (1965-1985)
- HN DC 393475, deleted 1986.

Rokeach, Milton
- DC D721200
- SN Born 27 December 1918 - died 25 October 1988.
- HN Formerly (1968-1985) DC 393800, Rokeach, M.

Rokkan, Stein
- DC D721250
- SN Born 4 July 1921 - died 1979.
- HN Added, 1989.

Role Ambiguity
- DC D721350
- HN Added, 1986.
- BT Ambiguity
- RT Occupational Roles
- Role Conflict
- Roles
- Self Concept
- Social Identity
- Status Inconsistency

Role Conflict
- DC D721500
- HN Added, 1986.
- BT Conflict
- RT Alienation
- Congruence (Psychology)
- Role Ambiguity
- Role Conflict
- Roles
- Self Concept
- Sex Roles
- Social Identity
- Status Inconsistency
- Working Mothers

Role Models
- DC D721700
- HN Added, 1986.
- UF Models (Role)
- RT Childhood Factors
- Imitation
- Models
- Occupational Roles
- Roles
- Sex Roles
- Significant Others
- Social Influence
- Socialization
- Womens Roles

Role Playing
- DC D721800
- HN Formerly (1985) DC 395000.
- RT Counseling
- Psychotherapy
- Simulation

Role Satisfaction
- DC D721900
- HN Added, 1989.
- BT Satisfaction
- RT Job Satisfaction
- Life Satisfaction
- Roles

Role Transition
- Use Life Stage Transitions

Roles
- DC D722100
- SN A context-dependent term for the rule-governed patterns of expectations and corresponding behaviors prevailing in society, and learned through the process of socialization. Select a more specific entry or coordinate with other terms when possible.
- UF Social Role/Social Roles (1963-1985)
- NT Family Role
- Occupational Roles
- Sex Roles
- Sick Role
- State Role
- RT Ascription
- Behavior
- Function
- Individuals
- Life Stage Transitions
- Norms
- Parenthood
- Role Ambiguity
- Role Conflict
- Role Models
- Role Satisfaction
- Social Function
- Social Relations
- Social Status
- Social Types
- Womens Roles

Roman Catholicism
- DC D722400
- HN Formerly (1963-1985) part of DC 395600, Roman Catholic/Roman Catholics/Roman Catholicism.
- BT Catholicism
- RT Confession
- Papacy
- Protestant Reformation
- Roman Catholics
- Saints

Roman Catholics
- DC D722700
- HN Formerly (1963-1985) part of DC 395600, Roman Catholic/Roman Catholics/Roman Catholicism.
- BT Catholics
- NT Franciscans
- Jesuits
- RT Dominicans (Clergy)
- Papacy
- Roman Catholicism

Romance Languages
- DC D723000
- HN Added, 1986.
- UF Catalan (Language)
- French (Language)
- Italian (Language)
- Portuguese (Language)
- Romanian (Language)
- Spanish (Language)
- BT Indoeuropean Languages
- NT Latin

Romance/Romances/Romantic (1968-1985)
- HN DC 395270.
- Use Love

Romances (Fiction)
- Use Fiction

Romani

Romani
- Use Gypsies

Romania
- DC D723300
- HN Formerly (1964-1985) DC 397650, Rumania/Rumanian/Rumanians.
- UF Rumania
- BT Balkan States
  Eastern Europe
- NT Bucharest, Romania

Romanian (Language)
- Use Romance Languages

Romanticism
- DC D723400
- HN Formerly (1964-1985) DC 395300.
- BT Artistic Styles
- RT Art History
  Literature
  Music
  Rationalism
  Sociology of Art
  Visual Arts

Rome, Italy
- DC D723600
- HN Formerly (1963-1985) DC 395400, Rome, Italy/Roman/Romans.
- BT Italy

Roper Public Opinion Research Center (1964-1985)
- HN DC 395690, deleted 1986.

Rorschach Test (1963-1985)
- HN DC 396000.
- Use Projective Techniques

Rotation (1964-1985)
- HN DC 397150, deleted 1986.

Rousseau, Jean-Jacques
- DC D723900
- SN Born 28 June 1712 - died 2 July 1778.
- HN Formerly (1963-1985) DC 397215, Rousseau, J. J.

Royalty
- DC D724200
- HN Formerly (1963-1985) DC 397240, Royal/Royalty.
- RT Aristocracy
  Monarchy

RSFSR
- Use Russian Soviet Federated Socialist Republic

Ru/Ur (1963-1985)
- HN DC 399000, deleted 1986. See now Rural Urban Differences, Rural to Urban Migration, or other appropriate "Rural" or "Urban" terms.

Rule/Rules (1964-1985)
- HN DC 397375, deleted 1986. See now Norms, Standards, Regulation, or appropriate "Political" terms.

Ruling Class
- DC D724500
- HN Formerly (1963-1985) DC 397500, Ruling/Rulings.
- UF Establishment/Establishments (1971-1985)
- RT Aristocracy
  Elites

Ruling Class (cont'd)
- RT Government
  Oligarchy
  Political Elites
  Political Power
  Power Elite
  Privilege
  Social Class
  Upper Class

Rumania
- Use Romania

Rumors
- DC D724800
- HN Formerly (1963-1985) DC 397700, Rumor/Rumors.
- RT Conversation
  Interpersonal Communication
  Messages
  Scandals
  Truth

Runaways
- DC D725100
- HN Formerly (1964-1985) DC 397950, Runaway.
- UF Adult Runaways
  Juvenile Runaways
- RT Adolescents
  Delinquency
  Deviant Behavior
  Dropouts
  Family Relations
  Parent Child Relations

Running/Jogging (1983-1985)
- HN DC 397990.
- Use Sports

Rural Areas
- DC D725400
- HN Formerly (1963-1985) DC 398400, Rural.
- RT Agrarian Structures
  Agriculture
  Extension Services
  Geographic Regions
  Nonmetropolitan Areas
  Rural Communities
  Rural Crime
  Rural Development
  Rural Education
  Rural Population
  Rural Poverty
  Rural Sociology
  Rural to Urban Migration
  Rural Urban Continuum
  Rural Urban Differences
  Rural Women
  Rural Youth
  Rurality
  Ruralization
  Urban Areas
  Urban Fringe
  Urban to Rural Migration
  Villages

Rural Communities
- DC D725700
- HN Added, 1986.
- UF Agricultural Communities
  Farming Communities
- BT Communities
- RT Peasants
  Rural Areas
  Rural Population
  Rural Poverty
  Rural Sociology
  Villages

Rural

Rural Crime
- DC D726000
- HN Added, 1986.
- BT Crime
- RT Rural Areas
  Urban Crime

Rural Development
- DC D726300
- HN Formerly (1984-1985) DC 399100.
- BT Development
- RT Agribusiness
  Agricultural Development
  Agricultural Policy
  Community Development
  Development Policy
  Development Programs
  Development Strategies
  Economic Development
  Extension Services
  Land Reform
  Land Use
  Regional Development
  Rural Areas
  Rural Poverty
  Urban Development

Rural Education
- DC D726600
- HN Added, 1986.
- BT Education
- RT Educational Systems
  Rural Areas

Rural Life
- Use Rurality

Rural Poor
- Use Rural Poverty

Rural Population
- DC D726900
- HN Added, 1986.
- BT Population
- RT Agricultural Workers
  Family Farms
  Farmers
  Internal Migration
  Population Distribution
  Population Growth
  Residents
  Rural Areas
  Rural Communities
  Rural Poverty
  Rural to Urban Migration
  Rural Women
  Rural Youth
  Urban Population
  Urban to Rural Migration

Rural Poverty
- DC D727200
- HN Added, 1986.
- UF Rural Poor
- BT Poverty
- RT Low Income Areas
  Rural Areas
  Rural Communities
  Rural Development
  Rural Population
  Urban Poverty

Rural Sociology
- DC D727500
- HN Formerly (1963-1985) DC 399230.
- BT Sociology
- RT Rural Areas
  Rural Communities
  Urban Sociology

Rural

Rural to Urban Migration
- **DC** D727800
- **HN** Added, 1986.
- **BT** Migration
- **RT** Internal Migration
  Rural Areas
  Rural Population
  Urban Areas
  Urban Population
  Urban to Rural Migration
  Urbanization

Rural Urban Comparisons
- **Use** Rural Urban Differences

Rural Urban Continuum
- **DC** D728100
- **SN** The range along which all communities can be placed, according to the degree to which they may be characterized as more rural or more urban.
- **HN** Added, 1986.
- **UF** Continuum (1963-1985)
  Folk Urban Continuum (1963-1985)
  Urban Rural Continuum
- **RT** Community Size
  Lifestyle
  Rural Areas
  Rural Urban Differences
  Urban Areas
  Urban Fringe

Rural Urban Differences
- **DC** D728400
- **SN** Used in analyses in which a social problem or phenomenon is explained as a consequence or correlate of contrasting features of urban and rural locales.
- **HN** Added, 1986.
- **UF** Rural Urban Comparisons
  Urban Rural Differences
- **BT** Differences
- **RT** Comparative Sociology
  Gemeinschaft And Gesellschaft
  Lifestyle
  Regional Differences
  Rural Areas
  Rural Urban Continuum
  Rurality
  Urban Areas
  Urbanism

Rural Urban Fringe
- **Use** Urban Fringe

Rural Women
- **DC** D728700
- **HN** Added, 1986.
- **BT** Females
- **RT** Rural Areas
  Rural Population

Rural Youth
- **DC** D729000
- **HN** Added, 1986.
- **UF** Farm Youth
  Peasant Youth
- **BT** Youth
- **RT** Rural Areas
  Rural Population
  Youth Employment

Ruralism
- **Use** Rurality

Rurality
- **DC** D729300
- **HN** Formerly (1966-1985) DC 399330.
- **UF** Rural Life
  Ruralism
- **RT** Everyday Life
  Lifestyle
  Localism
  Rural Areas
  Rural Urban Differences
  Urbanism

Ruralization
- **DC** D729600
- **HN** Formerly (1977-1985) DC 399360.
- **BT** Social Processes
- **RT** Rural Areas
  Urban to Rural Migration
  Urbanization

Rurban (1971-1985)
- **HN** DC 399369.
- **Use** Urban Fringe

Russell, Bertrand Arthur William
- **DC** D729900
- **SN** Born 18 May 1872 - died 2 February 1970.
- **HN** Formerly (1967-1985) DC 399380, Russell, Bertrand.

Russia
- **Use** Union of Soviet Socialist Republics

Russia/Russian/Russians (1963-1985)
- **HN** DC 399385, deleted 1986. See now Union of Soviet Socialist Republics, Russian Soviet Federated Socialist Republic, or Slavic Languages.

Russian Cultural Groups
- **Use** Soviet Union Cultural Groups

Russian Soviet Federated Socialist Republic
- **DC** D730200
- **HN** Added, 1986.
- **UF** RSFSR
- **BT** Union of Soviet Socialist Republics

Rwanda
- **DC** D730500
- **HN** Formerly (1968-1985) DC 399440, Rwanda/Rwandaese.
- **BT** Sub Saharan Africa

Saba
- **DC** D730800
- **HN** Added, 1986.
- **BT** Caribbean

Sabotage (1978-1985)
- **HN** DC 399465, deleted 1986.

Sacraments (1978-1985)
- **HN** DC 399470.
- **Use** Religious Rituals

Sacred Literature
- **Use** Religious Literature

Sacredness
- **DC** D731100
- **HN** Formerly (1963-1985) DC 399480, Sacred/Sacredness.
- **UF** Sanctity (1964-1985)
- **RT** Mana
  Places of Worship

Saint

Sacredness (cont'd)
- **RT** Religions
  Religious Beliefs
  Religious Literature
  Saints
  Secularization
  Shrines

Sacrifice (1985)
- **HN** DC 399481, deleted 1986.

Sacrificial Rites
- **DC** D731400
- **HN** Formerly (1965-1985) DC 399482.
- **UF** Blood Sacrifices
  Human Sacrifices
- **BT** Religious Rituals
- **RT** Cannibalism
  Deities
  Paganism
  Worship

Sadhus
- **DC** D731700
- **SN** Mendicant, ascetic, Hindu holy men.
- **HN** Formerly (1978-1985) DC 399490.
- **BT** Hindus
- **RT** Asceticism
  Hinduism

Sadism/Sadistic (1966-1985)
- **HN** DC 399493.
- **Use** Sexual Deviation

Sadomasochism (1985)
- **HN** DC 399495.
- **Use** Sexual Deviation

Safety
- **DC** D732000
- **HN** Formerly (1963-1985) DC 399500.
- **NT** Occupational Safety And Health
- **RT** Accidents
  Behavior
  Consumerism
  Fire
  Hazards
  Health
  Injuries
  Protection
  Sanitation
  Security
  Traffic
  Vulnerability

Sahlins, Marshall David
- **DC** D732300
- **SN** Born 27 December 1930 - .
- **HN** Formerly (1985) DC 399516, Sahlins, Marshall.

Sail/Sails/Sailor/Sailors/Sailing (1963-1985)
- **HN** DC 399517.
- **Use** Shipping Industry

Saint Barthelemy
- **DC** D732600
- **HN** Added, 1986.
- **BT** Caribbean

Saint Eustatius
- **DC** D732900
- **HN** Added, 1986.
- **BT** Caribbean

Saint Sardinia

Saint Kitts Nevis
- DC D733200
- HN Added, 1986. Prior to 1986 use Nevis, British West Indies (DC 298490).
- BT Caribbean

Saint Lucia
- DC D733500
- HN Added, 1986.
- BT Caribbean

Saint Martin
- DC D733800
- HN Added, 1986.
- BT Caribbean

Saint Simon, Claude Henri de Rouvroy
- DC D734000
- SN Born 17 October 1760 - died 19 May 1825.
- HN Formerly (1963-1985) DC 399545, Saint Simon/Saint Simonists.

Saint Vincent
- DC D734100
- HN Added, 1986.
- BT Caribbean

Sainthood
- Use Saints

Saints
- DC D734400
- HN Added, 1986.
- UF Canonization
     Hagiography (1978-1985)
     Sainthood
     Sanctification
     St. Augustine (1967-1985)
     St. Thomas Aquinas (1964-1985)
- RT Prayer
     Roman Catholicism
     Sacredness
     Worship

Salaries
- DC D734700
- HN Formerly (1963-1985) DC 399600, Salary/Salaried/Salaries.
- BT Compensation
- RT Income
     Income Distribution
     Professional Workers
     Wages

Sales
- DC D735000
- HN Formerly (1983-1985) DC 399603.
- UF Selling (1963-1985)
- RT Advertising
     Business
     Consumerism
     Consumers
     Exchange (Economics)
     Marketing
     Products
     Purchasing
     Retail Industry
     Sales Workers
     Stores
     Trade

Sales Workers
- DC D735300
- HN Formerly (1964-1985) DC 399605, Salesmen.
- BT White Collar Workers
- RT Merchants
     Retail Industry
     Sales

Salience
- DC D735400
- SN Quality of being perceived as prominent or particularly relevant, especially regarding variables with particular explanatory or descriptive importance.
- HN Formerly (1972-1985) DC 399800, Salient/Salience.
- RT Expectations
     Experience
     Influence
     Perceptions
     Values

Salvation
- DC D735600
- HN Formerly (1963-1985) DC 400175.
- RT Baptism
     Mahdis
     Messianic Figures
     Messianic Movements
     Religious Beliefs
     Religious Conversion
     Sins
     Soul

Samoa/Samoan/Samoans (1963-1985)
- HN DC 400800, deleted 1986. See now American Samoa or Western Samoa.

Sampling
- DC D735750
- HN Formerly (1963-1985) DC 401000, Sample/Samples/Sampling.
- NT Random Samples
- RT Data Collection
     Error of Measurement
     Experiments
     Methodology (Data Collection)
     Multivariate Analysis
     Parameters (Statistics)
     Probability
     Quantitative Methods
     Reliability
     Research Design
     Research Methodology
     Social Science Research
     Statistical Bias
     Statistics
     Surveys
     Verification
     Weighting

Samurai
- DC D735900
- HN Formerly (1963-1985) DC 403100.
- RT Asian Cultural Groups
     Feudalism
     Militarism

San Diego, California
- DC D736200
- HN Formerly (1980-1985) DC 403180, San Diego, Calif.
- BT California

San Francisco, California
- DC D736500
- HN Formerly (1964-1985) DC 403200, San Francisco, Calif.
- BT California

San Juan, Puerto Rico
- DC D736600
- HN Added, 1989.
- BT Puerto Rico

San Marino
- DC D736800
- HN Added, 1986.
- BT Western Europe
- RT Italy

Sanctification
- Use Saints

Sanctions
- DC D737100
- HN Formerly (1963-1985) DC 403125, Sanction/Sanctions/Sanctioning.
- NT Punishment
     Rewards
- RT Awards
     Behavior
     Censorship
     Feedback
     Law
     Norms
     Social Control
     Social Response
     Social Values
     Taboos

Sanctity (1964-1985)
- HN DC 403130.
- Use Sacredness

Sanitation
- DC D737400
- HN Formerly (1963-1985) DC 403210, Sanitation/Sanitary.
- UF Community Sanitation
     Industrial Sanitation
- RT Epidemiology
     Health
     Hygiene
     Occupational Safety And Health
     Public Health
     Safety

Sanskrit
- Use Indic Languages

Santa Cruz Islands
- DC D737700
- HN Added, 1986.
- BT Melanesia

Santo Domingo, Dominican Republic
- DC D738000
- HN Formerly (1964-1985) DC 403257.
- BT Dominican Republic

Sao Paulo, Brazil
- DC D738300
- HN Formerly (1964-1985) DC 403260.
- BT Brazil

Sao Tome And Principe
- DC D738600
- HN Added, 1986.
- BT Sub Saharan Africa

Sapir, Edward
- DC D738900
- SN Born 26 January 1884 - died 4 February 1939.
- HN Formerly (1967-1985) DC 403262.

Sardinia
- DC D739200
- HN Formerly (1964-1985) DC 403265, Sardinia/Sardinian/Sardinians.
- BT Italy

Sartre, Jean-Paul
- **DC** D739500
- **SN** Born 21 June 1905 - died 15 April 1980.
- **HN** Formerly (1963-1985) DC 403270, Sartre, J.-P.

Saskatchewan
- **DC** D739800
- **HN** Added, 1986.
- **BT** Canada

Satan (1964-1985)
- **HN** DC 403290.
- **Use** Devils

Satellites (1963-1985)
- **HN** DC 403315, deleted 1986. See now Telecommunications or Space Technology.

Satire
- **DC** D740100
- **HN** Formerly (1965-1985) DC 403340, Satire/Satirical.
- **UF** Caricature/Caricatures (1969-1985)
- **RT** Cartoons
  Comics (Publications)
  Literature

Satisfaction
- **DC** D740400
- **SN** A context-dependent term for an individual's positive assessment of self or circumstances. Select a more specific entry or coordinate with other terms.
- **HN** Formerly (1963-1985) DC 403350.
- **UF** Fulfillment (1969-1985)
- **BT** Attitudes
- **NT** Community Satisfaction
  Job Satisfaction
  Life Satisfaction
  Marital Satisfaction
  Role Satisfaction
- **RT** Discontent
  Emotions
  Happiness
  Improvement
  Needs
  Quality
  Self Esteem

Saudi Arabia
- **DC** D740700
- **HN** Formerly (1963-1985) DC 403410, Saudi Arabia/Saudi Arabian/Saudi Arabians.
- **BT** Arab Countries
  Middle East

Savanna/Savannas (1969-1985)
- **HN** DC 403465, deleted 1986.

Saving
- **DC** D741000
- **HN** Formerly (1965-1985) DC 403550, Saving/Savings.
- **UF** Thrift
- **RT** Accumulation
  Banking
  Capital
  Consumption
  Finance
  Income
  Money
  Wealth

Scalability (1978-1985)
- **HN** DC 403620.
- **Use** Scales

Scale Items
- **Use** Items (Measures)

Scales
- **DC** D741200
- **HN** Formerly (1963-1985) DC 403700, Scale/Scales.
- **UF** Edwards Personal Preference Scale (1966-1985)
  Multidimensional Scaling
  Rating Scales
  Scalability (1978-1985)
  Scaling (1963-1985)
  Unfolding Technique (1984-1985)
  Unidimensional Scaling
- **BT** Measures (Instruments)
- **NT** F Scale
  Guttman Scales
  Social Desirability Scales
- **RT** Attitude Measures
  Factor Structure
  Indexes (Measures)
  Interval Measurement
  Items (Measures)
  Magnitude Estimation
  Nominal Measurement
  Ordinal Measurement
  Ranking
  Rating
  Scores
  Weighting

Scales (Attitude)
- **Use** Attitude Measures

Scaling (1963-1985)
- **HN** DC 404000.
- **Use** Scales

Scalogram (1964-1985)
- **HN** DC 404030.
- **Use** Guttman Scales

Scandals
- **DC** D741260
- **HN** Formerly (1972-1985) DC 404045, Scandal/Scandals/Scandalous.
- **NT** Watergate Scandal
- **RT** Corruption
  Offenses
  Public Opinion
  Rumors

Scandinavia
- **DC** D741300
- **HN** Formerly (1963-1985) DC 404050, Scandinavia/Scandinavian/Scandinavians.
- **UF** Nordic Countries (1964-1985)
- **BT** Western Europe
- **NT** Denmark
  Faeroe Islands
  Finland
  Greenland
  Iceland
  Lapland
  Norway
  Sweden

Scapegoating
- **DC** D741450
- **SN** Process by which blame, anger, and aggression are displaced onto innocent, usually less powerful, groups or individuals.
- **HN** Formerly (1967-1985) DC 404075, Scapegoat/Scapegoats.

Scapegoating (cont'd)
- **UF** Witch Hunting
- **RT** Hostility
  Labeling
  Stereotypes
  Stigma
  Symbolism

Scarcity
- **DC** D741600
- **HN** Formerly (1963-1985) DC 404080.
- **UF** Shortages
- **BT** Economic Conditions
- **RT** Commodities
  Consumption
  Deprivation
  Economic Problems
  Famine
  Natural Disasters
  Resources

Scenario/Scenarios (1984-1985)
- **HN** DC 404092.
- **Use** Forecasting

Schedules (Interview)
- **Use** Interview Schedules

Scheler, Max
- **DC** D741900
- **SN** Born 22 August 1874 - died 19 May 1928.
- **HN** Formerly (1964-1985) DC 404125, Scheler, M.

Schism
- **DC** D742100
- **HN** Added, 1989.
- **BT** Cleavage
- **NT** Photian Schism
- **RT** Apostasy
  Extremism
  Movements
  Partisanship
  Polarization
  Political Defection
  Political Ideologies
  Political Parties
  Religions
  Religious Beliefs
  Religious Doctrines
  Religious Orthodoxy
  Sectarianism
  Social Conflict
  Social Unrest

Schizophrenia
- **DC** D742200
- **SN** Group of mental disorders characterized by varying combinations of symptoms such as bizarre behavior, delusions, hallucinations, incoherence, and catatonia.
- **HN** Formerly (1963-1985) DC 404200, Schizophrenia/Schizophrenic/Schizophrenics.
- **UF** Dementia Praecox
- **BT** Psychosis
- **RT** Autism
  Depersonalization
  Mental Illness
  Mental Patients
  Paranoia

Scholarly Journals
- **Use** Journals

Scholarly

Scholarly Societies
  Use Professional Associations

Scholarship
  DC D742500
  HN Formerly (1963-1985) DC 404900, Scholar/Scholars/Scholarly/Scholarship.
  RT Academic Achievement
     Academic Careers
     Authorship
     College Faculty
     Discourse
     Dissertations
     Fellowships And Scholarships
     Historiography
     Intellectuals
     Journals
     Knowledge
     Learning
     Objectivity
     Research
     Writing for Publication

Scholastic (1963-1985)
  HN DC 404910, deleted 1986. See now appropriate "Academic" terms.

Scholastic Achievement
  Use Academic Achievement

School Absenteeism
  Use Absenteeism

School Administration
  Use Educational Administration

School Attendance
  DC D742800
  HN Added, 1986.
  BT Attendance
  RT Dropouts
     Enrollment
     Truancy

School Boards
  DC D743100
  HN Formerly (1965-1985) DC 405100, School Board.
  UF Boards of Education
  BT Governing Boards
  RT Educational Administration
     Educational Policy
     School Districts
     Schools

School Books
  Use Textbooks

School Curriculum
  Use Curriculum

School Desegregation
  DC D743400
  HN Added, 1986.
  UF Busing (1981-1985)
     School Integration
  BT Desegregation
  RT Schools

School Districts
  DC D743500
  HN Added, 1986.
  UF Local Education Agencies
  BT Districts
  RT Geographic Regions
     Local Government
     Public Schools
     School Boards
     Schools
     Superintendents

School Guidance
  Use Guidance

School Integration
  Use School Desegregation

School Leavers
  Use Dropouts

School Performance
  Use Academic Achievement

School Reform
  Use Educational Reform

School Superintendents
  Use Superintendents

School Truancy
  Use Truancy

Schools
  DC D743700
  HN Formerly (1963-1985) DC 405000, School/Schools.
  BT Facilities
  NT Colleges
     Elementary Schools
     Private Schools
     Public Schools
     Secondary Schools
  RT Admissions
     Curriculum
     Dropouts
     Education
     Educational Administration
     Educational Programs
     Educational Systems
     Enrollment
     Institutions
     Principals
     School Boards
     School Desegregation
     School Districts
     Socialization Agents
     Students
     Teachers
     Teaching

Schools of Philosophy
  Use Philosophical Doctrines

Schumpeter, Joseph Alois
  DC D744000
  SN Born 8 February 1883 - died 8 January 1950.
  HN Formerly (1964-1985) DC 409900, Schumpeter, J.

Schutz, Alfred
  DC D744300
  SN Born 13 April 1899 - died 20 May 1959.
  HN Formerly (1963-1985) DC 409750.

Schweitzer, Albert
  DC D744600
  SN Born 14 January 1875 - died 4 September 1965.
  HN Formerly (1963-1985) DC 409925.

Science
  DC D744900
  HN Formerly (1963-1985) DC 410000, Science/Sciences.
  BT Science And Technology
  RT Behavioral Sciences
     Cosmology
     Epistemological Doctrines
     Formalism

Scientific

Science (cont'd)
  RT Natural Sciences
     Physical Sciences
     Postulates
     Propositions
     Rationalism
     Science Policy
     Scientific Development
     Scientific Discoveries
     Scientific Knowledge
     Scientific Method
     Scientific Research
     Scientific Technological Revolution
     Scientists
     Social Sciences
     Sociology of Science
     Technology
     Theories

Science And Technology
  DC D745200
  HN Formerly (1985) DC 410200, Science & Technology.
  UF Technology And Science
  NT Science
     Technology
  RT Innovations
     Intellectual History
     Knowledge
     Scientific Discoveries
     Scientific Technological Revolution
     Sociology of Science
     Technological Innovations
     Technological Progress

Science Fiction
  Use Fiction

Science Policy
  DC D745500
  HN Added, 1986.
  BT Policy
  RT Economic Policy
     Science
     Scientific Development
     Scientific Research

Scientific Community
  DC D745800
  HN Added, 1986.
  RT Communities
     Elites
     Engineers
     Intelligentsia
     Scientists
     Sociology of Science
     Technology Transfer

Scientific Creationism
  Use Creationism

Scientific Development
  DC D745950
  HN Added, 1986.
  BT Development
  RT Economic Development
     Progress
     Science
     Science Policy
     Scientific Discoveries
     Scientific Technological Revolution
     Technological Progress
     Revolutions

Scientific Disciplines
  Use Academic Disciplines

Scientific

Scientific Discoveries
- **DC** D746100
- **HN** Added, 1986.
- **RT** Discovery
  - Innovations
  - Inventions
  - Patents
  - Research And Development
  - Science
  - Science And Technology
  - Scientific Development
  - Scientific Knowledge
  - Scientific Research
  - Scientific Technological Revolution
  - Technological Change
  - Technological Innovations
  - Technological Progress

Scientific Knowledge
- **DC** D746400
- **HN** Added, 1986.
- **BT** Knowledge
- **RT** Science
  - Scientific Discoveries
  - Scientific Research
  - Scientific Technological Revolution
  - Sociology of Knowledge
  - Sociology of Science
  - Technology
  - Technology Transfer

Scientific Management
- **DC** D746500
- **HN** Added, 1986.
- **UF** Taylor, N.W./Taylorism (1969-1985)
- **BT** Management
- **RT** Division of Labor
  - Labor Process
  - Labor Relations
  - Leninism
  - Productivity
  - Rationalization
  - Work Organization

Scientific Medicine
- **Use** Medicine

Scientific Method
- **DC** D746550
- **SN** Accumulation of knowledge based on observation, experimentation, and logic. Replicability of results by independent researchers using the same procedures is considered a key factor.
- **HN** Formerly (1985) DC 410400.
- **BT** Empirical Methods
- **RT** Deduction
  - Experiments
  - Generalization
  - Induction
  - Objectivity
  - Science
  - Scientific Research

Scientific Research
- **DC** D746700
- **HN** Formerly (1963-1985) part of DC 410380, Scientific/Scientism/Scienticity/Scientization.
- **BT** Research
- **NT** Medical Research
- **RT** Astronomy
  - Bioethics
  - Biology
  - Biotechnology
  - Chemistry
  - Ecology
  - Eugenics

Scientific Research (cont'd)
- **RT** Geology
  - Laboratories
  - Medicine
  - Physics
  - Physiology
  - Quantitative Methods
  - Research And Development
  - Research Ethics
  - Science
  - Science Policy
  - Scientific Discoveries
  - Scientific Knowledge
  - Scientific Method
  - Scientific Technological Revolution
  - Space Technology
  - Technology
  - Technology Assessment

Scientific Technological Revolution
- **DC** D747000
- **SN** Dramatic changes throughout society initiated by key scientific and technological breakthroughs such as the perfection of the steam engine in the eighteenth century.
- **HN** Added, 1986. Formerly (1963-1985) part of DC 390800, Revolution/Revolutions/Revolutionary.
- **UF** Revolution (Scientific Technological)
  - Technological Scientific Revolution
- **BT** Revolutions
- **RT** Computers
  - Economic Development
  - Information
  - Microcomputers
  - Modernization
  - Progress
  - Science
  - Science And Technology
  - Scientific Development
  - Scientific Discoveries
  - Scientific Knowledge
  - Scientific Research
  - Social Revolution
  - Sociology of Science
  - Technological Change
  - Technological Progress
  - Technology
  - Worker Machine Relationship

Scientists
- **DC** D747300
- **SN** Coordinate with a specific scientific discipline to locate information about personnel in that discipline, eg, for Chemists use Scientists and Chemistry.
- **HN** Formerly (1963-1985) DC 410700, Scientist/Scientists.
- **BT** Professional Workers
- **RT** Brain Drain
  - Engineers
  - Expert Witnesses
  - Experts
  - Natural Sciences
  - Physical Sciences
  - Researchers
  - Science
  - Scientific Community
  - Social Scientists

Scope (1971-1985)
- **HN** DC 410790, deleted 1986.

Second

Scores
- **DC** D747500
- **HN** Formerly (1963-1985) DC 410800, Score/Scores/Scoring.
- **UF** Scoring
- **BT** Data
- **RT** Correlation
  - Error of Measurement
  - Grades (Scholastic)
  - Items (Measures)
  - Measurement
  - Measures (Instruments)
  - Scales
  - Tests
  - Weighting

Scoring
- **Use** Scores

Scotland
- **DC** D747600
- **HN** Formerly (1963-1985) DC 410825, Scotland/Scottish.
- **BT** Great Britain
  - United Kingdom
  - Western Europe
- **NT** Glasgow, Scotland

Sculpture
- **Use** Visual Arts

Sculpture/Sculptor/Sculptors (1964-1985)
- **HN** DC 410850, deleted 1986. See now Visual Arts or Artists.

Search (1971-1985)
- **HN** DC 410855, deleted 1986. See now Job Search or Help Seeking Behavior.

Search And Rescue Operations
- **Use** Disaster Relief

Seasonal Variations
- **DC** D747900
- **HN** Formerly (1964-1985) DC 410860, Season/Seasons/Seasonal.
- **RT** Cyclical Processes
  - Differences
  - Environmental Factors
  - Time Series Analysis
  - Weather

Seattle, Washington
- **DC** D748200
- **HN** Formerly (1963-1985) DC 410875, Seattle, Wash.
- **BT** Washington (State)

Seclusion (1972-1985)
- **HN** DC 410883.
- **Use** Social Isolation

Second Language Learning
- **DC** D748500
- **HN** Added, 1986.
- **UF** Foreign Language Learning
- **BT** Learning
- **RT** Bilingual Education
  - Bilingualism
  - Educational Policy
  - Language
  - Monolingualism
  - Multilingualism

Second

Second/Secondary (1972-1985)
- HN DC 410888, deleted 1986. See now specific terms.

Secondary Analysis
- DC D748650
- SN The re-analysis of empirical data previously compiled by another researcher for a different study.
- HN Added, 1986.
- BT Analysis
- RT Aggregate Data
  Data Collection
  Research

Secondary Education
- DC D748800
- HN Added, 1986.
- UF Secondary Grades
- BT Education
- RT Adult Education
  High School Students
  High Schools
  Junior High Schools
  Secondary Schools
  Vocational Education

Secondary Grades
- Use Secondary Education

Secondary Schools
- DC D749100
- HN Formerly (1963-1985) DC 410890, Secondary School/Secondary Schools.
- BT Schools
- NT High Schools
  Junior High Schools
- RT Curriculum
  High School Students
  Secondary Education
  Teachers

Secrecy
- DC D749200
- HN Formerly (1963-1985) part of DC 410910, Secret/Secrets/Secrecy.
- RT Espionage
  National Security
  Secret Societies

Secret Societies
- DC D749250
- HN Formerly (1963-1985) part of DC 410910, Secret/Secrets/Secrecy.
- UF Ku Klux Klan (1964-1985)
- BT Associations
- RT Religious Brotherhoods
  Religious Rituals
  Secrecy
  Traditional Societies

Secretion/Secretions (1964-1985)
- HN DC 410920, deleted 1986.

Sectarianism
- DC D749325
- SN Narrow adherence to a religious sect, political party, school of thought, or social group.
- HN Formerly (1967-1985) DC 410935.
- RT Bias
  Ethnocentrism
  Factionalism
  Partisanship
  Political Affiliation
  Political Ideologies
  Religious Orientations
  Schism

Sectarianism (cont'd)
- RT Social Attitudes
  Social Conflict
  Worldview

Sectors (Economic)
- Use Economic Sectors

Sects
- DC D749300
- HN Formerly (1963-1985) DC 410930, Sect/Sects.
- RT Churches
  Countercultures
  Cults
  Denominations
  Religions
  Religious Fundamentalism

Secularism
- Use Secularization

Secularization
- DC D749400
- HN Formerly (1971-1985) DC 410990, Secular/Secularism/Secularization.
- UF Secularism
- BT Social Processes
- RT Church State Relationship
  Churches
  Civil Religion
  Creationism
  Modernization
  Rationalization
  Religion Politics Relationship
  Religions
  Religiosity
  Religious Beliefs
  Religious Cultural Groups
  Religious Movements
  Religious Orthodoxy
  Sacredness

Security
- DC D749700
- SN State of safety and stability in which protective measures are taken to insure against danger, fear, or uncertainty.
- HN Formerly (1963-1985) DC 411000, Security/Securities.
- UF Insecurity (1966-1985)
- NT National Security
- RT Certainty
  Control
  Crime Prevention
  Fear
  Law Enforcement
  Needs
  Protection
  Risk
  Safety
  Stability
  Threat
  Vulnerability

Sedatives
- Use Tranquilizing Drugs

Sedition (1964-1985)
- HN DC 411080, deleted 1986.

Seeking Help
- Use Help Seeking Behavior

Segmentation (1965-1985)
- HN DC 411185, deleted 1986. See now Labor Market Segmentation or Social Segmentation.

Self

Segregation
- DC D750000
- HN Formerly (1963-1985) DC 411200, Segregation/Segregated/Segregationist/Segregationists.
- NT Desegregation
  Occupational Segregation
  Racial Segregation
  Residential Segregation
- RT Discrimination
  Inequality
  Marginality
  Racism
  Separatism
  Social Control

Seismology/Seismological (1969-1985)
- HN DC 411400, deleted 1986.

Select/Selective/Selectivity/Selection/Selecting (1963-1985)
- HN DC 412000, deleted 1986. See now Choices, Mate Selection, or Selection Procedures.

Selection Procedures
- DC D750200
- HN Added, 1986.
- BT Methods
- RT Choices
  Decision Making
  Mate Selection

Selective Service (Military)
- Use Draft (Military)

Self (1963-1985)
- HN DC 413000, deleted 1986. See now Consciousness and specific "Self" terms.

Self Actualization
- DC D750300
- SN Processes of realizing one's potentialities, capacities, and talents; of accepting oneself; and of integrating or harmonizing one's motives.
- HN Formerly (1966-1985) DC 013200, Actualist/Actualists/Actuality/Actualization.
- UF Actualization (Self)
  Self Realization
- RT Aspiration
  Help Seeking Behavior
  Individualism
  Individuals
  Intellectual Development
  Life Satisfaction
  Mental Health
  Personality
  Self Concept
  Self Expression
  Sensitivity Training

Self Assertion
- Use Assertiveness

Self Assessment
- Use Self Evaluation

Self Care
- DC D750600
- HN Added, 1986.
- RT After Care
  Coping
  Deinstitutionalization
  Elderly
  Health Care

Self

Self Care (cont'd)
- RT Illness
- Rehabilitation

Self Centeredness
- Use Egocentrism

Self Concept
- DC D750900
- HN Formerly (1985) DC 413050.
- UF Body Image
- Personal Identity
- Self Image
- Self Perception
- BT Identity
- NT Self Esteem
- RT Aspiration
- Attribution
- Cognitive Dissonance
- Congruence (Psychology)
- Delay of Gratification
- Depersonalization
- Egocentrism
- Honor
- Images
- Individuals
- Locus of Control
- Personality
- Reference Groups
- Relative Deprivation
- Role Ambiguity
- Role Conflict
- Self Actualization
- Self Evaluation
- Self Presentation
- Sex Role Identity
- Significant Others
- Social Identity
- Social Status

Self Confidence
- Use Self Esteem

Self Congruence
- Use Congruence (Psychology)

Self Destructive Behavior
- DC D751000
- HN Added, 1989.
- UF Self Injurious Behavior
- Self Mutilation
- Suicide Attempts
- BT Behavior
- NT Suicide
- RT Deviant Behavior

Self Determination
- DC D751100
- HN Formerly (1963-1985) part of DC 131140, Determinant/Determination/Determinism/Deterministic.
- RT Autonomy
- Black Power
- Foreign Policy
- Minority Groups
- Nationalism
- Opportunities
- Political Movements
- Political Participation
- Sovereignty

Self Disclosure
- DC D751200
- HN Formerly (1984-1985) DC 133030, Disclosure/Disclosures.
- UF Disclosure (Individuals)
- RT Anonymity
- Confidentiality

Self Disclosure (cont'd)
- RT Individuals
- Interpersonal Communication
- Intimacy
- Psychotherapy
- Self Expression
- Self Help

Self Employment
- DC D751300
- HN Added, 1989.
- BT Employment
- RT Entrepreneurship
- Home Workplaces
- Small Businesses

Self Esteem
- DC D751500
- HN Formerly (1984-1985) DC 413090.
- UF Esteem (1963-1985)
- Pride (1968-1985)
- Self Confidence
- BT Self Concept
- RT Cognitive Dissonance
- Happiness
- Human Dignity
- Individuals
- Interpersonal Relations
- Narcissism
- Personality Traits
- Recognition (Achievement)
- Respect
- Satisfaction
- Self Evaluation
- Self Presentation
- Sensitivity Training

Self Evaluation
- DC D751650
- HN Added, 1986.
- UF Self Assessment
- BT Evaluation
- RT Peer Review
- Self Concept
- Self Esteem

Self Expression
- DC D751800
- HN Formerly (1963-1985) DC 164500, Expression/Expressions/Expressive/Expressiveness.
- UF Emotional Expression
- Expressivity
- RT Assertiveness
- Conversation
- Creativity
- Interpersonal Communication
- Nonverbal Communication
- Self Actualization
- Self Disclosure
- Self Presentation

Self Help
- DC D752100
- SN Support or development programs conducted by and for the participants, usually with the philosophy that such approaches are preferable to those run by government agencies or professional groups.
- HN Formerly (1984-1985) DC 414020.
- UF Mutual Help
- RT Behavior Modification
- Group Therapy
- Help Seeking Behavior
- Individuals
- Self Disclosure
- Self Help Groups

Semantics

Self Help Groups
- DC D752150
- SN Community-based organizations for mutual support in coping with various adversities or personal problems, usually functioning outside of mainstream professional systems and public service agencies.
- HN Added, 1989.
- UF Support Groups
- BT Groups
- RT Group Therapy
- Help Seeking Behavior
- Helping Behavior
- Self Help
- Support Networks

Self Image
- Use Self Concept

Self Injurious Behavior
- Use Self Destructive Behavior

Self Interest
- Use Individualism

Self Love
- Use Narcissism

Self Management in Industry
- Use Worker Control

Self Mutilation
- Use Self Destructive Behavior

Self Perception
- Use Self Concept

Self Presentation
- DC D752200
- HN Formerly (1984-1985) DC 345323, Presentation/Presentations.
- RT Assertiveness
- Impression Management
- Self Concept
- Self Esteem
- Self Expression
- Social Interaction
- Social Perception

Self Realization
- Use Self Actualization

Selling (1963-1985)
- HN DC 415000.
- Use Sales

Semantic Differential
- DC D752300
- SN An attitude scale that measures the subjective meaning of phenomena (persons, institutions, concepts, political issues) to an individual. The subject rates selected phenomena on a 7-point scale consisting of opposite adjectives (eg, valuable-worthless).
- HN Added, 1986. Formerly (1963-1985) part of DC 416000, Semantic/Semantics.
- BT Attitude Measures
- RT Personality Measures

Semantics
- DC D752400
- HN Formerly (1963-1985) part of DC 416000, Semantic/Semantics.
- BT Linguistics
- Semiotics
- RT Definitions
- Discourse Analysis

Semi

Semantics (cont'd)
- RT Etymology
    - Grammar
    - Pragmatics
    - Words

Semi Arid Lands
- Use Arid Zones

Seminarians
- DC D752700
- HN Formerly (1968-1985) DC 416204, Seminarian/Seminarians/Seminary.
- UF Seminary Students
- BT College Students
- RT Christianity
    - Clergy
    - Religious Education

Seminars
- DC D753000
- HN Formerly (1964-1985) DC 416200, Seminar.
- RT Congresses And Conventions
    - Courses
    - Educational Programs
    - Meetings
    - Symposia
    - Workshops (Courses)

Seminary Students
- Use Seminarians

Semiology
- Use Semiotics

Semiotics
- DC D753300
- SN Theory or study of signs and symbols, dealing especially with their function in language, and comprising syntactics, semantics, and pragmatics.
- HN Formerly (1967-1985) DC 416210, Semiotic/Semiotics/Semiology/Semiological.
- UF Semiology
- BT Linguistics
    - Philosophy
- NT Pragmatics
    - Semantics
- RT Definitions
    - Hermeneutics
    - Language
    - Marxist Aesthetics
    - Signs
    - Structuralism
    - Symbolism
    - Verbal Communication

Semitic Languages
- DC D753600
- HN Formerly (1964-1985) DC 416230, Semitic.
- UF Amharic
    - Arabic
    - Hebrew Language
- BT Languages
- RT Arab Cultural Groups
    - Jewish Cultural Groups

Senate/Senates (1964-1985)
- HN DC 416340.
- Use Legislative Bodies

Senator/Senators/Senatorial (1963-1985)
- HN DC 416350.
- Use Legislators

Senegal
- DC D753900
- HN Formerly (1963-1985) DC 416405, Senegal/Senegalese.
- BT Sub Saharan Africa

Senescence (1979-1985)
- HN DC 416420, deleted 1986. See now Aging, Elderly, or Geriatrics.

Senile Dementia
- Use Senility

Senility
- DC D754200
- HN Formerly (1981-1985) DC 416437, Senile/Senility.
- UF Senile Dementia
- RT Aging
    - Alzheimer's Disease
    - Brain
    - Mental Illness

Senior Citizen/Senior Citizens (1984-1985)
- HN DC 416439.
- Use Elderly

Seniority
- DC D754500
- HN Formerly (1964-1985) DC 416440.
- BT Status
- RT Academic Tenure
    - Employment
    - Job Change
    - Personnel Policy
    - Promotion (Occupational)
    - Workers

Sensation/Sensational/Sensationalism/Sensationalists (1963-1985)
- HN DC 416650, deleted 1986.

Sense Organs
- Use Sensory Systems

Sense/Senses/Sensuous/Sensuousness (1964-1985)
- HN DC 416700, deleted 1986. See now Common Sense or Sensory Systems.

Sensitivity Training
- DC D754800
- HN Added, 1986.
- UF Erhard Seminar Training (EST) (1983-1985)
    - Human Relations Training
    - T Groups
- BT Training
- RT Group Dynamics
    - Group Therapy
    - Interpersonal Relations
    - Self Actualization
    - Self Esteem
    - Treatment

Sensory Systems
- DC D754900
- HN Added, 1986.
- UF Perceptual Systems
    - Sense Organs
    - Smell (Sense)
    - Taste (Sense)
    - Touch (Sense)
- BT Systems
- NT Hearing
    - Vision
- RT Experience
    - Hallucinations
    - Human Body
    - Pain
    - Physical Contact

Sermons

Sentencing
- DC D755100
- HN Formerly (1964-1985) DC 417030, Sentence/Sentences/Sentencing.
- BT Judicial Decisions
- RT Criminal Proceedings
    - Imprisonment
    - Offenders
    - Plea Bargaining
    - Probation
    - Restitution (Corrections)

Sentiment/Sentiments (1963-1985)
- HN DC 417050.
- Use Attitudes

Seoul, South Korea
- DC D755300
- HN Added, 1989.
- BT South Korea

Separation (1964-1985)
- HN DC 417480, deleted 1986. See now Divorce or Marital Disruption.

Separation (Marital)
- Use Marital Disruption

Separatism
- DC D755400
- HN Formerly (1964-1985) DC 417485, Separatism/Separatist/Separatists.
- BT Political Ideologies
- RT American Indian Reservations
    - Apartheid
    - Cleavage
    - Plural Societies
    - Regionalism
    - Segregation

Sephardic Jews
- Use Jewish Cultural Groups

Sequence/Sequential (1963-1985)
- HN DC 417525, deleted 1986.

Serbia, Yugoslavia
- DC D755700
- HN Formerly (1963-1985) DC 417536, Serbia, Yugoslavia/Serbian/Serbians.
- BT Yugoslavia

Serbs (1966-1985)
- HN DC 417540, deleted 1986. See now European Cultural Groups.

Serendipity (1972-1985)
- HN DC 417560.
- Use Discovery

Serf/Serfs/Serfdom (1970-1985)
- HN DC 417580.
- Use Peasants

Serial Murder
- Use Homicide

Serial/Serials/Serialized (1964-1985)
- HN DC 417585, deleted 1986.

Series (Time)
- Use Time Series Analysis

Sermons
- DC D756000
- HN Formerly (1969-1985) DC 417595, Sermon.
- UF Homilies
    - Preaching
- BT Religious Rituals
- RT Clergy
    - Evangelism
    - Religious Literature

Servants

Servants
  Use Domestics

Service Industries
  DC D756300
  HN Added, 1986.
  BT Industry
  NT Banking
      Real Estate Industry
  RT Accounting
      Deindustrialization
      Domestics
      Insurance
      Postindustrial Societies
      White Collar Workers

Servicemen
  Use Military Personnel

Services
  DC D756600
  SN A context-dependent term; select a more specific entry or coordinate with other terms.
  HN Formerly (1963-1985) DC 417660, Service/Services.
  NT Community Services
      Human Services
      Public Services
  RT Access
      Activities
      Advocacy
      Agencies
      Consultants
      Delivery Systems
      Program Implementation
      Programs
      Resources
      Social Networks
      Support

Set/Sets/Settings (1963-1985)
  HN DC 418000.
  Use Environment

Settlement Patterns
  DC D756900
  HN Added, 1986.
  RT Colonization
      Immigrants
      Land Settlement
      Migration
      Migration Patterns
      Population Distribution
      Residential Patterns

Settlers
  DC D757200
  HN Formerly (1963-1985) part of DC 418800, Settlement/Settler/Settlers.
  UF Pioneer/Pioneers (1965-1985)
  RT Colonization
      Frontiers
      Homesteading
      Immigrants
      Land Settlement

Seventeenth Century
  DC D757500
  HN Formerly (1985) DC 418850.
  BT Time Periods
  RT Renaissance

Sex
  DC D757800
  SN Use limited to analyses of gender. Do not confuse with Sexual Intercourse or Sex Differences.
  HN Formerly (1963-1985) DC 419000, Sex/Sexes/Sexism/Sexist/Sexists.

Sex (cont'd)
  UF Gender/Genders (1972-1985)
  BT Physical Characteristics
  RT Biology
      Demographic Characteristics
      Females
      Group Composition
      Males
      Sex Differences
      Sex Roles

Sex Changes
  Use Transsexualism

Sex Differences
  DC D758100
  SN Used in analyses in which a social problem or phenomenon is explained as a consequence or correlate of the differences between males and females. These differences may be biological or stem from sex-role socialization.
  HN Formerly (1964-1985) DC 420000.
  UF Gender Differences (1984-1985)
  BT Differences
  RT Age Differences
      Individual Differences
      Occupational Segregation
      Physical Characteristics
      Sex
      Sex Roles
      Sex Stereotypes
      Sexual Behavior
      Sexual Inequality

Sex Education
  DC D758400
  HN Formerly (1985) DC 420100.
  BT Marriage And Family Education
  RT Sex Information
      Sexual Behavior

Sex Information
  DC D758700
  HN Formerly (1985) DC 420150, Sex Information/Sex Knowledge.
  UF Sex Knowledge
  RT Birth Control
      Gynecology
      Sex Education
      Sexual Reproduction

Sex Knowledge
  Use Sex Information

Sex Preferences (Children)
  Use Child Sex Preferences

Sex Role Attitudes
  DC D759000
  SN See also Sex Role Orientations.
  HN Added, 1986.
  BT Attitudes
  RT Child Sex Preferences
      Feminization
      Parental Attitudes
      Sex Role Identity
      Sex Role Orientations
      Sex Roles
      Sex Stereotypes
      Sexism
      Sexual Behavior
      Sexual Inequality
      Sexuality
      Womens Rights
      Working Mothers
      Working Women

Sex

Sex Role Identity
  DC D759300
  SN Refers to self-definition in terms of sex-role characteristics and related lifestyles. The term is often measured on the basis of traditional definitions of masculinity and femininity, resulting in the categories of heterosexual, homosexual, androgynous, and undifferentiated. Closely related to Sex Role Orientations.
  HN Added, 1986.
  UF Gender Identity
  BT Identity
  RT Androgyny
      Females
      Males
      Self Concept
      Sex Role Attitudes
      Sex Role Orientations
      Sex Roles
      Sexual Preferences

Sex Role Orientations
  DC D759600
  SN Refers to preferences for sex-stereotyped behaviors. The basic orientations usually cited are traditional versus nontraditional masculine and feminine roles. The term is also used in reference to homosexual lifestyles. See also Sex Role Identity.
  HN Added, 1986.
  BT Orientation
  RT Sex Role Attitudes
      Sex Role Identity
      Sex Roles

Sex Role Stereotypes
  Use Sex Stereotypes

Sex Roles
  DC D759900
  HN Formerly (1964-1985) DC 421000, Sex Role/Sex Roles.
  UF Male Roles
      Mens Roles
  BT Roles
  NT Womens Roles
  RT Androgyny
      Bisexuality
      Females
      Femininity
      Feminism
      Males
      Masculinity
      Opposite Sex Relations
      Role Conflict
      Role Models
      Sex
      Sex Differences
      Sex Role Attitudes
      Sex Role Identity
      Sex Role Orientations
      Sex Stereotypes
      Sexual Division of Labor
      Sexual Inequality

Sex Segregated Occupations
  Use Occupational Segregation

Sex Stereotypes
  DC D760200
  SN Beliefs about typical male or female behavior, usually based on overgeneralization and applied unfairly.
  HN Added, 1986.
  UF Gender Stereotypes
      Sex Role Stereotypes
  BT Stereotypes
  RT Females
      Males

Sexism

Sex Stereotypes (cont'd)
- RT Nontraditional Occupations
  - Occupational Segregation
  - Sex Differences
  - Sex Role Attitudes
  - Sex Roles
  - Sexism
  - Sexual Inequality

Sexism
- DC D760500
- HN Formerly (1985) DC 421150, Sexism/Sexist. Prior to 1985 use Sex/Sexes/Sexism/Sexist/Sexists (DC 419000).
- UF Chauvinism/Chauvinistic (1977-1985)
- BT Discrimination
- RT Bias
  - Feminism
  - Occupational Segregation
  - Prejudice
  - Sex Role Attitudes
  - Sex Stereotypes
  - Sexual Harassment
  - Sexual Inequality
  - Social Attitudes
  - Womens Rights

Sexual Abstinence
- Use Celibacy

Sexual Abuse
- DC D760700
- HN Added, 1986.
- BT Abuse
- NT Child Sexual Abuse
- RT Child Abuse
  - Family Violence
  - Rape
  - Sexual Assault

Sexual Arousal
- DC D760800
- HN Added, 1986.
- UF Arouse/Arousal/Aroused (1963-1985)
  - Excitation (1963-1985)
- BT Sexual Behavior
- RT Eroticism
  - Masturbation
  - Orgasm
  - Sexual Intercourse

Sexual Assault
- DC D761100
- HN Added, 1986.
- BT Assault
- NT Rape
- RT Sexual Abuse
  - Sexual Harassment
  - Victims

Sexual Behavior
- DC D761400
- HN Formerly (1964-1985) DC 421400.
- BT Behavior
  - Sexuality
- NT Bisexuality
  - Celibacy
  - Extramarital Sexuality
  - Frigidity
  - Incest
  - Masturbation
  - Orgasm
  - Premarital Sex
  - Promiscuity
  - Sexual Arousal
  - Sexual Deviation

Sexual Behavior (cont'd)
- NT Sexual Dysfunction
  - Sexual Intercourse
  - Transsexualism
  - Transvestism
- RT Couples
  - Courtship
  - Dating (Social)
  - Eroticism
  - Guilt
  - Heterosexuality
  - Homosexual Relationships
  - Homosexuality
  - Instinct
  - Prostitution
  - Sex Differences
  - Sex Education
  - Sex Role Attitudes
  - Sexual Permissiveness
  - Single Persons
  - Strippers
  - Taboos
  - Venereal Diseases
  - Virginity
  - Young Adults

Sexual Deviation
- DC D761700
- HN Formerly (1964-1985) DC 421700.
- UF Exhibitionism
  - Masochism (1984-1985)
  - Nymphomania/Nymphomaniac/Nymphomaniacs (1965-1985)
  - Sadism/Sadistic (1966-1985)
  - Sadomasochism (1985)
- BT Deviance
  - Sexual Behavior
- NT Sodomy
- RT Deviant Behavior
  - Incest
  - Oedipal Complex
  - Sexuality

Sexual Division of Labor
- DC D762000
- HN Added, 1986.
- UF Family Division of Labor
  - Womens Work
- BT Division of Labor
- RT Homemakers
  - Housework
  - Income Inequality
  - Labor Market Segmentation
  - Nontraditional Occupations
  - Occupational Roles
  - Occupational Segregation
  - Sex Roles

Sexual Dysfunction
- DC D762300
- HN Added, 1986.
- BT Sexual Behavior
- RT Disorders
  - Frigidity
  - Sexual Intercourse

Sexual Harassment
- DC D762600
- HN Added, 1986.
- UF Harass/Harassment (1981-1985)
- RT Abuse
  - Offenses
  - Opposite Sex Relations
  - Sexism
  - Sexual Assault
  - Victimization

Sexuality

Sexual Inequality
- DC D762900
- HN Formerly (1985) DC 422030.
- UF Gender Inequality (1985)
  - Sexual Stratification
- BT Inequality
- RT Females
  - Feminism
  - Opposite Sex Relations
  - Sex Differences
  - Sex Role Attitudes
  - Sex Roles
  - Sex Stereotypes
  - Sexism
  - Social Inequality

Sexual Intercourse
- DC D763200
- HN Formerly (1985) DC 422050.
- UF Coitus/Coital (1963-1985)
  - Intercourse (1963-1985)
- BT Sexual Behavior
- RT Extramarital Sexuality
  - Incest
  - Orgasm
  - Premarital Sex
  - Rape
  - Sexual Arousal
  - Sexual Dysfunction
  - Sexual Reproduction
  - Sexuality
  - Sodomy

Sexual Permissiveness
- DC D763500
- HN Formerly (1964-1985) DC 328660, Permissiveness.
- UF Permissiveness (Sexual)
- RT Attitudes
  - Extramarital Sexuality
  - Premarital Sex
  - Promiscuity
  - Sexual Behavior

Sexual Preferences
- DC D763800
- HN Added, 1986.
- BT Preferences
- RT Bisexuality
  - Heterosexuality
  - Homosexual Relationships
  - Homosexuality
  - Sex Role Identity
  - Sexual Preferences
  - Sexuality

Sexual Reproduction
- DC D764100
- HN Formerly (1985) DC 422060.
- RT Artificial Insemination
  - Biology
  - Birth
  - Fertility
  - Gynecology
  - Pregnancy
  - Reproductive Technologies
  - Sex Information
  - Sexual Intercourse

Sexual Stratification
- Use Sexual Inequality

Sexuality
- DC D764400
- HN Formerly (1963-1985) DC 422000, Sexual/Sexuality/Sexually.
- UF Human Sexuality
  - Libido/Libidinal (1963-1985)
- NT Bisexuality
  - Heterosexuality

Seychelles

Sexuality (cont'd)
- NT Homosexuality
  Sexual Behavior
- RT Extramarital Sexuality
  Frigidity
  Personality Traits
  Physical Contact
  Pornography
  Sex Role Attitudes
  Sexual Deviation
  Sexual Intercourse
  Sexual Preferences
  Transsexualism

Seychelles
- DC D764700
- HN Added, 1986.
- BT Sub Saharan Africa

Shaman (1963-1985)
- HN DC 422115.
- Use Shamanism

Shamanism
- DC D765000
- HN Added, 1986.
- UF Shaman (1963-1985)
- RT Divination
  Faith Healing
  Magic
  Priests
  Religious Beliefs
  Religious Rituals
  Supernatural
  Traditional Medicine
  Traditional Societies

Shame
- DC D765300
- HN Formerly (1964-1985) DC 422125, Shame/Shaming.
- BT Emotions
- RT Conscience
  Embarrassment
  Guilt
  Honor
  Morality

Shantytowns
- Use Slums

Sharecropping
- DC D765600
- HN Formerly (1969-1985) DC 422255, Sharecropper/Sharecroppers/Sharecropping.
- BT Agrarian Structures
- RT Land Tenure
  Plantations

Shared Custody
- Use Child Custody

Sharing
- DC D765900
- HN Formerly (1969-1985) DC 422253, Share/Sharing.
- BT Social Behavior
- RT Altruism
  Cooperation
  Reciprocity
  Turn Taking

Sheltered Workshops
- Use Workshops (Manufacturing)

Shelters
- DC D766200
- HN Formerly (1966-1985) DC 422278, Shelter/Shelters/Sheltered.
- UF Refuge (1979-1985)
- BT Facilities
- RT Assistance
  Battered Women
  Buildings
  Housing
  Skid Row

Sherif, Muzafer
- DC D766500
- SN Born 29 July 1906 - died 16 October 1988.
- HN Formerly (1969-1985) DC 422285, Sherif, M.

Sherman Act (1981-1985)
- HN DC 422290.
- Use Statutes

Shevky-Bell Theories (1972-1985)
- HN DC 422326.
- Use Social Area Analysis

Shift (Language)
- Use Language Shift

Shift Work
- DC D766800
- HN Formerly (1963-1985) DC 422340, Shifts.
- BT Work
- RT Work Organization
  Working Hours

Shigellosis (1964-1985)
- HN DC 422350.
- Use Diseases

Shintoism
- DC D767100
- HN Formerly (1985) DC 422385, Shinto/Shintoism.
- BT Religions
- RT Ancestor Worship
  Asian Cultural Groups

Shipping Industry
- DC D767400
- HN Formerly (1963-1985) DC 422420, Ship/Ships/Shipping.
- UF Maritime (1965-1985)
  Merchant Marines (1985)
  Sail/Sails/Sailor/Sailors/Sailing (1963-1985)
- BT Industry
- RT Exports And Imports
  Longshoremen
  Oceans
  Transportation

Shock
- DC D767700
- SN Reaction to physical, emotional, or social trauma.
- HN Formerly (1977-1985) DC 422500.
- RT Crises
  Cultural Conflict
  Injuries
  Responses
  Stress
  Symptoms

Shooting
- Use Hunting

Shop/Shopping (1964-1985)
- HN DC 422875, deleted 1986. See now Purchasing or Stores.

Shoplifting
- DC D768000
- HN Formerly (1964-1985) DC 422876, Shoplift/Shoplifter/Shoplifters/Shoplifting.
- BT Larceny
- RT Juvenile Delinquency

Short Stories
- DC D768300
- HN Added, 1986. Formerly (1963-1985) part of DC 446500, Story/Stories.
- BT Fiction
- RT Books

Shortages
- Use Scarcity

Shrines
- DC D768600
- HN Formerly (1971-1985) DC 422935, Shrine/Shrines.
- RT Pilgrimages
  Places of Worship
  Religious Rituals
  Sacredness

Shutdowns (Industrial)
- Use Plant Closure

Siam/Siamese (1964-1985)
- HN DC 422960.
- Use Thailand

Sib/Sibs/Sibship/Sibships (1963-1985)
- HN DC 422975.
- Use Siblings

Siberia
- DC D768900
- HN Formerly (1963-1985) DC 422987, Siberia, USSR.
- BT Union of Soviet Socialist Republics
- RT Arctic Regions

Siblings
- DC D769200
- HN Formerly (1963-1985) DC 423000, Sibling/Siblings.
- UF Brother/Brothers (1985)
  Sib/Sibs/Sibship/Sibships (1963-1985)
  Sister/Sisters (1985)
- NT Twins
- RT Birth Order
  Birth Spacing
  Children
  Daughters
  Family Life
  Family Structure
  Kinship
  Parent Child Relations
  Relatives
  Sons
  Stepfamily

Sicily
- DC D769500
- HN Formerly (1965-1985) DC 423045, Sicily, Italy/Sicilian/Sicilians.
- BT Italy

Sick Role
- **DC** D769800
- **HN** Added, 1986.
- **BT** Roles
- **RT** Illness
  Illness Behavior
  Patients
  Practitioner Patient Relationship

Sickness (1963-1985)
- **HN** DC 423065.
- **Use** Illness

Sierra Leone
- **DC** D770100
- **HN** Formerly (1965-1985) DC 423170.
- **BT** Sub Saharan Africa

Sight
- **Use** Vision

Sign Language
- **Use** Manual Communication

Signal/Signals/Signaling (1963-1985)
- **HN** DC 423500, deleted 1986. See now Signs, Messages, or Nonverbal Communication.

Significance (Statistical)
- **Use** Statistical Significance

Significant Others
- **DC** D770300
- **SN** In symbolic interactionism, individuals representing the reference groups that constitute social identity. May be used more narrowly for role models or love interests.
- **HN** Added, 1986.
- **RT** Childhood Factors
  Family
  Friendship
  Influence
  Peers
  Reference Groups
  Role Models
  Self Concept
  Socialization
  Spouses

Signs
- **DC** D770400
- **HN** Formerly (1963-1985) DC 423200, Sign/Signs.
- **RT** Collective Representation
  Communication
  Culture
  Linguistics
  Meaning
  Messages
  Nonverbal Communication
  Semiotics
  Social Determination of Meaning
  Symbolism

Sikhism
- **DC** D770600
- **HN** Added, 1989.
- **BT** Religions
- **RT** Sikhs

Sikhs
- **DC** D770650
- **HN** Added, 1989.
- **BT** Religious Cultural Groups
- **RT** Sikhism

Silence
- **DC** D770700
- **HN** Added, 1986.
- **UF** Quiet (1980-1985)
- **RT** Noise
  Nonverbal Communication

Similarity
- **DC** D771100
- **HN** Formerly (1963-1985) DC 424200, Similarity/Similarities.
- **RT** Agreement
  Conformity
  Convergence Theory
  Differences
  Social Cohesion
  Uniformity

Simmel, Georg
- **DC** D771000
- **SN** Born 1 March 1858 - died 26 September 1918.
- **HN** Formerly (1963-1985) DC 424250, Simmel, G.

Simulation
- **DC** D771200
- **HN** Formerly (1963-1985) DC 424340, Simulate/Simulated/Simulation/Simulator.
- **BT** Methods
- **RT** Computer Assisted Research
  Game Theory
  Models
  Role Playing

Simultaneous Translation
- **Use** Translation

Sindi (Language)
- **Use** Indic Languages

Singapore
- **DC** D771300
- **HN** Formerly (1963-1985) DC 424355.
- **BT** Southeast Asia

Single (1981-1985)
- **HN** DC 424371, deleted 1986. See now Single Persons or Single Parent Family.

Single Fathers
- **DC** D771500
- **HN** Added, 1989.
- **BT** Fathers
  Single Persons
- **RT** Child Custody
  Divorce
  Family Structure
  Mother Absence
  Single Parent Family

Single Parent Family
- **DC** D771600
- **HN** Added, 1986.
- **UF** One Parent Family
- **BT** Family
- **RT** Child Custody
  Divorce
  Family Size
  Family Stability
  Family Structure
  Father Absence
  Female Headed Households
  Mother Absence
  Parenthood
  Single Fathers
  Single Persons
  Unwed Mothers

Single Persons
- **DC** D771900
- **HN** Added, 1986.
- **UF** Bachelor/Bachelors/Bachelorhood (1969-1985)
  Spinster/Spinsters/Spinsterhood (1976-1985)
  Unmarried (1963-1985)
- **NT** Single Fathers
- **RT** Cohabitation
  Dating (Social)
  Marital Status
  Marriage
  Premarital Sex
  Sexual Behavior
  Single Parent Family
  Unwed Mothers
  Virginity
  Young Adults

Sinhala (Language)
- **Use** Indic Languages

Sinhalese (1964-1985)
- **HN** DC 424400, deleted 1986. See now Asian Cultural Groups.

Sinotibetan Languages
- **Use** Oriental Languages

Sins
- **DC** D772200
- **HN** Formerly (1971-1985) DC 424347, Sin/Sins/Sinful.
- **RT** Confession
  Evil
  Morality
  Religious Beliefs
  Salvation
  Taboos

Sister/Sisters (1985)
- **HN** DC 424471.
- **Use** Siblings

Sisters (Clergy)
- **Use** Nuns

Sit-In/Sit-Ins (1963-1985)
- **HN** DC 424480.
- **Use** Protest Movements

Situation
- **DC** D772500
- **SN** A context-dependent term; select a more specific entry or coordinate with other terms.
- **HN** Formerly (1963-1985) DC 424500, Situation/Situations/Situational.
- **UF** Situational Factors
  Social Situation
- **BT** Social Environment
- **RT** Impression Formation
  Impression Management
  Social Behavior
  Social Factors
  Social Interaction
  Social Perception
  Universalism-Particularism

Situational Factors
- **Use** Situation

Situses
- **DC** D772800
- **SN** Segments of society differentiated from other segments on the basis of criteria that do not involve rank or hierarchical evaluation, eg, distinctions of sex, clan membership, and occupations of equal esteem.

Sixteenth   **Smelser**

Situses (cont'd)
- **HN** Formerly (1963-1985) DC 424600.
- **RT** Clans
  - Occupational Structure
  - Occupations
  - Social Stratification
  - Social Structure
  - Status

Sixteenth Century
- **DC** D773100
- **HN** Formerly (1985) DC 424700.
- **BT** Time Periods
- **RT** Renaissance

Size
- **DC** D773400
- **HN** Formerly (1963-1985) DC 424800, Size/Sizes.
- **NT** Community Size
  - Family Size
  - Group Size
  - Organization Size
- **RT** Small Businesses
  - Small Farms
  - Small Groups

Skepticism
- **DC** D773600
- **HN** Formerly (1970-1985) DC 425560, Skeptic/Skeptics/Skepticism.
- **BT** Attitudes
  - Epistemological Doctrines
- **RT** Agnosticism
  - Beliefs
  - Certainty
  - Cynicism
  - Dogmatism
  - Knowledge
  - Truth

Skid Row
- **DC** D773700
- **HN** Formerly (1981-1985) DC 425900.
- **RT** Central Cities
  - Homelessness
  - Low Income Areas
  - Poverty
  - Shelters
  - Slums

Skilled Labor
- **Use** Work Skills

Skills
- **DC** D774000
- **HN** Formerly (1964-1985) DC 426000, Skill/Skills/Skilled.
- **BT** Ability
- **NT** Work Skills
- **RT** Behavior
  - Gifted
  - Human Resources
  - Performance
  - Qualifications
  - Training

Skin
- **DC** D774300
- **HN** Formerly (1972-1985) DC 426505.
- **RT** Human Body

Skinner, Burrhus Frederic
- **DC** D774400
- **SN** Born 20 March 1904 - .
- **HN** Formerly (1964-1985) DC 426510, Skinner, B. F./Skinnerian.

Skolnick, Jerome Herbert
- **DC** D774600
- **SN** Born 21 March 1931 - .
- **HN** Formerly (1972-1985) DC 426525, Skolnick, Jerome.

Slang
- **DC** D774900
- **HN** Formerly (1971-1985) DC 426530.
- **UF** Argot (1968-1985)
  - Street Vernacular
- **BT** Vocabularies
- **RT** Dialects
  - Language Usage
  - Language Varieties
  - Subcultures

Slav/Slavs/Slavic (1964-1985)
- **HN** DC 427800, deleted 1986. See now European Cultural Groups or Slavic Languages.

Slavery
- **DC** D775200
- **HN** Formerly (1963-1985) DC 427500, Slave/Slaves/Slavery.
- **UF** Abolition/Abolitionist/Abolitionists (1972-1985)
- **RT** Blacks
  - Economic Systems
  - Exploitation
  - Freedom
  - Human Rights
  - Modes of Production
  - Oppression
  - Ownership

Slavic Languages
- **DC** D775500
- **HN** Added, 1986.
- **BT** Indoeuropean Languages

Sleep
- **DC** D775800
- **HN** Formerly (1963-1985) DC 428000, Sleep/Sleeping.
- **RT** Dreams
  - Fatigue
  - Health

Slovenia, Yugoslavia
- **DC** D776100
- **HN** Formerly (1968-1985) DC 428261.
- **BT** Yugoslavia

Slums
- **DC** D776400
- **HN** Formerly (1964-1985) DC 428300, Slum/Slums.
- **UF** Favela/Favelas (1972-1985)
  - Rancherio (1968-1985)
  - Shantytowns
- **BT** Low Income Areas
- **RT** Central Cities
  - Ghettos
  - Housing
  - Low Income Groups
  - Poverty
  - Skid Row
  - Urban Areas
  - Urban Renewal

Small (1963-1985)
- **HN** DC 428320, deleted 1986. See now specific terms.

Small, Albion Woodbury
- **DC** D776700
- **SN** Born 1854 - died 1926.
- **HN** Formerly (1972-1985) DC 428340, Small, Albion W.

Small Arms
- **Use** Firearms

Small Businesses
- **DC** D777000
- **HN** Added, 1986.
- **BT** Enterprises
- **RT** Business
  - Cottage Industries
  - Entrepreneurship
  - Family Businesses
  - Home Workplaces
  - Minority Businesses
  - Organization Size
  - Self Employment
  - Size

Small Farms
- **DC** D777300
- **HN** Added, 1986.
- **UF** Minifundia/Minifundismo (1971-1985)
  - Small Scale Farming
- **BT** Farms
- **RT** Agrarian Structures
  - Agricultural Economics
  - Agricultural Technology
  - Crofting
  - Family Farms
  - Part Time Farming
  - Size

Small Group Research
- **Use** Group Research

Small Groups
- **DC** D777600
- **HN** Formerly (1984-1985) DC 200000, Group, Small. Prior to 1984 use Group/Groups/Grouping/Groupism (DC 197700) and Small (DC 428320).
- **BT** Groups
- **NT** Dyads
  - Triads
- **RT** Cliques
  - Group Dynamics
  - Group Norms
  - Group Size
  - Interpersonal Communication
  - Interpersonal Relations
  - Microsociology
  - Size
  - Social Behavior
  - Social Cohesion
  - Social Interaction
  - Sociometric Analysis

Small Scale Farming
- **Use** Small Farms

Small Town (1964-1985)
- **HN** DC 428355.
- **Use** Towns

Smell (Sense)
- **Use** Sensory Systems

Smelser, Neil Joseph
- **DC** D777900
- **SN** Born 22 July 1930 - .
- **HN** Formerly (1965-1985) DC 428378, Smelser, N. J.

Smiling

Smiling (1965-1985)
- **HN** DC 428490.
- **Use** Nonverbal Communication

Smith Act (1964-1985)
- **HN** DC 428495.
- **Use** Statutes

Smith, Adam
- **DC** D778200
- **SN** Born 5 June 1723 - died 17 July 1790.
- **HN** Formerly (1967-1985) DC 428500.

Smog
- **Use** Air Pollution

Smoker/Smokers (1969-1985)
- **HN** DC 428590.
- **Use** Smoking

Smoking
- **DC** D778500
- **HN** Formerly (1964-1985) DC 428600.
- **UF** Cigarette/Cigarettes (1964-1985)
  Smoker/Smokers (1969-1985)
  Tobacco (1975-1985)
- **RT** Behavior
  Cancer
  Drug Use
  Habits
  Health

Sober/Sobriety (1972-1985)
- **HN** DC 428700, deleted 1986. See now Alcohol Use or Temperance Movements.

Sociability
- **DC** D778800
- **HN** Formerly (1963-1985) DC 428800, Sociable/Sociability.
- **BT** Social Behavior
- **RT** Celebrations
  Interpersonal Relations
  Peer Relations
  Personality Traits
  Primary Groups
  Public Behavior
  Social Contact
  Social Participation
  Visitation

Social (1963-1985)
- **HN** DC 428900, deleted 1986.

Social Acceptance
- **DC** D779100
- **HN** Formerly (1963-1985) DC 429000.
- **BT** Acceptance
- **RT** Affiliation Need
  Approval
  Individual Collective Relationship
  Interpersonal Relations
  Needs
  Rejection
  Social Response
  Stigma

Social Action
- **DC** D779400
- **HN** Formerly (1963-1985) DC 429080.
- **BT** Action
- **NT** Collective Action
- **RT** Action Research
  Action Theory
  Activism
  Affirmative Action
  Agitation

Social Action (cont'd)
- **RT** Boycotts
  Charities
  Citizen Participation
  Civil Rights Organizations
  Community Involvement
  Contributions (Donations)
  Disorders
  Intervention
  Movements
  Political Action
  Protest Movements
  Social Change
  Social Goals
  Social Interest
  Social Movements
  Social Participation
  Social Problems
  Social Processes
  Social Reform
  Social Responsibility
  Society
  Structuration
  Voluntarism
  Youth Movements

Social Administration/Social Administrator (1963-1985)
- **HN** DC 429095, deleted 1986. See now Public Administration or Social Planning.

Social Agencies
- **DC** D779700
- **HN** Formerly (1964-1985) DC 429099, Social Agency/Social Agencies.
- **BT** Agencies
- **NT** Human Service Organizations
- **RT** Charities
  Community Mental Health Centers
  Information And Referral Services
  Social Services
  Social Work

Social Agitation
- **Use** Agitation

Social Alliance/Social Alliances (1985)
- **HN** DC 429110.
- **Use** Alliance

Social Anthropology
- **DC** D780000
- **HN** Formerly (1984-1985), DC 429114.
- **UF** Cultural Anthropology
  Ethnobiology (1985)
- **BT** Anthropology
- **RT** Crosscultural Analysis
  Cultural Relativism
  Culture
  Customs
  Ethnic Groups
  Ethnography
  Ethnolinguistics
  Ethnology
  Linguistics
  Traditions

Social Approval
- **Use** Approval

Social Area Analysis
- **DC** D780200
- **HN** Added, 1986.
- **UF** Shevky-Bell Theories (1972-1985)
- **BT** Analysis
- **RT** Census
  Human Ecology
  Socioeconomic Status
  Urban Areas

Social

Social Attitudes
- **DC** D780300
- **SN** A context-dependent term for the thoughts, feelings, perceptions, opinions, or mind-set of individuals or groups toward or about other members of society or social problems. See also Attitudes, which includes explicitly psychological meanings of the term.
- **HN** Formerly (1963-1985) DC 429125.
- **BT** Attitudes
- **NT** Cosmopolitanism
  Ethnocentrism
  Localism
  Nativism
  Regionalism
  Traditionalism
- **RT** Acceptance
  Activism
  Ageism
  Alienation
  Altruism
  Apathy
  Approval
  Beliefs
  Dissent
  Egocentrism
  Elitism
  Impression Formation
  Language Attitudes
  Modernity
  Optimism
  Pessimism
  Political Attitudes
  Political Socialization
  Prejudice
  Progressivism
  Public Opinion
  Racial Differences
  Racism
  Rejection
  Sectarianism
  Sexism
  Social Change
  Social Distance
  Social Environment
  Social Perception
  Social Values
  Tolerance

Social Background
- **DC** D780600
- **SN** The sum of sociocultural influences used to explain or place specific social problems or behaviors in context, including family characteristics, social class, ethnicity, etc.
- **HN** Formerly (1963-1985) DC 429175.
- **UF** Background/Backgrounds (1963-1985)
  Family Background
- **RT** Childhood Factors
  Ethnicity
  Individual Differences
  Social Class
  Social Factors
  Socioeconomic Factors
  Socioeconomic Status

Social Behavior
- **DC** D780900
- **SN** A context-dependent term for actions attributed to individuals or groups that are described or explained by reference to social causes and consequences. See also Behavior, which includes explicitly psychological meanings of the term.
- **HN** Formerly (1963-1985) DC 429300.

Social

Social Behavior (cont'd)
- **BT** Behavior
- **NT** Acceptance
  Aggression
  Altruism
  Ambivalence
  Approval
  Assertiveness
  Collective Behavior
  Competition
  Compliance
  Conformity
  Cooperation
  Disengagement
  Encouragement
  Help Seeking Behavior
  Obedience
  Rejection
  Resistance
  Respect
  Sharing
  Sociability
  Turn Taking
- **RT** Alliance
  Anger
  Anomie
  Attribution
  Behavior Problems
  Conflict
  Countercultures
  Dating (Social)
  Discrimination
  Egalitarianism
  Emotions
  Exchange Theory
  Group Dynamics
  Group Norms
  Hostility
  Impression Management
  Institutionalization (Social)
  Interpersonal Communication
  Machiavellianism (Personality)
  Manipulation
  Negotiation
  Norms
  Organizational Behavior
  Participation
  Peer Influence
  Praxeology
  Privacy
  Public Behavior
  Reciprocity
  Responsibility
  Risk
  Situation
  Small Groups
  Social Change
  Social Control
  Social Facts
  Social Influence
  Social Interaction
  Social Networks
  Social Perception
  Social Pressure
  Social Responsibility
  Social Support
  Sociobiology
  Support
  Teamwork
  Territoriality
  Trust
  Universalism-Particularism

Social Bias
- **Use** Prejudice

Social Boundaries
- **Use** Boundaries

Social Casework (1963-1985)
- **HN** DC 429500.
- **Use** Social Work

Social Change
- **DC** D781200
- **SN** A context-dependent term for the processes by which societies and other large social structures and groups evolve historically. Closely related to Social Processes and Social Development.
- **HN** Formerly (1963-1985) DC 429700.
- **UF** Societal Change
- **BT** Change
- **NT** Social Progress
- **RT** Action Research
  Activism
  Agitation
  Change Agents
  Community Change
  Convergence Theory
  Cooptation
  Cultural Change
  Desegregation
  Development
  Economic Change
  Entropy
  Figuration Sociology
  Futures (of Society)
  Industrialization
  Marxist Analysis
  Middletown Studies
  Modernization
  Movements
  Political Movements
  Revolutions
  Social Action
  Social Attitudes
  Social Behavior
  Social Conditions
  Social Conflict
  Social Development
  Social Disorganization
  Social Dynamics
  Social Equilibrium
  Social Evolution
  Social History
  Social Impact Assessment
  Social Integration
  Social Movements
  Social Planning
  Social Processes
  Social Reform
  Social Revolution
  Social Structure
  Social Unrest
  Society
  Technological Change

Social Class
- **DC** D781500
- **SN** A context-dependent term for levels in human populations stratified by wealth, privilege, modes of labor, way of life, and other sociocultural factors. Social problems are often explained or described with reference to social-class variables, for which there are numerous labels and analytic modes.
- **HN** Formerly (1963-1985) DC 429800, Social Class/Social Classes.
- **BT** Groups
- **NT** Lower Class
  Middle Class

Social Class (cont'd)
- **NT** Upper Class
  Working Class
- **RT** Class Analysis
  Class Consciousness
  Class Differences
  Class Formation
  Class Identity
  Class Politics
  Class Relations
  Class Society
  Class Struggle
  Elites
  Family Work Relationship
  Income Inequality
  Language Social Class Relationship
  Poverty
  Ruling Class
  Social Background
  Social Closure
  Social Distance
  Social Factors
  Social Inequality
  Social Mobility
  Social Status
  Social Stratification
  Social Structure
  Socioeconomic Status

Social Class Analysis
- **Use** Class Analysis

Social Cleavage
- **Use** Cleavage

Social Closure
- **DC** D781800
- **SN** Maximization of the power and advantages of social groups or classes through the use of exclusionary codes that restrict access to economic opportunities and other rewards to group members, thus closing access to outsiders.
- **HN** Added, 1986.
- **BT** Closure
- **RT** Access
  Boundary Maintenance
  Discrimination
  Labor Market Segmentation
  Opportunities
  Rewards
  Social Class
  Social Control
  Social Environment

Social Cohesion
- **DC** D782100
- **SN** The strength of an organization over time, as determined by interrelated and interdependent roles, and success in socializing new members and achieving goals.
- **HN** Formerly (1963-1985) DC 429840.
- **UF** Cohesion/Cohesive/Cohesiveness (1963-1985)
  Group Cohesion
  Social Solidarity (1969-1985)
  Solidarity (Social)
  Unity (1963-1985)
- **BT** Social Processes
- **RT** Anomie
  Assimilation
  Cleavage
  Collective Representation
  Communities
  Consensus
  Cooptation
  Group Dynamics

Social

Social Cohesion (cont'd)
- RT Group Norms
- Groups
- Organizational Dissolution
- Primary Groups
- Similarity
- Small Groups
- Social Disorganization
- Social Environment
- Social Equilibrium
- Social Groups
- Social Identity
- Social Integration
- Social Interaction
- Social Order
- Society
- Solidarity Movements

Social Conditioning
- Use Conditioning

Social Conditions
- DC D782400
- SN Quality of the social environment prevailing at a given place and time, particularly as this affects social problems, behaviors, and attitudes.
- HN Formerly (1963-1985) DC 429850, Social Condition/Social Conditions.
- NT Social Unrest
- RT Community Satisfaction
- Discontent
- Economic Conditions
- Life Satisfaction
- Living Conditions
- Quality of Life
- Social Change
- Social Conflict
- Social Criticism
- Social Development
- Social Environment
- Social Factors
- Social Impact Assessment
- Social Inequality
- Social Movements
- Social Structure
- Social Unrest
- Society
- Socioeconomic Factors
- Unemployment

Social Conflict
- DC D782700
- SN A context-dependent term for strife owing to absence of consensus among social actors and to inherently contradictory forces in relations between individuals, social classes, strata, and other groups.
- HN Formerly (1963-1985) DC 429875, Social Conflicts.
- BT Conflict
- NT Class Struggle
- Feuds
- RT Civil Disorders
- Cleavage
- Conflict Theory
- Cultural Conflict
- Disputes
- Dissent
- Factionalism
- Intergroup Relations
- Organizational Dissolution
- Polarization
- Protest Movements
- Schism
- Sectarianism
- Social Change
- Social Conditions

Social Conflict (cont'd)
- RT Social Criticism
- Social Disorganization
- Social Order
- Social Power
- Social Problems
- Social Unrest
- Tension

Social Conflict Theory
- Use Conflict Theory

Social Conformity (1969-1985)
- HN DC 429880.
- Use Conformity

Social Consciousness
- DC D783000
- HN Formerly (1965-1985) DC 429900.
- BT Consciousness
- NT Class Consciousness
- Social Perception
- Worker Consciousness
- RT Political Behavior
- Social Values

Social Construction (1984-1985)
- HN DC 429910.
- Use Social Determination of Meaning

Social Contact
- DC D783300
- SN Implies that social structural factors determine or condition availability for social interaction; for example, those with similar or adjacent social status have more opportunity for social contact than those from widely separated social groupings.
- HN Added, 1986.
- UF Intergroup Contact
- Interpersonal Contact
- RT Associations
- Communities
- Culture Contact
- Intergroup Relations
- Interpersonal Relations
- Loneliness
- Membership
- Neighbors
- Physical Contact
- Primary Groups
- Sociability
- Social Groups
- Social Interaction
- Social Isolation
- Social Life
- Social Networks
- Social Participation
- Spatial Behavior
- Visitation

Social Contagion Theory
- Use Contagion Theory

Social Context
- Use Social Environment

Social Contradictions
- Use Contradictions

Social Control
- DC D783600
- SN Refers to the regulatory institutions of society, particularly the law enforcement and judicial systems and how they operate. The term encompasses rule-enforcement at all levels and implies an inherent need for social order.
- HN Formerly (1963-1985) DC 429925, Social Control/Social Controls.

Social Control (cont'd)
- BT Control
- RT Behavior
- Caste Systems
- Compliance
- Conformity
- Discipline
- Government Regulation
- Law Enforcement
- Majority Groups
- Norms
- Power Elite
- Power Structure
- Punishment
- Rewards
- Sanctions
- Segregation
- Social Behavior
- Social Closure
- Social Environment
- Social Facts
- Social Influence
- Social Order
- Social Pressure
- Social Relations
- Social Structure
- Social Values
- State Power
- Structuration
- Taboos

Social Correlates (1964-1985)
- HN DC 429975.
- Use Social Factors

Social Criticism
- DC D783900
- SN A form of social analysis or theory, often associated with the Frankfurt school, principally concerned with criticizing institutions defined and supported by the capitalist mode of production.
- HN Formerly (1964-1985) DC 429980.
- UF Criticism (Social)
- BT Criticism
- RT Activism
- Dissent
- Marxism
- Progressivism
- Protest Movements
- Social Conditions
- Social Conflict
- Social Disorganization
- Social Theories

Social Darwinism
- DC D784100
- HN Added, 1986.
- BT Evolutionary Theories
- RT Competition
- Darwinism
- Eugenics
- Genetics
- Racial Relations
- Social Evolution
- Social Theories

Social Democracy
- DC D784200
- HN Formerly (1964-1985) DC 429990, Social Democrat/Social Democracy.
- RT Democracy
- Political Ideologies
- Political Parties
- Socialism
- Welfare State

Social

Social Desirability
- **DC** D784500
- **HN** Formerly (1963-1985) DC 430000.
- **UF** Desirability (1968-1985)
- **RT** Acceptance
  Approval
  Attractiveness
  Expectations
  Personality Traits
  Social Desirability Scales
  Social Influence
  Social Values
  Socioeconomic Status

Social Desirability Scales
- **DC** D784520
- **HN** Formerly (1985) DC 430500, Social Desirability Scale.
- **BT** Scales
- **RT** Attitude Measures
  Social Desirability

Social Determination of Meaning
- **DC** D784600
- **SN** Encompasses discussions of how knowledge is shaped by social and cultural factors.
- **HN** Added, 1986.
- **UF** Social Construction (1984-1985)
  Social Meaning (1985)
- **BT** Social Processes
- **RT** Collective Representation
  Meaning
  Relativism
  Signs
  Social Facts
  Social Reality
  Symbolism

Social Development
- **DC** D784800
- **SN** A context-dependent term for the relative progress made by societies worldwide in evolving social institutions that are effective in solving domestic and international social problems. See also Child Development, which is preferred for subject matter related to developmental psychology.
- **HN** Formerly (1964-1985) DC 430600, Social Development/Social Developments.
- **BT** Development
- **RT** Developmental Stages
  Economic Development
  Social Change
  Social Conditions
  Social Evolution
  Social Processes
  Social Progress

Social Disorganization
- **DC** D785100
- **SN** Long-term and widespread deterioration of social order and control in a population.
- **HN** Formerly (1963-1985) 430750.
- **UF** Disorganization (1963-1985)
  Fragmentation (1964-1985)
- **BT** Social Structure
- **RT** Civil Disorders
  Crime
  Deviance
  Norms
  Organizational Dissolution
  Reconstruction
  Social Change
  Social Cohesion

Social Disorganization (cont'd)
- **RT** Social Conflict
  Social Criticism
  Social Equilibrium
  Social Order
  Social Processes
  Social Unrest
  Socioeconomic Factors

Social Distance
- **DC** D785400
- **SN** Perceived or actual social separation between individuals or groups, as measured by degree of prejudice or sympathetic understanding between them.
- **HN** Formerly (1963-1985) DC 431000.
- **UF** Distance (1963-1985)
  Distance (Social)
- **RT** Intergroup Relations
  Marginality
  Prejudice
  Social Attitudes
  Social Class
  Social Integration
  Social Isolation
  Social Status
  Social Stratification
  Social Structure
  Sociometric Analysis
  Tolerance

Social Drinking
- **Use** Alcohol Use

Social Dynamics
- **DC** D785700
- **SN** A context-dependent term for broadly conceived forces of change in populations and social circumstances. Select a more specific entry if possible.
- **HN** Formerly (1963-1985) DC 431150.
- **UF** Dynamics (Social)
- **NT** Group Dynamics
- **RT** Communities
  Individual Collective Relationship
  Social Change
  Social Function
  Social History
  Social Interaction
  Social Networks
  Social Processes
  Social Relations
  Social Structure
  Social Systems
  Society
  State Society Relationship

Social Ecology
- **Use** Human Ecology

Social Elites
- **Use** Elites

Social Environment
- **DC** D786000
- **SN** Network of social relationships and activities surrounding social phenomena.
- **HN** Added, 1986.
- **UF** Social Context
- **BT** Environment
- **NT** Situation
  Social Isolation
- **RT** Quality of Life
  Social Attitudes
  Social Closure
  Social Cohesion

Social Environment (cont'd)
- **RT** Social Conditions
  Social Control
  Social Factors
  Social Inequality
  Social Influence
  Social Integration
  Social Life
  Social Pressure
  Social Space
  Social Structure
  Social Support
  Work Environment

Social Equilibrium
- **DC** D786700
- **SN** Closely related to Social Cohesion. The term implies lack of social conflict or social disorganization.
- **HN** Added, 1986.
- **UF** Disequilibrium (1971-1985)
  Equilibrium/Equilibration (1963-1985)
  Homeostasis/Homeostatic (1966-1985)
  Social Stability
- **RT** Action Theory
  Balance Theory
  Functionalism
  Social Change
  Social Cohesion
  Social Disorganization
  Social Order
  Social Systems
  Sociocultural Factors
  Socioeconomic Factors
  Stability
  Systems Theory

Social Evolution
- **DC** D786300
- **SN** Closely related to Social Development. The term implies an analogy between social and biological phenomena. Compare with Cultural Change.
- **HN** Formerly (1963-1985) DC 431300.
- **BT** Social Processes
- **RT** Cultural Change
  Differentiation
  Evolution
  Evolutionary Theories
  Historical Development
  Historical Materialism
  Historicism
  History
  Social Change
  Social Darwinism
  Social Development
  Social History
  Social Progress
  Social Structure
  Society
  Utopias

Social Exchange
- **Use** Exchange Theory

Social Factors
- **DC** D786600
- **SN** A context-dependent term for sets of sociological variables used to describe or explain social problems. Closely related to Social Conditions and Social Background.
- **HN** Formerly (1963-1985) DC 431400.
- **UF** Social Correlates (1964-1985)
- **RT** Biological Factors
  Psychosocial Factors

Social

Social Factors (cont'd)
- RT Situation
- Social Background
- Social Class
- Social Conditions
- Social Environment
- Social Mobility
- Social Planning
- Socialization Agents
- Society
- Sociocultural Factors
- Sociodemographic Factors
- Socioeconomic Factors

Social Facts
- DC D786500
- SN Patterns of a social nature that have explanatory significance and that are discernible in quantitative data.
- HN Added, 1986.
- UF Social Phenomena
- BT Phenomena
- RT Formalism
- Methodological Individualism
- Social Behavior
- Social Control
- Social Determination of Meaning
- Social Interaction
- Social Reality

Social Force/Social Forces (1963-1985)
- HN DC 431450, deleted 1986. See now Social Factors or Social Influence.

Social Function
- DC D786900
- SN A context-dependent term for the characteristics of social systems, structures, institutions, or processes that serve organizational purposes.
- HN Formerly (1963-1985) DC 431550, Social Function/Social Functioning/Social Functions.
- BT Function
- RT Roles
- Social Dynamics
- Social Institutions
- Social Networks
- Social Systems

Social Geography
- Use Geography

Social Goals
- DC D787200
- HN Formerly (1963-1985) DC 431580, Social Goal/Social Goals.
- BT Goals
- RT Public Policy
- Social Action
- Social Justice
- Social Movements
- Social Policy
- Social Progress
- Social Reform
- Social Values
- Society

Social Gospel Movement
- DC D787500
- SN International movement, strongest from 1890 to 1920, that applied Christian moral norms to social issues emerging with industrialization and the working classes.
- HN Added, 1986.
- BT Religious Movements

Social Group Work
- Use Group Work

Social Groups
- DC D787800
- SN A context-dependent term for sub-populations whose members have one or more social characteristics in common.
- HN Formerly (1963-1985) DC 431600, Social Group/Social Groups/Social Grouping.
- BT Groups
- NT Primary Groups
- RT Affiliation Need
- Cultural Groups
- Group Composition
- Group Norms
- Individual Collective Relationship
- Interpersonal Relations
- Neighbors
- Organizations (Social)
- Social Cohesion
- Social Contact
- Social Influence
- Social Interaction
- Social Life
- Social Status
- Womens Groups

Social History
- DC D788100
- HN Formerly (1964-1985) DC 431650.
- BT History
- RT Culture
- Historicism
- Intellectual History
- Social Change
- Social Dynamics
- Social Evolution
- Social Progress
- Social Revolution
- Sociocultural Factors
- Sociology

Social Identity
- DC D788400
- SN Sense of belonging to socially defined groups.
- HN Added, 1986.
- BT Identity
- RT Affiliation Need
- Anonymity
- Class Identity
- Cosmopolitanism
- Cultural Identity
- Group Identity
- Interpersonal Relations
- Localism
- Professional Identity
- Reference Groups
- Role Ambiguity
- Role Conflict
- Self Concept
- Social Cohesion
- Social Perception

Social Impact Assessment
- DC D788600
- HN Formerly (1985) DC 431667.
- BT Evaluation
- RT Economic Factors
- Quality of Life
- Social Change
- Social Conditions
- Social Indicators
- Socioeconomic Factors
- Technology Assessment

Social Indicators
- DC D788700
- SN Characteristics used as indexes of the quality of life of social groups. The term is associated with a movement in the social sciences of the late 1950s and 1960s to provide reliable data on social development processes.
- HN Formerly (1972-1985) DC 431685.
- BT Indexes (Measures)
- RT Futures (of Society)
- Life Satisfaction
- Prediction
- Quality of Life
- Social Impact Assessment
- Society
- Socioeconomic Factors
- Standard of Living
- Trends

Social Inequality
- DC D789000
- SN The condition that results when a social group is underprivileged compared with another.
- HN Formerly (1984-1985) DC 431693.
- BT Inequality
- RT Black White Differences
- Class Differences
- Distributive Justice
- Elitism
- Human Rights
- Minority Groups
- Poverty
- Privilege
- Sexual Inequality
- Social Class
- Social Conditions
- Social Environment
- Social Justice
- Social Mobility
- Social Stratification
- Society
- Socioeconomic Status
- Subordination

Social Influence
- DC D789300
- SN A context-dependent term for the capacity to impact or be impacted by social forces such as norms, role expectations, and other conditions of participation in social institutions and cultural groups.
- HN Formerly (1963-1985) DC 431700.
- BT Influence
- NT Peer Influence
- RT Conformity
- Criticism
- Opinion Leaders
- Power Elite
- Prestige
- Reputation
- Role Models
- Social Behavior
- Social Control
- Social Desirability
- Social Environment
- Social Groups
- Social Integration
- Social Participation
- Social Power
- Social Pressure
- Social Status
- Social Values
- Society

Social

Social Institutions
- **DC** D789500
- **SN** A context-dependent term denoting specific social structures, more or less formalized through tradition, planning, or other social processes, that respond to and express human needs and aspirations.
- **HN** Formerly (1963-1985) DC 431775, Social Institution/Social Institutions.
- **BT** Institutions
- **NT** Education
  Family
  Government
  Law
  Marriage
  Religions
- **RT** Institutionalization (Social)
  Norms
  Organizations (Social)
  Social Function
  Social Order
  Social Revolution
  Social Structure
  Social Systems
  Society
  Traditions

Social Insurance Systems
- **Use** Social Security

Social Integration
- **DC** D789600
- **SN** A context-dependent term encompassing the processes by which social groups merge with one another or by which individuals come to identify themselves with sociocultural groups.
- **HN** Formerly (1963-1985) DC 431900.
- **UF** Integrate/Integrated/Integration/ Integrative (1963-1985)
  Integration (Social)
- **BT** Social Processes
- **RT** Acculturation
  Assimilation
  Crosscultural Analysis
  Cultural Change
  Desegregation
  Discrimination
  Ethnic Groups
  Ethnic Relations
  Immigrants
  Indigenous Populations
  Intercultural Communication
  Intergroup Relations
  Intermarriage
  Nativism
  Social Change
  Social Cohesion
  Social Distance
  Social Environment
  Social Influence
  Social Isolation
  Social Segmentation
  Social Systems
  Socialization
  Society
  Subcultures

Social Interaction
- **DC** D789900
- **SN** A context-dependent term encompassing behaviors characterized by mutual awareness of interactants over time.
- **HN** Formerly (1963-1985) DC 432000.
- **UF** Encounter/Encounters (1971-1985)
  Face to Face (1963-1985)

Social Interaction (cont'd)
- **UF** Interpersonal Interaction
- **BT** Interaction
- **NT** Group Dynamics
- **RT** Aggression
  Assertiveness
  Communicative Action
  Communities
  Competition
  Conversation
  Conversational Analysis
  Cooperation
  Emotions
  Ethnomethodology
  Exchange Theory
  Gift Giving
  Group Composition
  Impression Formation
  Impression Management
  Individual Collective Relationship
  Interactionism
  Interpersonal Attraction
  Interpersonal Relations
  Loneliness
  Personal Space
  Primary Groups
  Psychodynamics
  Self Presentation
  Situation
  Small Groups
  Social Behavior
  Social Cohesion
  Social Contact
  Social Dynamics
  Social Facts
  Social Groups
  Social Life
  Social Perception
  Social Processes
  Structural-Functional Analysis
  Symbolic Interactionism
  Universalism-Particularism

Social Interest
- **DC** D790200
- **HN** Formerly (1964-1985) DC 432006.
- **BT** Interests
- **RT** Activism
  Altruism
  Charities
  Contributions (Donations)
  Foundations
  Helping Behavior
  Nonprofit Organizations
  Social Action
  Social Participation

Social Isolation
- **DC** D790500
- **HN** Formerly (1963-1985) DC 432065.
- **UF** Deprivation (Social)
  Isolate/Isolates (1964-1985)
  Isolation/Isolationism/Isolationist (1963-1985)
  Seclusion (1972-1985)
- **BT** Social Environment
- **RT** Affiliation Need
  Alienation
  American Indian Reservations
  Anomie
  Deprivation
  Disengagement
  Indigenous Populations
  Individual Collective Relationship
  Loneliness
  Marginality
  Social Contact
  Social Distance

Social Isolation (cont'd)
- **RT** Social Integration
  Social Participation
  Social Segmentation
  Society

Social Justice
- **DC** D790800
- **HN** Formerly (1984-1985) DC 432096.
- **BT** Justice
- **RT** Civil Rights
  Egalitarianism
  Equality
  Human Rights
  Inequality
  Social Goals
  Social Inequality
  Social Reform
  Social Responsibility
  Social Welfare
  Society

Social Legislation (1963-1985)
- **HN** DC 432128.
- **Use** Legislation

Social Life
- **DC** D791100
- **HN** Formerly (1963-1985) DC 432135.
- **BT** Life
- **RT** Celebrations
  Dating (Social)
  Everyday Life
  Family Life
  Friendship
  Life Satisfaction
  Lifestyle
  Social Contact
  Social Environment
  Social Groups
  Social Interaction
  Social Participation
  Social Space
  Society

Social Maladaptation (1964-1985)
- **HN** DC 432140.
- **Use** Adjustment

Social Marginality
- **Use** Marginality

Social Meaning (1985)
- **HN** DC 432140.
- **Use** Social Determination of Meaning

Social Mobility
- **DC** D791400
- **SN** The movement of an individual or group from one social class, stratum, or status to another, upward or downward in a social stratification system, or "horizontally" from one geographical location to another.
- **HN** Formerly (1963-1985) DC 432145.
- **UF** Class Mobility
  Intragenerational Mobility
  Upward Mobility
  Vertical Mobility
- **BT** Mobility
- **NT** Intergenerational Mobility
  Occupational Mobility
- **RT** Achievement
  Demography
  Educational Attainment
  Elitism
  Embourgeoisement
  Generational Differences
  Geographic Mobility

Social

Social Mobility (cont'd)
- RT Proletarianization
- Social Class
- Social Factors
- Social Inequality
- Social Status
- Social Stratification
- Socioeconomic Status
- Status Attainment

Social Morphology (1964-1985)
- HN DC 432160.
- Use Social Structure

Social Movements
- DC D791700
- SN Collective activities with spontaneous origins that acquire institutional structure over time; they generally emerge in the context of some form of perceived social injustice and center around specific causes and/or charismatic leaders.
- HN Formerly (1963-1985) DC 432170.
- BT Movements
- NT Environmentalism
  - Feminism
  - Nativistic Movements
  - Protest Movements
- RT Activism
  - Agitation
  - Black Power
  - Civil Rights
  - Collective Behavior
  - Countermovements
  - Human Rights
  - Interest Groups
  - Millenarianism
  - Political Movements
  - Religious Movements
  - Social Action
  - Social Change
  - Social Conditions
  - Social Goals
  - Social Problems
  - Social Processes
  - Social Reform
  - Social Revolution
  - Womens Rights
  - Youth Movements

Social Networks
- DC D792000
- SN Forms of social organization characterized by common interests and communication patterns among interactants, particularly those distributed widely in geographical terms.
- HN Formerly (1967-1985) DC 432175, Social Network/Social Networks/Social Networking.
- BT Networks
- NT Kinship Networks
- RT Centrality
  - Communication
  - Exchange Theory
  - Interpersonal Relations
  - Network Analysis
  - Services
  - Social Behavior
  - Social Contact
  - Social Dynamics
  - Social Function
  - Social Services
  - Social Structure
  - Social Support
  - Social Systems
  - Sociometric Analysis

Social Norms (1985)
- HN DC 432180.
- Use Norms

Social Order
- DC D792300
- SN A context-dependent term denoting coherence and continuity in the social environment, and rational cooperation among individuals and social institutions.
- HN Formerly (1963-1985) DC 432185.
- UF Order (Social)
- RT Conflict Theory
  - Law Enforcement
  - Social Cohesion
  - Social Conflict
  - Social Control
  - Social Disorganization
  - Social Equilibrium
  - Social Institutions
  - Social Structure
  - Social Theories

Social Organization/Social Organizations (1972-1985)
- HN DC 432192, deleted 1986. See now Organizations (Social), Social Agencies, or Social Structure.

Social Participation
- DC D792600
- HN Formerly (1984-1985) DC 432200.
- UF Involvement (Social)
  - Participation, Social (1964-1985)
- BT Participation
- RT Affiliation Need
  - Associations
  - Clubs
  - Disengagement
  - Sociability
  - Social Action
  - Social Contact
  - Social Influence
  - Social Interest
  - Social Isolation
  - Social Life

Social Patterns (1963-1985)
- HN DC 432220, deleted 1986.

Social Perception
- DC D792900
- SN A context-dependent term for individual cognitive orientations toward social phenomena, particularly in the contexts of social interaction and public opinion.
- HN Formerly (1963-1985) DC 432230.
- UF Interpersonal Perception
  - Person Perception
- BT Social Consciousness
- NT Impression Formation
- RT Anonymity
  - Attribution
  - Credibility
  - Cynicism
  - Impression Management
  - Labeling
  - Perceptions
  - Self Presentation
  - Situation
  - Social Attitudes
  - Social Behavior
  - Social Identity
  - Social Interaction
  - Social Space
  - Social Types
  - Universalism-Particularism

Social Phenomena
- Use Social Facts

Social Philosophy
- DC D793200
- HN Formerly (1963-1985) DC 432235.
- BT Philosophy
- RT Social Theories
  - Society

Social Planning
- DC D793500
- HN Formerly (1963-1985) DC 432238.
- BT Planning
- RT Economic Planning
  - Family Planning
  - Local Planning
  - Social Change
  - Social Factors
  - Social Policy
  - Social Progress
  - Social Reform
  - Society
  - State Planning

Social Policy
- DC D793800
- HN Formerly (1971-1985) DC 432239.
- BT Policy
- NT Criminal Justice Policy
  - Family Policy
  - Health Policy
  - Housing Policy
  - Population Policy
  - Welfare Policy
- RT Antipoverty Programs
  - Apartheid
  - Desegregation
  - Educational Policy
  - Government Policy
  - Law
  - Policy Implementation
  - Policy Making
  - Public Policy
  - Public Services
  - Social Goals
  - Social Planning
  - Social Problems
  - Social Security
  - Tolerance
  - Welfare State

Social Position (1964-1985)
- HN DC 432240.
- Use Social Status

Social Power
- DC D794100
- HN Added, 1986.
- BT Power
- RT Authority
  - Community Power
  - Elites
  - Exchange Theory
  - Family Power
  - Intelligentsia
  - Leadership
  - Privilege
  - Social Conflict
  - Social Influence
  - Upper Class

Social Pressure
- DC D794400
- HN Formerly (1963-1985) DC 432250.
- BT Pressure
- RT Conformity
  - Peer Influence

Social Pressure (cont'd)
RT Social Behavior
Social Control
Social Environment
Social Influence
Society
Uniformity

Social Problems
DC D794700
SN A context-dependent term for any perceived adversity or pattern of injustice with social causes, definitions, consequences, or possible solutions.
HN Formerly (1963-1985) DC 432260, Social Problem/Social Problems.
BT Problems
RT Crime
Deprivation
Disasters
Discrimination
Economic Problems
Etiology
Family Conflict
Family Violence
Government Policy
Hazards
Homelessness
Labor Disputes
Overpopulation
Poverty
Prejudice
Refugees
Social Action
Social Conflict
Social Movements
Social Policy
Social Reform
Social Welfare
Social Work
Unemployment
World Problems

Social Processes
DC D795000
SN A context-dependent term covering the complex, interrelated changes in social phenomena over time, seen as analytically distinct from biological, psychological, and environmental processes. Closely related to Social Change; see also Social Structure.
HN Formerly (1963-1985) DC 432285, Social Process/Social Processes.
NT Acculturation
Assimilation
Bureaucratization
Deindustrialization
Embourgeoisement
Group Formation
Industrialization
Militarization
Modernization
Polarization
Professionalization
Proletarianization
Rationalization
Ruralization
Secularization
Social Cohesion
Social Determination of Meaning
Social Evolution
Social Integration
Social Segmentation
Socialization
Structuration
Suburbanization
Unionization

Social Processes (cont'd)
NT Urbanization
RT Boundary Maintenance
Class Formation
Cultural Change
Differentiation
Formation
Futures (of Society)
Institutionalization (Social)
Social Action
Social Change
Social Development
Social Disorganization
Social Dynamics
Social Interaction
Social Movements
Social Reality
Social Reform
Social Revolution
Social Structure
Society
Specialization

Social Programs
DC D795300
HN Formerly (1984-1985) DC 432289.
BT Programs
NT Antipoverty Programs
RT Government Policy
Program Implementation
Social Reform
Social Services

Social Progress
DC D795600
HN Formerly (1963-1985) DC 432293.
UF Societal Progress
BT Progress
Social Change
RT Futures (of Society)
History
Social Development
Social Evolution
Social Goals
Social History
Social Planning
Social Reform
Social Values
Society

Social Psychiatry
DC D795900
SN Branch of psychiatry focusing on the role of environmental, social, cultural, and economic factors in the causes, incidence, and manifestations of mental disorders.
HN Formerly (1963-1985) DC 432300, Social Psychiatry/Social Psychiatrist.
BT Psychiatry
RT Forensic Psychiatry
Social Psychology

Social Psychology
DC D796200
HN Formerly (1963-1985) DC 432500, Social Psychology/Social Psychologist/Social Psychological.
BT Psychology
RT Balance Theory
Chicago School of Sociology
Criminology
Group Dynamics
Interactionism
Psychopathology
Social Psychiatry
Sociology
Symbolic Interactionism

Social Reality
DC D796500
SN Comparable to Social Facts, this term emphasizes the involvement of human cognitions in creating social phenomena.
HN Formerly (1965-1985) DC 432575.
RT Everyday Life
Family Life
Reality
Social Determination of Meaning
Social Facts
Social Processes
Social Reproduction
Social Theories
Society
Worldview

Social Reform
DC D796800
HN Formerly (1963-1985) DC 432585, Social Reform/Social Reformers.
BT Reform
RT Affirmative Action
Land Reform
New Deal
Political Ideologies
Revolutions
Social Action
Social Change
Social Goals
Social Justice
Social Movements
Social Planning
Social Problems
Social Processes
Social Programs
Social Progress
Society
Welfare Reform

Social Reinforcement
Use Reinforcement

Social Rejection
Use Rejection

Social Relations
DC D797100
SN A context-dependent term for interrelations among social roles, groups, and institutions. For relations among individuals, see Interpersonal Relations.
HN Formerly (1963-1985) DC 432600, Social Relations/Social Relationships.
NT Business Society Relationship
Church State Relationship
Intergroup Relations
Kinship
Military Civilian Relations
Police Community Relations
Public Sector Private Sector Relations
Religion Politics Relationship
State Society Relationship
RT Civil Society
Exchange Theory
Gemeinschaft And Gesellschaft
Paternalism
Patronage
Philosophical Doctrines
Reification
Roles
Social Control
Social Dynamics
Social Relations

Social

Social Relations of Production
  Use Forces And Relations of Production
Social Reproduction
  DC D797400
  SN The tendency of social institutions, classes, and strata to maintain the status quo over time and across generations, especially when vested economic interests and privileges are at stake in an established mode of production.
  HN Formerly (1985) DC 432610.
  RT Cultural Transmission
     Marxist Sociology
     Social Reality
     Social Structure
     Socialization
     Society
     Structuration

Social Research (1963-1985)
  HN DC 432640.
  Use Social Science Research
Social Response
  DC D797700
  HN Formerly (1985) DC 432655.
  UF Community Response
     Public Response
     Societal Reaction
  BT Responses
  RT Acceptance
     Collective Behavior
     Crises
     Dissent
     Information And Referral Services
     Labeling
     Public Support
     Rejection
     Sanctions
     Social Acceptance
     Strangers

Social Responsibility
  DC D798000
  HN Formerly (1963-1985) DC 432660, Social Responsibility/Social Responsibilities.
  BT Responsibility
  RT Citizenship
     Ethics
     Helping Behavior
     Social Action
     Social Behavior
     Social Justice
     Social Services
     State Intervention

Social Revolution
  DC D798300
  SN Economic, ideological, normative, or other changes having widespread impact on a society.
  HN Formerly (1963-1985) DC 432670.
  BT Revolutions
  RT Cultural Change
     Culture Contact
     Modernization
     Scientific Technological Revolution
     Social Change
     Social History
     Social Institutions
     Social Movements
     Social Processes
     Social Theories
     Society

Social Role/Social Roles (1963-1985)
  HN DC 432685.
  Use Roles
Social Science Education
  DC D798600
  HN Added, 1986.
  BT Education
  NT International Studies
     Social Studies
     Social Work Education
     Sociology Education
  RT Curriculum
     Social Sciences

Social Science Research
  DC D798900
  HN Added, 1986.
  UF Behavioral Science Research
     Social Research (1963-1985)
  BT Research
  NT Ethnomethodology
     Market Research
     Psychological Research
     Public Opinion Research
     Sociological Research
  RT Action Research
     Communication Research
     Community Research
     Educational Research
     Family Research
     Frankfurt School
     Group Research
     Historiography
     Interdisciplinary Approach
     Life History
     Life Tables
     Marxist Analysis
     Mathematics
     Middle Range Theories
     Organizational Research
     Paradigms
     Policy Research
     Psychohistory
     Research Methodology
     Sampling
     Social Sciences
     Social Scientists
     Surveys
     Theoretical Problems
     Verstehen
     Victimology

Social Sciences
  DC D799200
  HN Formerly (1963-1985) DC 432700, Social Science/Social Sciences/Social Scientific.
  UF Human Sciences
  NT Anthropology
     Behavioral Sciences
     Economics
     Geography
     Gerontology
     History
     Law
     Policy Science
     Political Science
     Sociology
     Topography
  RT Academic Disciplines
     Medicine
     Science
     Social Science Education
     Social Science Research
     Social Scientists
     Social Studies
     Theory Practice Relationship

Social Scientists
  DC D799500
  HN Formerly (1963-1985) DC 432760, Social Scientist/Social Scientists.
  UF Behavioral Scientists
     Geographer/Geographers (1967-1985)
  BT Professional Workers
  NT Anthropologists
     Economists
     Historians
     Sociologists
  RT Psychologists
     Researchers
     Scientists
     Social Science Research
     Social Sciences

Social Security
  DC D799800
  HN Formerly (1963-1985) DC 432800.
  UF Social Insurance Systems
  RT Benefits
     Elderly
     Medicare
     New Deal
     Pensions
     Retirement
     Social Policy
     Welfare State

Social Segmentation
  DC D799900
  SN A characteristic of societies with highly differentiated social systems and divisions of labor in which groups become separated into sub-groupings with minimal opportunities for interaction and community building.
  HN Added, 1986.
  BT Social Processes
  RT Anomie
     Cleavage
     Factionalism
     Group Formation
     Intergroup Relations
     Labor Market Segmentation
     Polarization
     Social Integration
     Social Isolation
     Social Stratification
     Social Structure
     Specialization
     Subcultures

Social Services
  DC D800100
  HN Formerly (1963-1985) DC 432805, Social Service/Social Services.
  BT Human Services
  NT Foster Care
     Welfare Services
  RT Assistance
     Caregivers
     Community Services
     Emergencies
     Human Service Organizations
     Interdisciplinary Approach
     Social Agencies
     Social Networks
     Social Programs
     Social Responsibility
     Social Welfare
     Social Work

Social

Social Situation
- Use Situation

Social Solidarity (1969-1985)
- HN DC 432830.
- Use Social Cohesion

Social Space
- DC D800400
- SN Refers to social perceptions of the physical environment as a factor in analyses of social interaction and relations.
- HN Added, 1986.
- BT Space
- RT Primary Groups
  Reference Groups
  Social Environment
  Social Life
  Social Perception

Social Stability
- Use Social Equilibrium

Social Status
- DC D800700
- SN A context-dependent term for the relative prestige of an individual or group and the hierarchical position of a social role in a social structure or stratification system. Closely related to Socioeconomic Status.
- HN Formerly (1963-1985) DC 432850.
- UF Class Status
  Social Position (1964-1985)
- BT Status
- NT Occupational Status
  Socioeconomic Status
- RT Ascription
  Caste Systems
  Elites
  Initiation Rites
  Life Satisfaction
  Marginality
  Marital Status
  Peer Groups
  Peers
  Prestige
  Privilege
  Quality of Life
  Reputation
  Roles
  Self Concept
  Social Class
  Social Distance
  Social Groups
  Social Influence
  Social Mobility
  Social Stratification
  Social Structure
  Status Attainment
  Status Inconsistency
  Subordination

Social Stigma
- Use Stigma

Social Strains (1965-1985)
- HN DC 432910, deleted 1986.

Social Stratification
- DC D801000
- SN A context-dependent term denoting the tendency for societies to organize themselves hierarchically by social class or caste.
- HN Formerly (1963-1985) DC 432920.
- UF Class Stratification
  Ranking (Social)

Social Stratification (cont'd)
- UF Societal Stratification
- BT Social Structure
  Stratification
- RT Boundaries
  Caste Systems
  Class Analysis
  Class Society
  Differentiation
  Elitism
  Functionalism
  Income Inequality
  Situses
  Social Class
  Social Distance
  Social Inequality
  Social Mobility
  Social Segmentation
  Social Status
  Society
  Socioeconomic Status
  Status
  Wealth

Social Structure
- DC D801300
- SN A context-dependent term for social phenomena (both specific institutions and societies as wholes) viewed in terms of their interrelated structural characteristics. See also Organizations (Social) and Social Processes.
- HN Formerly (1963-1985) DC 433000, Social Structure/Social Structures.
- UF Class Structure
  Organization, Social (1964-1985)
  Social Morphology (1964-1985)
- BT Structure
- NT Social Disorganization
  Social Stratification
  Structuration
- RT Balance Theory
  Base And Superstructure
  Boundaries
  Caste Systems
  Center And Periphery
  Centrality
  Class Analysis
  Class Society
  Community Structure
  Convergence Theory
  Economic Structure
  Elites
  Equality
  Family Structure
  Formalism
  Functionalism
  Kinship
  Majority Groups
  Marginality
  Minority Groups
  Organizational Structure
  Organizations (Social)
  Power Structure
  Situses
  Social Change
  Social Class
  Social Conditions
  Social Control
  Social Distance
  Social Dynamics
  Social Environment
  Social Evolution
  Social Institutions
  Social Networks
  Social Order
  Social Processes

Social Structure (cont'd)
- RT Social Reproduction
  Social Segmentation
  Social Status
  Social Systems
  Social Theories
  Society
  Structural Models
  Structural-Functional Analysis
  Structuralism
  Verstehen

Social Studies
- DC D801600
- HN Formerly (1963-1985) DC 433175.
- BT Social Science Education
- RT Curriculum
  Social Sciences

Social Support
- DC D801900
- HN Formerly (1983-1985) DC 433182.
- UF Support Systems
- BT Support
- RT Affiliation Need
  Employment Assistance Programs
  Encouragement
  Friendship
  Human Services
  Primary Groups
  Social Behavior
  Social Environment
  Social Networks

Social Systems
- DC D802200
- SN A context-dependent term referring broadly to the form of social and economic organization prevailing in a society and to the characteristics of constituent sub-systems.
- HN Formerly (1963-1985) DC 433200, Social System/Social Systems.
- BT Systems
- NT Caste Systems
- RT Boundary Maintenance
  Economic Systems
  Holism
  Political Ideologies
  Political Systems
  Social Dynamics
  Social Equilibrium
  Social Function
  Social Institutions
  Social Integration
  Social Networks
  Social Structure
  Social Theories
  Society
  Structural-Functional Analysis
  Structuralism
  Systems Theory

Social Theories
- DC D802500
- SN A context-dependent term for theories that focus on social phenomena. In contexts where Social Theories is closely related to Sociological Theory, select the latter.
- HN Formerly (1963-1985) DC 433325, Social Theory/Social Theories.
- BT Theories
- NT Action Theory
  Balance Theory
  Conflict Theory
  Contagion Theory
  Convergence Theory
  Critical Theory

Social

Social Theories (cont'd)
- NT Dialectical Materialism
- Exchange Theory
- Middle Range Theories
- Organicism
- Systems Theory
- RT Biosocial Theory
- Evolutionary Theories
- Functionalism
- History of Sociology
- Marxist Analysis
- Materialism
- Methodological Individualism
- Progressivism
- Social Criticism
- Social Darwinism
- Social Order
- Social Philosophy
- Social Reality
- Social Revolution
- Social Structure
- Social Systems
- Socialization
- Society
- Sociological Theory
- Sociology
- Structural-Functional Analysis
- Teleology
- Universalism-Particularism
- Voluntarism

Social Types
- DC D802600
- SN The unconventional roles in a sociocultural system (ie, those not defined in terms of major social institutions but well known in everyday life). Examples include playboys, hippies, street people, highbrows, etc.
- HN Added, 1986.
- BT Types
- RT Ideal Types
- Labeling
- Roles
- Social Perception
- Stereotypes

Social Understanding
Use Verstehen

Social Unit (1964-1985)
- HN DC 433400, deleted 1986.

Social Unrest
- DC D802700
- HN Formerly (1985) DC 433440.
- UF Civil Unrest
- BT Social Conditions
- RT Agitation
- Civil Disorders
- Discontent
- Dissent
- Intergroup Relations
- Protest Movements
- Schism
- Social Change
- Social Conditions
- Social Conflict
- Social Disorganization
- Tension

Social Values
- DC D802800
- SN Patterns of feelings and judgments about right vs wrong, good vs bad, strength vs weakness, and acceptance vs rejection. In Marxist analysis, values are seen as determined by the society's economic mode of production.

Social Values (cont'd)
- HN Formerly (1984-1985) DC 433480.
- BT Values
- RT Aesthetics
- Altruism
- Anomie
- Beliefs
- Censorship
- Civilization
- Cultural Values
- Egalitarianism
- Human Dignity
- Humanitarianism
- Ideologies
- Internalization
- Morality
- Norms
- Political Ideologies
- Prestige
- Priorities
- Quality of Life
- Reference Groups
- Sanctions
- Social Attitudes
- Social Consciousness
- Social Control
- Social Desirability
- Social Goals
- Social Influence
- Social Progress
- Socialization
- Technology Assessment
- Traditionalism

Social Visitation
Use Visitation

Social Welfare
- DC D803100
- HN Formerly (1963-1985) DC 433500.
- RT Benefits
- Social Justice
- Social Problems
- Social Services
- Social Work
- Welfare Policy
- Welfare Services
- Welfare State

Social Welfare Policy
Use Welfare Policy

Social Work
- DC D803400
- HN Formerly (1963-1985) DC 433700.
- UF Casework/Caseworker/Caseworkers (1963-1985)
- Social Casework (1963-1985)
- NT Clinical Social Work
- Group Work
- RT Counseling
- Criminal Justice
- Helping Behavior
- Information And Referral Services
- Intervention
- Permanency Planning
- Psychology
- Rehabilitation
- Social Agencies
- Social Problems
- Social Services
- Social Welfare
- Social Work Cases
- Social Work Education
- Social Workers
- Treatment Methods

Socialist

Social Work Cases
- DC D803700
- HN Added, 1986.
- UF Cases (Social Work)
- RT Disposition
- Social Work

Social Work Education
- DC D804000
- HN Added, 1986.
- BT Social Science Education
- RT Doctoral Programs
- Social Work
- Sociology Education
- Undergraduate Programs

Social Workers
- DC D804300
- HN Formerly (1963-1985) DC 433850, Social Worker/Social Workers.
- UF Psychiatric Social Workers
- BT Professional Workers
- RT Caregivers
- Client Relations
- Correctional Personnel
- Counseling
- Psychologists
- Psychotherapy
- Social Work

Socialism
- DC D804600
- HN Formerly (1963-1985) DC 433890.
- BT Economic Systems
- Political Ideologies
- RT Capitalism
- Collectivism
- Communism
- Marxism
- Marxist Economics
- Revisionism
- Social Democracy
- Socialist Parties
- Socialist Societies
- Syndicalism
- Utopias

Socialist Countries
Use Socialist Societies

Socialist Parties
- DC D804900
- HN Added, 1986.
- BT Political Parties
- RT Communist Parties
- Labor Parties
- Left Wing Politics
- Socialism
- Socialist Societies

Socialist Societies
- DC D805200
- HN Added, 1986.
- UF Socialist Countries
- Socialist/Socialistic (1963-1985)
- BT Society
- RT Capitalist Societies
- Communist Societies
- Liberal Democratic Societies
- Marxism
- Marxist Sociology
- Political Ideologies
- Socialism
- Socialist Parties

236

Socialist

Socialist/Socialistic (1963-1985)
- HN DC 433900.
- Use Socialist Societies

Socialization
- DC D805500
- SN The process of acquiring social roles, identity, and the skills necessary to function socially. It is a life-long process, but often refers to activity in the formative years, in concert with biological and cognitive maturation. See also Child Development and Childrearing Practices.
- HN Formerly (1964-1985) DC 433910.
- BT Social Processes
- NT Internalization
    Political Socialization
    Prisonization
    Professional Socialization
- RT Adjustment
    Child Development
    Childrearing Practices
    Conformity
    Cultural Transmission
    Education
    Group Identity
    Individuals
    Learning
    Peer Influence
    Personality
    Reference Groups
    Religious Orientations
    Role Models
    Significant Others
    Social Integration
    Social Reproduction
    Social Theories
    Social Values
    Socialization Agents

Socialization Agents
- DC D805800
- SN Individuals, groups, or institutions under whose influence or direction one learns to participate in or conform with society. May include parents, family, schools, churches, mass media, etc.
- HN Formerly (1963-1985) part of DC 020250, Agent/Agents.
- UF Agents (Socialization)
- RT Cultural Transmission
    Peers
    Schools
    Social Factors
    Socialization

Socialized (1970-1985)
- HN DC 434890, deleted 1986.

Socialized Medicine
- DC D805900
- SN Health care systems funded and administered by the state.
- HN Added, 1989.
- UF National Health Service
- BT Medicine
- NT Medicaid
    Medicare
- RT Health Care
    Health Insurance
    Health Planning
    Health Policy
    Health Services
    Public Health

Socially Deviant Behavior
- Use Deviant Behavior

Societal (1963-1985)
- HN DC 433950, deleted 1986.

Societal Assessment of Technology
- Use Technology Assessment

Societal Change
- Use Social Change

Societal Progress
- Use Social Progress

Societal Reaction
- Use Social Response

Societal Stratification
- Use Social Stratification

Society
- DC D806100
- SN A context-dependent term for organized human activity at varying levels of complexity and specificity. Select a more specific entry or coordinate with other terms.
- HN Formerly (1963-1985) DC 434400, Society/Societies.
- NT Bourgeois Societies
    Capitalist Societies
    Civil Society
    Class Society
    Communist Societies
    Complex Societies
    Industrial Societies
    Liberal Democratic Societies
    Mass Society
    Modern Society
    Plural Societies
    Postindustrial Societies
    Socialist Societies
    Traditional Societies
    Western Society
- RT Business Society Relationship
    Civilization
    Countries
    Cultural Groups
    Culture
    Economic Systems
    Futures (of Society)
    Groups
    Individual Collective Relationship
    Macrosociology
    Political Systems
    Social Action
    Social Change
    Social Cohesion
    Social Conditions
    Social Dynamics
    Social Evolution
    Social Factors
    Social Goals
    Social Indicators
    Social Inequality
    Social Influence
    Social Institutions
    Social Integration
    Social Isolation
    Social Justice
    Social Life
    Social Philosophy
    Social Planning
    Social Pressure
    Social Processes
    Social Progress
    Social Reality
    Social Reform

Sociocultural

Society (cont'd)
- RT Social Reproduction
    Social Revolution
    Social Stratification
    Social Structure
    Social Systems
    Social Theories
    Sociocultural Factors
    Sociology
    State Society Relationship

Society for Psych Study of Social Issues/SPSSI (1970-1985)
- HN DC 434420. Abbreviated here due to character restrictions. Formerly used in indexing under its full name Society for the Psychological Study of Social Issues/SPSSI.
- Use Professional Associations

Society Individual Relationship
- Use Individual Collective Relationship

Society Islands
- DC D806400
- HN Added, 1986.
- BT French Polynesia
- NT Tahiti

Society of Friends
- Use Quakers

Society of Jesus
- Use Jesuits

Society, The, of (1963-1985)
- HN DC 434100.
- Use Traditional Societies

Socio (1963-1985)
- HN DC 434550, deleted 1986. See now specific "Socio" and "Social" terms.

Sociobiology
- DC D806700
- SN Study of the biological basis of social behavior.
- HN Formerly (1977-1985) DC 434559.
- UF Biosociology
- BT Behavioral Sciences
    Biology
- RT Biosocial Theory
    Darwinism
    Ethology
    Evolution
    Evolutionary Theories
    Genetics
    Social Behavior
    Sociology

Sociocultural Factors
- DC D807000
- SN A context-dependent term encompassing sets of variables used to describe or explain social phenomena. Closely related to Socioeconomic Factors, the term emphasizes the cultural attributes of populations (eg, ethnicity, language, religion, kinship, and belief systems).
- HN Formerly (1984-1985) DC 434567, Sociocultural.
- RT Biological Factors
    Black White Differences
    Civilization
    Cultural Change
    Cultural Groups
    Cultural Relativism
    Culture
    Environmental Factors

Sociodemographic

Sociocultural Factors (cont'd)
- RT Ethnicity
  Ethnography
  Ethnology
  Influence
  Language Social Class Relationship
  Social Equilibrium
  Social Factors
  Social History
  Society
  Socioeconomic Factors
  Sociolinguistics
  Western Civilization

Sociodemographic Factors
- DC D807300
- SN A context-dependent term for sets of variables used to describe or explain social phenomena. Closely related to Socioeconomic Factors, the term emphasizes statistical data (eg, from censuses) on population-wide variables (eg, migration patterns, fertility).
- HN Formerly (1985) DC 434570, Sociodemographic.
- RT Biological Factors
  Demographic Change
  Demographic Characteristics
  Demography
  Environmental Factors
  Geography
  Social Factors
  Socioeconomic Factors

Socioeconomic Class
  Use Socioeconomic Status

Socioeconomic Factors
- DC D807600
- SN A context-dependent term covering many of the variables used to describe and explain social phenomena. Closely related to Socioeconomic Status, the term emphasizes income level and social class variables.
- HN Formerly (1963-1985) DC 434455, Socioeconomic.
- RT Economic Factors
  Influence
  Social Background
  Social Conditions
  Social Disorganization
  Social Equilibrium
  Social Factors
  Social Impact Assessment
  Social Indicators
  Sociocultural Factors
  Sociodemographic Factors
  Socioeconomic Status
  Standard of Living
  Sustenance Organization

Socioeconomic Level
  Use Socioeconomic Status

Socioeconomic Status
- DC D807900
- SN A context-dependent term encompassing all the key variables used in sociological analyses, including age, sex, income, religion, social class, occupation, etc.
- HN Formerly (1984-1985) DC 434500.
- UF Socioeconomic Class
  Socioeconomic Level
- BT Social Status
- RT Affluence
  Class Differences

Socioeconomic Status (cont'd)
- RT Demographic Characteristics
  Disadvantaged
  Income Inequality
  Quality of Life
  Relative Deprivation
  Social Area Analysis
  Social Background
  Social Class
  Social Desirability
  Social Inequality
  Social Mobility
  Social Stratification
  Socioeconomic Factors

Socioeconomically Disadvantaged
  Use Disadvantaged

Sociogram/Sociograms (1972-1985)
- HN DC 434680.
- Use Sociometric Analysis

Sociography
- DC D808200
- SN The descriptive analysis of specific social relations in a specific environment.
- HN Formerly (1963-1985) DC 434700, Sociography/Sociographic.
- RT Sociological Research
  Sociology

Sociolinguistics
- DC D808500
- SN Study of the effects of the social and cultural context on the structure and use of language, and of the effects of early linguistic influences on patterns of social relations.
- HN Formerly (1979-1985) DC 434760, Sociolinguistic/Sociolinguistics.
- BT Linguistics
- NT Ethnolinguistics
  Language Planning
- RT Bilingualism
  Code Switching
  Communicative Action
  Dialects
  Diglossia
  Grammar
  Hermeneutics
  Kinship Terminology
  Language Attitudes
  Language Maintenance
  Language Policy
  Language Shift
  Language Social Class Relationship
  Language Usage
  Language Varieties
  Monolingualism
  Multilingualism
  Naming Practices
  Pragmatics
  Psycholinguistics
  Sociocultural Factors
  Sociology

Sociological Associations
- DC D808800
- HN Added, 1986.
- UF American Sociological Association (1963-1985)
- BT Professional Associations
- RT Sociology

Sociology

Sociological History
  Use History of Sociology

Sociological Research
- DC D809100
- SN Since the concept is pervasive in the sociological literature, this term should be selected infrequently. Select a related entry if possible or coordinate with other terms.
- HN Formerly (1963-1985) DC 434820, Sociological.
- BT Social Science Research
- RT Chicago School of Sociology
  Community Research
  Family Research
  Macrosociology
  Metasociology
  Microsociology
  Organizational Research
  Sociography
  Sociology

Sociological Theory
- DC D809400
- SN The corpus of explicit knowledge produced by sociologists to describe and explain social phenomena.
- HN Formerly (1985) DC 434845.
- BT Theories
- RT Biosocial Theory
  Chicago School of Sociology
  Critical Theory
  Evolutionary Theories
  Figuration Sociology
  Formalism
  Formalization (Theoretical)
  Frankfurt School
  Gemeinschaft And Gesellschaft
  Marxist Analysis
  Marxist Sociology
  Metasociology
  Methodological Individualism
  Middle Range Theories
  Paradigms
  Positivism
  Psychoanalytic Interpretation
  Realism (Philosophy)
  Social Theories
  Sociology
  Structuralism
  Symbolic Interactionism
  Systems Theory
  Teleology
  Theory Practice Relationship
  Verstehen
  Voluntarism

Sociologists
- DC D809700
- HN Formerly (1963-1985) DC 434880, Sociologist/Sociologists.
- BT Social Scientists
- RT Researchers
  Sociology

Sociologizing/Sociologism (1963-1985)
- HN DC 434980, deleted 1986.

Sociology
- DC D810000
- SN Scientific study of society and its elements, which emerged as a discipline in the nineteenth century through the works of August Comte, Emile Durkheim, Max Weber, and Karl Marx.
- HN Formerly (1963-1985) DC 435000.

Sociology

Sociology (cont'd)
- BT Social Sciences
- NT Applied Sociology
  - Bourgeois Sociology
  - Comparative Sociology
  - Criminology
  - Demography
  - Environmental Sociology
  - Figuration Sociology
  - Humanistic Sociology
  - Industrial Sociology
  - Interpretive Sociology
  - Macrosociology
  - Marxist Sociology
  - Mathematical Sociology
  - Medical Sociology
  - Microsociology
  - Military Sociology
  - Organizational Sociology
  - Political Sociology
  - Radical Sociology
  - Regional Sociology
  - Rural Sociology
  - Sociology of Art
  - Sociology of Education
  - Sociology of Knowledge
  - Sociology of Law
  - Sociology of Leisure
  - Sociology of Literature
  - Sociology of Religion
  - Sociology of Science
  - Sociology of Sports
  - Sociology of Work
  - Urban Sociology
  - Visual Sociology
- RT Behavioral Sciences
  - Chicago School of Sociology
  - Ethnomethodology
  - History of Sociology
  - Human Ecology
  - Metasociology
  - Social History
  - Social Psychology
  - Social Theories
  - Society
  - Sociobiology
  - Sociography
  - Sociolinguistics
  - Sociological Associations
  - Sociological Research
  - Sociological Theory
  - Sociologists
  - Sociology Education

Sociology Education
- DC D810300
- HN Added, 1986.
- UF Teaching Sociology (1985)
- BT Social Science Education
- RT College Majors
  - Doctoral Programs
  - Social Work Education
  - Sociology
  - Undergraduate Programs

Sociology of Art
- DC D810600
- HN Added, 1986.
- BT Sociology
- RT Aesthetics
  - Art
  - Art History
  - Artistic Styles
  - Romanticism
  - Sociology of Literature

Sociology of Education
- DC D810900
- HN Formerly (1985) DC 435100.
- BT Sociology
- RT Education
  - Educational Ideologies
  - Educational Research
  - Educational Systems

Sociology of Knowledge
- DC D811200
- SN Study of the relationship between systems of thought (eg, scientific, religious, philosophical, aesthetic, political, or legal) and social and cultural factors.
- HN Formerly (1985) DC 435200.
- BT Sociology
- RT Concepts
  - Epistemological Doctrines
  - Epistemology
  - Formalization (Theoretical)
  - Historicism
  - Ideologies
  - Intellectual History
  - Interpretive Sociology
  - Knowledge
  - Phenomenology
  - Relativism
  - Scientific Knowledge
  - Sociology of Science

Sociology of Law
- DC D811500
- HN Added, 1986.
- UF Legal Sociology
- BT Sociology
- RT Adversary Legal System
  - Criminology
  - Jurisprudence
  - Law
  - Legal Profession
  - Legal System
  - Political Sociology

Sociology of Leisure
- DC D811800
- HN Added, 1986.
- BT Sociology
- RT Leisure
  - Recreation
  - Sociology of Sports

Sociology of Literature
- DC D812100
- HN Added, 1986.
- BT Sociology
- RT Aesthetics
  - Literary Criticism
  - Literature
  - Sociology of Art

Sociology of Medicine
- Use Medical Sociology

Sociology of Occupations
- Use Sociology of Work

Sociology of Organizations
- Use Organizational Sociology

Sociology of Religion
- DC D812400
- HN Added, 1986.
- BT Sociology
- RT Religions
  - Religious Beliefs
  - Religious Cultural Groups

Sociology of Science
- DC D812700
- HN Added, 1986.
- BT Sociology
- RT Adoption of Innovations
  - Appropriate Technologies
  - Mathematics
  - Revolutions
  - Science
  - Science And Technology
  - Scientific Community
  - Scientific Knowledge
  - Scientific Technological Revolution
  - Sociology of Knowledge

Sociology of Sports
- DC D813000
- HN Added, 1986.
- BT Sociology
- RT Sociology of Leisure
  - Sports

Sociology of Work
- DC D813300
- HN Added, 1986.
- UF Sociology of Occupations
  - Work Sociology
- BT Sociology
- RT Industrial Sociology
  - Occupations
  - Organizational Sociology
  - Work

Sociometric Analysis
- DC D813400
- SN The quantitative study of small-group social relations, using methods that assess personal preference, rejection, or indifference of group members with respect to each other.
- HN Formerly (1963-1985) DC 437000, Sociometry/Sociometric.
- UF Sociogram/Sociograms (1972-1985)
  - Sociometry
- BT Quantitative Methods
- RT Graph Theory
  - Group Dynamics
  - Group Research
  - Network Analysis
  - Small Groups
  - Social Distance
  - Social Networks

Sociometry
- Use Sociometric Analysis

Sociopathic Personality
- DC D813600
- SN Personality characterized by aggressive, impulsive, sometimes violent behavior, through failure to internalize social and ethical standards, such as those concerning personal and property rights.
- HN Formerly (1972-1985) DC 437060, Sociopath/Sociopathy/Sociopathic.
- UF Antisocial Personality
  - Psychopathic Personality
- BT Personality
- RT Crime
  - Deviant Behavior
  - Disorders
  - Emotionally Disturbed
  - Juvenile Delinquency

Socioprofessional

Socioprofessional Orientations
  Use Professional Orientations

Socrates/Socratic (1966-1985)
  HN DC 437280.
  Use Ancient Greek Philosophy

Sodomy
  DC D813900
  HN Formerly (1971-1985) DC 437400, Sodomy/Sodomist/Sodomists.
  BT Sexual Deviation
  RT Homosexuality
     Sexual Intercourse

Sofia, Bulgaria
  DC D814000
  HN Added, 1989.
  BT Bulgaria

Software (Computers)
  Use Computer Software

Soil Conservation
  DC D814200
  HN Formerly (1963-1985) DC 437500.
  UF Erosion (1965-1985)
  BT Conservation
  RT Agricultural Policy
     Agricultural Technology
     Agriculture
     Ecology
     Human Ecology
     Irrigation
     Land
     Land Use
     Natural Resources

Solar Energy
  DC D814500
  HN Formerly (1983-1985) DC 437590, Solar.
  BT Energy
  RT Appropriate Technologies
     Electricity
     Energy Conservation
     Energy Policy
     Radiation

Soldier/Soldiers (1963-1985)
  HN DC 437600.
  Use Military Personnel

Solicitor General (1969-1985)
  HN DC 437666, deleted 1986.

Solidarity (1963-1985)
  HN DC 437700, deleted 1986. See now Social Cohesion or Solidarity Movements.

Solidarity Movements
  DC D814800
  HN Added, 1986.
  UF Movements (Solidarity)
     Polish Solidarity Movement
  RT Collective Action
     Feminism
     Labor Movements
     Social Cohesion
     Worker Consciousness

Solidarity (Social)
  Use Social Cohesion

Solomon Islands
  DC D815100
  HN Formerly (1972-1985) DC 437725.
  BT Melanesia

Somali/Somaliland (1963-1985)
  HN DC 437750.
  Use Djibouti

Somalia
  DC D815400
  HN Formerly (1982-1985) DC 437751, Somalia/Somalian.
  BT Sub Saharan Africa

Somatic (1969-1985)
  HN DC 437760, deleted 1986. See now Illness, Neurosis, or Human Body.

Song/Songs (1964-1985)
  HN DC 437858.
  Use Music

Sons
  DC D815700
  HN Formerly (1964-1985) DC 437850, Son/Sons.
  BT Males
  RT Child Sex Preferences
     Children
     Daughters
     Parent Child Relations
     Siblings

Sorcery (1963-1985)
  HN DC 437885.
  Use Witchcraft

Sorel, Georges
  DC D816000
  SN Born 2 November 1847 - died 28 August 1922.
  HN Formerly (1968-1985) DC 437900, Sorel, G.

Sorokin, Pitirim Alexandrovitch
  DC D816300
  SN Born 21 January 1889 - died 10 February 1968.
  HN Formerly (1963-1985) DC 437910, Sorokin, P. A.

Sorority/Sororities (1970-1985)
  HN DC 437917.
  Use Fraternities And Sororities

Soul
  DC D816600
  HN Formerly (1964-1985) DC 437930.
  RT Animism
     Death
     Death Attitudes
     Death Rituals
     Dualism
     Ghosts
     Mind
     Religious Beliefs
     Salvation
     Spirit Possession
     Spirits

Sound Image Recordings
  Use Recordings

Sound/Sounds (1965-1985)
  HN DC 437950, deleted 1986. See now Speech, Noise, or Recordings.

Source/Sources (1963-1985)
  HN DC 438275, deleted 1986.

South

Sources of Information
  Use Information Sources

South Africa
  DC D816900
  HN Formerly (1963-1985) DC 438353.
  UF Republic of South Africa
     Union of South Africa/Republic of South Africa (1963-1985)
  BT Sub Saharan Africa
  NT Cape Town, South Africa
     Johannesburg, South Africa
     Pretoria, South Africa

South America
  DC D817200
  HN Formerly (1963-1985) DC 438355.
  BT Latin America
  NT Argentina
     Bolivia
     Brazil
     Chile
     Colombia
     Ecuador
     French Guiana
     Guyana
     Paraguay
     Peru
     Surinam
     Uruguay
     Venezuela
  RT Amazon
     Andes
     Falkland Islands

South American Cultural Groups
  Use Latin American Cultural Groups

South American Indian Languages
  Use Amerindian Languages

South Asia
  DC D817500
  HN Added, 1986. Prior to 1986 use Asia (DC 039500) or specific countries or regions.
  BT Asia
  NT Bangladesh
     Bhutan
     Himalayan States
     India
     Nepal
     Pakistan
     Sri Lanka
  RT Southeast Asia

South Asian Cultural Groups
  DC D817600
  SN Cultural groups of the Indian subcontinent.
  HN Added, 1989.
  BT Asian Cultural Groups
  RT Southeast Asian Cultural Groups

South Atlantic Ocean
  DC D817800
  HN Added, 1986. Prior to 1986 use Atlantic (DC 043565).
  BT Atlantic Ocean
  RT Falkland Islands
     North Atlantic Ocean

South Carolina
  DC D818100
  HN Formerly (1968-1985) DC 438365.
  BT Southern States
     United States of America
  RT Appalachia

South Dakota
- **DC** D818400
- **HN** Formerly (1968-1985) DC 438370.
- **BT** Midwestern States
  United States of America

South Korea
- **DC** D818700
- **HN** Formerly (1984-1985) DC 438372, South Korea/South Koreans. Prior to 1984 use Korea/Korean/Koreans (DC 248200).
- **BT** Far East
- **NT** Seoul, South Korea

South Pacific Ocean
- **DC** D819000
- **HN** Formerly (1963-1985) DC 438375, South Pacific.
- **BT** Pacific Ocean
- **RT** North Pacific Ocean

South Vietnam
- **Use** Vietnam

South West Africa
- **Use** Namibia

Southeast Asia
- **DC** D819300
- **HN** Formerly (1984-1985) DC 438380.
- **BT** Asia
- **NT** Burma
  Indonesia
  Kampuchea
  Laos
  Malaysia
  Papua New Guinea
  Philippines
  Singapore
  Thailand
  Vietnam
- **RT** Indochina
  South Asia

Southeast Asian Cultural Groups
- **DC** D819400
- **HN** Added, 1989.
- **BT** Asian Cultural Groups
- **RT** South Asian Cultural Groups

Southern African Cultural Groups
- **DC** D819500
- **HN** Added, 1989.
- **BT** African Cultural Groups
- **RT** North African Cultural Groups

Southern Baptist Church
- **Use** Baptists

Southern Christian Leadership Conference/SCLC (1969-1985)
- **HN** DC 438385.
- **Use** Civil Rights Organizations

Southern Rhodesia
- **Use** Zimbabwe

Southern States
- **DC** D819900
- **HN** Formerly (1963-1985) part of DC 438350, South/Southern.
- **BT** States (Political Subdivisions)
- **NT** Alabama
  Arkansas
  Florida
  Georgia
  Kentucky
  Louisiana

Southern States (cont'd)
- **NT** Mississippi
  North Carolina
  South Carolina
  Tennessee
  Virginia
  West Virginia
- **RT** North And South
  United States of America

Sovereignty
- **DC** D820500
- **HN** Formerly (1965-1985) DC 438400, Sovereign/Sovereignty.
- **RT** Authority
  Autonomy
  Political Power
  Self Determination
  State

Soviet American Relations
- **DC** D820600
- **HN** Added, 1989.
- **BT** International Relations
- **RT** Cold War
  East and West
  Foreign Policy
  Peaceful Coexistence
  Union of Soviet Socialist Republics
  United States of America

Soviet Union
- **Use** Union of Soviet Socialist Republics

Soviet Union Cultural Groups
- **DC** D820700
- **HN** Added, 1989.
- **UF** Russian Cultural Groups
- **BT** Cultural Groups
- **RT** Asian Cultural Groups
  European Cultural Groups

Soviet/Soviets (1963-1985)
- **HN** DC 438425.
- **Use** Union of Soviet Socialist Republics

Space
- **DC** D820800
- **HN** Formerly (1963-1985) DC 438500, Space/Spatial/Spatio.
- **NT** Extraterrestrial Space
  Personal Space
  Social Space
- **RT** Boundaries
  Crowding
  Environment
  Population Density
  Space And Time
  Spatial Analysis
  Spatial Behavior

Space And Time
- **DC** D821100
- **HN** Added, 1986.
- **UF** Time And Space
- **RT** Concepts
  Space
  Time

Space Exploration
- **Use** Space Technology

Space Technology
- **DC** D821400
- **HN** Added, 1986.
- **UF** Astronautics
  Space Exploration
  Spacecraft
- **BT** Technology
- **RT** Armaments
  Astronomy

Space Technology (cont'd)
- **RT** Engineering
  Extraterrestrial Space
  Physical Sciences
  Physics
  Scientific Research
  Unidentified Flying Objects

Spacecraft
- **Use** Space Technology

Spain
- **DC** D821700
- **HN** Formerly (1963-1985) DC 439150, Spain/Spanish.
- **BT** Mediterranean Countries
  Western Europe
- **NT** Basque Provinces
  Barcelona, Spain
  Catalonia, Spain
  Madrid, Spain

Spanish Americans
- **Use** Hispanic Americans

Spanish (Language)
- **Use** Romance Languages

Spatial Analysis
- **DC** D822000
- **HN** Added, 1986.
- **UF** Spatial Distribution
  Spatial Organization
- **BT** Analysis
- **RT** Cognitive Mapping
  Distribution
  Geographic Distribution
  Space

Spatial Behavior
- **DC** D822300
- **HN** Added, 1986.
- **BT** Behavior
- **RT** Interaction
  Personal Space
  Physical Contact
  Social Contact
  Space

Spatial Distribution
- **Use** Spatial Analysis

Spatial Organization
- **Use** Spatial Analysis

Speaking (1970-1985)
- **HN** DC 439300, deleted 1986. See now Speech or Ethnolinguistic Groups.

Speaking in Tongues
- **Use** Glossolalia

Special Education
- **DC** D822600
- **HN** Added, 1986.
- **BT** Education
- **RT** Gifted
  Handicapped

Special Interest Groups
- **Use** Interest Groups

Specialists
- **DC** D822900
- **HN** Formerly (1963-1985) DC 439400, Specialist/Specialists.
- **NT** Advisors
  Consultants
  Experts
- **RT** Occupations
  Professional Workers
  Specialization

Specialization

Specialization
- DC D823200
- HN Formerly (1963-1985) DC 439500.
- NT Division of Labor
- RT Complex Societies
  Differences
  Differentiation
  Occupations
  Social Processes
  Social Segmentation
  Specialists
  Work

Species (1966-1985)
- HN DC 439800, deleted 1986.

Specificity
- DC D823300
- HN Formerly (1969-1985) DC 439810, Specificity/Specification/Specifications.
- RT Generalization

Spectator Violence
- Use Sports Violence

Spectators
- DC D823500
- HN Formerly (1972-1985) DC 439870, Spectator/Spectators.
- BT Groups
- RT Audiences
  Sports Participation
  Sports Violence

Speculation/Speculations (1971-1985)
- HN DC 439875, deleted 1986.

Speech
- DC D823800
- HN Formerly (1963-1985) DC 440000, Speech/Speeches.
- UF Intonation (1964-1985)
  Voice (1971-1985)
- RT Discourse
  Language
  Language Acquisition
  Language Disorders
  Language Usage
  Linguistics
  Morphology (Language)
  Phonetics
  Pragmatics
  Rhetoric
  Verbal Accounts
  Verbal Communication

Speed/Speeding (1965-1985)
- HN DC 443000, deleted 1986.

Spencer, Herbert
- DC D824100
- SN Born 27 April 1820 - died 8 December 1903.
- HN Formerly (1963-1985) DC 443020.

Spending
- Use Expenditures

Spinoza, Baruch
- DC D824400
- SN Born 24 November 1632 - died 20 February 1677.
- HN Formerly (1970-1985) DC 443100, Spinoza, B.

Spinster/Spinsters/Spinsterhood (1976-1985)
- HN DC 443110.
- Use Single Persons

Spirit Possession
- DC D824700
- SN Psychic event during which a person acts as though another personality has entered his or her body and has taken control.
- HN Formerly (1963-1985) part of DC 340522, Possession/Possessions.
- UF Demonic Possession
- RT Demons
  Devils
  Evil
  Soul
  Spirits
  Voodooism
  Witchcraft

Spirits
- DC D825000
- HN Formerly (1963-1985) DC 443150, Spirit/Spirits/Spiritism.
- NT Demons
  Ghosts
- RT Ancestor Worship
  Animism
  Devils
  Ghost Dances
  Soul
  Spirit Possession
  Spiritualism
  Supernatural

Spiritual (1966-1985)
- HN DC 443190, deleted 1986. See now specific "Church" or "Religion" terms.

Spiritualism
- DC D825300
- HN Formerly (1963-1985) DC 443200, Spiritualist/Spiritualists/Spiritualism.
- BT Philosophical Doctrines
- RT Divination
  Ghosts
  Occultism
  Parapsychology
  Spirits
  Supernatural
  Superstitions

Spiro, Melford Elliot
- DC D825600
- SN Born 26 April 1920 - .
- HN Formerly (1967-1985) DC 443220, Spiro, M. E.

Split Labor Market Theory
- Use Labor Market Segmentation

Sponsorship
- DC D825800
- HN Formerly (1969-1985) DC 443290, Sponsor/Sponsorship.
- BT Support
- RT Assistance
  Financial Support
  Grants
  Immigration
  Patronage

Spontaneity
- DC D825825
- HN Formerly (1972-1985) DC 443340, Spontaneous/Spontaneity.
- BT Behavior
- RT Collective Behavior
  Compulsivity
  Flexibility
  Impulsiveness
  Instinct

Spontaneous Abortion
- Use Miscarriage

Sports
- DC D825900
- HN Formerly (1964-1985) DC 443450, Sport/Sporting/Sports.
- UF Athletics
  Running/Jogging (1983-1985)
  Sportsmanship (1965-1985)
- BT Activities
- NT College Sports
  Professional Sports
- RT Amateurs
  Athletes
  Games
  Leisure
  Olympic Games
  Physical Contact
  Sociology of Sports
  Sports Participation
  Sports Teams
  Sports Violence

Sports Participation
- DC D826200
- HN Added, 1986.
- BT Participation
- RT Spectators
  Sports

Sports Teams
- DC D826500
- HN Added, 1986.
- UF Athletic Teams
- BT Teams
- RT Clubs
  Sports

Sports Violence
- DC D826800
- SN Violence among athletes and by spectators during sports events.
- HN Added, 1986.
- UF Spectator Violence
- BT Violence
- RT Mass Media Violence
  Professional Sports
  Spectators
  Sports

Sportsmanship (1965-1985)
- HN DC 443525.
- Use Sports

Spouse Abuse
- DC D827100
- SN Physical or mental abuse of a marital partner.
- HN Added, 1986.
- UF Wife Abuse (1985)
- BT Abuse
  Family Violence
- RT Battered Women
  Child Abuse
  Elder Abuse
  Husbands
  Marriage
  Wives

Spouses

Spouses
- **DC** D827400
- **HN** Formerly (1964-1985) DC 443575, Spouse/Spousal.
- **UF** Marriage Partners
  Married Couples
- **NT** Husbands
  Wives
- **RT** Couples
  Marital Relations
  Marriage
  Mate Selection
  Parents
  Significant Others

Spying
  Use Espionage

Squatters
- **DC** D827700
- **HN** Formerly (1984-1985) DC 443656, Squatters/Squatting.
- **RT** Homelessness
  Housing
  Land Settlement

Sri Lanka
- **DC** D828000
- **HN** Formerly (1975-1985) DC 443657.
- **UF** Ceylon/Ceylonese (1963-1985)
- **BT** South Asia

Srole, Leo
- **DC** D828300
- **SN** Born 8 October 1908 - .
- **HN** Formerly (1972-1985) DC 443660.

St. Augustine (1967-1985)
- **HN** DC 399525.
- **Use** Saints

St. Louis, Missouri
- **DC** D828600
- **HN** Formerly (1964-1985) DC 399535, St. Louis, Mo.
- **BT** Missouri

St. Thomas Aquinas (1964-1985)
- **HN** DC 399559.
- **Use** Saints

Stability
- **DC** D828700
- **HN** Formerly (1963-1985) DC 443675, Stable/Stability/Stabilization.
- **UF** Continuity/Continuities/Continuous (1963-1985)
  Discontinuous/Discontinuance/Discontinuity (1964-1985)
  Fluctuation/Fluctuations (1964-1985)
  Instability (1963-1985)
- **NT** Family Stability
- **RT** Change
  Control
  Cooptation
  Permanency Planning
  Relations
  Security
  Social Equilibrium
  Uniformity

Staff/Staffing (1963-1985)
- **HN** DC 443800, deleted 1986. See now Personnel Management, Occupations, or Workers.

Stage/Stages (1963-1985)
- **HN** DC 443838.
- **Use** Developmental Stages

Stages of Development
  Use Developmental Stages

Stalinism
- **DC** D828750
- **HN** Formerly (1963-1985) DC 443860, Stalin, J./Stalinism.
- **BT** Marxism
- **RT** Agricultural Collectives
  Bolshevism
  Communism
  Leninism

Standard of Living
- **DC** D828900
- **HN** Formerly (1964-1985) DC 443925.
- **UF** Living Standard
- **BT** Standards
- **RT** Affluence
  Consumption
  Economic Conditions
  Economics
  Gross National Product
  Income
  Income Distribution
  Life Satisfaction
  Living Conditions
  Poverty
  Prices
  Quality of Life
  Social Indicators
  Socioeconomic Factors
  Wages

Standards
- **DC** D828950
- **HN** Formerly (1963-1985) DC 443920, Standard/Standards/Standardized/Standardization.
- **NT** Standard of Living
- **RT** Achievement
  Criteria
  Ethics
  Evaluation
  Measurement
  Norms
  Performance
  Principles
  Quality
  Tests
  Validity
  Values

Staphylococcus (1963-1985)
- **HN** DC 444140, deleted 1986.

Starvation
- **DC** D829200
- **HN** Formerly (1970-1985) DC 444190.
- **RT** Famine
  Hunger
  Malnutrition
  Suffering

State
- **DC** D829500
- **HN** Formerly (1963-1985) part of DC 444225, State/States.
- **UF** Nation State
- **NT** Welfare State
- **RT** Authority
  Autonomy
  Base And Superstructure
  Church State Relationship
  Constitutions

State (cont'd)
- **RT** Countries
  Government
  Hegemony
  Legitimacy
  Legitimation
  National Security
  Political Ideologies
  Political Philosophy
  Political Science
  Political Systems
  Politics
  Public Sector
  Revolutions
  Sovereignty
  State Formation
  State Planning
  State Power
  State Role
  State Society Relationship

State Capitalism
- **DC** D829800
- **SN** Substantial state intervention in economic activities, especially those involving key industries.
- **HN** Added, 1986.
- **BT** Capitalism
- **RT** Economic Systems

State Finance
  Use Public Finance

State Formation
- **DC** D830100
- **HN** Added, 1986.
- **BT** Formation
- **RT** Nationalism
  State

State Intervention
- **DC** D830200
- **HN** Added, 1986.
- **UF** Government Intervention
- **BT** Intervention
- **RT** Community Involvement
  Government Regulation
  Social Responsibility
  State Role

State Mental Hospitals
  Use Mental Hospitals

State Officials
  Use Public Officials

State Planning
- **DC** D830400
- **HN** Added, 1986.
- **UF** Government Planning
  State Plans
- **BT** Planning
- **RT** Economic Planning
  Local Planning
  Social Planning
  State
  State Role

State Plans
  Use State Planning

State Power
- **DC** D830700
- **HN** Added, 1986.
- **BT** Power
- **RT** Authority
  Censorship
  Compulsory Participation
  Hegemony

State

State Power (cont'd)
- RT Imperialism
- Nationalization
- Political Power
- Repression (Political)
- Social Control
- State
- State Society Relationship

State Role
- DC D831000
- HN Added, 1986.
- BT Roles
- RT State
- State Intervention
- State Planning
- State Society Relationship

State Security
- Use National Security

State Society Relationship
- DC D831300
- HN Added, 1986.
- BT Social Relations
- RT Church State Relationship
- Citizens
- Civil Society
- Corporatism
- General Public
- Government
- Government Regulation
- Military Civilian Relations
- Police Community Relations
- Public Sector Private Sector Relations
- Social Dynamics
- Society
- State
- State Power
- State Role

Statement/Statements (1972-1985)
- HN DC 444247, deleted 1986.

States (Political Subdivisions)
- DC D831600
- HN Formerly (1963-1985) part of DC 444225, State/States.
- NT Midwestern States
- Northern States
- Southern States
- Western States
- RT Borders
- Counties
- Federal Government
- Geographic Regions
- Governors
- Provinces
- Regional Movements

Statesman/Statesmen/Stateship (1963-1985)
- HN DC 444245, deleted 1986.

Statistical Analysis
- Use Quantitative Methods

Statistical Bias
- DC D831700
- HN Added, 1986.
- BT Bias
- RT Error of Measurement
- Methodology (Data Analysis)
- Quantitative Methods
- Research Design Error
- Research Responses
- Sampling
- Statistics
- Validity

Statistical Data
- Use Data

Statistical Distributions
- Use Frequency Distributions

Statistical Estimation
- Use Estimation

Statistical Inference
- DC D831775
- HN Added, 1986.
- UF Inferential Statistics
- BT Methodology (Data Analysis)
- Quantitative Methods
- RT Estimation
- Factor Analysis
- Forecasting
- Generalization
- Hypotheses
- Inference
- Multivariate Analysis
- Parameters (Statistics)
- Probability
- Statistical Significance
- Statistics
- Variance (Statistics)

Statistical Measurement
- Use Statistics

Statistical Significance
- DC D831850
- HN Formerly (1963-1985) part of DC 423800, Significance/Significant.
- UF Significance (Statistical)
- BT Methodology (Data Analysis)
- RT Chi Square Test
- Correlation
- Hypotheses
- Probability
- Quantitative Methods
- Statistical Inference
- Statistics
- Variance (Statistics)

Statistical Tables
- Use Tables

Statisticians
- DC D831900
- HN Formerly (1963-1985) DC 444398, Statistician/Statisticians.
- BT Professional Workers

Statistics
- DC D832000
- HN Formerly (1963-1985) DC 444400, Statistics/Statistical/Statistically.
- UF Statistical Measurement
- BT Mathematics
- RT Census
- Chi Square Test
- Computation
- Correlation
- Data
- Estimation
- Frequency Distributions
- Graphs
- Matrices
- Mean
- Measurement
- Median
- Methodology (Data Analysis)
- Parameters (Statistics)
- Prediction
- Probability
- Quantitative Methods
- Rates

Statutes

Statistics (cont'd)
- RT Research
- Research Methodology
- Sampling
- Statistical Bias
- Statistical Inference
- Statistical Significance
- Tables
- Trends
- Variance (Statistics)

Stature (1965-1985)
- HN DC 444700.
- Use Body Height

Status
- DC D832200
- SN A context-dependent term for hierarchical position. Select a more specific entry or coordinate with other terms. In sociological contexts where Status is closely related to Social Status, select the latter.
- HN Formerly (1963-1985) DC 444800, Status/Statuses.
- NT Marital Status
- Seniority
- Social Status
- Tenure
- RT Differences
- Hierarchy
- Ranking
- Situses
- Social Stratification
- Stratification

Status Attainment
- DC D832500
- SN Social status improvement through upward social mobility. Do not confuse with Social Status.
- HN Added, 1986.
- UF Status Level
- BT Attainment
- RT Social Mobility
- Social Status

Status Inconsistency
- DC D832800
- SN A term coined by Gerhard Emmanuel Lenski to describe the incompatibility among an individual's different statuses (eg, a highly educated person who is employed in a low-paying, non-prestigious occupation).
- HN Formerly (1967-1985) DC 227630, Inconsistency/Inconsistencies.
- UF Inconsistency (Status)
- RT Congruence (Psychology)
- Role Ambiguity
- Role Conflict
- Social Status

Status Level
- Use Status Attainment

Statutes
- DC D833100
- HN Formerly (1965-1985) DC 444900, Statute/Statutes/Statutory.
- UF Acts (Statutes)
- Civil Codes
- Laws (Statutes)
- Manpower Development & Training Act (1965-1985)
- Sherman Act (1981-1985)
- Smith Act (1964-1985)
- Taft Hartley Act (1969-1985)
- BT Legislation
- RT Constitutional Amendments

Stealing

Stealing (1964-1985)
- **HN** DC 444915.
- **Use** Larceny

Steel Industry
- **Use** Metal Industry

Steel Making
- **Use** Metallurgical Technology

Stem Family
- **DC** D833400
- **SN** A family consisting of either a nuclear family and one or more relatives, or two nuclear families of consecutive generations. Also, a family in which a son chosen by the father inherits the family estate.
- **HN** Formerly (1983-1985) DC 444970.
- **BT** Family

Stepchildren/Stepkin (1963-1985)
- **HN** DC 444990.
- **Use** Stepfamily

Stepfamily
- **DC** D833700
- **HN** Added, 1986.
- **UF** Stepchildren/Stepkin (1963-1985)
- **BT** Family
- **RT** Adopted Children
  Family Relations
  Fathers
  Foster Children
  Marriage
  Mothers
  Parent Child Relations
  Parents
  Remarriage
  Siblings

Stereotypes
- **DC** D834000
- **SN** Simplified, rigid, and often negatively biased conceptions of others based on presumed ethnic or group characteristics, applied erroneously to individual members.
- **HN** Formerly (1963-1985) DC 445000, Stereotype/Stereotypes/Stereotyped/Stereotyping.
- **BT** Types
- **NT** Sex Stereotypes
- **RT** Anti-Semitism
  Attitudes
  Discrimination
  Ethnocentrism
  Ideal Types
  Identity
  Labeling
  Prejudice
  Scapegoating
  Social Types

Sterility/Fertility (1966-1985)
- **HN** DC 445200
- **Use** Childlessness

Sterilization
- **DC** D834300
- **HN** Formerly (1963-1985) DC 445300.
- **RT** Birth Control
  Castration
  Intrauterine Devices
  Surgery
  Vasectomy

Stigma
- **DC** D834600
- **HN** Formerly (1965-1985) DC 445395, Stigma/Stigmatize/Stigmatized/Stigmatization.
- **UF** Social Stigma
- **RT** Coping
  Deviance
  Labeling
  Rejection
  Scapegoating
  Social Acceptance

Stillbirth/Stillbirths/Stillborn (1974-1985)
- **HN** DC 445396.
- **Use** Infant Mortality

Stimulation (1965-1985)
- **HN** DC 445400.
- **Use** Stimuli

Stimuli
- **DC** D834900
- **HN** Formerly (1963-1985) DC 445700, Stimulus/Stimuli.
- **UF** Stimulation (1965-1985)
- **RT** Behaviorism
  Conditioning
  Deprivation
  Responses

Stinchcombe, Arthur L.
- **DC** D835200
- **SN** Born 16 May 1933 - .
- **HN** Formerly (1969-1985) DC 445780.

Stochastic Models
- **DC** D835400
- **SN** Statistical models for the probability of the occurrence of an event over time as a function of previous occurrences. See also Markov Process.
- **HN** Formerly (1963-1985) DC 445800, Stochastic.
- **UF** Process Models (Stochastic)
- **BT** Models
- **NT** Markov Process
- **RT** Probability
  Time Series Analysis

Stock Farming
- **Use** Animal Husbandry

Stockholm, Sweden
- **DC** D835450
- **HN** Added, 1989.
- **BT** Sweden

Stoicism (1964-1985)
- **HN** DC 445900.
- **Use** Ancient Greek Philosophy

Stone Age
- **Use** Prehistory

Stores
- **DC** D835500
- **HN** Formerly (1964-1985) DC 446460, Store/Stores.
- **UF** Department Stores
  Retail Stores
  Supermarket/Supermarkets (1963-1985)
- **BT** Facilities
- **RT** Consumers
  Merchants
  Retail Industry
  Sales

Stress

Storytelling
- **DC** D835800
- **HN** Added, 1986. Formerly (1963-1985) part of DC 446500, Story/Stories.
- **RT** Narratives
  Reading

Stouffer, Samuel Andrew
- **DC** D835900
- **SN** Born 6 June 1900 - died 1960.
- **HN** Formerly (1963-1985) DC 446550, Stouffer, Samuel.

Strain/Strains (1963-1985)
- **HN** DC 446600, deleted 1986. See now Conflict or Stress.

Strangers
- **DC** D836100
- **HN** Formerly (1963-1985) DC 446610, Stranger/Strangers.
- **RT** Assimilation
  Foreigners
  Newcomers
  Social Response

Strata/Stratum (1970-1985)
- **HN** DC 446850.
- **Use** Stratification

Strategies
- **DC** D836200
- **HN** Formerly (1963-1985) DC 446700, Strategy/Strategies/Strategic.
- **BT** Methods
- **NT** Development Strategies
- **RT** Change
  Management
  Planning
  Policy Making
  Reform

Stratification
- **DC** D836300
- **HN** Formerly (1964-1985) DC 446800, Stratify/Stratified/Stratification.
- **UF** Strata/Stratum (1970-1985)
- **BT** Structure
- **NT** Social Stratification
- **RT** Classification
  Groups
  Hierarchy
  Inequality
  Status

Strauss, Anselm Leonard
- **DC** D836400
- **SN** Born 18 December 1916 - .
- **HN** Formerly (1979-1985) DC 446900, Strauss, A. L.

Street Vernacular
- **Use** Slang

Stress
- **DC** D836700
- **HN** Formerly (1963-1985) DC 447000, Stress/Stresses.
- **NT** Occupational Stress
  Psychological Stress
- **RT** Ambiguity
  Coping
  Crises
  Crowding
  Diseases
  Environment
  Health
  Life Events
  Physiology
  Pressure
  Shock
  Threat

Strikes

Strikes
- DC D837000
- HN Formerly (1963-1985) DC 447700, Strike/Strikes.
- BT Labor Disputes
- RT Boycotts
  Labor Relations
  Unions

Strippers
- DC D837300
- HN Formerly (1972-1985) DC 447750, Strip/Stripper/Strippers/Striptease.
- UF Striptease Artists
- RT Sexual Behavior

Striptease Artists
- Use Strippers

Striving (1972-1985)
- HN DC 447800.
- Use Aspiration

Structural (1963-1985)
- HN DC 448125, deleted 1986. See now Structure or Structural-Functional Analysis.

Structural Models
- DC D837425
- SN Abstract representations used to simplify and aid comprehension of structural systems.
- HN Added, 1986.
- BT Models
- RT Graphs
  Social Structure
  Structure

Structural-Functional Analysis
- DC D837400
- HN Formerly (1963-1985) DC 448135, Structural-Functional/Theory/Analysis.
- BT Analysis
- RT Conflict Theory
  Functionalism
  Social Interaction
  Social Structure
  Social Systems
  Social Theories

Structuralism
- DC D837450
- SN A method of analysis that emphasizes the unobservable, underlying frameworks of observable social phenomena.
- HN Formerly (1964-1985) DC 448140.
- UF Structuralist (1968-1985)
- BT Epistemological Doctrines
- RT Existentialism
  Linguistics
  Marxist Aesthetics
  Marxist Sociology
  Modes of Production
  Myths
  Psychology
  Realism (Philosophy)
  Semiotics
  Social Structure
  Social Systems
  Sociological Theory
  Teleology

Structuralist (1968-1985)
- HN DC 448145.
- Use Structuralism

Structuration
- DC D837475
- SN Production or reproduction of social structure by specific participants or forces in the course of social action. The concept was introduced and explicated by Anthony Giddens in 1984.
- HN Added, 1989.
- BT Social Processes
  Social Structure
- RT Action Theory
  Interpretive Sociology
  Social Action
  Social Control
  Social Reproduction
  Verstehen

Structure
- DC D837500
- SN A context-dependent term; select a more specific entry or coordinate with other terms. In sociological contexts where Structure is closely related to Social Structure, select the latter.
- HN Formerly (1963-1985) DC 448150, Structure/Structures/Structuring/Structured.
- UF Configuration/Configurations/Configurational (1963-1985)
  Formal Structure
  Informal Structure
  Organization (Structure)
- NT Community Structure
  Economic Structure
  Factor Structure
  Family Structure
  Hierarchy
  Occupational Structure
  Organizational Structure
  Power Structure
  Social Structure
  Stratification
  Work Organization
- RT Agrarian Structures
  Classification
  Design
  Morphology (Language)
  Structural Models
  Systems

Struggle/Struggles (1963-1985)
- HN DC 448190.
- Use Class Struggle

Student Achievement
- Use Academic Achievement

Student Attitudes
- DC D837600
- HN Added, 1986.
- UF Student Opinion
- BT Attitudes
- RT Student Behavior
  Student Teacher Relationship
  Students

Student Behavior
- DC D837900
- HN Added, 1986.
- BT Behavior
- RT Discipline
  Student Attitudes
  Students

Student, College (1985)
- HN DC 448300.
- Use College Students

Student Evaluation of Teachers
- Use Teacher Evaluation

Student, Graduate (1985)
- HN DC 448500.
- Use Graduate Students

Student, High School (1985)
- HN DC 448600.
- Use High School Students

Student, Medical (1985)
- HN DC 448700.
- Use Medical Students

Student Movements
- Use Youth Movements

Student Opinion
- Use Student Attitudes

Student Teacher Relationship
- DC D838200
- HN Added, 1986.
- UF Pupil Teacher Relationship
  Teacher Student Interaction
- BT Interpersonal Relations
- RT Classroom Environment
  Grades (Scholastic)
  Guidance
  Helping Behavior
  Student Attitudes
  Students
  Teacher Attitudes
  Teachers

Students
- DC D838500
- HN Formerly (1963-1985) DC 448200, Student/Students.
- UF Pupils
- NT College Students
  Elementary School Students
  High School Students
  Married Students
- RT Absenteeism
  Academic Achievement
  Academic Aptitude
  Classroom Environment
  Dropouts
  Education
  Educational Attainment
  Educational Opportunities
  Educational Plans
  Educational Research
  Enrollment
  Fellowships And Scholarships
  Graduates
  Placement
  Private Schools
  Public Schools
  Schools
  Student Attitudes
  Student Behavior
  Student Teacher Relationship
  Teacher Evaluation
  Tracking (Education)

Study/Studies (1963-1985)
- HN DC 449000, deleted 1986. See now appropriate "Curriculum" or "Research" terms.

Sturzo, Luigi
- **DC** D838800
- **SN** Born 26 November 1871 - died 8 August 1959.
- **HN** Formerly (1964-1985) DC 450000, Sturzo, Don Luigi.

Styles
- **DC** D838950
- **HN** Formerly (1963-1985) DC 450100, Style/Styles.
- **NT** Artistic Styles
  Lifestyle
  Management Styles
- **RT** Behavior

Stylistic (1968-1985)
- **HN** DC 450200, deleted 1986. See now Artistic Styles, Styles, or Linguistics.

Sub Saharan Africa
- **DC** D839100
- **HN** Formerly (1963-1985) part of DC 399515, Sahara.
- **BT** Africa
- **NT** Angola
  Benin
  Botswana
  Burkina Faso
  Burundi
  Cameroons
  Cape Verde Islands
  Central African Republic
  Chad
  Comoro Islands
  Congo
  Djibouti
  Equatorial Guinea
  Ethiopia
  Gabon
  Gambia
  Ghana
  Guinea
  Guinea Bissau
  Ivory Coast
  Kenya
  Lesotho
  Liberia
  Madagascar
  Malawi
  Mali
  Mauritania
  Mauritius
  Mozambique
  Namibia
  Niger
  Nigeria
  Reunion
  Rwanda
  Sao Tome And Principe
  Senegal
  Seychelles
  Sierra Leone
  Somalia
  South Africa
  Swaziland
  Tanzania
  Togo
  Uganda
  Zaire
  Zambia
  Zimbabwe
- **RT** North Africa

Subcaste (1984-1985)
- **HN** DC 450400.
- **Use** Caste Systems

Subcultures
- **DC** D839400
- **SN** Social enclaves within the larger culture with distinctly different beliefs, values, and behaviors.
- **HN** Formerly (1963-1985) DC 450450, Subculture/Subcultures.
- **BT** Cultural Groups
- **NT** Countercultures
- **RT** Acculturation
  Assimilation
  Cleavage
  Crosscultural Analysis
  Cultural Identity
  Cultural Pluralism
  Cultural Values
  Ethnic Groups
  Ethnic Relations
  Intercultural Communication
  Prison Culture
  Religious Brotherhoods
  Religious Cultural Groups
  Slang
  Social Integration
  Social Segmentation

Subject/Subjects (1963-1985)
- **HN** DC 450535, deleted 1986. See now Research Subjects or Curriculum and its associated terms.

Subjectivity
- **DC** D839550
- **SN** Refers to personal, individual experience. Subjectivity often infers bias and lack of scientific validity, but if many individuals share the same subjective experience it becomes culturally objective reality.
- **HN** Formerly (1963-1985) DC 450538, Subjective/Subjectivity/Subjectivist/Subjectivism.
- **RT** Bias
  Cultural Relativism
  Experience
  Individuals
  Objectivity
  Personality
  Reflexivity

Subliminal (1965-1985)
- **HN** DC 450560, deleted 1986.

Submission/Submissive (1972-1985)
- **HN** DC 450565.
- **Use** Subordination

Subnormality (1965-1985)
- **HN** DC 450570.
- **Use** Mentally Retarded

Subordination
- **DC** D839700
- **HN** Formerly (1964-1985) DC 450585, Subordinate/Subordinates/Subordination.
- **UF** Deference (1963-1985)
  Inferiority (1964-1985)
  Submission/Submissive (1972-1985)
- **RT** Dependency (Psychology)
  Dominance
  Passiveness
  Social Inequality
  Social Status
  Superior Subordinate Relationship

Subsidies
- **DC** D840000
- **HN** Formerly (1969-1985) DC 450595, Subsidy/Subsidies.
- **BT** Financial Support
- **NT** Food Stamps
- **RT** Government Spending
  Grants
  Loans
  Payments

Subsistence Economy
- **DC** D840300
- **HN** Formerly (1964-1985) DC 450600, Subsistence.
- **RT** Agricultural Economics
  Economic Structure
  Economic Systems
  Economic Underdevelopment
  Economics
  Traditional Societies

Substance Abuse
- **DC** D840600
- **HN** Formerly (1984-1985) DC 450616.
- **BT** Abuse
- **NT** Alcohol Abuse
  Drug Abuse
- **RT** Drinking Behavior
  Drugs
  Eating Disorders

Substantivist-Formalist Debate (1970-1985)
- **HN** DC 450620, deleted 1986.

Suburban Areas
- **Use** Suburbs

Suburbanization
- **DC** D840900
- **HN** Formerly (1963-1985) DC 450675.
- **BT** Social Processes
- **RT** Suburbs
  Urban to Rural Migration
  Urbanization

Suburbs
- **DC** D841200
- **HN** Formerly (1963-1985) DC 450630, Suburb/Suburbs/Suburban/Suburbanism.
- **UF** Suburban Areas
- **BT** Communities
- **RT** Annexation
  Central Cities
  Cities
  Community Structure
  Commuting (Travel)
  Geographic Regions
  Metropolitan Areas
  New Towns
  Suburbanization
  Urban Areas
  Urban Fringe
  Urban to Rural Migration
  Zoning

Success
- **DC** D841500
- **HN** Formerly (1963-1985) DC 450700, Success/Successes.
- **BT** Performance
- **RT** Achievement
  Aspiration
  Effectiveness
  Evaluation
  Failure
  Goals

Succession / Support

Success (cont'd)
- RT Motivation
- Organizational Effectiveness
- Prestige
- Quality

Succession (1963-1985)
- HN DC 450710.
- Use Inheritance And Succession

Sudan
- DC D841800
- HN Formerly (1963-1985) DC 450850.
- BT Arab Countries
- North Africa

Sudanic Languages
- Use African Languages

Suez Canal (1963-1985)
- HN DC 450895, deleted 1986.

Suffering
- DC D842100
- HN Formerly (1969-1985) DC 450896, Suffer/Suffering.
- RT Emotions
- Grief
- Pain
- Psychological Distress
- Starvation

Suffrage (1964-1985)
- HN DC 450900.
- Use Voting Rights

Sugar (1963-1985)
- HN DC 451900.
- Use Food

Suggestions (1963-1985)
- HN DC 452200, deleted 1986.

Suicidal Behavior
- Use Suicide

Suicide
- DC D842400
- HN Formerly (1963-1985) DC 452500, Suicide/Suicides/Suicidal.
- UF Suicidal Behavior
- NT Jonestown Mass Suicide
- Self Destructive Behavior
- RT Death
- Fatalities
- Mortality Rates

Suicide Attempts
- Use Self Destructive Behavior

Sumatra, Indonesia (1963-1985)
- HN DC 452575.
- Use Indonesia

Summit Meeting/Summit Meetings (1966-1985)
- HN DC 452590, deleted 1986.

Sumner, William Graham
- DC D842700
- SN Born 30 October 1840 - died 12 April 1910.
- HN Formerly (1964-1985) DC 452600, Sumner, W. G.

Sun (1969-1985)
- HN DC 452610, deleted 1986. See now Solar Energy, Weather, or appropriate "Environment" terms.

Superego
- HN DC 452700.
- Use Conscience

Supererogation (1964-1985)
- HN DC 452720, deleted 1986.

Superheroes
- Use Heroes

Superintendents
- DC D843000
- HN Formerly (1964-1985) DC 452740.
- UF School Superintendents
- BT Administrators
- RT Educational Administration
- Public Officials
- School Districts

Superior Subordinate Relationship
- DC D843300
- HN Formerly (1972-1985) DC 452750, Superior/Superiors/Superiority.
- UF Superordinate Subordinate Relationship
- BT Interpersonal Relations
- RT Dominance
- Leadership
- Management Styles
- Managers
- Obedience
- Organizational Structure
- Paternalism
- Patronage
- Personnel Management
- Subordination
- Supervision
- Work Environment

Superiority
- Use Dominance

Supermarket/Supermarkets (1963-1985)
- HN DC 452772.
- Use Stores

Supernatural
- DC D843600
- HN Formerly (1963-1985) DC 452780, Supernatural/Supernaturalism.
- RT Divination
- Evil Eye
- Fetishism
- Ghost Dances
- Ghosts
- Hallucinations
- Magic
- Mana
- Occultism
- Parapsychology
- Shamanism
- Spirits
- Spiritualism
- Superstitions
- Voodooism
- Witchcraft

Superordinate Subordinate Relationship
- Use Superior Subordinate Relationship

Superstitions
- DC D843900
- HN Formerly (1964-1985) DC 452950, Superstition/Superstitions.
- BT Beliefs
- NT Evil Eye
- RT Divination
- Folk Culture

Superstitions (cont'd)
- RT Ghosts
- Magic
- Religious Beliefs
- Spiritualism
- Supernatural
- Taboos

Superstructure/Superstructures (1972-1985)
- HN DC 452960.
- Use Base And Superstructure

Supervision
- DC D844200
- HN Formerly (1963-1985) DC 453000.
- RT Coordination
- Job Performance
- Management
- Management Styles
- Personnel Management
- Superior Subordinate Relationship
- Work Organization
- Workers

Supervisor/Supervisors/Supervisory (1963-1985)
- HN DC 453050.
- Use Managers

Supervisory Styles
- Use Management Styles

Supply (1964-1985)
- HN DC 453058.
- Use Supply And Demand

Supply And Demand
- DC D844500
- HN Added, 1986.
- UF Demand/Demands (1963-1985)
- Supply (1964-1985)
- RT Economic Factors
- Economic Theories
- Economics
- Exchange (Economics)
- Inflation
- Labor Supply
- Market Economy
- Markets
- Prices
- Production Consumption Relationship
- Trade

Supply of Labor
- Use Labor Supply

Support
- DC D844800
- HN Formerly (1963-1985) DC 453065, Support/Supports/Supported/Supporting/Supportive.
- NT Financial Support
- Public Support
- Social Support
- Sponsorship
- RT Assistance
- Employee Assistance Programs
- Services
- Social Behavior
- Support Groups
- Support Networks

Support Groups
- Use Self Help Groups

Support Networks
- **DC** D845100
- **SN** The pattern formed by a person's sources of social support, often dispersed geographically.
- **HN** Added, 1986.
- **RT** Self Help Groups
  Support
  Support Groups

Support Systems
- **Use** Social Support

Supposition (1964-1985)
- **HN** DC 453068.
- **Use** Postulates

Suppression (1969-1985)
- **HN** DC 453070.
- **Use** Repression (Political)

Supreme Court (1963-1985)
- **HN** DC 453090.
- **Use** United States Supreme Court

Surgery
- **DC** D845400
- **HN** Formerly (1963-1985) DC 453100.
- **UF** Appendectomy (1967-1985)
- **BT** Treatment
- **NT** Abortion
  Castration
  Circumcision
  Genital Mutilation
  Organ Transplantation
  Vasectomy
- **RT** Health Care
  Medical Decision Making
  Medicine
  Sterilization

Surinam
- **DC** D845700
- **HN** Formerly (1968-1985) DC 453111.
- **BT** South America

Surnames
- **Use** Naming Practices

Surplus Labor
- **Use** Labor Supply

Surplus Value
- **Use** Labor Theory of Value

Surplus/Surpluses (1964-1985)
- **HN** DC 453125, deleted 1986.

Surrender (1963-1985)
- **HN** DC 453145, deleted 1986.

Surrogate Parents
- **DC** D845725
- **HN** Formerly (1985) DC 453170, Surrogate.
- **BT** Parents
- **RT** Artificial Insemination
  Childlessness
  Foster Care
  Parenthood

Surveillance (1972-1985)
- **HN** DC 453190, deleted 1986.

Survey Research (1985)
- **HN** DC 453300.
- **Use** Surveys

Survey Responses
- **Use** Research Responses

Surveys
- **DC** D845750
- **HN** Formerly (1963-1985) DC 453200, Survey/Surveys.
- **UF** Survey Research (1985)
- **BT** Methodology (Data Collection)
- **NT** Mail Surveys
  Opinion Polls
  Telephone Surveys
- **RT** Attitude Measures
  Data Collection
  Fieldwork
  Interviews
  Market Research
  Measures (Instruments)
  Public Opinion Research
  Questionnaires
  Research
  Research Design
  Research Methodology
  Research Responses
  Respondents
  Sampling
  Social Science Research

Survival
- **DC** D845800
- **HN** Formerly (1964-1985) DC 453320.
- **UF** Survivor/Survivors/Survivorship (1970-1985)
- **RT** Accidents
  Child Mortality
  Civil Defense
  Death
  Disaster Relief
  Disasters
  Environmental Protection
  Genocide
  Hazards
  Health Policy
  Holocaust
  Infant Mortality
  Longevity
  National Security
  Natural Disasters
  Overpopulation
  Preservation
  Widowhood

Survivor/Survivors/Survivorship (1970-1985)
- **HN** DC 453325.
- **Use** Survival

Suspicion (1966-1985)
- **HN** DC 453330.
- **Use** Trust

Sustenance Organization
- **DC** D845900
- **HN** Formerly (1964-1985) DC 453332, Sustenance.
- **BT** Economic Structure
- **RT** Demographic Change
  Economic Sectors
  Human Ecology
  Production
  Socioeconomic Factors

Sutherland, Edwin Hardin
- **DC** D846000
- **SN** Born 1883 - died 1950.
- **HN** Formerly (1963-1985) DC 453333, Sutherland, E. H.

Swahili
- **DC** D846300
- **HN** Formerly (1983-1985) DC 453334a.
- **BT** African Languages

Swaziland
- **DC** D846600
- **HN** Formerly (1978-1985) DC 453334b.
- **BT** Sub Saharan Africa

Sweden
- **DC** D846900
- **HN** Formerly (1963-1985) DC 453335, Sweden/Swedish.
- **BT** Scandinavia
  Western Europe
- **NT** Stockholm, Sweden

Swedish (Language)
- **Use** Germanic Languages

Sweetheart (1977-1985)
- **HN** DC 453355, deleted 1986.

Swing/Swinger/Swingers/Swinging (1970-1985)
- **HN** DC 453370.
- **Use** Extramarital Sexuality

Switching (Language)
- **Use** Code Switching

Switzerland
- **DC** D847200
- **HN** Formerly (1963-1985) DC 453375, Switzerland/Swiss.
- **BT** Western Europe
- **NT** Geneva, Switzerland

Sydney, Australia
- **DC** D847300
- **HN** Added, 1989.
- **BT** Australia

Symbiotic Relations
- **DC** D847400
- **HN** Formerly (1964-1985) DC 453385, Symbiosis.
- **BT** Relations
- **RT** Attachment
  Cybernetics
  Interaction
  Interpersonal Relations
  Psychodynamics
  Reciprocity
  Technology
  Worker Machine Relationship

Symbolic Interactionism
- **DC** D847500
- **SN** Based on the social philosophy of George Herbert Mead, a sociological perspective that explains the role of linguistic interaction in developing a social identity and functioning according to shared norms and values.
- **HN** Formerly (1984-1985) DC 453450, Symbolic Interaction/Symbolic Interactionism/Symbolic Interactionist.
- **BT** Interactionism
- **RT** Action
  Action Theory
  Chicago School of Sociology
  Communicative Action
  Dramaturgical Approach
  Ethnomethodology
  Idealism
  Labeling
  Negotiation

Symbolic Interactionism (cont'd)
- **RT** Nonverbal Communication
  Phenomenology
  Pragmatism
  Social Interaction
  Social Psychology
  Sociological Theory

Symbolic Logic
- **Use** Logic

Symbolism
- **DC** D847800
- **HN** Formerly (1963-1985) DC 453400, Symbol/Symbols/Symbology/Symbolism/Symbolization.
- **RT** Art
  Collective Representation
  Images
  Language
  Literature
  Meaning
  Metaphors
  Rituals
  Scapegoating
  Semiotics
  Signs
  Social Determination of Meaning

Sympathy/Sympathetic (1964-1985)
- **HN** DC 453670.
- **Use** Compassion

Symposia
- **DC** D848100
- **HN** Formerly (1963-1985) DC 453700, Symposium/Symposiums/Symposia.
- **UF** Colloquium/Colloquia (1969-1985)
  Symposiums
- **RT** Congresses And Conventions
  Institutes
  Meetings
  Seminars
  Workshops (Courses)

Symposiums
- **Use** Symposia

Symptoms
- **DC** D848400
- **HN** Formerly (1963-1985) DC 453800, Symptom/Symptoms/Symptomatic/Symptomatology.
- **NT** Fatigue
  Pain
- **RT** Illness
  Physical Characteristics
  Shock

Synagogues
- **DC** D848700
- **HN** Formerly (1965-1985) DC 453840, Synagogue/Synagogues.
- **BT** Places of Worship
- **RT** Jews
  Judaism

Synchronic/Synchronism (1971-1985)
- **HN** DC 453850, deleted 1986.

Syncretism
- **DC** D849000
- **SN** The union of distinct or conflicting elements drawn from different philosophical, religious, or cultural systems into a new whole or system.
- **HN** Formerly (1964-1985) DC 453855.
- **BT** Religious Beliefs
- **RT** Cults
  Manicheism

Syncretism (cont'd)
- **RT** Paganism
  Religions
  Religious Conversion
  Religious Rituals
  Taoism

Syndicalism
- **DC** D849300
- **SN** Anarchistic movement, originating in France and lasting through the first half of the twentieth century, advocating abolition of the capitalist order by the working class through strikes and violence.
- **HN** Formerly (1964-1985) DC 453860, Syndicalism/Syndicalist.
- **BT** Political Ideologies
- **RT** Anarchism
  Class Politics
  Corporatism
  Labor Movements
  Socialism
  Unions

Syndicates/Syndicated (1964-1985)
- **HN** DC 453865, deleted 1986.

Syndrome/Syndromes (1978-1985)
- **HN** DC 453865a, deleted 1986.

Synergy (1964-1985)
- **HN** DC 453866.
- **Use** Cooperation

Syntax (1978-1985)
- **HN** DC 453866b.
- **Use** Grammar

Synthesis
- **DC** D849450
- **HN** Formerly (1964-1985) DC 453867.
- **RT** Cognition
  Dialectics
  Generalization
  Knowledge
  Principles

Synthetic (1970-1985)
- **HN** DC 453868, deleted 1986.

Syphilis
- **Use** Venereal Diseases

Syracuse, N.Y. (1964-1985)
- **HN** DC 453870, deleted 1986.

Syria
- **DC** D849600
- **HN** Formerly (1964-1985) DC 453885, Syria/Syrian/Syrians.
- **BT** Arab Countries
  Mediterranean Countries
  Middle East
- **NT** Damascus, Syria

Systematic/Systematics (1964-1985)
- **HN** DC 453930, deleted 1986. See now Systems Theory or Systems.

Systematize/Systematization/Systematizes (1971-1985)
- **HN** DC 453932, deleted 1986.

Systemic (1964-1985)
- **HN** DC 453935, deleted 1986.

Systems
- **DC** D849650
- **SN** A context-dependent term; select a more specific entry or coordinate with other terms. In sociological contexts where Systems is closely related to Social Systems, select the latter.
- **HN** Formerly (1963-1985) DC 453900, System/Systems.
- **NT** Delivery Systems
  Economic Systems
  Educational Systems
  Legal System
  Political Systems
  Sensory Systems
  Social Systems
- **RT** Computers
  Philosophical Doctrines
  Structure
  Systems Theory

Systems Theory
- **DC** D849700
- **SN** An intellectual orientation to many scientific disciplines that stresses the analysis of the organization of interconnected parts of an entity, rather than the study of its separate units.
- **HN** Formerly (1963-1985) DC 192400, General Systems Theory.
- **UF** General Systems Theory
- **BT** Social Theories
- **RT** Communicative Action
  Entropy
  Functionalism
  Holism
  Social Equilibrium
  Social Systems
  Sociological Theory
  Systems
  Teleology
  Voluntarism

Szasz, Thomas Stephen
- **DC** D849900
- **SN** Born 15 April 1920 - .
- **HN** Formerly (1969-1985) DC 453937, Szasz, T.

Szczepanski, Jan
- **DC** D849950
- **SN** Born 14 September 1913 - .
- **HN** Formerly (1969-1985) DC 453939, Szczepanski, J.

T Groups
- **Use** Sensitivity Training

Tables
- **DC** D850050
- **HN** Formerly (1963-1985) DC 453940, Table/Tables.
- **UF** Statistical Tables
  Tabular Data
- **NT** Life Tables
- **RT** Contingency Analysis
  Data
  Frequency Distributions
  Graphs
  Matrices
  Statistics

Tables (Life)
- **Use** Life Tables

Taboos
- **DC** D850200
- **HN** Formerly (1963-1985) DC 453960, Taboo/Taboos.

Taboos (cont'd)
- **UF** Tabus
- **BT** Norms
- **RT** Cannibalism
  Customs
  Incest
  Intermarriage
  Sanctions
  Sexual Behavior
  Sins
  Social Control
  Superstitions
  Traditions
  Words

Tabular Data
- **Use** Tables

Tabulation/Tabulations (1964-1985)
- **HN** DC 453990, deleted 1986.

Tabus
- **Use** Taboos

Tactics (1963-1985)
- **HN** DC 454080, deleted 1986.

Taft Hartley Act (1969-1985)
- **HN** DC 454140.
- **Use** Statutes

Tahiti
- **DC** D850500
- **HN** Formerly (1964-1985) DC 454155, Tahiti/Tahitian/Tahitians.
- **BT** Society Islands

Taipei, Taiwan
- **DC** D850800
- **HN** Formerly (1969-1985) DC 454171.
- **BT** Taiwan

Taiwan
- **DC** D851100
- **HN** Formerly (1963-1985) DC 454178.
- **UF** Formosa/Formosan/Formosans (1965-1985)
- **BT** Far East
- **NT** Taipei, Taiwan

Takeovers (Corporate)
- **Use** Mergers

Talent (1963-1985)
- **HN** DC 454200.
- **Use** Ability

Talmud
- **Use** Rabbinical Literature

Tamil (1964-1985)
- **HN** DC 454245, deleted 1986. See now Dravidian Languages or Asian Cultural Groups.

Tamil (Language)
- **Use** Dravidian Languages

Tanganyika/Tanganyikan/Tanganyikans (1963-1985)
- **HN** DC 454255.
- **Use** Tanzania

Tanzania
- **DC** D851400
- **HN** Formerly (1968-1985) DC 454290, Tanzania/Tanzanian/Tanzanians.
- **UF** Tanganyika/Tanganyikan/Tanganyikans (1963-1985)
- **BT** Sub Saharan Africa

Tao
- **Use** Taoism

Taoism
- **DC** D851700
- **HN** Formerly (1963-1985) DC 454295, Tao/Taoism/Taoist.
- **UF** Tao
- **BT** Religions
- **RT** Syncretism

Tape Recordings
- **Use** Recordings

Tarde, Gabriel
- **DC** D852000
- **SN** Born 12 March 1834 - died 13 May 1904.
- **HN** Formerly (1973-1985) DC 454450.

Tariff/Tariffs (1963-1985)
- **HN** DC 454475.
- **Use** Exports And Imports

Task Organization
- **Use** Work Organization

Task Oriented Groups
- **DC** D852300
- **HN** Formerly (1963-1985) DC 454550, Task-Oriented Group Situation.
- **BT** Groups
- **RT** Teamwork

Task Performance
- **DC** D852600
- **HN** Added, 1986.
- **BT** Performance
- **RT** Job Performance
  Tasks

Tasks
- **DC** D852900
- **SN** Specific pieces or components of work, usually comprising part of a larger work function or role.
- **HN** Formerly (1963-1985) DC 454500, Task/Tasks.
- **UF** Work Tasks
- **BT** Activities
- **RT** Division of Labor
  Job Characteristics
  Occupational Roles
  Occupational Structure
  Task Performance
  Work
  Work Organization

Tasmania
- **DC** D853200
- **HN** Formerly (1969-1985) DC 454560, Tasmania, Australia/Tasmanian/Tasmanians.
- **BT** Australia

Tasmanian Languages
- **Use** Austronesian Languages

Taste (1965-1985)
- **HN** DC 454600.
- **Use** Preferences

Taste (Sense)
- **Use** Sensory Systems

Tattoo/Tattoos/Tattooing (1964-1985)
- **HN** DC 454740, deleted 1986.

Tau (1964-1985)
- **HN** DC 454750, deleted 1986.

Tavern/Taverns (1966-1985)
- **HN** DC 454760.
- **Use** Eating And Drinking Establishments

Tavistock Institute of Human Relations (1963-1985)
- **HN** DC 454770, deleted 1986.

Taxation
- **DC** D853500
- **HN** Formerly (1963-1985) DC 454790, Tax/Taxes/Taxation.
- **UF** Taxes
- **RT** Finance
  Fiscal Policy
  Government
  Income
  Public Finance

Taxes
- **Use** Taxation

Taxonomy/Taxonomies/Taxonomic/Taxonomical (1963-1985)
- **HN** DC 454855.
- **Use** Classification

Taylor, N.W./Taylorism (1969-1985)
- **HN** DC 454900.
- **Use** Scientific Management

Teacher Attitudes
- **DC** D853800
- **HN** Added, 1986.
- **UF** Instructor Attitudes
- **BT** Attitudes
- **RT** Student Teacher Relationship
  Teachers

Teacher Education
- **DC** D853850
- **HN** Added, 1989.
- **BT** Education
- **RT** Graduate Schools
  Teachers
  Teaching

Teacher Evaluation
- **DC** D853900
- **HN** Added, 1986.
- **UF** Faculty Evaluation
  Student Evaluation of Teachers
- **BT** Evaluation
- **RT** Students
  Teachers
  Teaching

Teacher Student Interaction
- **Use** Student Teacher Relationship

Teachers
- **DC** D854100
- **HN** Formerly (1963-1985) DC 455200, Teacher/Teachers.
- **UF** Instructors
- **BT** Professional Workers
- **NT** College Faculty
- **RT** Academic Tenure
  Classroom Environment
  Education
  Principals
  Schools
  Secondary Schools
  Student Teacher Relationship
  Teacher Attitudes
  Teacher Education
  Teacher Evaluation
  Teaching

Teaching

Teaching
- DC D854400
- HN Formerly (1963-1985) DC 455300.
- UF Instruction
  Pedagogy/Pedagogic/Pedagogical (1964-1985)
- NT Computer Assisted Instruction
- RT Curriculum
  Education
  Explanation
  Learning
  Reading
  Schools
  Teacher Education
  Teacher Evaluation
  Teachers
  Teaching Methods

Teaching Aids
- Use Teaching Methods

Teaching Freedom
- Use Academic Freedom

Teaching Machines (1964-1985)
- HN DC 455350.
- Use Computer Assisted Instruction

Teaching Methods
- DC D854700
- HN Added, 1986.
- UF Instructional Methods
  Teaching Aids
  Teaching Techniques
- BT Methods
- RT Computer Assisted Instruction
  Learning
  Teaching

Teaching Sociology (1985)
- HN DC 455450.
- Use Sociology Education

Teaching Techniques
- Use Teaching Methods

Teams
- DC D855000
- HN Formerly (1963-1985) DC 456760, Team/Teams.
- BT Groups
- NT Sports Teams
- RT Teamwork

Teamsters (1981-1985)
- HN DC 456780.
- Use Unions

Teamwork
- DC D855300
- HN Formerly (1963-1985) DC 456800.
- BT Work
- RT Cooperation
  Group Decision Making
  Interdisciplinary Approach
  Peer Relations
  Social Behavior
  Task Oriented Groups
  Teams

Technical Assistance
- DC D855600
- HN Formerly (1963-1985) part of DC 456812, Technical.
- UF Peace Corps (1964-1985)
- BT Assistance
- RT Appropriate Technologies
  Developing Countries
  Economic Development

Technical Assistance (cont'd)
- RT Human Resources
  International Cooperation
  International Relations
  Technological Progress
  Technology
  Technology Transfer

Technical Progress
- Use Technological Progress

Technicians
- DC D855900
- HN Formerly (1963-1985) DC 456813, Technician/Technicians.
- BT Paraprofessional Workers

Technique/Techniques (1963-1985)
- HN DC 456815.
- Use Methods

Technocracy
- DC D856200
- SN Government by an elite social class of technical experts or according to structural constraints placed on the political process by technology.
- HN Formerly (1963-1985) DC 456850, Technocracy/Technocratic.
- BT Political Systems
- RT Meritocracy
  Oligarchy

Technological Change
- DC D856500
- HN Added, 1986.
- UF Technological Development
- BT Change
- NT Technological Progress
- RT Agricultural Mechanization
  Cultural Change
  Dislocated Workers
  Economic Change
  Government Policy
  High Technology Industries
  Industrial Automation
  Industrialization
  Information
  Inventions
  Modernization
  Obsolescence
  Scientific Discoveries
  Scientific Technological Revolution
  Social Change
  Technological Innovations
  Technology
  Technology Assessment
  Technology Transfer

Technological Development
- Use Technological Change

Technological Innovations
- DC D856800
- HN Added, 1986.
- BT Innovations
- RT Adoption of Innovations
  High Technology Industries
  Industrial Development
  Inventions
  Patents
  Research And Development
  Science And Technology
  Scientific Discoveries
  Technological Change
  Technological Progress
  Technology

Technology

Technological Obsolescence
- Use Obsolescence

Technological Progress
- DC D857100
- HN Added, 1986.
- UF Technical Progress
- BT Progress
  Technological Change
- RT Adoption of Innovations
  Appropriate Technologies
  Cybernetics
  Economic Development
  Economic History
  Forces And Relations of Production
  Futures (of Society)
  Inventions
  Obsolescence
  Quality of Life
  Science And Technology
  Scientific Development
  Scientific Discoveries
  Scientific Technological Revolution
  Technical Assistance
  Technological Innovations
  Technology
  Technology Assessment

Technological Scientific Revolution
- Use Scientific Technological Revolution

Technology
- DC D857400
- HN Formerly (1963-1985) DC 456860, Technology/Technological/Technologically.
- UF Applied Sciences
  Hydraulic (1977-1985)
- BT Science And Technology
- NT Agricultural Technology
  Appropriate Technologies
  Automation
  Biotechnology
  Cybernetics
  Electronic Technology
  Engineering
  Information Technology
  Medical Technology
  Metallurgical Technology
  Space Technology
- RT Culture
  Economics
  High Technology Industries
  Industry
  Inventions
  Labor Process
  Research Applications
  Resources
  Science
  Scientific Knowledge
  Scientific Research
  Scientific Technological Revolution
  Symbiotic Relations
  Technical Assistance
  Technological Change
  Technological Innovations
  Technological Progress
  Technology Assessment
  Technology Transfer
  Telecommunications
  Tools
  Western Society

Technology And Science
- Use Science And Technology

252

Technology … Tennessee

Technology Assessment
- **DC** D857700
- **HN** Formerly (1979-1985) DC 456870.
- **UF** Assessment of Technology
  Societal Assessment of Technology
- **BT** Evaluation
- **RT** Appropriate Technologies
  Engineering
  Ethics
  Scientific Research
  Social Impact Assessment
  Social Values
  Technological Change
  Technological Progress
  Technology
  Technology Transfer

Technology Transfer
- **DC** D858000
- **SN** Export of technological innovations from their place of origin to other countries, especially to foster social development.
- **HN** Added, 1986.
- **RT** Adoption of Innovations
  Appropriate Technologies
  Automation
  Diffusion
  Economic Development
  Economic Policy
  High Technology Industries
  Industrialization
  Information Dissemination
  Innovations
  International Cooperation
  Inventions
  Modernization
  Patents
  Research Applications
  Scientific Community
  Scientific Knowledge
  Technical Assistance
  Technological Change
  Technology
  Technology Assessment

Teen Magazines
- **Use** Magazines

Teenage/Teenagers (1963-1985)
- **HN** DC 456900.
- **Use** Adolescents

Teheran, Iran
- **DC** D858300
- **HN** Formerly (1968-1985) DC 456915.
- **BT** Iran

Teilhard de Chardin, Pierre
- **DC** D858600
- **SN** Born 1 May 1881 - died 10 April 1955.
- **HN** Formerly (1983-1985) DC 456918, Teilard de Chardin, Pierre.

Tel Aviv, Israel
- **DC** D858800
- **HN** Added, 1989.
- **BT** Israel

Telanthropus (1969-1985)
- **HN** DC 456929.
- **Use** Prehistoric Man

Telecommunications
- **DC** D858900
- **HN** Added, 1986.
- **UF** Broadcast Communications
  Communications Systems
  Communications Technology
  Electronic Communications
  Telegraph/Telegraphic (1967-1985)
- **NT** Radio
  Telephone Communications
  Television
- **RT** Audiovisual Media
  Communication
  Communication Research
  Communications Technology
  Computers
  Electronic Technology
  Information Technology
  Information Theory
  Mass Media
  Publicity
  Technology

Telegraph/Telegraphic (1967-1985)
- **HN** DC 456940.
- **Use** Telecommunications

Telegu (Language)
- **Use** Dravidian Languages

Teleology
- **DC** D859100
- **SN** Belief that phenomena evolve according to fixed inherent processes, purposefully toward preordained end-states.
- **HN** Formerly (1964-1985) DC 456955, Teleology/Teleological.
- **BT** Philosophical Doctrines
- **RT** Epistemology
  Functionalism
  Metaphysics
  Social Theories
  Sociological Theory
  Structuralism
  Systems Theory

Telephone Communications
- **DC** D859200
- **HN** Formerly (1964-1985) DC 456970, Telephone/Telephones.
- **BT** Telecommunications
- **RT** Conversation
  Counseling
  Interpersonal Communication
  Telephone Surveys

Telephone Surveys
- **DC** D859300
- **HN** Added, 1986.
- **BT** Surveys
- **RT** Computer Assisted Research
  Interviews
  Telephone Communications

Televangelism
- **Use** Evangelism

Television
- **DC** D859500
- **HN** Formerly (1963-1985) DC 457000, Television/Televised.
- **UF** Broadcast Television
  Cable Television
  TV
- **BT** Mass Media
  Telecommunications
- **RT** Actors
  Cartoons
  Electronic Technology
  Fictional Characters
  Journalism
  Mass Media Effects

Television (cont'd)
- **RT** Mass Media Violence
  News Media
  Popular Culture
  Programming (Broadcast)
  Radio
  Television Viewing
  Videotape Recordings

Television Coverage
- **Use** News Coverage

Television Industry
- **Use** Entertainment Industry

Television Programming
- **Use** Programming (Broadcast)

Television Viewing
- **DC** D859800
- **HN** Added, 1986.
- **BT** Activities
- **RT** Audiences
  Leisure
  Mass Media Effects
  Programming (Broadcast)
  Television

Television Violence
- **Use** Mass Media Violence

Temperament (1968-1985)
- **HN** DC 457700.
- **Use** Personality

Temperance Movements
- **DC** D860100
- **HN** Formerly (1966-1985) DC 458000, Temperance.
- **BT** Movements
- **RT** Alcohol Use
  Alcoholism
  Drunkenness

Temple/Temples (1970-1985)
- **HN** DC 458200.
- **Use** Places of Worship

Temporal/Temporality (1966-1985)
- **HN** DC 458300.
- **Use** Time

Tenancy (1964-1985)
- **HN** DC 459000.
- **Use** Land Tenure

Tenants
- **DC** D860400
- **HN** Formerly (1966-1985) DC 459050.
- **UF** Renters
- **RT** Housing
  Landlord Tenant Relations
  Landlords
  Public Housing
  Rental Housing
  Rents

Tendency/Tendencies (1963-1985)
- **HN** DC 459600.
- **Use** Trends

Tennessee
- **DC** D860700
- **HN** Formerly (1963-1985) DC 459750.
- **BT** Southern States
  United States of America
- **RT** Appalachia

Tension

Tension
- DC D861000
- HN Formerly (1963-1985) DC 460000, Tension/Tensions.
- RT Anxiety
  Crises
  Emotions
  Hostility
  Intergroup Relations
  Interpersonal Relations
  Psychological Stress
  Social Conflict
  Social Unrest
  Threat

Tenure
- DC D861300
- HN Formerly (1963-1985) DC 460150.
- BT Status
- NT Academic Tenure
  Land Tenure
- RT Employment
  Housing
  Property
  Workers

Tenure (Academic)
- Use Academic Tenure

Tenure (Land)
- Use Land Tenure

Terminal Care (1981-1985)
- HN DC 460260, deleted 1986. See now Hospices or Terminal Illness.

Terminal Care Facilities
- Use Hospices

Terminal Illness
- DC D861600
- HN Formerly (1981-1985) DC 460270.
- BT Illness
- RT Cancer
  Death
  Dying
  Euthanasia
  Hospices

Termination (Employees)
- Use Dismissal

Termination of Treatment
- DC D861700
- HN Added, 1986.
- RT Discharge
  Health Care Utilization
  Treatment
  Treatment Compliance

Terminology
- DC D861900
- HN Formerly (1963-1985) DC 460300, Terminology/Terminological.
- UF Nomenclature (1964-1985)
- BT Words
- NT Kinship Terminology
- RT Definitions
  Language
  Vocabularies

Terrain
- Use Topography

Territorial Annexation
- Use Annexation

Territorial Boundaries
- Use Borders

Territoriality
- DC D862200
- HN Formerly (1963-1985) DC 460450, Territory/Territories/Territorial/Territoriality.
- BT Behavior
- RT Borders
  Boundaries
  Personal Space
  Social Behavior

Territories (Geographic)
- Use Geographic Regions

Terrorism
- DC D862500
- HN Formerly (1963-1985) DC 460600, Terror/Terrorism.
- BT Political Violence
- RT Assassination
  Bombs
  Guerrillas
  Hostages
  Mau Mau Rebellion
  Nihilism
  Torture
  World Problems

Test Bias
- DC D862700
- HN Added, 1986.
- UF Cultural Test Bias
- BT Bias
- RT Ethnic Groups
  Tests
  Validity

Test Items
- Use Items (Measures)

Testimony
- DC D862800
- HN Formerly (1965-1985) DC 461485.
- BT Evidence (Legal)
- RT Expert Witnesses
  Lie Detection
  Trials
  Verbal Accounts
  Witnesses

Testing (1963-1985)
- HN DC 461450.
- Use Tests

Tests
- DC D862900
- HN Formerly (1963-1985) DC 461000, Test/Tests.
- UF Examination/Examinations (1966-1985)
  Testing (1963-1985)
- BT Measures (Instruments)
- NT Achievement Tests
  Intelligence Tests
- RT Evaluation
  Items (Measures)
  Measurement
  Scores
  Standards
  Test Bias

Texas
- DC D863100
- HN Formerly (1964-1985) DC 461965.
- BT United States of America
  Western States
- NT Dallas, Texas
  Houston, Texas

Theoretical

Text/Texts (1963-1985)
- HN DC 461985, deleted 1986. See now Textbooks or Content Analysis.

Textbooks
- DC D863400
- HN Formerly (1964-1985) DC 462000, Textbook/Textbooks.
- UF Readers (Texts)
  School Books
- RT Readability
  Readership
  Reading

Textile Industry
- DC D863700
- HN Formerly (1963-1985) DC 462790, Textile/Textiles.
- UF Cloth Manufacturing
- BT Manufacturing Industries
- RT Garment Industry

Thai Languages
- Use Oriental Languages

Thailand
- DC D864000
- HN Formerly (1963-1985) DC 464030, Thai/Thais/Thailand.
- UF Siam/Siamese (1964-1985)
- BT Southeast Asia
- NT Bangkok, Thailand

Thaumaturgical (1964-1985)
- HN DC 464032, deleted 1986.

Theater Arts
- DC D864300
- HN Formerly (1963-1985) DC 464035, Theater/Theatrical.
- UF Acting (Dramatic)
  Opera/Operatic (1973-1985)
  Performing Arts
- BT Fine Arts
- NT Drama
- RT Actors
  Art
  Audiences
  Dance
  Films

Theft (Larceny)
- Use Larceny

Theme/Themes/Thematic (1963-1985)
- HN DC 464040, deleted 1986.

Theology
- DC D864400
- HN Formerly (1963-1985) DC 464080, Theology/Theological/Theologian/Theologians.
- BT Philosophy
- RT Ethics
  God (Judeo-Christian)
  Metaphysics
  Religions
  Religious Beliefs
  Religious Doctrines
  Religious Literature

Theoretical (1963-1985)
- HN DC 464120, deleted 1986. See now Theories and its associated terms.

Theoretical

Theoretical Issues
- **Use** Theoretical Problems

Theoretical Problems
- **DC** D864425
- **SN** Use limited to discussion and debate emphasizing the theoretical ramifications of new ideas or findings.
- **HN** Added, 1986.
- **UF** Conceptual Issues
  Theoretical Issues
- **BT** Problems
- **RT** Methodological Problems
  Research Design
  Social Science Research
  Theories
  Theory Formation
  Theory Practice Relationship

Theories
- **DC** D864450
- **HN** Formerly (1963-1985) DC 464200, Theory/Theories/Theorem/Theorizing.
- **NT** Biosocial Theory
  Demographic Transition Theory
  Economic Theories
  Evolutionary Theories
  Graph Theory
  Information Theory
  Organization Theory
  Social Theories
  Sociological Theory
- **RT** Concepts
  Formalization (Theoretical)
  Game Theory
  Generalization
  Ideal Types
  Ideologies
  Knowledge
  Methodology (Philosophical)
  Models
  Phenomena
  Postulates
  Principles
  Propositions
  Research
  Science
  Theoretical Problems
  Theory Formation
  Theory Practice Relationship
  Verification

Theories of the Middle Range
- **Use** Middle Range Theories

Theorist/Theorists/Theoretician (1964-1985)
- **HN** DC 464135, deleted 1986. See now appropriate "Theory" terms.

Theory Development
- **Use** Theory Formation

Theory Formation
- **DC** D864475
- **HN** Added, 1986.
- **UF** Theory Development
- **BT** Formation
  Methodology (Philosophical)
- **NT** Formalization (Theoretical)
- **RT** Cognition
  Concept Formation
  Discovery
  Generalization
  Heuristics
  Phenomena
  Research Methodology
  Revolutions
  Theoretical Problems
  Theories
  Theory Practice Relationship

Theory of Action
- **Use** Action Theory

Theory Practice Relationship
- **DC** D864500
- **HN** Added, 1986.
- **UF** Application of Theories
  Practice Theory Relationship
  Theory Praxis Relationship
- **BT** Relations
- **RT** Methods
  Praxis
  Research Applications
  Social Sciences
  Sociological Theory
  Theoretical Problems
  Theories
  Theory Formation

Theory Praxis Relationship
- **Use** Theory Practice Relationship

Theory (Psychoanalytic)
- **Use** Psychoanalytic Interpretation

Therapeutic Methods
- **Use** Treatment Methods

Therapist Client Relationship
- **Use** Client Relations

Therapists
- **DC** D864600
- **HN** Formerly (1963-1985) DC 464280, Therapist/Therapists.
- **UF** Psychotherapist/Psychotherapists (1966-1985)
- **BT** Professional Workers
- **RT** Client Relations
  Health Professions
  Psychiatrists
  Psychologists
  Treatment

Therapy/Therapeutic (1963-1985)
- **HN** DC 464300.
- **Use** Treatment

Thermonuclear Energy
- **Use** Nuclear Energy

Thesis/Theses (1966-1985)
- **HN** DC 464390, deleted 1986.

Things
- **Use** Inanimate Objects

Thinking
- **DC** D864900
- **HN** Formerly (1963-1985) DC 464400.
- **UF** Thought (1963-1985)
- **BT** Cognition
- **NT** Reasoning
- **RT** Concepts
  Imagination
  Mind

Third World (1969-1985)
- **HN** DC 464472.
- **Use** Developing Countries

Thomas, William Isaac
- **DC** D865200
- **SN** Born 1863 - died 1947.
- **HN** Formerly (1963-1985) DC 464520, Thomas, W. I.

Time

Thought (1963-1985)
- **HN** DC 464560.
- **Use** Thinking

Thought Control
- **Use** Brainwashing

Threat
- **DC** D865500
- **HN** Formerly (1963-1985) DC 464600, Threat/Threats.
- **UF** Danger (1966-1985)
- **RT** Abuse
  Aggression
  Anxiety
  Conflict
  Crises
  Hazards
  Hostility
  Risk
  Security
  Stress
  Tension
  Vulnerability

Threshold/Thresholds (1963-1985)
- **HN** DC 464605, deleted 1986.

Thrift
- **Use** Saving

Tibet
- **DC** D865800
- **SN** A province of the Peoples Republic of China.
- **HN** Formerly (1963-1985) DC 464700, Tibet/Tibetan/Tibetans.
- **BT** Peoples Republic of China

Tillich, Paul Johannes
- **DC** D866100
- **SN** Born 20 August 1886 - died 22 October 1965.
- **HN** Formerly (1964-1985) DC 464950, Tillich, Paul.

Tilly, Charles
- **DC** D866200
- **SN** Born 27 May 1929 - .
- **HN** Added, 1989.

Time
- **DC** D866400
- **HN** Formerly (1963-1985) DC 465000.
- **UF** Duration
  Temporal/Temporality (1966-1985)
- **NT** Time Periods
- **RT** Age
  Calendars
  Chronologies
  Cyclical Processes
  Evolution
  Future Orientations
  Futures (of Society)
  Limitations
  Obsolescence
  Space And Time
  Time Utilization
  Trends
  Work Leisure Relationship
  Working Hours

Time And Space
- **Use** Space And Time

Time Periods
- **DC** D866700
- **HN** Formerly (1963-1985) Period/Periods/Periodicity.
- **UF** Century/Centuries (1963-1985)

Time

Time Periods (cont'd)
- UF Periods (Time)
- BT Time
- NT Antiquity
  Eighteenth Century
  Enlightenment
  Middle Ages
  Nineteenth Century
  Prehistory
  Renaissance
  Seventeenth Century
  Sixteenth Century
  Twentieth Century
  Victorian Period
- RT Chronologies
  History
  Modernity

Time Series Analysis
- DC D866850
- SN Method involving the use of a statistical series ordered sequentially in time, for example, a learning curve or hospital admission rates. Often applied to methods of forecasting.
- HN Added, 1986. Prior to 1986 use Time (DC 465000) and Series (DC 417590).
- UF Series (Time)
- BT Analysis
- RT Econometric Analysis
  Forecasting
  Panel Data
  Regression Analysis
  Seasonal Variations
  Stochastic Models
  Trends

Time Utilization
- DC D867000
- SN Allocation, expenditure, or management of work or leisure time by individuals or groups.
- HN Added, 1986.
- UF Management of Time
- BT Utilization
- RT Efficiency
  Leisure
  Management
  Productivity
  Time

Timing (1963-1985)
- HN DC 465600, deleted 1986. See now First Birth Timing or Marriage Timing.

Tip/Tipping (1963-1985)
- HN DC 465650.
- Use Compensation

Tithing
- DC D867300
- SN Practice of donating a part of one's property or income, traditionally one tenth, to the church.
- HN Formerly (1972-1986) DC 465713, Tithe/Tithes/Tithing.
- BT Religious Rituals
- RT Churches
  Financial Support

Tito, J./Titoism (1965-1985)
- HN DC 465720, deleted 1986. See now Yugoslavia or Marxism.

Tobacco (1975-1985)
- HN DC 465750.
- Use Smoking

Tobago/Tobagonian/Tobagonians (1964-1985)
- HN DC 465755.
- Use Trinidad And Tobago

de Tocqueville, Alexis Charles Henri Maurice Clerel
- DC D867600
- SN Born 29 July 1805 - died 16 April 1859.
- HN Formerly (1967-1985) DC 131155, De Tocqueville, Alexis.

Togetherness (1964-1985)
- HN DC 465785, deleted 1986.

Togo
- DC D867900
- HN Formerly (1964-1985) DC 465795, Togo/Togolese.
- BT Sub Saharan Africa

Toilet (1966-1985)
- HN DC 465800, deleted 1986.

Tokelau Islands
- DC D868200
- HN Added, 1986.
- BT Polynesia

Tokenism
- DC D868500
- HN Formerly (1983-1985) DC 465765, Token/Tokenism.
- BT Desegregation
- RT Affirmative Action
  Equality

Tokyo, Japan
- DC D868800
- HN Formerly (1963-1985) DC 465850.
- BT Japan

Tolerance
- DC D869100
- HN Formerly (1963-1985) DC 465900, Tolerance/Tolerant/Toleration.
- BT Attitudes
- RT Ethics
  Personality Traits
  Political Attitudes
  Prejudice
  Religious Attitudes
  Religious Beliefs
  Social Attitudes
  Social Distance
  Social Policy
  Values

Tonga
- DC D869400
- HN Formerly (1965-1985) DC 465975, Tonga/Tongaland.
- BT Polynesia

Tonnies, Ferdinand
- DC D869700
- SN Born 26 July 1855 - died 11 March 1936.
- HN Formerly (1966-1985) DC 466000, Tonnies, F.

Totemism

Tools
- DC D870000
- HN Formerly (1964-1985) DC 466300, Tool/Tools.
- RT Artifacts
  Labor Process
  Machinery
  Material Culture
  Materials
  Resources
  Technology
  Weapons

Topography
- DC D870300
- SN Science or practice of graphically representing the natural and man-made features of an area to show their relative positions and elevations.
- HN Formerly (1963-1985) DC 466400, Topography/Topographical/Topographology.
- UF Landforms
  Terrain
- BT Social Sciences
- RT Demography
  Earth (Planet)
  Geography
  Islands
  Mountain Regions
  Oceans

Tornado (1978-1985)
- HN DC 466550.
- Use Natural Disasters

Toronto, Ontario
- DC D870600
- HN Formerly (1963-1985) DC 466552.
- BT Ontario

Torture
- DC D870900
- HN Formerly (1982-1985) DC 466628.
- NT Brainwashing
- RT Abuse
  Coercion
  Human Rights
  Political Violence
  Punishment
  Terrorism

Tory/Tories/Toryism (1963-1985)
- HN DC 466640.
- Use Conservatism

Total/Totality (1972-1985)
- HN DC 466695, deleted 1986.

Totalitarianism
- DC D871200
- HN Formerly (1963-1985) DC 466700, Totalitarian/Totalitarianism.
- BT Political Ideologies
- RT Authoritarianism (Political Ideology)
  Communism
  Dictatorship
  Fascism
  Maoism
  Oppression

Totemism
- DC D871500
- HN Formerly (1963-1985) DC 466875, Totem/Totemism/Totemistic/Totemic.
- RT Animism
  Cannibalism

Touch / Traditions

Totemism (cont'd)
- RT Clans
-     Religions

Touch (Sense)
- Use Sensory Systems

Touching
- Use Physical Contact

Toulouse, France (1963-1985)
- HN DC 467300, deleted 1986.

Touraine, Alain
- DC D871800
- SN Born 3 August 1925 - .
- HN Formerly (1967-1985) DC 467340, Touraine, A.

Tourism
- DC D872100
- HN Formerly (1964-1985) DC 467350, Tourism/Tourist/Tourists.
- RT Hotels
-     Recreation
-     Recreational Facilities
-     Transportation
-     Travel

Towns
- DC D872400
- HN Formerly (1963-1985) DC 467400, Town/Towns.
- UF Small Town (1964-1985)
- BT Communities
- NT Boom Towns
-     New Towns
- RT Cities
-     Community Size
-     Villages

Toxic Substances
- DC D872700
- HN Formerly (1984-1985) DC 467500, Toxic/Toxin.
- UF Poisons
-     Toxins
- NT Pesticides
- RT Hazards
-     Health
-     Lead Poisoning
-     Poisoning
-     Pollution
-     Public Health
-     Wastes

Toxins
- Use Toxic Substances

Trachoma (1964-1985)
- HN DC 467608.
- Use Diseases

Tracking (Education)
- DC D872900
- SN Placement of students in more or less advanced classes or programs based on results of aptitude tests or subjective perceptions of their abilities.
- HN Formerly (1972-1985) DC 467609, Track/Tracked/Tracking.
- RT Ability
-     Academic Aptitude
-     Education Work Relationship
-     Educational Programs
-     Occupational Choice
-     Placement
-     Students
-     Vocational Education

Trade
- DC D873000
- HN Formerly (1963-1985) DC 468150.
- UF Commerce (1963-1985)
- RT Business
-     Center And Periphery
-     Commodities
-     Consumption
-     Economics
-     European Economic Community
-     Exchange (Economics)
-     Exports And Imports
-     Finance
-     International Economic Organizations
-     Market Economy
-     Marketing
-     Markets
-     Products
-     Protectionism
-     Purchasing
-     Retail Industry
-     Sales
-     Supply And Demand
-     World Economy

Trade Unions
- Use Unions

Traditional Medicine
- DC D873300
- SN Methods of healing used in traditional societies, usually having a spiritual basis and characterized by treatment of the whole person. Do not confuse with Holistic Medicine, which refers to modern methods based partly on traditional medicine.
- HN Formerly (1985) DC 468310.
- UF Folk Medicine
-     Healing (Traditional)
- BT Medicine
- RT Faith Healing
-     Folk Culture
-     Folklore
-     Medical Pluralism
-     Medical Technology
-     Plants (Botanical)
-     Shamanism

Traditional Societies
- DC D873600
- SN Coordinate with geographical descriptors to locate tribes and traditional peoples, for example research on the Asante can be retrieved using Traditional Societies and Ghana.
- HN Formerly (1963-1985) DC 434100, Society, The, of.
- UF Archaism/Archaic (1964-1985)
-     Nonindustrial Societies
-     Precapitalist Societies
-     Primitive/Primitives/Primitivism (1963-1985)
-     Society, The, of (1963-1985)
-     Tribalism (1963-1985)
- BT Society
- NT Agrarian Societies
-     Hunting And Gathering Societies
-     Nomadic Societies
-     Pastoral Societies
-     Peasant Societies
- RT Aboriginal Australians
-     African Cultural Groups
-     American Indian Reservations
-     American Indians
-     Ancestor Worship
-     Animism
-     Cargo Cults
-     Caste Systems

Traditional Societies (cont'd)
- RT Chieftaincies
-     Civilization
-     Clans
-     Common Lands
-     Cultural Change
-     Cultural Groups
-     Cultural Values
-     Culture
-     Customs
-     Drum Languages
-     Ethnic Groups
-     Ethnography
-     Ethnology
-     Folk Culture
-     Gemeinschaft And Gesellschaft
-     Gypsies
-     Indigenous Populations
-     Initiation Rites
-     Kinship
-     Mana
-     Masks
-     Material Culture
-     Modernization
-     Paganism
-     Prehistory
-     Rituals
-     Secret Societies
-     Shamanism
-     Subsistence Economy
-     Traditionalism
-     Traditions
-     Villages
-     Voodooism

Traditionalism
- DC D873900
- HN Formerly (1963-1985) part of DC 468300, Tradition/Traditions/Traditional/Traditionalism.
- BT Social Attitudes
- RT Adoption of Innovations
-     Authoritarianism (Psychology)
-     Conservatism
-     Cultural Change
-     Ethnicity
-     Judeo-Christian Tradition
-     Modernity
-     Political Attitudes
-     Postmodernism
-     Religions
-     Social Values
-     Traditional Societies
-     Traditions

Traditions
- DC D874200
- HN Formerly (1963-1985) part of DC 468300, Tradition/Traditions/Traditional/Traditionalism.
- RT Adoption of Innovations
-     Behavior
-     Common Sense
-     Cultural Values
-     Culture
-     Customs
-     Ethnography
-     Ethnology
-     Folk Culture
-     Folklore
-     Law
-     Norms
-     Rites of Passage
-     Rituals
-     Social Anthropology
-     Social Institutions
-     Taboos
-     Traditional Societies

Traffic   Treatment

Traditions (cont'd)
- RT Traditionalism

Traffic
- DC D874500
- HN Formerly (1963-1985) DC 468500.
- RT Accidents
  - Air Transportation
  - Automobiles
  - Highways
  - Public Transportation
  - Safety
  - Transportation

Tragedy (Drama)
- Use Drama

Tragedy/Tragedies/Tragedian (1966-1985)
- HN DC 468525, deleted 1986. See now Drama or Grief.

Training
- DC D874800
- HN Formerly (1963-1985) DC 469000, Training/Trainer.
- NT Job Training
  - Professional Training
  - Sensitivity Training
- RT Education
  - Educational Programs
  - Skills
  - Workshops (Courses)

Training Programs
- Use Educational Programs

Trains
- Use Railroads

Traits (Personality)
- Use Personality Traits

Tranquilizing Drugs
- DC D875100
- HN Formerly (1975-1985) DC 470700, Tranquilizers.
- UF Sedatives
- BT Drugs

Transaction/Transactions/Transactional (1964-1985)
- HN DC 470800, deleted 1986. See now Interaction or Trade.

Transcendental Meditation
- DC D875400
- SN Used for the specific religious movement and for meditation as a form of recreation or method for self-improvement.
- HN Formerly (1969-1985) DC 470860, Transcendental.
- UF Meditation (Transcendental)
- RT Behavior Modification
  - Consciousness

Transfer (1963-1985)
- HN DC 470900, deleted 1986. See now Information Dissemination, Diffusion, Technology Transfer, or Income Distribution.

Transference (Psychology)
- DC D875700
- SN Displacement of an emotion or affective attitude from one person onto another.
- HN Formerly (1964-1985) DC 471000.
- UF Countertransference

Transference (Psychology) (cont'd)
- UF Psychotherapeutic Transference
- RT Clients
  - Psychotherapy

Transform/Transformation/Transformational (1963-1985)
- HN DC 471100, deleted 1986. See now Change or Development and their associated terms.

Transgression (1974-1985)
- HN DC 471150, deleted 1986.

Transition (Life)
- Use Life Stage Transitions

Transition Theory (Demographic)
- Use Demographic Transition Theory

Transition/Transitions/Transitional (1963-1985)
- HN DC 471200, deleted 1986.

Translation
- DC D876000
- HN Formerly (1963-1985) DC 471400, Translating/Translation.
- UF Free Translation
  - Machine Translation
  - Simultaneous Translation
- RT Bilingualism
  - Communication
  - Definitions
  - Explanation
  - Languages
  - Linguistics
  - Meaning

Transmission (1963-1985)
- HN DC 471500, deleted 1986. See now Cultural Transmission, Diffusion, or Information Dissemination.

Transnational Corporation (1985)
- HN DC 471550.
- Use Multinational Corporations

Transnational Groups (1972-1985)
- HN DC 471600.
- Use Multinational Corporations

Transplant/Transplants/Transplanted (1972-1985)
- HN DC 471660.
- Use Organ Transplantation

Transportation
- DC D876300
- HN Formerly (1963-1985) DC 471700.
- NT Air Transportation
  - Public Transportation
- RT Automobiles
  - Highways
  - Industry
  - Railroads
  - Shipping Industry
  - Tourism
  - Traffic
  - Travel

Transsexualism
- DC D876600
- SN Personality orientations in which individuals perceive themselves as belonging to the opposite biological sex.
- HN Formerly (1972-1985) DC 472100, Transsexual/Transsexuals/Transsexualism.

Transsexualism (cont'd)
- UF Sex Changes
- BT Sexual Behavior
- RT Bisexuality
  - Homosexuality
  - Lesbianism
  - Sexuality
  - Transvestism

Transvestism
- DC D876900
- SN Habitual cross-dressing, usually in order to pass for a person of the opposite sex in public places, and sexual arousal from such activities. Do not confuse with Transsexualism.
- HN Formerly (1964-1985) DC 472200, Transvestite/Transvestites/Transvestism.
- BT Sexual Behavior
- RT Couvade
  - Transsexualism

Trapping
- Use Hunting

Trash
- Use Wastes

Travel
- DC D877200
- HN Formerly (1964-1985) DC 472225.
- NT Commuting (Travel)
- RT Activities
  - Geographic Mobility
  - Pilgrimages
  - Tourism
  - Transportation

Treaties
- DC D877500
- HN Formerly (1963-1985) DC 472335.
- RT American Indian Reservations
  - Foreign Policy
  - International Alliances
  - International Law
  - International Relations

Treatment
- DC D877800
- SN A context-dependent term for client/patient-oriented activities in medical and psychiatric contexts. Select a more specific entry or coordinate with other terms.
- HN Formerly (1963-1985) DC 472400.
- UF Therapy/Therapeutic (1963-1985)
- NT Conjoint Therapy
  - Detoxification
  - Faith Healing
  - Family Therapy
  - Group Therapy
  - Psychotherapy
  - Surgery
- RT Counseling
  - Crisis Intervention
  - Dental Care
  - Diagnosis
  - Health Services
  - Helping Behavior
  - Hospitalization
  - Informed Consent
  - Justice
  - Medical Decision Making
  - Medications
  - Medicine
  - Practitioner Patient Relationship
  - Professional Malpractice
  - Rehabilitation

Treatment (cont'd)
- **RT** Sensitivity Training
  Termination of Treatment
  Therapists
  Treatment Compliance
  Treatment Methods
  Treatment Programs

Treatment Compliance
- **DC** D878100
- **HN** Added, 1986.
- **UF** Medical Compliance
- **BT** Compliance
- **RT** Health Behavior
  Health Care
  Illness Behavior
  Medical Decision Making
  Prevention
  Termination of Treatment
  Treatment

Treatment Methods
- **DC** D878300
- **HN** Added, 1989.
- **UF** Therapeutic Methods
- **BT** Methods
- **RT** Client Relations
  Intervention
  Practitioner Patient Relationship
  Rehabilitation
  Social Work
  Treatment
  Treatment Programs

Treatment Programs
- **DC** D878400
- **HN** Formerly (1984-1985) DC 472407.
- **UF** Rehabilitation Programs
- **BT** Programs
- **RT** After Care
  Deinstitutionalization
  Detoxification
  Drug Addiction
  Employee Assistance Programs
  Intervention
  Methadone Maintenance
  Placebo Effect
  Program Evaluation
  Program Implementation
  Rehabilitation
  Residential Institutions
  Treatment
  Treatment Methods

Trends
- **DC** D878500
- **HN** Formerly (1963-1985) DC 472420, Trend/Trends.
- **UF** Tendency/Tendencies (1963-1985)
- **RT** Analysis
  Change
  Development
  Forecasting
  Historical Development
  Indexes (Measures)
  Quantitative Methods
  Social Indicators
  Statistics
  Time
  Time Series Analysis

Triads
- **DC** D878700
- **HN** Formerly (1963-1985) DC 472455, Triad/Triads/Triadic.
- **BT** Small Groups
- **RT** Dyads

Trials
- **DC** D879000
- **HN** Formerly (1963-1985) DC 472460, Trial/Trials.
- **BT** Legal Procedure
- **RT** Courts
  Criminal Proceedings
  Defendants
  Due Process
  Evidence (Legal)
  Insanity Defense
  Judges
  Juries
  Litigation
  Pretrial Release
  Prosecutors
  Testimony
  Verdicts
  Witnesses

Tribalism (1963-1985)
- **HN** DC 472480.
- **Use** Traditional Societies

Trinidad And Tobago
- **DC** D879600
- **HN** Added, 1986.
- **UF** Tobago/Tobagonian/Tobagonians (1964-1985)
  Trinidad/Trinidadian/Trinidadians (1963-1985)
- **BT** Caribbean

Trinidad/Trinidadian/Trinidadians (1963-1985)
- **HN** DC 472575.
- **Use** Trinidad And Tobago

Trobriand Islands
- **DC** D879900
- **HN** Formerly (1978-1985) DC 472585, Trobriand Islands, New Zealand.
- **BT** Papua New Guinea

Troeltsch, Ernst
- **DC** D880200
- **SN** Born 1865 - died 1923.
- **HN** Formerly (1964-1985) DC 472586.

Tropical Regions
- **DC** D880500
- **HN** Formerly (1963-1985) part of DC 472590, Tropic/Tropics/Tropical.
- **UF** Forests (Tropical)
  Tropics
- **BT** Geographic Regions
- **RT** Arctic Regions
  Arid Zones
  Earth (Planet)
  Mountain Regions

Tropics
- **Use** Tropical Regions

Trotsky, Leon
- **DC** D880800
- **SN** Born 8 November 1879 - died 21 August 1940.
- **HN** Formerly (1967-1985) DC 472594.

Troubadors
- **Use** Poets

Truancy
- **DC** D881100
- **HN** Formerly (1970-1985) DC 472595, Truant/Truants/Truancy.
- **UF** School Truancy
- **RT** Absenteeism
  Deviant Behavior
  Dropouts
  School Attendance

Truck (1964-1985)
- **HN** DC 472596, deleted 1986.

Trust
- **DC** D881400
- **HN** Formerly (1963-1985) DC 472600.
- **UF** Confidence (1975-1985)
  Distrust (1966-1985)
  Suspicion (1966-1985)
- **RT** Credibility
  Emotions
  Interpersonal Relations
  Optimism
  Social Behavior

Trusteeship (1964-1985)
- **HN** DC 472620, deleted 1986.

Truth
- **DC** D881700
- **HN** Formerly (1965-1985) DC 472700.
- **RT** Accuracy
  Beliefs
  Credibility
  Deception
  Errors
  Ethics
  Fallacies
  Justice
  Morality
  Objectivity
  Phenomena
  Pragmatism
  Reality
  Rumors
  Skepticism
  Validity
  Values
  Verification

Tuamotu Archipelago
- **DC** D882000
- **HN** Added, 1986.
- **BT** French Polynesia

Tuberculosis
- **DC** D882300
- **HN** Formerly (1963-1985) DC 472800.
- **BT** Diseases

Tubuai Islands
- **DC** D882600
- **HN** Added, 1986.
- **BT** French Polynesia

Tunisia
- **DC** D882900
- **HN** Formerly (1963-1985) DC 472870, Tunisia/Tunisian/Tunisians.
- **BT** Arab Countries
  Mediterranean Countries
  North Africa

Turkey
- **DC** D883200
- **HN** Formerly (1963-1985) DC 472890, Turkey/Turkish.
- **UF** Anatolia, Turkey (1963-1985)
- **BT** Balkan States
  Mediterranean Countries
  Middle East
  Western Europe
- **NT** Istanbul, Turkey

Turks And Caicos Islands
- **DC** D883500
- **HN** Added, 1986.
- **BT** Caribbean

Turn

Turn Taking
- DC D883600
- HN Added, 1989.
- BT Social Behavior
- RT Cooperation
      Coordination
      Reciprocity
      Sharing

Turnover
- Use Labor Turnover

TV
- Use Television

Twentieth Century
- DC D883800
- HN Formerly (1985) DC 472965.
- BT Time Periods
- RT Modern Society
      World War I
      World War II

Twins
- DC D884100
- HN Formerly (1963-1985) DC 473000, Twin/Twins.
- BT Siblings
- RT Birth
      Children
      Family

Two Party System (1963-1985)
- HN DC 473650.
- Use Political Parties

Types
- DC D884250
- SN A context-dependent term; select a more specific entry or coordinate with other terms.
- HN Formerly (1963-1985) DC 473700, Type/Types.
- UF Archetype/Archetypes/Archetypical (1975-1985)
- BT Classification
- NT Ideal Types
      Social Types
      Stereotypes
- RT Constructs
      Typology

Typification/Typifications (1971-1985)
- HN DC 473725, deleted 1986. See now Stereotypes or Labeling.

Typography
- Use Printing

Typology
- DC D884300
- HN Formerly (1963-1985) DC 473750, Typology/Typologies/Typological.
- BT Classification
- RT Analysis
      Models
      Types

Tyranny (1964-1985)
- HN DC 473800.
- Use Despotism

UFOs
- Use Unidentified Flying Objects

Uganda
- DC D884400
- HN Formerly (1963-1985) DC 473915.
- BT Sub Saharan Africa
- NT Kampala, Uganda

Ukrainian Soviet Socialist Republic
- DC D884700
- HN Formerly (1963-1985) DC 473950, Ukraine, USSR/Ukrainian/Ukrainians.
- BT Union of Soviet Socialist Republics

Ulster
- Use Northern Ireland

UN
- Use United Nations

Uncertainty (1964-1985)
- HN DC 474300.
- Use Certainty

Unconscious (Psychology)
- DC D885000
- HN Formerly (1963-1985) DC 475000, Unconscious/Unconsciousness.
- RT Consciousness
      Mind
      Psychoanalytic Interpretation

Underdeveloped Countries (1985)
- HN DC 475110.
- Use Developing Countries

Underdevelopment (Economic)
- Use Economic Underdevelopment

Underemployment
- DC D885300
- SN Employment in jobs for which the worker is overqualified or that provide less than full-time work schedules.
- HN Formerly (1965-1985) DC 475175.
- BT Employment
- RT Labor Market
      Labor Supply
      Part Time Employment
      Unemployment
      Work Skills

Undergraduate Programs
- DC D885600
- HN Formerly (1963-1985) part of DC 475250, Undergraduate/Undergraduates.
- BT Higher Education
- RT Baccalaureate Degrees
      College Majors
      Colleges
      Community Colleges
      Educational Programs
      Internship Programs
      Social Work Education
      Sociology Education
      Undergraduate Students
      Universities

Undergraduate Students
- DC D885900
- HN Formerly (1963-1985) part of DC 475250, Undergraduate/Undergraduates.
- BT College Students
- RT Baccalaureate Degrees
      College Graduates
      Undergraduate Programs

Underground Economy
- Use Informal Sector

Underground Movements
- DC D886200
- HN Formerly (1972-1985) DC 475349, Underground/Undergrounds.
- UF Underground Resistance Movements (1972-1985)
- BT Political Movements
- RT Movements
      Revolutions
      War

Unidentified

Underground Resistance Movements (1972-1985)
- HN DC 475350.
- Use Underground Movements

Undernourishment (1965-1985)
- HN DC 475500.
- Use Malnutrition

Underprivileged (1963-1985)
- HN DC 475575.
- Use Disadvantaged

Understanding (1967-1985)
- HN DC 475600.
- Use Comprehension

Undocumented Immigrants
- DC D886500
- HN Formerly (1984-1985) DC 475650, Undocumented Worker.
- UF Illegal Alien/Illegal Aliens (1985)
- BT Immigrants
- RT Borders
      Foreign Workers
      Labor Migration
      Migration
      Refugees

Unemployed Youth
- Use Youth Employment

Unemployment
- DC D886800
- HN Formerly (1963-1985) DC 475700, Unemployed/Unemployment.
- BT Employment
- RT Depression (Economics)
      Dislocated Workers
      Dismissal
      Economic Problems
      Education Work Relationship
      Employability
      Employment Changes
      Job Search
      Labor Force Participation
      Labor Policy
      Occupational Qualifications
      Poverty
      Social Conditions
      Social Problems
      Underemployment
      Unemployment Rates

Unemployment Rates
- DC D887100
- HN Added, 1986.
- BT Rates
- RT Demography
      Unemployment

UNESCO
- Use United Nations Educational, Scientific & Cultural Org

Unfolding Technique (1984-1985)
- HN DC 475875.
- Use Scales

Unidentified Flying Objects
- DC D887400
- HN Added, 1986.
- UF UFOs
- RT Extraterrestrial Space
      Space Technology

Unidimensional

Unidimensional Scaling
- Use Scales

Unification Church
- DC D887700
- HN Added, 1986. Formerly (1983-1985) part of DC 276616, Moon, Sun Myung/Moonies.
- UF Moonies
- BT Cults

Uniform Crime Reporting
- Use Crime Rates

Uniformity
- DC D887800
- HN Formerly (1963-1985) DC 475950, Uniform/Uniformity.
- RT Conformity
  Deviance
  Differences
  Norms
  Regulation
  Similarity
  Social Pressure
  Stability

Uniforms
- Use Clothing

Unify/Unified/Unification (1963-1985)
- HN DC 475900, deleted 1986. See now Unification Church, Alliance, or State Formation.

Unilineality
- DC D888000
- SN The principle of descent that recognizes only male, or female, ancestors in determining kinship.
- HN Formerly (1963-1985) DC 475985, Unilineal.
- BT Descent
- NT Matrilineality
  Patrilineality
- RT Cognatic Descent
  Kinship

Union Management Relations (1963-1985)
- HN DC 477000.
- Use Labor Relations

Union of South Africa/Republic of South Africa (1963-1985)
- HN DC 477060.
- Use South Africa

Union of Soviet Socialist Republics
- DC D888300
- HN Formerly (1963-1985) DC 477075, Union of Soviet Socialist Republics/USSR.
- UF Russia
  Soviet Union
  Soviet/Soviets (1963-1985)
- BT Eastern Europe
- NT Armenian Soviet Socialist Republic
  Estonian Soviet Socialist Republic
  Latvian Soviet Socialist Republic
  Kiev, Union of Soviet Socialist Republics
  Leningrad, Union of Soviet Socialist Republics
  Moscow, Union of Soviet Socialist Republics
  Russian Soviet Federated Socialist Republic
  Siberia
  Ukrainian Soviet Socialist Republic
  Uzbek Soviet Socialist Republic
- RT Soviet American Relations

Union Organization
- Use Unionization

Unionism
- Use Unionization

Unionization
- DC D888600
- HN Formerly (1964-1985) DC 476500, Unionized/Unionization.
- UF Union Organization
  Unionism
- BT Social Processes
- RT Industrialization
  Labor Movements
  Unions

Unions
- DC D888900
- HN Formerly (1963-1985) DC 476000, Union/Unions/Unionism.
- UF American Fed of Labor & Cong of Ind Orgs (1963-1985)
  Congress of Industrial Organizations/CIO (1969-1985)
  International Ladies' Garment Workers Union (1970-1985)
  Labor Unions
  Teamsters (1981-1985)
  Trade Unions
  United Auto Workers (1964-1985)
  United Mine Workers (1964-1985)
- BT Organizations (Social)
- RT Blue Collar Workers
  Business
  Collective Bargaining
  Employers Associations
  Guilds
  Industrial Democracy
  Labor
  Labor Disputes
  Labor Force
  Labor Movements
  Labor Parties
  Labor Relations
  Strikes
  Syndicalism
  Unionization
  Workers
  Working Class

Unit/Units (1963-1985)
- HN DC 477082, deleted 1986.

Unitarians
- DC D889200
- HN Formerly (1964-1985) DC 477090, Unitarian/Unitarians/Unitarianism.
- BT Protestants
- RT Protestantism

United Arab Emirates
- DC D889500
- HN Added, 1986.
- BT Arab Countries
  Middle East

United Arab Republic (1963-1985)
- HN DC 477100.
- Use Egypt

United Auto Workers (1964-1985)
- HN DC 477108.
- Use Unions

United Kingdom
- DC D889800
- SN England, Scotland, Wales, and Northern Ireland.
- HN Formerly (1963-1985) DC 477140, United Kingdom/UK.

United

United Kingdom (cont'd)
- BT Western Europe
- NT England
  Great Britain
  Northern Ireland
  Scotland
  Wales

United Mine Workers (1964-1985)
- HN DC 477180.
- Use Unions

United Nations
- DC D890100
- HN Formerly (1963-1985) DC 477150, United Nations/UN.
- UF UN
  United Nations Internat Childrens Emergency Fund (1963-1985)
  World Health Organization (1963-1985)
- BT International Organizations
- NT United Nations Educational, Scientific & Cultural Org
- RT International Alliances
  International Relations

United Nations Educational, Scientific & Cultural Org
- DC D890400
- HN Formerly (1963-1985) DC 477170, United Nations Educational, Scientific & Cultural Organization - UNESCO.
- UF UNESCO
- BT United Nations

United Nations Internat Childrens Emergency Fund (1963-1985)
- HN DC 477172. Abbreviated here due to character restrictions. Formerly used in indexing under its full name United Nations International Children's Emergency Fund/UNICEF.
- Use United Nations

United States of America
- DC D890700
- HN Formerly (1963-1985) DC 477200, United States/US.
- UF US
  USA
- BT North America
- NT Alabama
  Alaska
  Arizona
  Arkansas
  California
  Colorado
  Connecticut
  Delaware
  Florida
  Georgia
  Hawaii
  Idaho
  Illinois
  Indiana
  Iowa
  Kansas
  Kentucky
  Louisiana
  Maine
  Maryland
  Massachusetts
  Michigan
  Minnesota
  Mississippi
  Missouri
  Montana
  Nebraska

United

United States of America (cont'd)
- **NT** Nevada
  New Hampshire
  New Jersey
  New Mexico
  New York
  North Carolina
  North Dakota
  Ohio
  Oklahoma
  Oregon
  Pennsylvania
  Rhode Island
  South Carolina
  South Dakota
  Tennessee
  Texas
  Utah
  Vermont
  Virginia
  Washington, D.C.
  Washington (State)
  West Virginia
  Wisconsin
  Wyoming
- **RT** Midwestern States
  Northern States
  Southern States
  Soviet American Relations
  Western States

United States Supreme Court
- **DC** D891000
- **HN** Added, 1986.
- **UF** Supreme Court (1963-1985)
- **BT** Courts
- **RT** Judicial Decisions
  Legal Procedure

Unity (1963-1985)
- **HN** DC 477300.
- **Use** Social Cohesion

Universal Pragmatics
- **Use** Pragmatics

Universal Primary Education Programs
- **Use** Literacy Programs

Universalism-Particularism
- **DC** D891250
- **SN** A pattern variable in Talcott Parsons's structural functionalism that deals with the problem of whether a person regards another person as a member or representative of a social category or as an individual.
- **HN** Formerly (1963-1985) part of DC 477400, Universal/Universals/Universalism/Universality.
- **UF** Particularism/Particularistic (1965-1985)
- **BT** Orientation
- **RT** Situation
  Social Behavior
  Social Interaction
  Social Perception
  Social Theories

Universals of Culture
- **Use** Cultural Universals

Universe (1963-1985)
- **HN** DC 477450, deleted 1986.

Universities
- **DC** D891300
- **HN** Formerly (1963-1985) DC 477500, University/Universities.
- **UF** Harvard University (1964-1985)
- **BT** Colleges
- **RT** Academic Departments
  College Faculty
  College Sports
  College Students
  Doctoral Programs
  Higher Education
  Medical Schools
  Postdoctoral Programs
  Undergraduate Programs

University Departments
- **Use** Academic Departments

University Disciplines
- **Use** Academic Disciplines

University Graduates
- **Use** College Graduates

University Students
- **Use** College Students

Unmarried (1963-1985)
- **HN** DC 477600.
- **Use** Single Persons

Unskilled (1963-1985)
- **HN** DC 477680.
- **Use** Manual Workers

Untouchable/Untouchables/Untouchability (1963-1985)
- **HN** DC 477720.
- **Use** Caste Systems

Unwanted Pregnancy
- **DC** D891500
- **HN** Added, 1989.
- **BT** Pregnancy
- **RT** Abortion
  Adolescents
  Illegitimacy
  Incest
  Rape
  Unwed Mothers

Unwed Mothers
- **DC** D891600
- **HN** Added, 1986. Prior to 1986 use Unmarried (DC 477600).
- **BT** Mothers
- **RT** Adolescents
  Birth
  Family Relations
  Father Absence
  Female Headed Households
  Marriage
  Parent Child Relations
  Parents
  Premarital Sex
  Single Parent Family
  Single Persons
  Unwanted Pregnancy

UPE Campaigns
- **Use** Literacy Programs

Upper Class
- **DC** D891900
- **HN** Added, 1986.
- **BT** Social Class
- **RT** Aristocracy
  Economic Elites

Urban

Upper Class (cont'd)
- **RT** Elites
  Intelligentsia
  Ruling Class
  Social Power
  Wealth

Upper Paleolithic (1963-1985)
- **HN** DC 477800.
- **Use** Prehistory

Upper Volta (1971-1985)
- **HN** DC 477810.
- **Use** Burkina Faso

Upward Mobility
- **Use** Social Mobility

Uralic Language (1965-1985)
- **HN** DC 477900.
- **Use** Oriental Languages

Urban Areas
- **DC** D892200
- **HN** Formerly (1963-1985) DC 478000, Urban.
- **NT** Metropolitan Areas
- **RT** Air Pollution
  Annexation
  Cities
  City Planning
  Geographic Regions
  Neighborhoods
  Population Density
  Rural Areas
  Rural to Urban Migration
  Rural Urban Continuum
  Rural Urban Differences
  Slums
  Social Area Analysis
  Suburbs
  Urban Crime
  Urban Development
  Urban Fringe
  Urban Policy
  Urban Population
  Urban Poverty
  Urban Renewal
  Urban Sociology
  Urban to Rural Migration
  Urbanism
  Urbanization

Urban Crime
- **DC** D892500
- **HN** Added, 1986.
- **BT** Crime
- **RT** Drug Trafficking
  Rural Crime
  Urban Areas
  Urban Poverty

Urban Development
- **DC** D892800
- **HN** Added, 1986.
- **BT** Development
- **RT** Cities
  City Planning
  Community Development
  Development Policy
  Development Programs
  Development Strategies
  Economic Development
  Industrial Development
  Land Use
  Neighborhood Change
  Public Transportation
  Regional Development
  Rural Development

Urban Development (cont'd)
- **RT** Urban Areas
  Urban Policy
  Urban Renewal
  Urbanization

Urban Education
- **DC** D893100
- **HN** Added, 1986.
- **BT** Education
- **RT** Educational Systems

Urban Fringe
- **DC** D893400
- **HN** Formerly (1963-1985) DC 188850, Fringe.
- **UF** Rural Urban Fringe
  Rurban (1971-1985)
- **RT** Rural Areas
  Rural Urban Continuum
  Suburbs
  Urban Areas

Urban Life
- **Use** Urbanism

Urban Neighborhoods
- **Use** Neighborhoods

Urban Planning
- **Use** City Planning

Urban Policy
- **DC** D893700
- **HN** Added, 1986.
- **BT** Policy
- **RT** Cities
  Housing Policy
  Urban Areas
  Urban Development
  Welfare Policy

Urban Poor
- **Use** Urban Poverty

Urban Population
- **DC** D894000
- **HN** Added, 1986.
- **UF** Urban Residents
  Urbanites (1964-1985)
- **BT** Population
- **RT** Internal Migration
  Population Distribution
  Population Growth
  Residents
  Rural Population
  Rural to Urban Migration
  Urban Areas
  Urban to Rural Migration

Urban Poverty
- **DC** D894300
- **HN** Added, 1986.
- **UF** Inner City Poverty
  Urban Poor
- **BT** Poverty
- **RT** Central Cities
  Homelessness
  Rural Poverty
  Urban Areas
  Urban Crime

Urban Renewal
- **DC** D894600
- **HN** Formerly (1963-1985) DC 383580, Renewal.
- **RT** Antipoverty Programs
  Central Cities
  Cities

Urban Renewal (cont'd)
- **RT** City Planning
  Community Change
  Community Development
  Improvement
  Relocation
  Slums
  Urban Areas
  Urban Development

Urban Residents
- **Use** Urban Population

Urban Rural Continuum
- **Use** Rural Urban Continuum

Urban Rural Differences
- **Use** Rural Urban Differences

Urban Sociology
- **DC** D894900
- **HN** Formerly (1985) DC 478020.
- **BT** Sociology
- **RT** Chicago School of Sociology
  Cities
  Rural Sociology
  Urban Areas

Urban to Rural Migration
- **DC** D895200
- **HN** Added, 1986.
- **BT** Migration
- **RT** Internal Migration
  Return Migration
  Rural Areas
  Rural Population
  Rural to Urban Migration
  Ruralization
  Suburbanization
  Suburbs
  Urban Areas
  Urban Population

Urbanism
- **DC** D895500
- **SN** The forms of social interaction and culture peculiar to cities, characterized by impersonality, greater division of labor, economic interdependence, high mobility, the increased importance of technology and mass media, and the lack of primary relationships.
- **HN** Formerly (1963-1985) DC 478040, Urbanism/Urbanity.
- **UF** Urban Life
- **RT** Cities
  Commuting (Travel)
  Cosmopolitanism
  Everyday Life
  Lifestyle
  Rural Urban Differences
  Rurality
  Urban Areas

Urbanites (1964-1985)
- **HN** DC 478130.
- **Use** Urban Population

Urbanization
- **DC** D895800
- **HN** Formerly (1963-1985) DC 478150, Urbanization/Urbanized/Urbanizing.
- **BT** Social Processes
- **RT** Cities
  Community Change
  Economic Development
  Industrial Societies
  Industrialization

Urbanization (cont'd)
- **RT** Mass Society
  Modern Society
  Modernization
  Postindustrial Societies
  Rural to Urban Migration
  Ruralization
  Suburbanization
  Urban Areas
  Urban Development

Uruguay
- **DC** D896100
- **HN** Formerly (1963-1985) DC 478300, Uruguay/Uruguayan/Uruguayans.
- **BT** South America
- **NT** Montevideo, Uruguay

US
- **Use** United States of America

USA
- **Use** United States of America

Usury (1965-1985)
- **HN** DC 478400, deleted 1986.

Utah
- **DC** D896400
- **HN** Formerly (1963-1985) DC 478420.
- **BT** United States of America
  Western States

Uterus/Uterine (1965-1985)
- **HN** DC 478425, deleted 1986.

Utilitarianism
- **DC** D896600
- **SN** A social philosophy, usually associated with Jeremy Bentham and John Stuart Mill, that considers pleasure and the satisfaction of individual wants as the only moral value, and the greatest happiness of the greatest number of people as the aim of human conduct.
- **HN** Formerly (1963-1985) DC 478445, Utilitarian/Utilitarians/Utilitarianism.
- **BT** Philosophical Doctrines
- **RT** Ethics
  Exchange Theory
  Hedonism
  Liberalism
  Morality
  Norms

Utilization
- **DC** D896700
- **HN** Formerly (1963-1985) DC 478470, Utility/Utilization.
- **NT** Health Care Utilization
  Land Use
  Time Utilization
- **RT** Consumption

Utopias
- **DC** D896850
- **SN** Visionary systems of social perfection toward which human society is evolving, especially according to socialist philosophies.
- **HN** Formerly (1963-1985) DC 478485, Utopia/Utopias/Utopian/Utopianism.
- **RT** Evolutionary Theories
  Historical Materialism
  Literature
  Marxism
  Millenarianism
  Social Evolution

Utopias (cont'd)
- RT Socialism

Uttar Pradesh, India
- DC D897000
- HN Formerly (1963-1985) DC 478510.
- BT India

Uxorilocal (1977-1985)
- HN DC 478530.
- Use Matrilocal Residence

Uzbek Soviet Socialist Republic
- DC D897300
- HN Formerly (1975-1985) DC 478540, Uzbekistan, USSR.
- BT Union of Soviet Socialist Republics

Vacation/Vacations (1963-1985)
- HN DC 478550, deleted 1986. See now Leisure or Tourism.

Vaccination
- DC D897600
- HN Formerly (1963-1985) DC 478560, Vaccine/Vaccines/Vaccination.
- UF Immunization
- RT Diseases
  Epidemiology
  Health
  Health Services
  Public Health

Vagrants/Vagrancy (1967-1985)
- HN DC 478585, deleted 1986. See now Homelessness or Offenses.

Valence (1964-1985)
- HN DC 478595, deleted 1986.

Validation
- Use Validity

Validity
- DC D897800
- HN Formerly (1963-1985) DC 478600, Validity/Validation.
- UF Validation
- RT Accuracy
  Correlation
  Empiricism
  Fallacies
  Generalization
  Inference
  Logic
  Measurement
  Measures (Instruments)
  Quantitative Methods
  Regression Analysis
  Reliability
  Research Design Error
  Research Methodology
  Standards
  Statistical Bias
  Test Bias
  Truth
  Variables
  Weighting

Value (Economics)
- DC D897900
- HN Formerly (1963-1985) part of DC 479000, Value/Values/Valuation/Valuations.
- RT Costs
  Economic Theories
  Economics
  Exchange (Economics)
  Labor Process

Value (Economics) (cont'd)
- RT Labor Theory of Value
  Marxist Economics
  Money
  Political Economy
  Prices
  Property
  Wealth

Value Free Sociology
- Use Value Neutrality

Value Neutrality
- DC D898200
- SN The avoidance by social scientists of personal value judgments concerning research and policy formation. See also Objectivity.
- HN Formerly (1964-1985) part of DC 298475, Neutralism/Neutrality/Neutralist/Neutralists.
- UF Value Free Sociology
  Wertfreiheit
- BT Objectivity
- RT Cultural Relativism
  Empirical Methods
  Research Ethics
  Research Methodology
  Values

Value Orientations
- DC D898500
- SN Predispositions toward similar sets of values, particularly Social Values concerning ethics or morals.
- HN Added, 1986.
- BT Orientation
- RT Cultural Relativism
  Machiavellianism (Personality)
  Morality
  Religious Orientations
  Values

Values
- DC D898800
- SN A context-dependent term; select a more specific entry or coordinate with other terms. In contexts where Values is closely related to Social Values, select the latter.
- HN Formerly (1963-1985) DC 479000, Value/Values/Valuation/Valuations.
- UF Axiology (1971-1985)
  Ideals
- NT Cultural Values
  Social Values
  Work Values
- RT Beliefs
  Conscience
  Ethics
  Freedom
  Ideologies
  Judgment
  Justice
  Morality
  Objectivity
  Praxeology
  Principles
  Relevance
  Salience
  Standards
  Tolerance
  Truth
  Value Neutrality
  Value Orientations

Van den Berghe, Pierre Louis
- DC D899000
- SN Born 30 January 1933 - .
- HN Added, 1989.

Vancouver, British Columbia
- DC D899100
- HN Added, 1986.
- BT British Columbia

Vandalism
- DC D899400
- HN Formerly (1963-1985) DC 479100.
- BT Offenses

Variability (1963-1985)
- HN DC 479200.
- Use Differences

Variables
- DC D899550
- HN Formerly (1963-1985) DC 479300, Variable/Variables/Variableness.
- UF Dependent Variables
  Independent Variables
  Predictor Variables
- RT Contingency Analysis
  Correlation
  Data
  Experiments
  Measurement
  Multivariate Analysis
  Path Analysis
  Quantitative Methods
  Research Design
  Validity

Variance Analysis
- Use Variance (Statistics)

Variance (Statistics)
- DC D899600
- SN Conversion of the total variance (a function of the standard deviation) of a set of random variables into component variables associated with pre-defined factors.
- HN Formerly (1963-1985) part of DC 479500, Variance/Variant/Variation.
- UF Analysis of Variance
  ANOVA
  Covariance/Covariable (1963-1985)
  Variance Analysis
- BT Methodology (Data Analysis)
- RT Correlation
  Factor Analysis
  Frequency Distributions
  Multivariate Analysis
  Probability
  Quantitative Methods
  Regression Analysis
  Statistical Inference
  Statistical Significance
  Statistics

Varieties (Language)
- Use Language Varieties

Vasectomy
- DC D899700
- HN Formerly (1963-1985) DC 479800.
- BT Surgery
- RT Birth Control
  Intrauterine Devices
  Sterilization

Vatican
- **DC** D900000
- **HN** Formerly (1964-1985) DC 479840.
- **UF** Holy See
  Papal State
  Vatican City
- **BT** Western Europe
- **RT** Italy
  Papacy

Vatican City
- **Use** Vatican

Veblen, Thorstein Bunde
- **DC** D900300
- **SN** Born 30 July 1857 - died 3 August 1929.
- **HN** Formerly (1964-1985) DC 479860, Veblen, Thorstein.

Vegetation
- **Use** Plants (Botanical)

Vendettas
- **Use** Feuds

Venereal Diseases
- **DC** D900600
- **HN** Formerly (1965-1985) DC 479875, Venereal Disease.
- **UF** Gonorrhea
  Herpes Simplex Genitalis
  Syphilis
- **BT** Diseases
- **RT** Genitals
  Sexual Behavior

Venezuela
- **DC** D900900
- **HN** Formerly (1963-1985) DC 479880, Venezuela/Venezuelan/Venezuelans.
- **BT** South America
- **NT** Caracas, Venezuela

Venice, Italy (1975-1985)
- **HN** DC 479890, deleted 1986.

Verbal Accounts
- **DC** D901100
- **SN** Informal descriptions, explanations, or interpretations of events given by social actors, especially research subjects.
- **HN** Added, 1989.
- **BT** Reports
- **RT** Narratives
  Oral History
  Speech
  Testimony
  Verbal Communication
  Writing

Verbal Communication
- **DC** D901200
- **HN** Added, 1986.
- **UF** Verbal/Verb (1963-1985)
- **BT** Communication
- **NT** Conversation
  Letters (Correspondence)
- **RT** Conversational Analysis
  Debate
  Discourse
  Discussion
  Interpersonal Communication
  Language
  Linguistics
  Narratives
  Nonverbal Communication
  Reading

Verbal Communication (cont'd)
- **RT** Semiotics
  Speech
  Verbal Accounts
  Writing

Verbal Reinforcement
- **Use** Reinforcement

Verbal/Verb (1963-1985)
- **HN** DC 479900.
- **Use** Verbal Communication

Verdicts
- **DC** D901500
- **HN** Formerly (1972-1985) DC 480040, Verdict/Verdicts.
- **UF** Acquit/Acquittal/Acquitting (1965-1985)
  Jury Decisions
- **BT** Decisions
- **RT** Criminal Proceedings
  Judicial Decisions
  Juries
  Litigation
  Trials

Verification
- **DC** D901650
- **HN** Formerly (1963-1985) DC 480065, Verify/Verified/Verifiability/Verification.
- **RT** Accuracy
  Empirical Methods
  Evaluation
  Experiments
  Falsification
  Hypotheses
  Replication
  Research Design
  Research Methodology
  Sampling
  Theories
  Truth

Vermont
- **DC** D901800
- **HN** Formerly (1974-1985) DC 480085.
- **BT** Northern States
  United States of America

Vernacular (1978-1985)
- **HN** DC 480100, deleted 1986. See now Dialects or Slang.

Verse (1967-1985)
- **HN** DC 480111.
- **Use** Poetry

Verstehen
- **DC** D901900
- **SN** Methodological viewpoint that emphasizes subjective states of mind and interpretations of action by the actors studied. Compare with Hermeneutics, which emphasizes interpretation of action in the context of the individual's Worldview.
- **HN** Formerly (1965-1985) DC 480115.
- **UF** Interpretive Method
  Social Understanding
- **RT** Action Theory
  Analysis
  Comprehension
  Critical Theory
  Empathy
  Hermeneutics
  Historicism
  Ideal Types

Verstehen (cont'd)
- **RT** Interpretive Sociology
  Meaning
  Methodological Individualism
  Methodology (Philosophical)
  Naturalism
  Phenomenology
  Positivism
  Qualitative Methods
  Social Science Research
  Social Structure
  Sociological Theory
  Structuration

Vertical (1969-1985)
- **HN** DC 480165, deleted 1986.

Vertical Mobility
- **Use** Social Mobility

Vested (1969-1985)
- **HN** DC 480190, deleted 1986.

Veterans
- **DC** D902100
- **HN** Formerly (1963-1985) DC 480300, Veteran/Veterans.
- **RT** Military Officers
  Military Personnel
  Military Service
  War

Veterans Administration (1963-1985)
- **HN** DC 480375.
- **Use** Government Agencies

Vico, Giovanni Battista
- **DC** D902400
- **SN** Born 23 June 1668 - died 27 January 1744.
- **HN** Formerly (1970-1985) DC 480390, Vico, G.

Victim Compensation
- **Use** Restitution (Corrections)

Victim Offender Relations
- **DC** D902600
- **HN** Added, 1989.
- **UF** Offender Victim Relations
- **BT** Interpersonal Relations
- **RT** Crime
  Offenders
  Rape
  Restitution (Corrections)
  Victimization
  Victims

Victimization
- **DC** D902700
- **SN** The experience of being personally subjected to acts of crime or violence.
- **HN** Formerly (1965-1985) part of DC 480400, Victim/Victims/Victimization.
- **RT** Abuse
  Battered Women
  Child Sexual Abuse
  Crime
  Elder Abuse
  Family Violence
  Fear of Crime
  Sexual Harassment
  Victim Offender Relations
  Victimology
  Violence
  Vulnerability

Victimology / Visual

Victimology
- DC D903000
- SN Research centered on victims of crime or abuse.
- HN Formerly (1983-1985) DC 480412.
- BT Criminology
- RT Fear of Crime
  Social Science Research
  Victimization

Victims
- DC D903300
- HN Formerly (1965-1985) part of DC 480400, Victim/Victims/Victimization.
- UF Crime Victims
- RT Battered Women
  Child Abuse
  Elder Abuse
  Hostages
  Rape
  Restitution (Corrections)
  Sexual Assault
  Victim Offender Relations
  Witnesses

Victorian Period
- DC D903600
- HN Formerly (1963-1985) DC 480420.
- BT Time Periods
- RT Nineteenth Century

Videos
- Use Videotape Recordings

Videotape Recordings
- DC D903900
- HN Formerly (1981-1985) DC 480430, Videotape.
- UF Videos
- BT Methodology (Data Collection)
  Recordings
- RT Films
  Music
  Programming (Broadcast)
  Television

Vienna, Austria
- DC D904200
- HN Formerly (1963-1985) DC 480450, Vienna, Austria/Viennese.
- BT Austria

Vietnam
- DC D904500
- HN Formerly (1963-1985) DC 480475, Vietnam/Vietnamese.
- UF North Vietnam
  South Vietnam
- BT Southeast Asia
- NT Hanoi, Vietnam
  Ho Chi Minh City, Vietnam
- RT Indochina

Vietnam War
- DC D904800
- HN Formerly (1984-1985) DC 480479.
- BT War

Vietnamese (Language)
- Use Oriental Languages

View/Views/Viewer/Viewers (1969-1985)
- HN DC 480482, deleted 1986. See now Audiences or Opinions.

Viewers
- Use Audiences

Vigilance Committees
- Use Vigilantism

Vigilantees
- Use Vigilantism

Vigilantism
- DC D904900
- HN Added, 1989.
- UF Vigilance Committees
  Vigilantees
- RT Anarchism
  Criminal Justice
  Due Process
  Extremism
  Law Enforcement
  Legal System
  Punishment
  Right Wing Politics

Villages
- DC D905100
- HN Formerly (1963-1985) DC 480540, Village/Villages/Villagers.
- BT Communities
- RT Community Size
  Rural Areas
  Rural Communities
  Towns
  Traditional Societies

Violate/Violates/Violation/Violations (1970-1985)
- HN DC 480575, deleted 1986. See now appropriate "Offenders," "Crime," or "Law" terms.

Violence
- DC D905400
- HN Formerly (1963-1985) DC 480600, Violence/Violent.
- UF Fight/Fights/Fighter/Fighters/Fighting (1975-1985)
- NT Assault
  Civil Disorders
  Combat
  Family Violence
  Mass Media Violence
  Political Violence
  Sports Violence
- RT Abuse
  Aggression
  Behavior
  Coercion
  Conflict
  Disorders
  Hostility
  Interaction
  Nonviolence
  Offenses
  Victimization
  War

Virgin Islands
- DC D905700
- HN Formerly (1971-1985) DC 480630, Virgin Islands/Virgin Islander/Virgin Islanders.
- BT Caribbean

Virginia
- DC D906000
- HN Formerly (1963-1985) DC 480620, Virginia/Virginian/Virginians.
- BT Southern States
  United States of America
- RT Appalachia

Virginity
- DC D906300
- HN Formerly (1964-1985) DC 480615, Virgin/Virgins/Virginity.
- RT Celibacy
  Marriage
  Sexual Behavior
  Single Persons

Virilocal Residence
- Use Patrilocal Residence

Virtue (1963-1985)
- HN DC 480682.
- Use Morality

Virus (1966-1985)
- HN DC 480685, deleted 1986.

Vision
- DC D906600
- HN Formerly (1964-1985) part of DC 480700, Vision/Visual/Visibility.
- UF Sight
- BT Sensory Systems
- RT Blind
  Eye Contact
  Hearing
  Optometry

Visions (1964-1985)
- HN DC 480850, deleted 1986.

Visit/Visits (1964-1985)
- HN DC 480860, deleted 1986.

Visitation
- DC D906900
- HN Formerly (1976-1985) DC 480880.
- UF Conjugal Visitation
  Social Visitation
  Visitation Rights
- RT Child Custody
  Sociability
  Social Contact

Visitation Rights
- Use Visitation

Visitor/Visitors (1965-1985)
- HN DC 480885, deleted 1986. See now Visitation or Tourism.

Visits (Medical)
- Use Health Care Utilization

Visual Arts
- DC D907200
- HN Added, 1986.
- UF Draw/Draws/Drawing/Drawings (1972-1985)
  Painting/Paintings (1963-1985)
  Sculpture
- BT Fine Arts
- NT Crafts
- RT Architecture
  Art
  Art History
  Films
  Museums
  Photographs
  Printing
  Romanticism

Visual Sociology
- DC D907300
- HN Added, 1986.
- BT Sociology

Vital Statistics (1963-1985)
  HN DC 481590, deleted 1986. See now Rates and its associated terms.

Vocabularies
  DC D907500
  SN Stock of words used by a language, group, individual, or specific work.
  HN Formerly (1963-1985) DC 481700, Vocabulary.
  NT Slang
  RT Code Switching
     Definitions
     Literacy
     Reading
     Terminology
     Words

Vocabulary of Kinship
  Use Kinship Terminology

Vocal Music
  Use Music

Vocation/Vocations (1963-1985)
  HN DC 481900.
  Use Occupations

Vocational (1963-1985)
  HN DC 481970, deleted 1986. See now appropriate "Occupational" or "Vocational" terms.

Vocational Choice
  Use Occupational Choice

Vocational Education
  DC D907800
  HN Added, 1986.
  UF Vocational Training
  BT Education
  RT Apprenticeships
     Curriculum
     Guidance
     Job Training
     Occupational Qualifications
     Occupations
     Polytechnic Schools
     Secondary Education
     Tracking (Education)
     Vocational Rehabilitation

Vocational Guidance
  Use Guidance

Vocational Rehabilitation
  DC D908100
  HN Added, 1986.
  BT Rehabilitation
  RT Vocational Education
     Workshops (Manufacturing)

Vocational Training
  Use Vocational Education

Voice (1971-1985)
  HN DC 482000.
  Use Speech

Volition/Volitional (1965-1985)
  HN DC 482050.
  Use Will

Voltaire, Francois-Marie Arouet de
  DC D908400
  SN Born 21 November 1694 - died 30 May 1778.
  HN Formerly (1973-1985) DC 482100, Voltaire, F.

Volume (Sound)
  Use Noise

Voluntarism
  DC D908600
  SN Doctrine that free will is the primary determining factor in human action. Contrast with Determinism.
  HN Formerly (1963-1985) DC 482140, Voluntary/Voluntarism.
  BT Philosophical Doctrines
  RT Action Theory
     Determinism
     Indeterminism
     Social Action
     Social Theories
     Sociological Theory
     Systems Theory
     Will

Voluntary Associations (1985)
  HN DC 482150.
  Use Associations

Volunteerism
  Use Volunteers

Volunteers
  DC D908700
  HN Formerly (1963-1985) DC 482200, Volunteer/Volunteers.
  UF Volunteerism
  RT Activism
     Activities
     Altruism
     Charities
     Contributions (Donations)
     Human Services
     Nonprofit Organizations
     Participation

Von Wiese (und Kaiserswaldau), Leopold
  DC D908900
  SN Born 2 December 1876 - died 11 January 1969.
  HN Formerly (1964-1985) DC 482250, Von Wiese, L.

Voodooism
  DC D909000
  HN Formerly (1963-1985) DC 482260, Voodoo/Voodooism.
  UF Hoodoo (1964-1985)
  RT Ancestor Worship
     Evil
     Magic
     Occultism
     Spirit Possession
     Supernatural
     Traditional Societies
     Witchcraft

Vote/Votes (1963-1985)
  HN DC 482320.
  Use Voting

Voters
  DC D909300
  HN Formerly (1963-1985) part of DC 482400, Voting/Voter/Voters.
  UF Electorate (1963-1985)
  RT Citizens
     Elections
     Majorities (Politics)
     Political Attitudes
     Political Behavior
     Political Power
     Voting

Voting
  DC D909600
  HN Formerly (1963-1985) part of DC 482400, Voting/Voter/Voters.
  UF Vote/Votes (1963-1985)
  RT Citizenship
     Civil Rights
     Democracy
     Elections
     Political Action
     Political Participation
     Political Representation
     Referendum
     Voters
     Voting Behavior
     Voting Rights

Voting Behavior
  DC D909900
  HN Added, 1986.
  UF Condorcet Paradox (1969-1985)
     Electoral Behavior
  BT Political Behavior
  RT Elections
     Opinion Polls
     Political Attitudes
     Voting

Voting Rights
  DC D910200
  HN Added, 1986.
  UF Suffrage (1964-1985)
  BT Civil Rights
  RT Elections
     Voting

Vulnerability
  DC D910350
  HN Formerly (1984-1985) DC 482600.
  RT Risk
     Safety
     Security
     Threat
     Victimization

Wages
  DC D910500
  HN Formerly (1963-1985) DC 483200, Wage/Wages.
  UF Pay (Wages)
  BT Compensation
  NT Minimum Wage
  RT Employment
     Income
     Income Distribution
     Income Inequality
     Piecework
     Salaries
     Standard of Living
     Workers

Wake Island
  DC D910800
  HN Added, 1986.
  BT Micronesia

Wales
  DC D911100
  HN Formerly (1963-1985) DC 483400, Wales/Welsh.
  BT Great Britain
     United Kingdom
     Western Europe

Wall Street (1963-1985)
  HN DC 483520, deleted 1986.

Wallerstein, Immanuel Maurice
- **DC** D911400
- **SN** Born 28 September 1930 - .
- **HN** Added, 1986.

Walloon/Walloons (1970-1985)
- **HN** DC 483560, deleted 1986. See now European Cultural Groups or Romance Languages.

War
- **DC** D911700
- **HN** Formerly (1963-1985) DC 483700, War/Wars/Warfare.
- **UF** International War
  Warfare
- **NT** Civil War
  Nuclear War
  Vietnam War
  World War I
  World War II
- **RT** Aggression
  Alliance
  Armaments
  Armed Forces
  Borders
  Civil Defense
  Cold War
  Combat
  Conflict
  Defense Spending
  Draft (Military)
  Feuds
  Foreign Policy
  History
  Imperialism
  International Conflict
  International Relations
  Invasion
  Militarism
  Militarization
  Military Personnel
  Military Service
  National Security
  Patriotism
  Peace
  Peace Movements
  Prisoners of War
  Reconstruction
  Refugees
  Underground Movements
  Veterans
  Violence
  World Problems

War Prisoners
- **Use** Prisoners of War

Ward, Lester Frank
- **DC** D912000
- **SN** Born 18 June 1841 - died 18 April 1913.
- **HN** Formerly (1964-1985) DC 483878, Ward, Lester F.

Wards (Hospital)
- **Use** Hospital Wards

Warfare
- **Use** War

Warsaw, Poland
- **DC** D912300
- **HN** Formerly (1963-1985) DC 484200.
- **BT** Poland

Washington, D.C.
- **DC** D912600
- **HN** Formerly (1963-1985) DC 484300.
- **UF** District of Columbia
- **BT** United States of America

Washington (State)
- **DC** D912900
- **HN** Formerly (1963-1985) DC 484250, Washington, state.
- **BT** United States of America
  Western States
- **NT** Seattle, Washington

Wastes
- **DC** D913200
- **HN** Formerly (1984-1985) DC 484400, Waste.
- **UF** Refuse
  Trash
- **RT** Air Pollution
  Conservation
  Ecology
  Environmental Protection
  Human Ecology
  Poisoning
  Pollution
  Pollution Control
  Public Health
  Radiation
  Toxic Substances
  Water Supply

Water Resources
- **Use** Water Supply

Water Supply
- **DC** D913500
- **HN** Formerly (1963-1985) DC 485615.
- **UF** Water Resources
- **BT** Natural Resources
- **RT** Animal Husbandry
  Conservation
  Ecology
  Energy
  Energy Conservation
  Irrigation
  Pollution
  Wastes

Watergate Scandal
- **DC** D913800
- **SN** Events leading to the resignation of US President Richard Nixon.
- **HN** Formerly (1977-1985) DC 485605, Watergate.
- **BT** Scandals
- **RT** Corruption
  Presidents

Watering
- **Use** Irrigation

Watts, Los Angeles (1968-1985)
- **HN** DC 485630.
- **Use** Los Angeles, California

Way of Life (1985)
- **HN** DC 485625.
- **Use** Lifestyle

Wealth
- **DC** D914100
- **HN** Formerly (1963-1985) DC 485800, Wealth/Wealthy.
- **RT** Accumulation
  Affluence
  Capital
  Consumption

Wealth (cont'd)
- **RT** Economic Elites
  Economics
  Elites
  Finance
  Gross National Product
  Income
  Income Distribution
  Income Inequality
  Investment
  Money
  Ownership
  Poverty
  Profits
  Property
  Saving
  Social Stratification
  Upper Class
  Value (Economics)

Weapons
- **DC** D914400
- **HN** Formerly (1963-1985) DC 486000, Weapon/Weapons.
- **BT** Armaments
- **NT** Bombs
  Firearms
  Nuclear Weapons
- **RT** Tools

Weather
- **DC** D914700
- **HN** Formerly (1963-1985) DC 486470.
- **UF** Rain/Rainfall (1983-1985)
- **RT** Earth (Planet)
  Ecology
  Environmental Factors
  Geographic Regions
  Meteorology
  Natural Disasters
  Seasonal Variations

Webb, Sidney James, Lord Passfield
- **DC** D914750
- **SN** Born 13 July 1859 - died 13 October 1947.
- **HN** Formerly (1963-1985) DC 486480, Webb, S. & B.

Weber, Max
- **DC** D914800
- **SN** Born 21 April 1864 - died 14 June 1920.
- **HN** Formerly (1963-1985) DC 486500, Weber, M./Weberian.

Weddings
- **DC** D915000
- **HN** Formerly (1963-1985) DC 489150, Wedding/Weddings.
- **UF** Marriage Rites
- **BT** Rituals
- **RT** Celebrations
  Marriage

Weeklies (1963-1985)
- **HN** DC 489200, deleted 1986. See now Newspapers or Periodicals.

Weeklies (Newspapers)
- **Use** Newspapers

Weekly Periodicals
- **Use** Periodicals

Weight (1963-1985)
- **HN** DC 489300.
- **Use** Body Weight

Weighting
- **DC** D915200
- **SN** A statistical sampling technique whereby unequal probabilities are adjusted to indicate their relative importance.
- **HN** Formerly (1975-1985) DC 489500.
- **RT** Items (Measures)
  Measures (Instruments)
  Sampling
  Scales
  Scores
  Validity

Welfare Dependency
- **DC** D915250
- **HN** Added, 1989.
- **BT** Dependency (Psychology)
- **RT** Employment
  Motivation
  Welfare Recipients
  Welfare Services
  Work Attitudes

Welfare Families
- **Use** Welfare Recipients

Welfare Policy
- **DC** D915300
- **HN** Added, 1986.
- **UF** Social Welfare Policy
- **BT** Social Policy
- **RT** Family Policy
  Government Policy
  Housing Policy
  Low Income Groups
  Social Welfare
  Urban Policy
  Welfare Reform
  Welfare Services
  Welfare State

Welfare Recipients
- **DC** D915600
- **HN** Formerly (1971-1985) part of DC 374400, Recipients.
- **UF** Welfare Families
- **RT** Benefits
  Dependents
  Disability Recipients
  Disadvantaged
  Low Income Groups
  Welfare Dependency
  Welfare Services

Welfare Reform
- **DC** D915700
- **HN** Added, 1989.
- **BT** Reform
- **RT** Social Reform
  Welfare Policy
  Welfare Services
  Welfare State

Welfare Services
- **DC** D915900
- **HN** Formerly (1963-1985) DC 489725, Welfare.
- **UF** AFDC/Aid for Families of Dependent Children (1965-1985)
  Relief Services
- **BT** Social Services
- **NT** Child Welfare Services
- **RT** Antipoverty Programs
  Benefits
  Family Policy
  Low Income Groups
  Medicaid
  Poverty

Welfare Services (cont'd)
- **RT** Public Housing
  Social Welfare
  Welfare Dependency
  Welfare Policy
  Welfare Recipients
  Welfare Reform

Welfare State
- **DC** D916200
- **HN** Added, 1986. Prior to 1986 use Welfare (DC 489725) and State (DC 444225).
- **BT** State
- **RT** Liberal Democratic Societies
  Liberalism
  Public Services
  Social Democracy
  Social Policy
  Social Security
  Social Welfare
  Welfare Policy
  Welfare Reform

Well Being
- **DC** D916500
- **HN** Formerly (1965-1985) DC 489780.
- **RT** Adjustment
  Affluence
  Coping
  Deprivation
  Happiness
  Health
  Life Satisfaction
  Mental Health
  Morale
  Needs
  Quality of Life

Wellness
- **Use** Health

Weltanschauung
- **Use** Worldview

Wertfreiheit
- **Use** Value Neutrality

West And East
- **Use** East And West

West Bengal, India
- **DC** D916800
- **HN** Added, 1986.
- **BT** India

West Berlin
- **Use** Berlin, Federal Republic of Germany

West Germany
- **Use** Federal Republic of Germany

West Indian/West Indians (1963-1985)
- **HN** DC 489820, deleted 1986. See now Latin American Cultural Groups.

West Indies
- **Use** Caribbean

West Virginia
- **DC** D917100
- **HN** Formerly (1969-1985) DC 489824, West Virginia/West Virginian/West Virginians.
- **BT** Southern States
  United States of America
- **RT** Appalachia

Westermarck, Edward Alexander
- **DC** D917400
- **SN** Born 20 November 1862 - died September 1939.
- **HN** Formerly (1963-1985) DC 489817, Westermarck, Edward.

Western Civilization
- **DC** D917700
- **HN** Added, 1986.
- **UF** Occidental Civilization
- **BT** Civilization
- **RT** Christianity
  European Cultural Groups
  Industrial Societies
  Judaism
  Judeo-Christian Tradition
  Sociocultural Factors

Western Europe
- **DC** D918000
- **HN** Formerly (1984-1985) DC 160274, Europe, West/Western Europe.
- **BT** Europe
- **NT** Andorra
  Austria
  Azores
  Baltic States
  Belgium
  Canary Islands
  Channel Islands
  Cyprus
  Denmark
  England
  Faeroe Islands
  Federal Republic of Germany
  Finland
  France
  Germany
  Gibraltar
  Great Britain
  Greece
  Iceland
  Ireland
  Italy
  Lapland
  Liechtenstein
  Luxembourg
  Madeira
  Malta
  Monaco
  Netherlands
  Northern Ireland
  Norway
  Portugal
  San Marino
  Scandinavia
  Scotland
  Spain
  Sweden
  Switzerland
  Turkey
  United Kingdom
  Vatican
  Wales
- **RT** Eastern Europe

Western Samoa
- **DC** D918300
- **HN** Added, 1986. Prior to 1986 use Samoa (DC 400800).
- **BT** Polynesia

Western Society
- **DC** D918600
- **HN** Formerly (1963-1985) part of DC 489800, West/Western/Westernization.
- **BT** Society
- **RT** Bourgeois Societies
  Capitalist Societies

Western

Western Society (cont'd)
- RT East And West
- Industrialism
- Liberal Democratic Societies
- Modern Society
- Popular Culture
- Postindustrial Societies
- Technology

Western States
- DC D918900
- HN Added, 1986.
- BT States (Political Subdivisions)
- NT Arizona
- California
- Colorado
- Idaho
- Montana
- Nevada
- New Mexico
- Oklahoma
- Oregon
- Texas
- Utah
- Washington (State)
- Southwestern States
- Wyoming
- RT United States of America

White Black Differences
- Use Black White Differences

White Collar Crime
- DC D919200
- SN Offenses committed by persons of high social status, usually in connection with their employment, and that generally involve fraud, embezzlement, or financial misdealing.
- HN Added, 1986. Prior to 1986 use White-collar (DC 489850) and Crime (DC 119100).
- BT Crime
- RT Corruption
- Fraud

White Collar Workers
- DC D919500
- SN Non-manual, non-managerial salaried workers engaged in clerical, administrative, sales, and technical occupations. Sometimes synonymous with New Middle Class. Contrasted with Blue Collar Workers.
- HN Formerly (1963-1985) part of DC 489850, White-Collar.
- BT Workers
- NT Clerical Workers
- Paraprofessional Workers
- Sales Workers
- RT Blue Collar Workers
- New Middle Class
- Occupational Classifications
- Occupations
- Professional Workers
- Service Industries

Whites
- DC D919800
- HN Formerly (1963-1985) DC 489845, White/Whites.
- UF Caucasian/Caucasians (1966-1985)
- RT Anglo Americans
- Black White Differences
- Black White Relations
- Ethnic Groups
- Race

Whorf, Benjamin Lee
- DC D920100
- SN Born 1897 - died 1941.
- HN Formerly (1966-1985) DC 489867.

Whyte, William Foote
- DC D920400
- SN Born 27 June 1914 - .
- HN Formerly (1976-1985) DC 489870, Whyte, W. F.

Widowhood
- DC D920700
- SN The loss of a spouse by death. Includes widows and widowers.
- HN Formerly (1963-1985) DC 489872, Widow/Widowed/Widowhood/Widower/Widowers.
- RT Death
- Elderly
- Elderly Women
- Life Stage Transitions
- Marital Disruption
- Marital Status
- Marriage
- Remarriage
- Survival

Wife Abuse (1985)
- HN DC 489883.
- Use Spouse Abuse

Wilderness
- Use Natural Environment

Will
- DC D921000
- HN Formerly (1965-1985) DC 489895.
- UF Volition/Volitional (1965-1985)
- RT Action
- Consciousness
- Indeterminism
- Intentionality
- Mind
- Voluntarism

Windigo Psychosis
- Use Cannibalism

Windward Islands
- Use Caribbean

Wiretapping (1970-1985)
- HN DC 489915, deleted 1986.

Wirth, Louis
- DC D921300
- SN Born 1897 - died 1952.
- HN Formerly (1969-1985) DC 489930.

Wisconsin
- DC D921600
- HN Formerly (1963-1985) DC 489940.
- BT Midwestern States
- United States of America

Witch Hunting
- Use Scapegoating

Witchcraft
- DC D921900
- HN Formerly (1963-1985) DC 489960, Witch/Witchcraft.
- UF Sorcery (1963-1985)
- Witches
- RT Cults
- Demons
- Devils
- Evil
- Evil Eye

Womens

Witchcraft (cont'd)
- RT Fetishism
- Magic
- Occultism
- Parapsychology
- Spirit Possession
- Supernatural
- Voodooism

Witches
- Use Witchcraft

Withdrawal (1964-1985)
- HN DC 489970, deleted 1986.

Witnesses
- DC D922200
- HN Formerly (1963-1985) DC 489980, Witness/Witnesses.
- UF Eyewitnesses
- NT Expert Witnesses
- RT Defendants
- Evidence (Legal)
- Testimony
- Trials
- Victims

Wittgenstein, Ludwig Joseph Johann
- DC D922500
- SN Born 26 April 1889 - died 29 April 1951.
- HN Formerly (1979-1985) DC 489985, Wittgenstein, L.

Wives
- DC D922800
- HN Formerly (1963-1985) DC 489880, Wife/Wives.
- UF Married Women
- BT Spouses
- RT Homemakers
- Husbands
- Marital Relations
- Mothers
- Spouse Abuse

Wolff, Kurt Heinrich
- DC D923100
- SN Born 20 May 1912 - .
- HN Formerly (1969-1985) DC 489992, Wolff, Kurt H.

Woman/Women (1963-1985)
- HN DC 490000.
- Use Females

Womens Clubs
- Use Womens Groups

Womens Education
- DC D923400
- HN Added, 1986.
- BT Education
- RT Females
- Feminism
- Working Women

Womens Groups
- DC D923700
- HN Added, 1986.
- UF National Organization for Women/NOW (1977-1985)
- Womens Clubs
- Womens Organizations
- BT Groups
- RT Females
- Feminism
- Social Groups

Womens

Womens Liberation Movement
   Use Feminism

Womens Organizations
   Use Womens Groups

Womens Rights
   DC D924000
   HN Added, 1986.
   UF Equal Rights for Women
   BT Human Rights
   RT Civil Rights
        Females
        Feminism
        Sex Role Attitudes
        Sexism
        Social Movements

Womens Roles
   DC D924100
   HN Added, 1988.
   UF Female Roles
   BT Sex Roles
   RT Androgyny
        Females
        Femininity
        Feminism
        Role Conflict
        Role Models
        Professional Women
        Working Mothers
        Working Women

Womens Work
   Use Sexual Division of Labor

Words
   DC D924300
   HN Formerly (1963-1985) DC 491750, Word/Words/Wording.
   UF Neologism/Neologisms (1970-1985)
   NT Terminology
   RT Definitions
        Etymology
        Language
        Morphology (Language)
        Semantics
        Taboos
        Vocabularies

Work
   DC D924600
   SN A context-dependent term for the expenditure of effort to accomplish tasks or solve problems. Select a more specific entry or coordinate with other terms.
   HN Formerly (1963-1985) DC 492000, Work/Works/Working.
   NT Housework
        Piecework
        Shift Work
        Teamwork
   RT Education Work Relationship
        Employment
        Family Work Relationship
        Job Characteristics
        Job Performance
        Job Requirements
        Labor
        Labor Force
        Labor Process
        Labor Productivity
        Occupational Aspiration
        Occupational Classifications
        Occupational Structure
        Quality of Working Life
        Sociology of Work
        Specialization

Work (cont'd)
   RT Tasks
        Work Attitudes
        Work Environment
        Work Experience
        Work Groups
        Work Humanization
        Work Leisure Relationship
        Work Organization
        Work Orientations
        Work Skills
        Work Values
        Worker Attitudes
        Workers
        Working Hours
        Workplaces

Work Attitudes
   DC D924900
   SN Attitudes toward work. Do not confuse with Worker Attitudes.
   HN Added, 1986.
   UF Job Attitudes
   BT Attitudes
   NT Professionalism
   RT Employment
        Family Work Relationship
        Job Satisfaction
        Morale
        Motivation
        Organizational Commitment
        Welfare Dependency
        Work
        Work Humanization
        Work Orientations
        Work Values
        Worker Attitudes
        Workers

Work Characteristics
   Use Job Characteristics

Work Choice
   Use Occupational Choice

Work Collectives
   Use Collectives

Work Environment
   DC D925200
   HN Formerly (1985) DC 492200.
   UF Organizational Climate
        Working Conditions
   BT Environment
   RT Biotechnology
        Employment
        Home Workplaces
        Job Characteristics
        Job Performance
        Job Satisfaction
        Labor Relations
        Living Conditions
        Management Styles
        Occupational Safety And Health
        Occupational Stress
        Personnel Management
        Personnel Policy
        Quality of Working Life
        Social Environment
        Superior Subordinate Relationship
        Work
        Work Humanization
        Worker Machine Relationship
        Working Hours
        Workplaces

Work Ethic
   Use Protestant Ethic

Work Experience
   DC D925500
   HN Added, 1986.
   BT Experience
   RT Career Patterns
        Employability
        Job Requirements
        Occupational Qualifications
        Work
        Youth Employment

Work Force
   Use Labor Force

Work Groups
   DC D925800
   HN Added, 1986.
   BT Groups
   RT Group Dynamics
        Human Relations Movement
        Organizations (Social)
        Work
        Work Humanization

Work Humanization
   DC D926100
   HN Added, 1986.
   UF Labor Humanization
   BT Humanization
   RT Employee Assistance Programs
        Human Relations Movement
        Industrial Automation
        Job Satisfaction
        Labor
        Labor Process
        Quality of Working Life
        Work
        Work Attitudes
        Work Environment
        Work Groups
        Work Organization
        Worker Machine Relationship

Work Leisure Relationship
   DC D926400
   HN Added, 1986.
   BT Relations
   RT Family Work Relationship
        Leisure
        Time
        Work
        Working Hours

Work Life Quality
   Use Quality of Working Life

Work Organization
   DC D926700
   HN Added, 1986.
   UF Task Organization
        Work Structure
   BT Structure
   RT Division of Labor
        Industrial Enterprises
        Industrial Management
        Organizational Structure
        Scientific Management
        Shift Work
        Supervision
        Tasks
        Work
        Work Humanization
        Workers
        Working Hours

Work

Work Orientations
- DC D927000
- HN Added, 1986.
- BT Orientation
- NT Professional Orientations
- RT Education Work Relationship
  - Job Satisfaction
  - Labor Force Participation
  - Occupational Aspiration
  - Organizational Development
  - Protestant Ethic
  - Work
  - Work Attitudes
  - Work Values

Work Qualifications
- Use Occupational Qualifications

Work Requirements
- Use Job Requirements

Work Roles
- Use Occupational Roles

Work Safety
- Use Occupational Safety And Health

Work Satisfaction
- Use Job Satisfaction

Work Skills
- DC D927300
- HN Added, 1986.
- UF Job Skills
  - Skilled Labor
- BT Skills
- RT Employability
  - Employment
  - Job Characteristics
  - Job Requirements
  - Job Training
  - Labor Market
  - Manual Workers
  - Occupational Classifications
  - Occupational Qualifications
  - Occupational Status
  - Underemployment
  - Work
  - Workers

Work Sociology
- Use Sociology of Work

Work Structure
- Use Work Organization

Work Tasks
- Use Tasks

Work Values
- DC D927600
- HN Added, 1986.
- BT Values
- RT Job Satisfaction
  - Occupational Aspiration
  - Professional Orientations
  - Professionalism
  - Protestant Ethic
  - Work
  - Work Attitudes
  - Work Orientations

Work Week
- Use Working Hours

Worker Attitudes
- DC D927900
- HN Added, 1986.
- BT Attitudes
- RT Family Work Relationship
  - Work
  - Work Attitudes
  - Worker Machine Relationship
  - Workers

Worker Consciousness
- DC D928200
- HN Added, 1986.
- BT Social Consciousness
- RT Class Consciousness
  - Class Politics
  - Labor Movements
  - Solidarity Movements
  - Workers

Worker Control
- DC D928500
- SN The process by which an organization's employees exercise and are fully responsible for their own management decisions.
- HN Added, 1986.
- UF Industrial Self Management
  - Self Management in Industry
- BT Control
  - Industrial Democracy
- RT Worker Ownership

Worker Dismissal
- Use Dismissal

Worker Machine Relationship
- DC D928800
- SN The mutual effects between humans and the machines they operate, especially as studied for purposes of improving machine design and work environment.
- HN Added, 1986.
- UF Man Machine Relationship
- BT Relations
- RT Biotechnology
  - Industrial Automation
  - Industrial Workers
  - Machinery
  - Manufacturing Industries
  - Office Automation
  - Quality of Working Life
  - Scientific Technological Revolution
  - Symbiotic Relations
  - Work Environment
  - Work Humanization
  - Worker Attitudes
  - Workers

Worker Mobility
- Use Job Change

Worker Ownership
- DC D929100
- HN Added, 1986.
- UF Employee Ownership
- BT Ownership
- RT Enterprises
  - Industrial Democracy
  - Worker Control
  - Workers

Worker Participation
- DC D929400
- SN The process by which employees take part in management decision making, usually in industrial organizations. May vary in degree and kind of participation, depending on political or social environment.
- HN Added, 1986.
- UF Participative Management
- BT Industrial Democracy
  - Participation
- RT Management
  - Participative Decision Making
  - Representation

Working

Workers
- DC D929700
- HN Formerly (1963-1985) DC 492500, Worker/Workers.
- UF Employee/Employees (1963-1985)
- NT Blue Collar Workers
  - Dislocated Workers
  - Foreign Workers
  - Migrant Workers
  - Professional Workers
  - White Collar Workers
  - Working Women
- RT Employers
  - Employee Assistance Programs
  - Employment
  - Enterprises
  - Homemakers
  - Human Resources
  - Job Performance
  - Job Satisfaction
  - Labor
  - Labor Disputes
  - Labor Force
  - Labor Market
  - Labor Movements
  - Labor Policy
  - Labor Productivity
  - Labor Relations
  - Labor Supply
  - Occupational Roles
  - Occupational Structure
  - Occupations
  - Pensions
  - Personnel Management
  - Quality of Working Life
  - Retirement
  - Seniority
  - Supervision
  - Tenure
  - Unions
  - Wages
  - Work
  - Work Attitudes
  - Work Organization
  - Work Skills
  - Worker Attitudes
  - Worker Consciousness
  - Worker Machine Relationship
  - Worker Ownership
  - Working Class

Workers Compensation Insurance
- DC D930000
- SN Insurance that provides medical benefits and continued income for employees injured in work-related accidents.
- HN Added, 1986.
- BT Insurance
- RT Disability Recipients
  - Health Insurance
  - Injuries
  - Occupational Safety And Health

Workers Movements
- Use Labor Movements

Working Class
- DC D930300
- SN Unskilled, semiskilled, and skilled nonprofessional workers considered as a class.
- HN Formerly (1985) DC 493100.
- BT Social Class
- RT Blue Collar Workers
  - Capitalist Societies
  - Class Politics
  - Class Struggle

Working Class (cont'd)
- **RT** Embourgeoisement
  - Industrial Workers
  - Labor Force
  - Labor Movements
  - Low Income Groups
  - Lower Class
  - Masses
  - Peasants
  - Proletarianization
  - Proletariat
  - Unions
  - Workers

Working Conditions
- **Use** Work Environment

Working Hours
- **DC** D930600
- **HN** Added, 1986.
- **UF** Flexible Working Hours
  - Hours of Work
  - Work Week
- **RT** Employment
  - Job Characteristics
  - Labor Productivity
  - Part Time Employment
  - Personnel Policy
  - Shift Work
  - Time
  - Work
  - Work Environment
  - Work Leisure Relationship
  - Work Organization

Working Mothers
- **DC** D930800
- **HN** Added, 1989.
- **UF** Maternal Employment
- **BT** Mothers
  - Working Women
- **RT** Childrearing Practices
  - Cottage Industries
  - Dual Career Family
  - Employment
  - Family Work Relationship
  - Female Headed Households
  - Home Workplaces
  - Parent Child Relations
  - Parental Attitudes
  - Role Conflict
  - Sex Role Attitudes
  - Womens Roles

Working Women
- **DC** D930900
- **HN** Added, 1986.
- **UF** Maternal Employment
- **BT** Females
  - Workers
- **NT** Professional Women
  - Working Mothers
- **RT** Cottage Industries
  - Dual Career Family
  - Employment
  - Female Headed Households
  - Feminism
  - Home Workplaces
  - Labor Force
  - Labor Force Participation
  - Labor Market Segmentation
  - Nontraditional Occupations
  - Occupational Roles
  - Occupational Segregation
  - Occupational Status
  - Sex Role Attitudes
  - Womens Education
  - Womens Roles

Workplaces
- **DC** D931200
- **HN** Formerly (1983-1985) DC 492540, Workplace/Workplaces.
- **NT** Home Workplaces
- **RT** Commuting (Travel)
  - Enterprises
  - Factories
  - Labor
  - Occupational Safety And Health
  - Residence
  - Work
  - Work Environment
  - Workshops (Manufacturing)

Works of Art
- **Use** Art

Workshop (1971-1985)
- **HN** DC 492550, deleted 1986. See now Workshops (Courses) or Workshops (Manufacturing).

Workshops (Courses)
- **DC** D931500
- **HN** Added, 1986. Prior to 1986 use Workshop (DC 492550).
- **RT** Courses
  - Educational Programs
  - Seminars
  - Symposia
  - Training

Workshops (Manufacturing)
- **DC** D931800
- **HN** Added, 1986. Prior to 1986 use Workshop (DC 492550).
- **UF** Sheltered Workshops
- **BT** Factories
- **RT** Job Training
  - Manufacturing Industries
  - Vocational Rehabilitation
  - Workplaces

World (1963-1985)
- **HN** DC 493340, deleted 1986. See now appropriate "International" or "World" terms.

World Bank
- **Use** International Economic Organizations

World Congress of Sociology (1970-1985)
- **HN** DC 493342.
- **Use** Congresses And Conventions

World Councils
- **Use** Councils

World Economy
- **DC** D932100
- **HN** Added, 1986. Prior to 1986 use World (DC 493340) and Economy/Economies (DC 145200).
- **UF** International Economy
- **RT** Dependency Theory
  - Economic Conditions
  - Economic Planning
  - Economic Policy
  - Economic Structure
  - Economic Systems
  - Economic Underdevelopment
  - Economics
  - Exports And Imports
  - Foreign Aid
  - International Division of Labor
  - International Economic Organizations
  - International Relations

World Economy (cont'd)
- **RT** Multinational Corporations
  - Protectionism
  - Public Debt
  - Trade
  - World System Theory

World Health Organization (1963-1985)
- **HN** DC 493350.
- **Use** United Nations

World Population
- **DC** D932400
- **HN** Added, 1986.
- **BT** Population
- **RT** Demography
  - Overpopulation
  - Population Distribution
  - Population Growth

World Problems
- **DC** D932700
- **HN** Added, 1986.
- **UF** Global Problems
  - International Problems
- **BT** Problems
- **RT** Disarmament
  - Economic Problems
  - Economic Underdevelopment
  - Famine
  - Human Rights
  - Hunger
  - International Relations
  - Overpopulation
  - Pollution
  - Poverty
  - Refugees
  - Social Problems
  - Terrorism
  - War

World System Theory
- **DC** D933000
- **SN** The view that the development and underdevelopment of nations are not isolated phenomena and should be studied in the context of the world economy.
- **HN** Added, 1986.
- **UF** Capitalist World System
- **BT** Economic Theories
- **RT** Capitalism
  - Center And Periphery
  - Dependency Theory
  - Developing Countries
  - Economic Policy
  - Exploitation
  - World Economy

World War I
- **DC** D933300
- **HN** Formerly (1964-1985) DC 493370.
- **BT** War
- **RT** Twentieth Century

World War II
- **DC** D933600
- **HN** Formerly (1964-1985) DC 493400.
- **UF** Nuremberg Tribunal (1976-1985)
- **BT** War
- **RT** Concentration Camps
  - Genocide
  - Holocaust
  - Twentieth Century

Worldview
- **DC** D933700
- **SN** The philosophy of life or outlook on the world of an individual or a specific social group. A synonym for worldvision and the German *Weltanschauung*.
- **HN** Formerly (1984-1985) DC 493365.
- **UF** Ethos (1963-1985)
  Weltanschauung
- **BT** Perceptions
- **RT** Beliefs
  Common Sense
  Culture
  Cynicism
  Hermeneutics
  Ideologies
  Interpretive Sociology
  Lifestyle
  Methodology (Philosophical)
  Optimism
  Pessimism
  Sectarianism
  Social Reality

Worship
- **DC** D933900
- **HN** Formerly (1963-1985) DC 493440.
- **NT** Ancestor Worship
- **RT** Cults
  Deities
  Fetishism
  Liturgy
  Places of Worship
  Prayer
  Religions
  Religious Beliefs
  Religious Rituals
  Sacrificial Rites
  Saints

Writers
- **DC** D934200
- **HN** Formerly (1963-1985) DC 493485, Writer/Writers.
- **UF** Authors
- **BT** Professional Workers
- **NT** Poets
- **RT** Authorship
  Editors
  Journalists
  Literature
  Publications
  Publishing Industry
  Writing
  Writing for Publication

Writing
- **DC** D934500
- **HN** Formerly (1964-1985) DC 493500, Writing/Writings.
- **BT** Literacy
- **NT** Writing for Publication
- **RT** Authorship
  Language
  Letters (Correspondence)
  Literacy Programs
  Verbal Accounts
  Verbal Communication
  Writers

Writing for Publication
- **DC** D934800
- **HN** Added, 1986.
- **UF** Publication Productivity
- **BT** Writing
- **RT** Articles
  Authorship

Writing for Publication (cont'd)
- **RT** Books
  Journalism
  Journals
  Periodicals
  Publications
  Publishing Industry
  Scholarship
  Writers

Wyoming
- **DC** D935100
- **HN** Formerly (1976-1985) DC 493575.
- **BT** United States of America
  Western States

Xenophile/Xenophobic/Xenophobia (1978-1985)
- **HN** DC 493650.
- **Use** Phobias

X-ray (1968-1985)
- **HN** DC 493700, deleted 1986.

Yemen Arab Republic
- **DC** D935400
- **HN** Added, 1986. Prior to 1986 use Yemen/Yemenite/Yemenites (DC 493880).
- **BT** Arab Countries
  Middle East

Yemen (Peoples Democratic Republic)
- **DC** D935700
- **HN** Added, 1986. Prior to 1986 use Yemen/Yemenite/Yemenites (DC 493880).
- **UF** Aden (1972-1985)
- **BT** Arab Countries
  Middle East

Yemen/Yemenite/Yemenites (1966-1985)
- **HN** DC 493880, deleted 1986. See now Yemen (Peoples Democratic Republic) or Yemen Arab Republic.

Yoga
- **DC** D936000
- **HN** Formerly (1964-1985) DC 493935.
- **RT** Hinduism
  Religious Rituals

Young (1964-1985)
- **HN** DC 493940, deleted 1986.

Young Adults
- **DC** D936300
- **SN** Persons aged 18 to 30.
- **HN** Formerly (1985) DC 493960.
- **BT** Adults
  Age Groups
- **RT** Adolescents
  College Students
  Marriage Timing
  Married Students
  Sexual Behavior
  Single Persons
  Youth

Young Men's-Women's Christian Assn/YM & YWCA (1964-1985)
- **HN** DC 494100. Abbreviated here due to character restrictions. Formerly used in indexing under its full name Young Men's-Women's Christian Association/YM & YWCA.
- **Use** Associations

Youth
- **DC** D936600
- **HN** Formerly (1963-1985) DC 494500, Youth/Youths/Youthful.
- **NT** Rural Youth
- **RT** Adolescents
  Age Groups
  Childhood
  Educational Plans
  Elderly
  Juvenile Delinquency
  Parent Child Relations
  Young Adults
  Youth Culture
  Youth Employment
  Youth Movements
  Youth Organizations

Youth Culture
- **DC** D936800
- **HN** Added, 1989.
- **UF** Punk (1985)
- **BT** Culture
- **RT** Adolescents
  Countercultures
  Popular Culture
  Youth
  Youth Movements
  Youth Organizations

Youth Diversion Programs
- **Use** Delinquency Prevention

Youth Employment
- **DC** D936900
- **HN** Added, 1986.
- **UF** Unemployed Youth
  Youth Unemployment
- **BT** Employment
- **RT** Adolescents
  Delinquency Prevention
  Part Time Employment
  Rural Youth
  Work Experience
  Youth

Youth Movements
- **DC** D937100
- **HN** Added, 1986.
- **UF** Student Movements
- **BT** Movements
- **RT** Political Movements
  Social Action
  Social Movements
  Youth
  Youth Culture

Youth Organizations
- **DC** D937200
- **HN** Added, 1986.
- **BT** Organizations (Social)
- **RT** Adolescents
  Clubs
  Gangs
  Youth
  Youth Culture

Youth Unemployment
- **Use** Youth Employment

Yucatan, Mexico (1964-1985)
- **HN** DC 494800, deleted 1986.

Yugoslavia
- **DC** D937500
- **HN** Formerly (1963-1985) DC 495000, Yugoslav/Yugoslavs/Yugoslavia.
- **BT** Balkan States
  Eastern Europe
- **NT** Croatia, Yugoslavia
  Montenegro, Yugoslavia
  Serbia, Yugoslavia
  Slovenia, Yugoslavia

Yukon
- **DC** D937800
- **HN** Formerly (1964-1985) DC 495100.
- **BT** Canada
- **RT** Arctic Regions

Zadruga (1970-1985)
- **HN** DC 495300, deleted 1986.

Zaire
- **DC** D938100
- **HN** Formerly (1972-1985) DC 495310.
- **BT** Sub Saharan Africa
- **NT** Kinshasa, Zaire

Zambia
- **DC** D938400
- **HN** Formerly (1968-1985) DC 495322, Zambia/Zambian/Zambians.
- **UF** Northern Rhodesia
- **BT** Sub Saharan Africa

Zamindari/Zamindaris (1963-1985)
- **HN** DC 495350, deleted 1986.

Zen Buddhism
- **DC** D938700
- **HN** Formerly (1965-1985) DC 495450, Zen.
- **BT** Buddhism
- **NT** Lamaism

Zimbabwe
- **DC** D939000
- **HN** Formerly (1981-1985) DC 495540.
- **UF** Southern Rhodesia
- **BT** Sub Saharan Africa

Zionism
- **DC** D939300
- **HN** Formerly (1963-1985) DC 495550, Zion/Zionism/Zionist/Zionists.
- **BT** Religious Movements
- **RT** Aliyah
  Jews
  Movements

Znaniecki, Florian
- **DC** D939600
- **SN** Born 1882 - died 1958.
- **HN** Formerly (1964-1985) DC 495735, Znaniecki, F.

Zodiac
- **Use** Astrology

Zoning
- **DC** D939900
- **HN** Formerly (1963-1985) DC 495800, Zone/Zones/Zoning.
- **RT** City Planning
  Districts
  Land Use
  Suburbs

Zoroastrianism
- **DC** D940200
- **HN** Formerly (1968-1985) DC 496025, Zoroaster/Zoroastrian/Zoroastrianism.
- **UF** Mazdaism
- **BT** Religions

Zurich, Switzerland
- **HN** DC 496500, deleted 1986.

ROTATED DESCRIPTOR DISPLAY

Addis **Ababa,** Ethiopia
Ability
Aboriginal Australians
Abortion
Father **Absence**
Mother **Absence**
Absenteeism
Abstraction
Abuse
Alcohol **Abuse**
Child **Abuse**
Child Sexual **Abuse**
Drug **Abuse**
Elder **Abuse**
Sexual **Abuse**
Spouse **Abuse**
Substance **Abuse**
Academic Achievement
Academic Aptitude
Academic Careers
Academic Degrees
Academic Departments
Academic Disciplines
Academic Freedom
Academic Tenure
Acceptance
Social **Acceptance**
Access
Accidents
Accountability
Accountants
Accounting
Verbal **Accounts**
Acculturation
Accumulation
Accuracy
Academic **Achievement**
Achievement
Achievement Tests
Occupational **Achievement**
Recognition **(Achievement)**
Lysergic **Acid** Diethylamide
Acquired Immune Deficiency Syndrome
Language **Acquisition**
Action
Action Research
Action Theory
Affirmative **Action**
Collective **Action**
Communicative **Action**
Political **Action**
Political **Action** Committees
Social **Action**
Activism
Activities
Cultural **Activities**
Actors
Self **Actualization**
Drug **Addiction**
Addis Ababa, Ethiopia
Adjustment
Marital **Adjustment**
Adler, Alfred
Carter **Administration**
Educational **Administration**
Public **Administration**
Reagan **Administration**
Administrators
Admissions
Adolescents
Adopted Children
Adoption of Innovations

Adorno, Theodor Wiesengrund
Adult Children
Adult Development
Adult Education
Adults
Middle Aged **Adults**
Young **Adults**
Adversary Legal System
Advertising
Advisors
Advisory Committees
Advocacy
Aesthetics
Marxist **Aesthetics**
Affective Illness
Affiliation Need
Political **Affiliation**
Affinity (Kinship)
Affirmative Action
Affluence
Afghanistan
Kabul, **Afghanistan**
Africa
Cape Town, South **Africa**
Johannesburg, South **Africa**
North **Africa**
Pretoria, South **Africa**
South **Africa**
Sub Saharan **Africa**
African Cultural Groups
African Languages
Central **African** Republic
North **African** Cultural Groups
Southern **African** Cultural Groups
After Care
Age
Age Differences
Age Groups
Middle **Aged** Adults
Ageism
Agencies
Government **Agencies**
Social **Agencies**
Change **Agents**
Socialization **Agents**
Middle **Ages**
Aggregate Data
Aggression
Aging
Agitation
Agnosticism
Agrarian Societies
Agrarian Structures
Agreement
Agribusiness
Agricultural Collectives
Agricultural Development
Agricultural Economics
Agricultural Enterprises
Agricultural Mechanization
Agricultural Policy
Agricultural Production
Agricultural Research
Agricultural Technology
Agricultural Workers
Agriculture
Foreign **Aid**
Air Pollution
Air Transportation
Buenos **Aires,** Argentina
Alabama
Alaska
Albania

Alberta   ROTATED DESCRIPTOR DISPLAY   **Architects**

Alberta	Network **Analysis**
Alcohol Abuse	Path **Analysis**
Alcohol Use	Policy **Analysis**
Alcoholic Beverages	Principal Components **Analysis**
Alcoholism	Psychometric **Analysis**
Porto **Alegre**, Brazil	Regression **Analysis**
Alexander, Jeffrey C.	Secondary **Analysis**
Algeria	Social Area **Analysis**
Algiers, **Algeria**	Sociometric **Analysis**
Algiers, Algeria	Spatial **Analysis**
Algorithms	Structural-Functional **Analysis**
Alienation	Time Series **Analysis**
Alimony	**Anarchism**
Alinsky, Saul David	**Ancestor** Worship
Aliyah	**Ancient** Greek Philosophy
Alliance	**Andes**
International **Alliances**	**Andhra** Pradesh, India
Allocation	**Andorra**
Resource **Allocation**	**Androgyny**
Allport, Gordon Willard	Los **Angeles**, California
Alternative Approaches	**Anger**
Althusser, Louis	**Anglicans**
Altitude Effects	**Anglo** Americans
Altruism	**Angola**
Alzheimer's Disease	**Anguilla**
Amateurs	**Animal** Human Relations
Amazon	**Animal** Husbandry
Ambiguity	**Animals**
Role **Ambiguity**	**Animism**
Ambivalence	**Annexation**
Constitutional **Amendments**	**Annulment**
Central **America**	**Anomie**
Latin **America**	**Anonymity**
North **America**	**Anorexia** Nervosa
South **America**	**Antarctica**
United States of **America**	**Anthropologists**
American Indian Reservations	**Anthropology**
American Indians	Social **Anthropology**
American Samoa	**Antigua**
Latin **American** Cultural Groups	Netherlands **Antilles**
North **American** Cultural Groups	**Antinuclear** Movements
Soviet **American** Relations	**Antipoverty** Programs
Anglo **Americans**	**Antiquity**
Hispanic **Americans**	**Anti-Semitism**
Mexican **Americans**	**Antwerp**, Belgium
Amerindian Languages	**Anxiety**
Amish	**Apartheid**
Amniocentesis	**Apathy**
Amsterdam, Netherlands	**Aphasia**
Anabaptists	**Apocalypse**
Analogy	**Apostasy**
Analysis	**Appalachia**
Class **Analysis**	Job **Application**
Cluster **Analysis**	Research **Applications**
Cohort **Analysis**	**Applied** Sociology
Comparative **Analysis**	Legislative **Apportionment**
Componential **Analysis**	**Apprenticeships**
Content **Analysis**	Dramaturgical **Approach**
Contingency **Analysis**	Interdisciplinary **Approach**
Conversational **Analysis**	Alternative **Approaches**
Crosscultural **Analysis**	**Appropriate** Technologies
Dimensional **Analysis**	**Appropriation**
Discourse **Analysis**	**Approval**
Discriminant **Analysis**	Academic **Aptitude**
Econometric **Analysis**	**Arab** Countries
Factor **Analysis**	**Arab** Cultural Groups
Latent Structure **Analysis**	United **Arab** Emirates
Linear **Analysis**	Yemen **Arab** Republic
Loglinear **Analysis**	Saudi **Arabia**
Marxist **Analysis**	**Arbitration**
Methodology (Data **Analysis**)	**Archaeology**
Multiple Regression **Analysis**	Tuamotu **Archipelago**
Multivariate **Analysis**	**Architects**

Architecture — ROTATED DESCRIPTOR DISPLAY — Bali

	Architecture
	Archival Research
	Archives
	Arctic Regions
Social	Area Analysis
Low Income	Areas
Metropolitan	Areas
Nonmetropolitan	Areas
Rural	Areas
Urban	Areas
	Arendt, Hannah
	Argentina
Buenos Aires,	Argentina
	Arid Zones
	Aristocracy
	Arizona
Phoenix,	Arizona
	Arkansas
	Armaments
	Armed Forces
	Armenian Soviet Socialist Republic
	Aron, Raymond Claude Ferdinand
Sexual	Arousal
	Arrests
	Arson
	Art
	Art History
Sociology of	Art
	Arthritis
	Articles
	Artifacts
	Artificial Insemination
	Artificial Intelligence
	Artisans
	Artistic Styles
	Artists
Fine	Arts
Theater	Arts
Visual	Arts
	Aruba
	Asceticism
	Asch, Solomon Elliott
	Ascription
	Asia
South	Asia
Southeast	Asia
	Asian Cultural Groups
South	Asian Cultural Groups
Southeast	Asian Cultural Groups
	Aspiration
Occupational	Aspiration
	Assassination
	Assault
Sexual	Assault
	Assertiveness
Needs	Assessment
Risk	Assessment
Social Impact	Assessment
Technology	Assessment
	Assimilation
	Assistance
Employee	Assistance Programs
Technical	Assistance
Computer	Assisted Instruction
Computer	Assisted Research
	Associations
Employers	Associations
Professional	Associations
Sociological	Associations
	Astrology
	Astronomy
	Atheism

	Athens, Greece
	Athletes
	Atlanta, Georgia
	Atlantic Ocean
North	Atlantic Ocean
South	Atlantic Ocean
	Attachment
	Attainment
Educational	Attainment
Status	Attainment
	Attendance
Church	Attendance
School	Attendance
	Attention
	Attitude Change
	Attitude Measures
	Attitudes
Death	Attitudes
Environmental	Attitudes
Language	Attitudes
Parental	Attitudes
Political	Attitudes
Religious	Attitudes
Sex Role	Attitudes
Social	Attitudes
Student	Attitudes
Teacher	Attitudes
Work	Attitudes
Worker	Attitudes
Interpersonal	Attraction
	Attractiveness
	Attribution
	Attrition
	Audiences
	Audiovisual Media
	Australasia
	Australasian Cultural Groups
	Australia
Brisbane,	Australia
Canberra,	Australia
Melbourne,	Australia
Sydney,	Australia
Aboriginal	Australians
	Austria
Vienna,	Austria
	Austronesian Languages
	Authoritarianism (Political Ideology)
	Authoritarianism (Psychology)
	Authority
	Authorship
	Autism
	Autobiographical Materials
	Automation
Industrial	Automation
Office	Automation
	Automobile Industry
	Automobiles
	Autonomy
Tel	Aviv, Israel
	Avoidance
	Awards
	Azores
	Baccalaureate Degrees
	Bachofen, Johann Jakob
Social	Background
	Baghdad, Iraq
	Bahaism
	Bahamas
	Bahrain
	Balance Theory
	Bales, Robert Freed
	Bali

Balkan   ROTATED DESCRIPTOR DISPLAY   **Bourgeoisie**

Balkan States	Alcoholic **Beverages**
Baltic States	**Bhutan**
Baltimore, Maryland	**Bias**
Banditry	Statistical **Bias**
Banfield, Edward Christie	Test **Bias**
Bangkok, Thailand	**Bible**
Bangladesh	**Bibliographies**
Banking	**Biculturalism**
Bankruptcy	**Bihar,** India
Data **Banks**	**Bilingual** Education
Baptism	**Bilingualism**
Baptists	**Binet,** Alfred
Barbados	**Bioethics**
Barbuda	**Biographies**
Barcelona, Spain	**Biological** Factors
Collective **Bargaining**	**Biological** Sciences
Plea **Bargaining**	**Biology**
Saint **Barthelemy**	**Biomedicine**
Barthes, Roland	**Biosocial** Theory
Base And Superstructure	**Biotechnology**
Basque Provinces	**Birth**
Bateson, Gregory	**Birth** Control
Battered Women	**Birth** Order
Becker, Howard Saul	**Birth** Spacing
Beggary	First **Birth** Timing
Behavior	**Bisexuality**
Behavior Modification	Guinea **Bissau**
Behavior Problems	**Black** Community
Collective **Behavior**	**Black** Family
Deviant **Behavior**	**Black** Muslims
Drinking **Behavior**	**Black** Power
Health **Behavior**	**Black** White Differences
Help Seeking **Behavior**	**Black** White Relations
Helping **Behavior**	**Blacks**
Illness **Behavior**	**Blau,** Peter Michael
Mass **Behavior**	**Blind**
Organizational **Behavior**	**Bloch,** Ernst
Political **Behavior**	**Blood**
Public **Behavior**	**Blood** Groups
Religious **Behavior**	**Blood** Pressure
Self Destructive **Behavior**	**Blue** Collar Workers
Sexual **Behavior**	**Blumer,** Herbert George
Social **Behavior**	Governing **Boards**
Spatial **Behavior**	School **Boards**
Student **Behavior**	**Boas,** Franz
Voting **Behavior**	Legislative **Bodies**
Behavioral Sciences	**Body** Height
Behaviorism	**Body** Weight
Well **Being**	Human **Body**
Beirut, Lebanon	**Bogota,** Colombia
Antwerp, **Belgium**	**Bolivia**
Belgium	**Bolshevism**
Brussels, **Belgium**	**Bombay,** India
Beliefs	**Bombs**
Religious **Beliefs**	Napoleon **Bonaparte**
Belize	**Book** Reviews
Bell, Daniel	**Books**
Bellah, Robert N.	**Boom** Towns
Bendix, Reinhard	**Borders**
Benedict, Ruth Fulton	**Boredom**
Benefits	**Borgatta,** Edgar F.
Bengal	**Borstal**
West **Bengal,** India	**Boston,** Massachusetts
Benin	Plants **(Botanical)**
Berger, Peter	**Botswana**
Bergson, Henri Louis	**Boulding,** Kenneth Ewart
Berlin, Federal Republic of Germany	**Boundaries**
	Boundary Maintenance
Berlin, German Democratic Republic	**Bourdieu,** Pierre
	Bourgeois Ideologies
Berlin, Germany	**Bourgeois** Societies
Berlin, Sir Isaiah	**Bourgeois** Sociology
Bermuda	**Bourgeoisie**

280

ROTATED DESCRIPTOR DISPLAY

Boycotts ... **Cerebral**

                Boycotts
                Brahmins
                Brain
                Brain Drain
                Brainwashing
                Brand Names
                Brazil
Porto Alegre, **Brazil**
Rio de Janeiro, **Brazil**
Sao Paulo, **Brazil**
                Breast Feeding
                Bridewealth
                Brisbane, Australia
Great **Britain**
                British Columbia
Vancouver, **British** Columbia
Programming (**Broadcast**)
Religious **Brotherhoods**
New **Brunswick**
                Brussels, Belgium
                Buber, Martin
                Bucharest, Romania
                Buddhism
Zen **Buddhism**
                Buddhists
                Budgets
                Buenos Aires, Argentina
                Buffalo, New York
                Buildings
                Bulgaria
Sofia, **Bulgaria**
                Bulimia
                Bureaucracy
                Bureaucratization
                Burglary
                Burials
                Burke, Edmund
                Burkina Faso
                Burma
Rangoon, **Burma**
                Burt, Sir Cyril Lodowic
                Burundi
                Business
                Business Cycles
                Business Society Relationship
Family **Businesses**
Minority **Businesses**
Small **Businesses**
                Businessmen
                Cabala
                Cadres
Turks And **Caicos** Islands
                Cairo, Egypt
                Calcutta, India
New **Caledonia**
                Calendars
                California
Los Angeles, **California**
San Diego, **California**
San Francisco, **California**
                Calvinism
                Calvinists
                Cameroons
Political **Campaigns**
                Camping
Concentration **Camps**
                Camus, Albert
                Canada
                Canary Islands
                Canberra, Australia
                Cancer
                Candidates
                Cannibalism

                Canons
                Cantril, Albert Hadley
                Cape Town, South Africa
                Cape Verde Islands
                Capital
                Capital Punishment
Human **Capital**
                Capitalism
Monopoly **Capitalism**
State **Capitalism**
                Capitalist Societies
                Caplow, Theodore
                Caracas, Venezuela
After **Care**
Child **Care** Services
Day **Care**
Dental **Care**
Foster **Care**
Health **Care**
Health **Care** Utilization
Home Health **Care**
Primary Health **Care**
Self **Care**
                Career Criminals
                Career Patterns
Dual **Career** Family
Academic **Careers**
                Careers
                Caregivers
                Cargo Cults
                Caribbean
                Caribbean Cultural Groups
North **Carolina**
South **Carolina**
                Caroline Islands
                Carter Administration
                Cartoons
                Case Studies
Legal **Cases**
Social Work **Cases**
                Caste Systems
                Castration
                Catalonia, Spain
                Categorical Data
                Cathari
                Catholicism
Roman **Catholicism**
                Catholics
Roman **Catholics**
                Causal Models
                Causality
                Cayman Islands
                Celebrations
                Celibacy
                Cemeteries
                Censorship
                Census
                Center And Periphery
                Centers
Community Mental Health **Centers**
                Central African Republic
                Central America
                Central Cities
                Central Government
                Centrality
                Centralization
Eighteenth **Century**
Nineteenth **Century**
Seventeenth **Century**
Sixteenth **Century**
Twentieth **Century**
                Cerebral Palsy

Certainty ROTATED DESCRIPTOR DISPLAY Coast

	Certainty		**Church** State Relationship
	Certification	Unification	**Church**
	Chad		**Churches**
	Chance		**Cicourel,** Aaron V.
Attitude	**Change**		**Cincinnati,** Ohio
	Change		**Circumcision**
	Change Agents		**Citations** (References)
Community	**Change**	Central	**Cities**
Cultural	**Change**		**Cities**
Demographic	**Change**		**Citizen** Participation
Economic	**Change**		**Citizens**
Job	**Change**		**Citizenship**
Neighborhood	**Change**		**City** Planning
Organizational	**Change**	Ho Chi Minh	**City,** Vietnam
Social	**Change**	Kansas	**City,** Missouri
Technological	**Change**	Mexico	**City,** Mexico
Employment	**Changes**	New York	**City,** New York
	Channel Islands		**Civil** Defense
Client	**Characteristics**		**Civil** Disobedience
Demographic	**Characteristics**		**Civil** Disorders
Interviewer	**Characteristics**		**Civil** Religion
Job	**Characteristics**		**Civil** Rights
Physical	**Characteristics**		**Civil** Rights Organizations
Fictional	**Characters**		**Civil** Service
	Charisma		**Civil** Society
	Charities		**Civil** War
	Cheating	Military	**Civilian** Relations
	Chemical Industry		**Civilization**
	Chemistry	Western	**Civilization**
	Chi Square Test		**Clans**
Ho	**Chi** Minh City, Vietnam		**Class** Analysis
	Chicago, Illinois		**Class** Consciousness
	Chicago School of Sociology		**Class** Differences
	Chieftaincies		**Class** Formation
	Child Abuse		**Class** Identity
	Child Care Services		**Class** Politics
	Child Custody		**Class** Relations
	Child Development		**Class** Society
	Child Mortality		**Class** Struggle
	Child Neglect	Language Social	**Class** Relationship
	Child Sex Preferences	Lower	**Class**
	Child Sexual Abuse	Middle	**Class**
	Child Support	New Middle	**Class**
	Child Welfare Services	Ruling	**Class**
Parent	**Child** Relations	Social	**Class**
	Childhood	Upper	**Class**
	Childhood Factors	Working	**Class**
	Childlessness		**Classification**
	Childrearing Practices	Occupational	**Classifications**
Adopted	**Children**		**Classroom** Environment
Adult	**Children**		**Clausewitz,** Karl von
	Children		**Cleavage**
Foster	**Children**		**Clergy**
Only	**Children**	Dominicans	**(Clergy)**
Preschool	**Children**	Ministers	**(Clergy)**
	Chile		**Clerical** Workers
	China		**Cleveland,** Ohio
Peking, Peoples			**Client** Characteristics
Republic of	**China**		**Client** Relations
Peoples Republic of	**China**		**Clients**
	Chiropractors		**Clinical** Social Work
Occupational	**Choice**		**Clinics**
Rational	**Choice**		**Cliques**
	Choices		**Closure**
	Chou En-lai	Plant	**Closure**
Jesus	**Christ**	Social	**Closure**
	Christianity		**Clothing**
	Christians		**Clubs**
	Christmas		**Cluster** Analysis
	Chronic Illness		**Coal**
	Chronologies		**Coalition** Formation
	Church Attendance		**Coalitions**
	Church Membership	Ivory	**Coast**

ROTATED DESCRIPTOR DISPLAY

Cocaine — Confucianism

	Cocaine
	Code Switching
	Codes of Conduct
	Coding
	Coercion
Peaceful	**Coexistence**
	Cognatic Descent
	Cognition
	Cognitive Development
	Cognitive Dissonance
	Cognitive Mapping
	Cohabitation
Social	**Cohesion**
	Cohort Analysis
	Cold War
	Coleman, James Samuel
Blue	**Collar** Workers
White	**Collar** Crime
White	**Collar** Workers
Data	**Collection**
Methodology (Data	**Collection**)
	Collective Action
	Collective Bargaining
	Collective Behavior
	Collective Representation
Individual	**Collective** Relationship
Agricultural	**Collectives**
	Collectives
Industrial	**Collectives**
	Collectivism
	Collectivization
	College Faculty
	College Graduates
	College Majors
	College Sports
	College Students
	Colleges
Community	**Colleges**
	Collins, Randall
Bogota,	**Colombia**
	Colombia
	Colonialism
	Colonization
	Colorado
Denver,	**Colorado**
British	**Columbia**
Vancouver, British	**Columbia**
	Combat
	Comics (Publications)
	Commissions
	Commitment
Organizational	**Commitment**
Advisory	**Committees**
	Committees
Political Action	**Committees**
	Commodities
	Common Lands
	Common Sense
	Communes
	Communication
	Communication Research
Intercultural	**Communication**
Interpersonal	**Communication**
Manual	**Communication**
Nonverbal	**Communication**
Verbal	**Communication**
Telephone	**Communications**
	Communicative Action
	Communism
	Communist Parties
	Communist Societies
	Communities
Fishing	**Communities**

Retirement	**Communities**
Rural	**Communities**
Black	**Community**
	Community Change
	Community Colleges
	Community Development
	Community Involvement
	Community Mental Health
	Community Mental Health Centers
	Community Organizations
	Community Power
	Community Research
	Community Satisfaction
	Community Services
	Community Size
	Community Structure
European Economic	**Community**
Police	**Community** Relations
Scientific	**Community**
	Commuting (Travel)
	Comoro Islands
	Compadrazgo
	Comparative Analysis
	Comparative Sociology
	Compassion
	Compensation
Workers	**Compensation** Insurance
	Competence
	Competition
	Complementary Needs
	Complex Organizations
	Complex Societies
Oedipal	**Complex**
	Compliance
Treatment	**Compliance**
	Componential Analysis
Principal	**Components** Analysis
Group	**Composition**
	Comprehension
	Compulsivity
	Compulsory Participation
	Computation
	Computer Assisted Instruction
	Computer Assisted Research
	Computer Software
	Computers
	Comte, Auguste Isidore-Marie-Francois-Xavier
	Concentration Camps
	Concept Formation
Self	**Concept**
	Concepts
	Conditioning
Economic	**Conditions**
Living	**Conditions**
Social	**Conditions**
	Condorcet, Marie Jean Antoine Nicolas de Caritat
Codes of	**Conduct**
	Confession
	Confidentiality
	Conflict
	Conflict Resolution
	Conflict Theory
Cultural	**Conflict**
Family	**Conflict**
International	**Conflict**
Interpersonal	**Conflict**
Role	**Conflict**
Social	**Conflict**
	Conformity
	Confucianism

ROTATED DESCRIPTOR DISPLAY

                       Congenitally Handicapped
                       Congo
                       Congregations
                       Congresses And Conventions
                       Congruence (Psychology)
                       Conjoint Therapy
                       Connecticut
        Hartford, **Connecticut**
                       Consanguinity
                       Conscience
                       Conscientious Objectors
           Class **Consciousness**
                       Consciousness
          Social **Consciousness**
        Worker **Consciousness**
                       Consensus
     Informed **Consent**
                       Conservation
       Energy **Conservation**
         Soil **Conservation**
                       Conservatism
                       Constitutional Amendments
                       Constitutions
                       Constraints
                       Construction Industry
                       Constructs
                       Consultants
  Professional **Consultation**
                       Consumerism
                       Consumers
                       Consumption
       Energy **Consumption**
  Production **Consumption** Relationship
       Culture **Contact**
          Eye **Contact**
     Physical **Contact**
       Social **Contact**
                       Contagion Theory
         Cost **Containment**
                       Content Analysis
                       Contingency Analysis
  Rural Urban **Continuum**
                       Contracts
                       Contradictions
                       Contributions (Donations)
        Birth **Control**
                       Control
          Gun **Control**
     Locus of **Control**
     Pollution **Control**
       Social **Control**
      Worker **Control**
Congresses And **Conventions**
                       Convents
                       Convergence Theory
                       Conversation
                       Conversational Analysis
     Religious **Conversion**
                       Cook Islands
                       Cooley, Charles Horton
                       Cooperation
 International **Cooperation**
                       Cooperatives
                       Cooptation
                       Coordination
                       Copenhagen, Denmark
                       Copernicus, Nicolaus
                       Coping
                       Copyrights
                       Corporal Punishment
                       Corporations
  Multinational **Corporations**
                       Corporatism

                       Correctional Personnel
                       Correctional System
     Juvenile **Correctional** Institutions
   Restitution **(Corrections)**
                       Correlation
      Letters **(Correspondence)**
                       Corruption
                       Corsica
                       Coser, Lewis Alfred
                       Cosmology
                       Cosmopolitanism
                       Cost Containment
                       Costa Rica
                       Costs
       Housing **Costs**
                       Cottage Industries
                       Councils
                       Counseling
                       Countercultures
                       Countermovements
                       Counties
         Arab **Countries**
                       Countries
   Developing **Countries**
 Mediterranean **Countries**
                       Couples
                       Coups d'Etat
                       Courses
     Workshops **(Courses)**
United States Supreme **Court**
                       Courts
      Juvenile **Courts**
                       Courtship
                       Cousin Marriage
                       Couvade
          News **Coverage**
                       Crafts
                       Creationism
                       Creativity
                       Credibility
                       Credit
                       Cremation
                       Creolized Languages
                       Crime
                       Crime Prevention
                       Crime Rates
     Fear of **Crime**
   Organized **Crime**
        Rural **Crime**
        Urban **Crime**
 White Collar **Crime**
                       Criminal Justice
                       Criminal Justice Policy
                       Criminal Proceedings
       Career **Criminals**
                       Criminology
                       Crises
     Economic **Crises**
                       Crisis Intervention
                       Criteria
                       Critical Theory
                       Criticism
      Literary **Criticism**
       Social **Criticism**
                       Croatia, Yugoslavia
                       Croce, Benedetto
                       Crofting
                       Crosscultural Analysis
                       Crowding
                       Crowds
                       Crozier, Michel
        Santa **Cruz** Islands
                       Cuba

Cuba   ROTATED DESCRIPTOR DISPLAY   **Denmark**

Havana, **Cuba**	Methodology (**Data** Collection)
Cargo **Cults**	Panel **Data**
Cults	**Dating** (Social)
African **Cultural** Groups	**Daughters**
Arab **Cultural** Groups	**Davis**, Kingsley
Asian **Cultural** Groups	**Day** Care
Australasian **Cultural** Groups	**de** Beauvoir, Simone
Caribbean **Cultural** Groups	Rio **de** Janeiro, Brazil
Cultural Activities	**de** Tocqueville, Alexis Charles
Cultural Change	Henri Maurice Clerel
Cultural Conflict	**Deacons**
Cultural Groups	**Deaf**
Cultural Identity	New **Deal**
Cultural Pluralism	**Deans**
Cultural Relativism	**Death**
Cultural Transmission	**Death** Attitudes
Cultural Universals	**Death** Rituals
Cultural Values	**Debate**
European **Cultural** Groups	Public **Debt**
Jewish **Cultural** Groups	**Debts**
Latin American **Cultural** Groups	**Decentralization**
Middle Eastern **Cultural** Groups	**Deception**
North African **Cultural** Groups	**Decision** Making
North American **Cultural** Groups	**Decision** Models
Oceanic **Cultural** Groups	Group **Decision** Making
Religious **Cultural** Groups	Medical **Decision** Making
South Asian **Cultural** Groups	Participative **Decision** Making
Southeast Asian **Cultural** Groups	**Decisions**
Southern African **Cultural** Groups	Judicial **Decisions**
Soviet Union **Cultural** Groups	Fertility **Decline**
United Nations	**Decolonization**
Educational, Scientific	**Decriminalization**
& **Cultural** Org	**Deduction**
Culture	Political **Defection**
Culture Contact	**Defendants**
Folk **Culture**	Civil **Defense**
Material **Culture**	**Defense** Mechanisms
Organizational **Culture**	**Defense** Spending
Political **Culture**	Insanity **Defense**
Popular **Culture**	Repression (**Defense** Mechanism)
Prison **Culture**	Acquired Immune **Deficiency** Syndrome
Youth **Culture**	**Definitions**
Curacao	Operational **Definitions**
Curiosity	**DeGaulle**, Charles Andre Joseph
Curriculum	Academic **Degrees**
Child **Custody**	Baccalaureate **Degrees**
Customs	Doctoral **Degrees**
Cybernetics	Masters **Degrees**
Life **Cycle**	**Deindustrialization**
Business **Cycles**	**Deinstitutionalization**
Cyclical Processes	**Deities**
Cynicism	**Delaware**
Cyprus	**Delay** of Gratification
Czechoslovakia	**Delhi**, India
Prague, **Czechoslovakia**	**Delinquency**
Washington, **D.C.**	**Delinquency** Prevention
Dahrendorf, Ralf	Juvenile **Delinquency**
Dairy Farms	**Delivery** Systems
North **Dakota**	Supply And **Demand**
South **Dakota**	**Democracy**
Dallas, Texas	Industrial **Democracy**
Damascus, Syria	Social **Democracy**
Dance	Berlin, German **Democratic** Republic
Ghost **Dances**	German **Democratic** Republic
Darwinism	Liberal **Democratic** Societies
Social **Darwinism**	Yemen (Peoples **Democratic** Republic)
Aggregate **Data**	**Demographic** Change
Categorical **Data**	**Demographic** Characteristics
Data	**Demographic** Transition Theory
Data Banks	**Demography**
Data Collection	**Demons**
Data Processing	Copenhagen, **Denmark**
Methodology (**Data** Analysis)	**Denmark**

285

Denominations — ROTATED DESCRIPTOR DISPLAY — Disruption

	Denominations
Population	**Density**
	Dental Care
	Dental Students
	Dentistry
	Dentists
	Denver, Colorado
	Denzin, Norman K.
Academic	**Departments**
	Departments
	Dependency (Psychology)
	Dependency Theory
Welfare	**Dependency**
	Dependents
	Depersonalization
	Depression (Economics)
	Depression (Psychology)
	Deprivation
Relative	**Deprivation**
	Derrida, Jacques
	Descartes, Rene
Cognatic	**Descent**
	Descent
	Description
	Desegregation
School	**Desegregation**
Military	**Desertion**
	Design
Environmental	**Design**
Research	**Design**
Research	**Design** Error
Social	**Desirability**
Social	**Desirability** Scales
	Despotism
Self	**Destructive** Behavior
Lie	**Detection**
	Detention
Self	**Determination**
Social	**Determination** of Meaning
	Determinism
	Deterrence
	Detoxification
	Detroit, Michigan
	Developing Countries
Adult	**Development**
Agricultural	**Development**
Child	**Development**
Cognitive	**Development**
Community	**Development**
	Development
	Development Policy
	Development Programs
	Development Strategies
Economic	**Development**
Energy	**Development**
Historical	**Development**
Industrial	**Development**
Intellectual	**Development**
Moral	**Development**
Organizational	**Development**
Psychological	**Development**
Regional	**Development**
Research And	**Development**
Rural	**Development**
Scientific	**Development**
Social	**Development**
Urban	**Development**
	Developmental Stages
	Deviance
	Deviant Behavior
Sexual	**Deviation**
Intrauterine	**Devices**
	Devils

	Dewey, John
	Dharma
	Diabetes
	Diagnosis
	Dialectical Materialism
	Dialectics
	Dialects
	Dictatorship
	Diderot, Denis
San	**Diego,** California
	Diet
Lysergic Acid	**Diethylamide**
Age	**Differences**
Black White	**Differences**
Class	**Differences**
	Differences
Generational	**Differences**
Individual	**Differences**
Racial	**Differences**
Regional	**Differences**
Rural Urban	**Differences**
Sex	**Differences**
Semantic	**Differential**
	Differentiation
	Diffusion
	Diglossia
Human	**Dignity**
	Dilemmas
	Dilthey, Wilhelm Christian Ludwig
	Dimensional Analysis
	Diplomacy
Inner And Other	**Directedness**
Interlocking	**Directorates**
	Directors
Learning	**Disabilities**
	Disability Recipients
	Disadvantaged
	Disarmament
	Disaster Relief
	Disasters
Natural	**Disasters**
	Discharge
	Discipline
Academic	**Disciplines**
Self	**Disclosure**
	Discontent
	Discourse
	Discourse Analysis
Scientific	**Discoveries**
	Discovery
	Discretion
	Discretionary Power
	Discriminant Analysis
	Discrimination
Employment	**Discrimination**
	Discussion
Alzheimer's	**Disease**
	Diseases
Heart	**Diseases**
Venereal	**Diseases**
	Disengagement
	Dislocated Workers
	Dismissal
Civil	**Disobedience**
Civil	**Disorders**
	Disorders
Eating	**Disorders**
Language	**Disorders**
Social	**Disorganization**
	Disposition
	Disputes
Labor	**Disputes**
Marital	**Disruption**

Dissemination — ROTATED DESCRIPTOR DISPLAY — Education

Information	**Dissemination**
	Dissent
	Dissertations
Organizational	**Dissolution**
Cognitive	**Dissonance**
Social	**Distance**
Psychological	**Distress**
	Distribution
Geographic	**Distribution**
Income	**Distribution**
Population	**Distribution**
Frequency	**Distributions**
	Distributive Justice
	Districts
School	**Districts**
Emotionally	**Disturbed**
	Divination
	Division of Labor
International	**Division** of Labor
Sexual	**Division** of Labor
	Divorce
	Djibouti
	Doctoral Degrees
	Doctoral Programs
Epistemological	**Doctrines**
Philosophical	**Doctrines**
Religious	**Doctrines**
	Documentation
	Documents
Records	**(Documents)**
	Dogmatism
	Dolmen
	Domestics
	Domhoff, George William
	Dominance
	Dominant Ideologies
Santo	**Domingo,** Dominican Republic
	Dominica
	Dominican Republic
Santo Domingo,	**Dominican** Republic
	Dominicans (Clergy)
Contributions	**(Donations)**
	Downs Syndrome
	Dowry
	Draft (Military)
Brain	**Drain**
	Drama
	Dramaturgical Approach
	Dravidian Languages
	Dreams
	Drinking Behavior
Eating And	**Drinking** Establishments
Drunk	**Driving**
	Dropouts
	Drug Abuse
	Drug Addiction
	Drug Trafficking
	Drug Use
	Drugs
Narcotic	**Drugs**
Psychedelic	**Drugs**
Tranquilizing	**Drugs**
	Drum Languages
	Drunk Driving
	Drunkenness
	Du Bois, William Edward Burghardt
	Dual Career Family
	Dual Economy
	Dualism
	Due Process
	Duncan, Otis Dudley
	Durkheim, Emile

	Dyads
	Dying
Group	**Dynamics**
Social	**Dynamics**
Sexual	**Dysfunction**
	Earth (Planet)
	East And West
Far	**East**
Middle	**East**
	Easter Island
	Eastern Europe
Middle	**Eastern** Cultural Groups
	Eating And Drinking Establishments
	Eating Disorders
	Ecclesiastical Law
	Ecological Models
	Ecology
Human	**Ecology**
	Econometric Analysis
	Economic Change
	Economic Conditions
	Economic Crises
	Economic Development
	Economic Elites
	Economic Factors
	Economic History
	Economic Models
	Economic Planning
	Economic Policy
	Economic Problems
	Economic Sectors
	Economic Structure
	Economic Systems
	Economic Theories
	Economic Underdevelopment
European	**Economic** Community
International	**Economic** Organizations
Agricultural	**Economics**
Depression	**(Economics)**
	Economics
Exchange	**(Economics)**
Home	**Economics**
Keynesian	**Economics**
Marxist	**Economics**
Value	**(Economics)**
	Economists
Dual	**Economy**
Market	**Economy**
Political	**Economy**
Subsistence	**Economy**
World	**Economy**
	Ecuador
	Ecumenical Movement
	Ecumenism
	Editorials
	Editors
Adult	**Education**
Bilingual	**Education**
	Education
	Education Work Relationship
Elementary	**Education**
Higher	**Education**
Marriage And Family	**Education**
Moral	**Education**
Multicultural	**Education**
Preschool	**Education**
Primary	**Education**
Religious	**Education**
Rural	**Education**
Secondary	**Education**
Sex	**Education**
Social Science	**Education**

Education ROTATED DESCRIPTOR DISPLAY Ethnic

Social Work **Education**
Sociology **Education**
Sociology of **Education**
Special **Education**
Teacher **Education**
Tracking **(Education)**
Urban **Education**
Vocational **Education**
Womens **Education**
Educational Administration
Educational Attainment
Educational Ideologies
Educational Opportunities
Educational Plans
Educational Policy
Educational Programs
Educational Reform
Educational Research
Educational Systems
United Nations **Educational,** Scientific & Cultural Org
Prince **Edward** Island
Placebo **Effect**
Effectiveness
Organizational **Effectiveness**
Altitude **Effects**
Effects
Mass Media **Effects**
Efficiency
Egalitarianism
Egocentrism
Egoism
Cairo, **Egypt**
Egypt
Eighteenth Century
Einstein, Albert
Eisenstadt, Shmuel Noah
El Salvador
Elder Abuse
Elderly
Elderly Women
Elections
Electricity
Electronic Technology
Elementary Education
Elementary School Students
Elementary Schools
Elias, Norbert
Power **Elite**
Economic **Elites**
Elites
Political **Elites**
Elitism
Gilbert And **Ellice** Islands
Embarrassment
Embourgeoisement
Emergencies
Emergency Medical Services
Emigration
United Arab **Emirates**
Emotionally Disturbed
Emotions
Empathy
Empires
Empirical Methods
Empiricism
Employability
Employee Assistance Programs
Employers
Employers Associations
Employment
Employment Changes
Employment Discrimination

Employment Opportunities
Part Time **Employment**
Self **Employment**
Youth **Employment**
Encouragement
Endogamy
Energy
Energy Conservation
Energy Consumption
Energy Development
Energy Policy
Nuclear **Energy**
Solar **Energy**
Investigations (Law **Enforcement)**
Law **Enforcement**
Engels, Friedrich
Engineering
Engineers
England
London, **England**
English Language
Enlightenment
Enrollment
Agricultural **Enterprises**
Enterprises
Industrial **Enterprises**
Entertainment Industry
Entrepreneurship
Entropy
Classroom **Environment**
Environment
Home **Environment**
Natural **Environment**
Social **Environment**
Work **Environment**
Environmental Attitudes
Environmental Design
Environmental Factors
Environmental Protection
Environmental Sociology
Environmentalism
Epidemics
Epidemiology
Epilepsy
Episcopalians
Epistemological Doctrines
Epistemology
Equality
Equatorial Guinea
Social **Equilibrium**
Equity
Erikson, Erik Homburger
Eroticism
Error of Measurement
Research Design **Error**
Errors
Eskimos
Esperanto
Espionage
Eating And Drinking **Establishments**
Real **Estate** Industry
Self **Esteem**
Estimation
Magnitude **Estimation**
Estonian Soviet Socialist Republic
Protestant **Ethic**
Ethics
Professional **Ethics**
Research **Ethics**
Addis Ababa, **Ethiopia**
Ethiopia
Ethnic Groups
Ethnic Identity

Ethnic Minorities
Ethnic Neighborhoods
Ethnic Relations
Ethnicity
Ethnocentrism
Ethnography
Ethnolinguistic Groups
Ethnolinguistics
Ethnology
Ethnomethodology
Ethology
Etiology
Etymology
Etzioni, Amitai Werner
Eugenics
Eurasia
Eastern **Europe**
Europe
Western **Europe**
European Cultural Groups
European Economic Community
Saint **Eustatius**
Euthanasia
Evaluation
Evaluation Research
Program **Evaluation**
Self **Evaluation**
Teacher **Evaluation**
Evangelism
Evans-Pritchard, Sir Edward Evan
Life **Events**
Everyday Life
Evidence (Legal)
Evil
Evil Eye
Evolution
Social **Evolution**
Evolutionary Theories
Exchange (Economics)
Exchange Theory
Executives
Existence
Existentialism
Expectations
Expenditures
Experience
Work **Experience**
Experiments
Expert Witnesses
Experts
Explanation
Exploitation
Exports And Imports
Self **Expression**
Expropriation
Extended Family
Extension Services
Extramarital Sexuality
Extrasensory Perception
Extraterrestrial Space
Extremism
Evil **Eye**
Eye Contact
Eysenck, Hans Jurgen
F Scale
Facilities
Recreational **Facilities**
Factionalism
Factor Analysis
Factor Structure
Factories
Biological **Factors**
Childhood **Factors**

Economic **Factors**
Environmental **Factors**
Political **Factors**
Psychological **Factors**
Psychosocial **Factors**
Social **Factors**
Sociocultural **Factors**
Sociodemographic **Factors**
Socioeconomic **Factors**
Social **Facts**
College **Faculty**
Fads
Faeroe Islands
Failure
Faith Healing
Falkland Islands
Fallacies
Falsification
Familism
Black **Family**
Dual Career **Family**
Extended **Family**
Family
Family Businesses
Family Conflict
Family Farms
Family Life
Family Planning
Family Policy
Family Power
Family Relations
Family Research
Family Role
Family Size
Family Stability
Family Structure
Family Therapy
Family Violence
Family Work Relationship
Marriage And **Family** Education
Matrifocal **Family**
Nuclear **Family**
Single Parent **Family**
Stem **Family**
Famine
Fanon, Frantz
Fantasy
Far East
Farmers
Part Time **Farming**
Dairy **Farms**
Family **Farms**
Farms
Small **Farms**
Fascism
Fashions
Burkina **Faso**
Fatalism
Fatalities
Fate
Father Absence
Fathers
Single **Fathers**
Fatigue
Fear
Fear of Crime
Fecundity
Berlin, **Federal** Republic of Germany
Federal Government
Federal Republic of Germany
Frankfurt, **Federal** Republic of Germany
Russian Soviet **Federated** Socialist Republic
Federations

289

Feedback — ROTATED DESCRIPTOR DISPLAY — **Geographic**

	Feedback
Breast	**Feeding**
	Feeding Practices
	Fellowships And Scholarships
	Female Headed Households
	Female Offenders
	Females
	Femininity
	Feminism
	Feminization
	Ferguson, Adam
	Fertility
	Fertility Decline
	Festinger, Leon
	Festivals
	Fetishism
	Fetus
	Feudalism
	Feuds
	Feyerabend, Paul Karl
	Fiction
	Fictional Characters
	Fieldwork
Fire	**Fighters**
	Figuration Sociology
Messianic	**Figures**
	Fiji Islands
	Filial Responsibility
	Films
	Finance
Public	**Finance**
	Financial Support
	Fine Arts
	Finland
Helsinki,	**Finland**
	Fire
	Fire Fighters
	Firearms
	Firms
	First Birth Timing
	Fiscal Policy
	Fishermen
	Fishing
	Fishing Communities
Physical	**Fitness**
	Flanders
	Flexibility
	Florida
Miami,	**Florida**
	Fluoridation
Unidentified	**Flying** Objects
	Folk Culture
	Folklore
	Food
	Food Industry
	Food Preparation
	Food Stamps
Labor	**Force**
Labor	**Force** Participation
Armed	**Forces**
	Forces And Relations of Production
Paramilitary	**Forces**
	Forecasting
	Foreign Aid
	Foreign Policy
	Foreign Workers
	Foreigners
	Foremen
	Forensic Psychiatry
	Forestry
	Formalism
	Formalization (Theoretical)
Class	**Formation**
Coalition	**Formation**
Concept	**Formation**
	Formation
Group	**Formation**
Impression	**Formation**
State	**Formation**
Theory	**Formation**
	Foster Care
	Foster Children
	Foucault, Michel
	Foundations
	France
Paris,	**France**
	Franciscans
San	**Francisco**, California
	Frankfurt, Federal Republic of Germany
	Frankfurt School
	Fraternities And Sororities
	Fraud
Academic	**Freedom**
	Freedom
	French Guiana
	French Polynesia
	Frequency Distributions
	Freud, Anna
	Freud, Sigmund
	Freudian Psychology
	Friendship
	Frigidity
Urban	**Fringe**
	Fromm, Erich
	Frontiers
	Frustration
	Fuels
	Function
Social	**Function**
	Functionalism
Religious	**Fundamentalism**
	Funerals
	Future Orientations
	Futures (of Society)
	Gabon
	Gadamer, Hans Georg
	Galbraith, John Kenneth
	Gambia
	Gambling
	Game Theory
	Games
Olympic	**Games**
	Gandhi, Mohandas Karamchand
	Gangs
	Gardening
	Garfinkel, Harold
	Garment Industry
	Garvey, Marcus Moziah
Hunting And	**Gathering** Societies
	Gehlen, Arnold
	Gemeinschaft And Gesellschaft
	Genealogy
	General Public
	Generalization
	Generational Differences
	Genetics
	Geneva, Switzerland
	Genital Mutilation
	Genitals
	Genius
	Genocide
	Gentiles
	Geographic Distribution
	Geographic Mobility

Geographic ROTATED DESCRIPTOR DISPLAY **Gusfield**

Geographic Regions	Athens, **Greece**
Geography	**Greece**
Geology	Ancient **Greek** Philosophy
Geopolitics	**Greenland**
Atlanta, **Georgia**	**Grenada**
Georgia	**Grief**
Geriatrics	**Grievances**
Berlin, **German** Democratic Republic	**Gross** National Product
German Democratic Republic	**Group** Composition
Germanic Languages	**Group** Decision Making
Berlin, Federal Republic of **Germany**	**Group** Dynamics
	Group Formation
Berlin, **Germany**	**Group** Identity
Federal Republic of **Germany**	**Group** Norms
Frankfurt, Federal Republic of **Germany**	**Group** Research
	Group Size
Germany	**Group** Therapy
Gerontocracy	**Group** Work
Gerontology	African Cultural **Groups**
Gemeinschaft And **Gesellschaft**	Age **Groups**
Gestalt Psychology	Arab Cultural **Groups**
Ghana	Asian Cultural **Groups**
Ghettos	Australasian Cultural **Groups**
Ghost Dances	Blood **Groups**
Ghosts	Caribbean Cultural **Groups**
Gibraltar	Cultural **Groups**
Giddens, Anthony	Ethnic **Groups**
Gift Giving	Ethnolinguistic **Groups**
Gifted	European Cultural **Groups**
Gilbert And Ellice Islands	**Groups**
Gini, Corrado	Interest **Groups**
Gift **Giving**	Jewish Cultural **Groups**
Glaser, Daniel	Latin American Cultural **Groups**
Glasgow, Scotland	Low Income **Groups**
Glazer, Nathan	Majority **Groups**
Glossolalia	Middle Eastern Cultural **Groups**
Goals	Minority **Groups**
Social **Goals**	North African Cultural **Groups**
God (Judeo-Christian)	North American Cultural **Groups**
Godparenthood	Oceanic Cultural **Groups**
Goethe, Johann Wolfgang von	Peer **Groups**
Goffman, Erving	Primary **Groups**
Goldmann, Lucien	Reference **Groups**
Goodman, Leo A.	Religious Cultural **Groups**
Public **Goods**	Self Help **Groups**
Social **Gospel** Movement	Small **Groups**
Gouldner, Alvin Ward	Social **Groups**
Governing Boards	South Asian Cultural **Groups**
Central **Government**	Southeast Asian Cultural **Groups**
Federal **Government**	Southern African Cultural **Groups**
Government	Soviet Union Cultural **Groups**
Government Agencies	Task Oriented **Groups**
Government Policy	Womens **Groups**
Government Regulation	Work **Groups**
Government Spending	Population **Growth**
Local **Government**	**Guadeloupe**
Governors	**Guam**
Grades (Scholastic)	**Guardianship**
Graduate Schools	**Guatemala**
Graduate Students	**Guerrillas**
College **Graduates**	French **Guiana**
Graduates	**Guidance**
Graffiti	**Guilds**
Grammar	**Guilt**
Gramsci, Antonio	Equatorial **Guinea**
Grandchildren	**Guinea**
Grandparents	**Guinea** Bissau
Grants	Papua New **Guinea**
Graph Theory	**Gujarat,** India
Graphology	**Gun** Control
Graphs	**Gurvitch,** Georges
Delay of **Gratification**	**Gusfield,** Joseph Robert
Great Britain	

291

ROTATED DESCRIPTOR DISPLAY

Guttman, Louis
Guttman Scales
Guyana
Gynecology
Gypsies
Habermas, Jurgen
Habits
Haiti
Hallucinations
New Hampshire
Congenitally Handicapped
Handicapped
Physically Handicapped
Hands
Hanoi, Vietnam
Happiness
Sexual Harassment
Hartford, Connecticut
Hassidim
Hassidism
Hate
Hauser, Robert Mason
Havana, Cuba
Hawaii
Hazards
Project Head Start
Female Headed Households
Heads of Households
Faith Healing
Community Mental Health
Community Mental Health Centers
Health
Health Behavior
Health Care
Health Care Utilization
Health Insurance
Health Maintenance Organizations
Health Planning
Health Policy
Health Problems
Health Professions
Health Services
Home Health Care
Mental Health
Mental Health Services
Occupational Safety And Health
Primary Health Care
Public Health
Hearing
Heart
Heart Diseases
Hedonism
Hegel, Georg Wilhelm Friedrich
Hegemony
Heidegger, Martin
Body Height
Help Seeking Behavior
Self Help
Self Help Groups
Helping Behavior
Helsinki, Finland
Heresy
Hermeneutics
Heroes
Heroin
Heterogeneity
Heterosexuality
Heuristics
Hierarchy
High School Students
High Schools
High Technology Industries
Junior High Schools

Higher Education
Highways
Himalayan States
Hinduism
Hindus
Hiring Practices
Hiroshima, Japan
Hispanic Americans
Historians
Historical Development
Historical Materialism
Historicism
Historiography
Art History
Economic History
History
History of Sociology
Intellectual History
Life History
Oral History
Social History
Hitler, Adolph
Ho Chi Minh City, Vietnam
Hobbes, Thomas
Holidays
Holism
Holistic Medicine
Hollingshead, August deBelmont
Holocaust
Homans, George Caspar
Home Economics
Home Environment
Home Health Care
Home Ownership
Home Workplaces
Homelessness
Homemakers
Nursing Homes
Homesteading
Homicide
Homogamy
Homogeneity
Homosexual Relationships
Homosexuality
Honduras
Hong Kong
Honor
Horkheimer, Max
Hormones
Horowitz, Irving Louis
Hospices
Hospital Wards
Hospitalization
Hospitals
Mental Hospitals
Hostages
Hostels
Hostility
Hotels
Working Hours
Female Headed Households
Heads of Households
Households
Housework
Housing
Housing Costs
Housing Market
Housing Policy
Public Housing
Rental Housing
Houston, Texas
Animal Human Relations
Human Body

Human   ROTATED DESCRIPTOR DISPLAY   Industry

Human Capital	**Impression** Formation
Human Dignity	**Impression** Management
Human Ecology	**Imprisonment**
Human Nature	**Improvement**
Human Relations Movement	**Impulsiveness**
Human Resources	**Inanimate** Objects
Human Rights	**Inbreeding**
Human Service Organizations	**Incentives**
Human Services	**Incest**
Humanism	**Income**
Humanistic Sociology	**Income** Distribution
Humanitarianism	**Income** Inequality
Humanities	**Income** Maintenance Programs
Humanization	Low **Income** Areas
Work **Humanization**	Low **Income** Groups
Hume, David	Status **Inconsistency**
Humor	**Independence**
Hungary	**Indeterminism**
Hunger	**Indexes** (Measures)
Hunting	Andhra Pradesh, **India**
Hunting And Gathering Societies	Bihar, **India**
Animal **Husbandry**	Bombay, **India**
Husbands	Calcutta, **India**
Husserl, Edmund	Delhi, **India**
Hutterites	Gujarat, **India**
Hygiene	**India**
Hypnosis	Kerala, **India**
Hypotheses	Madras, **India**
Hysteria	Punjab, **India**
Iceland	Rajasthan, **India**
Idaho	Uttar Pradesh, **India**
Ideal Types	West Bengal, **India**
Idealism	American **Indian** Reservations
Class **Identity**	**Indiana**
Cultural **Identity**	**Indianapolis,** Indiana
Ethnic **Identity**	American **Indians**
Group **Identity**	**Indic** Languages
Identity	Social **Indicators**
National **Identity**	**Indigenous** Populations
Professional **Identity**	**Individual** Collective Relationship
Sex Role **Identity**	**Individual** Differences
Social **Identity**	**Individualism**
Ideological Struggle	Methodological **Individualism**
Bourgeois **Ideologies**	**Individuals**
Dominant **Ideologies**	**Indochina**
Educational **Ideologies**	**Indoctrination**
Ideologies	**Indoeuropean** Languages
Political **Ideologies**	**Indonesia**
Authoritarianism	Jakarta, **Indonesia**
(Political **Ideology)**	**Induction**
Ignorance	**Industrial** Automation
Illegitimacy	**Industrial** Collectives
Chicago, **Illinois**	**Industrial** Democracy
Illinois	**Industrial** Development
Affective **Illness**	**Industrial** Enterprises
Chronic **Illness**	**Industrial** Management
Illness	**Industrial** Production
Illness Behavior	**Industrial** Societies
Mental **Illness**	**Industrial** Sociology
Terminal **Illness**	**Industrial** Workers
Images	**Industrialism**
Imagination	**Industrialization**
Imitation	Cottage **Industries**
Immigrants	High Technology **Industries**
Undocumented **Immigrants**	Manufacturing **Industries**
Immigration	Service **Industries**
Acquired **Immune** Deficiency Syndrome	Automobile **Industry**
Social **Impact** Assessment	Chemical **Industry**
Imperialism	Construction **Industry**
Implementation	Entertainment **Industry**
Policy **Implementation**	Food **Industry**
Program **Implementation**	Garment **Industry**
Exports And **Imports**	**Industry**

293

Industry   ROTATED DESCRIPTOR DISPLAY   **Islands**

Metal **Industry**	Social **Interest**
Mining **Industry**	**Interests**
Petroleum **Industry**	**Intergenerational** Mobility
Publishing **Industry**	**Intergenerational** Relations
Real Estate **Industry**	**Intergroup** Relations
Retail **Industry**	**Interlocking** Directorates
Shipping **Industry**	**Intermarriage**
Textile **Industry**	**Internal** Migration
Income **Inequality**	**Internalization**
Inequality	**International** Alliances
Sexual **Inequality**	**International** Conflict
Social **Inequality**	**International** Cooperation
Infant Mortality	**International** Division of Labor
Infanticide	**International** Economic Organizations
Infants	
Premature **Infants**	**International** Law
Inference	**International** Organizations
Statistical **Inference**	**International** Relations
Inflation	**International** Studies
Influence	**Internationalism**
Peer **Influence**	**Internship** Programs
Social **Influence**	**Interorganizational** Networks
Lunar **Influences**	**Interorganizational** Relations
Influenza	**Interpersonal** Attraction
Informal Sector	**Interpersonal** Communication
Information	**Interpersonal** Conflict
Information And Referral Services	**Interpersonal** Relations
Information Dissemination	Psychoanalytic **Interpretation**
Information Processing	**Interpretive** Sociology
Information Sources	**Interval** Measurement
Information Technology	Crisis **Intervention**
Information Theory	**Intervention**
Sex **Information**	State **Intervention**
Informed Consent	**Interview** Schedules
Inheritance And Succession	**Interviewer** Characteristics
Initiation Rites	**Interviews**
Injuries	**Intimacy**
Inner And Other Directedness	**Intrauterine** Devices
Adoption of **Innovations**	**Intuition**
Innovations	**Invasion**
Technological **Innovations**	**Inventions**
Insanity Defense	Minnesota Multiphasic Personality **Inventory**
Artificial **Insemination**	
Instinct	**Investigations** (Law Enforcement)
Institutes	**Investment**
Institutionalization (Persons)	Community **Involvement**
Institutionalization (Social)	**Iowa**
Institutions	**Iran**
Juvenile Correctional **Institutions**	Teheran, **Iran**
Residential **Institutions**	Baghdad, **Iraq**
Social **Institutions**	**Iraq**
Computer Assisted **Instruction**	**Ireland**
Measures **(Instruments)**	Northern **Ireland**
Health **Insurance**	**Irrationality**
Insurance	**Irrigation**
Workers Compensation **Insurance**	**Islam**
Social **Integration**	**Islamic** Law
Intellectual Development	Easter **Island**
Intellectual History	Prince Edward **Island**
Intellectuals	Rhode **Island**
Artificial **Intelligence**	Wake **Island**
Intelligence	Canary **Islands**
Intelligence Tests	Cape Verde **Islands**
Intelligentsia	Caroline **Islands**
Intentionality	Cayman **Islands**
Interaction	Channel **Islands**
Social **Interaction**	Comoro **Islands**
Interactionism	Cook **Islands**
Symbolic **Interactionism**	Faeroe **Islands**
Sexual **Intercourse**	Falkland **Islands**
Intercultural Communication	Fiji **Islands**
Interdisciplinary Approach	Gilbert And Ellice **Islands**
Interest Groups	**Islands**

Line **Islands**	Criminal **Justice**
Mariana **Islands**	Criminal **Justice** Policy
Marquesas **Islands**	Distributive **Justice**
Marshall **Islands**	**Justice**
Midway **Islands**	Juvenile **Justice**
Phoenix **Islands**	Social **Justice**
Santa Cruz **Islands**	**Juvenile** Correctional Institutions
Society **Islands**	**Juvenile** Courts
Solomon **Islands**	**Juvenile** Delinquency
Tokelau **Islands**	**Juvenile** Justice
Trobriand **Islands**	**Juvenile** Offenders
Tubuai **Islands**	**Kabul**, Afghanistan
Turks And Caicos **Islands**	**Kampala**, Uganda
Virgin **Islands**	**Kampuchea**
Social **Isolation**	**Kansas**
Israel	**Kansas** City, Missouri
Jerusalem, **Israel**	**Kant**, Immanuel
Tel Aviv, **Israel**	**Karachi**, Pakistan
Istanbul, Turkey	**Karma**
Italy	**Kentucky**
Milan, **Italy**	**Kenya**
Naples, **Italy**	**Kerala**, India
Rome, **Italy**	**Keynesian** Economics
Items (Measures)	**Khaldoun**, Ibn
Ivory Coast	**Kibbutz**
Jainism	**Kierkegaard**, Soren Aabye
Jakarta, Indonesia	**Kiev**, Union of Soviet Socialist Republics
Jamaica	
Rio de **Janeiro**, Brazil	**Kindergarten**
Janowitz, Morris	**King**, Martin Luther
Hiroshima, **Japan**	United **Kingdom**
Japan	**Kinsey**, Alfred Charles
Tokyo, **Japan**	**Kinshasa**, Zaire
Jealousy	Affinity **(Kinship)**
Jehovah's Witnesses	**Kinship**
Jensen, Arthur Robert	**Kinship** Networks
New **Jersey**	**Kinship** Terminology
Jerusalem, Israel	Saint **Kitts** Nevis
Jesuits	**Knowledge**
Jesus Christ	Scientific **Knowledge**
Jesus Movement	Sociology of **Knowledge**
Jewish Cultural Groups	**König**, René
Jews	Hong **Kong**
Job Application	**Koran**
Job Change	North **Korea**
Job Characteristics	Seoul, South **Korea**
Job Performance	South **Korea**
Job Requirements	**Kuala** Lumpur, Malaysia
Job Satisfaction	**Kuhn**, Manford H.
Job Search	**Kuhn**, Thomas Samuel
Job Training	**Kuwait**
Multiple **Jobholding**	**Labeling**
Johannesburg, South Africa	Division of **Labor**
Jokes	International Division of **Labor**
Jonestown Mass Suicide	**Labor**
Jordan	**Labor** Disputes
Journalism	**Labor** Force
Journalists	**Labor** Force Participation
Journals	**Labor** Market
San **Juan**, Puerto Rico	**Labor** Market Segmentation
Judaism	**Labor** Migration
God **(Judeo-Christian)**	**Labor** Movements
Judeo-Christian Tradition	**Labor** Parties
Judges	**Labor** Policy
Judgment	**Labor** Process
Moral **Judgment**	**Labor** Productivity
Judicial Decisions	**Labor** Relations
Judiciary	**Labor** Supply
Jung, Carl Gustav	**Labor** Theory of Value
Junior High Schools	**Labor** Turnover
Juries	Sexual Division of **Labor**
Jurisdiction	**Laboratories**
Jurisprudence	**Lacan**, Jacques Marie Emile

ROTATED DESCRIPTOR DISPLAY

Lactation
Lagos, Nigeria
Lahore, Pakistan
Laity (Religious)
Lamaism
Land
Land Ownership
Land Reform
Land Settlement
Land Tenure
Land Use
Landlord Tenant Relations
Landlords
Common **Lands**
English **Language**
Language
Language Acquisition
Language Attitudes
Language Disorders
Language Maintenance
Language Planning
Language Policy
Language Shift
Language Social Class Relationship
Language Usage
Language Varieties
Morphology **(Language)**
Second **Language** Learning
African **Languages**
Amerindian **Languages**
Austronesian **Languages**
Creolized **Languages**
Dravidian **Languages**
Drum **Languages**
Germanic **Languages**
Indic **Languages**
Indoeuropean **Languages**
Languages
Oriental **Languages**
Romance **Languages**
Semitic **Languages**
Slavic **Languages**
Sri **Lanka**
Laos
Lapland
Larceny
Latent Structure Analysis
Latin
Latin America
Latin American Cultural Groups
Latvian Soviet Socialist Republic
Laughter
Ecclesiastical **Law**
International **Law**
Investigations **(Law** Enforcement)
Islamic **Law**
Law
Law Enforcement
Sociology of **Law**
Lawyers
Laymen
Lazarsfeld, Paul Felix
Le Play, Pierre Guillaume Frederic
Lead Poisoning
Opinion **Leaders**
Leadership
Learning
Learning Disabilities
Second Language **Learning**
Beirut, **Lebanon**
Lebanon
Lebenswelt

Lee, Alfred McClung
Lefebvre, Henri
Left Wing Politics
Adversary **Legal** System
Evidence **(Legal)**
Legal Cases
Legal Procedure
Legal Profession
Legal System
Legislation
Legislative Apportionment
Legislative Bodies
Legislators
Legitimacy
Legitimation
Leibnitz, Gottfried Wilhelm
Leisure
Sociology of **Leisure**
Work **Leisure** Relationship
Leningrad, Union of Soviet Socialist Republics
Leninism
Lenski, Gerhard Emmanuel
Sierra **Leone**
Leprosy
Lesbianism
Lesotho
Letters (Correspondence)
Leukemia
Levi-Strauss, Claude
Levy-Bruhl, Lucien
Lewin, Kurt
Liability
Liberal Democratic Societies
Liberalism
Liberia
Libertarians
Libraries
Libya
Licenses
Lie Detection
Liechtenstein
Everyday **Life**
Family **Life**
Life
Life Cycle
Life Events
Life History
Life Plans
Life Satisfaction
Life Stage Transitions
Life Tables
Quality of **Life**
Quality of Working **Life**
Social **Life**
Lifestyle
Likert, Rensis
Lima, Peru
Limitations
Line Islands
Lineage
Linear Analysis
Linguistic Minorities
Linguistics
Lipset, Seymour Martin
Literacy
Literacy Programs
Literary Criticism
Literature
Literature Reviews
Rabbinical **Literature**
Religious **Literature**
Sociology of **Literature**

Litigation　　ROTATED DESCRIPTOR DISPLAY　　Maryland

	Litigation
	Littering
	Liturgy
	Livestock
	Living Conditions
Standard of	**Living**
	Loans
	Lobbying
	Local Government
	Local Planning
	Local Politics
	Localism
	Locke, John
	Locus of Control
	Lodz, Poland
	Logic
	Loglinear Analysis
	Lombroso, Cesare
	London, England
	Loneliness
	Longevity
	Longitudinal Studies
	Longshoremen
	Los Angeles, California
St.	**Louis,** Missouri
Wirth,	**Louis**
	Louisiana
New Orleans,	**Louisiana**
	Love
	Low Income Areas
	Low Income Groups
	Lowenthal, Leo
	Lower Class
	Loyalty
Saint	**Lucia**
	Luhmann, Niklas
	Lukacs, Georg
Kuala	**Lumpur,** Malaysia
	Lunar Influences
	Luther, Martin
	Lutherans
	Luxembourg
	Luxemburg, Rosa
	Lynching
	Lynd, Robert Staughton
	Lysergic Acid Diethylamide
	Macao
	Machiavellianism (Personality)
Worker	**Machine** Relationship
	Machinery
	Macrosociology
	Madagascar
	Madeira
	Madras, India
	Madrid, Spain
	Magazines
	Maghreb
	Magic
	Magnitude Estimation
	Mahdis
	Mail Surveys
	Maine
Boundary	**Maintenance**
Health	**Maintenance** Organizations
Income	**Maintenance** Programs
Language	**Maintenance**
	Maintenance
Methadone	**Maintenance**
	Majorities (Politics)
	Majority Groups
College	**Majors**
Decision	**Making**
Group Decision	**Making**
Medical Decision	**Making**
Participative Decision	**Making**
Policy	**Making**
	Malawi
Kuala Lumpur,	**Malaysia**
	Malaysia
	Males
	Mali
	Malinowski, Bronislaw Kaspar
	Malnutrition
Professional	**Malpractice**
	Malta
	Malthus, Thomas Robert
Prehistoric	**Man**
	Mana
Impression	**Management**
Industrial	**Management**
	Management
	Management Styles
Personnel	**Management**
Resource	**Management**
Scientific	**Management**
	Managers
	Managua, Nicaragua
	Manicheism
	Manila, Philippines
	Manipulation
	Manitoba
	Mannheim, Karl
	Manual Communication
	Manual Workers
	Manufacturing Industries
Workshops	**(Manufacturing)**
	Mao Tse-tung
	Maoism
Cognitive	**Mapping**
	Marcuse, Herbert
	Marginality
	Mariana Islands
	Marijuana
San	**Marino**
	Marital Adjustment
	Marital Disruption
	Marital Relations
	Marital Satisfaction
	Marital Status
Housing	**Market**
Labor	**Market**
Labor	**Market** Segmentation
	Market Economy
	Market Research
	Marketing
	Markets
	Markov Process
	Marquesas Islands
Cousin	**Marriage**
	Marriage
	Marriage And Family Education
	Marriage Patterns
	Marriage Timing
	Married Students
	Marshall Islands
Saint	**Martin**
	Martindale, Donald Albert
	Martinique
	Marx, Karl
	Marxism
	Marxist Aesthetics
	Marxist Analysis
	Marxist Economics
	Marxist Sociology
Baltimore,	**Maryland**
	Maryland

Masculinity   ROTATED DESCRIPTOR DISPLAY   **Middle**

Masculinity	**Medical** Sociology
Masks	**Medical** Students
Maslow, Abraham Harold	**Medical** Technology
Jonestown **Mass** Suicide	**Medicare**
Mass Behavior	**Medications**
Mass Media	Holistic **Medicine**
Mass Media Effects	**Medicine**
Mass Media Violence	Socialized **Medicine**
Mass Society	Traditional **Medicine**
Boston, **Massachusetts**	Transcendental **Meditation**
Massachusetts	**Mediterranean** Countries
Masses	**Meetings**
Masters Degrees	**Melanesia**
Masturbation	**Melbourne,** Australia
Mate Selection	Church **Membership**
Material Culture	**Membership**
Dialectical **Materialism**	**Memory**
Historical **Materialism**	**Menarche**
Materialism	**Mennonites**
Autobiographical **Materials**	**Menopause**
Materials	**Menstruation**
Raw **Materials**	Community **Mental** Health
Reference **Materials**	Community **Mental** Health Centers
Mathematical Models	**Mental** Health
Mathematical Sociology	**Mental** Health Services
Mathematics	**Mental** Hospitals
Matriarchy	**Mental** Illness
Matrices	**Mental** Patients
Matrifocal Family	**Mentally** Retarded
Matrilineality	**Merchants**
Matrilocal Residence	**Mergers**
Matza, David	**Meritocracy**
Mau Mau Rebellion	**Merleau-Ponty,** Maurice
Mauritania	**Merton,** Robert King
Mauritius	**Messages**
Mauss, Marcel	**Messianic** Figures
Mayans	**Messianic** Movements
Mayors	**Mestizos**
McCarthyism	**Metal** Industry
McLuhan, Herbert Marshall	**Metallurgical** Technology
Mead, George Herbert	**Metaphors**
Mead, Margaret	**Metaphysics**
Mean	**Metasociology**
Meaning	**Meteorology**
Social Determination of **Meaning**	**Methadone** Maintenance
Means-Ends Rationality	Scientific **Method**
Error of **Measurement**	**Methodists**
Interval **Measurement**	**Methodological** Individualism
Measurement	**Methodological** Problems
Nominal **Measurement**	**Methodology** (Data Analysis)
Ordinal **Measurement**	**Methodology** (Data Collection)
Attitude **Measures**	**Methodology** (Philosophical)
Indexes **(Measures)**	Research **Methodology**
Items **(Measures)**	Empirical **Methods**
Measures (Instruments)	**Methods**
Personality **Measures**	Qualitative **Methods**
Repression (Defense **Mechanism)**	Quantitative **Methods**
Defense **Mechanisms**	Teaching **Methods**
Agricultural **Mechanization**	Treatment **Methods**
Audiovisual **Media**	**Metropolitan** Areas
Mass **Media**	**Mexican** Americans
Mass **Media** Effects	**Mexico**
Mass **Media** Violence	**Mexico** City, Mexico
News **Media**	New **Mexico**
Median	**Miami,** Florida
Mediation	**Michels,** Robert
Medicaid	Detroit, **Michigan**
Emergency **Medical** Services	**Michigan**
Medical Decision Making	**Microcomputers**
Medical Model	**Micronesia**
Medical Pluralism	**Microsociology**
Medical Research	**Middle** Aged Adults
Medical Schools	**Middle** Ages

ROTATED DESCRIPTOR DISPLAY

	Middle Class
	Middle East
	Middle Eastern Cultural Groups
	Middle Range Theories
New	**Middle** Class
	Middleman Minorities
	Middletown Studies
	Midway Islands
	Midwestern States
	Midwifery
	Migrant Workers
	Migrants
Internal	**Migration**
Labor	**Migration**
	Migration
	Migration Patterns
Return	**Migration**
Rural to Urban	**Migration**
Urban to Rural	**Migration**
	Milan, Italy
	Militarism
	Militarization
Draft	**(Military)**
	Military Civilian Relations
	Military Desertion
	Military Officers
	Military Personnel
	Military Regimes
	Military Service
	Military Sociology
	Mill, John Stuart
	Millenarianism
	Mills, Charles Wright
	Mind
	Mineral Resources
	Miners
Ho Chi	**Minh** City, Vietnam
	Minimum Wage
	Mining Industry
	Ministers (Clergy)
	Minneapolis, Minnesota
Minneapolis,	**Minnesota**
	Minnesota
	Minnesota Multiphasic Personality Inventory
Ethnic	**Minorities**
Linguistic	**Minorities**
Middleman	**Minorities**
	Minority Businesses
	Minority Groups
	Miscarriage
	Missionaries
	Mississippi
Kansas City,	**Missouri**
	Missouri
St. Louis,	**Missouri**
Geographic	**Mobility**
Intergenerational	**Mobility**
	Mobility
Occupational	**Mobility**
Residential	**Mobility**
Social	**Mobility**
	Mobilization
Resource	**Mobilization**
Medical	**Model**
Causal	**Models**
Decision	**Models**
Ecological	**Models**
Economic	**Models**
Mathematical	**Models**
	Models
Prediction	**Models**
Role	**Models**
Stochastic	**Models**
Structural	**Models**
	Modern Society
	Modernity
	Modernization
	Modes of Production
Behavior	**Modification**
	Monaco
	Monarchy
	Monasteries
	Monasticism
	Money
	Mongolia
	Monks
	Monogamy
	Monolingualism
	Monopolies
	Monopoly Capitalism
	Montana
	Montenegro, Yugoslavia
	Montesquieu, Charles Louis de Secondat
	Montevideo, Uruguay
	Montreal, Quebec
	Montserrat
	Monuments
	Moore, Barrington
	Moore, Wilbert Ellis
	Moral Development
	Moral Education
	Moral Judgment
	Morale
	Morality
	Morbidity
	Morgan, Lewis Henry
	Mormons
	Morocco
	Morphology (Language)
Child	**Mortality**
Infant	**Mortality**
	Mortality Rates
	Mosca, Gaetano
	Moscow, Union of Soviet Socialist Republics
	Mother Absence
	Mothers
Unwed	**Mothers**
Working	**Mothers**
	Motivation
Profit	**Motive**
	Mountain Regions
Ozark	**Mountains**
Ecumenical	**Movement**
Human Relations	**Movement**
Jesus	**Movement**
Social Gospel	**Movement**
Antinuclear	**Movements**
Labor	**Movements**
Messianic	**Movements**
	Movements
Nativistic	**Movements**
Peace	**Movements**
Political	**Movements**
Protest	**Movements**
Regional	**Movements**
Religious	**Movements**
Social	**Movements**
Solidarity	**Movements**
Temperance	**Movements**
Underground	**Movements**
Youth	**Movements**
	Moynihan, Daniel Patrick
	Mozambique

Multicultural — ROTATED DESCRIPTOR DISPLAY — Obedience

Multicultural Education	Saint Kitts **Nevis**
Multilingualism	Buffalo, **New** York
Multinational Corporations	**New** Brunswick
Minnesota **Multiphasic** Personality Inventory	**New** Caledonia
Multiple Jobholding	**New** Deal
Multiple Regression Analysis	**New** Hampshire
Multivariate Analysis	**New** Jersey
Murdock, George Peter	**New** Mexico
Museums	**New** Middle Class
Music	**New** Orleans, Louisiana
Musicians	**New** Towns
Black **Muslims**	**New** York
Muslims	**New** York City, New York
Genital **Mutilation**	**New** Zealand
Myrdal, Karl Gunnar	Papua **New** Guinea
Mysticism	**Newcomb,** Theodore Mead
Myths	**Newcomers**
Brand **Names**	**Newfoundland**
Namibia	**News** Coverage
Naming Practices	**News** Media
Naples, Italy	**Newspapers**
Napoleon Bonaparte	Managua, **Nicaragua**
Narcissism	**Nicaragua**
Narcotic Drugs	**Niebuhr,** Reinhold H.
Narratives	**Nietzsche,** Friedrich Wilhelm
Nasser, Gamal Abdal	**Niger**
Gross **National** Product	Lagos, **Nigeria**
National Identity	**Nigeria**
National Security	**Nihilism**
Nationalism	**Nineteenth** Century
Nationalization	**Nisbet,** Robert Alexander
United **Nations**	**Nixon,** Richard Milhous
United **Nations** Educational, Scientific & Cultural Org	**Noise**
Nativism	**Nomadic** Societies
Nativistic Movements	**Nominal** Measurement
Natural Disasters	**Nominalism**
Natural Environment	**Nonmetropolitan** Areas
Natural Resources	**Nonprofit** Organizations
Natural Sciences	**Nontraditional** Occupations
Naturalism	**Nonverbal** Communication
Human **Nature**	**Nonviolence**
Nazism	Group **Norms**
Nebraska	**Norms**
Affiliation **Need**	**North** Africa
Complementary **Needs**	**North** African Cultural Groups
Needs	**North** America
Needs Assessment	**North** American Cultural Groups
Child **Neglect**	**North** And South
Negotiation	**North** Atlantic Ocean
Nehru, Jawaharlal	**North** Carolina
Neighborhood Change	**North** Dakota
Ethnic **Neighborhoods**	**North** Korea
Neighborhoods	**North** Pacific Ocean
Neighbors	**Northern** Ireland
Nepal	**Northern** States
Anorexia **Nervosa**	**Northwest** Territories
Amsterdam, **Netherlands**	**Norway**
Netherlands	Oslo, **Norway**
Netherlands Antilles	**Nova** Scotia
Network Analysis	**Novels**
Interorganizational **Networks**	**Nuclear** Energy
Kinship **Networks**	**Nuclear** Family
Networks	**Nuclear** Reactors
Social **Networks**	**Nuclear** War
Support **Networks**	**Nuclear** Weapons
Neurology	**Nudity**
Neurosis	**Nuns**
Neuroticism	**Nuptiality**
Neutralism	**Nurses**
Value **Neutrality**	**Nursing** Homes
Neutralization Theory	**Nurturance**
Nevada	**Nutrition**
	Obedience

Obesity — ROTATED DESCRIPTOR DISPLAY — Pain

Obesity
Obituaries
Objectivity
Conscientious **Objectors**
Inanimate **Objects**
Unidentified Flying **Objects**
Obligation
Obscenity
Observation
Participant **Observation**
Obsolescence
Occultism
Occupational Achievement
Occupational Aspiration
Occupational Choice
Occupational Classifications
Occupational Mobility
Occupational Qualifications
Occupational Roles
Occupational Safety And Health
Occupational Segregation
Occupational Status
Occupational Stress
Occupational Structure
Promotion **(Occupational)**
Nontraditional **Occupations**
Occupations
Atlantic **Ocean**
North Atlantic **Ocean**
North Pacific **Ocean**
Pacific **Ocean**
South Atlantic **Ocean**
South Pacific **Ocean**
Oceania
Oceanic Cultural Groups
Oceans
Oedipal Complex
Victim **Offender** Relations
Female **Offenders**
Juvenile **Offenders**
Offenders
Offenses
Office Automation
Military **Officers**
Public **Officials**
Cincinnati, **Ohio**
Cleveland, **Ohio**
Ohio
Oklahoma
Oligarchy
Oligopolies
Olympic Games
Oman
Ombudsmen
Only Children
Ontario
Ottawa, **Ontario**
Toronto, **Ontario**
Ontology
Operational Definitions
Opiates
Opinion Leaders
Opinion Polls
Public **Opinion**
Public **Opinion** Research
Opinions
Educational **Opportunities**
Employment **Opportunities**
Opportunities
Opposite Sex Relations
Oppression
Optimism
Optometry

Oral History
Birth **Order**
Social **Order**
Religious **Orders**
Ordinal Measurement
Oregon
Portland, **Oregon**
United Nations Educational, Scientific & Cultural **Org**
Organ Transplantation
Organicism
Organization Size
Organization Theory
Sustenance **Organization**
Work **Organization**
Organizational Behavior
Organizational Change
Organizational Commitment
Organizational Culture
Organizational Development
Organizational Dissolution
Organizational Effectiveness
Organizational Power
Organizational Research
Organizational Sociology
Organizational Structure
Civil Rights **Organizations**
Community **Organizations**
Complex **Organizations**
Health Maintenance **Organizations**
Human Service **Organizations**
International Economic **Organizations**
International **Organizations**
Nonprofit **Organizations**
Organizations (Social)
Youth **Organizations**
Organized Crime
Orgasm
Oriental Languages
Orientation
Future **Orientations**
Professional **Orientations**
Religious **Orientations**
Sex Role **Orientations**
Value **Orientations**
Work **Orientations**
Task **Oriented** Groups
New **Orleans,** Louisiana
Orphans
Ortega y Gasset, Jose
Religious **Orthodoxy**
Orwell, George
Osgood, Charles Egerton
Oslo, Norway
Ossowski, Stanislav
Ossuaries
Inner And **Other** Directedness
Significant **Others**
Ottawa, Ontario
Outpatients
Overpopulation
Home **Ownership**
Land **Ownership**
Ownership
Worker **Ownership**
Ozark Mountains
North **Pacific** Ocean
Pacific Ocean
South **Pacific** Ocean
Pacifism
Paganism
Pain

301

Pakistan   ROTATED DESCRIPTOR DISPLAY   **Philosophy**

Karachi, **Pakistan**	Sao **Paulo,** Brazil
Lahore, **Pakistan**	**Payments**
Pakistan	**Peace**
Palestine	**Peace** Movements
Palestinians	**Peaceful** Coexistence
Cerebral **Palsy**	**Peasant** Rebellions
Pan-Africanism	**Peasant** Societies
Panama	**Peasants**
Panchayats	**Pediatrics**
Panel Data	**Peer** Groups
Papacy	**Peer** Influence
Papua New Guinea	**Peer** Relations
Paradigms	**Peer** Review
Paraguay	**Peers**
Paramedical Personnel	**Peking,** Peoples Republic of China
Parameters (Statistics)	**Penal** Reform
Paramilitary Forces	**Pennsylvania**
Paranoia	Philadelphia, **Pennsylvania**
Paraprofessional Workers	Pittsburgh, **Pennsylvania**
Parapsychology	**Penology**
Parent Child Relations	**Pensions**
Single **Parent** Family	**Pentecostalists**
Parental Attitudes	Peking, **Peoples** Republic of China
Parenthood	**Peoples** Republic of China
Parents	Yemen **(Peoples** Democratic Republic)
Surrogate **Parents**	Extrasensory **Perception**
Pareto, Vilfredo	Social **Perception**
Paris, France	**Perceptions**
Parishioners	Job **Performance**
Park, Robert Ezra	**Performance**
Parks	Task **Performance**
Parole	Victorian **Period**
Parsons, Talcott	**Periodicals**
Part Time Employment	Time **Periods**
Part Time Farming	Center And **Periphery**
Participant Observation	**Permanency** Planning
Citizen **Participation**	Sexual **Permissiveness**
Compulsory **Participation**	**Peronism**
Labor Force **Participation**	**Personal** Space
Participation	Machiavellianism **(Personality)**
Political **Participation**	Minnesota Multiphasic **Personality** Inventory
Social **Participation**	**Personality**
Sports **Participation**	**Personality** Measures
Worker **Participation**	**Personality** Traits
Participative Decision Making	Sociopathic **Personality**
Universalism- **Particularism**	**Personhood**
Communist **Parties**	Correctional **Personnel**
Labor **Parties**	Military **Personnel**
Political **Parties**	Paramedical **Personnel**
Socialist **Parties**	**Personnel** Management
Partisanship	**Personnel** Policy
Rites of **Passage**	Institutionalization **(Persons)**
Passion Plays	Single **Persons**
Passiveness	**Persuasion**
Pastoral Societies	Lima, **Peru**
Pastors	**Peru**
Patents	**Pessimism**
Paternalism	**Pesticides**
Path Analysis	**Petroleum**
Practitioner **Patient** Relationship	**Petroleum** Industry
Mental **Patients**	**Pets**
Patients	**Pharmacists**
Patriarchy	**Pharmacy**
Patrilineality	**Phenomena**
Patrilocal Residence	**Phenomenology**
Patriotism	**Philadelphia,** Pennsylvania
Patronage	**Philanthropy**
Career **Patterns**	Manila, **Philippines**
Marriage **Patterns**	**Philippines**
Migration **Patterns**	**Philosophers**
Residential **Patterns**	Methodology **(Philosophical)**
Settlement **Patterns**	**Philosophical** Doctrines
Pauling, Linus Carl	Ancient Greek **Philosophy**

Philosophy — ROTATED DESCRIPTOR DISPLAY — Population

Philosophy	Foreign **Policy**
Political **Philosophy**	Government **Policy**
Realism (**Philosophy**)	Health **Policy**
Social **Philosophy**	Housing **Policy**
Phobias	Labor **Policy**
Phoenix, Arizona	Language **Policy**
Phoenix Islands	Personnel **Policy**
Phonetics	**Policy**
Photian Schism	**Policy** Analysis
Photographs	**Policy** Implementation
Physical Characteristics	**Policy** Making
Physical Contact	**Policy** Research
Physical Fitness	**Policy** Science
Physical Sciences	Population **Policy**
Physically Handicapped	Public **Policy**
Physicians	Science **Policy**
Physics	Social **Policy**
Physiocrats	Urban **Policy**
Physiology	Welfare **Policy**
Piaget, Jean	**Poliomyelitis**
Piecework	Authoritarianism (**Political** Ideology)
Pilgrimages	**Political** Action
Pittsburgh, Pennsylvania	**Political** Action Committees
Placebo Effect	**Political** Affiliation
Placement	**Political** Attitudes
Places of Worship	**Political** Behavior
Plague	**Political** Campaigns
Earth (**Planet**)	**Political** Culture
Planners	**Political** Defection
City **Planning**	**Political** Economy
Economic **Planning**	**Political** Elites
Family **Planning**	**Political** Factors
Health **Planning**	**Political** Ideologies
Language **Planning**	**Political** Movements
Local **Planning**	**Political** Participation
Permanency **Planning**	**Political** Parties
Planning	**Political** Philosophy
Social **Planning**	**Political** Power
State **Planning**	**Political** Representation
Educational **Plans**	**Political** Science
Life **Plans**	**Political** Socialization
Plant Closure	**Political** Sociology
Plantations	**Political** Systems
Plants (Botanical)	**Political** Violence
Play	Repression (**Political**)
Role **Playing**	States (**Political** Subdivisions)
Passion **Plays**	**Politicians**
Plea Bargaining	Class **Politics**
Plural Societies	Left Wing **Politics**
Cultural **Pluralism**	Local **Politics**
Medical **Pluralism**	Majorities (**Politics**)
Pluralism	**Politics**
Poetry	Religion **Politics** Relationship
Poets	Right Wing **Politics**
Poggi, Gianfranco	Opinion **Polls**
Lead **Poisoning**	Air **Pollution**
Poisoning	**Pollution**
Lodz, **Poland**	**Pollution** Control
Poland	**Polyandry**
Warsaw, **Poland**	**Polyarchy**
Polanyi, Karl Paul	**Polygamy**
Polanyi, Michael	**Polygyny**
Polarization	French **Polynesia**
Police	**Polynesia**
Police Community Relations	**Polytechnic** Schools
Agricultural **Policy**	**Popper**, Karl Raimund
Criminal Justice **Policy**	**Popular** Culture
Development **Policy**	**Population**
Economic **Policy**	**Population** Density
Educational **Policy**	**Population** Distribution
Energy **Policy**	**Population** Growth
Family **Policy**	**Population** Policy
Fiscal **Policy**	Rural **Population**

303

ROTATED DESCRIPTOR DISPLAY

Population — Profiles

Urban **Population**	**Prices**
World **Population**	**Priests**
Indigenous **Populations**	**Primary** Education
Populism	**Primary** Groups
Pornography	**Primary** Health Care
Portland, Oregon	**Primates**
Porto Alegre, Brazil	**Prince** Edward Island
Portugal	**Principal** Components Analysis
Positivism	**Principals**
Spirit **Possession**	Sao Tome And **Principe**
Postdoctoral Programs	**Principles**
Postindustrial Societies	**Printing**
Postmodernism	**Priorities**
Postulates	**Prison** Culture
Potlatches	**Prisoners**
Poverty	**Prisoners** of War
Rural **Poverty**	**Prisonization**
Urban **Poverty**	**Prisons**
Black **Power**	**Privacy**
Community **Power**	**Private** Schools
Discretionary **Power**	**Private** Sector
Family **Power**	Public Sector **Private** Sector Relations
Organizational **Power**	**Privatization**
Political **Power**	**Privilege**
Power	**Probability**
Power Elite	**Probation**
Power Structure	**Problem** Solving
Social **Power**	Behavior **Problems**
State **Power**	Economic **Problems**
Theory **Practice** Relationship	Health **Problems**
Childrearing **Practices**	Methodological **Problems**
Feeding **Practices**	**Problems**
Hiring **Practices**	Social **Problems**
Naming **Practices**	Theoretical **Problems**
Practitioner Patient Relationship	World **Problems**
Andhra **Pradesh,** India	Legal **Procedure**
Uttar **Pradesh,** India	Selection **Procedures**
Pragmatics	Criminal **Proceedings**
Pragmatism	Due **Process**
Prague, Czechoslovakia	Labor **Process**
Praxeology	Markov **Process**
Praxis	Cyclical **Processes**
Prayer	Social **Processes**
Preachers	Data **Processing**
Prediction	Information **Processing**
Prediction Models	Gross National **Product**
Child Sex **Preferences**	Agricultural **Production**
Preferences	Forces And Relations of **Production**
Residential **Preferences**	Industrial **Production**
Sexual **Preferences**	Modes of **Production**
Pregnancy	**Production**
Unwanted **Pregnancy**	**Production** Consumption Relationship
Prehistoric Man	
Prehistory	Labor **Productivity**
Prejudice	**Productivity**
Premarital Sex	**Products**
Premature Infants	Legal **Profession**
Food **Preparation**	**Professional** Associations
Presbyterians	**Professional** Consultation
Preschool Children	**Professional** Ethics
Preschool Education	**Professional** Identity
Self **Presentation**	**Professional** Malpractice
Preservation	**Professional** Orientations
Presidents	**Professional** Socialization
Blood **Pressure**	**Professional** Sports
Pressure	**Professional** Training
Social **Pressure**	**Professional** Women
Prestige	**Professional** Workers
Pretoria, South Africa	**Professionalism**
Pretrial Release	**Professionalization**
Crime **Prevention**	Health **Professions**
Delinquency **Prevention**	**Professions**
Prevention	**Profiles**

304

ROTATED DESCRIPTOR DISPLAY

Profit Motive
Profits
Program Evaluation
Program Implementation
Programming (Broadcast)
Antipoverty **Programs**
Development **Programs**
Doctoral **Programs**
Educational **Programs**
Employee Assistance **Programs**
Income Maintenance **Programs**
Internship **Programs**
Literacy **Programs**
Postdoctoral **Programs**
Programs
Social **Programs**
Treatment **Programs**
Undergraduate **Programs**
Progress
Social **Progress**
Technological **Progress**
Progressivism
Project Head Start
Projective Techniques
Proletarianization
Proletariat
Promiscuity
Promotion (Occupational)
Propaganda
Property
Property Rights
Prophecy
Propositions
Prosecutors
Proselytism
Prostitution
Environmental **Protection**
Protection
Protectionism
Protest Movements
Protestant Ethic
Protestant Reformation
Protestantism
Protestants
Proudhon, Pierre-Joseph
Basque **Provinces**
Provinces
Prussia
Psychedelic Drugs
Psychiatric Research
Psychiatrists
Forensic **Psychiatry**
Psychiatry
Social **Psychiatry**
Psychoanalysis
Psychoanalytic Interpretation
Psychodynamics
Psychohistory
Psycholinguistics
Psychological Development
Psychological Distress
Psychological Factors
Psychological Research
Psychological Stress
Psychologists
Authoritarianism **(Psychology)**
Congruence **(Psychology)**
Dependency **(Psychology)**
Depression **(Psychology)**
Freudian **Psychology**
Gestalt **Psychology**
Psychology
Recognition **(Psychology)**
Social **Psychology**
Transference **(Psychology)**
Unconscious **(Psychology)**
Psychometric Analysis
Psychopathology
Psychosis
Psychosocial Factors
Psychotherapy
Puberty
General **Public**
Public Administration
Public Behavior
Public Debt
Public Finance
Public Goods
Public Health
Public Housing
Public Officials
Public Opinion
Public Opinion Research
Public Policy
Public Relations
Public Schools
Public Sector
Public Sector Private Sector Relations
Public Services
Public Support
Public Transportation
Writing for **Publication**
Comics **(Publications)**
Publications
Publicity
Publishing Industry
Puerto Rico
San Juan, **Puerto** Rico
Capital **Punishment**
Corporal **Punishment**
Punishment
Punjab, India
Purchasing
Purdah
Puritans
Qatar
Quakers
Occupational **Qualifications**
Qualifications
Qualitative Methods
Quality
Quality of Life
Quality of Working Life
Quantitative Methods
Montreal, **Quebec**
Quebec
Questionnaires
Quotas
Rabbinical Literature
Rabbis
Race
Racial Differences
Racial Relations
Racial Segregation
Racism
Radcliffe-Brown, Alfred Reginald
Radiation
Radical Sociology
Radicalism
Radio
Railroads
Rajasthan, India
Random Samples
Randomness
Middle **Range** Theories

ROTATED DESCRIPTOR DISPLAY

	Rangoon, Burma
	Ranking
	Rape
	Rapport
	Rastafarians
Crime	**Rates**
Mortality	**Rates**
	Rates
Unemployment	**Rates**
	Rating
	Rational Choice
	Rationalism
Means-Ends	**Rationality**
	Rationality
	Rationalization
	Ratios
	Raw Materials
Nuclear	**Reactors**
	Readability
	Readership
	Reading
	Reagan Administration
	Real Estate Industry
	Realism (Philosophy)
	Reality
Social	**Reality**
	Reasoning
Mau Mau	**Rebellion**
Peasant	**Rebellions**
	Rebellions
	Recidivism
Disability	**Recipients**
Welfare	**Recipients**
	Reciprocity
	Recognition (Achievement)
	Recognition (Psychology)
	Reconstruction
	Recordings
Videotape	**Recordings**
	Records (Documents)
	Recreation
	Recreational Facilities
	Recruitment
	Reductionism
	Redundancy
	Reference Groups
	Reference Materials
Citations	**(References)**
	Referendum
Information And	**Referral** Services
	Referral
	Reflexivity
Educational	**Reform**
Land	**Reform**
Penal	**Reform**
	Reform
Social	**Reform**
Welfare	**Reform**
Protestant	**Reformation**
	Refugees
Military	**Regimes**
	Regional Development
	Regional Differences
	Regional Movements
	Regional Sociology
	Regionalism
Arctic	**Regions**
Geographic	**Regions**
Mountain	**Regions**
Tropical	**Regions**
	Registration
Multiple	**Regression** Analysis
	Regression Analysis
Government	**Regulation**
	Regulation
	Rehabilitation
Vocational	**Rehabilitation**
	Reich, Wilhelm
	Reification
	Reinforcement
	Rejection
Animal Human	**Relations**
Black White	**Relations**
Class	**Relations**
Client	**Relations**
Ethnic	**Relations**
Family	**Relations**
Forces And	**Relations** of Production
Human	**Relations** Movement
Intergenerational	**Relations**
Intergroup	**Relations**
International	**Relations**
Interorganizational	**Relations**
Interpersonal	**Relations**
Labor	**Relations**
Landlord Tenant	**Relations**
Marital	**Relations**
Military Civilian	**Relations**
Opposite Sex	**Relations**
Parent Child	**Relations**
Peer	**Relations**
Police Community	**Relations**
Public	**Relations**
Public Sector Private Sector	**Relations**
Racial	**Relations**
	Relations
Researcher Subject	**Relations**
Social	**Relations**
Soviet American	**Relations**
Symbiotic	**Relations**
Victim Offender	**Relations**
Business Society	**Relationship**
Church State	**Relationship**
Education Work	**Relationship**
Family Work	**Relationship**
Individual Collective	**Relationship**
Language Social Class	**Relationship**
Practitioner Patient	**Relationship**
Production Consumption	**Relationship**
Religion Politics	**Relationship**
State Society	**Relationship**
Student Teacher	**Relationship**
Superior Subordinate	**Relationship**
Theory Practice	**Relationship**
Work Leisure	**Relationship**
Worker Machine	**Relationship**
Homosexual	**Relationships**
	Relative Deprivation
	Relatives
Cultural	**Relativism**
	Relativism
Pretrial	**Release**
	Relevance
	Reliability
Disaster	**Relief**
Civil	**Religion**
	Religion Politics Relationship
Sociology of	**Religion**
	Religions
	Religiosity
Laity	**(Religious)**
	Religious Attitudes
	Religious Behavior
	Religious Beliefs

ROTATED DESCRIPTOR DISPLAY

Religious ... **Rights**

Religious Brotherhoods	Market **Research**
Religious Conversion	Medical **Research**
Religious Cultural Groups	Organizational **Research**
Religious Doctrines	Policy **Research**
Religious Education	Psychiatric **Research**
Religious Fundamentalism	Psychological **Research**
Religious Literature	Public Opinion **Research**
Religious Movements	**Research**
Religious Orders	**Research** And Development
Religious Orientations	**Research** Applications
Religious Orthodoxy	**Research** Design
Religious Revivalism	**Research** Design Error
Religious Rituals	**Research** Ethics
Relocation	**Research** Methodology
Remarriage	**Research** Responses
Renaissance	**Research** Subjects
Urban **Renewal**	Scientific **Research**
Rental Housing	Social Science **Research**
Rents	Sociological **Research**
Replication	**Researcher** Subject Relations
Reports	**Researchers**
Collective **Representation**	American Indian **Reservations**
Political **Representation**	Matrilocal **Residence**
Representation	Patrilocal **Residence**
Repression (Defense Mechanism)	**Residence**
Repression (Political)	**Residential** Institutions
Sexual **Reproduction**	**Residential** Mobility
Social **Reproduction**	**Residential** Patterns
Reproductive Technologies	**Residential** Preferences
Armenian Soviet Socialist **Republic**	**Residential** Segregation
Berlin, Federal **Republic** of Germany	**Residents**
Berlin, German Democratic **Republic**	**Resistance**
Central African **Republic**	Conflict **Resolution**
Dominican **Republic**	**Resource** Allocation
Estonian Soviet Socialist **Republic**	**Resource** Management
Federal **Republic** of Germany	**Resource** Mobilization
Frankfurt, Federal **Republic** of Germany	Human **Resources**
German Democratic **Republic**	Mineral **Resources**
Latvian Soviet Socialist **Republic**	Natural **Resources**
Peking, Peoples **Republic** of China	**Resources**
Peoples **Republic** of China	**Respect**
Russian Soviet Federated Socialist **Republic**	**Respondents**
Santo Domingo, Dominican **Republic**	Social **Response**
Ukrainian Soviet Socialist **Republic**	Research **Responses**
Uzbek Soviet Socialist **Republic**	**Responses**
Yemen (Peoples Democratic **Republic**)	Filial **Responsibility**
Yemen Arab **Republic**	**Responsibility**
Kiev, Union of Soviet Socialist **Republics**	Social **Responsibility**
Leningrad, Union of Soviet Socialist **Republics**	**Restitution** (Corrections)
Moscow, Union of Soviet Socialist **Republics**	**Retail** Industry
Republics	Mentally **Retarded**
Union of Soviet Socialist **Republics**	**Retirement**
Reputation	**Retirement** Communities
Job **Requirements**	**Return** Migration
Action **Research**	**Reunion**
Agricultural **Research**	Peer **Review**
Archival **Research**	Book **Reviews**
Communication **Research**	Literature **Reviews**
Community **Research**	**Revisionism**
Computer Assisted **Research**	Religious **Revivalism**
Educational **Research**	Scientific Technological **Revolution**
Evaluation **Research**	Social **Revolution**
Family **Research**	**Revolutions**
Group **Research**	**Rewards**
	Rhetoric
	Rhode Island
	Costa **Rica**
	Puerto **Rico**
	San Juan, Puerto **Rico**
	Riesman, David
	Right Wing Politics
	Civil **Rights**
	Civil **Rights** Organizations

Rights — ROTATED DESCRIPTOR DISPLAY — Schools

Human **Rights**
Property **Rights**
Rights
Voting **Rights**
Womens **Rights**
Rio de Janeiro, Brazil
Riots
Risk
Risk Assessment
Initiation **Rites**
Rites of Passage
Sacrificial **Rites**
Death **Rituals**
Religious **Rituals**
Rituals
Robbery
Rokeach, Milton
Rokkan, Stein
Family **Role**
Role Ambiguity
Role Conflict
Role Models
Role Playing
Role Satisfaction
Sex **Role** Attitudes
Sex **Role** Identity
Sex **Role** Orientations
Sick **Role**
State **Role**
Occupational **Roles**
Roles
Sex **Roles**
Womens **Roles**
Roman Catholicism
Roman Catholics
Romance Languages
Bucharest, **Romania**
Romania
Romanticism
Rome, Italy
Rousseau, Jean-Jacques
Skid **Row**
Royalty
Ruling Class
Rumors
Runaways
Rural Areas
Rural Communities
Rural Crime
Rural Development
Rural Education
Rural Population
Rural Poverty
Rural Sociology
Rural to Urban Migration
Rural Urban Continuum
Rural Urban Differences
Rural Women
Rural Youth
Urban to **Rural** Migration
Rurality
Ruralization
Russell, Bertrand Arthur William
Russian Soviet Federated Socialist Republic
Rwanda
Saba
Sacredness
Sacrificial Rites
Sadhus
Occupational **Safety** And Health
Safety
Sub **Saharan** Africa

Sahlins, Marshall David
Saint Barthelemy
Saint Eustatius
Saint Kitts Nevis
Saint Lucia
Saint Martin
Saint Simon, Claude Henri de Rouvroy
Saint Vincent
Saints
Salaries
Sales
Sales Workers
Salience
El **Salvador**
Salvation
American **Samoa**
Western **Samoa**
Random **Samples**
Sampling
Samurai
San Diego, California
San Francisco, California
San Juan, Puerto Rico
San Marino
Sanctions
Sanitation
Santa Cruz Islands
Santo Domingo, Dominican Republic
Sao Paulo, Brazil
Sao Tome And Principe
Sapir, Edward
Sardinia
Sartre, Jean-Paul
Saskatchewan
Satire
Community **Satisfaction**
Job **Satisfaction**
Life **Satisfaction**
Marital **Satisfaction**
Role **Satisfaction**
Satisfaction
Saudi Arabia
Saving
F **Scale**
Guttman **Scales**
Scales
Social Desirability **Scales**
Watergate **Scandal**
Scandals
Scandinavia
Scapegoating
Scarcity
Interview **Schedules**
Scheler, Max
Photian **Schism**
Schism
Schizophrenia
Scholarship
Fellowships And **Scholarships**
Grades **(Scholastic)**
Chicago **School** of Sociology
Elementary **School** Students
Frankfurt **School**
High **School** Students
School Attendance
School Boards
School Desegregation
School Districts
Elementary **Schools**
Graduate **Schools**
High **Schools**

308

ROTATED DESCRIPTOR DISPLAY

Schools … **Sexual**

Junior High **Schools**
Medical **Schools**
Polytechnic **Schools**
Private **Schools**
Public **Schools**
Schools
Secondary **Schools**
Schumpeter, Joseph Alois
Schutz, Alfred
Schweitzer, Albert
Policy **Science**
Political **Science**
Science
Science And Technology
Science Policy
Social **Science** Education
Social **Science** Research
Sociology of **Science**
Behavioral **Sciences**
Biological **Sciences**
Natural **Sciences**
Physical **Sciences**
Social **Sciences**
Scientific Community
Scientific Development
Scientific Discoveries
Scientific Knowledge
Scientific Management
Scientific Method
Scientific Research
Scientific Technological Revolution
United Nations Educational, **Scientific** & Cultural Org
Scientists
Social **Scientists**
Scores
Nova **Scotia**
Glasgow, **Scotland**
Scotland
Job **Search**
Seasonal Variations
Seattle, Washington
Second Language Learning
Secondary Analysis
Secondary Education
Secondary Schools
Secrecy
Secret Societies
Sectarianism
Informal **Sector**
Private **Sector**
Public **Sector**
Public **Sector** Private Sector Relations
Public Sector Private **Sector** Relations
Economic **Sectors**
Sects
Secularization
National **Security**
Security
Social **Security**
Help **Seeking** Behavior
Labor Market **Segmentation**
Social **Segmentation**
Occupational **Segregation**
Racial **Segregation**
Residential **Segregation**
Segregation
Mate **Selection**
Selection Procedures
Self Actualization
Self Care
Self Concept

Self Destructive Behavior
Self Determination
Self Disclosure
Self Employment
Self Esteem
Self Evaluation
Self Expression
Self Help
Self Help Groups
Self Presentation
Semantic Differential
Semantics
Seminarians
Seminars
Semiotics
Semitic Languages
Anti- **Semitism**
Senegal
Senility
Seniority
Common **Sense**
Sensitivity Training
Sensory Systems
Sentencing
Seoul, South Korea
Separatism
Serbia, Yugoslavia
Time **Series** Analysis
Sermons
Civil **Service**
Human **Service** Organizations
Military **Service**
Service Industries
Child Care **Services**
Child Welfare **Services**
Community **Services**
Emergency Medical **Services**
Extension **Services**
Health **Services**
Human **Services**
Information And Referral **Services**
Mental Health **Services**
Public **Services**
Services
Social **Services**
Welfare **Services**
Land **Settlement**
Settlement Patterns
Settlers
Seventeenth Century
Child **Sex** Preferences
Opposite **Sex** Relations
Premarital **Sex**
Sex
Sex Differences
Sex Education
Sex Information
Sex Role Attitudes
Sex Role Identity
Sex Role Orientations
Sex Roles
Sex Stereotypes
Sexism
Child **Sexual** Abuse
Sexual Abuse
Sexual Arousal
Sexual Assault
Sexual Behavior
Sexual Deviation
Sexual Division of Labor
Sexual Dysfunction
Sexual Harassment

309

Sexual   ROTATED DESCRIPTOR DISPLAY   Social

                        Sexual Inequality   Language **Social** Class Relationship
                        Sexual Intercourse   Organizations **(Social)**
                        Sexual Permissiveness   **Social** Acceptance
                        Sexual Preferences   **Social** Action
                        Sexual Reproduction   **Social** Agencies
            Extramarital **Sexuality**   **Social** Anthropology
                        Sexuality   **Social** Area Analysis
                        Seychelles   **Social** Attitudes
                        Shamanism   **Social** Background
                        Shame   **Social** Behavior
                        Sharecropping   **Social** Change
                        Sharing   **Social** Class
                        Shelters   **Social** Closure
                        Sherif, Muzafer   **Social** Cohesion
             Language **Shift**   **Social** Conditions
                        Shift Work   **Social** Conflict
                        Shintoism   **Social** Consciousness
                        Shipping Industry   **Social** Contact
                        Shock   **Social** Control
                        Shoplifting   **Social** Criticism
                        Short Stories   **Social** Darwinism
                        Shrines   **Social** Democracy
                        Siberia   **Social** Desirability
                        Siblings   **Social** Desirability Scales
                        Sicily   **Social** Determination of Meaning
                        Sick Role   **Social** Development
                        Sierra Leone   **Social** Disorganization
           Statistical **Significance**   **Social** Distance
                        Significant Others   **Social** Dynamics
                        Signs   **Social** Environment
                        Sikhism   **Social** Equilibrium
                        Sikhs   **Social** Evolution
                        Silence   **Social** Factors
                        Similarity   **Social** Facts
                        Simmel, Georg   **Social** Function
                        Simulation   **Social** Goals
                        Singapore   **Social** Gospel Movement
                        Single Fathers   **Social** Groups
                        Single Parent Family   **Social** History
                        Single Persons   **Social** Identity
                        Sins   **Social** Impact Assessment
                        Situation   **Social** Indicators
                        Situses   **Social** Inequality
                        Sixteenth Century   **Social** Influence
         Community **Size**   **Social** Institutions
             Family **Size**   **Social** Integration
              Group **Size**   **Social** Interaction
      Organization **Size**   **Social** Interest
                        Size   **Social** Isolation
                        Skepticism   **Social** Justice
                        Skid Row   **Social** Life
                        Skills   **Social** Mobility
               Work **Skills**   **Social** Movements
                        Skin   **Social** Networks
                        Skinner, Burrhus Frederic   **Social** Order
                        Skolnick, Jerome Herbert   **Social** Participation
                        Slang   **Social** Perception
                        Slavery   **Social** Philosophy
                        Slavic Languages   **Social** Planning
                        Sleep   **Social** Policy
                        Slovenia, Yugoslavia   **Social** Power
                        Slums   **Social** Pressure
                        Small, Albion Woodbury   **Social** Problems
                        Small Businesses   **Social** Processes
                        Small Farms   **Social** Programs
                        Small Groups   **Social** Progress
                        Smelser, Neil Joseph   **Social** Psychiatry
                        Smith, Adam   **Social** Psychology
                        Smoking   **Social** Reality
                        Sociability   **Social** Reform
            Clinical **Social** Work   **Social** Relations
               Dating **(Social)**   **Social** Reproduction
Institutionalization **(Social)**   **Social** Response

Social — ROTATED DESCRIPTOR DISPLAY — South

Social Responsibility
Social Revolution
Social Science Education
Social Science Research
Social Sciences
Social Scientists
Social Security
Social Segmentation
Social Services
Social Space
Social Status
Social Stratification
Social Structure
Social Studies
Social Support
Social Systems
Social Theories
Social Types
Social Unrest
Social Values
Social Welfare
Social Work
Social Work Cases
Social Work Education
Social Workers
Socialism
Armenian Soviet **Socialist** Republic
Estonian Soviet **Socialist** Republic
Kiev, Union of Soviet **Socialist** Republics
Latvian Soviet **Socialist** Republic
Leningrad, Union of Soviet **Socialist** Republics
Moscow, Union of Soviet **Socialist** Republic
Russian Soviet Federated **Socialist** Republics
Socialist Parties
Socialist Societies
Ukrainian Soviet **Socialist** Republic
Union of Soviet **Socialist** Republics
Uzbek Soviet **Socialist** Republic
Political **Socialization**
Professional **Socialization**
Socialization
Socialization Agents
Socialized Medicine
Agrarian **Societies**
Bourgeois **Societies**
Capitalist **Societies**
Communist **Societies**
Complex **Societies**
Hunting And Gathering **Societies**
Industrial **Societies**
Liberal Democratic **Societies**
Nomadic **Societies**
Pastoral **Societies**
Peasant **Societies**
Plural **Societies**
Postindustrial **Societies**
Secret **Societies**
Socialist **Societies**
Traditional **Societies**
Business **Society** Relationship
Civil **Society**
Class **Society**
Futures (of **Society**)
Mass **Society**
Modern **Society**
Society
Society Islands
State **Society** Relationship
Western **Society**
Sociobiology

Sociocultural Factors
Sociodemographic Factors
Socioeconomic Factors
Socioeconomic Status
Sociography
Sociolinguistics
Sociological Associations
Sociological Research
Sociological Theory
Sociologists
Applied **Sociology**
Bourgeois **Sociology**
Chicago School of **Sociology**
Comparative **Sociology**
Environmental **Sociology**
Figuration **Sociology**
History of **Sociology**
Humanistic **Sociology**
Industrial **Sociology**
Interpretive **Sociology**
Marxist **Sociology**
Mathematical **Sociology**
Medical **Sociology**
Military **Sociology**
Organizational **Sociology**
Political **Sociology**
Radical **Sociology**
Regional **Sociology**
Rural **Sociology**
Sociology
Sociology Education
Sociology of Art
Sociology of Education
Sociology of Knowledge
Sociology of Law
Sociology of Leisure
Sociology of Literature
Sociology of Religion
Sociology of Science
Sociology of Sports
Sociology of Work
Urban **Sociology**
Visual **Sociology**
Sociometric Analysis
Sociopathic Personality
Sodomy
Sofia, Bulgaria
Computer **Software**
Soil Conservation
Solar Energy
Solidarity Movements
Solomon Islands
Problem **Solving**
Somalia
Sons
Sorel, Georges
Sorokin, Pitirim Alexandrovitch
Fraternities And **Sororities**
Soul
Information **Sources**
Cape Town, **South** Africa
Johannesburg, **South** Africa
North And **South**
Pretoria, **South** Africa
Seoul, **South** Korea
South Africa
South America
South Asia
South Asian Cultural Groups
South Atlantic Ocean
South Carolina
South Dakota
South Korea

311

South   ROTATED DESCRIPTOR DISPLAY   Structure

South Pacific Ocean	**State**
Southeast Asia	**State** Capitalism
Southeast Asian Cultural Groups	**State** Formation
Southern African Cultural Groups	**State** Intervention
Southern States	**State** Planning
Sovereignty	**State** Power
Armenian **Soviet** Socialist Republic	**State** Role
Estonian **Soviet** Socialist Republic	**State** Society Relationship
Kiev, Union of **Soviet** Socialist Republics	Washington **(State)**
Latvian **Soviet** Socialist Republic	Welfare **State**
Leningrad, Union of **Soviet** Socialist Republics	Balkan **States**
Moscow, Union of **Soviet** Socialist Republics	Baltic **States**
Russian **Soviet** Federated Socialist Republic	Himalayan **States**
	Midwestern **States**
Soviet American Relations	Northern **States**
Soviet Union Cultural Groups	Southern **States**
Ukrainian **Soviet** Socialist Republic	**States** (Political Subdivisions)
Union of **Soviet** Socialist Republics	United **States** of America
Uzbek **Soviet** Socialist Republic	United **States** Supreme Court
Extraterrestrial **Space**	Western **States**
Personal **Space**	**Statistical** Bias
Social **Space**	**Statistical** Inference
Space	**Statistical** Significance
Space And Time	**Statisticians**
Space Technology	Parameters **(Statistics)**
Birth **Spacing**	**Statistics**
Barcelona, **Spain**	Variance **(Statistics)**
Catalonia, **Spain**	Marital **Status**
Madrid, **Spain**	Occupational **Status**
Spain	Social **Status**
Spatial Analysis	Socioeconomic **Status**
Spatial Behavior	**Status**
Special Education	**Status** Attainment
Specialists	**Status** Inconsistency
Specialization	**Statutes**
Specificity	**Stem** Family
Spectators	**Stepfamily**
Speech	Sex **Stereotypes**
Spencer, Herbert	**Stereotypes**
Defense **Spending**	**Sterilization**
Government **Spending**	**Stigma**
Spinoza, Baruch	**Stimuli**
Spirit Possession	**Stinchcombe**, Arthur L.
Spirits	**Stochastic** Models
Spiritualism	**Stockholm**, Sweden
Spiro, Melford Elliot	**Stores**
Sponsorship	Short **Stories**
Spontaneity	**Storytelling**
College **Sports**	**Stouffer**, Samuel Andrew
Professional **Sports**	**Strangers**
Sociology of **Sports**	Development **Strategies**
Sports	**Strategies**
Sports Participation	Social **Stratification**
Sports Teams	**Stratification**
Sports Violence	**Strauss**, Anselm Leonard
Spouse Abuse	Occupational **Stress**
Spouses	Psychological **Stress**
Chi **Square** Test	**Stress**
Squatters	**Strikes**
Sri Lanka	**Strippers**
Srole, Leo	**Structural** Models
St. Louis, Missouri	**Structural-Functional** Analysis
Family **Stability**	**Structuralism**
Stability	**Structuration**
Life **Stage** Transitions	Community **Structure**
Developmental **Stages**	Economic **Structure**
Stalinism	Factor **Structure**
Food **Stamps**	Family **Structure**
Standard of Living	Latent **Structure** Analysis
Standards	Occupational **Structure**
Project Head **Start**	Organizational **Structure**
Starvation	Power **Structure**
Church **State** Relationship	Social **Structure**

Structure   ROTATED DESCRIPTOR DISPLAY   Technology

Structure	Stockholm, **Sweden**
Agrarian **Structures**	**Sweden**
Class **Struggle**	Code **Switching**
Ideological **Struggle**	Geneva, **Switzerland**
Student Attitudes	**Switzerland**
Student Behavior	**Sydney**, Australia
Student Teacher Relationship	**Symbiotic** Relations
College **Students**	**Symbolic** Interactionism
Dental **Students**	**Symbolism**
Elementary School **Students**	**Symposia**
Graduate **Students**	**Symptoms**
High School **Students**	**Synagogues**
Married **Students**	**Syncretism**
Medical **Students**	**Syndicalism**
Students	Acquired Immune Deficiency **Syndrome**
Undergraduate **Students**	Downs **Syndrome**
Case **Studies**	**Synthesis**
International **Studies**	Damascus, **Syria**
Longitudinal **Studies**	**Syria**
Middletown **Studies**	Adversary Legal **System**
Social **Studies**	Correctional **System**
Sturzo, Luigi	Legal **System**
Artistic **Styles**	World **System** Theory
Management **Styles**	Caste **Systems**
Styles	Delivery **Systems**
Sub Saharan Africa	Economic **Systems**
Subcultures	Educational **Systems**
States (Political **Subdivisions**)	Political **Systems**
Researcher **Subject** Relations	Sensory **Systems**
Subjectivity	Social **Systems**
Research **Subjects**	**Systems**
Superior **Subordinate** Relationship	**Systems** Theory
Subordination	**Szasz**, Thomas Stephen
Subsidies	**Szczepanski**, Jan
Subsistence Economy	Life **Tables**
Substance Abuse	**Tables**
Toxic **Substances**	**Taboos**
Suburbanization	**Tahiti**
Suburbs	**Taipei**, Taiwan
Success	Taipei, **Taiwan**
Inheritance And **Succession**	**Taiwan**
Sudan	Turn **Taking**
Suffering	**Tanzania**
Jonestown Mass **Suicide**	**Taoism**
Suicide	**Tarde**, Gabriel
Sumner, William Graham	**Task** Oriented Groups
Superintendents	**Task** Performance
Superior Subordinate Relationship	**Tasks**
Supernatural	**Tasmania**
Superstitions	**Taxation**
Base And **Superstructure**	Student **Teacher** Relationship
Supervision	**Teacher** Attitudes
Labor **Supply**	**Teacher** Education
Supply And Demand	**Teacher** Evaluation
Water **Supply**	**Teachers**
Child **Support**	**Teaching**
Financial **Support**	**Teaching** Methods
Public **Support**	Sports **Teams**
Social **Support**	**Teams**
Support	**Teamwork**
Support Networks	**Technical** Assistance
United States **Supreme** Court	**Technicians**
Surgery	Projective **Techniques**
Surinam	**Technocracy**
Surrogate Parents	Scientific **Technological** Revolution
Mail **Surveys**	**Technological** Change
Surveys	**Technological** Innovations
Telephone **Surveys**	**Technological** Progress
Survival	Appropriate **Technologies**
Sustenance Organization	Reproductive **Technologies**
Sutherland, Edwin Hardin	Agricultural **Technology**
Swahili	Electronic **Technology**
Swaziland	

Technology — ROTATED DESCRIPTOR DISPLAY — Transvestism

High **Technology** Industries	**Theory** Formation
Information **Technology**	**Theory** Practice Relationship
Medical **Technology**	World System **Theory**
Metallurgical **Technology**	**Therapists**
Science And **Technology**	Conjoint **Therapy**
Space **Technology**	Family **Therapy**
Technology	Group **Therapy**
Technology Assessment	**Thinking**
Technology Transfer	**Thomas**, William Isaac
Teheran, Iran	**Threat**
Teilhard de Chardin, Pierre	**Tibet**
Tel Aviv, Israel	**Tillich**, Paul Johannes
Telecommunications	**Tilly**, Charles
Teleology	Part **Time** Employment
Telephone Communications	Part **Time** Farming
Telephone Surveys	Space And **Time**
Television	**Time**
Television Viewing	**Time** Periods
Temperance Movements	**Time** Series Analysis
Landlord **Tenant** Relations	**Time** Utilization
Tenants	First Birth **Timing**
Tennessee	Marriage **Timing**
Tension	**Tithing**
Academic **Tenure**	Trinidad And **Tobago**
Land **Tenure**	**Togo**
Tenure	**Tokelau** Islands
Terminal Illness	**Tokenism**
Termination of Treatment	**Tokyo**, Japan
Kinship **Terminology**	**Tolerance**
Terminology	Sao **Tome** And Principe
Territoriality	**Tonga**
Northwest **Territories**	**Tonnies**, Ferdinand
Terrorism	**Tools**
Chi Square **Test**	**Topography**
Test Bias	**Toronto**, Ontario
Testimony	**Torture**
Achievement **Tests**	**Totalitarianism**
Intelligence **Tests**	**Totemism**
Tests	**Touraine**, Alain
Dallas, **Texas**	**Tourism**
Houston, **Texas**	Cape **Town**, South Africa
Texas	Boom **Towns**
Textbooks	New **Towns**
Textile Industry	**Towns**
Bangkok, **Thailand**	**Toxic** Substances
Thailand	**Tracking** (Education)
Theater Arts	**Trade**
Theology	Judeo-Christian **Tradition**
Formalization **(Theoretical)**	**Traditional** Medicine
Theoretical Problems	**Traditional** Societies
Economic **Theories**	**Traditionalism**
Evolutionary **Theories**	**Traditions**
Middle Range **Theories**	**Traffic**
Social **Theories**	Drug **Trafficking**
Theories	Job **Training**
Action **Theory**	Professional **Training**
Balance **Theory**	Sensitivity **Training**
Biosocial **Theory**	**Training**
Conflict **Theory**	Personality **Traits**
Contagion **Theory**	**Tranquilizing** Drugs
Convergence **Theory**	**Transcendental** Meditation
Critical **Theory**	Technology **Transfer**
Demographic Transition **Theory**	**Transference** (Psychology)
Dependency **Theory**	Demographic **Transition** Theory
Exchange **Theory**	Life Stage **Transitions**
Game **Theory**	**Translation**
Graph **Theory**	Cultural **Transmission**
Information **Theory**	Organ **Transplantation**
Labor **Theory** of Value	Air **Transportation**
Neutralization **Theory**	Public **Transportation**
Organization **Theory**	**Transportation**
Sociological **Theory**	**Transsexualism**
Systems **Theory**	**Transvestism**

ROTATED DESCRIPTOR DISPLAY

Travel — Vienna

Commuting **(Travel)**
Travel
Treaties
Termination of **Treatment**
Treatment
Treatment Compliance
Treatment Methods
Treatment Programs
Trends
Triads
Trials
Trinidad And Tobago
Trobriand Islands
Troeltsch, Ernst
Tropical Regions
Trotsky, Leon
Truancy
Trust
Truth
Tuamotu Archipelago
Tuberculosis
Tubuai Islands
Tunisia
Istanbul, **Turkey**
Turkey
Turks And Caicos Islands
Turn Taking
Labor **Turnover**
Twentieth Century
Twins
Ideal **Types**
Social **Types**
Types
Typology
Kampala, **Uganda**
Uganda
Ukrainian Soviet Socialist Republic
Unconscious (Psychology)
Economic **Underdevelopment**
Underemployment
Undergraduate Programs
Undergraduate Students
Underground Movements
Undocumented Immigrants
Unemployment
Unemployment Rates
Unidentified Flying Objects
Unification Church
Uniformity
Unilineality
Kiev, **Union** of Soviet Socialist Republics
Leningrad, **Union** of Soviet Socialist Republics
Moscow, **Union** of Soviet Socialist Republics
Soviet **Union** Cultural Groups
Union of Soviet Socialist Republics
Unionization
Unions
Unitarians
United Arab Emirates
United Kingdom
United Nations
United Nations Educational, Scientific & Cultural Org
United States of America
United States Supreme Court
Universalism-Particularism
Cultural **Universals**
Universities

Social **Unrest**
Unwanted Pregnancy
Unwed Mothers
Upper Class
Rural to **Urban** Migration
Rural **Urban** Continuum
Rural **Urban** Differences
Urban Areas
Urban Crime
Urban Development
Urban Education
Urban Fringe
Urban Policy
Urban Population
Urban Poverty
Urban Renewal
Urban Sociology
Urban to Rural Migration
Urbanism
Urbanization
Montevideo, **Uruguay**
Uruguay
Language **Usage**
Alcohol **Use**
Drug **Use**
Land **Use**
Utah
Utilitarianism
Health Care **Utilization**
Time **Utilization**
Utilization
Utopias
Uttar Pradesh, India
Uzbek Soviet Socialist Republic
Vaccination
Validity
Labor Theory of **Value**
Value (Economics)
Value Neutrality
Value Orientations
Cultural **Values**
Social **Values**
Values
Work **Values**
Van den Berghe, Pierre Louis
Vancouver, British Columbia
Vandalism
Variables
Variance (Statistics)
Seasonal **Variations**
Language **Varieties**
Vasectomy
Vatican
Veblen, Thorstein Bunde
Venereal Diseases
Caracas, **Venezuela**
Venezuela
Verbal Accounts
Verbal Communication
Cape **Verde** Islands
Verdicts
Verification
Vermont
Verstehen
Veterans
Vico, Giovanni Battista
Victim Offender Relations
Victimization
Victimology
Victims
Victorian Period
Videotape Recordings
Vienna, Austria

315

ROTATED DESCRIPTOR DISPLAY

Hanoi, **Vietnam**	**Welfare** Services
Ho Chi Minh City, **Vietnam**	**Welfare** State
Vietnam	**Well** Being
Vietnam War	East And **West**
Television **Viewing**	**West** Bengal, India
Vigilantism	**West** Virginia
Villages	**Westermarck**, Edward Alexander
Saint **Vincent**	**Western** Civilization
Family **Violence**	**Western** Europe
Mass Media **Violence**	**Western** Samoa
Political **Violence**	**Western** Society
Sports **Violence**	**Western** States
Violence	Black **White** Differences
Virgin Islands	Black **White** Relations
Virginia	**White** Collar Crime
West **Virginia**	**White** Collar Workers
Virginity	**Whites**
Vision	**Whorf**, Benjamin Lee
Visitation	**Whyte**, William Foote
Visual Arts	**Widowhood**
Visual Sociology	**Will**
Vocabularies	Left **Wing** Politics
Vocational Education	Right **Wing** Politics
Vocational Rehabilitation	**Wirth**, Louis
Voltaire, Francois-Marie Arouet de	**Wisconsin**
Voluntarism	**Witchcraft**
Volunteers	Expert **Witnesses**
Von Wiese (und Kaiserswaldau), Leopold	Jehovah's **Witnesses**
	Witnesses
Voodooism	**Wittgenstein**, Ludwig Joseph Johann
Voters	
Voting	**Wives**
Voting Behavior	**Wolff**, Kurt Heinrich
Voting Rights	Battered **Women**
Vulnerability	Elderly **Women**
Minimum **Wage**	Professional **Women**
Wages	Rural **Women**
Wake Island	Working **Women**
Wales	**Womens** Education
Wallerstein, Immanuel Maurice	**Womens** Groups
Civil **War**	**Womens** Rights
Cold **War**	**Womens** Roles
Nuclear **War**	**Words**
Prisoners of **War**	Clinical Social **Work**
Vietnam **War**	Education **Work** Relationship
War	Family **Work** Relationship
World **War** I	Group **Work**
World **War** II	Shift **Work**
Ward, Lester Frank	Social **Work**
Hospital **Wards**	Social **Work** Cases
Warsaw, Poland	Social **Work** Education
Seattle, **Washington**	Sociology of **Work**
Washington, D.C.	**Work**
Washington (State)	**Work** Attitudes
Wastes	**Work** Environment
Water Supply	**Work** Experience
Watergate Scandal	**Work** Groups
Wealth	**Work** Humanization
Nuclear **Weapons**	**Work** Leisure Relationship
Weapons	**Work** Organization
Weather	**Work** Orientations
Webb, Sidney James, Lord Passfield	**Work** Skills
	Work Values
Weber, Max	**Worker** Attitudes
Weddings	**Worker** Consciousness
Body **Weight**	**Worker** Control
Weighting	**Worker** Machine Relationship
Child **Welfare** Services	**Worker** Ownership
Social **Welfare**	**Worker** Participation
Welfare Dependency	Agricultural **Workers**
Welfare Policy	Blue Collar **Workers**
Welfare Recipients	Clerical **Workers**
Welfare Reform	Dislocated **Workers**

316

Foreign **Workers**
Industrial **Workers**
Manual **Workers**
Migrant **Workers**
Paraprofessional **Workers**
Professional **Workers**
Sales **Workers**
Social **Workers**
White Collar **Workers**
Workers
Workers Compensation Insurance
Quality of **Working** Life
Working Class
Working Hours
Working Mothers
Working Women
Home **Workplaces**
Workplaces
Workshops (Courses)
Workshops (Manufacturing)
World Economy
World Population
World Problems
World System Theory
World War I
World War II
Worldview
Ancestor **Worship**
Places of **Worship**
Worship
Writers
Writing
Writing for Publication
Wyoming
Yemen (Peoples Democratic Republic)
Yemen Arab Republic
Yoga
Buffalo, New **York**
New **York**
New York City, New **York**
Young Adults
Rural **Youth**
Youth
Youth Culture
Youth Employment
Youth Movements
Youth Organizations
Croatia, **Yugoslavia**
Montenegro, **Yugoslavia**
Serbia, **Yugoslavia**
Slovenia, **Yugoslavia**
Yugoslavia
Yukon
Kinshasa, **Zaire**
Zaire
Zambia
New **Zealand**
Zen Buddhism
Zimbabwe
Zionism
Znaniecki, Florian
Arid **Zones**
Zoning

sa Classification Scheme

0100 methodology & research technology
- 0103 methodology (conceptual & epistemological)
- 0104 research methods
- 0105 statistical methods
- 0161 models: mathematical & other

0200 sociology: history & theory
- 0202 of professional interest (teaching sociology)
- 0206 history & present state of sociology
- 0207 theories, ideas, & systems
- 0267 macrosociology: analysis of whole societies
- 0285 comparative & historical sociology

0300 social psychology
- 0309 interaction within (small) groups
- 0312 personality & culture
- 0322 leadership
- 0364 deviance
- 0373 cognitive/interpretive sociologies, symbolic interactionism & ethnomethodology

0400 group interactions
- 0410 interaction between (large) groups (race relations, ethnicity, & inter-ethnic relations)

0500 culture and social structure
- 0508 social organizations
- 0513 culture
- 0514 social anthropology

0600 complex organization
- 0621 jobs, work organization, workplaces, & unions
- 0623 military sociology
- 0624 bureaucratic structure/organizational sociology
- 0665 social network analysis
- 0674 voluntary associations
- 0686 modes of production, employment patterns, social division of labor

0700 social change & economic development
- 0715 social change & economic development
- 0749 market structures & consumer behavior
- 0770 capitalism/socialism — world systems

0800 mass phenomena
- 0826 social movements
- 0827 public opinion
- 0828 communication
- 0829 collective behavior
- 0842 sociology of leisure/tourism
- 0850 mass culture
- 0869 sociology of sports

0900 political sociology/interactions
- 0911 interactions between societies, nations, & states
- 0925 voting, parties, political systems

1000 social differentiation
- 1019 social stratification/mobility
- 1020 sociology of occupations & professions

1100 rural sociology & agriculture
- 1116 rural sociology (village, agriculture)

1200 urban sociology
- 1218 urban sociology

1300 sociology of language & the arts
- 1330 sociology of language/sociolinguistics
- 1331 sociology of art (creative & performing)
- 1375 sociology of literature

1400 sociology of education
- 1432 sociology of education

1500 sociology of religion
- 1535 sociology of religion

1600 social control
- 1636 sociology of law
- 1653 police, penology & correctional problems

1700 sociology of science
- 1734 sociology of science
- 1772 sociology of technology

1800 demography & human biology
- 1837 demography (population studies)
- 1844 human biology/sociobiology

1900 the family & socialization
- 1976 socialization
- 1938 sociology of the child
- 1939 adolescence & youth
- 1940 sociology of sexual behavior
- 1977 birth control (abortion, contraception, fertility, & childbearing)
- 1941 sociology of the family
- 1978 sociology of death & dying

2000 sociology of health & medicine
- 2045 sociology of medicine (public health)
- 2046 social psychiatry (mental health)
- 2079 substance use/abuse & compulsive behaviors (drug abuse, addiction, alcoholism, gambling, eating disorders, etc.)

2100 social problems & social welfare
- 2143 social gerontology
- 2147 sociology of crime & victimology
- 2148 applied sociology
- 2151 juvenile delinquency
- 2187 social service programs/delivery systems

2200 sociology of knowledge
- 2233 sociology of knowledge
- 2252 history of ideas

2300 community development
- 2317 sociology of communities & regions

2400 policy, planning, forecasting
- 2454 planning & forecasting
- 2460 social indicators
- 2462 policy sciences

2500 radical sociology
- 2555 radical sociology
- 2580 critical sociology

2600 environmental interactions
- 2656 environmental interactions
- 2681 disaster studies
- 2682 social geography

2700 studies in poverty
- 2757 studies in poverty

2800 studies in violence
- 2858 studies in violence
- 2884 terrorism

2900 feminist/gender studies
- 2959 feminist studies
- 2983 sociology of gender & gender relations

3000 marxist sociology
- 3063 marxist sociology

3100 clinical sociology
- 3166 clinical sociology

3200 sociology of business
- 3268 sociology of business

3300 visual sociology
- 3371 visual sociology

Bibliography

Abercrombie, Nicholas, Hill, Stephen, and Turner, Bryan S. *The Penguin Dictionary of Sociology.* Harmondsworth, Middlesex: Penguin Books, 1984.

Aitchison, Jean, comp. *UNESCO Thesaurus.* 2 vols. Paris: UNESCO, 1977.

Angeles, Peter A. *Dictionary of Philosophy.* New York: Barnes and Noble, 1981.

Beck, Carl, Dym, Eleanor D., and McKechnie, J. Thomas, eds. *Political Science Thesaurus.* Washington, DC: American Political Science Association, 1975.

Bernsdorf, Wilhelm, and Knospe, Horst, eds. *Internationales Soziologenlexikon.* 2 vols. Stuttgart: Ferdinand Enke Verlag, 1980-1984.

Black, Henry Campbell. *Black's Law Dictionary.* 5th edition. St. Paul: West Publishing Co., 1979.

Bottomore, Tom. *A Dictionary of Marxist Thought.* Cambridge: Harvard University Press, 1983.

Bridgwater, William, and Kurtz, Seymour, eds. *The Columbia Encyclopedia.* 3rd edition. New York: Columbia University Press, 1963.

Crim, Keith, Bullard, Roger A., Shinn, Larry D., eds. *Abingdon Dictionary of Living Religions.* Nashville: Parthenon Press, 1981.

Ducrot, Oswald, and Todorov, Tzvetan, *Encyclopedic Dictionary of the Sciences of Language.* Baltimore: Johns Hopkins University Press, 1983.

Durr, W.T., Rosenberg, Paul M., comps. *The Urban Information Thesaurus: A Vocabulary for Social Documentation.* Westport, CT: Greenwood Press, 1977.

Eidelberg, Ludwig, M.D., ed. *Encyclopedia of Psychoanalysis.* New York: Free Press, 1968.

English, Horace B., and English, Ava Champney. *A Comprehensive Dictionary of Psychological and Psychoanalytical Terms.* New York: David MacKay Co., 1958.

Flew, Antony. *A Dictionary of Philosophy.* New York: St. Martins Press, 1979.

Gentz, William H. *The Dictionary of Bible and Religion.* Nashville: Abingdon Press, 1973.

Good, Carter V. *Dictionary of Education.* New York: McGraw-Hill, 1959.

Gould, Julius, and Kolb, William L., eds. *A Dictionary of the Social Sciences.* New York: Free Press, 1964.

Hays, William L. *Statistics.* 3rd edition. New York: Holt, Rinehart and Winston, 1981.

Herbert, Miranda C., and McNeil, Barbara, eds. *Biography and Genealogy Master Index.* 2nd edition. 8 vols. Detroit: Gale Research Co., Book Tower, 1980.

Hinsie, Leland E., and Campbell, Robert J. *Psychiatric Dictionary.* New York: Oxford University Press, 1975.

Hoult, Thomas Ford. *Dictionary of Modern Sociology.* Totowa, NJ: Littlefield, Adams and Co., 1977.

Jaques Cattell Press, ed. *American Men and Women of Science: Social and Behavioral Sciences.* 13th edition. New York: R.R. Bowker, 1978.

Jeffers, Robert J., and Lehiste, Ilse. *Principles and Methods for Historical Linguistics.* Cambridge: MIT Press, 1979.

Johnston, R.J., et al. *Dictionary of Human Geography.* New York: Free Press, 1981.

Kuper, Adam, and Kuper, Jessica. *The Social Science Encyclopedia.* London: Routledge and Kegan Paul, 1985.

Labovitz, Sanford. *An Introduction to Sociological Concepts.* New York: John Wiley and Sons, 1977.

Levin, Jack, and Spates, James L. *Starting Sociology.* 3rd edition. New York: Harper and Row, 1985.

Lieber, Arthur S. *The Penguin Dictionary of Psychology.* Harmondsworth, Middlesex: Penguin Books, 1985.

Longman Dictionary of Psychology and Psychiatry. Longman: New York, 1984.

Mann, Michael, ed. *The Macmillan Student Encyclopedia of Sociology.* London: Macmillan Press, 1983.

McKee, James B. *Sociology: The Study of Society.* New York: Holt, Rinehart and Winston, 1981.

Mitchell, G. Duncan, ed. *A New Dictionary of the Social Sciences.* Routledge and Kegan Paul, 1979.

Moore, W.G., *A Dictionary of Geography.* 5th edition. Harmondsworth, Middlesex: Penguin Books, 1977.

National Criminal Justice Thesaurus. Rockville, MD: U.S. Department of Justice, National institute of Justice, 1985.

National Library of Medicine (U.S.). Medical Subject Headings — Annotated Alphabetic List, 1982. Washington, DC: U.S. Department of Commerce, National Technical Information Service, 1981.

Pei, Mario, and Gaynor, Frank. *Dictionary of Linguistics.* Totowa, NJ: Littlefield, Adams and Co., 1980.

Perry, John A., and Perry, Erna K. *Contemporary Society: An Introduction to Social Science.* 4th edition. New York: Harper and Row, 1984.

Rand McNally. *Cosmopolitan World Atlas.* Chicago: Rand McNally, 1978.

Random House. *The Random House Dictionary of the English Language.* New York: Random House, 1966.

Rosenberg, Jerry M. *Dictionary of Business and Management.* New York: John Wiley and Sons, 1978.

Rubin, Herbert J. *Applied Social Research.* Columbus, OH: Charles E. Merrill, 1983.

Scruton, Roger. *A Dictionary of Political Thought.* New York: Hill and Wang, 1982.

Sills, David L., ed. *International Encyclopedia of the Social Sciences. Vol. 18, Biographical Supplement.* New York: Free Press, 1979.

Sloan, Harold S., and Zurcher, Arnold J. *Dictionary of Economics.* New York: Barnes and Noble, 1970.

Stetler, Susan L., ed. *Biography Almanac. Vol. 1, Biographies.* Detroit: Gale Research Co., Book Tower, 1983.

Sullivan, Thomas J., and Thompson, Kenrick S. *Sociology: Concepts, Issues and Applications.* New York: John Wiley and Sons, 1984.

Theodorson, George A., and Theodorson, Achilles G. *A Modern Dictionary of Sociology.* New York: Barnes and Noble, 1969.

Thesaurus of ERIC Descriptors, 10th Edition. Phoenix, Ariz: Oryx Press, 1984.

UNESCO Secretariat, and de Padirac, B., comps. *SPINES Thesaurus. Vol. 1, Rules, Conventions, Directions for Use, and Auxiliary Devices*. Paris: UNESCO Press, 1976.

van de Merwe, Caspar. *Thesaurus of Sociological Research Terminology*. Rotterdam: Rotterdam University Press, 1974.

Vander Zanden, James W. *Social Psychology, 3rd edition*. New York: Random House, 1984.

Viet, Jean. *Thesaurus for Information Processing in Sociology*. Paris: Mouton, 1971.

Webster's New Biographical Dictionary. Springfield, MA: Merriam-Webster, 1983.

Webster's Third New International Dictionary. Springfield, MA: G. and C. Merriam Co., 1966.

Williams, Raymond. *Keywords: A Vocabulary of Culture and Society. Revised edition*. New York: Oxford University Press, 1983.

Woods, Lawrence J., MacQuibben, Mary, Goldschmidt, Eva, and Bartenbach, Wilhelm K., eds. *PAIS Subject Headings*. New York: Public Affairs Information Service, 1984.

Yule, John-David, ed. *Concise Encyclopedia of Science and Technology*. New York: Crescent Books, 1979.

Yule, John-David, ed. *Concise Encyclopedia of the Sciences*. New York: Facts on File, 1978.

Zadrozny, John T. *Dictionary of Social Science*. Washington, DC: Public Affairs Press, 1959.

Notes

Notes